Textbook on
Immigration and Asylum Law

....

Third edition

Gina Clayton
BA (Hons), LLM

OXFORD
UNIVERSITY PRESS

OXFORD
UNIVERSITY PRESS

Great Clarendon Street, Oxford OX2 6DP

Oxford University Press is a department of the University of Oxford.
It furthers the University's objective of excellence in research, scholarship,
and education by publishing worldwide in

Oxford New York

Auckland Cape Town Dar es Salaam Hong Kong Karachi
Kuala Lumpur Madrid Melbourne Mexico City Nairobi
New Delhi Shanghai Taipei Toronto

With offices in

Argentina Austria Brazil Chile Czech Republic France Greece
Guatemala Hungary Italy Japan Poland Portugal Singapore
South Korea Switzerland Thailand Turkey Ukraine Vietnam

Oxford is a registered trade mark of Oxford University Press
in the UK and in certain other countries

Published in the United States
by Oxford University Press Inc., New York

British Library Cataloguing in Publication Data

Data available

Library of Congress Cataloging in Publication Data

Clayton, Gina.
    Textbook on immigration and asylum law / Gina Clayton.—3rd ed.
      p. cm.
    Includes index.
    ISBN-13: 978–0–19–923866–8
    1. Emigration and immigration law—Great Britain.   2. Asylum, Right
of—Great Britain.   I. Title.
    KD4134.C63 2008
    342.4108'2—dc22   2008018978

Typeset by Newgen Imaging Systems (P) Ltd., Chennai, India
Printed in Great Britain
on acid-free paper by
Ashford Colour Press Ltd, Gosport, Hampshire

ISBN 978–0–19–923866–8

1 3 5 7 9 10 8 6 4 2

OUTLINE CONTENTS

DETAILED CONTENTS

PREFACE

The landscape of immigration law is undergoing a fundamental change. The sheer frequency of legislation is no longer news, it has become a feature of the landscape that rules, both statutory and non-statutory, change frequently and their mass and complexity are multiplying. Since the last edition of this book the Immigration, Asylum and Nationality Act 2006 has gained Royal Assent, and before it is fully implemented the UK Borders Act 2007 is also on the statute book, itself laying out elements of a programme of change. A new Bill is promised for the autumn. This is the way of it – a relay race of legislation which has been accelerating since 1999.

Now, however, the institutional basis and the concept of immigration control are changing. The foundation was laid in the Immigration and Asylum Act 1999, which separated the grant of leave from the port of entry, meaning that leave to enter could potentially be granted anywhere. At the time of the second edition of this book, a more dispersed system was already developing, through the grant of leave to enter by entry clearance, juxtaposed controls in France and Belgium, and the development of a network of airline liaison officers. Now technological developments are turning immigration control into an act of co-ordinated policing, and this is institutionalised through the creation of the UK Border Agency. The new agency unites customs and excise with immigration, security and policing. Entry clearance applications across the world entail biometric data being checked against databases and watch lists, across the new unified security operation. Entry at the port will in due course be similarly technologically led, though the capacity of the technology to deliver the government's dream in the proposed timescale is still in doubt.

The other dimension, also prefigured in the 1999 Act, is that of control *within* the border. This also seems set to take a quantum leap. The UK Borders Act requires all non-EEA nationals in the UK to hold a biometric identity card. This intensified monitoring through both the internal and external expansion of immigration control is no doubt driven in part by anxieties about terrorism. Of more practical relevance to more people is that immigration status is becoming and will become increasingly a criterion of access to a range of social benefits; local authorities, non-governmental organisations and health trusts: all are being recruited to the business of monitoring the entitlements of the foreigner. Add to this the limited rights granted to EEA nationals from the new EU member states, and the result is a society whose fault lines of privilege run increasingly, though not exclusively, along national, ethnic and racial lines. The surprise is not that this happens, but that it is where we are heading rather than what we are trying to leave behind.

The creation of the UK Border Agency meshes with the root and branch reforms in the Home Office initiated by Home Secretary John Reid. This appears to be a programme of real change, introducing new casework methods, an inspectorate, and a committee of experts to assess the UK's needs for migrant labour. Economic migration has come back up the political agenda. The take-up of work in the UK by new EU nationals has had an impact on the availability of low paid work and thus on the opportunities to enter for work for non-EU migrants. The government issued a welcome to the highly skilled, only to withdraw it again in many cases by a dramatic reduction in entry for international medical graduates and by changes to the Highly Skilled Migrants Programme. The new points-based system for entry for work and study is launched on 29 February 2008 for applicants within the UK, and begins abroad in April with applications from India. Simultaneously, rights of appeal will be withdrawn from these applicants.

One reform follows fast upon another. Language tests for nationality were followed by language tests for settlement and now possibly even for entry in the case of spouses. An increase in powers to deprive people of British nationality is followed by proposals for graded conditional citizenship. The government is engaged, alongside all this, in a project to 'simplify' immigration law, and promises a Bill in November this year which will consolidate all existing immigration legislation.

In the face of all this and more, what to do with a textbook for law students? This edition not only updates but also revises the second edition. A new chapter on policy includes part of the material on executive power from the old chapter 1, increased coverage of the institution of the Home Office and new sections on the treatment of asylum seekers and on the media. Both these subjects are powerfully related to immigration law and policy. Although this remains a book about UK law, and that is a limitation, the international context is also introduced. All the coverage of foundation subjects in the first section of the book remains tantalisingly brief. It is certain that it will not satisfy experts, but I hope that it will raise the curiosity of learners. In accordance with the institutional changes, the chapters on entry and on the extension of immigration control have been merged, so that technological developments and the process of exporting the border are integrated with the legal stages of gaining entry. The appeals chapter has been expanded by the addition of a section on judicial review, and material on the human rights jurisdiction has been taken from the human rights chapter into an expanded section on human rights appeals. The substantive human rights material remains in its own chapter, though as a defence against removal or deportation it is in the new chapter 18, where material on challenging deportation and removal has been combined.

My thanks are more than ever due to other people. Gemma Manning has contributed much of the research and some clarity of structure and expression to chapter 12. Bernard Ryan gave full and helpful comments on chapter 6. Thanks to both, and to Prakash Shah for his support, Helena Wray and Mahmud Quayum for helping with my last-minute questions, Helen Swann at OUP for her patience, clarity and persistence. My sincere thanks to the anonymous reviewers for comments on the second edition. I am very grateful for their interest in developing this book and I hope they see here the effect of their contribution. All the shortcomings and any errors remain my responsibility. I have endeavoured to state the law as at January 2008, though references to some later developments are also included. Reference should be made to the Online Resource Centre for significant changes to the law between January 2008 and the date of publication. Finally, thanks to all those good friends who have once again tolerated my absence and obsession, and to my husband Mike Fitter. Words are inadequate to express what I owe to him, but without his generosity I doubt this book would be here.

Gina Clayton
February 20 2008

GUIDE TO USING THE BOOK

There are a number of features throughout the textbook designed to help you in your studies.

SUMMARY

This chapter traces an outline history of British natio explains by reference to particular groups of people t present categories of British nationality. The developm been largely a history of progressive exclusion, based Recent developments are discussed in which there is zenship, both in that formal discrimination on the gr reduced, and in that groups of people formerly exclu

---

Chapter summaries provide an overview of what will be addressed in each chapter, so you are aware of the key learning outcomes for each topic.

 Key Case

Case C-16/05 *The Queen (Tum and Dari)* v *SSHD*

Mr Tum and Mr Dari were Turkish nationals who ent cations. Pending the outcome of their asylum applic admission, which is a provisional permission to be in granted entry. The asylum claims were unsuccessful, them to European countries through which they h

---

Key case boxes highlight important cases in each subject area and provide a valuable summary of the significant points to note.

QUESTIONS

1 How do you think the Immigration (Leave substance and nature of immigration contr

2 What would you consider to be appropriate and who do you think should make that de present law?

3 What do you think are the reasons for limi person can switch?

 online resource centre For guidance on answering questions, visit w

---

At the end of each chapter is a selection of questions. These allow you to check your understanding of the topics covered, and help you engage fully with the material in preparation for further study, writing essays, and answering exam questions.

Guidance on answering these questions is available on the Online Resource Centre: **www.oxfordtextbooks.co.uk/orc/clayton3e**

FURTHER READING

Barnard, C. (2007) *The Substantive Law of the EU: The Fo* University Press).

Carlier, J-Y (2005) 'Case Note on *Chen*', (2005) *Common*

Craig, P. and de Burca, G. (2007) *EU Law: text, cases and* University Press).

Currie, S. (2006) ' "Free" movers? The post-accession ex *European Law Review*, April, pp. 207–299.

Guild, E. (ed.) (1999) *The Legal Framework and Social Con*

Each chapter concludes with a list of recommended further reading.

These suggestions include books and journal articles, and will help to supplement your knowledge and develop your understanding of the subjects covered.

ONLINE RESOURCE CENTRE

This book is accompanied by an Online Resource Centre – a website providing free and easy-to-use resources designed to support the book.
www.oxfordtextbooks.co.uk/orc/clayton3e

> 'Clayton is able to keep the reader up to date with the textbook's on-line companion website, which is easily accessible and very useful in this particular area'
>
> *Legal Information Management*

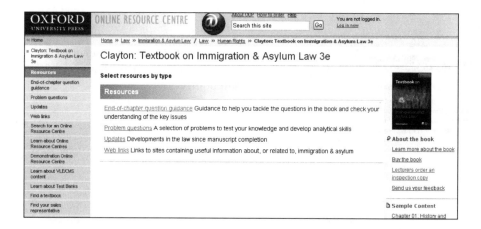

- **Twice-yearly updates** provide easy access to changes and developments in the law, helping you stay up-to-date in this fast-moving area

- **Problem questions** develop your analytical skills and let you put your knowledge to the test

- **Guidance on how to answer end-of-chapter questions** helps you engage with the material covered and check your understanding of the key issues

- **A selection of web links** helps you research topics of particular interest to you

TABLE OF EUROPEAN LEGISLATION

TABLE OF INTERNATIONAL LEGISLATION

TABLE OF UK SECONDARY
LEGISLATION

TABLE OF PRIMARY
LEGISLATION

TABLE OF CASES

LIST OF ABBREVIATIONS

AITOCA	Asylum and Immigration (Treatment of Claimants etc) Act 2004
AIT	Asylum and Immigration Tribunal
API	Asylum Policy Instructions
APU	Asylum Policy Update
ARC	asylum registration card
BDTC	British dependent territories citizenship
BIA	Border and Immigration Agency
BIOT	British Indian Ocean Territory
BNA	British Nationality Act
BN(O)	British national (overseas)
BOC	British overseas citizen
BOTA	British Overseas Territory Act
BOTC	British overseas territories citizen
BPP	British protected person
CAT	Convention Against Torture
CEDW	Convention on the Elimination of All Forms of Discrimination Against Women
CERD	Convention on Ending Racial Discrimination
CO	Crown Office
CRC	Convention on the Rights of the Child
CRE	Commission for Racial Equality
CUKC	citizen of the UK and Colonies
DL	Discretionary leave
ECHR	European Convention on Human Rights
ECtHR	European Court of Human Rights
EESC	European Economic and Social Committee
ELR	exceptional leave to remain
EWCA	England and Wales Court of Appeal
FGM	female genital mutilation
HLR	Housing Law Reports
HP	Humanitarian protection
HRLR	Human Rights Law Reports
IAA	Immigration and Asylum Act 1999
IANA	Immigration, Asylum and Nationality Act 2006
IANL	Immigration, Asylum and Nationality Law
IAT	Immigration Appeal Tribunal

ICCPR   International Covenant on Civil and Political Rights
IDI   Immigration Directorate Instructions
ILR   indefinite leave to remain
IND   Immigration and Nationality Directorate
INLP   Immigration and Nationality Law and Practice
INLR   Immigration and Nationality Law Reports

JCWI   Joint Council for the Welfare of Immigrants

NAM   New Asylum Model
NIAA   Nationality Immigration and Asylum Act 2002
NI   Nationality Instructions

SEF   Statement of Evidence Form
SIS   Schengen Information Systems

Introduction

The notion of a textbook might be taken to imply that there is a standard body of legal knowledge which can be imparted with neutrality and understood in isolation from its context. Nowhere is this less true than in immigration law. To use the words of Legomsky, 'Ensconced as it is in sensitive and controversial policy considerations, immigration law is an area in which the need to place legal doctrine within its larger social and political context is especially acute' (*Immigration and the Judiciary* 1987:5).

As a legal textbook, although this book does not examine in detail the historical and political circumstances, it does introduce the historical and political context in which the law arises. It gives the historical context of many of the topics covered, and includes references to political debates and some of the current research into the social dimensions of migration. This is not comprehensive, but is an encouragement to the reader to pursue some of these matters further using the wealth of literature in this area, and reference should be made to reading lists at the end of each chapter and to the bibliography at the end of the book.

The key themes will be seen to emerge across different sections and chapters of the book. For instance, the current focus on security and prevention of terrorism lies behind the e-borders scheme described in chapter 7, the detention provisions in chapter 15, and deprivation of nationality in chapter 3. Suspicion of asylum seekers and their motives – connected with the security issue also – is apparent in the material in chapter 12 on the asylum process and in chapter 15 on exclusion and criminalization. The integration agenda, also appearing as a form of control on private life, appears in chapter 9 on family life as well as chapter 3 on nationality. The managed migration programme is, of course, a major theme of the chapter on work (chapter 11), but its influence is also apparent in the material on entry in chapter 7. The recurrent reiteration of executive dominance of the whole area is apparent throughout, though particularly in the account of appeals and challenges (chapter 8), removals and deportation (chapters 16 and 17) and detention and the asylum process (chapters 15 and 12). No doubt more will occur to the reader.

Section 1 sets the foundation for the rest of the book. Chapter 1 gives an outline of the historical development of immigration law in the UK, and an introduction to the sources of immigration law, including discussion of the immigration rules and their special status. Chapter 2 introduces some policy issues, many of which provide themes that run throughout the book. The patterns of executive control are disclosed, and the current emphasis on both security and integration – though as reflected in legal provisions, integration translates into something more like surveillance. Chapter 3 explains who is subject to immigration control by looking at who has the right of abode in the UK and at key aspects of British nationality law. Chapter 4 deals with the application of the Human Rights Act to immigration and asylum law by looking at the content of the rights and their scope of application. The approach of this book is to look at the law through the prism of that Act, and the human rights dimension is addressed in each chapter as it arises.

Section 2 covers the European dimension. Chapter 5 sets out some of the framework issues arising from European membership, explaining how Europeans and non-Europeans are treated differently in the legal structures. Chapter 6 describes the rights of entry of European nationals and others through European free movement provisions for workers.

Section 3 deals with the system of immigration control. Chapter 7 follows the process of entering the UK by examining the legal hurdles encountered before and on arrival, discusses the powers of decision-making held by immigration and entry clearance officers, and concludes with an explanation of the kinds of leave that can be obtained. It integrates an examination of the new e-borders scheme, and the way in which the UK is extending its borders into other countries as part of the changing nature of immigration control, which is becoming more akin to policing. Chapter 8 outlines the structure of the appeals system and examines the grounds of appeal and the ways in which judicial review is used to challenge some of the exercises of executive power in the immigration system.

Section 4 examines the main legal bases for obtaining entry to the UK in immigration law. There is a chapter devoted to joining family members for those who are settled and temporarily resident. A chapter examines the rapidly changing area of entry for work and business, and one chapter deals with entry for temporary purposes such as study or holidays.

Section 5 is concerned with asylum claims. Chapter 12 considers the process of making an asylum claim and the special procedures such as fast tracking and certification of claims which enable claims to be decided in a minimum time and with minimum opportunity for challenge. It also examines the issues which are special to refugee appeals. Chapter 13 is devoted to an examination of the criteria which must be fulfilled in order to attain refugee status. Chapter 14 considers criminalization particularly of asylum seekers, and the laws which allow them to be excluded from protection because of what they have or are alleged to have done.

Section 6 is about enforcement. Chapter 15 concerns the grounds for immigration detention and the means of challenging it. The book ends with three short chapters on deportation, removal, and ways of challenging these enforced departures. Removal ends the book as it is the end of the process. In a sense, however, it brings us back to the beginning, as the capacity to remove those with no claim in law to stay is currently seen as a key to the credibility and power of the executive to carry out its policy.

SECTION 1

Laying the foundations

1

History and sources of immigration law

SUMMARY

This chapter divides into two parts. The first gives a brief history of immigration law in the UK, focusing on key legislative developments and noting the themes which arise in that history. The second part introduces the reader to the sources of immigration law, including the immigration rules and concessions.

1.1 Introduction

One of the reasons for having at least a passing acquaintance with the history is that themes repeat themselves over time, and it is possible to gain a greater perspective and understanding when we know that the current trend is not new. Particular kinds of legal provisions are created, abolished, and then recreated. For instance, sanctions on airlines for carrying passengers who do not carry full documents were introduced in the latter part of the twentieth century by the Immigration (Carriers Liability) Act 1987, but in 1905 the Aliens Act had provided for fines to be levied on carriers of unauthorised passengers.

Bevan identified nine themes in UK immigration policy: lack of planning, the Commonwealth, the importance of the European Community, international law, bipartisan policy, concern for civil liberties, race relations, the question of assimilation or diversity and the use of language (1986:22–28). These themes are still visible and important in the twenty-first century, though the balance has changed since 1986. We would now need to add the preoccupation with deterring false asylum claims and terrorism. Each of these will emerge to varying degrees in the course of this book. In enabling us to see that the issues of today are not new, a historical perspective creates the possibility of learning from history.

1.1.1 Attitudes to immigration

Every history of immigration shows that in Britain each new group of arrivals has been regarded with suspicion and hostility. Allegations against Jews at the turn of the twentieth century, West Indians in the 1950s, people from the Asian subcontinent in the 1960s, and in the 1990s, and at the turn of the twenty-first century, against asylum seekers, are all remarkably similar: 'every mass immigrant group was liable to be pronounced unconventional, unclean, unprincipled and generally unwelcome'

(Jones in Juss 1993:71). To this we can add that they are accused of being inveterate liars and scrounging from, or alternatively taking the jobs of, native British people, sometimes even the last two at the same time.

A linked phenomenon is the assertion that the issue is not one of race but of numbers. This is strongly correlated with a political objective of assimilation rather than diversity. If an immigrant group gains sufficient strength in numbers it is thought that it will have more capacity to retain an identity distinct from that of the host population. Interestingly, while denying that the control of entry is to do with race, it is generally said that it is to do with race relations. Politicians often justify a curb on immigration by saying that it is good for race relations. The basis for this is the numbers idea again, and the goal of assimilation. Immigrant groups are thought to be assimilable in small numbers (see for instance the report of Political and Economic Planning discussed in Dummett and Nicol 1990:174). In larger numbers they are said to generate resentment in the host population. Established immigrant groups have also sometimes supported this line of argument though others have opposed any form of immigration controls. Examples of the latter are the action of Jewish trade unions in the nineteenth century and the Indian, West Indian and Pakistani Workers' Association in the twentieth century, (see Cohen, Humphries and Mynott 2002).

The link between immigration and race relations was enshrined in government in the former Home Affairs Select Committee on Race Relations and Immigration. Just by way of example, this Committee's report of 1990 asserted that 'the effectiveness and fairness of immigration controls affect both the maintenance of good race relations at home and Britain's standing in the world'. The European Court of Human Rights did not accept this argument for the maintenance of immigration rules that discriminated against women (*Abdulaziz, Cabales and Balkandali* (1985) 7 EHRR 471). The Commission did not accept that the restriction on the entry of husbands was justifiable on the grounds advanced by the government, which included the protection of employment opportunities for the indigenous population and the maintenance of 'public tranquillity'. The numbers involved were so small that the effect on the employment situation was insignificant, and no link had been demonstrated between excluding such men and 'good race relations'. The effect could equally be the reverse, in that although the rules addressed the fears of some members of the population, they could create resentment in others, particularly the immigrant population which would regard the rules as unfair (para *77*). The Court endorsed the Commission's view (para 81).

Protection of race relations is often advanced as a reason for government policy. However, Lester and Bindman say that this thinking is an expression of 'the ambivalence of public policies. One face confronts the stranger at the gate; the other is turned towards the stranger within' (1972:13–14). Roy Hattersley discovered that he was wrong to make the connection between race relations and immigration:

Good community relations are not encouraged by the promotion of the idea that the entry of one more black immigrant into this country will be so damaging to the national interest that husbands must be separated from their wives, children denied the chance to look after their aged parents and sisters prevented from attending their brothers' weddings. It is measures like the Asylum and Immigration Bill – and the attendant speeches – which create the impression that we cannot 'afford to let them in'. And if we cannot afford to let them in, then those of them who are already here must be...doing harm. (The Guardian 26 February 1996)

1.2 **History of immigration law**

In studying immigration we are focusing on movement *into* a country, in this case the UK. However, this is only one small part of a worldwide movement of peoples which has gone on since time immemorial. Until at least around 1994 (Home Affairs Committee, Fifth Report 2005–06, para 8), Britain was a country of net emigration; in other words, more people left the UK than entered it. Many of the people who have come to the UK have been from areas with a long history of migration, and in paying attention to their arrival in the UK we are only selecting a tiny portion of history.

A complex body of statute and case law governing entry into the UK is a twentieth century phenomenon. Before this there was not a developed body of law, but there were numerous provisions controlling the movement of aliens. Aliens are defined as people who do not owe allegiance to the Crown; in other words they are not citizens of the UK nor of any territory in the control of the UK. Sometimes sweeping measures have been employed; for example, in 1290 Edward I, following an increasing campaign of hatred against Jews, expelled all Jews from England. Some of those expelled would have been aliens, and some British subjects. The latter, according to Magna Carta, had a right to remain in the kingdom and travel freely in and out; the royal decree was illegal as well as immoral, but there was no remedy.

Measures controlling the movement of aliens were often connected with hostilities with other countries. In the sixteenth century, when England was at war with Spain, Ireland gave assistance to the Spaniards, and Ireland and England were in continual conflict. There were by this time a significant number of Irish people resident in England. As Dummett and Nicol comment, regardless of the individual views or affiliations of these people, Queen Elizabeth I issued a proclamation that 'no manner of person born in the realm of Ireland . . . shall remain in the realm' (1990:45). The Irish were either expelled from England or imprisoned. Again in 1793, a statute was passed to control the entry of aliens, this time directed towards travellers from France; following the French Revolution it was feared they might stir up similar fervour in England. While some echoes of these earlier practices may be detected in modern law, by and large the immigration law of the last 100 years is a very different creature from the Royal Proclamations of Edward and Elizabeth.

The beginning of modern-day immigration control can be traced to the persecution of Jews in Eastern Europe at the end of the nineteenth century. From being an envied and romanticized minority as they had been in the nineteenth century, Jews once again became a target of violence and hostility. Many took refuge in Western Europe, including England. However, such movements of hatred are not generally confined within national boundaries, and the new arrivals found themselves also the subject of a campaign in Britain. They were concentrated in areas of poor housing and working conditions, and popular prejudice could regard them as having created these conditions rather than suffering from them alongside other workers. Here is an instance of the characteristics identified by Jones and many other writers as linked with immigrants. As mentioned earlier, both in former times and later in the twentieth century, immigrants are associated with overcrowded housing, disease, crime, and either taking jobs and keeping down wages, or refusing to work and taking up welfare provision.

A campaign against alien workers followed, and the government responded by setting up a Royal Commission to investigate the effect of immigrant workers upon housing and employment conditions and upon public health and morals, the allegations being that they were unclean and spread disease and crime.

The conclusion of the Royal Commission was that there was no threat to the jobs and working conditions of British workers, and immigrants did not create poverty, disease, and crime. There was a slightly higher rate of crime among some alien groups, though Dummett and Nicol suggest that 'the figures were crude and took no account of social class' (1990:101), and immigrants were living in overcrowded housing. The balance of the report was not obviously in favour of immigration control; nevertheless, the Royal Commission recommended control. The result was the Aliens Act 1905, the first major piece of modern immigration legislation. This Act marked the inception of the immigration service and the appeals system. It set up an inspectorate which operated at ports of entry to the UK. It was called the Aliens Inspectorate and its officers (the first immigration officers) had the power to refuse entry to aliens who were considered 'undesirable'. Undesirability was defined as lacking in the means to support oneself and dependants, and lacking in the capacity to acquire such means; mentally ill; likely through ill health to become dependent on the public welfare system or to endanger the health of others; or as having been previously expelled or convicted abroad of an extraditable nonpolitical crime. As a result of successful argument in Parliament, those opposed to controls on aliens had managed to limit the inspectorate's powers to those who travelled on the cheapest tickets (steerage class) on immigrant ships, which were defined as those carrying more than twenty aliens. These categories bear a striking similarity to the requirements for entry in modern-day immigration rules. Under present rules, all categories of entrant are required to show that they will not be reliant on public funds, long-term entrants are required to undergo a medical examination (HC 395 para 36) and the commission of criminal offences may give grounds for deportation (Immigration Act 1971 s 3(5)(a)). Note also that the standards in the Act do not clearly correspond to the findings of the Royal Commission; instead they compromise between averting real problems which had been identified and pandering to fears which had been shown to be unfounded. The overall effect is somewhat mitigated by the arguments in Parliament of those concerned with civil liberties. Here we see a reflection of Bevan's themes of lack of planning and bipartisan policy, the latter meaning that political parties would tend to take opposing positions on immigration (though it would also be true to say that it is an issue which does not always split on party lines). The combination of these two factors led to legislation with a confused purpose.

The Act also marked the beginning of an appeals system, by providing for Immigration Appeals Boards. They were set up in every major port of entry and immigrants refused leave to enter had a right of appeal to them.

As we have seen in relation to earlier conflicts with France and Spain, war has been used to impose severe restrictions upon foreigners. During the First World War, the Aliens Restriction Act 1914 s 1 gave the Secretary of State a great deal of power to regulate the entry, stay, and deportation of aliens, and even to pass regulations 'on any other matters which appear necessary or expedient with a view to the safety of the realm'. The Aliens Restrictions (Amendment) Act 1919 extended these wartime powers to apply at any time, subject to a yearly review. This was the pattern also with Prevention of Terrorism Acts, introduced in 1974 as an emergency measure subject to annual review, but culminating in a permanent Terrorism Act in 2000. The effects of the 1919 Act were far reaching. Not only did the wide powers given to the Secretary of State for wartime now also apply in peacetime, the Act also set the pattern, as Bevan describes, for the legal structure of immigration control. The legislation, like many modern statutes, was skeletal in form, having few substantive provisions but giving wide powers to the Secretary of State to make rules.

The 1919 Act was followed by the Aliens Order of 1920, which laid out the more detailed control of aliens and initiated today's system of work permits. Both passports and work permits grew out of wartime controls, as before 1914 it was possible to travel between a number of countries without a passport.

The Second World War had a very significant effect upon patterns of immigration to the UK. War was declared at a time when the Commonwealth was a strong bond which held together a number of nations in allegiance to the monarch of the UK. The UK was regarded by many as the 'mother country'. The fact that British and Commonwealth soldiers were fighting alongside one another contributed to the development of the idea of family, a sense of partnership, and belonging. Additionally, some Commonwealth service people had contributed to the war effort by doing essential work in the UK and so developed real familiarity with Britain. The media talked in terms of loyalty and gratitude to other Commonwealth citizens. This sense of belonging was not a thought-out policy based on a concept of rights enforceable by individuals, but more of a pleasing sentiment which was not expected to have any legal effect.

The reality of post-war entry to the UK was somewhat different. Spencer (1997) describes the deliberations of an interdepartmental working party set up in 1948, and also the later work of a committee of the Ministry of Labour, to consider where there were labour shortages and whether citizens from Commonwealth countries could or should be recruited to make up any shortfall. Writers differ as to the extent of any labour shortage and of recruitment policies aimed at remedying such shortage. The main focus was on the West Indies, and the question of whether workers should be recruited from there. Spencer reports negative conclusions as far as the recruitment of West Indians was concerned; they were not considered suitable workers or acceptable to the unions in the UK. Spencer also reports a refusal by the unions to co-operate with a recruitment scheme, and a preference by the government committees for workers from the continent of Europe. The reasons for this preference were that European workers would be easier to integrate and easier to return when no longer needed. The latter is in part because European workers would not have any claim as British subjects whereas Caribbean workers would. That Europeans would be regarded as easier to integrate could be surprising in view of the fact that English would be a native language for Caribbean workers though not for any European. However, Spencer's analysis of the Cabinet papers of the time, now released under the 30-year rule, strongly suggests that colour was at the root of the government's objection to West Indian workers. An analysis of Cabinet papers of the following few years relating to attempts to restrain immigration in the early 1950s reveals the same concerns (Carter, Harris, and Joshi 1987).

All the authors mentioned above, whose work is based on Cabinet papers, recount obstructive practices that were instituted in the Caribbean, West Africa, India, and Pakistan, making it more difficult for citizens of those countries to travel to Britain despite their being Commonwealth citizens. Examples of tactics employed were the delay in issuing passports and the omission of the reference to British subject status on travel documents, even though the holder was entitled to such a reference.

The passage of the British Nationality Act in 1948 did not affect right of entry into the UK; it dealt with nationality rather than immigration. However, it did so in a rather theoretical sense, being more a matter of labelling than of delivering enforceable rights. Indeed it was not within the contemplation of those who produced this legislation that the millions of Commonwealth citizens and citizens of the UK and Colonies would attempt to use their theoretical right to enter the UK. This Act will be considered in more detail in the chapter on nationality. In terms of this brief history, it both expressed the rather theoretical and symbolic idea that legislators had of the meaning of British subject status, and began the division between citizens of independent Commonwealth countries and other British subjects, which laid the foundation for the later development of immigration control.

Despite the disincentives mentioned above, immigration into Britain continued. There were opportunities for work, and these were attractive. By far the largest number of entrants was from Ireland and the countries known as the Old Commonwealth, i.e. Australia, Canada, and New Zealand. Immigration from the Caribbean was also rising, though not keeping pace with Ireland and the old Commonwealth. Until the release of the Cabinet papers relating to the 1950s, it was widely believed that there was a disproportionate rise in that period of immigration from the Caribbean and of social problems associated with this immigration. The popular account also entailed that the government was dedicated to retaining the rights of British subjects from the Caribbean to enter the UK, but then as social problems escalated, reluctantly they were forced to legislate in the form of the Commonwealth Immigrants Act 1962 to restrict the right of some Commonwealth citizens. Political speeches of the time focused on the familiar theme of numbers. A certain number of immigrants, it was asserted, could be assimilated – in other words absorbed – into the majority culture in Britain without noticeable impact or making demands. Beyond that number they became unassimilable. The studies mentioned above suggest a contrary view, namely that in working parties established specifically to consider the role of 'coloured' workers, the link of immigrants with social problems was not proven, and immigrants from the West Indies were far outnumbered by those from Ireland and the old Commonwealth. The initiative to control black immigration seemed to come, not from the identification of a social problem, but from an independent agenda within the Home Office and Cabinet Office. The government moved to impose a quota system on immigrants from the West Indies. However, official descriptions of them became more favourable after arrivals increased from India and Pakistan. Those who were formerly lazy were now industrious and English-speaking, and it was the South Asians who were 'unassimilable'. The British government succeeded in obtaining co-operation from West Indian, Indian and Pakistani governments to restrain migration, and Paul comments:

The range of administrative methods used by territories of origin and the United Kingdom to prevent colonial migration was so extensive that one might suggest that those migrants who did succeed in obtaining a passport, completing an English language interview, bearing up to scrutiny and accepting the propaganda at its true value were indeed hardy souls. (1997:153)

After years of political debate and manoeuvring the Commonwealth Immigrants Act was finally passed in 1962. The significance of the Act was immense. For the first time there was a restriction on the rights of certain Commonwealth citizens to come to the UK.

The Act distinguished between Commonwealth citizens based on parentage. Those who were born in the UK or Ireland or who held a passport issued by the government of those countries would not be subject to immigration control; others would. The immigration control consisted of conditions that a Commonwealth citizen would have to satisfy to gain entry. Whether these conditions were satisfied was to be determined by an immigration officer who was given a wide measure of discretion.

One of the peculiar features of British immigration law, to which we shall return time and again, is the heavy reliance on formerly unpublished instructions, guidelines, and concessions. These less formal sources in practice determine the outcome of applications. In the course of the implementation of the Commonwealth Immigrants Act 1962, it was made clear by internal guidance that the discretion given to immigration officers to refuse entry on the basis that requirements were not met, would not be applied in practice to immigrants from Canada, Australia, or New Zealand. The system of control that was established therefore discriminated at two levels against black would-be entrants. Initially, the terms of the Act itself, while neutral on their face as regards race or colour, were based on a requirement of birth in the UK or possession of a passport issued by the UK government, both of which would be satisfied more often in practice by white people. At the second level of internal instructions, the discrimination was closer to being explicit. As with the Jews in the thirteenth century, though more subtly, the distinction was made on the basis of ethnicity, not nationality.

For the Commonwealth citizens subject to immigration control, a three-tier system of work vouchers was instituted. Dummett and Nicol comment that this founded a bureaucratic system for processing immigration rather than a method of controlling it. The actual effect of the Commonwealth Immigrants Act was very different from the government's intention. There was a substantial rise in immigration from the Indian sub-continent in particular around the time of the 1962 Act. The Act has often been presented as the response to this increased immigration, but as Spencer (1997) and Bevan (1986) recount, it is more likely to have caused it. Spencer suggests four ways in which the Commonwealth Immigrants Act actually encouraged immigration, as follows.

First, the build-up to the legislation had taken years. The proposal to restrict immigration was therefore known long in advance and during the years 1960–62 this created a rush to 'beat the ban'.

Second, prior to the 1962 Act, those who had come from the Indian subcontinent to Britain were mainly men who had come for a temporary period to work, and to send money back to their families. Often this was in a tradition in their original locality, and they came to Britain because at that time there was a good chance of employment particularly in the textile industry in the north. These men's travels were therefore not immigration as it is sometimes understood 40 years later, i.e. they had not come to settle. The 1962 Act made it less likely that men retiring from this role could be replaced by younger relatives as the work voucher system would not have favoured their entry. The tendency of the Act therefore was to encourage those men to apply for leave to remain in the UK.

Following on from the last point, the Act permitted unification of families, and so for the men who had come as sojourners, the provisions of the Act combined to make remaining in the UK and being joined by their families the more viable option. It might be said (though Spencer does not make this point) that the Act encouraged and established the growth of an immigrant population modelled on British assumptions of working and family life, rather than an understanding of what migration meant to those who were doing it.

Spencer's final point is made also by Dummett and Nicol (1990): that the Act established a regime that regulated and therefore to a degree allowed people to enter the UK, namely the system of entry control and work vouchers.

The 1962 Act was formative in that it laid the foundation of the distinction between entry as a right and entry subject to the fulfilment of conditions, and did so by using the criterion of connection with the UK. The particular history of this Act reminds us not to take at face value assertions of cause and effect in relation to legislation; it also introduces the role of internal guidance in the operation of immigration law.

The history of the Commonwealth Immigrants Act 1968 is discussed by many writers including Shah, P. (2000), Bevan (1986), and Dummett and Nicol (1990). It provides a stark illustration of the difference between immigration policy based on loyalty to those whom the Empire and then the Commonwealth gave the status of British subject, and immigration policy based on fear of admission of numbers of non-white people. The key events were the independence of, first, Kenya and, later, Uganda and Tanzania. Each of these countries at independence had an established minority population which had come from the Indian sub-continent, some of whom had been introduced into East Africa by Britain which, as colonial power, had employed them on construction projects. Many had left India before its independence and before the creation of Pakistan, and their only citizenship was that of the UK and Colonies. The East African countries, on attaining independence, pursued a policy of Africanization that required residents to demonstrate their allegiance to the new state. Many Asians either did not fulfil the conditions for acquiring the new citizenship or did not register within the time limit, preferring to wait and see how their fortunes were likely to go in the new regime before committing themselves. Some may have been reluctant to lose their British connection. For many of those who did not acquire the new citizenship, serious consequences ensued. They lost their employment or their livelihood, and sought to use whatever protection their citizenship of the UK and Colonies could offer them. Their passports had been issued by the British High Commission and, therefore, under the 1962 Act they were not subject to immigration control. They had, as British subjects, right of entry into the UK. Inflated figures of likely entrants were quoted in the media, and the Commonwealth Immigrants Act 1968 was rushed through Parliament. The new Act provided that British subjects would be free from immigration control only if they, or at least one of their parents or grandparents, had been born, adopted, registered, or naturalized in the UK. The issue of a passport by a British High Commission thus ceased to be a qualification for entry free of control. For those subject to control, another voucher system was introduced. This one was based on tight quotas, reflecting the government's contention that numbers were the problem.

The story of the East African Asians illustrates how a British government was prepared to mix together issues of nationality and immigration. This is one of the themes identified by Bevan. While the East African Asians retained their CUKC (citizen of the UK and Colonies) status, it was in effect worthless as it no longer conferred a right of entry to their country of nationality.

The issue of colour (which was the terminology then used, and which was quite accurate) continued to dominate public debate about immigration. When the Immigration Act 1971 was passed, the racial definition of those with rights of entry and those without was complete. While the Immigration and Asylum Act 1999 and Nationality,

Immigration and Asylum Act 2002 have made substantial changes to the immigration process and the rights of immigrants, the 1971 Act remains the source of Home Office and immigration officers' powers to make decisions on entry, stay, and deportation. Its significance in terms of the history we are now tracing is its division of the world into patrials and non-patrials. Previously, UK law had divided the world into British subjects and aliens. This was the fundamental category which determined whether a person had right of entry into the UK. Legislation then, as we have seen, restricted the rights of some British subjects to the extent that these rights became practically worthless. The Immigration Act 1971 gave right of abode in the UK to those it defined as 'patrials'. These were:

(i)   citizens of the UK and Colonies who had that citizenship by birth, adoption, naturalization, or registration in the UK;

(ii) citizens of the UK and Colonies whose parent or grandparent had that citizenship by those same means at the time of the birth of the person in question;

(iii) citizens of the UK and Colonies with five years' ordinary residence in the UK;

(iv) Commonwealth citizens whose parent was born or adopted in the UK before their birth;

(v)   Commonwealth citizens married to a patrial man.

Commonwealth citizens who had been settled in the UK for five years when the Act came into force (1 January 1973) also had the right to register and thus possibly the right of abode. More detail is given of these provisions in chapter 2. Others, including British citizens without the necessary tie of parentage, would be subject to immigration controls. Apart from the five-year residence qualification, the right to live in the UK and to enter free from immigration control was determined by birth or parentage, not by nationality. The British Nationality Act 1981 carried this classification into British nationality law, and it is still the case that there are some, though a dwindling number, of British nationals who do not have a right of entry to the UK.

On the same day that the Immigration Act 1971 came into force, the UK entered the European Community. One of the cornerstones upon which the EC is built is freedom of movement, not only of goods but also of workers and their families. Despite this timing, the Immigration Act made no reference to European membership or the principle of freedom of movement. It continues to be the case up to the present that UK immigration law has developed quite separately from European law on freedom of movement (*R v IAT and Surinder Singh ex p SSHD* [1992] Imm AR 565) and that, at the same time that immigration restrictions were confirmed for Commonwealth citizens with a traditional allegiance to Britain, a new category of privilege was created for European nationals. The free movement rights of EU nationals are now implemented in UK law by the Immigration (European Economic Area) Regulations 2006, SI 2006/1003.

Primary immigration, that is of people coming to establish a life on their own rather than to join family members, virtually ceased with the Acts of 1968 and 1971; nevertheless in the 1980s the general trend in immigration provisions remained towards increasing restriction. Attention switched from primary immigration to family settlement, and more demanding rules for the entry of spouses were introduced. These raised such a political storm that, most unusually, there was a debate in Parliament concerning new immigration rules (see discussion in chapter 9).

On the whole, however, toward the end of the twentieth century, immigration policy (as distinct from asylum) did not play such a prominent part in the political life of the UK as it did previously. The Labour government's abolition of the infamous primary purpose rule in 1997 was a reversal of one of the most punitive provisions on family settlement (again see chapter 9) and the reduced tension around immigration and increased awareness of rights made this possible. The increasingly restrictive nature of immigration law did not arise from concerns about immigration as such, but from concerns about increased asylum claims. The rapid growth of a visa regime, now affecting travellers from potentially any country in the world, is an example of this (see chapter 7). The Immigration and Asylum Act 1999 made significant inroads into the rights of appeal of those alleged to be in breach of immigration law, but this was to address the backlog of cases at the Home Office and to expedite the removal of unsuccessful asylum seekers. The backlog, rather than issues of entry and entitlement, became the immigration scandal of the late 1990s in its own right.

The other major development in immigration law in the last 20 years has been the introduction of internal controls. This entails the devolution to housing officers, benefits officers, employers, registrars of births, marriages, and deaths, and airline officials of decisions concerning immigration status. These decisions then determine entitlement to a civil benefit such as housing or employment. Juss dates the introduction of these provisions from the first report of the Select Committee on Race Relations and Immigration in 1978. The effect has been to exclude from social benefits those people who have, or who may have, or who may be thought to have, a questionable immigration status. These provisions are predicated on the idea that there is a negative impact on Britain's housing and welfare system from immigrants who have deceived their way into the system – an idea we have seen at work earlier in the twentieth century.

Both the development of internal controls and the reduction of appeal rights ride on the back of the issue which has attracted public attention in the 1990s – that of asylum. The bulk of the case law reported in the Immigration Appeal Reports for some years concerned asylum rather than immigration issues. There was an escalation of legislation principally aimed at controlling asylum seekers: the Asylum and Immigration Appeals Act 1993, Asylum and Immigration Act 1996, Immigration and Asylum Act 1999, Nationality, Immigration and Asylum Act 2002, the bizarrely named Asylum and Immigration (Treatment of Claimants etc) Act 2004, and the Immigration, Asylum and Nationality Act 2006. However, although the target group is different, the themes are recognizable.

The 1993 Act introduced an appeal right for asylum seekers, but also the concept of a claim 'without foundation' (Sch 2 para 5). Again, this is based on the idea of a potential entrant as dishonest. Claims so certified would attract only limited appeal rights, the government's avowed intention being to speed through the system claims which could be identified at an early stage as unmeritorious. This provision is based not only on the idea of the deceptive applicant but also on addressing the backlog. Juss gives a stinging account of the origins of the 1993 Act in which he suggests that the problem of the backlog was self-inflicted, resulting from a recruitment freeze in the Immigration and Nationality Department (IND). Opportunities for applicants to manipulate the system arose as a result of increasing delays, and these manipulations in turn extended the delays. His account may be borne out by the fact that the backlogs were effectively tackled in the year 2000 by recruiting extra personnel in IND.

Delay and cheating the system, and the relationship between the two, became the political issues of the 1990s. The alleged cheating was both at the point of entry (the concept of the 'bogus' asylum seeker) and after entry (the concept of the 'scrounger'). These ideas underlie further provisions in the Asylum and Immigration Act 1996 such as, for instance, the creation of a new offence of obtaining leave to remain by deception (s 4). The kinds of claims that would be subjected to restricted appeal rights (known then as the short procedure) were extended to include those from a designated country of origin. Designation, according to the promoting minister in Parliament, would be on the basis that there had been a high number of applications and a high number of refusals from that particular country and that there was, in general, no serious risk of persecution in that country (HC Col 703 (11 December 1995)). This provision has a similar basis to the 'without foundation' provision, that of expediting applications on the basis that they may be identified without full examination as being unmeritorious. Similar provisions followed in the 1999 Act ('manifestly unfounded') and in the 2002 Act ('clearly unfounded'). The list of designated countries became known as the White List. It was abandoned after a successful challenge, in *R v SSHD ex p Javed and Ali* [2001] Imm AR 529, to the inclusion of Pakistan because of known widespread discrimination against women and against Ahmadis, which had been accepted in the higher courts in the UK (*Shah and Islam v IAT and SSHD* [1999] Imm AR 283 and *Ahmed (Iftikhar) v Secretary of State for the Home Department* [2000] INLR 1). Where sectors of society could be said to be at risk, it could not be reasonable to say there was, in general, no serious risk of persecution. A new 'white list' was produced in the 2002 Act and has been extended by ministerial orders.

Section 2 of the 1996 Act also introduced a power to remove asylum seekers before their appeal is heard (a 'non-suspensive appeal') if they had travelled through a country which can be regarded as a 'safe third country'. These provisions, as mentioned earlier, arose from concern in Europe about asylum seekers being 'bounced around' Europe, i.e. shuttled from one country to another, each one declining to hear their asylum application but finding a reason to return them to another member state. The UK was a signatory to the Dublin Convention, the treaty by which EC countries sought to find a way of determining which state should hear an asylum application. However, as international law, this treaty was not binding in the UK directly in tribunals. It has now been superseded by a regulation, discussed in chapter 12.

Other provisions of the 1996 Act continued the dual themes of deception and internal controls. More criminal offences were devised, targeting the racketeering of those who arrange entry to the UK for gain (s 5), and more internal controls were set up, including recruiting employers into the system of detection of residents with potentially irregular immigration status (ss 8 and 9).

The history of immigration law is full of examples of legislation swiftly introduced to reverse higher court decisions. Section 11 of the 1996 Act was one such example. The Social Security (Persons from Abroad) Miscellaneous Amendment Regulations 1996, SI 1996/30, had removed benefits from almost everyone who was subject to immigration control. The regulations were declared *ultra vires* by Simon Brown LJ because they were beyond the tolerance level of a 'civilised nation'. 'Something so uncompromisingly draconian can only be achieved by primary legislation' (*R v Secretary of State for Social Security ex p JCWI* [1997] 1 WLR 275). As Macdonald puts it: 'The government duly obliged, enacting the condemned regulation as section 11 of the 1996 Act'(2001:9).

The Immigration and Asylum Act 1999 continued the trend by, according to Statewatch, 'hugely increasing surveillance, monitoring and compulsion.' Registrars of births, marriages, and deaths were brought into the internal control system (s 24). Penalties for carrying passengers without full documentation increased once again, being extended to include trains, buses, and coaches to cover entry via the Channel Tunnel (Part II of the Act). There were also provisions for penalizing private car and lorry drivers who carried clandestine entrants. Material support for asylum seekers was converted into a voucher system and a dispersal system which would distribute asylum seekers around the country (Part VI). Appeal rights were further curtailed, both for asylum seekers and other deportees (Part IV). Limited appeal rights for family visitors were reinstated. The 1990s had seen a massive increase of asylum seekers detained in detention centres and prisons. One of the anomalous features of immigration detention generally, including that of asylum seekers, is that it is not subject to any form of supervision by the courts, and there is no presumption of a right to bail, as there is when someone is charged with a criminal offence. In the 1999 Act the government took the opportunity, partially, to address this issue by introducing a routine bail hearing (Part III). However, these provisions were never implemented, and were repealed by the Nationality, Immigration and Asylum Act 2002. The 1999 Act contained the first statutory presumptions of the safety of a third country to which an asylum seeker could be returned. This appeared to be a government reaction to having the Secretary of State's certificates of safety issued under the 1996 Act regularly struck down by the courts. In the Immigration and Asylum Act 1999, s 11, the certificates in relation to European countries were made immune to judicial review by a statutory presumption that such countries were deemed safe. This proved unassailable (R (Thangasara) v SSHD [2002] UKHL 36).

The 1999 Act was proclaimed as a radical overhaul of the immigration and asylum system. It expressed the political agenda of its day – suspicion that there is a large volume of unmeritorious asylum claims; the cost of welfare benefits obtained by people who made such claims; the progressive extension of internal controls; the problem of backlog and delay in the system both before dealing with claims and before removal from the country of those who did not succeed; and the shifting of blame to the morally more acceptable targets of 'racketeers' rather than the obviously vulnerable asylum seekers. There was another influence at the time of debates on the 1999 Act, namely, the Human Rights Act 1998 (HRA), which had received Royal Assent but was not yet in force. The 1999 Act removed some rights to have an appeal heard in the UK. The counterbalance was to provide an in-country appeal on human rights grounds. The 1999 Act provided the first statutory right of appeal against immigration decisions on human rights grounds (s 65, now in the Nationality, Immigration and Asylum Act 2002 s 84). Further discussion of the implications of the introduction of the HRA is reserved for chapter 4.

1.2.1 Twenty-first century

Four immigration statutes have been passed already in this century, in an atmosphere of 'gathering storm in relations between the executive and judicial branches in the national constitution' (Rawlings 2005:380). There have also been three terrorism statutes, one of which (Prevention of Terrorism Act 2005) consists entirely of the most severe statutory curtailment of civil liberties seen in Great Britain since wartime internment. This came into existence to replace earlier even more restrictive measures applied to foreign nationals through a misuse of immigration powers (Anti-terrorism, Crime and Security Act 2001, Part IV).

Two major cases in the House of Lords arising from the same issue were heard by chambers of nine and seven Lords respectively, indicating the constitutional importance of the matters addressed, and reasserting the place of the judiciary as protectors of fundamental constitutional values. *A and others v SSHD* [2004] UKHL 56 concerned the direct challenge to the detentions under the Anti-terrorism, Crime and Security Act 2001, and *A v SSHD* [2005] UKHL 71 the question of whether evidence which could have been obtained by torture could be used in cases before the Special Immigration Appeals Commission.

At the same time as the 2004 judgment, the government was proposing to stop all immigration and asylum issues from being heard by the courts, whether on appeal or review, by means of a far-reaching ouster clause in the Asylum and Immigration (Treatment of Claimants, etc) Bill 2003 (AITOC). Such a move was unprecedented. Rawlings refers to it as part of a 'revenge package' from a government frustrated that the judiciary continued to develop and maintain the rights of asylum seekers in the face of government attempts to restrict them (2005:378).

At the time of the passing of the 1999 Act it was widely predicted there would be another immigration statute within three years, and so it turned out (see for this point and generally McKee). The Nationality, Immigration and Asylum Act 2002 was preceded by a White Paper: *Secure Borders, Safe Haven; Integration with Diversity in Modern Britain* (Cm 5387). The publication of the White Paper was announced by Home Secretary David Blunkett in the following terms:

The White Paper takes forward our agenda by offering an holistic and comprehensive approach to nationality, managed immigration, and asylum that recognises the interrelationship of each element in the system. No longer will we treat asylum seekers in isolation or fail to recognise that there must be alternative routes to entry into this country. (HC col 1028 7 February 2002)

The Act deals with changes to nationality law, the provision of accommodation centres for asylum seekers, restrictions on the asylum support system, the provision of removal centres and expansion of powers of detention and removal, extension and amendment of the carriers' liability scheme, and the introduction of further criminal offences. At least as much as the 1999 Act, this Act was dominated by objectives concerning the asylum system.

McKee refers to 'divergent and contradictory goals', specifically:

- to keep asylum seekers out, but to provide a welcome for genuine refugees;
- to integrate refugees and ethnic minorities into mainstream British culture, but to celebrate cultural diversity;
- to include a raft of authoritarian and repressive measures under the same anodyne umbrella of 'modernisation' as liberal measures to allow economic migration and facilitate easier travel. (2002:181)

Within the broad purposes identified by McKee, the Act and the White Paper have a number of underlying policy themes which may be characterized as:

1. developing an all-pervasive control system for asylum-seekers;
2. a controlled development of the possibility of entry for work;

3. the creation of a class of people without rights or status;

4. development of extra-territorial immigration control;

5. combating terrorism; and

6. the strengthening of executive power.

Taking each of these in turn: the all-pervasive control system is an attempt to repair the damaged credibility of the asylum system, an issue discussed more fully in the next chapter. Accommodation and removal centres were elements in this development. Restrictions on welfare support which made it conditional on reporting or residence also tightened the level of continuous control that the government is able to exercise over asylum seekers. Increased powers of detention and removal served the same purpose.

The second policy underlying the 2002 White Paper was a cautious encouragement of economic migration. This was the first evidence for decades that immigration policy might be directed towards encouragement of entry, and received a general welcome. Shah, R. (2002:315), for instance, saw this as evidence of 'a new dynamism' in the Home Office. However, this apparent shift in policy was not reflected in the 2002 Act. Extensions of various schemes permitting entry of workers were implemented by concessions and developments in administrative practice which, in some cases, resulted in changes to the immigration rules. The retention of government control over entry into the UK is presaged in the White Paper, para 12: 'We have taken steps to ensure that people with the skills and talents *we need* are able to come to the UK on a sensible and managed basis' (emphasis added). The retention of control and the words emphasized lend support to the argument of Cohen that such proposals represent nothing new; rather, they replicate a historical tendency to manipulate overseas labour, 'labour which can be turned on and off like a tap' (2002). Bevan made the same comment in relation to earlier provisions (1986:278). Scepticism it seems was warranted. A further White Paper in 2005 announced a tiered system of managed migration that aims to bring entry for work and study into a more routinized, bureaucratized system, dominated by immigration control. But this is to anticipate. The growth of a class of people without rights or status is evident in a number of disparate developments, and three provisions of the 2002 Act in particular are part of that development. Section 4 substantially extended the power of the Secretary of State to deprive a person of their British nationality. In the case of people who acquired their British nationality by naturalization or registration, there is no requirement to have regard to whether doing so will leave them stateless. In the case of others, although they may not strictly speaking be left stateless, as the Joint Parliamentary Committee on Human Rights pointed out:

deprivation of British citizenship would entail loss of British diplomatic protection; loss of status; loss of the ability to participate in the democratic process in the United Kingdom; and serious damage to reputation and dignity. The Home Office argument assumes that the real threat to human rights would derive from any subsequent decisions taken as part of the immigration control process. In that process, there would usually be adequate opportunity to ensure that effect is given to Convention rights, and that other rights are given appropriate weight. However, we are concerned about the wider implications of loss of British citizenship. (Parliamentary Joint Committee on Human Rights Session 2001–02 Seventeenth Report para 26)

While recognizing that there is no right to a nationality, the Committee was concerned about the consequences of statelessness, and that if the other country refused a passport, the alternative nationality would be 'an empty shell' (para 26). The Committee's report reveals that the civic limbo in which persons would find themselves was not recognized by the Home Office. The dangers of being left in a condition of no status or rights were sadly demonstrated after the case of *Ahmed* v *Austria* 24 EHRR 62. The European Court of Human Rights decided that the applicant could not be removed from the country as this would breach his human rights. However, the Austrian government did not issue him with a residence permit, and eventually, without any support or security, Mr Ahmed took his own life.

Section 76 of the 2002 Act enables the Secretary of State to revoke a person's indefinite leave to remain if the person 'is liable to deportation but cannot be deported for legal reasons'. The legal reasons which would prevent deportation are likely to be that the person would face a serious violation of their human rights in their country of origin and no other country is willing to accept them. Without indefinite leave to remain, a person may neither work nor claim benefits. They are without status and without means.

The 2002 Bill was amended in the House of Lords so that citizenship by birth (though not by application) could only be removed in reliance on acts committed after s 4 came into force (1 April 2003). However, indefinite leave to remain may be revoked in reliance on anything done before s 76 came into force (10 February 2003) and leave granted before that date may be revoked, giving the section retrospective effect.

Finally, s 67(2) in combination with its interpretation in *R v SSHD ex p Khadir (Appellant)* [2005] UKHL 39 means that a person who is granted temporary admission – a status without rights – may remain in that position for years, even though there is no possibility of being removed (see chapter 15). The status of temporary admission, on which many asylum seekers remain for years, is a bar to rights of many kinds. The government has maintained that people on temporary admission are not 'lawfully present' for the purpose of social security rules and housing rules. Arguments on this and other issues have even led to the legal fiction that people temporarily admitted are not present at all, let alone lawfully. This has been scotched in *Szoma v Secretary of State for the Department of Work and Pensions* [2005] UKHL 64, in which their Lordships held that the appellant was lawfully present. As a consequence, he was one of a small minority of those on temporary admission who are able to claim income support.

The concern with undocumented migrants both throughout Europe and further afield is marked by this paradox. Ever-increasing control measures are developed alongside measures to exclude some people from the system altogether. The Criminal Justice and Immigration Bill contains a further power of this kind, discussed below.

The development of extra-territorial immigration control is strongly signalled in the 2002 White Paper but barely appears in the Act. Most measures taken for this purpose are administrative arrangements whose statutory support appears elsewhere (e.g. the Channel Tunnel Act 1987). They include the posting of immigration officers abroad as airline liaison officers, and alongside their counterparts at European ports. They are aimed at deterring asylum claims and in policy terms are important. To these measures could be added the extension and amendment of provisions relating to the liability of carriers (lorry drivers, rail companies, and so on) for clandestine entrants hidden in their vehicles. These developments constitute a significant change in the nature of immigration control, and are discussed fully in chapter 7.

Combating terrorism is a thread which runs throughout legislation and government policy much more strongly since 11 September 2001. The Anti-terrorism, Crime and Security Act 2001 contains significant provisions affecting refugee claims, discussed in chapter 14, but the connection with prevention of terrorism is not explicit in the Immigration Acts. There are not, for instance, sections headed 'terrorism'. Nevertheless, in the 2002 Act, the strengthened and extended border controls, the new offences created, and the intensive monitoring of asylum seekers all have security as a background theme and objective (see McKee and Shah, R. 2002). A radical interpretive provision in the 2006 Act (discussed in chapter 14) has the same objective, as did the proposals to work the Prime Minister's 2005 set of 'unacceptable behaviours' into immigration and nationality law (see chapters 3 and 16). This trend is the 'Secure Borders' aspect of the 2002 White Paper's title. More directly, as discussed in chapter 14, s 72 enables members of organizations proscribed under the Terrorism Act 2000 to be excluded from refugee status. For a discussion of the effect of the 2001 Act on immigration and asylum see Blake and Hussain, *Immigration, Asylum and Human Rights* (2003, Chapter 7).

The welfare support provisions of the 2002 Act were among its most contentious provisions. Despite research suggesting that welfare policies are not an effective deterrent (Home Office Research Study 243, 2003), the government was dedicated to a path of reducing welfare provision. As welfare support is not covered as a subject in its own right in this book, the main issues will be outlined here. The crucial provision in the 2002 Act was s 55 which provided that the Secretary of State has no obligation to provide welfare support (money or accommodation) where a claim for asylum has not been made 'as soon as reasonably practicable' unless this is necessary to avoid a breach of the claimant's human rights. Challenges to denial of benefit multiplied in the High Court. In the first year of the Act judges made over 800 emergency orders for the payment of interim benefit (Sedley LJ annual Legal Action Group lecture November 2003). After people were refused support even when they claimed asylum on the day of their arrival in the UK, the case of *R (on the application of Q) v SSHD* [2003] EWCA Civ 364 considered the meaning of s 55. The Court of Appeal accepted that the asylum seeker's circumstances should be taken into account in determining what was 'as soon as reasonably practicable' and this could include advice given by someone arranging their passage. In January 2004 the government was obliged to introduce fairer procedures and a three-day period to allow people to find their way to relevant government offices (Macdonald and Webber 2005:868).

The government still pursued to the House of Lords the question of whether actual or imminent destitution would amount to a breach of Article 3 – the right to be free of inhuman or degrading treatment. The House of Lords found that it did (*R v SSHD ex p Adam, Limbuela and Tesema* [2005] UKHL 66; see further in chapter 4). Despite the inroads which court decisions at all levels have made into the operation of s 55 the Parliamentary Joint Committee on Human Rights reiterated their concern that

the levels of homelessness and destitution which reliable evidence indicates have in practice resulted from section 55 are very likely to breach both the obligation of progressive realisation of rights under Articles 9 and 11 International Covenant on Economic Social and Cultural Rights (since they represent a regression in the protection of these rights for asylum seekers), and the obligation to ensure minimal levels of the Covenant rights to the individuals affected by section 55. (JCHR Session 2005–06 Eighth Report HL paper 104 HC 850 para 121)

Welfare support continued to be a major preoccupation in the 2004 Act. The proposal in the consultation letter which preceded the Act which provoked the most opposition was that welfare support and accommodation should be withdrawn from failed asylum seekers with families. The 1999 Act had already withdrawn support from asylum seekers whose claim had failed, but it was not thought appropriate then to inflict destitution on children. In 2003 the government had a different solution – take the children into care. Section 9 enables support to be withdrawn once a claim has failed and appeals are exhausted in a case where the Secretary of State certifies that the claimant 'has failed without reasonable excuse to take reasonable steps to leave the UK voluntarily' (s 9 of the 2004 Act, inserting para 7A into Sch 3 of the 2002 Act). Section 10 drew almost as much criticism as it enables the Secretary of State to make regulations making continuation of accommodation for a failed asylum seeker dependent upon performing community service.

The Parliamentary Joint Committee on Human Rights noted that an asylum seeker 'who has exhausted their rights of appeal, cannot return to their country for reasons beyond their control and who has no other means of support is in an analogous position to a UK citizen or any other person in the UK who is entitled to emergency state assistance to prevent destitution' (Fourteenth Report 2003–04 HL 130/HC 828 para 18). An obligation to perform community service as a condition of receiving emergency social assistance was not, as claimed by the government 'a normal civic obligation'. On the contrary, it was 'without precedent or even analogy' (para 15). There was a significant risk of breach of Article 4(2) ECHR through forced or compulsory labour (para 16). Singling out asylum seekers would breach Article 14 as it was unjustifiably discriminatory (para 21), and a withdrawal of support if someone did not perform the labour could breach Article 3 by subjecting them to inhuman and degrading treatment (para 24).

In the event, s 10 has proved impossible to implement as no community organizations could be found who were willing to provide the community service in question. The YMCA, which considered it, was persuaded to change its mind.

A similar fate may be in store for s 9. The operation of s 9 was piloted in late 2005 in East London, Manchester and West Yorkshire. Organizations representing social workers lobbied against it as their members baulked at taking asylum seekers' children into care when this would not be in the children's best interests. The Joint Committee on Human Rights considered that it would be difficult to implement s 9 without breaches of Articles 3 and 8 (Session 2003–04 Fifth Report HL Paper 35 HC 304 para 45). Reports of children's charities and refugee organizations concluded that the pilot of s 9 had caused enormous distress and destitution. Many families' support had been wrongly ended when they still had the possibility of appeals. Families were considered to be at low risk of absconding, but some did disappear when faced with the prospect of parents being separated from children (Refugee Action and Refugee Council 2006).

The Immigration, Asylum and Nationality Act 2006 contains a provision enabling the Secretary of State by order to repeal s 9. The intention was that the minister would be able to do this once the pilot study was over (HL Debs 7 Feb 2006 cols 587–8). No government report of the pilot has yet been produced, and the government is still reserving its position (Joint Committee on Human Rights, Tenth Report 2006–07, para 94). The opposition of unions, professions and civil society to the implementation of ss 9 and 10 may have neutralized these provisions.

The Bill that preceded the AITOC Act 2004 contained a clause which would have prevented all higher courts from hearing any immigration or asylum case whether by way of appeal or review. The decisions that would be affected were all those which came before the Asylum and Immigration Tribunal. These might be, for instance, refusal of a visa for a married partner to enter the UK, or a determination of free movement rights under European Union law. The government's stated reason was to streamline the appeals process and end unmeritorious appeals, but the measure contained no means of separating the meritorious from the unmeritorious, and that decision is precisely the one the courts can make. In addition to the plain injustice to foreign nationals the development of international refugee law would be denied the contribution of the British House of Lords.

There was unanimous opposition from the legal establishment. The Law Society, Bar Council, Joint Parliamentary Committee on Human Rights and senior judiciary including two former Lord Chancellors agreed the ouster clause violated the rule of law. Matrix Chambers published an opinion quoting Lord Denning: 'If tribunals were at liberty to exceed their jurisdiction without any check by courts the rule of law would be at an end' (*ex p Gilmore* [1957] 1 QB 574 at 586). The government was forced to concede, and on introducing the Bill for its second reading in the House of Lords the Lord Chancellor Lord Falconer accepted that the ouster clause could not stand (HL Debs 15 March 2004 col 51).

The Bill contained other reforms of the appeals system which, after reformulation, gained acceptance in Parliament. The principal one was collapsing the former two-tier system of immigration appeals into one. This and the other features of the new system are discussed in chapter 8.

The 2004 Act added a number of enforcement powers. It is a fairly short miscellany of mainly punitive or enforcement measures, the Bill being referred to by Lord Lester as 'mean spirited and reactionary'. (2004:263) It received Royal Assent on 22 July 2004.

In February 2005 the White Paper entitled *Controlling our Borders: Making migration work for Britain* (Cm 6472) was announced as a 'five-year strategy for asylum and immigration'. The Immigration, Asylum and Nationality Act 2006 was said to provide the legislative base for implementing the proposals, but includes fresh initiatives not raised in the White Paper; it is apparent that the White Paper is not a five-year plan in any comprehensive sense. Much of its content referred to changes that had already been agreed or made. New proposals included:

- the introduction of a points system encompassed in four tiers for all migration for work or study, privileging the most skilled and ending settlement rights for the low skilled;
- detaining more failed asylum seekers;
- giving recognized refugees only temporary leave (five years);
- abolishing appeals against work and study immigration decisions;
- increasing use of new technology and intelligence co-ordination at borders, and re-introducing exit monitoring.

Most of these did not require legislation, and the majority of the 2006 Act provisions concern tightening enforcement powers, whether through immigration officers' powers or sanctions on employers.

The most radical and far-reaching proposals of *Controlling our Borders* were those to end appeal rights and to institute a comprehensive points system for work and study. The points-based system was modelled on that of other countries, for instance Australia, in which a certain number of points are required to gain entry, and these are gained for qualifications and other characteristics such as age, available money, and so on. Once published the points-based system consisted of five tiers to encompass all routes to entry for work and study. The vision promoted by the government was of a routinized system, with applications beginning with an online self-assessment form for the applicant to check whether they would qualify for entry. As each tier comes into effect, appeal rights for that tier will be removed (BIA Highly Skilled Migrants under the Points Based System: Statement of Intent 2007). All applications to enter for work will be made at overseas posts instead of through the current specialized system at Work Permits (UK) (see chapter 11). There will be no appeal against refusal for entry clearance for any purpose except family-related applications. The first stage of implementation, for highly skilled people, is due to start in March 2008. The five-tier system is discussed in chapter 11.

The right of appeal for visitors was removed by the 1993 Act, but s 4 of the 2006 Act is a far more radical step. It removes the right of appeal against refusal of entry clearance in all but specified visitor and dependant cases. Those who will retain the right of appeal are not defined in the statute but will be by regulations and will include family visitors. The new system will encompass students and all those who apply under the rules for reasons such as religious ministry, self-employment, or working holidays. The change is potentially enormous. There was advance warning of this in relation to students and work permit holders in the five-year strategy document, and a swell of opposition ensued, including from University Vice Chancellors and Principals (letter from Universities UK to Financial Times, Tuesday, 5 July 2005) but to no avail.

The government regards appeal rights as less important in the future because of the claimed quality of the new points system. In its briefing to the House of Lords Committee Stage of the Bill, ILPA quoted the then Shadow Home Secretary Rt. Hon. Tony Blair, MP, during the passage of the Asylum and Immigration Appeals Act 1993:

When a right of appeal is removed, what is removed is a valuable and necessary constraint on those who exercise original jurisdiction. That is true not merely of immigration officers but of anybody. The immigration officer who knows that his decision may be subject to appeal is likely to be a good deal more circumspect, careful and even handed than the officer who knows that his power of decision is absolute. That is simply, I fear, a matter of human nature, quite apart from anything else. (Commons Hansard, vol 213, col 43, 2.11.92)

The five-tier system extends the policy of end-to-end monitoring to all who enter for work and study. A key feature of the system is 'compliance checking': this involves checking with sponsors that migrants are here and are doing what their terms of entry permitted them to do, and checking on whether people have left the UK at the end of their permitted period of stay. Educational institutions will become sponsors of overseas students, and employers of their employees.

In the meantime, entry for work became less welcome after all. Romanian and Bulgarian workers are given more limited rights to work than A8 nationals, and the terms of entry for medical graduates and highly skilled workers were dramatically restricted during 2006 (see chapters 2 and 11). Families once again came under the government spotlight, as a certificate of approval scheme was introduced for marriages of foreign nationals (see chapter 9), and proposals issued to raise the age for marriage once again and introduce language testing for spouses.

The 2006 Act, in addition to removing rights of appeal as mentioned above, develops the provisions for information exchange between carriers and immigration control personnel, including a power for the Secretary of State or an immigration officer to compel disclosure to them of passenger lists. This is an element in the development of 'exporting the border', as introduced in the 2002 White Paper. The Act's other miscellaneous provisions are enforcement oriented, including a provision which makes it far easier to exclude people charged with terrorist-related offences from the protection of the Refugee Convention (s 54). As discussed above, the 2002 Act made it possible for the first time for people to lose British nationality acquired by birth or parentage. The 2006 Act made the grounds for this substantially easier, equating them with the grounds for deportation – simply that the deprivation of nationality was 'conducive to the public good' (s 56).

Continuing the control theme, *Controlling our Borders* introduced a 'new asylum model' (NAM), an administrative system designed to streamline applications and make greater use of detention. Two induction centres are already in place. The accommodation centres proposed in the 2002 Act did not prove viable, and this is another attempt to process as many asylum claims as possible while keeping the claimant in some form of detention or controlled accommodation. The NAM is in place for all new asylum decisions from March 2007 onwards. Its workings are discussed further in chapter 12. In tandem with the NAM, in July 2006 the Home Office announced that there was a 'legacy' of 450,000 cases that were outstanding and would not come within the NAM, and they undertook to clear this backlog within five years. A directorate has been set up within the Home Office to be proactive in achieving this. A case will be considered to have been concluded when the individual has left the UK or been granted leave to remain.

In parallel with the passage of the 2006 Act through Parliament the Home Affairs Committee was conducting an inquiry into immigration control. A number of the current reforms may be traced to their report. Perhaps their main message was that the immigration system was stuck in the era of seeing itself, and being seen, as concerned with preventing entry. The focus now needed to be different. Two aspects were important: facilitation of legitimate travel; and control of immigration after arrival in the country. When people's leave to remain expired, the government should be aware of that and able to act on it.

Also in 2006 the Home Office instituted a root and branch review of the immigration system, following the disclosure that foreign prisoners had been released without being considered for deportation. Although this was the trigger for the review, in fact it resulted in a programme of far-reaching reforms which is still ongoing. The major ones are discussed in the next chapter. An independent inspectorate has been set up, replacing some of the existing monitor roles. Most of the reforms did not need primary legislation, but the UK Borders Act 2007 was enacted to deal with some that did, and to introduce a scheme of biometric identity documents for foreign nationals.

Sections 5 to15 provide that any non-EEA national in the UK, whether lawfully resident or not, may be required to apply for a 'biometric immigration document'. This means any kind of document recording external physical characteristics including in particular fingerprints, features of the iris and digital photographs which may be scanned by facial recognition technology. Exactly who *is* required to apply for these documents is to be specified by the Secretary of State in regulations. The Secretary of State therefore has the power to determine whether these provisions apply to people with settled status, and could for instance require applications by people who are in the UK on a work permit, or as students, or applying for asylum. This is a precursor to the government's plan to introduce identity cards for all, for which the statutory framework was laid down in the Identity Cards Act 2006.

Section 19 removes the right to introduce new documentary evidence at appeals against a refusal to vary leave under the points-based system. This seems to be related to the Home Affairs Committee's point that an appeal was not the place to be considering documents that should have been submitted at the outset.

The 2007 Act introduces automatic deportation for those who have committed certain criminal offences (ss 32–39). Although the Home Affairs Committee endorsed this idea for 'serious criminals', it may be doubted whether all those caught by this provision could really be described as such (see chapter 16 for discussion). A further provision in the Criminal Justice and Immigration Bill 2007 removes all status from people who cannot be deported for legal reasons. This is to prevent the government from being obliged to give a protective status to people who have been convicted of a criminal offence, but cannot be returned to their home country because of feared human rights abuses. They will not be removed, but will be able to be kept in the UK without any right to claim any social benefits or to work. Despite this, the Bill also provides for powers to restrict their residence and work, and for electronic tagging. It seems that this is some steps short of the house arrest introduced under the Prevention of Terrorism Act's control orders, but more oppressive than mere temporary admission. It is another example of the government legislating to overturn a decision of the courts, this time the decision in the Afghan hijackers' case, discussed in chapters 2 and 8.

The 2006 Act gave increased powers of arrest to immigration officers. The 2007 Act gave them increased powers of detention. The 2006 Act created a duty for immigration, revenue and customs officers to share information. These steps contribute to the creation of the unified border force, announced by the Prime Minister in July 2007. This is a major new development in immigration control. Collaboration now seems to be the new direction, not only in the creation of a unified border force but also in the development of in-country immigration control. It is marked by an intensification of the engagement of many other governmental and non-governmental bodies in the business of 'migration management'. It looks as though, by the end of 2008, immigration control will be an intelligence-led, bureaucratic process, which might impact upon a foreign national in the UK at any point in life, and which will be experienced also outside the UK as a technologically dominated bureaucracy.

1.3 Sources of immigration law

There is no doubt that immigration control is an exercise of executive power; that is, it is exercised by the executive arm of government, in this case principally by the Home Secretary, Home Office civil servants, immigration officers, and entry clearance officers. Less clear are the source and limits of that power. Immigration law is, in a sense, all about the exercise of executive power and the limits upon it. A characteristic that will be encountered over and over again in the study of immigration law is the retention of discretion, which of course is less amenable to control than the application of specific rules. The discretionary nature of immigration law is at the root of much of the criticism that has been directed at it. While challenges to decisions and initiatives towards accountability and openness seek to put limits on the power of the executive, in other ways the scope to use discretion is continually reasserted. In order to ascertain the extent to which decisions can be challenged, it is necessary to consider the source of the power which is exercised. A purely statutory power is subject to public law constraints and the exercise of appeal rights; something with a more nebulous origin may be harder to control. So we will begin with that question – where does it come from?

1.3.1 **Prerogative origins?**

The right of nation states to control the entry and expulsion of foreign nationals is often said to be an essential aspect of sovereignty, which some regard as exercised under the prerogative (e.g. Glossop 2007). The prerogative was originally the power of the crown. The Bill of Rights 1689 decreed that the prerogative could not be extended any further and that statute could supersede the prerogative. From this time on, the prerogative had a residual character (see, for instance, Loveland, *Constitutional Law; Administrative Law and Human Rights: A Critical Introduction* 2003). In the present day, relevant prerogatives, if any, are at the disposal of the government, which now holds the authority of the crown for most purposes. There are personal prerogatives of the monarch such as dispensing certain honours, but we are not concerned with these.

The present extent of the prerogative has been a matter of argument even in quite recent times. In *R v Secretary of State ex p Northumbria Police Authority* [1989] QB 26, the Court of Appeal found that there was a prerogative to keep the peace even though it had not been written down anywhere. However, Vincenzi argues that there are specific recognized areas of prerogative power, not an amorphous pool which could be used for purposes convenient to the government (1992:300). Following *CCSU v Minister for the Civil Service* [1985] AC 374 (the GCHQ case) in which the House of Lords decided that the exercise of the prerogative was reviewable, a number of prerogative powers have been considered, and the reviewability of each decided as a separate question (see, e.g. *R v Secretary of State for Foreign and Commonwealth Affairs ex p Everett* [1989] QB 811 CA, *R v SSHD ex p Bentley* [1993] 4 All ER 442). This seems to support Vincenzi's argument. Indeed this approach seems to flow from Lord Diplock's list in the GCHQ case of potentially non-reviewable prerogative powers, and the question was not resolved in *ex p Northumbria Police Authority*.

Those prerogative powers which have been identified include matters such as the conduct of foreign affairs, the power to conduct the internal affairs of the civil service, and the issue of passports (Vincenzi, *Crown Powers, Subjects and Citizens* (1998)). It would be a brave person now who suggested that there was a major prerogative power left undiscovered, and in the area of immigration control it is reasonable to assume that whatever prerogative power exists is known about. Chapter 4 of Vincenzi's book explores the relationship between the prerogative and immigration control, and reference should be made to that for a full account. All the authorities agree that there is a prerogative power to deal with aliens, but there is disagreement over the extent of that power.

Immigration control in the UK is now largely governed by statute and immigration rules made pursuant to the statutory duty to do so (Immigration Act 1971 s 3(2)). The Immigration Act 1971, however, expressly reserves a prerogative power in mysterious terms: 'This Act shall not be taken to supersede or impair any power exercisable by Her Majesty in relation to aliens by virtue of her prerogative' (s 33(5)). In its reference only to aliens, the subsection conforms with the established view that the prerogative does not apply to those who owe allegiance to the Crown, that is, British and Commonwealth citizens (*DPP v Bhagwan* [1972] AC 60 and *R v IAT ex p Secretary of State for the Home Department* [1990] 3 All ER 652). However, what power over aliens does the section reserve? The whole Act and all subsequent immigration statutes, deal with those who are subject to immigration control. If there was a prerogative of immigration control, this would, as a normal rule, be in abeyance to the extent of the statutory power (*AG v de Keyser's Royal Hotel Ltd* [1920] AC 508). It would be both superseded and impaired. Section 33(5) is not thought to displace this rule. Immigration control is exercised pursuant to the statute and rules as indeed the rule of law requires. It is not empowered by a mysterious source which somehow lurks behind the rules. Vincenzi suggests that the only non-contentious prerogative in relation to aliens is to imprison enemy aliens, that is, nationals of those countries with whom the UK is at war. Macdonald in his 5th edition (2001:708) suggested there was a power to deport, and as we have seen, Edward and Elizabeth I behaved as though they thought so. However, this was in relation to aliens regarded as enemies, not those regarded as friends. In the 6th edition Macdonald has revised his views (2005:3) and, following the work of Shah and Vincenzi, adopts the view that there was no distinction in common law between the rights of subjects and friendly aliens. The first appearance of a reservation of a prerogative power was in the Aliens Restriction Act 1914, which, at a time of war, can be taken to have been referring to enemy aliens.

There is undoubtedly a power to make immigration decisions outside the immigration rules, but this can more simply derive from the powers in the statute to give or refuse leave to enter or remain (the Immigration Act 1971 ss 3A, 3B and 4), and there is no need to employ the prerogative as an explanation (Macdonald 1995:41). Glidewell LJ in *R v Secretary of State for the Home Department ex p Rajinder Kaur* [1987] Imm AR 278 took the view that this power to make decisions outside the rules is derived from the prerogative. However that case concerned a Commonwealth citizen, and Glidewell LJ cannot have been right in this. Vincenzi argues that immigration control cannot be a prerogative power because the concept of immigration control is a modern one, originating in the Aliens Act 1905. The prerogative, as we have seen, could not be extended after 1689.

If immigration control is seen as a 'prerogative power clothed in statute', its amenability to regulation is that much less. If it is seen as a purely statutory power, it must be exercised in accordance with the power granted by that statute and in accordance with principles of statutory interpretation, and not otherwise. Evans notes:

The reluctance of the courts to challenge the Executive's exercise of statutory powers on matters touching national security may also have been influenced by the Crown's claim that the exclusion and expulsion of aliens were within its prerogative, the scope of which was never definitely established, but which still maintains a shadowy existence alongside immigration control. (1983:422–3)

The conclusion here is that it is unlikely that the prerogative is the source of immigration control, but there has been a tendency in the courts and executive to treat it as though it was. This has enabled them to call upon a supposed reserve of undefined power to supplement explicit provisions.

1.3.1.1 *A modern equivalent?*

It is perhaps less likely now that inexplicable discretion will be attributed to the prerogative (though see chapter 11 for a theory of work permits), but there is a tendency to see behind immigration control, not the prerogative, but two other principles: sovereignty and the judgment of the executive. The first is explanatory and the second is justificatory.

Sovereignty in dealing with foreign nationals is curtailed by treaties to which the state is a party such as, in the UK's case, the European Convention on Human Rights and the 1951 UN Convention Relating to Refugees. In the age of internationalism, globalization, the development of international human rights norms, and an international criminal court, the nation state can no longer be properly regarded as the ultimate legal authority. It is well recognized that national legal authority must now be tempered by regard for international law, and that international regulation is a fact of life.

Ironically, it is through the Human Rights Act 1998, bringing the rights of the European Convention into UK law, that the idea of sovereignty seems to be making something of a comeback. In immigration cases in the ECHR, the court routinely begins its reasoning with the statement that states have the right, as a recognized principle of international law, and subject to their treaty obligations, to control the entry of non-nationals (see *Abdulaziz Cabales and Balkandali* (1985) 7 EHRR 471 para 67). This statement has an understandable place in the judgment of an international court, but has been transposed into the UK courts' and tribunals' reasoning in human rights cases. It is not inaccurate, but is unnecessary in the national context, where the task of the decision-maker is to apply and interpret law which is already made by the sovereign law-maker (Parliament) or is of a lesser status (immigration rules) or is case law which arises or can be argued to have a place in the jurisdiction. Sovereignty, if it arises at all, is being exercised, not challenged, and the reiteration of it in national courts has an effect similar to that noted by Evans in relation to the prerogative. This was demonstrated in *R v SSHD ex p Saadi, Maged, Osman and Mohammed* [2002] 1 WLR 3131, HL, in which the principle of sovereignty prevailed over human rights (see chapter 15). As Dauvergne comments, 'Migration law is transformed into the new last bastion of sovereignty' (2004:588), and correspondingly, sovereignty is invoked to buttress the state's right to control migration. A number of writers now argue that the territorial notion of sovereignty is also breaking down (e.g. Thomas and Kostakopoulou, Dauvergne), and that sovereignty is now exercised over people and information more than over territory. The shift in the UK's border control strategy could be argued to demonstrate just that.

Deference to the judgment of the executive no longer has the hold on case law that it had in the early days of the Human Rights Act, but is still sometimes asserted or implicit. The basic idea is that immigration control is a matter within the remit of the executive, so the judiciary should be reluctant to interfere with their judgment. This argument gained in importance as the courts and tribunals began to explore the application of qualified rights under the Human Rights Act, which require the decision-maker to judge the proportionality of the harm done to the individual against the public interest served. For instance, to remove someone from the country who is in breach of immigration law serves certain public interests but interferes with the individual's right to respect for their family and private life. This judgment involves the courts and tribunals in judging the merits of the case, and deference to the executive was argued to restrain the judiciary in this new role. This issue is discussed further in chapter 8. Current authority is that the idea of deference has been overused, and that it is not really a proper constitutional principle at all (*Huang and Kashmiri v SSHD* [2007] UKHL 11). The judiciary are competent to decide whether in a particular case they should give special weight to the Secretary of State's judgment or not. The existence, extent, and nature of this principle has been a subject of extensive debate in academic writing and judicial decisions. To argue for deference is not the same thing as to argue for a prerogative power, but the effect may be similar in that, in both instances, it is posited that there is an area of exercise of judgment which is somehow the special preserve of the government. For instance, in the case of indefinite detentions of foreign nationals the Court of Appeal deferred to the judgment of the executive that discrimination on grounds of nationality was necessary for security reasons (*A v SSHD* [2002] EWCA Civ 1502). In the House of Lords, Lord Bingham in particular set out the UK's obligations under international treaties as an important part of the reasons why this deference was not warranted (*A v SSHD* [2004] UKHL 56).

The prerogative is not a source to which there can be fresh recourse, whatever view is taken of its earlier extent. The search for a deeper principle continues, however, and part of the present debate is a re-examination of the rule of law (see e.g. Dauvergne; Harvey C. 2005; Poole; Bingham 2007 for a range of views).

1.3.2 Statutory origins

For the avoidance of doubt, the present-day legal source of the power of immigration control is statutory. The main statutes are the Immigration Act 1971, the Immigration and Asylum Act 1999, the Nationality, Immigration and Asylum Act 2002, the Asylum and Immigration (Treatment of Claimants etc) Act 2004, and the Immigration, Asylum and Nationality Act 2006, supplemented by the UK Borders Act 2007. All of these have been discussed above.

The fundamental legal authority for the power to control immigration is found in the Immigration Act 1971 s 4(1), which says:

The power under this Act to give or refuse leave to enter the United Kingdom shall be exercised by immigration officers, and the power to give leave to remain in the United Kingdom, or to vary any leave under section 3(3)(a) (whether as regards duration or conditions), shall be exercised by the Secretary of State.

Perhaps surprisingly, the statutes contain none of the specific provisions which govern whether a person may gain entry to the UK or leave to remain, although they do contain the basic grounds upon which they may be required to leave. The requirements to be met to gain entry or leave to remain are contained mainly in the immigration rules.

Immigration Act 1971, s 1(4) contains the only requirement as to their content, which is also the only statutory provision for content of entry requirements. They must

include provision for admitting (in such cases and subject to such restrictions as may be provided by the rules ...) persons coming for the purpose of taking employment, or for the purposes of study, or as visitors, or as dependants of persons lawfully in or entering the UK.

Section 3(2) provides that this

shall not be taken to require uniform provision to be made by the rules as regards admission of persons for a purpose or in a capacity specified in section 1(4) (and in particular, for this as well as other purposes of this Act, account may be taken of citizenship or nationality).

The rules are now voluminous and run into several hundreds. (Numbering stops at 395 but this is not indicative as many are divided into sub-rules: A to K and so on.) They were last consolidated in 1994, and are frequently amended in major or minor respects. The rules govern almost all immigration cases and also have an impact on asylum cases. They therefore contain the practical substance of immigration law.

1.3.3 Immigration rules

On reading the rules it is apparent that they are the language of the administrator rather than the lawyer. They are practical and descriptive, stating what action should be taken in given sets of circumstances. This being the case, they should not be treated as a legal text in the English tradition, namely as language which has been created with great precision and therefore must be interpreted strictly. The accepted approach (*Alexander v IAT* [1982] 2 All ER 766) to interpretation is:

These Rules are not to be construed with all the strictness applicable to the construction of a statute or a statutory instrument. They must be construed sensibly according to the natural meaning of the language which is employed (para 11).

The rules have become more specific over the years. They have also become more and more comprehensive, as matters formerly dealt with by concessions and policies are absorbed into the rules. However, the Home Affairs Committee has called for their redrafting and consolidation 'to provide a clear, comprehensive and realistic framework for decisions'. The Committee considered that they fall short of this currently, as they 'present a list of issues to be addressed rather than a list of criteria which you might or might not meet'. They also include a number of what might be called 'subjective' tests of intentionality (Fifth Report 2005–06).

The Committee also recognized that the rules will also require an exercise of judgment and, even if redrafted, it is unlikely that they could be applied mechanistically. As they currently stand there is considerable scope for judgment as to whether specified criteria are met, for instance whether maintenance for a spouse is adequate and the couple intend to live together as husband and wife. This is not a discretion in a pure sense, but it is a matter on which an entry clearance officer and an applicant could disagree. Consider, by way of comparison, an application for a welfare benefit. If the claimant's income is less than the applicable amount, the benefit must be paid. There might be a question about whether all assets have been disclosed, but on a given set of figures there is no judgment to be made: the claimant has an entitlement. In the event of being turned down for entry clearance, applicants cannot point to the rules and say 'you are wrong – I am entitled to entry clearance'; they can only argue about the strength of their evidence and the conclusions to be drawn from it.

This predictability or otherwise of decisions based on the rules will become even more significant under the new points-based system. The Home Affairs Committee report casts doubt on whether it will ever be possible to apply the rules in the routinized way upon which the government relies as a guarantee of the quality that would justify removing rights of appeal. The status of the immigration rules has been a subject of much legal argument. For most purposes there is no doubt that they are not subordinate legislation. They are made by the minister pursuant to a statutory duty to do so, and are subject to the negative resolution procedure in Parliament. In these respects they resemble delegated legislation. However, s 3(2) describes them as 'rules...to be followed in the administration of this Act', and this is how they have been regarded in case law. *Pearson v IAT* [1978] Imm AR 212 remains the authority that the Rules are not delegated legislation or rules of law, but rules of practice for the guidance of those who administer the Act. Despite this, the rules have a status well beyond that of normal administrative guidelines. *Pearson* also found that the rules, while not rules of law, have the force of law. Previous statutes provided that an adjudicator 'must allow an appeal if he considers that the decision or action against which the appeal is brought was not in accordance with the law or any immigration rules applicable to the case' (Immigration Act 1971 s 19 and Immigration and Asylum Act 1999 Sch 4 para 21). The current equivalent provision is differently phrased. The appeal must be allowed if the decision 'is not in accordance with the law (including immigration rules)' (Nationality, Immigration and Asylum Act 2002 s 86(3)(a)). This seems to represent a shift towards recognizing the rules as a form of law. In either form of words the immigration rules are treated by statute as though they have binding force. In ascertaining what is the law relating to a given situation, for instance, to discover whether an aged mother will be permitted to join her daughter in the UK, the first place to look is the rules. They provide the basic content of legal entitlement, even if they are not themselves of a legal character.

The rules are made by the minister, subject to the negative resolution procedure. They are therefore subject only to very limited parliamentary scrutiny, and if Parliament wants to reject them it must reject the rules as a whole: there is no provision for amendment. This has happened on very few occasions, the most notable perhaps being in December 1982 (HC col 355 15 December 1982) when the Labour Party opposition succeeded in defeating the Conservative government's proposed new marriage rules. These would have introduced a burden on the applicant to show that the marriage was genuine (later introduced anyway) and a two-year probationary period (defeated on that occasion but introduced on 1 April 2003 without parliamentary debate). In *Huang and Kashmiri v SSHD* [2007] UKHL 11 the House of Lords rejected an argument that the negative resolution procedure meant that the immigration rules were the product of democratic debate and compromise. The immigration rules are 'not the product of active debate in Parliament, where non-nationals seeking leave to enter or remain are not in any event represented' (para 17). This latter point was a rare, perhaps unique, instance of the judiciary noting that those most affected by the immigration rules have no say in their content.

Even though the rules are subject only to a limited parliamentary scrutiny they are subject to challenge by way of judicial review. The duty to make the rules is derived from statute, and so the minister cannot achieve by the rules anything which is outside the powers given in the Act. The rules are therefore in theory subject to challenge on the grounds of illegality, irrationality, and procedural impropriety (following Lord Diplock's classification in *CCSU v Minister for the Civil Service* [1985] AC 374). Unsuccessful attempts have been made to challenge the rules on the basis that they fetter discretion, this being an aspect of illegality (*R v Secretary of State for the Home Department ex p Rajinder Kaur* [1987] Imm AR 278). For the purpose of a challenge for irrationality, the rules are treated like by-laws, and so may only be struck down if they are 'impartial or unequal in their operation as between classes; manifestly unjust; made in bad faith; or involving such oppressive or gratuitous interference with the rights of those subject to them as could find no justification in the minds of reasonable persons' (*Kruse v Johnson* [1898] 2 QB 91). This has succeeded on one occasion, when the rule on admission of family dependants was challenged for its requirement that the elderly dependent relative, in order to gain entry, must be living at a standard substantially below that in their country. This discriminated against applicants in poor countries, for whom even a small amount of financial help would lift their standard of living above a low level for their country (*R v IAT ex p Manshoora Begum* [1986] Imm AR 385).

The rules are now also subject to challenge on a further ground of illegality, namely that the minister in making them has acted unlawfully under s 6 HRA as the rules breach Convention rights. On and after 2 October 2000 there has been a trend towards removing discrimination from the rules, presumably to avoid such challenges. The rules are also subject to directly applicable EC law, and in *The Queen on the application of Ezgi Payir* [2005] EWHC 1426 (Admin) the High Court made a declaration that rr 92–94 were unlawful insofar as they purported to exclude the right to an extension of stay for a Turkish au pair, contrary to Article 6 of Decision 1/80 of the Council of the

Association between the EU and Turkey. This outcome was upheld on a preliminary reference to the ECJ (Case C-294/06).

Although for most purposes the rules are not regarded as subordinate legislation, they may be for the purposes of the Human Rights Act. The Act defines subordinate legislation in s 21(1) as including 'rules...made under primary legislation'. It appears that this includes the immigration rules, and so the interpretive duty in HRA s 3 will apply. Even without this, those who implement the rules are public authorities under s 6 and their actions must be in accordance with the Convention. In effect, immigration rules must be applied in a way that upholds Convention rights; the only relevance of their being subordinate legislation would be if to uphold rights requires a strained construction of the rules. Section 3 would require this of subordinate legislation, but s 6 may not require it of a public body. Ultimately, as discussed above, if the rule conflicts with rights and cannot be interpreted by whatever means so as to deliver the rights, it may be struck down as being made in breach of s 6.

The judgment in *Huang* referred to above confirmed that not only are they not the fruit of democratic debate, the immigration rules also do not already embody human rights standards. The consideration of a human rights claim begins once an applicant has failed under the rules. Human rights standards are additional to the rules, which, as previously discussed, are simply guidance in the administration of the powers to grant and refuse leave to enter or remain.

1.3.4 **Policies and concessions**

Internal government instructions are highly influential in the implementation of immigration law as they guide immigration officers and Home Office officials in their response to individual cases. These may be of a formal or informal kind. Mention has already been made of the exclusion of black passport holders from the UK by means of internal government instructions which accompanied the Commonwealth Immigrants Act 1962. These, of course, were not the kind of instructions to which the public would have access. The secrecy which was a hallmark of immigration law has changed in recent years, and the body of internal instructions is now disclosed on the Home Office website. Internal instructions as they now exist may be divided into three kinds.

First, there are policy documents which give guidance on the exercise of a discretion. An example is DP3/96, a policy document which sets out situations when it will and will not be appropriate to exercise powers of removal and deportation in relation to people who have families in the UK. It is not comprehensive but it is far more detailed than the statute. The criteria for immigration detention are found entirely in guidance documents of this kind, disclosed on the IND website in the Operational Enforcement Manual.

Second, there is guidance on the application of the immigration rules. There is a comprehensive code of guidance on the application of the immigration rules known as the Immigration Directorate Instructions (IDIs). There is another for dealing with asylum claims, the Asylum Policy Instructions (APIs), which include summaries of the relevant law, and Nationality Instructions (NIs) which give similar guidance for dealing with nationality applications. Also published are notices given at intervals: Asylum Policy Updates, and Asylum Process Guidance. Frequent reference is made to relevant instructions throughout this book. They are a practical guide to how discretion is exercised.

Third, there are various kinds of concessions. One of the features of immigration law is the extent of provision which has been contained in discretionary practices outside the rules. Although the rules have become more and more comprehensive, they still do not cover every eventuality. In relation to some situations commonly encountered, there is standard practice which is known as a concession. Some concessions have been established for many years but never integrated into the immigration rules. An example of this was the grant of indefinite leave to remain to a person who attains refugee status. This had the appearance of established rule, as it was invariable practice for some years, but when practice was changed in August 2005, this could be done simply by an announcement. Such announcements may be given for instance by notice on the IND website, in Parliament, by letter to interested organizations.

Some concessions are announced in Parliament and devised in terms as detailed as an immigration rule. Examples here have been a concession for entry of unmarried partners, which was announced in Parliament on 10 October 1997 and a concession for spouses subject to domestic violence to obtain indefinite leave to remain, announced in Parliament on 16 June 1999. In these cases the concessions had the appearance of trial rules. They were both amended by later statements in Parliament, following representations about how they operated in practice (17 June 1999 and 26 November 2002 respectively), and incorporated into the immigration rules. The first of these two provisions raises issues of equality of treatment between married and unmarried and between heterosexual and homosexual couples. Strong and conflicting opinions are held about these questions, and it appears that the government was seeking a politically viable rule by experiment in order to achieve some level of equality by 2 October 2000 when the Human Rights Act came into force, though it has since been amended more than once. The trend is for concessions to be incorporated into the rules, and there is a long-term project to incorporate all concessions into a set of consolidated rules.

There are also temporary concessions directed towards periods of upheaval or emergency. An example of such a concession was the Home Office decision in July 1999 temporarily to suspend the return to the Republic of Congo of asylum seekers whose applications had been rejected, because of the civil war. Concessions may also be given in the form of procedural waivers where hardship would arise if strict procedure were insisted upon. For example, following the Humanitarian Evacuation Programme from Kosovo, Kosovan families in Britain were required to travel to Croydon for an asylum screening interview. This involved whole families, who were surviving on minimal resources, paying fares for transport and travelling perhaps with ill family members or small children. In June 2000 the Home Office decided that it would be sufficient for only the principal applicant to attend the asylum screening interview providing certain conditions were met.

What all these forms of guidance have in common is that if an individual comes within their terms they can expect to be treated in accordance with the policy. This may be enforced, depending on circumstances, either by appeal or judicial review, and these forms of redress are discussed in chapter 8. *R v SSHD ex p Amankwah* [1994] Imm AR 240 was the first case which held that if the policy was undisclosed, but its existence was known, then a decision which did not take the policy properly into account was unreasonable and unfair. The existence of a policy on marriage and deportation had become known by accident, having been referred to in a Home Office letter in a previous case.

Since then, policies have been gradually disclosed. At first, selected documents were sent to practitioner organizations. Now the majority of internal instructions of substance are available on the Home Office website. Much of the substantive detail is contained in annexes to IDIs, APIs and NIs, but the majority of these too are disclosed. In 2003 the government took the further step of putting on the website parts of the Operational Enforcement Manual which deals with detention and removal.

Now it is clear that the Home Office should apply the policy in a relevant case even if the individual is unaware of it (*SSHD v the Queen on the application of Rashid* [2005] EWCA Civ 744).

There may still be a question as to which version of a policy applies in a particular case. While policies and instructions are increasingly disclosed, there is also a growing tendency to no longer disclose their date. In *R (on the application of I and O) v SSHD* [2005] EWHC 1025 (Admin) the Home Office was unable to provide the exact date when a policy came into effect, though Owen J accepted an assurance that there was no material difference from the earlier policy (para 21).

Individual exceptions may be made, and as Macdonald describes (1995: 44–5), may become established concessions as the compassionate circumstances which led to their first being recognized are replicated in other cases. An established concession is a stronger basis from which to argue, as is apparent from the above, but if there is no such concession available it is possible to argue that the particular circumstances of the case warrant more lenient treatment than the rules seem to provide. Both the Home Office and immigration officers do on occasion agree to act more leniently than the rules provide. The source of this power has been discussed above, and is the Immigration Act 1971, not the prerogative.

1.3.5 Tribunal decisions

A specialist source of law in the immigration and asylum field is the body of case law emanating from what is now the Asylum and Immigration Tribunal (AIT). The structure of the tribunal and grounds of appeal to it are discussed more fully in chapter 8. Here we simply consider tribunal decisions as a source of law.

Recent studies by Buck (2006) and Thomas (2005) examine the unique phenomenon of the AIT and its case law. The early idea of tribunals, as fact-finding bodies which were somehow closer to the people and the facts than the courts could be, is a misleading picture of the AIT. Its characteristics are described by Thomas as: high volume; fact-based; compulsory (in that claimants have little alternative); no compromise is possible; serving public interest; not bound by usual rules of evidence; and an exceptionally high rate of challenge.

Buck notes that the intention of tribunal case law was that it would not be binding in the way that the decisions of higher courts are. Wade and Forsyth say that the tribunal's duty is to reach the 'right decision in the circumstances of the moment' (p 931). However, like other tribunals, the AIT has devised its own system of precedent and authority. There is a starring system, whereby the President may decide to designate certain tribunal decisions binding on certain issues. Although they are fact-finding tribunals, their decisions are often intricate works of legal reasoning, and sometimes run to scores of pages. Buck notes that, like courts, they apply 'concrete legal rules to facts' (p 464). Their decisions are not all reported, and there is now a practice direction which prevents unreported cases from being cited in tribunals except in defined circumstances. There is a system of factual precedents called country guidance cases, discussed in chapter 12.

Tribunal decisions may be accessed on the AIT website (www.ait.gov.uk) and by searching on www.bailii.org or the membership database of www.ein.org.uk.

1.4 Conclusion

Whether the focus of attention is the Jews in the nineteenth century, West Indians in the 1960s, East African Asians in the 1970s, or more recently asylum seekers, immigration legislation is passed with a target group in mind. The political agenda of the day moulds the law in a very direct way. The current targets probably fall into two: the illegally resident population, and terrorists. The first is a diverse group of people not abroad, but present in the UK, and mainly unaccounted for. The same could perhaps be said of the second group. The result is a concentration on security and the dissemination of points of immigration control through many aspects of life. Another key present aim, to regularize entry for work, can be met in the course of this.

QUESTIONS

1 What further themes can you identify arising from the history and development of immigration law? Are these the same as the ones identified by Bevan in 1986?

2 Are there any other mechanisms of democratic accountability that could or should be introduced into the process of dealing with immigration? Is it a matter for the government or the people?

3 Given the use and origin of the immigration rules, it appears that the Secretary of State both makes and implements much of immigration law. Is this a problem?

 online resource centre For guidance on answering questions, visit www.oxfordtextbooks.co.uk/orc/clayton3e.

FURTHER READING

Bevan, V. (1986) *The Development of British Immigration Law* (Beckenham: Croom Helm).

Bingham, Lord 'The Rule of Law' *Cambridge Law Journal* (2007) 66, pp. 67–85.

Carter, B., Harris, C., Joshi, S., *The 1951–55 Conservative Government and the Racialisation of Black Immigration* [1987] Policy Papers in Ethnic Relations no. 11 CREC.

Cohen, S., Humphries, B., and Mynott, E. (eds) (2002) *From Immigration Controls to Welfare Controls* (London: Routledge).

—— (2000) 'Never mind the racism...feel the quality' *Immigration and Nationality Law and Practice* vol. 14, no. 4, pp. 223–226.

Dauvergne, C. (2004) 'Sovereignty, Migration and the Rule of Law in Global Times' *Modern Law Review* vol. 67, no. 4, pp. 588–615.

Dummett, A. and Nicol, A. (1990) *Subjects, Citizens, Aliens and Others* (London: Weidenfeld and Nicolson).

Fryer, P. (1984) *Staying Power: The History of Black People in Britain* (London: Pluto).

Gillespie, J. 'Asylum and Immigration Act 1996: an outline of the new law' *Immigration and Nationality Law and Practice* vol. 10, no. 3, pp. 86–90.

Gilroy, P. (2002) *There Ain't no Black in the Union Jack* (London: Routledge).

Harvey, C. (2005) 'Judging Asylum' in Shah, P. (ed) *The Challenge of Asylum to Legal Systems* (London: Cavendish).

JCWI (2005) *Recognise Rights, Realize Benefits*, JCWI analysis of the five-year plan.

Juss, S. (1993) *Immigration, Nationality and Citizenship* (London: Mansell).

Layton-Henry, Z. (1992) *The Politics of Immigration* (Oxford: Blackwell).

Lester, A. 'The Human Rights Act 1998 – Five years on', *European Human Rights Law Review* [2004] Issue 3, pp. 258–271.

Macdonald, I. and Webber, F. (2005) *Macdonald's Immigration Law and Practice*, 6th edn (London: Butterworths) Chapter 1.

McKee, R. (2002) 'Fitting the bill? A survey of the main proposals in the Nationality, Immigration and Asylum Bill and some related developments' *Journal of Immigration, Asylum & Nationality Law* vol. 16, no. 3, pp. 181–188.

—— (2006) 'The Immigration, Asylum and Nationality Act 2006 and other developments' *Journal of Immigration, Asylum & Nationality Law* vol. 20, no. 2, pp. 86–93.

Moor, R. and Wallace, T. (1975) *Slamming the Door* (London: Martin Robertson and Co.).

Paul, K. (1997) *Whitewashing Britain: Race and Citizenship in the Postwar Era* (New York: Cornell).

Poole, T. (2005) 'Harnessing the power of the Past? Lord Hoffmann and the *Belmarsh Detainees* Case' *Journal of Law and Society* vol. 32 no. 4, pp. 534–561.

Rawlings, R. (2005) 'Review, Revenge and Retreat' *Modern Law Review* vol. 68, no. 3, pp. 378–410.

Refugee Action and Refugee Council (2006) *Inhuman and Ineffective – Section 9 in Practice*.

Shah, P. (2000) *Refugees, Race and the Legal Concept of Asylum in Britain* (London: Cavendish).

Shah, R. 'Secure Borders, Safe Haven' [2002] NLJ vol. 152, no. 7021, pp. 315–317.

Singh, R. (2004) 'Equality: the Neglected Virtue' EHRLR 2 141–157.

Spencer, I. (1997) *British Immigration Policy since 1945: The Making of Multi-Racial Britain* (London: Routledge).

Stevens, D. (1998) 'The Asylum and Immigration Act 1996: the erosion of the right to seek asylum' *Modern Law Review* vol. 61, no. 2, pp. 201–222.

—— (2001) 'The Immigration and Asylum Act 1999: a missed opportunity?' *Modern Law Review* vol. 64, no. 3, pp. 413–438.

—— (2004) 'The Nationality, Immigration and Asylum Act 2002: Secure Borders, Safe Haven?' *Modern Law Review* vol. 67, no. 4, pp. 616–631.

—— (2004) *UK Asylum Law and Policy* (London: Sweet & Maxwell), Chapters 1 and 2.

Steyn, Lord (2004) 'Dynamic Interpretation Amidst an Orgy of Statutes' *European Human Rights Law Review* Issue 3, pp. 245–257.

Thomas, R. 'Asylum appeals overhauled again' [2003] *Public Law* Summer pp. 260–271.

Vincenzi, C. (1992) 'Extra-statutory ministerial discretion in immigration law' *Public Law* Summer pp. 310–321.

—— (1998) *Crown Powers, Subjects and Citizens* (London: Cassell).

Virdee, S. (1999) 'England: Racism, Anti-racism and the Changing Position of Racialised Groups in Economic Relations' in Dale, G., and Cole, M. (eds) *The European Union and Migrant Labour* (Oxford: Berg).

2

Policy, politics and media

SUMMARY

This chapter is an introduction to some of the policy issues surrounding immigration law. These issues are raised so that as they appear, embedded within the law throughout this book, they may be more easily recognized. The role of the media is discussed here in more detail, because it is a force to be reckoned with in the moulding of immigration and asylum policy and is a powerful actor in the scene, though in discussing the law, usually an invisible one. Some of the provisions which govern the treatment in the UK of asylum seekers are also covered here. This, too, has no other place in this book, not being an aspect of the law of entry, but is a very important subject which affects and is affected by the climate of policy on entry, and is in itself a major human rights issue. The institution and operation of the Borders and Immigration Agency is introduced as both a tool and an expression of policy.

2.1 Introduction

In 2006, shortly after taking up his post as Home Secretary, John Reid opined that the immigration system was 'not fit for purpose'. His comment, publicly given and head-line-catching, implied that hearers would know what the purpose of the system was meant to be, but the drama of the statement obscures the assumption behind it – that there is a recognized or agreed purpose for the immigration system. The Home Affairs Committee, in a more measured introduction to the report of their inquiry into immigration control did pose the question, 'what is the purpose of the immigration system in the twenty-first century?' (HC 775 para 5).

The Border and Immigration Agency website states their purpose as to 'manage immigration in the interests of Britain's security, economic growth and social stability' (accessed 31/01/08). This is of course a general statement, but it is not a bland one. First, the concept of 'managing migration' rather than 'controlling it' is something which has developed at least in the language of the Home Office since 2002. At that date, the publication of the White Paper *Secure Borders, Safe Haven: Integration with Diversity in Modern Britain* Cm 5387 marked the beginning of a more positive and welcoming tone for economic migration. This did not necessarily bear the fruit that it promised. Nevertheless, in rhetoric there has been a movement from control to management and this has implications. The 'control' of immigration generally implies keeping people out. However, as the Home Affairs Committee said, the government departments responsible for immigration 'cannot simply be organisations designed to exclude people from the country'. Management instead of control implies dealing with a resource, something that is inherently beneficial, and while setting rules and processes for how to handle the resource, getting the best out of it. Immigration is also being managed 'in the interests of Britain' rather than in order to stop something. The Home Affairs Committee said that 'facilitating travel' with a 'high level of service' was an essential aspect of the system. Management also implies a less isolationist view of the purpose of the immigration system.

Responsibility for policy on immigration has traditionally been in the hands of the Home Office, although this is changing. A number of other parts of government have a significant part to play in migration policy: the Department of Education and Skills in relation to overseas students and registers of colleges; local authority social service departments in relation to children at risk; the Department for Business, Enterprise and Regulatory Reform in relation to illegal working; and so on. As a result of the Home Affairs Committee's recommendation a Cabinet sub-committee was created to remedy 'the absence of any place within government with overall responsibility ... for determining ... migration strategy'. It is a significant development that government as a whole takes responsibility for migration strategy. As the Home Affairs Committee observed, the Home Office is not in a position to exercise that function alone (para 561). The engagement of other departments gives a stronger flavour of management of all issues related to migration, rather than just border control.

BIA's statement of purpose is to 'manage immigration in the interests of Britain's security, economic growth and social stability'. These three objectives may be seen to underlie much of current policy, as we shall see. It is not surprising that as a part of the Home Office its purpose would be inward-looking, towards the UK and its interests. That of course is a primary role of government. However, migration is by its nature an international activity, and it is artificial to consider the purpose of a domestic immigration system in isolation from the wider purposes of migration, particularly if migration is to be 'managed' rather than 'controlled'.

The Department for International Development (DFID) is represented at the Cabinet sub-committee. A policy document from DFID recognizes:

migration and development are linked...The objectives of both fields are more likely to be achieved if migration and development policies begin to acknowledge the benefits and risks of migration for poor people and developing countries. (DFID 2007:33)

The economist John Maynard Keynes remarked that migration is 'the oldest action against poverty'. This idea is expounded upon in the DFID report, and in the 2005 report of the Global Commission on Migration convened to move 'beyond the political deadlock which had effectively paralysed international discussion on migration for more than a decade' (Grant 2006:13).

Moving beyond the deadlock involves recognizing that migration is a potential benefit for the host country, the country of origin, and the migrant themselves, and developing policies that enable all those benefits to flow freely. The Global Commission proposed that migration should become 'an integral part of national, regional and global strategies for economic growth'. Their recommendations included to prevent the benefit to states of origin from being lost, for instance through a 'brain drain', or taxation or appropriation of remittances – the money that migrants send home. The money sent in remittances is 'second only to foreign direct investment in developing countries. In some countries remittances can be higher than official development assistance' (DFID 2007:13). Migration also directly assists development and moving out of poverty by enhancing the skills, knowledge and earning capacity of migrants, but the benefit of this to their country of origin is not as great as it might be if those migrants do not return, or at least have flexibility of movement between countries.

The Global Commission on Migration set an ambitious objective:

Women, men and children should be able to realise their potential, meet their needs, exercise their human rights and fulfil their aspirations in their country of origin, and hence migrate out of choice rather than necessity. Those women and men who migrate and enter the global labour marker should be able to do so in a safe and authorised manner, and because they and their skills are valued and needed by the states and societies that receive them. (2005:11)

Globalization presents the UK's migration management system with a major challenge. There are more passenger journeys than ever before, and still increasing; over 100 million people now enter the UK each year. More people have an aspiration to work or study abroad, international companies need internationally mobile workers. The international dimension of policy cannot be ignored. Evidence to the Home Affairs Committee was that:

'the great contradiction in migration today is that it is a global issue that people try to manage at a national level' and 'the root causes of migration are so powerful – it is about underdevelopment, disparities in demographic processes, in development, and in democracy – that to an extent…immigration control is treating the symptom rather than the cause'. (para 7)

Castles affirms that 'international migration is an integral part of globalisation', but goes on to say that 'governments welcome economic flows – especially of finance and trade – but are more ambivalent on flows of people' (2007:12). As we look at the UK's law and policy we can expect to see that ambivalence.

Looking simply at institutional developments, the major direction of developing inter-departmental co-operation is security and identity and border management. From 2008, immigration control will be the business of a new unified UK Border Agency, combining former departments of the Home Office and the Inland Revenue. This body was launched, not by a departmental announcement, but by the Prime Minister, and the report which describes it emanates from the Cabinet Office (*Security in a Global Hub*, 2007). The objectives are to establish a new intelligence- and information-led form of immigration control, in which the use of biometric data within the UK, at the border, and abroad is an integral tool. Passenger information is checked against databases, all movements in and out are monitored, and decisions to admit or exclude are made primarily on the basis of that information. The workings of this system are described more fully in chapter 7.

With all these factors in mind, we now turn to the features of current policy.

2.2 'Fair, effective, transparent and trusted: rebuilding confidence in our immigration system'

Under this title in 2006 the former Home Secretary John Reid launched a major review of immigration policy in order to make it fit for purpose. But why does confidence need rebuilding, and what was it that made the system unfit? Given the purpose as now stated, we can expect that there were views that security, economic growth and social stability were not well served by the system.

2.2.1 **Security**

The regular policy statements issued as part of the ongoing review do not disclose what the problems are thought to be with security, but this issue has been high on the government and public agenda since the attacks on the World Trade Centre on 11 September 2001. The presence of terrorist networks in the UK, many of whose members were born abroad, brought allegations that the government did not know who was in the UK. Increasingly, immigration has become wrapped up with the anti-terrorism programme. The Anti-terrorism, Crime and Security Act 2001, the government's legislative response to the September 11 attacks, included a powerful instance of immigration law being inappropriately used in the anti-terrorism campaign. The legal provisions and their defeat in the House of Lords are described in chapter 15. Refugee law has been changed by the drive against terrorism, and the climate created by connecting the two has contributed towards the ease with which detention and criminalization have been visited upon asylum seekers. Chapters 14 and 15 of this book include a more detailed exploration of these matters.

Criticism of the immigration system was compounded on 26 July 2005 when, immediately after failed attempts at bombings in London, one of the suspects departed on Eurostar. This brought to public attention that there was no longer any monitoring of people leaving the country, as controls on departure had been abolished in 1998. The Prime Minister's statement on security on 5 August 2005 set out a number of anti-terror measures that would be taken. Some have since fallen by the wayside. However, the speech provides a guide to the security purpose of a number of immigration-related measures. These are remarkably wide. They reveal three main areas of action on law and legal policy which are relevant for our purposes:

- Extending grounds for deportation. Whilst the actual grounds proposed at that time did not materialize as such, the new offence of encouraging terrorism was introduced in the Terrorism Act 2006. The grounds have since been tightened for other reasons, as discussed below and in chapter 16.
- Action on nationality law. This included reviewing the oath of allegiance and language testing, and expanding the grounds for depriving naturalized British citizens of their nationality. These matters are discussed in chapter 3.
- Implementation of the e-borders scheme. This is an electronic system of immigration control, involving the collection and checking of biometric information, with the aim that this will eventually apply to all passengers. It is already partly in place at the beginning of 2008, and is discussed in chapter 7.

The Prime Minister also referred to expanding the use of control orders, saying that judges and Parliament had not always agreed with the government's anti-terrorism initiatives. This refers among other things to the defeat of the indefinite detention provisions by the House of Lords in *A v UK*, and their replacement by control orders. The implication is that the judiciary and Parliament will be more ready to go along with the government's ideas after the London bombings.

The creation of the UK Border Agency did not feature in the Prime Minister's speech. Indeed, although it had been talked about for some time, it did not feature in the UK Borders Act 2007 which was the major instrument for taking the reforms generated by the review of the immigration system through Parliament. The House of Commons research paper on the Bill states more than once that the Act does not propose a unified border force. As late as November 2006, debating in Parliament the Home Affairs Committee report, the Minister for Immigration, Nationality and Citizenship said that the 'reorganisation of three agencies on the front line into a single border force' was 'damaging, distracting and disruptive. That idea is outdated and is rooted in a concept of a frontier that is long past'. It should be consigned to 'the bin where it belongs' (2 Nov 2006, Column 182WH). However, on 25 July 2007 the Prime Minister made another statement about security, detailing the imminent operation of e-borders, and announcing that there would be a unified border force. By April 2008 it was in place. This Agency will operate the e-borders system, and is a fundamental reorganization of the work of what until April 2007 was an immigration department, the main reason for the whole operation being security.

2.2.2 Economic growth

This objective is mainly connected with entry to the UK for work, now a controversial issue. There are two main problems for government in relation to entry for work: attracting the people with the skills for which there is an unmet demand; and tackling illegal working. In certain areas, particularly low-skilled work, the government often wants to retain control of the entry of workers. If labour market conditions change, the government wants to be able to restrict entry also. The Global Commission commends the practices of some traditional countries of immigration in granting settlement to those who enter for work. Granting the right to stay often contributes to economic growth in the destination country and plays a role in meeting the needs of migrants. However, they also point out two disadvantages. One is that the public mood is not always welcoming, and may be less willing to accept long-term migrants. The other is that countries of origin stand to gain more if migrants return. Although it is difficult to devise programmes of temporary entry for work that protect migrant workers' rights, the Commission advises that this should be attempted as well as settlement routes. In such cases, workers' rights including access to proper working conditions, and information and to transfer employers should be respected (2005: 17–18).

These standards support the capacity of migration to alleviate poverty. If routes to work within the law are too restricted so that enterprising migrants are pushed into using illegal means, there is an overall loss. The individual migrant may suffer poor or dangerous living and working conditions, never be able to earn enough to pay off debts owed to smugglers or traffickers, let alone send home, and yet not be able to bring any of their troubles to the attention of the authorities because of their own illegal status. In the meantime, their country of origin may receive little or no benefit from their migration. The host country loses taxation, working conditions for other workers may be driven down, the immigration system is brought into disrepute, and migrants suffer from being associated with illegality. Where the rights of migrant workers are respected, their autonomy increases and they are able to leave abusive employers, send money home, return home when they are ready, or if they want to settle in the new country, are free to do so lawfully rather than 'disappearing' into the illegal economy (see Ryan MRN 2006).

The issues concerning entry for work are discussed in detail in chapter 11, and later in this chapter we examine a recent example of the government's current policy in relation to the entry of highly skilled migrants.

2.2.3 **Social stability**

Many issues could be brought together under this heading. They can probably be grouped into two main areas: integration of new minority populations, and the credibility of the immigration system.

Integration is not necessarily a matter of law, and this subject begins to go outside the remit of this book. There is a refugee integration strategy for instance, with which we are not concerned. However, the government has recently turned its attention towards the integration of other minorities, and legal changes and proposals have resulted. These changes and proposals are marked by a tendency to harmonize to a conception of British life that is based on the majority culture. They include the introduction of tests on English language and 'life in the UK', initially as a condition of obtaining British citizenship, but now also to obtain indefinite leave to remain. These changes are discussed in chapter 7. More recently the government has issued a consultation paper proposing that the minimum age to sponsor a spouse from abroad or to enter as one be raised to 21. Part of the reasoning for this is that the average age for marriage in the UK as a whole is a lot higher than it is among the settled immigrant population. 'Our proposal has to be judged against that in terms of whether it is reasonable or not' (*Marriage to Partners from Overseas* December 2007 para 2.9). Another consultation also proposes English language testing even for spouses before entry.

The credibility of the immigration system is a major subject for our purposes, as this is the question of the reliability or otherwise of the laws and legal systems governing immigration.

These are the main issues that have been said to undermine the credibility of the system:

- Chaotic administration, resulting in delays and incompetence including lost files;
- Failure to remove people who have no right to be in the UK;
- The presence of an unknown number of people with irregular immigration status;
- Racism;
- Poor decision-making, resulting in distress and long drawn-out appeals;
- The suspicion that the asylum system is being abused by people who have no genuine claim to asylum but go on appealing and cannot be removed.

When Home Secretary John Reid introduced his reforms, on the basis that the system was not fit for purpose, these must have been some of the issues that he intended to address. The stated objectives of the reforms are to:

- Strengthen borders; use tougher checks abroad so that only those with permission can travel to the UK; monitor who leaves 'so that we can take action against those who break the rules';
- Fast-track asylum decisions, removing those who fail, and integrating those who need protection;
- Enforce compliance with immigration laws, 'removing the most harmful people first and denying the privileges of Britain to those here illegally';

- 'Boost Britain's economy by bringing the right skills here from around the world, and ensuring that this country is easy to visit legally' (*Fair, effective, transparent and trusted*, July 2006).

These are not particularly new, and largely repeat those of the five-year strategy launched in 2005. John Reid launched the review when he first came into office, following the public outcry over the release of foreign national prisoners who had not been considered for deportation. An observer would be forgiven for thinking that this was due to 'weak laws' or possibly even the Human Rights Act. Neither of these was the case, and the problem was poor communication within the Home Office. Factors contributing to this included overload on those working in the system and an over-concentration on asylum issues at the expense of other Home Office work. The affair as treated in the media is discussed below. The introduction to the first policy document of the review says that thousands of workers in the immigration system were consulted over a six-week period in order to establish what change was needed. It is apparent from the document that internal management and organization of the Home Office was also in need of reform. The first area we consider in detail is the internal Home Office organization of immigration and asylum work.

2.3 Institutional basis of immigration control – an overview

The legal authority for the power to control immigration is given by Immigration Act 1971 s 4(1) to 'the Secretary of State'. The immigration legislation does not specify which Secretary of State this is, but as a matter of long-standing government policy and practice it has been the Home Secretary, and the Home Office is the government department with responsibility for immigration control. In *Pearson* v *IAT* [1978] Imm AR 212 the Court of Appeal held that the Secretary of State, referred to throughout the immigration statute, must 'by reason of the subject matter' be the Home Secretary.

The Home Office itself has internal divisions of responsibility. The immigration service, originally a separate service based at ports, became part of the Home Office, and immigration officers are appointed by the Secretary of State (Immigration Act 1971 Sch 2 para 1). The immigration, nationality, and asylum work of the Home Office has historically been carried out by an immigration department. Changes in the model of immigration control have been reflected in name and identity changes for this department, though until April 2007 its title principally referred to immigration and nationality, the last variation before April 2007 being the Immigration and Nationality Directorate (IND). Immigration officers are still based mainly at ports and airports, now not only in the UK but sometimes overseas. In June 2001, Work Permits (UK), which handled work permit applications, transferred from the Department of Education and Employment to the Home Office, and is based in Sheffield. Entry clearance officers, who make immigration decisions in British posts abroad, were historically responsible to the Foreign and Commonwealth Office rather than the Home Office. In 2000 the Home Office and Foreign Office set up a joint unit to manage entry clearance; initially called the Joint Entry Clearance Unit, then UKvisas.

When John Reid announced his review of the then Immigration and Nationality Directorate, the Minister for Immigration, Citizenship and Nationality told the Home

Affairs Committee inquiry that the review would look at strategic objectives, the core processes, culture and organization, and would devise action plans (HC 775 para 537).

The first published fruit of the review included an intention to 'make IND a more powerful agency, more clearly accountable to Parliament and the public'. The Home Affairs Committee report argued the case for a Cabinet Committee to take overall responsibility for immigration, as the issues it raises affect the work of so many departments and they had noted a lack of liaison and overall judgment about the balance between competing interests (para 561). Opposition parties went further and called for a single border force, uniting Customs and Excise, security and immigration. In early 2007 the Home Secretary announced that the Home Office would be split into two. The focus of the new Home Office was to be terrorism, retaining also responsibility for policing, security and immigration. This association of immigration with security and terrorism was already established in government pronouncements, but this was a very substantial institutionalization of that connection ('Terrorism focus for new-look Home Office', news.bbc.co.uk 29 March 2007). It was in sharp contrast to a division of the Home Office discussed in 2004, in which a department for justice would deal with all crime-related matters, and 'department for rights' with human rights, immigration and asylum, family law and civil disputes, freedom of information, constitutional reform, electoral law and devolution (HL Constitution Committee Session 2006–07 Sixth Report para 19).

In a transitional phase from April 2007 the IND became the Border and Immigration Agency, reflecting the shifting emphasis. This agency was divided into regions, as the rhetoric about security was matched with rhetoric about accountability. The BIA website explains the regional placing as giving 'freedom to put local delivery and relationships with local stakeholders at the heart of our work'. Strategic direction was divided into management areas: asylum; borders; enforcement; human resources and organizational development; managed migration; and resource management; and the Director of UKvisas was also given a seat on the board. The structure is shown diagrammatically at http://www.bia.homeoffice.gov.uk/sitecontent/documents/aboutus/ourorganisation/ BIAorganogram.pdf.

On 14 November 2007 the government announced the creation of the new unified border force, mentioned earlier, called the UK Border Agency. It incorporates the work of the BIA, UKvisas and border work of HM Revenue and Customs, and involves closer co-operation with the police Special Branch and with transport organizations and regulators. The report *Security in a Global Hub* proposes 'dual and symmetrical' lines of accountability to the Chancellor and the Home Secretary. The Foreign and Commonwealth Office is said to be another interested body, and a Foreign Office official will be on the board. Migration in this vision is more a matter of border security than of foreign relations. The border as envisaged is not a 'purely geographical entity' (para 6). Much of the improved security that the document promises is delivered by 'exporting the border'. This process is described more fully in chapter 7, where we follow the various processes of border crossing. It relies on biometric data and cross-database checking at entry clearance posts, and the establishment of juxtaposed controls in France and Belgium. *Security in a Global Hub* is an extensive document, describing a strategy of deterrence, intelligence sharing and an integrated operation of policing and immigration control. It proposes a visa waiver system on the US model, whereby a passenger is exempt from a visa requirement only if they have an electronically readable passport. Passengers will be checked electronically against databases and watch lists, either in advance through a visa application or at the border. Departure from the country will be monitored, as well as arrival. On 1 March 2008 the first regulations take effect which show in their heading: 'Immigration, Police, Revenue and Customs'. They create a duty to share information between these three bodies in relation to a range of matters including 'passenger information' and 'notification of non-EEA arrivals on a ship or aircraft' (Immigration, Asylum and Nationality Act 2006 (Duty to Share Information and Disclosure of Information for Security Purposes) Order 2008).

Meanwhile, an immigration case work review is underway, aiming to 'radically overhaul processes to simplify and standardise activities' and 'put in place an electronic case working system and support this with improved information and knowledge management systems' (BIA website visited 22/01/08).

The asylum decision-making system has also been radically changed and regionalized. The New Asylum Model, discussed in chapter 12, applies to all asylum claims made after April 2007. It applies the new principles of speed, simplicity and accountability by allocating an asylum case, after a screening interview, to a 'case owner' who then sees it through to a conclusion. As discussed in chapter 1, historically the immigration department has been criticized for inefficiency on a massive scale. The system involved multiple transfers of a file during the course of a claim, each transfer providing an opportunity for the file to be lost, for misunderstandings and information loss to occur, and for delay. It also minimized any sense of identification or ownership with the individual claimant. An example given in Home Office training material shows 34 file movements in one case, including some blank spots in the system where no-one would know what was happening or what should happen next (*The New Asylum Model*, Asylum Operational Policy Unit). The case owner system has the potential to change much of this. The National Asylum Support Service, which was set up by the Immigration and Asylum Act 1999 to take the major part of the responsibility for welfare support of asylum seekers, has been disbanded and is now regionally located as part of the New Asylum Model. Case owners must therefore deal with support issues as well as the asylum process.

In the New Asylum Model, as in other areas of government action in this programme of change, a desirable quality is introduced at one end of the process but not necessarily at the other. Speed became a highly prized quality, in response to problems caused by delay and the simple injustice of delay itself. The New Asylum Model has the potential to generate faster *and* better quality decision-making at the individual level of an asylum claim. At the level of implementation, speed has been prioritized, but case owners are not fully trained before starting their work. Quality is therefore jeopardized. See also below for the other and damaging effects of speedier initial decision-making, when this is treated in isolation from a larger-scale perspective on migration.

2.3.1 Speed and targets

The whole issue of speed and targets deserves a special mention here. These are high-profile features of the BIA's approach to dealing with the challenges it faces. Setting targets, publicizing them, meeting them and publicizing that activity has been a key tool for achieving the objective of 'Rebuilding confidence in our immigration system'. Targets are nearly always described in terms of numbers and time (e.g. 30,000 removals per year). The Home Affairs Committee identifies four problems with targets:

- Major political targets meant that other work may have been sidelined or even deliberately manipulated (para 572).

For instance, prioritizing asylum claims and asylum removals had created backlog in other areas, and contributed to the foreign prisoner issue not being acted on more quickly.

- Targets were set for one part of a system without considering the effects elsewhere.

  This includes a problem with numerical targets *per se* in that, if a target of dealing with 90 per cent of claims in a certain time is met, 'what happens to the remaining 10% is irrelevant from the point of view of meeting targets' (para 583); so a target culture can also contribute to a black hole into which more difficult cases disappear because nobody can afford to spend the time on them.

- Targets on speed had a negative impact on quality.

- Targets might be met, but still have no impact on the underlying objective because they were the wrong targets. They might be set because they could be met rather than because they were designed to address a problem.

The speed and targets culture goes hand in hand with accountability by frequent issue of press releases, directed to the objective of 'rebuilding confidence'. This is most strikingly exemplified by the minister's 'Milestones' speech of 14 January 2008:

By day 60, we will introduce big on the spot fines for employers who don't make the right checks and employ illegal immigrants.

By day 80, we will commence the introduction of our points system, so that only those individuals Britain needs can come here to work or study.

By day 100, we will introduce a single border force and introduce our new powers for frontline staff.

By day 180, I will confirm that we are on track to deport more foreign national prisoners than last year, and by day 200, give or take a fortnight, we will activate powers for the automatic deportation of foreign national prisoners.

By day 300, we will have expanded our detention capacity to boost to the number of spaces at the disposal of Agency enforcement teams, including building a new centre at Gatwick Airport.

By day 330, we will be issuing compulsory ID cards to foreign nationals.

2.4 Undocumented migrants and removal

The director of immigration enforcement and removals, when asked by the Home Affairs Committee how many illegal migrants there were in the UK, famously replied: 'I have not the faintest idea' (HC 775 para 74). The media seized upon this as evidence of government incompetence in numerous ways. The political credibility of the immigration and asylum system rests in part on the timely and humane departure of those who have no right to be here. However, there is much confusion and misinformation about who such people are, how many there are, and what harm their continued presence does, if any. The undocumented or 'irregular' population (thought to be around half a million) consists mainly of people who have overstayed their original leave, people who have entered clandestinely or on false documents without being detected, and people whose removal has been directed, but who have not left, such as asylum seekers whose claim has failed (see e.g. JCWI 2006). There are also many migrants who are legitimately in the UK but who are in breach of their conditions of stay, for instance by working. Irregular migrants include those who have been trafficked. So when figures, known or guessed at, are used in debating these matters, it is generally unknown who is included. Describing such people as 'illegal' carries connotations of criminality that are often quite inappropriate. 'Illegal immigrant' – the term beloved of the media – has no precise meaning. To describe someone as an illegal immigrant who has worked in breach of their conditions of stay is equivalent to describing someone who has committed a speeding offence as an 'illegal driver'.

The circumstances of people with irregular status are more various than imagination can encompass. For instance, the history that led to the Court of Appeal case of *Bibi and others v SSHD* [2007] EWCA Civ 740 was that a man had entered the UK in the 1960s using documents that were not his, and obtained a British passport in that identity. He had worked in the UK ever since, and made regular trips home to Bangladesh. It was only after his death when the rights of his family were affected that his deception came to light. He had probably lived and worked and paid taxes with nothing apparently to distinguish his situation from that of another naturalized British citizen. This man's situation was very different from that of the cockle-pickers who died in Morecambe Bay, and others who live in hiding because their illegal status and their, in effect, debt bondage to their traffickers means that they have no option but to hide from the authorities.

Evidence given to the Home Affairs Committee suggested that by far the largest number among undocumented migrants are people who have at some point been lawfully resident, and may still be so. A number of NGOs take the same view:

Anecdotal evidence suggests that pressures exist with the experiences of migration which buffet against plans and intentions to remain lawfully and which convert a minority of migrants into rule breakers and overstayers. Many of these pressures are financial, involving the discovery that recovery of the cost of the original investment in migration (visa fees, student fees, travel costs, legal advice and other facilitation, etc) is not as easily recoverable from the meagre wages available to migrants as had been thought. In other instances migrants will come under pressure from family abroad to remain to take full advantage of earnings opportunities which can be remitted abroad. In these cases migrants may be tempted to work more hours than permitted or overstay their leave in order to claim to the benefits of migration. (MRN 2007)

The weight of evidence and opinion is that action needs to be taken on many different fronts to tackle this problem, but that some regularization of existing irregular migrants and the protection of migrant workers' rights are important elements. Enforcement by removal is not the only strategy.

2.4.1 Carrying out forced removals

Even when a removal decision has been made and directions issued to carry it out, carrying this into effect is not a simple matter. The obstacles to removal are real, and not always appreciated by critics. As JCWI relates:

Removal of failed asylum seekers may be impeded for a variety of practical reasons, such as a lack of travel documents, a lack of co-operation from the authorities of the country of origin in issuing such documents, or because there are no safe routes of return, or simply because that country is unsafe to return to. (2006:17)

In addition to these reasons, Phuong discusses a host of other practical factors. Airlines may be reluctant to take people who are being removed against their will:

Each person to be removed from the UK is subject to a risk assessment in order to determine his suitability for escorted or unescorted removal via commercial air services...In any case, the

International Air Transport Association...has decided that the number of persons to be removed should be limited to one escorted and three unescorted on each flight'. (2005:124)

Additionally, many passengers do not like to see people forced onto a plane and 'may take their business to another airline' (2005:125). In Germany, under pressure from the public, Lufthansa decided it would not carry passengers who were resisting deportation (2005:125). Because of the limited flights to removal destinations and the growing reluctance of commercial airlines, governments including the UK have begun to use charter planes for returns. Clearly this is an expensive method, as planes with a capacity of hundreds of passengers may only carry a few dozen returnees at any one time (2005:125).

The Home Affairs Committee noted that, despite the tone of much public debate, public opinion is another factor which explains the low number of removals relative to government targets and the numbers of those who are liable in law to removal (para 418). (See also the section on media below.) Phuong notes that, although public opinion may be in favour of removals in the abstract, when it comes to people being removed by force, and sometimes even injured or killed in the attempt, especially if they know them personally or they 'seem likeable (especially if they are well educated and have small children) they can become quite opposed to a particular forced removal' (2005:126).

In almost any government statement of immigration policy objectives in recent years, 'increase removals' has appeared as a key item. The practical reality is that it is a hard and unpleasant business for all involved and often unfeasible. Phuong concludes that one should also ask 'why are there so many people to be removed in the first place?' She too speculates that limited routes to legal migration may be part of the reason, and that opening up economic migration could assist. The Global Commission on International Migration recommends: 'States should address the conditions that promote irregular migration by providing additional opportunities for regular migration and by taking action against employers who engage migrants with irregular status'. The Commission also recommends 'dialogue and cooperation among states' (2005:36). Other commentators too consider that action on illegal working would alleviate the problems of undocumented migrants. Ryan (2006) explains that giving migrants the same basic workers' rights as other employees could solve some of the problems of exploitation not only directly but also indirectly, and help resolve immigration irregularity at the same time. The Home Affairs Committee recommends that action is taken more swiftly when, for instance, leave is refused or an appeal lost, while people are still in contact with the system. They criticise the practice of removing families as a 'soft target'.

The conduct of removals is also a cause for concern. The Joint Committee on Human Rights heard evidence of small children taken out of their beds early in the morning by officials, bundled into cold vans and then into detention. There were also many instances of violence, for instance people on the way to removal being beaten in the back of vans. The Committee recommends that people should be properly prepared for removal and that the removals should be carried out with dignity (HL 81 HC 60 para 337).

2.5 'Transparent and trusted'

The current government reforms include a project to 'simplify' immigration law. The Home Affairs Committee recommended that the immigration rules be consolidated and their requirements made more objectively measurable. It is not yet apparent whether this opportunity will be taken. The rhetoric associated with this project and with the split of the BIA into regional offices is of a kind of democratization. The message is that the immigration system is to be run in a way that ordinary people understand. This aim or claim cuts across some very established practices and attitudes in immigration law, a chief one being the retention of discretion and executive control. An understanding of this underlying nature of immigration law and how it manifests not only in decisions but in the law-making process is an important context for developing knowledge of the law itself. In the current programme of reform the government has given no promise that fairness and transparency will apply to the decision as to *which* rules to apply to an individual, *whether* there should be rules of that kind, and *what* the content of them is. These matters have to date been reserved for government, either explicitly or implicitly. This can be seen in three main areas: the passage of legislation; the amendment and application of rules and policy; and the content of legislation.

2.5.1 **Passage of legislation**

The policy objectives preceding the 2002 and 2006 Acts were stated in terms indicating breadth of vision. The Nationality, Immigration and Asylum Act 2002 concerned citizenship, identity, and 'integration with diversity'; and the Immigration, Asylum and Nationality Act 2006 was said to provide the statutory basis for a new system of managed migration. These are long-term goals which warrant measured consideration in Parliament and full participation by organizations concerned with these matters. The objectives of the 2004 Act were not announced in a White Paper, but in a short consultation letter which set out few of the major proposals. In terms of its effect on principles and rights, the Bill was exceedingly draconian, and warranted democratic consideration of the most careful kind. However, the progress of these extensive and complex pieces of legislation was marked by indecent, or more to the point, undemocratic, haste. McKee's view of the 2002 legislation was that: 'The Bill's objectives have partly been prompted by heightened security concerns about security in the wake of September 11th', additionally by the wish to 'stem the flood of asylum seekers' (2002:181). Shah said the Bill's overall concern was with 'the promotion of a fortress UK' (2002:315). Certainly the progress of this and the 2004 Act had more of the flavour of an emergency. The effect of this was a democratic deficit in the legislative process.

Haste and lack of consultation often characterize the process of legislating on immigration and asylum issues. The 2003 AITOC Bill was introduced in November 2003, with minimal consultation and during the currency of a Home Affairs Committee inquiry into Asylum Applications. Their report was published in January 2004. The Committee had to break off its work to provide a response to the Bill, and said:

we have not had the benefit of a draft Bill, nor – in common with other interested parties – were we given more than a few weeks' notice of the proposals even in outline. In view of the fact that since March 2003 we have been conducting a major inquiry into asylum applications, we find this regrettable. (Home Affairs Committee Session 2003–04 Second Report HC 218 para 3)

At the same time the Constitutional Affairs Committee was preparing a report on Asylum and Immigration Appeals, published in February 2004. The Committee noted the contents of the AITOC Bill and said:

The new proposals do little to address the failings at the initial decision making level and the low level of Home Office representation at initial appeals, which must add to the delays in the system.

We think it unlikely that the abolition of a tier of appeal can by itself increase 'end to end' speed and achieve improvements in the quality of judicial decisions. We doubt whether many of the proposals contained in the new Bill are necessary to deal with the current issues in relation to asylum and immigration appeals. (Constitutional Affairs Committee Session 2003–04 Second Report HC 211 summary)

The Home Affairs Committee inquiry into immigration control, to whose report we have been referring, began in November 2005, more than half-way through the passage through Parliament of the Bill which was to set the legal framework for the implementing the government's five-year plan.

Since the inception of the Human Rights Act the Joint Parliamentary Committee on Human Rights has been charged with scrutiny of all legislation, and comments substantively on legislation affecting rights. In the passage of both the 2002 and 2004 Act there were late amendments which gave rise to significant human rights issues. Also on occasions the Home Office did not reply to the Committee's questions until crucial parliamentary stages had been passed. The Committee commented adversely on this practice in relation to the 2002 Act (JCHR Session 2001–02 Seventeenth Report para 4), but in relation to the 2004 Act 'we find ourselves once again in the very same position so soon after having made clear that such a practice undermines parliamentary scrutiny of legislation for compatibility with human rights' (JCHR Session 2003–04 Fourteenth Report HL 130 HC 828 para 3). Lord Lester in Parliament commented that an unfortunate effect of this lack of scrutiny is that 'the matter will end up in court' (HL Debs 6 July 2004 col 722) as has in fact happened on the very matter upon which that comment was made (regulations on marriage, discussed in chapter 9).

A practice of introducing late amendments on significant matters affects not only human rights scrutiny but also the opportunity for Members of Parliament to debate matters. Farbey (2003) discusses this practice in relation to the 2002 Act, including in relation to a provision which, as she said, became 'one of the most hotly debated in the Bill'. It was the proposal that the Secretary of State should be able to certify asylum claims 'clearly unfounded' and that this certificate should prevent any appeal from taking place in the UK. This late amendment prevented proper parliamentary scrutiny of the removal of appeal rights for people who, if they have been wrongly refused, may face the most serious human rights violations. This was announced after the end of the Commons Standing Committee, leaving any effective debate only to the House of Lords. A further amendment to this clause was one of many announced even after Committee stage in the House of Lords. This led to the unusual step of the Bill being sent back to the Lords Committee for further consideration.

Late amendments also prevent effective input from concerned and expert groups. Some provisions are on their face dry and obscure, and under pressure of time and without context or interpretation it is difficult to understand their very real impact on the lives of those affected. In another way also this damages democracy. Farbey quotes the Hansard Society Commission on the legal process: 'All citizens directly affected should be involved as fully and openly as possible in the processes by which statute law is prepared'. So governments 'should make every effort to get Bills in a form fit for enactment, without major alteration, before they are presented to Parliament'. These hasty processes 'increase the government's imprint on legislation at the expense of the imprint of citizens and Parliament'.

The 2006 Act removes appeal rights from most entry clearance applicants. The points system that would replace the existing system had not been published in any detail at the time of parliamentary debate on the Bill. Parliament was asked to take on trust that an as yet unseen and untried system would guarantee fair and objective decisions, warranting removal of the right of appeal. This made it difficult for Parliamentarians to debate the Bill effectively. Eventually, at report stage in the House of Lords the government agreed that the new tiered migration system would be published before their Lordships went on to the third reading, so that they could assess the safeguards for themselves. This was done only by publishing the outline in the document, 'A Points Based System: Making Migration Work for Britain', and the Bill was passed.

The 2006 policy review with which we have been concerned is partly implemented by the UK Borders Act 2007. The presentation of the Bill shared a quality with some previous legislation which was commented on by the Joint Committee for Human Rights – a lack of evidence for the legislation proposed. The JCHR noted that evidence for the necessity of legislation was not offered, but that it was based rather on 'assertion' in many instances, including when rights were adversely affected. In the UK Borders Act there is a power for immigration officers to detain people suspected of arrestable offences for three hours. The government explained that the reason was to prevent suspected offenders from escaping if there did not happen to be a police officer in the vicinity, but offered no evidence that this had ever happened.

The JCHR pointed out that without detail they were unable to examine whether the proposal for biometric identity cards for foreign nationals – a key part of the Bill – would breach human rights, though clearly there were high risks of discrimination if the cards were to be used to access services.

Lest we be tempted to think that haste and lack of consultation are purely modern practices, the requirement for entry certificates, which laid the foundation for the whole system of entry clearance, was a last-minute amendment to the Immigration (Appeals) Act 1969. The draconian Commonwealth Immigrants Act 1968, setting a racial basis for exclusion from Britain and for the immigration and nationality law of the future, was rushed through Parliament in only five days. One difference now is that statutes are prefaced with a declaration that they are compatible with the Human Rights Act (under HRA s 19), but often there has not been enough consideration of whether this is the case.

2.5.2 **Enabling provisions**

In her submission to the Joint Committee on Human Rights concerning the 2002 Bill, Dummett made one overriding point: 'the chief threat to human rights in the Bill appears to me to arise from the character it shares with all the immigration legislation of the twentieth century: it is an enabling Bill'. In this vast piece of legislation, consisting of 164 sections and 9 schedules, it seems extraordinary that much should still be left to the executive, but this is the case. Dummett's submission continues: 'Many of its provisions are vague and general, allowing for subsequent, more precise provisions contained in statutory instruments and rules. The nature of these precise provisions is to be to a very large extent discretionary'.

The same is true in the 2006 Act, which leaves determination of who may lose appeal rights to the Secretary of State (s 4) – a remarkable delegation by Parliament of the power to remove the common law right of access to a court. Discretion and lack of scrutiny are the hallmarks of executive power. Even as accountability and openness increase in the disclosure of guidance and policy, the power to actually make the rules is strongly retained by the executive.

The certificate of approval regime for marriages, declared unlawful by the High Court and Court of Appeal, was introduced by the 2004 Act in a skeletal form, and the exemptions from the scheme, including of settled people, were only introduced in regulations. The certification regime in the 2002 Act for declaring countries of origin 'safe' is also an enabling power. The Secretary of State may by order designate any country as 'safe', so preventing an appeal against refusal of asylum from taking place in the UK, though the conditions for making this designation have been tightened by the Asylum Procedures Directive 2005/85/EC (see chapter 12).

The requirement in the UK Borders Act 2007 for non-European nationals to have a biometric identity document (BID) is a departure from traditional practice in the UK and clearly a proposal that has much potential for discrimination in its application. The requirement will be introduced for groups of people, but who these are does not appear on the face of the Act. They will be determined by regulations made by the Secretary of State. In introducing the Bill in the House of Commons the minister said: 'As is right and proper, we will return to the House each time that we wish to extend the power to a new category of third-country national' (5 February 2007 col 595). However, the section contains no requirement for regulations to be laid before Parliament. Speculation in the Public Bill Committee was that removing such issues from the face of Bills was a way of avoiding scrutiny by the House of Lords (1 March Q291).

2.5.3 Amendment to rules and policy

A key element in transparency is knowing what rules will apply to one's case. There has recently been a spate of challenges, discussed in this book mainly in chapter 8, of the government practice of moving the goal posts. Here the Highly Skilled Migrants Programme is treated as a case study in that exercise of executive power in making policy. Whether it is an extreme example, or an indication of the direction of the new points-based system, only time will tell.

Economic migration is a key area which demonstrates amply the contradictions of present-day immigration policy-making. As discussed in chapter 1, the 2002 White Paper signalled a more positive attitude to entry to the UK for work, recognizing that the UK has a need for labour which will not otherwise be fulfilled. This reasoning still creates a utilitarian relationship with the migrant worker, but the White Paper was followed by a proliferation of schemes for entry, and there did seem to be a more welcoming tone for a while. The Highly Skilled Migrants Programme (HSMP) is a scheme for entry for work that was devised in 2002 in tune with the new style of welcome for migrant workers. Details are given more fully in chapter 11. As the name suggests, its aim was to attract 'high human capital individuals' (Cm 5387) and it was the first scheme in the UK to use a points basis for entry. As such it was a trial for the new points-based system.

One of the unique features of the scheme was that applicants did not need to have a job to come to. The point was to attract the most talented people. In order to qualify, applicants were required to sign an undertaking that they intended to make the UK their permanent home. An undertaking is a promise that is intended to be legally binding. Applicants would be given one year's leave in the first instance, then be able to apply for an extension of three years. After four years' residence they could apply for indefinite leave to remain. In order to qualify for the extension of three years, they would be required to show that they were 'lawfully economically active' or that they had 'taken all reasonable steps to become lawfully economically active' (Home Office guidance para 26.5, quoted in *AA v SSHD* [2008] UKAIT 00003). There were numerous revisions of the scheme. The appellants in *AA* gave up their jobs and homes and moved to the UK on the HSMP. Two of the three appellants were accompanied by their families. One had sold a family farm as well as his home. They all found work after their arrival, but were not yet able to secure jobs that matched their previous skills and experience, so they did not earn highly. During their first 12 months the government changed the terms of the scheme. More points were needed to get an extension, and the way these were acquired was changed so as to give a high weighting to money earned in the UK.

The appellants in *AA* were refused extensions and so would be required to leave the UK. The guidance upon which they had relied included a series of questions and answers which said:

24.9 Q: **What if the scheme changes?**
A: As with any immigration scheme we reserve the right to adapt some of the criteria or documentation associated with the scheme and will inform you via our websites of any such changes. All applications will be treated on the basis of the HSMP provisions at the time that they were submitted.

24.10 Q: **I have already applied successfully under HSMP. How does the revised HSMP affect me?**
A: Not at all. It is important to note that once you have entered under the programme you are in a category that has an avenue to settlement. Those who have already entered under HSMP will be allowed to stay and apply for settlement after four years' qualifying residence regardless of these revisions to HSMP. (*This referred to a previous set of revisions, not the ones that affected these appellants.*)

The tribunal regarded Q24.9 as fatal (though it was not the only fatal point) to the appellants' case, reading it as obviously meaning that applications for extensions would be treated on the basis of the rules then in force, rather than as meaning that an individual's path within the scheme would be governed by the rules in force when they entered it. The tribunal's understanding of the application process is from the perspective of someone who analyses or administers it. In a significant endorsement of an instrumental attitude to economic migration policy, they approved the following passage from the immigration judge:

the very basis upon which highly skilled migrants are admitted to the United Kingdom in the first place is intended, not primarily to be for the benefit of the migrant (although it may well, and usually will, coincidentally benefit him), but for the benefit of the economy of the United Kingdom. The corollary of this is that at the point that the state judges the net economic benefit to the United Kingdom of the continued presence of the migrant in the United Kingdom to be outweighed by other factors (the pressure on housing, the cost to public services and so forth) interference with the Article 8 right of the migrant becomes necessary in a democratic society. (*AA* para 109)

This is a classic statement of the attitude to economic migration described by Bevan (1986), in which the flow of migrant workers is turned on and off like a tap. The government's claim, endorsed by the tribunal, that they are free to change the rules and that those affected may not rely on their content, has been the subject of other unsuccessful challenges in the tribunal (see for instance *MO (Nigeria)* [2007] UKAIT 00057). The Parliamentary Joint Committee on Human Rights most unusually instituted an investigation into the changes in HSMP (see chapter 11). On this issue they said:

53. In the course of justifying its changes to the HSMP the Government has claimed that the Immigration Rules must be capable of being changed from time to time by the Government so that it can carry out its policies. It does not accept that there can be any legitimate expectation

about the criteria which will be applied to future applications for leave. In the Government's view, the only expectation which applicants should have is that the rules and policies which are in force when their application is decided will be correctly applied to them.

54. This is an exorbitant claim about the scope of the statutory power in the Immigration Act 1971 to make changes to the Immigration Rules. As we have pointed out above, it amounts to a claim that the power to change those Rules from time to time, and without warning, is wholly unfettered in legal terms. However, since changes to the Immigration Rules are capable of inter-fering with Convention rights (as the Government appears to accept the changes did here), this amounts to a claim to an uncontrollable discretion to interfere with Convention rights. (Session 2006–07 Twentieth Report)

They recommended a scrutiny and declaration process when rules interfere with human rights. Although the government accepted that the changes in the HSMP affected Article 8 rights, the tribunal in *AA* did not. In the early stages of the points-based sys-tem we therefore have a situation in which there is no transparency as to whether the rules will change after an application has been lodged.

The conclusion of this section is that there are indications that the government intends to keep close control over the content of law, policy and guidance. It may be doubted whether this will produce the simple, streamlined system that they depict. As MRN says:

The mistake here is to presume that transparency is the only thing required of rules and regulations, when there is also a pressing need that they should be fair and in accord with the fundamentals of social justice and human rights. If these elements are not in place it can be expected that high levels of tension and contestation of the legitimacy of the regulations will continue. (2007)

2.6 Immigration control within the borders

The government appears to be acting on the Home Affairs Committee's strong recom-mendation to the government to act on enforcement of immigration control *within* the UK.

2.6.1 Treatment of asylum seekers

Although the Committee criticized the lack of such enforcement their remit did not include asylum seekers. The treatment of asylum seekers is a way in which the govern-ment is carrying out its enforcement policies, and this brief tour of policy issues would be incomplete without some account of how this is happening.

This section also illustrates some of the human consequences of speedy decisions and targets, referred to earlier. The Tenth Report of the Parliamentary Joint Committee on Human Rights in Session 2006–07, *The Treatment of Asylum Seekers*, is an important document in the current immigration and asylum debate. The Committee explains the importance of their report in this way:

12. The treatment of asylum seekers is important for the men, women and children seeking asy-lum in the UK. But it is also important for those of us who are not asylum seekers. This is because the UK's approach to migration – and its treatment of asylum seekers in particular – says some-thing about the society we live in and the kind of country we want to be. The human rights principles and values of democratic societies must guide the country's behaviour towards asylum seekers and its relationships with other countries from asylum seekers originate.

Asylum seekers who have no other means of material support are entitled to a basic level of assistance (for adults, 70 per cent of the income support rate) and accommodation while their claim is being considered (Immigration and Asylum Act 1999 s 95). This can be refused if they do not claim asylum as soon as reasonably practicable after their arrival (Nationality, Immigration and Asylum Act 2002 s 55). As discussed in chapter 1, the application and interpretation of this section left hundreds (at least) of asylum seekers destitute. Following the *Limbuela* judgment, discussed in chapter 1, asylum seekers should no longer be denied support where they are destitute. In the JCHR enquiry, witnesses including from the Home Office confirmed that s 55 of the 2002 Act was still being used to deny support to people who had somewhere to sleep but no food. Also, anyone who took more than three days after arrival to claim might well not receive support. However, the difficulties of finding one's way to an unknown location in an unknown country, perhaps not speaking the language, and without the information that this journey was necessary and how to do it, were minimized or overlooked (para 78). The Committee concluded that the continued application of s 55 did not comply with the *Limbuela* judgment, that there were clear breaches of Article 3 ECHR, and that s 55 ought to be repealed.

Where an asylum claim has failed, as most do, entitlement to support under s 95 ends. An asylum seeker may then be able to claim support under s 4 of the 1999 Act if they have signed an agreement to go home, but the Secretary of State accepts that they are physically not able to leave, either because of illness or there is no viable route of return. Section 4 support consists of accommodation and vouchers to the value of £35 per week. However, if they are not willing to sign such an agreement, there will be no support unless they have children. Asylum seekers are not permitted to work, though they can apply for permission to work if an initial decision on their claim is outstanding for more than 12 months.

The Committee found that a disturbingly high number of people had not even obtained the support to which they were entitled because of inefficiency and incompetence. Examples of how the system worked included that people could only claim asylum at either Liverpool or Croydon between 9 am and 1 pm, Monday to Friday. This placed an impossible burden on people who did not know the country and had nowhere to stay overnight and no means to pay for a bed. For some people, the system had proved so daunting that they did not manage to get into it at all. Refugee Action gave evidence to the JCHR that these difficulties increased the likelihood of potential asylum seekers 'disappearing without engaging in the asylum process, as they simply may not make it to an asylum screening unit' (para 80).

As the JCHR found, 'the government's approach to asylum has, in large part, been based on the assumption that many of those who arrive in the UK and claim asylum are not genuinely in need of protection but rather are economic migrants seeking a better life for themselves and their families' (para 3). The Committee criticized the frequent moves of asylum seekers, interrupting children's schooling and causing other hardship, the use of vouchers to buy food and toiletries – once abandoned by the government as too degrading and inefficient but now revived – and the poor housing provided as the only option for asylum seekers, sometimes overcrowded with collapsing ceilings. With the prohibition on doing paid work, there was no escape from the degrading conditions. The Committee concluded:

The treatment of asylum seekers in a number of cases reaches the Article 3 threshold of inhuman and degrading treatment. This applies at all stages of the asylum process.

Then, most damningly:

> We have been persuaded by the evidence that the government has indeed been practising a deliberate policy of destitution of this highly vulnerable group. We believe that the deliberate use of inhumane treatment is unacceptable.

Research by the Joseph Rowntree Trust revealed that, among the 21 countries of origin represented by the destitute asylum seekers surveyed, those most strongly represented were known for conflict and human rights abuses. The largest groups were from Eritrea (25 per cent), Sudan (14 per cent) and Iran (12 per cent). This may in part be an indicator of the very real obstacles to return even when an individual asylum claim has failed. For such a person, fast progress through the asylum system may mean that they are plunged more rapidly into destitution or, one of the few options for survival, illegal working. Other options are charities, begging, sleeping rough or staying with friends. For the government, meeting targets of fast processing may mean an increase in the number of people who have no regular status but cannot be removed, a phenomenon which causes them much political embarrassment (see below), an increase in illegal working which they are pledged to reduce, or an increase in destitution for which they are also criticized.

The Joseph Rowntree research showed that some of the destitute asylum seekers in Leeds had been through the New Asylum Model. The same research showed that people may remain in the UK, destitute, for long periods. Fast *initial* decision-making may increase illegal working and poverty in another way. Asylum seekers cannot apply for permission to work unless the initial decision on their asylum claim is outstanding for more than 12 months. However, this does not apply to a delay in appeals. So an initial decision may be very fast, but then the appeal process drags on for years, and the opportunity to apply for permission to work is no longer available (JCHR para 77).

In October 2006 the Learning and Skills Council announced that funding for English classes would be ended for asylum seekers. After intensive lobbying by groups opposed to this step, in March 2007 the government modified its proposal, permitting funding for English for asylum seekers where they had been waiting for more than six months for their claim to be determined, and for those who were receiving basic support under 1999 Act s 4.

The Refugee Council commented:

> The removal of automatic ESOL and FE funding for asylum seekers is a major blow toward their ability to function and communicate effectively during the time when their claim is being considered. Asylum seekers are prevented from working and asylum support is only 70 per cent of the rate of income support. They cannot be expected to pay for English courses. We welcome the LSC's decision to continue funding for asylum seekers aged 16–18 and to reinstate eligibility if a person's claim or appeal is still outstanding after six months. However, our experience has confirmed the importance of early entry onto English language courses for all ages.
>
> English language brings greater self-sufficiency which, amongst other benefits, means less reliance on support services. It also allows people to make connections with the local community that they would not have otherwise. We are particularly concerned that these changes further disempower people who have already undergone significant loss. (ESOL and Further Education Funding Changes 2007/08 announced by the Learning and Skills Council. Briefing November 2007)

The message of this cut in funding is that asylum seekers do not need English language, and although, as the Refugee Council explains, even someone who is only in the UK for six months may be greatly assisted by knowing some English, it appears that the cut was made with the New Asylum Model in mind.

2.6.2 **Immigration control within the borders: tracking and tracing**

The introduction in the UK Borders Act of biometric identity documents (BIDs) for all foreign nationals appears to be a trial run for identity cards for all UK residents, the foundation for which is laid in the Identity Cards Act 2006. However, a policy paper in December 2006, the Borders, Immigration and Identity Action Plan, makes it clear that identification documents for foreign nationals resident in the UK are intended to be a continuous system with that of the e-borders which starts with entry clearance posts overseas.

The government says that cards will be introduced for different groups of people at a time. However, how these groups are selected is obviously an important question. Beynon (2007) discusses statements that have been made on this issue. To the JCHR, the government said that exact categories were still to be decided and would depend on updated risk assessments nearer the time. They had in mind categories based on evidence of abuse and other factors. The JCHR reminded the government in its recommendations that 'to be lawful it is vital that race or ethnicity plays no part in the profile used by the government to decide the order in which it phases implementation of the biometric immigration document' (13th report 2006–07 para 1.29). Beynon relates that Lord Bassam told the Lords' Grand Committee that those applying to renew their leave would be the first for implementation, but then in a later stage of the Bill's progress that the focus would be 'immigration leave categories within which the most harm is prevalent', starting with discretionary leave and humanitarian protection, marriage and other partnerships and students.

It seems that there will be no obligation to carry the BID, but as it will be used to gain access to services there is great potential for discrimination. Beynon reports a speech of the former Home Secretary at the launch of *Enforcing the Rules*, the March 2007 instalment of the reform programme, to the effect that BIDs are to be used to 'refine and upscale a project already in hand – the enforced destitution of irregular migrants such as failed asylum applicants and visa overstayers so as to encourage them to return to their sending countries' (2007:328).

The use of BIDs to access health care is in keeping with the government's current programme of attempting to end access to the National Health Service for various groups of foreign nationals, in particular failed asylum seekers. The JCHR has already commented on the infringements of basic rights that are occurring as vulnerable pregnant women are refused ante-natal care, and how this sometimes results in an emergency which could have been prevented when a woman is rushed to hospital.

The reference to 'harm' in the words of Lord Bassam above refers to another new policy idea, which is to categorize migrants in terms of 'harm'. This follows on the policy commitment to remove the most harmful first, and is perhaps a clumsy attempt to educate the public in the reality that not all irregular migrants are the same, as well as to show that efforts are being targeted. The unfortunate result is that migrants are associated with a sliding scale of how harmful they are. This is part of the *Enforcing the Rules* instalment of the reform strategy, which also, in conjunction with enforcement against illegal working, proposes that 'immigration crime partnerships' will be created across the country, consisting of local authorities, police, primary care trusts, government departments, private sector bodies – and the public. From 1 January 2007, Crimestoppers UK, the organization which publicizes details of people wanted for crime, is taking reports of illegal working. Employers, as discussed above and in chapter 11, will be the focus of enforcement activity. The aim seems to be to make combating illegal migration the responsibility of the whole of society.

2.7 **Media**

The final subject in this chapter is the media. They have been present, though without mention, in much of what has gone before. Policy is presented and framed in the way it is because the government expects that the media will publicize what they have said. Without the news media, many of the policy statements we have been discussing might not be made at all. Lord Woolf described the relationship between the media and the judiciary as one of a common interest, and a need to be independent of one another while also recognizing that each has some power to uphold the other's independence. The media and judiciary each act as a check on the power of government, particularly when that government has a large majority and can become 'impatient of interference and criticism' (2003). When there is tension in the relationship between the judiciary and executive, the media is an interested party.

Constitutional Reform Act 2005 s 3 affirms convention by requiring ministers to uphold the independence of the judiciary. The House of Lords Constitution Committee explained that this does not mean that ministers may not comment on individual cases. They may, but they should say that they disagree with the decision and that they will appeal if that is the case, and not imply that there is something wrong with the judge for making that decision (2006–07 Sixth Report para 40).

This convention has been infringed in immigration and asylum cases in recent years. In a number of cases the judge has come under personal attack. Even more than this, ministers have implied that there is something unconstitutional and anti-democratic in the judges upholding the rights of asylum seekers. Remarkably, in relation to *R (on the application of Q and M) v SSHD* [2003] 2 All ER 905, the then Home Secretary David Blunkett said that he would not put up with judges interfering with the democratic process in this way. The case was one of statutory interpretation, using the Human Rights Act to interpret the Nationality, Immigration and Asylum Act 2002. Commenting on Mr Blunkett's response, Geoffrey Bindman in the Independent newspaper in February 2003 pointed out that it is the constitutional task of the judiciary to interpret legislation, and in a democracy, judicial review is the essential constitutional check by the judiciary of the executive.

This personal attack on the judge was combined with misinformation in the case of *S v SSHD*, in which the government apparently used the media to publish a distorted account of a court case, with damaging results for the courts, the Human Rights Act and the appellants. This case was serious enough that, in combination with two other incidents, it prompted an enquiry by the JCHR.

The legal aspects of the case of *S* are dealt with in chapter 8. Briefly, this was the case of the nine people who had hijacked a plane as a desperate measure to leave Afghanistan. They were members of a group opposed to the government, and were in fear for various reasons, including that one member of their group had been tortured, killed, and then delivered to their door. After an eight-day hearing by a specially convened tribunal, their claims for asylum were turned down because of the crime they had committed by hijacking the plane, but it was held that they should have temporary protection because of their fears of human rights abuses. This would entail a grant of discretionary leave. They were convicted of the hijacking and served prison sentences, though later cleared by the Court of Appeal because the jury had been misdirected on the question of duress.

The government accepted before the tribunal that the appellants did not present any security risk to the UK, but refused to accept the ruling of the tribunal. They did not challenge it, but just kept the appellants on temporary admission, even though there was no basis in law for this. Discretionary leave, although temporary, would entitle them to work or claim benefits, neither of which they could do on temporary admission.

As the hijack itself was such a high-profile event, the media would be interested in the fate of the appellants, so anticipation of press coverage must have been in the government's mind in the conduct of this case. The question was whether the government was willing to take the lead in explaining to the public that the hijackers had paid the penalty in law for their criminal actions, what they had suffered, why they needed protection, and to take credit for Britain upholding its proud tradition of giving sanctuary, albeit temporary. Unfortunately they did nothing, leaving the appellants in limbo for 18 months.

When the case eventually came to the High Court, and Sullivan J ordered that the Secretary of State act lawfully and grant discretionary leave, the government appealed to the Court of Appeal. The High Court judgment was castigated in the press and by the Prime Minister as 'an abuse of common sense'. The response of the Prime Minister and Home Secretary implied that the High Court had only just decided that the claimants could not return for human rights reasons and that they were amazed and outraged by this, rather than acknowledging that the human rights decision had been made 18 months earlier and was no surprise. Their response also implied that these people had hijacked a plane and got off scot-free. Crucially, the Home Secretary commented in the press:

When decisions are taken which appear inexplicable or bizarre to the general public, it only reinforces the perception that the system is not working to protect or in favour of the vast majority of ordinary decent hard-working citizens in this country.

The media did not apparently notice that the 'ordinary decent hard-working citizens of this country' were not in any way adversely affected by the decision, but were being invoked in support of the indignation of the Home Secretary and Prime Minister. Over the next few days they picked up the case as a call to repeal the Human Rights Act. The *Daily Telegraph* contrasted the 'hijack at gunpoint' with the right to stay. There was no mention of the basis for the appellants' fear, nor the abuse of power by the Home Secretary. The press coverage painted the claimants as the villains of the piece, and the Home Secretary as amazed and outraged. Eventually the Court of Appeal applauded Sullivan J's judgment as 'impeccable'.

At the special inquiry by the Parliamentary Joint Human Rights Committee, the Lord Chancellor was asked whether he regarded Sullivan J's judgment as 'impeccable' or 'inexplicable and bizarre'. His response sets out a fairly standard piece of legal reasoning which implicitly endorses that it was 'impeccable'.

Comment has not all been in one direction. As discussed in chapter 1, earlier in the current decade there was a high level of tension between the executive and judicial branches of government. One indication of this was that senior judiciary broke their time-honoured tradition of not commenting on government policy. The battle over the proposed ouster clause in the AITOC Bill brought out the senior and retired judiciary in powerful opposition, not only in Parliament but also outside it. Lord Woolf's trenchant criticism in his Squire Centenary lecture marked a new point in executive/judicial relations. Lord Steyn was prepared to count himself out of hearing the challenge to the British government's role in detention in Guantanamo Bay, which he described as a 'legal black hole' (2004:256), in order to be free to warn publicly against an 'unprincipled and exorbitant executive response' (*The Independent* 26 November 2003).

The use of the media in relation to *S* was a low water mark. However, the release of foreign prisoners reported in 2006 was, if anything, a lower point. In this case, neither the judiciary nor the Human Rights Act had any part to play. Journalism revealed a failing in government, and the government then blamed the judiciary and the Human Rights Act. The story is best told in the words of the JCHR report:

22. When it came to light that a substantial number of foreign prisoners had been released at the end of their sentences without being considered for deportation, some of whom had re-offended, the then Home Secretary, Rt Hon Charles Clarke MP announced plans, in a statement to the House of Commons on 3 May 2006, to change the system governing deportation of foreign prisoners.

23. The new Home Secretary, Dr Reid, said in a newspaper article on 7 May: 'the vast majority of decent, law-abiding people...believe that it is wrong if court judgments put the human rights of foreign prisoners ahead of the safety of UK citizens. They believe that the Government and their wishes are often thwarted by the courts. They want the deportation for foreign nationals [sic] to be considered early in their sentence, and are aware that this was overruled by the courts' (*News of the World*).

The cause of the prisoners not being considered for deportation was actually a failure of communication between different parts of the Home Office, and nothing at all to do with the Human Rights Act. This was admitted by the government in evidence given to the JCHR enquiry. This admission of course gained almost no press coverage by comparison with the outcry over the release of the prisoners, which was full of misinformation of all kinds. After the assertion by the Home Secretary that the Human Rights Act was to blame, the Prime Minister followed up in Parliament with a speech referring to the government's plans to change the law on deportation, and said that the vast majority of people 'would be deported, irrespective of any claim that they have that the country they are returning to may not be safe' (HC debs 17 May 2006 col 990). The implication was not only that the Human Rights Act was to blame but also that the government had the power to legislate to override fundamental rights. The press coverage also implied that the prisoners *would* have been deported if they had been considered, but deportation is a discretion to be exercised on the merits of the individual case. There were said to be 1,000 prisoners freed without consideration of their cases, but the fact that this total was accumulated over seven years was lost from public view.

A serious result of the media outcry was that the government was under pressure to find and deport as many of the freed prisoners as they could. This meant that recently released foreign nationals, even if they would not normally be deported on the facts of their case, were at higher risk. One such case was that of Sakchai Makao, a popular young Thai man who had lived in Shetland most of his life. After one crime that was out of character he had served an eight-month prison sentence, but was welcomed back to Shetland. He was re-arrested for deportation in the aftermath of the foreign prisoners issue, but the islanders said he had been picked up as a 'soft target', and they campaigned for him to stay. The tribunal agreed he should.

Not only foreign nationals were at risk in this operation. Some of the alleged foreign national prisoners turned out to be British. It seemed that prisoners' nationality was not routinely checked (see Shah, R. 2007).

None of this was to do with the Human Rights Act or, in fact, the state of the law at all, but it was nevertheless a platform upon which the government could launch its idea of 'automatic' deportation for serious offences. In chapter 16 we discuss how automatic this actually is. Although the UK Borders Act 2007 has created a strong presumption in a wide range of criminal cases, even the strongest presumption cannot displace human rights, as the JCHR noted. Government representatives before the Committee were forced to agree.

The foreign national prisoners issue also provoked a published letter from the Prime Minister to the Home Secretary, in which he alleged that British courts overruled the government in a way that was inconsistent with other EU countries' interpretation of the ECHR. A parliamentary question and inquiries by the JCHR were unable to unearth any such case, but if they had, the implication that this would be somehow illegal, unethical or unconstitutional is simply wrong. Courts cannot judge more restrictively of rights than the ECHR, but the Human Rights Act is a domestic statute and the courts are free in law at least to develop a human rights jurisdiction that is stronger than that in Strasbourg. Neither do other EU countries have any binding or constitutional force in this matter. The suggestion was withdrawn before the JCHR, but again without media attention.

Sometimes of course the press itself misrepresents the law, and has also done this in a way that inaccurately disparages the Human Rights Act. An instance of this was press coverage of the case of Learco Chindamo, the young man who killed Philip Lawrence. A teenager killing a respected headteacher generated particularly strong feeling, and once again the Human Rights Act was wrongly credited with the fact that the Asylum and Immigration Tribunal held that he could not be deported. Chindamo, as an EU national, could only be deported 'on imperative grounds of public policy', which would not apply in this case where he was agreed not to present a future risk. Undeterred by facts, the *Daily Mail* and other newspapers reported that the Human Rights Act was the reason for the ruling which it described as 'profoundly stupid and amoral' (21 August 2007). The Shadow Home Secretary was apparently also taken in, saying that the case demonstrated 'a stark demonstration of the clumsy incompetence of this Government's human rights legislation'. In fact it was an EC Directive which bound the tribunal.

The concern in cases of this kind, and one reason that *S* and the foreign prisoners issue warranted investigation by the JCHR, was that such inaccurate reporting, and particularly when led by government, undermines attempts to build a human rights culture. It feeds racism, though this was not discussed by the JCHR, as the implication of the Home Secretary's remark, not voiced openly by him but quickly picked up on by newspapers such as the *Daily Mail*, is that human rights are delivered to failed asylum seekers in preference to long-term residents. There was no foundation for this in the cases in question.

The role and power of the press in creating a climate around asylum has been researched in a number of studies. This too is not new. Greenslade for the Institute of Public Policy Research shows that press reports have encouraged ill-feeling against migrants since the early part of the twentieth century, including anti-Jewish material in the newspapers of the late 1940s and press coverage of street fighting in Notting Hill in the 1950s, inaccurately reported as 'race riots'. The study shows how 'newspapers, either by exaggerating race disputes or covering them in such a way as to suggest that migrants were the cause of trouble, helped to set the political agenda which led to immigration legislation' (2005:17). A similar story may be told about disturbances in Brixton in 1981, also inaccurately dubbed 'race riots'. Greenslade gives up-to-date examples of misinformation in newspapers which directly resulted in violence. For instance, the misleading claim that 'luxury pads' were being prepared for asylum seekers resulted in homes being broken into and damaged before refugees had moved in.

In October 2003 the Press Complaints Commission issued a brief guidance note to editors about terminology. It explained, for instance, that an asylum seeker is 'someone currently seeking refugee status or humanitarian protection'. Consequently 'there can be no such thing in law as an "illegal asylum seeker"'. This guidance on terminology, while welcome, only scratched the surface. The JCHR recommended the PCC go further and provide practical guidance on professional practice of journalists in reporting matters of legitimate public interest, while not encroaching on free speech (para 366).

A study for the Information Centre about Asylum and Refugees in the UK (ICAR) assessed the impact of media and political images of refugees and asylum seekers on community relations in London (Media Image, Community Impact 2004). This report uses a range of methods and is a theoretically grounded study. It was inconclusive about the link between unbalanced press reporting and violence against asylum seekers. It did find under-reporting of violence against asylum seekers and refugees, and the frequent use of emotive language and inaccurate information. The writers noted that 'local papers were more likely than national ones to interpret their role as providing a balanced picture on issues that affect local people' (2004:98). This finding was repeated in a later study by ICAR of the effect of the Press Complaints Commission Guidelines (ICAR 2007).

The ICAR research found that during the period of the study (in 2005) only 1 per cent of newspaper articles contained inaccurate terminology such as 'illegal asylum seeker'. Of 2,000 articles assessed, 37 were singled out for further investigation and 'analysed for possible mixing of fact, comment and conjecture. Examples were found of misuse of statistics, stories whose main claims were misleading and misrepresentations of quotes or facts' (2007:12). The most inaccurate reporting was in the daily newspapers with the top six circulation figures. The most common theme in these papers was the system being 'out of control'. The study found 'most political reporting to be "tired, repetitive and unquestioning". Stories reflected the obsession with chaos, and failed to offer alternative perspectives'. Another finding was that regional papers ran more individual stories, which ICAR considered 'an important means of increasing understanding of how policies and attitudes affect real people' (2007:13). 'In particular, it is interesting that local concern about asylum seekers facing deportation featured highly' (2007:11). ICAR contrasted the sympathetic response in individual situations with the national political focus on the desirability of deportation.

This finding is important, given the enormous power attributed in the immigration and asylum field to an invisible factor called 'public opinion'. There is now a range of initiatives by NGOs and by individuals and community groups to tackle 'public opinion' directly by the provision of direct information about and contact with refugees and asylum seekers and their human experience. See for instance the Refugee Awareness Project originating in Refugee Action, in which local people and refugees talk and work together, and the City of Sanctuary movement, a faith-based initiative to build a climate of welcome. These and other initiatives working directly on this form of 'climate change' illustrate that public opinion and the question of accurate and inaccurate information is a major driver in the field of asylum policy.

As government solutions to an ill-defined problem proliferate, so do the solutions of civil society, migrants themselves, activists, and people at various levels of organization. The London-based Strangers into Citizens campaign commissioned a telephone poll of 1,004 British adults in April 2007. Of these, 66 per cent believed that undocumented migrants who have been in the UK for more than four years and pay taxes should be allowed to stay and not called 'illegal'. 67 per cent believed that asylum seekers should be allowed to work (Strangers into Citizens press release 24 April 2007).

An important role played by the media in immigration and asylum issues is in investigative journalism. Journalists have revealed many human stories and uncovered malpractice in government, for instance when a chief immigration officer was alleged to have pressurized an 18-year-old asylum seeker for sex in return for asylum status (Observer 21 May 2006). Sometimes also press reports from their country of origin may be an important source of evidence for asylum seekers. It is difficult to establish their claim outside their country, but they may be able to obtain newspaper reports through contacts or online, or occasionally witness statements from investigative journalists (for instance in *BK (DRC)* [2007] UKAIT 00098).

Some of the major human rights violations occurring in connection with migration have been uncovered by investigative journalists, for instance, the Joseph Rowntree Foundation note in their report on contemporary slavery a 'formidable body of work by investigative journalists' (2007:24) which has uncovered stories of trafficking adults and children for sex and other forms of forced labour, and abuse. John Pilger's film, Stealing a Nation, brought the little-known story of the Chagos Islanders (see chapter 3) into the mainstream media when it was shown on ITV.

2.8 **Conclusion**

This chapter just touches on some of the issues surrounding the making of legal policy. This is the edge of a very large field. Some other policy issues are addressed throughout this book as they arise.

QUESTIONS

1 How does the Highly Skilled Migrant Programme rate against the DFID standards for migration policy?
2 What elements would you like to see in a code of practice for the media on reporting on immigration and asylum issues?

 online resource centre For guidance on answering questions, visit www.oxfordtextbooks.co.uk/orc/clayton3e.

FURTHER READING

Beynon, R. (2007) 'The Compulsory Biometric Registration of Foreign Nationals in the UK: Policy Justifications and Potential Breaches of Human Rights' *Journal of Immigration, Asylum & Nationality Law* vol. 21 no.4, pp. 324–333.

Billings, P. and McDonald, I. (2007) 'The Treatment of Asylum Seekers in the UK' *Journal of Social Welfare and Family Law* vol. 29, no.1, March 2007, pp. 49–65.

Castles, Flynn, Lawson, Ryan et al. (2007) 'Towards a Progressive Immigration Policy' Migrant Rights Network.

DFID (2007) 'Moving out of poverty – making migration work better for poor people'.

Farbey, J. (2003) 'Lobbying Lessons' *Legal Action* January 2003, p. 6.

Global Commission on International Migration (2005) 'Migration in an Interconnected World: New Directions for Action'.

Grant, S. (2006) 'GCIM Report: Defining an "Ethical Compass" for International Migration Policy' *International Migration* vol.44 (1) pp. 13–19.

Greenslade, R. (2005) 'Seeking scapegoats' IPPR.

Home Office, *Borders, Immigration and Identity Action Plan* (Policy document, December 2006).

—— *Fair, effective, transparent and trusted: Rebuilding confidence in our immigration system* (Policy document, July 2006).

ICAR (2004) Media Image, Community Impact.

—— (2006) Reporting Asylum: the UK Press and the effectiveness of PCC Guidelines.

IPPR (2006) 'Irregular Migration in the UK'.

JCWI (2006) 'Recognising Rights, Recognising Political Realities: The case for Regularising Irregular Migrants'.

Migrants Rights Network (2007) 'Enforcement Policy: the Heart of Managed Migration?'.

Phuong, C. (2005) 'The removal of failed asylum seekers', *Legal Studies* vol. 25, no. 1, 117–141.

Shah, R. (2007) 'The FNP Saga' *Journal of Immigration, Asylum & Nationality Law* vol. 21 no.1, pp. 27–31.

Somerville, W. (2007) *Immigration under New Labour* (Bristol: Policy Press).

Woolf, Lord (2003) 'Should the Media and the Judiciary be on Speaking Terms?' www.judiciary. gov.uk/publications_media/speeches/pre_2004/lcj221003.htm

—— (2004) Squire Centenary Lecture: www.judiciary.gov.uk/publications_media/ speeches/2004/lcj030304.htm.

3

Nationality and right of abode

SUMMARY

This chapter traces an outline history of British nationality law from 1948 to the present. It explains by reference to particular groups of people the reasons for the development of the present categories of British nationality. The development of these categories is shown to have been largely a history of progressive exclusion, based on views of who 'belonged' to Britain. Recent developments are discussed in which there is a trend towards inclusion in British citizenship, both in that formal discrimination on the grounds of sex and birth status has been reduced, and in that groups of people formerly excluded have now reduced in number and so are included. The bases for obtaining British nationality by registration and naturalization are discussed, and finally, the powers to deprive a person of nationality, which suggest a new basis for inclusion and exclusion.

3.1 Introduction

The purpose of considering nationality law in a book on immigration and asylum is to give some context and meaning to the immigration law question, 'who has the right of abode?'. In other words, who has the right to enter the UK 'without let or hindrance' (Immigration Act 1971 s 1(1))? As will be seen, the answer to the question 'who has the right of abode?' is not the same in UK law as the answer to the question 'who is a British national?'. However, there is a substantial overlap, and some general idea of nationality principles is necessary.

As a result of legislation in 2002, the number of British nationals who do not have the option of right of abode has diminished. The 2002 legislation is itself the culmination of a process which may be summarized as one of gradual exclusion from the most favoured class of British nationality, which carries the right of abode, until the group remaining was so small that steps towards inclusion were finally taken. This brief account of British nationality is therefore also an account of a number of different routes which have led to British citizenship, and of the stories of inclusion and exclusion which have brought about the present situation. It is part of the historical introduction to immigration law, and reveals how immigration considerations have driven the law on nationality.

For greater depth of coverage, reference should be made to *Fransman's British Nationality Law* (2005), the definitive work.

3.1.1 **Nature of nationality and its development**

Nationality is a concept arising in international law, because a fundamental defining quality of a state is the power to determine who are its own nationals. The Council of Europe's European Convention on Nationality 1997 defines nationality as 'the legal bond between a person and a State'. Nationality is a legal relationship, and nationals of a State can look to that State for protection just as the State is entitled to look to its nationals for allegiance. In *Al-Rawi v SSHD* [2006] EWCA Civ 1279 the court held that this meant that the UK had the right to intervene with the USA about how British nationals on US territory were treated (in Guantanamo Bay). However, following *R (on the application of Abbassi) v Secretary of State for Foreign and Commonwealth Affairs* [2003] UKHRR 76, the court did not have the power to compel the government to do that in a particular way.

As noted in the 1997 Convention, nationality does not indicate a person's ethnic origin, as a state may be made up of many ethnicities either from its creation or by the process of immigration or both. An ethnic group, as defined in law for the purposes of the Race Relations Act 1976, involves a shared history and some of the practices we regard as culture, such as language or sometimes religious practice (*Mandla v DowellLee* [1983] 2 AC 548 HL). Thus Sikhs are an ethnic group, as are the English, and Roma (also called gypsies). However, the legal relationship with the state which is called British nationality may encompass all these and many other ethnic groups.

In the European Union, nationality of a member state also confers the benefits of citizenship of the European Union. However, the power to determine this remains with the member state, and the European Court of Justice does not take over the state's role in determining who are its nationals. For further discussion of this, see chapter 5 and Case C-192/99 *R v Secretary of State for the Home Department ex p Manjit Kaur*. The State, within international law limits, sets the criteria and procedures for how its nationality is gained or lost.

It is possible to hold dual nationality, providing the law of both states involved permits this, as UK law does.

Nationality law has consequences for immigration law. As explained by Juss (1993:48), 'those individuals who are nationals of a state are deemed . . . to be its citizens . . . and the state uses its immigration law to prevent the entry and residence of non-nationals'. From this we might expect that if we can determine who has British nationality then we can say that immigration law applies to those who are not British nationals. However, British nationality is not one but a number of different statuses each carrying different rights. Some British nationals are subject to immigration law, and European nationals are privileged over some British nationals in terms of rights to enter the UK. The status of British national does not always mean that the holder has a right in UK law to the protection of the UK or to enter the country. In some cases it has been a virtually empty status.

Because of this anomaly that not all British nationals have a right to enter the UK, the UK has not, to date, ratified Protocol 4 Article 3 ECHR which says 'No-one shall be deprived of the right to enter the territory of which he is a national'. Non-ratification of the provision does not mean that the standard it protects is irrelevant. Where European law is applicable, all the rights of the ECHR are imported, whether or not the respondent government has ratified them, and Protocol 4 was used (though unsuccessfully) in argument in *Manjit Kaur*. In both international and parliamentary debates (see e.g. that on the Commonwealth Immigrants Act 1968) Protocol 4 is a standard towards which the UK is expected to move.

In the White Paper *Bringing Rights Home* which introduced the Human Rights Act the Labour government which came to power in 1997 acknowledged that Protocol 4 contained important rights, and that it should be ratified 'if potential conflicts with our domestic law can be resolved' (para 4.11). Perhaps for similar reasons, the UK has also not yet ratified the European Convention on Nationality 1997. In addition to the disadvantages that still apply to some groups of British nationals, new powers in the Immigration, Asylum and Nationality Act 2006 to deprive British citizens of their nationality may put compliance with the Convention in question in relation to British citizens.

In *Harrison v SSHD* [2003] INLR 284 the Court of Appeal held that the right to be recognized as a British citizen was not a civil right within the meaning of Article 6 ECHR; thus the requirement of that Article for a fair hearing did not apply. However, Mr Harrison could apply to the court for a declaration of his citizenship and this hearing would follow normal requirements of fairness, so the finding has more symbolic than practical significance. It illustrates a phenomenon which will be encountered time and time again in this book, namely that in matters seen to be affecting the State's power to control its membership or borders, the courts are reluctant to imply private rights for an affected party. The application of Article 6 is considered more fully in chapter 4.

The UK, in common with some other European countries, has recently reformed its law of naturalization, creating more hurdles to acquiring nationality. There are also initiatives to infuse nationality with the idea of citizenship, a concept without content in the UK until 2002. The promotion of citizenship as a school subject, along with compulsory learning about life in the UK for intending British nationals, has begun to create an idea of a citizen as a participant in civic life. This idea of a citizen is increasingly linked with nationality, as in the terms of a current governmental review. Lord Goldsmith's 'Review of British Citizenship'was set up:

- to clarify the legal rights and responsibilities associated with British citizenship, in addition to those enjoyed under the Human Rights Act, as a basis for defining what it means to be a Citizen in Britain's open democratic society;
- to consider the difference between the different categories of British nationality;
- to examine the relationship between residence, citizenship and British national status and the incentives for long-term residents to become British citizens; and
- to explore the role of citizens and residents in civic society, including voting, jury service and other forms of civic participation.

In these aims, the law of nationality is mingled with the developing ideas of civic participation.

Nationality is increasingly treated as a status that must be earned. Hand in hand with that, it has become easier to lose one's British nationality for acts deemed to be against the public interest (see below).

The European Convention on Nationality includes a commitment to avoid statelessness, and a UN Convention also aims at the reduction of statelessness. Nevertheless, changes in the law are not always coherent in this aim. An Imiscoe policy brief of 2006 notes that in Europe 'nationality law has become a highly politicized matter' and 'reforms have become more frequent'. The UK is no exception. The political objectives sometimes conflict with the objective to reduce statelessness.

3.1.2 Brief history of British nationality law up to 1983

British nationality law is closely bound up with Britain's colonial history, and the law has changed as the former colonial relationships have changed. In order to understand the present categories of nationality status we need to look briefly at their historical development. For a fuller account, see for instance Fransman (2005), Shah, P. (2000), and Dummett and Nicol (1990).

Prior to the British Nationality Act 1948 the theoretical position was that all British subjects enjoyed the same status. Shah (2000:70) describes how the reality was somewhat different, in that non-white British subjects were already subject to restrictions and exclusions without reference to the right of abode which they supposedly enjoyed. In law, however, there was one status, that of British subject, and part of the myth of the Empire was that this status was the same wherever it was held or acquired.

As Commonwealth states gained independence they naturally wished to gain more control over their own citizenship and entry to their territories. In 1946 Canada precipitated legislative change in the UK by passing its own citizenship laws. Rather than have the rug pulled out from under it, the British government moved to legislate to accommodate both the desire of independent Commonwealth countries to control their own affairs and the myth of seamless equality (see Dummett and Nicol 1990:134–6). The 1948 Act divided British subjects into two main categories: citizens of the United Kingdom and Colonies (CUKCs) and citizens of independent Commonwealth countries. Thus, in independent Commonwealth countries, citizenship would give access to British subjecthood, rather than the other way round. Rather confusingly, all these people were called not only 'British subjects' but also 'Commonwealth citizens' (s 1(2)). There was a third category, that of British subjects without citizenship, for people who were potentially citizens of a Commonwealth country who did not actually gain citizenship when the country in question passed its citizenship laws or whose parent had lost their British subject status (BNA 1948 ss 13 and 16). It was intended to apply as a transitional status but in fact persisted for a dwindling group of people. While they did not become citizens of independent Commonwealth countries on independence, for instance because they did not meet residence conditions, at the same time they could not acquire CUKC status because they did not have the requisite connection with the UK or a colony. The government of Empire also created a distinction in status between those who were born in a colony (British subjects) and those who were born in a protectorate (British protected persons). A protectorate did not in theory fall within the rule of the common law, but in practice the British did not recognize a local ruler and exercised administrative control. The status of BPP was not transmitted to children, and is now held by very few people. However, the distinction had important repercussions for East African Asians in the 1960s (see Dummett and Nicol 1990:125–6 and 196–204 and Shah 2000:71).

CUKCs under the 1948 Act (ss 4 and 12) were people who were born, adopted, registered, or naturalized in the UK or Colonies or whose father was. Citizens of independent Commonwealth countries or of Ireland had a right to register as a CUKC if they had been resident in the UK or a colony for 12 months. These registration rights were gradually eroded, first by the Commonwealth Immigrants Act 1962, then by the 1971

Immigration Act. The 1948 Act made no immediate impact upon the immigration status of either group: CUKCs or citizens of independent Commonwealth countries. All retained a theoretical right to enter the UK. There was also movement between the two groups as citizens of independent Commonwealth countries resident in the UK could register as CUKCs as described above, and CUKCs would, if they met any necessary criteria, become citizens of independent Commonwealth countries when their home country gained independence.

As we have seen in chapter 1, the immigration statutes of the 1960s introduced immigration control for citizens of independent Commonwealth countries. This built upon the distinction created by the 1948 Act between two groups of British subjects. The 1971 Immigration Act used the categories of CUKC and citizen of independent Commonwealth country and the concept of familial connection introduced by the 1948 Act, to create different classes of immigration entitlement. These categories were imported directly into the nationality definitions set out by the British Nationality Act 1981. The 1971 Immigration Act therefore had a significant impact on the development of nationality law. The Act defines who has a right of abode and who does not. Most of those who retained right of abode when the Act was implemented on 1 January 1973 were CUKCs. Those who had the right of abode were referred to as 'patrial'. This was a term previously unknown in immigration law, and which, following the repeal of these provisions, is no longer used. Section 2 set out who were patrials. These were:

(i) CUKCs by birth, adoption, naturalization or registration in the UK (s 2(1)(a));
(ii) CUKCs whose parents or grandparents were CUKCs by birth, adoption, naturalization, or registration in the UK (s 2(1)(b));
(iii) CUKCs who had been ordinarily resident in the UK for five years (s 2(1)(c));
(iv) Commonwealth citizens with a parent born or adopted in the UK (s 2(1)(d));
(v) Commonwealth women married to patrial men (s 2(2)).

It may be seen, by comparing paragraphs (iv) and (v) above with the rest, that the ancestral connection for Commonwealth citizens needed to be closer than for CUKCs in order to obtain the right of abode.

At the time of implementation of the 1971 Immigration Act, nationality passed through men to the children of their marriage. A person who was born in the UK and Colonies would acquire that citizenship through their birth. However, a person born outside the UK and Colonies could only acquire CUKC status through their parents if their father had it and their parents were married. The CUKC citizenship so acquired was citizenship by descent, which could not pass to a child. Transmission of nationality outside the UK and Colonies could therefore only occur for one generation, and this is still the position under the 1981 Act, although some rights of registration help to remedy this deficit (see below). In *Bibi and others v SSHD* [2007] EWCA Civ 740 Mr Jabbar had entered the UK using someone else's identity. After five years of residence he registered as a CUKC in 1967. He had since died, and the application before the court was the claim of his widow and children that they had right of abode through his citizenship. The Court of Appeal held that his registration as a CUKC was void. The person identified on the documents had not been in the UK for five years, so no registration had taken place. Thus the family had no basis upon which to claim right of abode.

The British Nationality Act 1981, which commenced on 1 January 1983, now governs current British nationality law, together with amendments brought about by the British Overseas Territories Act 2002, the Nationality, Immigration and Asylum Act 2002 and Immigration, Asylum and Nationality Act 2006. Section 2 of the Immigration Act 1971 as set out above was repealed by the 1981 Act and replaced with the current s 2. This gives right of abode to:

(a) British citizens;

(b) Commonwealth citizens who immediately before the commencement of the 1981 Act had a right of abode in the UK under the old s 2.

Currently there are the following categories in British nationality law: British citizens, British Overseas Territories citizens, British Overseas citizens, British subjects, British nationals (Overseas), and British protected persons. We shall consider each of these categories in turn.

3.2 British citizenship under the British Nationality Act 1981

Holding British citizenship carries a right of abode in the UK and is the most privileged class of British nationality.

3.2.1 Acquisition by birth after commencement

Section 1 of the British Nationality Act 1981 (BNA 1981) deals with the acquisition of British citizenship by people born after the commencement of the Act on 1 January 1983. It provides that a person born in the UK after commencement is a British citizen if, at the time of their birth, their mother or father is a British citizen or settled in the UK. This changed the nature of the UK's nationality law in a very substantial way. It abolished the long-standing common law tradition, enacted in the 1948 Nationality Act, of *jus soli*. This Latin name means 'the right from the soil or land', and the common law rule was that anyone born on British soil was a British subject, regardless of their parents' nationality or whether they were just visiting or had lived in the UK all their lives. The BNA 1981 changed all this and gave the UK more in common with those countries which employ the rule not of *jus soli* but of *jus sanguinis*, i.e. 'the right of blood', meaning by inheritance rather than by birth. Parental connection with the UK, of increasing relevance in the earlier part of the twentieth century, from 1983 assumed a vital importance in the determination of a child's nationality. This change creates a risk of statelessness, as for instance a child of migrant workers or overseas students would not acquire British nationality.

The British Overseas Territories Act 2002 (BOTA) Sch 1 amended British Nationality Act s 1 so that since 21 May 2002 birth in an overseas territory also results in British citizenship if the child's parents are British or settled in the territory. Their parents are likely now to be British following BOTA s 3 (see below). British Overseas territories are currently: Anguilla, Bermuda, the British Antarctic Territory (so-called, although this is also claimed by Chile and Argentina and has no inhabitants), British Indian Ocean Territory, Cayman Islands, Falkland Islands, Gibraltar, Montserrat, Pitcairn, Henderson, Ducie and Oeno Islands, St Helena and Dependencies, Turks and Caicos Islands, and the Virgin Islands. The Sovereign base areas on Cyprus are British Overseas Territories, but birth there does not give rise to British citizenship. The BOTA is discussed more fully below.

Under BNA 1981 s 1 British citizenship is acquired by birth in the UK if the child's parents are either British or settled. To be settled means to be ordinarily resident in the UK without any immigration restrictions (Immigration Act 1971 s 33). Settlement is discussed more fully in chapter 7 and does not normally imply any particular

Table 1 Right of abode

Legislative era	Right of abode	Subject to immigration control
Pre-1948	All British subjects	Aliens
British Nationality Act 1948	All British subjects	Aliens
Commonwealth Immigrants Act 1962	Those born in the UK	Aliens
	Irish citizens	Commonwealth citizens with passports issued by colonial or Commonwealth government
	Commonwealth citizens (i.e. British subjects) with passports issued by UK government	
Commonwealth Immigrants Act 1968	Those born in the UK	Aliens
	Irish citizens	Commonwealth citizens with passports issued by colonial or Commonwealth government
	Commonwealth citizens (i.e. British subjects) with passports issued by UK government and whose parent or grandparent was born, naturalized or adopted in the UK	Commonwealth citizens with passports issued by UK government, but without parental connection
Immigration Act 1971	CUKCs born, naturalized or adopted in UK or with parent or grandparent born, adopted or naturalized in UK	Aliens
	CUKC resident in UK for five years	CUKCs without parental connection or residence
		Other commonwealth citizens without parent born in UK
	Other commonwealth citizens whose parent was born (only) in UK	Irish citizens (in theory subject to control but mainly exempt because of Common Travel Area)
	Commonwealth citizens married before 1 January 1973 to a man with right of abode	
British Nationality Act 1981	British Citizens	Aliens
	Commonwealth Citizens who had right of abode at commencement (1 January 1983)	Citizens of Commonwealth Countries
		British Overseas Citizens
		British Dependent Territories Citizens

nationality. European nationals exercising free movement rights in the UK used to be regarded as settled for nationality purposes, i.e. their child born in the UK could have British nationality. However, the Immigration (European Economic Area) Regulations, SI 2000/2326, limited the definition of European nationals who would be regarded as settled for nationality purposes, and this limitation is continued in the 2006 Regulations (SI 2006/1003) to apply to those who have acquired permanent residence under those regulations. Therefore children born to EEA nationals who are exercising EC rights in the UK will be British if born before 2 October 2000, but not if born after that date unless their parents have permanent residence.

3.2.2 Acquisition under the Act by those born before commencement

Section 11 of the British Nationality Act gave British citizenship to anyone born before commencement of the Act who was a CUKC with right of abode before the Act. In other words, it gave British citizenship to patrial CUKCs as defined in the old s 2 of the 1971 Act, discussed above. These were the people with a parental or grandparental connection with the UK who were citizens of the UK itself, or a colony, but not Commonwealth countries.

On 21 May 2002 British citizenship was also acquired by existing citizens of the British Overseas Territories listed above (British Overseas Territories Act 2002 s 3), whatever their date of birth.

3.2.3 British citizenship by descent

Where a person is born to British parents outside the United Kingdom, they are a British citizen by descent (BNA s 2). The essential characteristic of this status is that it cannot be passed to a child. It therefore means that if a British couple, A and B, go abroad, say to work, and have a child C while they are abroad, but later return, C's children, if born in the UK will be British, and the line of British citizenship continues unbroken. If however C stays abroad, or goes to work abroad herself and has children there, they will not be British unless their other parent is British otherwise than by descent. C's children have an entitlement to register as British if they meet the conditions set out below, but this ends with them, and is not available to their children. The provision maintains a distinction between those who are British and those who are settled. The children of a settled couple are British if born in the UK, but otherwise are not. The exception since 21 May 2002 is that birth in an overseas territory to British parents will now give rise to British citizenship otherwise than by descent (i.e. full British citizenship) regardless of whether the parents are settled in the UK or in the overseas territory where the birth takes place. British citizenship by descent in the overseas territories continues only for those who had that status before 2002.

3.2.4 British nationality in European law

For the purposes of EC law Britain has defined 'British nationals' as British citizens, British overseas territories citizens deriving their citizenship from Gibraltar (though since the British Overseas Territories Act 2002 s 3 came into force these people have been British citizens), and British subjects with the right of abode. This excludes British overseas citizens (see *Manjit Kaur*), British protected persons (see *R v SSHD ex p Upadhey*

Table 2 Effect of legislation determining immigration and nationality status

Legislation	Legal principle	Effect
Pre-1948	In theory all British subjects had the right to enter UK	In reality there was less travel than now, and informal means were used to control non-white entry
British Nationality Act 1948	Divided British subjects into CUKCs and Citizens of Independent Commonwealth Countries. British subjects also called Commonwealth Citizens	Laid foundation for distinctions to be made between CUKCs and other British subjects/ Commonwealth citizens
Commonwealth Immigrants Act 1962	Introduced first immigration control on Commonwealth citizens	Linking freedom from control to passports issued by UK government or birth in UK meant ex-patriate white British more likely to be exempt than non-white colonial or Commonwealth residents
Commonwealth Immigrants Act 1968	Parental connection with UK more fully established as basis for freedom from immigration control	Developing blood tie as basis of UK citizenship, many UK passport holders, esp. East African Asians, excluded
Immigration Act 1971	Parental or birth connection with UK becomes main means of establishing freedom from control. More generous provisions for CUKCs than for Commonwealth Citizens	Consolidating blood tie and effects of 1968 Act. In simultaneous legislation

European Nationals granted rights of free movement. |
| British Nationality Act 1981 | Birth in UK no longer enough for exemption from immigration control. Crucial emphasis on parentage

Citizens of Dependent Territories excluded | British Citizenship finally established, and on basis of earlier immigration law. Immigration law considerations have informed who is deemed fully British |
| British Overseas Territories Act 2002 | BDTCs renamed BOTCs, made BCs and given right of abode | Hong Kong's independence is now established. There are very few overseas territories left and British government grants right of abode to their citizens |

ILU vol 3 no 13) and Commonwealth citizens with right of abode. For discussion of these issues, see chapter 5.

3.3 Other categories of British nationality

The less privileged classes of British nationality were created to answer immigration concerns at particular moments in history, and can best be understood in the context of the UK's relationship with the groups who were the targets of the legislation.

3.3.1 **British Overseas Territories citizens**

In older documentation and in the British Nationality Act 1981 this nationality status is referred to as British Dependent Territories Citizenship; but in recognition that many territories are not dependent but thriving communities, (see White Paper, *Partnership for Progress and Prosperity* (Cm 4264)), they were renamed in s 1 British Overseas Territories Act 2002 as 'overseas' rather than 'dependent'. Since the 2002 Act came fully into force on 21 May 2002, the majority in this citizenship category have become British citizens.

On the face of it there seems to be little reason for retaining BOTC status at all, as most BOTCs became British citizens on 21 May 2002. One remaining function is that the 2002 Act does not amend the British Nationality Act in relation to naturaliza-tion. Therefore residence in an overseas territory can only lead to naturalization as a BOTC, not a British citizen (under the British Nationality (British Overseas Territories) Regulations 2007, SI 2007/3139). This prevents British citizenship from being attained by going to live in a British Overseas Territory. The Parliamentary debates also reveal another reason. Birth in the Sovereign base areas in Cyprus (Akrotiri and Dhekelia) gives only BOTC status, not British citizenship. Why should such children not be British citizens? The Foreign Office Minister replied, concerning the Cyprus bases, that according to the treaty with Cyprus which established them 'they are for use as mili-tary bases only, and not for the establishment of a wider community' (HC 22 November 2001 col 543). This is part of the answer. The rest is to be found in the proceedings of the Standing Committee, in the words of the same minister:

Hon. Members should also bear in mind that Cyprus is at an important crossroads between the middle east and Europe. We have already had difficult experiences with refugees from the middle east landing in Cyprus and claiming asylum in the bases. The potential to acquire British citizen-ship through the back door could be a huge pull factor and make us, and Cyprus, vulnerable to a large influx of asylum seekers. We want to avoid that if we can, because it would also undermine the military integrity of the bases . . . if we extended the treaty's provisions to cover the bases, there would not just be a handful of people who might be eligible for British citizenship. The fear is that more people would be attracted to go to Cyprus and make applications for asylum. (6 December 2001 Standing Committee D)

Here we see the development of trends as described in chapter 1. Whereas in the mid-twentieth century, a desire to curb non-white immigration drove immigration law and policy and that of nationality, in the late twentieth and early twenty-first centuries, a desire to curb asylum claims is the driver. This policy shapes not only immigration law, but also, as we see here, an otherwise incomprehensible and some would say, obscure, provision of nationality law.

3.3.1.1 *The status as it was created*

The category originally called British Dependent Territories Citizenship was created by the BNA 1981 for those people who were CUKCs by virtue of a close connection with what would have formerly been called a colony, then called a dependent terri-tory and now an overseas territory. The close connection was birth in the territory and at the time of the birth their father or mother was either a BDTC, or settled there, or in another overseas territory (BNA 1981 s 15). Under BNA s 23 a person became a BDTC on commencement if they were a CUKC before commencement by their birth, naturalization, or registration in a dependent territory or if their parent or grandparent had CUKC citizenship by one of these means. There are also provisions for naturalization and registration as BOTCs, and for obtaining BOT citizenship by descent if born outside the territories to a BOTC parent.

BOTC status can be passed through generations. It can also be acquired by descent by birth outside the territory in the same way as British citizenship and with the same consequences.

At the time of the passing of the British Nationality Act 1981 the promoting minister made it clear that all BDTCs were to have the same citizenship status, although this did not give them entry to other dependent territories. More significantly, it did not give them entry to Britain as BDTC status did not carry a right of abode. It may appear that the 1981 Act removed the right of abode from this group of CUKCs. However, as discussed earlier, the Commonwealth Immigrants Act 1968 and the Immigration Act 1971 had already restricted the right of abode to those with a British born, adopted, registered, or naturalized parent or grandparent. In practice therefore most CUKCs living in overseas territories would not have had a right of abode, and in relation to this group the 1981 Act did not do much more than crystallize into nationality law what was already the case in immigration law.

3.3.1.2 *Hong Kong*

In the 2002 Act BOTCs from all overseas territories apart from the Cyprus bases have become British citizens, with full rights of abode, with a limited exception in the case of the British Indian Ocean Territory, discussed further below. The reader might feel moved to ask why these rights could not have been accorded in 1983, instead of these British nationals going through 20 years of nationality wilderness. It is not possible to give a full answer to this question. There have been changes of government in the meantime, and the political climate is different in 2002 from that in 1981. The government has stated its wish to advance towards ratification of Protocol 4. Another relevant factor is certainly Hong Kong. During the Parliamentary debate on the 1981 Act, the question was raised of whether each dependent territory should have its own citizenship status. The government was opposed to this. Opposition members argued the case for Gibraltar and the Falklands, but it was noticeable that opposition parties conceded that Hong Kong was a special case, and no one was prepared to argue for concessions for Hong Kong. The anticipated return of the territory to China, due in 1997, gave rise to fears that many Hong Kong CUKCs would want to enter the UK rather than live under Chinese control. Dummett and Nicol's analysis is that: 'No British politician was ready to consider a redefinition of British nationality which would give right of abode in the UK to 2.6 million British Chinese in Hong Kong' (1990: 242). Before 1997 Macdonald said that:

The population of Hong Kong consists of some 3.2 million British Dependent Territories Citizens who will become Chinese nationals after 1997, 10, 000 who will not, 2 million Chinese nationals, 17, 000 British citizens with the right of abode, 150, 000 foreign nationals (ie not British or Chinese) and about 11, 000 stateless persons (mainly refugees from Vietnam). (1995:147)

The figures are slightly at variance but the point is clear. The right of abode in the UK would not be given to the people of Hong Kong.

However, the return to Chinese rule also created anxiety on the part of those who wanted to see these former British nationals protected. In anticipation of the return to

China, and in response to pressure various legislative measures were brought in to give some possibility of entry to the UK to a limited number of Hong Kong BDTCs. Article 4 of the Hong Kong (British Nationality) Order 1986 created a new category of citizenship: British national (overseas). This applied only to BDTCs who had that citizenship by virtue of birth, parentage, naturalization, or registration in Hong Kong. This status was not awarded automatically but only on application before a cut-off date.

BN(O) status does not carry any right of entry to the UK. It entitles the holder to a passport which shows a form of British citizenship and to registration as a British citizen after five years' lawful residence in the UK, providing the last year is free of immigration restrictions. This is the same right which is held by BOTCs and BOCs. It therefore only retains the registration right which Hong Kong BDTCs would have had anyway under s 4(1) BNA. It seems that most of those who were entitled to register as BN(O)s did so, although the vast majority were ethnically Chinese and therefore obtained Chinese nationality as well.

A more practically significant right was later given in the British Nationality (Hong Kong) Act 1997 to those who were ordinarily resident in Hong Kong immediately before 4 February 1997. If, by virtue of connection with Hong Kong, they held any of the categories of British nationality which do not carry a right of abode, or were a British protected person, and would otherwise be stateless, s 1 gave a right to register as British citizens after 1 July 1997. This would be full British citizen status carrying a right of abode. The effect was that neither ethnic Chinese nor those with a form of British nationality need become stateless as a result of the handover. A discretionary right to register was given to Hong Kong war widows. There was also a scheme for selecting key people in certain occupational classes and awarding British citizenship to them. This was under the British Nationality (Hong Kong) Act 1990, and the scheme is now closed.

The Nationality, Immigration and Asylum Act 2002 s 14 provides that no one may be registered as a BOTC by virtue of a connection with Hong Kong.

3.3.1.3 *Gibraltar and the Falkland Islands*

More favourable terms were granted to citizens of these two overseas territories. Under BNA 1981 s 5 Gibraltarians had a right to register as British citizens. They were also the only group of BDTCs who were included in the UK's declaration of British nationality for EU purposes. When the Falklands war broke out, the British Nationality (Falkland Islands) Act 1983 was passed, providing that anyone born in the Falklands after the date of commencement to a parent born or settled in the Falklands would be a British citizen. Following the British Overseas Territories Act the advantage to Gibraltarians and Falkland Islanders evaporates as all BOTCs become British citizens automatically, and obtain the rights of an EU citizen.

3.3.1.4 *Chagossians*

The story of the Chagossians is one of the more scandalous episodes in British colonial history. The term refers to the inhabitants of the Chagos Islands which form part of the British Indian Ocean Territory. This territory came into existence as a separate dependent territory in 1965, having up to that time been governed as part of the then British colony of Mauritius. Mauritius became independent in 1968. The separation of the BIOT, however, had less to do with Mauritian independence than with the USA's desire for a military base in the Indian Ocean. They identified Diego Garcia, the largest Chagos island, as a suitable site, and the British government was persuaded that it would be acceptable to give the island over to the Americans for this use, removing those who lived there. They were removed by various tactics including forcible eviction. The majority were displaced to Mauritius, though some to the Seychelles and other locations. This forcible displacement finally faced a legal challenge in the UK's Divisional Court in *R v Secretary of State for the Foreign and Commonwealth Office ex p Bancoult* [2001] 2 WLR 1219. The court found that 'a power to make laws for the "peace, order and good government" of a territory...required its people to be governed, not removed', and Mr Bancoult won the right for the Chagossians to return.

In the Standing Committee debate on the British Overseas Territories Bill the Foreign Office minister stated that 'such treatment would be impossible today' (HC Standing Committee D 6 December 2001). Nevertheless, it took some lobbying, the case of *Bancoult,* and an amendment to the Bill before those Chagossians who had lost the opportunity of BDTC status were included in the provisions of the 2002 Act. As nationality prior to the 1981 Act passed only through married fathers, those born to Chagossian (CUKC) mothers but whose father was not Chagossian (say, for instance, Mauritian, as was highly likely in the circumstances) after the enforced exile but before the 1981 Act, did not obtain CUKC status. If they had been born in the Chagos Islands they would have been CUKCs by birth. Section 6 of the British Overseas Territories Act 2002 provides that a person born in these circumstances between 26 April 1969 and 1 January 1983 will obtain British citizenship by descent. This puts them in the same position as they would have been if their citizenship had been transmitted through their mother, but not the same position as if the exile had never happened, as in this case they would have become British Citizens under the 2002 Act like other BOTCs. The government's justification for this at the time was that they were now free to return to the Chagos Islands. If they did so their children will be British citizens. If they did not, there would be no reason for them to have any more enduring form of British citizenship than any other British citizen who chooses to stay abroad.

Practical plans for their return were slow to materialize, and a government feasibility study suggested the low-lying islands would not be habitable. On 10 June 2004, hidden behind the publicity given to European and local election day, two Orders in Council were signed by the Queen relating to the Chagos Islands. The British Indian Ocean Territory (Constitution) Order appointed a Commissioner to rule over the territory and stated as a constitutional principle that no person has any right of abode in the territory or has unrestricted access to any part of it. The British Indian Ocean Territory (Immigration) Order provided for a system of permits to visit the islands, decisions being appealable only to the Commissioner. These orders were made under the Royal Prerogative and, in the words of Baroness Symons 'restore the legal position to what it had been understood to be before the High Court decision' in *ex p Bancoult* (HL Debs 15 June 2004 col WS27). The executive had overturned the judicial decision and stopped the repopulation of the islands. This undermined the justification offered by the government for limiting the nationality entitlement of Ilois people born between 1969 and 1981, as they have no right of return to enable them to pass British citizenship to their children. The announcement of the prerogative orders provoked outrage in a number of quarters including in Mauritius, where the government threatened to withdraw from the Commonwealth to enable it to sue the UK in the International Court of Justice. On 7 July an early day motion secured a debate in the House of Commons at which the Minister had an opportunity to defend the government's reasons. He also took this opportunity to disclose that two days earlier the government had amended its declaration accepting the jurisdiction of the International Court of Justice to exclude not only current Commonwealth countries (an existing exception retained by a number of Commonwealth members) but also former Commonwealth countries. In other words, Mauritius would not be able to sue at any time.

The orders were challenged by judicial review and once again found unlawful (*R (Bancoult) v SSFCA* [2006] EWHC 1038 (Admin)). The government appealed but lost again in the Court of Appeal (*Secretary of State for Foreign and Commonwealth Affairs v The Queen (on the application of Bancoult)* [2007] EWCA Civ 498). The Secretary of State argued that an Order in Council was not subject to judicial review. The prerogative orders were made nominally by the Queen in a process even less open to scrutiny than secondary legislation as there was no debate in the Privy Council on the matter. The Queen signed the orders on the advice of a single minister, as by constitutional convention she was bound to do. The Court of Appeal held that it was a fiction to regard these orders as acts of the monarch. They were in reality acts of the executive and as such subject to judicial review. The Court held that, like the ordinance that was successfully challenged in 2000, the prerogative power exercised by the Orders in Council was not in reality an act of governance at all, let alone one for peace and good order. For the population of the Chagos Islands, the case concerned 'not its governance, but its elimination as a population' (para 66). There was no relevant change of circumstance since the ministerial assurance after the 2000 Divisional Court decision that the Chagossians would be allowed to return home. The prerogative orders that once again removed their right were a defeat of a substantive legitimate expectation and were 'so profoundly unfair...as to amount to an abuse of power' (para 73). The government is appealing to the House of Lords, who granted leave to appeal on condition that the government paid all the costs, regardless of the outcome (see Times Online 9 November 2007: 'Islanders who wait in vain for justice and a paradise lost').

See http://ukwatch.net/article/diego_garcia_-_crime_against_humanity%3F for an argument that the government's treatment of the Chagossians amounts to a crime against humanity.

Another curious exception is Ascension Island, which is part of the territory of St Helena, and like Diego Garcia is devoted largely to military use. Here, no one has a right of abode. A Foreign Office promise to grant this was revoked in early 2006, and St Helenian British citizens must leave Ascension Island on retirement.

3.3.2 **British overseas citizens**

This kind of nationality was created by the BNA 1981 s 26. It was to consist of those CUKCs who did not at commencement obtain British citizenship or British Dependent Territories citizenship. It carries no right of abode in the UK, and the number of people holding this status is diminishing as it cannot be transmitted to children.

Those most affected by the creation of BOC status were people of Asian origin living in East African countries. The situation of people from India and Pakistan who had moved to Kenya and Uganda has been briefly described in chapter 1. The legislative history reveals one of the longest-running human rights issues in UK nationality and immigration law.

Following the British Nationality Act 1948, as previously described, British subjects were divided into CUKCs and citizens of independent Commonwealth countries. Some people who came, or whose parents came, originally from Commonwealth countries which became independent did not obtain citizenship of those countries when they passed their citizenship laws because they were not able for instance to meet residence conditions. Such was the situation of people from South Asia living in East Africa, who did not obtain citizenship of their country of origin. Accordingly this group were not citizens of independent Commonwealth countries, although when for instance Kenya and Uganda became independent, they were living in independent Commonwealth countries. They were CUKCs, or British subjects without citizenship, and as such had a right of abode in the UK. Yet others were British Protected Persons if they originated from protectorates rather than what were then colonies. The 1962 Commonwealth Immigrants Act retained CUKCs' exemption from immigration control providing they had a UK passport issued by the UK government rather than the government of a colony. One issued by a High Commission would suffice for this, so once their country of residence became independent, passports issued by the High Commission in those countries would give the right of abode in the UK.

The independence statutes of East African countries gave Asian people a difficult choice. They had a two-year period in which to decide whether to opt for citizenship of their African country of residence. After this they would lose that option and thus their right to live in that country. Kenya and Uganda began to pursue policies of Africanization, which involved favouring their own citizens in economic and civic matters. In anticipation of increasing discrimination, and in reliance on the possibility of using their right of abode in the UK, the vast majority chose to retain their CUKC or even BPP status, and not opt for Kenyan or Ugandan citizenship.

The 1968 Commonwealth Immigrants Act, however, divided CUKCs into those who could enter the UK without restriction, and those who could not. The line of inclusion was drawn around those who had a British parent or grandparent, born, adopted, registered, or naturalized in the UK. The value of a UK passport for those without such parental connections suddenly diminished. They were subject to a voucher scheme which operated on a quota system, so they might or might not be able to gain entry to the UK. The Act took away the right of abode for the majority of East African Asians. They were thus left with no country in which they had any right to live.

Section 1 of the 1968 Act was the subject of the challenge before the European Commission of Human Rights in *East African Asians v UK* (1981) 3 EHRR 76. The successful basis of the claim was that the Act was racially discriminatory and that such treatment was degrading and thus in breach of Article 3 of the Convention. This decision was of historic importance in, first, finding as fact that the statute was passed with a racial motive. This was strenuously denied by the government on the basis that requiring a familial connection had nothing to do with colour but only with defining who 'belongs' to the UK. However, the evidence for this emerges clearly from the Cabinet papers and other official records of the time, which refer to 'coloured' immigration (see Lester 2002).

The second significant aspect of the Commission's decision is the finding that racial discrimination can amount to a breach of Article 3 in itself. If it is sufficiently severe it amounts to degrading treatment. This does away with the need to identify another Convention right in respect of which discrimination may be alleged under Article 14 (see chapter 4 for further discussion of these Articles). If the UK had ratified Protocol 4 of the Convention the applicants would have had a virtually unanswerable case under Protocol 4, being nationals denied entry, and also under Article 14 read with Protocol 4. This course was not open to them, and the actual decision could be said to have greater significance because of the use of Article 3.

All this of course is immigration law rather than nationality law, however it is necessary history to understand the category of BOC under the BNA 1981. The decision of the Commission was answered by the UK government increasing the number of vouchers available under the quota system. This compromise was accepted by the Council of Europe's Committee of Ministers. East African Asian CUKCs thus remained without a right of abode, but with a greater chance of obtaining entry to the UK through the voucher system.

It will be apparent from the foregoing that East African Asians did not have the necessary connection with the UK to obtain British Citizenship on 1 January 1983, nor with an overseas territory to become a BDTC. Accordingly under the BNA 1981 they obtained the residual status of BOC with no right of abode and no transmission to children.

There was a significant lobby to include them in what became the 2002 British Overseas Territories Act, but this failed. A Private Member's Bill was proposed to fill this deficit, but did not receive government support. East African Asians thus remained BOCs without right of abode while citizens of overseas territories attained full British citizenship. The government gave as a reason for not including BOCs in the 2002 Act that many had access to or had acquired dual nationality, or had access to the UK through the voucher scheme. The assertion of dual nationality is generally correct as regards the most numerous group of people who have BOC status, namely those of Malaysian nationality living in Singapore, but not East African Asians, who could only use the discretionary voucher system. However, on 4 March 2002 the voucher scheme was abolished by announcement in Parliament without any prior warning. The reason given was that it was not much used (Angela Eagle, Minister of State for Home Office HC 5 Mar 2002 col 162W), though evidence given in *ECO Mumbai v NH (India)* [2007] EWCA Civ 1330 para 6 was that there were 500 applications per year at that stage.

The matter was finally addressed by a late amendment to the Nationality, Immigration and Asylum Bill 2002 to provide that BOCs have a right to register as British citizens if they have no other nationality or have not deprived themselves of such nationality after 4 July 2002 when the provision (s 4B inserted in BNA 1981) was announced. In *The Queen on the application of Shah* [2004] EWHC 2733 (Admin) the claimant was a BOC who applied for a BOC passport in 2001, but was erroneously refused by the High Commission. He applied in 2003 for registration as a British citizen under s 4B but was refused on the ground that he had Indian nationality. In Indian law he would have lost his Indian nationality if the High Commission had acted correctly and granted a BOC passport. He renewed his application in 2004. Lightman J refused permission to move for judicial review of the 2004 refusal on the basis that s 4B did not permit any discretion to be exercised on the ground of injustice to the applicant and it was too late to compel a remedy for the 2001 mistake. The Court of Appeal agreed it was too late. If the court now ordered a correction of the 2001 decision, Mr Shah would lose his Indian citizenship, but there was a Catch 22 as this would mean that he would have taken a step to divest himself of another citizenship after July 2002 and so be unable to avail himself of British Nationality Act 1981 s 4B (*R (on the application of Shah) v SSHD* CA Civ 21/6/05, unreported).

The present position for BOCs may be summarized as follows:

(a) BOCs who have no other nationality may register as British citizens.

(b) If they do so, unlike other British citizens, they do not have the option of dual nationality.

(c) They may not relinquish another nationality in order to gain British nationality.

(d) Those who entered under the voucher system or can otherwise obtain leave to enter, have a right to register after five years' residence.

(e) This applies also for a dual national (see s 4 below).

(f) Dependants of former BOCs now BCs may apply to enter the UK under the usual family rules for settlement, which are more stringent than the rules for families under the voucher scheme.

(g) Any qualifying person may become a British citizen, whereas only heads of families could obtain vouchers under that scheme.

The abolition of the special voucher scheme and creation of a right to register was accompanied by an assertion that no one would be worse off because of the scheme's abolition and that the provisions were intended to right a historic wrong. However, there were no transitional provisions to ensure that individuals did not suffer, and the changes have thrown up numerous problems.

In *ECO Mumbai v NH* the sponsor was a BOC who registered as a British Citizen under the new provisions in 2003. She returned to India to support the entry clearance of her husband and son, but her son, who had just turned 18, was refused. The Court of Appeal endorsed the AIT's decision, which was interesting not only in its outcome but also in the matters that it took into account. The son could not succeed under the immigration rules, but his application was upheld under the right to respect for family life (Human Rights Act Article 8). This right may only be lawfully interfered with by the state to the extent that the interference is proportionate to the public benefit from doing so, and necessary in a democratic society (Article 8.2, see chapter 4). The AIT, endorsed by the Court of Appeal, took into account that the 'families like this had been prevented for over 30 years from settling in the country of which some or all of their members once were, and are now again, citizens' (CA, para 21). They were prevented from settling by legislation which was racially discriminatory. The sponsor was then prevented from coming to the UK because the UK's response to the finding of racial discrimination was the voucher scheme which discriminated against women (para 18, quoting AIT para 34). The sponsor's husband was not a BOC, and as a married woman she was not accepted as a head of household. The legislation of 2002 was intended to right a historic wrong. These were the historic wrongs that she suffered. It would not be proportionate now to stand on the letter of the law and refuse entry to her dependent son who had only just turned 18, and who would, if she had been a voucher holder, have entered with her. What was necessary in a democratic society was 'consideration of all the circumstances including the previous history of any previous wrongful act' (AIT quoted in para 18).

The immigration rules on special voucher holders remained for six months after the abolition of the scheme in 2002. In *HT (Special voucher holder – dependants) India* [2007] UKAIT 00031 the tribunal held that this did not mean that applications could still be made by dependants after the ending of the scheme. It was abolished (without notice) on the day of the announcement in Parliament, and the rules which remained in force did so for the purpose of outstanding applications, but did not allow new applications, even for dependants. This meant that dependants who would have been able to gain entry under the scheme lost that right immediately. This decision predates that in *ECO Mumbai v NH (India)*, and though the point is slightly different it may now be called into question.

The UK's declaration on nationality for purposes of EU memberhips still excludes BOCs. Therefore BOCs do not, by virtue of that status, obtain citizenship of the European Union (*Manjit Kaur*), though following the new s 4B, the discrimination inherent in this situation is much reduced.

3.3.3 British subjects under the Act

This name is given by the 1981 Act to the people known under earlier nationality statutes as British subjects without citizenship. If such people acquire any other citizenship they lose their British subject status. In addition to those mentioned in the historical section above, this group includes some Irish citizens who exercised a right to retain their British subject status. They have right of abode in the UK by virtue of the Common Travel Area (see chapter 7) though most others do not. The new right to register under BNA 1981 s 4B applies also to this group.

3.3.4 British protected persons

Earlier reference has been made to this status. Before the majority of countries under British rule obtained independence it applied to millions of people; now there are very few. They too have the new right to register under BNA 1981 s 4B.

3.4 Registration

This is a means of obtaining British nationality by application, rather than by place of birth or parentage. Registration may be an entitlement, unlike naturalization, which is always discretionary, although Immigration, Asylum and Nationality Act 2006 s 58 imports a requirement of good character, and thus an element of judgement except in the case of children under ten. Those who are entitled to register as British citizens are:

(a) Children of a British citizen by descent, if either the child and both parents have lived in the UK for three years prior to the date of the application (BNA 1981 s 3(5)) or application is made for registration within twelve months of the child's birth, and providing at least one of the parents was a British citizen otherwise than by descent (s 3(2) and (3)). This is the provision referred to above which limits the transmission of citizenship by descent to one generation by birth and a second generation by registration. In the case of the second entitlement, the British parent by descent must also have lived in the UK for at least three years prior to the birth (s 3(3)). In the case of registration under s 3(5), i.e. where the child and parents have returned to live in the UK for three years, both parents must consent to the registration. If the parents are divorced or legally separated or one has died, the three-year residence requirement only applies to one parent. It may be seen that these rules provide a mixture of *jus soli* and *jus sanguinis*. Where a British citizen by descent returns to the UK and lives here with their child, this demonstrates an intention to make the UK their home, which gives the child a kind of restored *jus soli*. They have not actually been born in the UK, but their presence here and that of their family suggests that they should be treated as though they were. Where the child themselves is not resident, a stronger blood tie with the UK is required (s 3(3)).

(b) British overseas Territories citizens, British nationals (overseas), British overseas citizens, British subjects under the 1981 Act, and British protected persons, so long as they have been resident in the UK for five years, are entitled to register as British citizens under BNA 1981 s 4. As mentioned earlier, since the British Overseas Territories Act 2002, the only BOTCs who remain to use the right to register are those who have naturalized in the overseas territories or who are BOTCs solely by virtue of birth in a Cyprus base (unlikely to be the case as the parent's nationality will generally have superseded this). The rest will be British citizens automatically. BOCs, BPPs, and British subjects under the Act who have no other nationality can now register under s 4B without the five-year residence condition, but note that this does not apply to British Nationals (Overseas). Residents of Hong Kong have still not won the rights now attained by the East Africans Asians and the Chagossians.

(c) Gibraltarians used to have a right to register under BNA s 5. This has become unnecessary since BOTA s 3 has come into force.

(d) Children born in the UK whose parent becomes British or settled, providing the application is made while they are still minors (BNA s 1(3)).

(e) Children born in the UK who live here until they are 10 years old (BNA s 1(4)).

(f) Persons born stateless in the UK, providing they have lived in the UK for five years at the date of the application and apply before they reach the age of 22 (BNA Sch 2 para 3, as amended by the Nationality, Immigration and Asylum Act 2002).

The Secretary of State has a discretion under BNA s 3(1) to register any minor. A child registered under s 3(1) is a British citizen by descent if one of their parents was British at the time of their birth (s 14(1)(c)). This discretion may be used to fill gaps in the entitlements listed above, for instance where a child has been adopted abroad by British parents. Nationality Instructions Chapter 9 gives guidance on the exercise of the discretion. Section 9.15.2 says 'the most important criterion is that the child's future should clearly be seen to lie in the UK'. If the child and family seem to have an established way of life in the UK then the Home Office 'should accept at face value that the child intends to live here'. The parents' immigration status is relevant to this. Where the mother had indefinite leave and had applied for British Citizenship, the Home Office was wrong to place emphasis on the fact that the father's leave was still limited. He had also applied for indefinite leave to remain. The reason it had not yet been granted was delay in the Home Office, and his application showed where the children's future lay (*R (on the application of Ali) v SSHD* [2007] EWHC 1983 (Admin)).

3.5 Naturalization

This is another process of obtaining British nationality by application, and while there are conditions which must be fulfilled, there is no entitlement to naturalization. It is an exercise of discretion by the Secretary of State. As an exercise of discretion subject to statutory requirements and published criteria, it is open to judicial review on usual administrative law grounds. This is discussed further at the end of this chapter.

The requirements which must be fulfilled in order to qualify to apply for naturalization are found in BNA 1981 s 6 and Sch 1. Applications may only be made by persons of 'full age and capacity'. So, the applicant must be at least 18 years of age.

3.5.1 **Capacity**

Full capacity is defined in BNA 1981 s 50(11) as 'not of unsound mind'. The Nationality Instructions Ch 18 Annex A says that the question is whether the applicant is sufficiently mentally competent to know that they want to become British citizens. Where applicants have lodged their own applications, it should be assumed that they meet the requirement 'unless there is information on the Home Office papers to cast doubt on this'. By Immigration, Asylum and Nationality Act 2006, s 49, the Secretary of State may waive the capacity requirement 'if he thinks it in the applicant's best interests'. This is a very minimal standard compared with the demanding approach of the new tests of knowledge of English language and life in the UK, but this too may be waived in suitable cases (see below).

3.5.2 **Period of residence**

Naturalization requires a period of residence in the UK. The qualifying period is three years for a person married to or in a civil partnership with a British citizen (s 6(2)) and otherwise it is five years (s 6(1)). Schedule 1 allows a certain period of absence from the UK without jeopardizing the application. For a s 6(1) application this is 450 days, providing that not more than 90 of these days are in the last 12 months. For a s 6(2) application the permitted days' absence is 270, again providing not more than 90 of these are in the last 12 months. In addition to this, the Secretary of State has a discretion to waive fulfilment of the residence requirement. However, as the NI says, that discretion cannot be exercised 'in such a way as, virtually, to ignore these requirements'. The Home Office has a tariff, set out in NI Ch 18 Annex B paras 4 and 5 for periods of excess absences which will normally be accepted.

Apart from limited exceptions, the NI says that there is no discretion to waive the requirement for presence at the beginning of the qualifying period. The common sense reason for this is clear: if the applicant was not here at the beginning of the period then it is in fact a shorter period, and it would be difficult to find another suitable marker to start the period running. Where the applicant arrived, say on 10 March 1997, went abroad for the month of May, then lived in the UK continuously and submitted an application for naturalization during May 2002 on the basis that they have now lived in the UK for at least five years, they do not meet the requirement to be physically present on the date five years before the application was submitted. NI Ch 18 Annex B allows for the application form to be returned to the applicant to be re-signed and dated for a date when the requirement will be met, providing the date is only missed by a maximum of two months either way (para 3.3).

3.5.3 **Type of residence**

Residence during the majority of the qualifying period is only required to be physical presence, not a particular immigration status. However, at the date of application a spouse or civil partner, and for the last year of residence a s 6(1) applicant, must be free of immigration restrictions on their stay (Sch 1 para 1(2)(b)). Residence must also not have been in breach of immigration laws (1(2)(d)), though once again there is a discretion to regard periods so spent as lawful (para 2(d)). NI Ch 18 Annex B para 8.10 gives examples of when the Home Office would normally exercise discretion to disregard a breach, for instance when an application form was submitted in time but incorrectly completed. The discretion would not normally be exercised 'when the breach was substantial and deliberate' or could affect the good character requirement (see below). Clearly in between these extremes there are countless other situations, and in particular asylum seekers and refugees are affected as they may have been forced to enter illegally and then spend years waiting for their claim to be determined. The Nationality, Immigration and Asylum Act 2002 s 11 defines time spent in breach of immigration laws as including any time when a person 'does not have leave to enter or remain in United Kingdom', which seems to include periods of waiting for the determination of even a successful application. Such an interpretation would breach Article 34 of the UN Convention on Refugees which provides that naturalization procedures for successful refugees should be expedited so that they can be more fully assimilated into the host community. NI Annex B para 8.7 explains that, where someone claims asylum on arrival, time spent on temporary admission does not count as time spent in breach of immigration laws. They will not be held to be in breach until they have exhausted the appeal process, their temporary admission has been revoked, and leave to enter refused. However, if they have claimed after having entered illegally, discretion may be exercised to regard all their residence as illegal, unless and until they are given leave to enter. The distinction between the two groups is not necessarily an easy one to make.

There is a special provision concerning periods spent in detention or on temporary admission (as to which, see chapter 15). BNA 1981 Sch 1 gives a discretion to regard periods of 'technical absence' as residence for naturalization purposes. This is generally used for members of the forces and diplomatic staff. People in detention without leave, and those on temporary admission, are physically present in the UK but in immigration law they are not legally present. NI 9.7 says that if at the end of detention or temporary admission the person was given leave to enter, their time in detention or on temporary admission should count as residence, but not if they are removed or depart voluntarily.

3.5.4 Good character requirement

Schedule 1 para 1(1)(b) requires 'that he is of good character'. The Act gives no further explanation as to how this requirement should be interpreted. Home Office guidance is to be found in NI Ch 18 Annex D. Criminal activity is clearly an indication that the person may be regarded as not of good character, however not all criminal activity will debar an applicant. The Home Office applies the Rehabilitation of Offenders Act 1974 for this purpose, and in Northern Ireland the Rehabilitation of Offenders (Northern Ireland) Order 1978. On 5 December 2007 the Home Secretary made an announcement that henceforth, unspent convictions would generally debar an application. Some offences can never be spent under the statutory provisions. The Home Office used to look in these cases for a period clear of offending, but have not suggested what their approach will be now. The whole issue is discretionary. The question used to be whether it seems that the person intends to abide by the law (para 2.1), but the Home Secretary's announcement suggests that the goal posts have moved.

The Home Office confirmed to Bindmans solicitors, in a letter dated 4 September 2001, that homelessness of itself did not put a person's good character in doubt. Other matters which should not be held against the applicant include 'Eccentricity, including beliefs, appearance and lifestyle' (para 5.2). Notoriety may be a reason to refuse an application, taking account of 'anticipated public reaction' (para 5.4).

3.5.5 Language requirement

This requirement came into the public spotlight with the publication, in February 2002, of the White Paper, *Secure Borders, Safe Haven* (Cm 5387). The White Paper proposed that applicants for British citizenship should be required to demonstrate a level of language proficiency in English, Welsh, or Scottish Gaelic, these being regarded as the British languages. The BNA 1981 in fact already required that the applicant 'had sufficient knowledge of the English, Welsh or Scottish Gaelic language' (Sch 1 para 1(1)(c)). As the White Paper observed, this was assumed to be the case unless there was evidence to the contrary. The new proposal was for actual testing of language ability as in other countries cited in the White Paper, for instance Australia, Canada, France, Germany, and the USA. The proposal came into being in the Nationality, Immigration and Asylum Act 2002 as an addition to the rule-making powers in BNA s 41, enabling rules to be made 'for determining whether a person has sufficient knowledge of a language for the purpose of an application for naturalization' (s 1(3)). Accordingly, the British Nationality (General) (Amendment) Regulations 2005, SI 2005/2785 provide that the level of language qualification is ESOL (English for Speakers of Other Languages) level 3. Someone who is already fluent in the English language may meet the language requirement by taking and passing the test on Life in the UK (see next section). Someone not yet fluent to ESOL level 3 is required to learn and pass a separate language test.

Schedule 1 BNA 1981 contains provision for waiving the language requirement if 'because of the applicant's age or physical or mental condition it would be unreasonable to expect him to fulfil it' (para 2(e)). The 2002 Act does not repeal this provision and so exemption may be given to ill or elderly people or those with learning difficulties. The measure has been controversial, not because there is doubt about the value of fluency in British languages, but because of concern about the alienating effects of compulsion.

3.5.6 Knowledge of British society

This was a highly contentious provision in the 2002 Act in s 1(1), adding a requirement 'that he has sufficient knowledge about life in the United Kingdom', backed up with an addition to the rule-making power to enable this to be assessed as for language. The proposal was a manifestation of the government's policy mentioned at the beginning of this chapter to make citizenship a meaningful concept, and link it with nationality. The phrase 'life in the United Kingdom' suggests something about habits and practices, usual ways of behaving, and so on. This suggests culture and raises connotations of ethnicity rather than nationality. In a state made up of many ethnicities this raises the question of whose life the candidate for naturalization should know about. In the words of Jim Marshall MP in the Second reading debate in the House of Commons, is the measure concerned 'to improve civic participation and awareness' or to 'promote cultural uniformity' (HC 24 April 2002 col 366)? Answers may be found in *Life in the United Kingdom: A Journey to Citizenship,* the handbook produced by the 'Life in the United Kingdom' Advisory Group which was set up to advise the Home Secretary on implementation of these proposals. A critique of the handbook from a South Asian perspective noted the relative absence of information in the book that would be useful to immigrants, and the invisibility of minority ethnic groups, the writing seeming to come from a perspective of being 'born and bred' in the UK with little attention paid to crucial issues of racism and religion other than Christianity (Noor 2007). A second and expanded edition in 2007 recognizes that 'immigration and diversity' and history are important (Kiwan 2007). Contributions to the Citizenship Review reveal that the thinking behind the new naturalization process is at least in part a vision of education and integration, but its impact is unresearched (Kiwan 2007).

There is a programme of studies which can accompany the handbook for all applicants for naturalization. Knowledge of life in the UK is a requirement for applications for naturalization made after 1 November 2005 when s 1(1) and (2) came into force. Since April 2007 this is also part of the requirements for indefinite leave to remain (see chapter 7).

3.5.7 **Pledge**

Along with the requirement for knowledge of British society was the institution of a pledge to be taken as well as the oath of allegiance, which is the formal moment at which new citizenship is acquired. Contrary to what an observer might glean from much of the media discussion at the time of the 2002 Bill, the oath of allegiance to the monarchy had always been part of obtaining citizenship. However, it was administered by a commissioner for oaths (usually a solicitor) or magistrate, in private and without ceremony.

The additional pledge, in Sch 1 to the 2002 Act, is as follows:

I will give my loyalty to the United Kingdom and respect its rights and freedoms. I will uphold its democratic values. I will observe its laws faithfully and fulfil my duties and obligations as a British Citizen.

This is administered in formal ceremonies for nationality applications made after 1 January 2004.

Part of the legacy of the focus on immigration considerations as a basis for nationality law is that the 'duties and obligations' of a British citizen have never been identified and most people who are British by birth or descent would have no idea what these are. It is therefore debatable whether those who acquire their nationality by a formal process should be asked to promise to fulfil them. The formal ceremonies, after an initial blaze of publicity, have largely become a matter of routine once more (Rimmer 2007).

3.5.8 **Intention to live in UK**

The final requirement for naturalization is that the applicant intends to make their future home in the UK (Sch 1 para 1 (1)(d)). Where the applicant has an established home in the UK, or there is no reason to doubt this intention, then it will be regarded as met (NI Ch 18 Annex F para 2). An intention to travel should not debar the applicant unless it appears that they do not intend to return.

3.6 Discrimination

Nationality law has been riddled with inequality on grounds of sex and birth status.

Prior to the 1981 Act, citizenship could pass only through a married father. The 1981 Act provided for citizenship to pass through the mother also, and this applied to the citizenship of British Dependent Territories as well as British citizenship. This was a substantial move towards equality.

Even following the 1981 Act, children could not obtain British citizenship from their father if their parents were unmarried. This state of affairs was challenged in *R on the application of Montana v SSHD* [2001] 1 WLR 552 CA. The appellant was a British citizen who had a son born in Norway to a Norwegian mother. The couple were not married and the relationship had ended. As the child was born outside the UK he would have been British by descent if his parents had been married, however, s 50 BNA defined 'father' to exclude an unmarried father. The appellant applied to have his child registered as a British citizen under the discretionary power in s 3. When his application was turned down he applied for judicial review of the Secretary of State's decision. The basis for the Secretary of State's refusal was that the child had insufficient connection with the UK. The appellant's argument was that the child would have British citizenship if his parents had been married, so the exercise of the Secretary of State's discretion was in breach of human rights, namely, Article 8, the right to respect for private and family and Article 14, freedom from discrimination in relation to Convention rights. The Court of Appeal held that common nationality was not a requirement of family life, so Article 8 was not engaged. It considered that there was no true comparison between those who obtained citizenship under s 2, by descent, and those who did so by registration under s 3, and therefore there was no discrimination.

Nationality, Immigration and Asylum Act 2002 s 9 addresses the disparity between married and unmarried fathers. 'Father' is redefined to include not only married fathers but also those treated as the father of a child under the Human Fertilisation and Embryology Act 1990 and any other person 'who satisfies prescribed requirements as to proof of paternity'. These are either:

- naming the father on the child's birth certificate within one year of their birth, or
- proving the matter to the Secretary of State's satisfaction by 'any evidence which [the Secretary of State] considers to be relevant, including, but not limited to' DNA test reports and court orders. (British Nationality (Proof of Paternity) Regulations 2006, SI 2006/1496)

In other provisions of the BNA, which had previously excluded unmarried fathers from being defined as a parent, the exclusions are removed.

The 2002 Act s 13 also offers a remedy for those born between 7 February 1961 and 1 January 1983 who would have been British by descent if, at the time of their birth, nationality could pass through a woman. They now have a right to register as British. Mr Hicks in the case discussed below benefited from this provision.

The 2002 Act brings nationality decisions fully within the ambit of the Race Relations Act 1976. The Race Relations (Amendment) Act 2000 had made a partial exclusion for nationality functions as it did for immigration functions, however the 2002 Act s 6 takes nationality out of that exclusion, and so nationality functions are now included within the general duty on public authorities to avoid race discrimination.

3.7 **Deprivation of nationality**

The 2002 and 2006 Acts contain significant extensions of the Secretary of State's powers to deprive a person of their citizenship. The BNA 1981 provided in s 40 for citizens who obtained their citizenship by naturalization or registration, to be deprived of it if the Secretary of State was satisfied that the person had been guilty of 'disloyalty or disaffection to Her Majesty', helping an enemy in time of war, or a criminal offence within five years of obtaining citizenship. Additionally, the Secretary of State had to be satisfied that it was conducive to the public good to deprive the person of their nationality and that they would not become stateless as a consequence. In *SSHD v Hicks* [2006] EWCA Civ 400 the court held that the Secretary of State could not rely on Mr Hicks' receiving terrorist training in Pakistan and Afghanistan, including with known terrorists, as evidence of his disaffection, because at that time he was not a British citizen. As he owed no duty of allegiance he could not breach it. The respondent was an Australian citizen detained in Guantanamo Bay, who after the 2002 legislative reforms acquired a right under BNA 1981 s 4C to register as a British citizen by descent because his mother was British. He applied in 2005, and the Secretary of State proposed to deprive him of that citizenship simultaneously with granting it. It was agreed, however, that the original 1981 version of the section applied, and in 2000 and 2001 when he was in Afghanistan Mr Hicks owed no duty to the British Crown.

The 2002 Act replaced this section with two new powers. The first is to deprive any person of their citizenship, whether or not this is acquired by registration or naturalization, and all classes of British nationality are included. The basis for so doing is that 'the Secretary of State is satisfied that the person has done anything seriously prejudicial to the vital interests of the UK or a British Overseas Territory' (new s 40(2)). This is the first power granted to the Secretary of State to remove nationality obtained by birth. The implications of this are considerable. There is nothing to govern who decides what are the vital interests of the UK or what this phrase ought to mean. The removal by executive action of citizenship obtained by birth or parentage is an extraordinary exercise of power by the government. This power is restricted in that it cannot be used if the Secretary of State is satisfied that the order would make the person stateless. In other words, though it can remove citizenship acquired by birth, it can only be used in relation to a dual national.

Although this subsection was open to a politicized or subjective interpretation it was in line with the 1961 UN Convention on the Reduction of Statelessness. The standard it represents is certainly higher than that in a new s 40(2) which has replaced it

(Immigration, Asylum and Nationality Act 2006 s 56). This provides that citizenship may be removed 'if the Secretary of State is satisfied that deprivation is conducive to the public good'. There is no requirement for reasonable grounds, and although administrative law imports a requirement of reasonableness into the Secretary of State's decision this means that an appeal would have the rather limited scope of a judicial review. There is no requirement for any particular kind of behaviour by the person who loses their nationality, nor any specific risk that they must present. The criterion is the same as that for deportation, which means that on the face of the law British citizenship offers little protection against deportation for dual nationals. The government indicated that the kind of behaviour which could found deprivation of citizenship under this subsection would include that in the 'list of unacceptable behaviours' made public by the Home Secretary on 24 August 2005 (Standing Committee E 27 October 2005 col 254). These were part of the government's public strategy to counter terrorism after the London bombings of 7 July 2005 (see chapter 16).

The second new power under the 2002 Act (undisturbed by the 2006 Act) retains the power of the old s 40 to deprive a person of nationality obtained by registration or naturalization if this has been obtained by fraud, false representation, or concealment of a material fact (s 40(3)). However, unlike the old s 40, in this case the Secretary of State apparently does not have to have regard as to whether the person will be left stateless.

These powers demonstrate a new attitude to nationality. It has become more conditional upon conduct. In the case of people who have obtained their nationality by registration or naturalization the possibility that they could be left stateless if they have obtained it by fraud conveys a powerful message. The Nationality Instructions Chapter 55 give an account of the difference between fraud which means that nationality will be taken away, and fraud which means that the original grant of nationality was a nullity – i.e. had no effect. In *Bibi and others v SSHD* [2007] EWCA Civ 740 discussed above, the grant was a nullity because Mr Jabbar took on the identity of another person, so a grant of nationality to him did not happen. If he had falsified certain details, such as the time he had spent in the UK, the grant of nationality would have taken effect. He could have been deprived of it once the fraud came to light, but he would have actually been a British Citizen in the interim. In some cases (though problematic on the facts of that case as he had died) this difference could affect the rights of relatives.

The International Covenant on Civil and Political Rights Art 24 (3) provides a right to a nationality, and avoidance of statelessness is one of the objectives of the European Convention on Nationality 1997, according to its preamble. Its Article 4 provides that the rules of each State Party should be based on the principles that everyone has a right to a nationality and that statelessness should be avoided.

As mentioned in chapter 1, the Parliamentary Joint Committee on Human Rights raised these concerns with the Home Office, particularly 'loss of British diplomatic protection; loss of status; loss of the ability to participate in the democratic process in the United Kingdom; and serious damage to reputation and dignity' (Joint Committee on Human Rights Session 2001–02 Seventeenth Report para 26). The Home Office, somewhat disingenuously, replied that the person would have another nationality and so the harm to them would be limited, but did not mention that this may not be the case where nationality is removed because of fraud.

Deprivation of nationality has in the past been rare. There has been one deprivation order since 1973 and ten between 1948 and 1973. Lord Filkin in parliamentary debate said that it would continue to be used only in the most serious and flagrant cases (HL 9 October 2002 col 279). The first attempted use of the new 2002 Act power was in relation to Sheikh Abu Hamza, the controversial cleric at the Finsbury Park mosque in London. The attempted deprivation order is still subject to challenge and Abu Hamza is serving a prison sentence for criminal charges.

The 2006 Act also carries a new power to deprive someone of their right of abode where this is held without citizenship. This is to be exercised if the secretary of state 'thinks' that the person's deportation or exclusion would be for the public good (s 57), restoring the use of subjective wording that was a feature of the 2002 Act at Bill stage, but defeated then.

3.8 Challenging nationality decisions

Under the old s 40 a proposal to make an order depriving a person of their citizenship could be referred to a committee of inquiry. The 2002 Act introduced a full right of appeal to the tribunal, but not if the Secretary of State certifies that the decision was taken wholly or partly in reliance on information which in his opinion should not be made public in the interests of national security, or the relationship between the UK and another country, or is 'otherwise in the public interest'. This is a very wide ground, and given the grounds for deprivation in s 40(2) there is potential for it to apply in almost any case. In these cases an appeal will lie to the Special Immigration Appeals Commission. As discussed in chapter 8, the proceedings of this Commission may be closed to the public and evidence may be withheld from the appellant.

Under the BNA there is no appeal against a refusal of naturalization or registration, and this remains unchanged. The Act has however provided some increased rights for aggrieved applicants. It repeals s 44(2) and (3) which provided that no reasons should be given for discretionary nationality decisions. In practice this had already become a discredited provision as in Mohammed Al Fayed's well-known challenge to the Home Secretary's refusal of his naturalization application, the Court of Appeal held that in some cases the Secretary was under a duty to give the applicant notice of the reasons for refusal (*Fayed v SSHD* [1997] 1 All ER 228). The Secretary of State followed this with an announcement in Parliament that reasons would generally be given and this is in accordance with the 1997 Convention. The method of legal challenge to a refusal of naturalization is judicial review on usual administrative law grounds on the basis of reasons given. In practice if an application fails through not meeting the factual criteria, the remedy would be to re-apply when the criteria were met, or point out the Home Office error if there had been one.

3.9 **Conclusion**

This chapter has sought to show that the UK's nationality law has been strongly influenced by its relationships with its former colonies and by the desire to restrict immigration from the majority of these. From the early part of the twentieth century, when millions of people could claim the status of British subject and the theoretical right of abode that went with this, we have now come to a time when only the status of British citizen carries the right of abode. Obtaining this by birth is restricted to those with a close connection with the UK or its few remaining overseas territories. The process of changing the basis of entitlement seems to be coming to an end, but some people, particularly British Overseas citizens, have had to fight long and hard not to be entirely left out of the concluding arrangements of the empire.

A new phase was heralded by the Nationality, Immigration and Asylum Act 2002. The Act demonstrates the exclusive power of the State, as noted at the beginning of this chapter, to determine who are its nationals. In earlier legislation the government was preoccupied with the question of who 'belonged' and this was seen in terms largely of birth and parentage. In this and the 2006 legislation, the State's power of determination is turned in a new direction, testing allegiance not by blood line but by conduct and participation as a citizen. As one era ends, a new one is dawning.

QUESTIONS

1 Are the UK's nationality laws closer to a principle of *jus soli* or *jus sanguinis?* Whichever you think, what elements can you find in UK nationality law of the other principle? How do registration and naturalization fit into this?

2 Is it possible to give content to the idea of 'belonging' to a country? How would you do it?

 online resource centre For guidance on answering questions, visit www.oxfordtextbooks.co.uk/orc/clayton3e.

FURTHER READING

Dummett, A., Nicol, A. (1990) *Subjects, Citizens, Aliens and Others* (London: Weidenfeld and Nicolson), Chapter 7.

Fransman L. *Fransman's British Nationality Law* (2005) 3rd edn (London: Butterworths) – the major authoritative work, for reference on all issues.

Imiscoe Policy brief (2006) 'The Acquisition and Loss of Nationality in 15 EU States: results of the comparative project NATAC'.

JCWI (2006) *Immigration, Nationality and Refugee Law Handbook* 6th edn. (London: JWCI).

Kiwan, D. (2007) 'Becoming a British Citizen: A Learning Journey', Goldsmith Citizenship Review, Ministry of Justice.

Lester, A. 'Thirty Years On: The *East African Asians* Case Revisited' [2002] *Public Law* Spring 52–72.

Noor, O. 'Review of life in the UK' [2007] *Journal of Immigration, Asylum and Nationality Law* vol. 21 no. 2, pp. 166–168.

Paul, K. (1997) *Whitewashing Britain: race and citizenship in the postwar era* (New York: Cornell) Chapter 1.

Pilger, J. (2004) 'Stealing a Nation' – documentary film about the Chagos Islanders.

Rimmer, M. (2007) 'The Future of Citizenship Ceremonies', Goldsmith Citizenship Review, Ministry of Justice.

Sawyer, C. 'A losing ticket in the lottery of life: expelling British children' [2004] *Public Law* Winter pp. 750–758.

Sawyer, C. 'Civis europeanus sum: the citizenship rights of the children of foreign parents' [2005] *Public Law* Autumn pp. 477–484.

Shah, P. (2000) *Refugees, Race and the Legal Concept of Asylum* (London: Cavendish), Chapter 5.

Shah, R. 'Special voucher scheme abolished' [2003] *Journal of Immigration, Asylum & Nationality Law* vol. 16, no. 2, pp. 108–110.

—— 'A Wrong Righted: full status for Britain's "other citizens"' [2003] *Journal of Immigration, Asylum & Nationality Law* vol. 17, no. 1, pp. 19–24.

The Overseas Territories White Paper and Protocol 4 of the ECHR – the ILPA response *Journal of Immigration, Asylum & Nationality* vol. 14, no. 3, pp. 142–150.

The Stationery Office (2007). 'Life in the United Kingdom: A Journey to Citizenship' 2nd edn.

Tomkins, A. 'Magna Carta, Crown and Colonies' [2001] *Public Law* Autumn pp. 571–585.

White, R. M. (2002) 'Immigration, Nationality, Citizenship and the meaning of naturalisation: Brubaker, the United Kingdom EU citizens, third country nationals and the European Union' *Northern Ireland Law Quarterly* vol. 53 no. 3, pp. 288–319.

Woollacott, S. (2005) 'Persons Granted British Citizenship, 2004', Home Office Statistical Bulletin 08/05.

4

....

Immigration law and human rights

SUMMARY

This chapter discusses the effects of the Human Rights Act 1998 on immigration law in the UK, including the effect on unsuccessful asylum claimants. It begins by noting the relationship between immigration law and human rights, then gives an introduction to the operation of the Human Rights Act. There is a more detailed discussion of the application of the Act to immigration law and the application of Article 3 and Article 8 to immigration situations, particularly removal from the UK, and there is briefer treatment of the remaining Articles.

4.1 Introduction

4.1.1 Relationship between immigration law and human rights

There is an obvious connection between migration and human rights. In moving between countries fundamental rights are often being exercised, for instance to be reunited with one's family or to be free from torture or discrimination. Some accounts of human rights would include the right to freedom of movement itself, or the right to work. Immigration law enforcement may involve violations of other rights; for instance, people who are not even suspected of crime can be detained under immigration powers. However, there is no human right to move to a particular country. States have the right to a system of law which, within the constraints of international law, regulates who may enter. Whatever the origins of that power, which we briefly considered in chapter 1, immigration law is primarily concerned with defining and giving enforceable substance to it. It has been concerned with regulating the numbers, origin, and material and other circumstances of those to whom entry will be granted, not primarily with the protection of their rights.

In the context of migration and human rights, seeking asylum is a special case as an application for asylum is an application for a specialized form of international human rights protection. This chapter is not concerned with making an asylum claim, which is dealt with in section 5 of this book, but is concerned with the application of human rights law in the UK in immigration decision-making, including to a person whose asylum claim has failed. In fact, many human rights claims heard by the immigration appellate bodies are made by people whose asylum claims have been unsuccessful.

The commencement of the Human Rights Act on 2 October 2000 marked a new era. From that date onwards, human rights could be relied upon as the basis of legal argument, and this offers the potential to give a greater equality of arms between the executive and the individual. However, the actual delivery of human rights depends on many factors. Within the legal system, human rights are only powerful tools for individuals to the extent that rules of law permit human rights arguments to be fully considered by decision-makers. For instance, it is of limited use to have a right to respect for family life if no appeal body can decide freely for itself whether the right has been violated. This issue is considered in the chapter on appeals. Economic and political pressures may mean that human rights law does not save an individual from acute suffering (as in many AIDS cases, see *N v SSHD* [2005] UKHL 31); the government may legislate to restrict the delivery of rights (as in Nationality, Immigration and Asylum Act 2002 s 55 and the Criminal Justice and Immigration Bill 2007); the interpretation of human rights standards may still leave people in difficult situations without redress (e.g. the family divided as in *AM v ECO Ethiopia* [2007] UKAIT 00058). Sometimes, human rights law is not engaged at all to protect a vulnerable person (e.g. *AL (Serbia)* [2006] EWCA Civ 1619). Human rights are an important step in bringing human interests and needs into the legal arena but are certainly not a panacea.

4.1.2 Development of immigration law and human rights

International human rights law has already played an important role in immigration cases in UK courts as, even before the Human Rights Act 1998, there was a body of opinion that international human rights norms could be relied upon in argument in UK courts as they formed part of customary international law (see, e.g., Hunt, *Using Human Rights Law in English Courts*, (1998) 29). An early example of the use of human rights norms in the UK was *R v Miah* [1974] 1 WLR 683, where Stephenson LJ held that a penal provision of the Immigration Act 1971 could not have retrospective effect as this would violate human rights treaty provisions.

However, political positions on immigration matters have also had a restrictive effect on human rights law. When the UK first ratified the ECHR, it did not immediately grant the individual right of petition to people who were aggrieved because of an infringement of their Convention rights. This meant that although the UK was a party to the Convention in international law, no one in the UK's jurisdiction who suffered an infringement of their rights could actually go to the Court of Human Rights and complain. In 1966, some 13 years after the Convention came into force, the UK granted the individual right of petition. The delay may be attributed to the government's fear of the applications that would arise from overseas territories, of which Britain had 42 in 1953 when the Convention was ratified. Macdonald cites a reply of a minister in Parliament on the question of individual petition: 'among emerging communities political agitators thrive and one may well imagine the use which political agitators would make of the right of individual petition' (Blake and Fransman (1999:vii). By the end of 1966, the number of overseas territories had dropped to twenty-four.

The expectation that relations with non-British citizens would give rise to human rights cases did seem to be borne out; the first case to be taken to the ECtHR from the UK was an immigration case: a challenge to the refusal of admission to a 12-year-old boy who was coming to the UK to join his father (*Alam v UK* Application 2991/66 The Times, 12 October 1967).

Further in relation to the UK's endorsement of the ECHR, as discussed in the previous chapter, the UK has not ratified Protocol 4 because of its inability to comply on account of the position of British overseas citizens.

One of the earliest and most influential cases decided by the European Court of Human Rights (ECtHR) in the field of immigration law is *Abdulaziz, Cabales and Balkandali v UK*.

Key Case

Abdulaziz, Cabales and Balkandali v UK (1985) 7 EHRR 471

Three women who were settled in the UK challenged the immigration rules then in force (HC 394) on the basis that they discriminated against women. The rules allowed virtually automatic admission of wives of British men, but there were more hurdles to be overcome for the husbands of British women.

The ECtHR found that the rules were discriminatory. The British government's response to this was to alter the rules to make the more restrictive process applicable to wives as well as husbands. The inequality between the sexes was thus rectified, but British citizens of different ethnic origins were more sharply differentiated as more people who have family connections abroad are likely to want to marry someone from abroad. The Court considered this question in relation to Mrs Balkandali who was a British citizen born outside the UK, but concluded that the government was not obliged to provide equal rights between citizens of different ethnic origins. They said: 'there are in general persuasive social reasons for giving special treatment to those whose link with a country stems from birth within it' (para 88).

Abdulaziz established the principle that Convention rights, and in this case the right to respect for family life (Art 8), do apply to a State's immigration decisions. The court did not accept the government's assertion that immigration was catered for by Protocol 4 and so the other articles would not apply. They made the following important statement:

the right of a foreigner to enter or remain in a country was not as such guaranteed by the Convention, but immigration controls had to be exercised consistently with Convention obligations, and the exclusion of a person from a State where members of his family were living might raise an issue under Article 8. (para 59)

Despite the UK government's conservative response to *Abdulaziz,* this principle remains a crucial foundation of the relationship between immigration decisions and human rights. The ECtHR acknowledged the long-established principle that a state has the right to control the entry of non-nationals, but that this right is *subject to its treaty obligations.* It is not unfettered.

One might then ask, to what treaty obligations is it subject? Primarily, we shall be concerned with the European Convention on Human Rights. However, many other treaties may be relevant in immigration and asylum cases. Examples are the International Covenant on Civil and Political Rights (ICCPR), the Convention on Ending Racial Discrimination (CERD), the Convention on the Elimination of All Forms of Discrimination Against Women (CEDAW), the Convention Against Torture (CAT) and the Convention on the Rights of the Child (CRC). Human rights principles may also be drawn from the deliberations of bodies whose work is to develop human rights, for instance the United Nations Commission on Human Rights. Case law from other jurisdictions where there are constitutionally enshrined rights is relevant, including in particular from Commonwealth jurisdictions and judgments of the Privy Council.

The conventional understanding in the period immediately preceding the Human Rights Act was that international treaties including the ECHR could not be relied upon unless the statute or other legal provision being applied was unclear or ambiguous (*R v SSHD ex p Brind* [1991] 1 AC 696). However, at an earlier stage the courts had on occasions seemed to assume that Parliament would not legislate in a way that was contrary to its treaty obligations (e.g. *Miah*). Reference could therefore be made to treaty standards without further justification. The courts had also made use of the ECHR to interpret and develop the common law. Well before the HRA, some judges were prepared to give full weight to Convention rights, some regarded them as relevant in judicial review but a matter for the executive to assess, and some as not relevant at all. Although the Human Rights Act introduced a new legal order, similar underlying attitudes continue, some judges regarding human rights as to be invoked only in special circumstances, some regarding human rights as an integral part of the legal order. This latter approach also divides into those who regard them as so integral that they are already implied in legal provisions, so no further attention is needed, and those who regard them as so fundamental as to require active respect delivered in the outcome of a case.

R (Mahmood) v SSHD [2001] 1 WLR 840 was a key case in immigration law based on the law in force during the period between Royal Assent and commencement of the Human Rights Act. It concerned the removal of someone who had entered the UK illegally, had remained for some time, and was now working, married, and had children in the UK. This is a situation frequently encountered in immigration law which involves a clash between immigration enforcement and the right to respect for family life. Indeed, it is perhaps the most typical encounter between these two conflicting principles, and we shall meet it in many forms in the course of this book. The majority of the Court of Appeal (Laws LJ, with May LJ agreeing) declined to approach the case on the basis that the Act was in force, but said it would have made no difference if they had.

This view espoused by Laws and May LJJ, that the common law already embodies the values of the Convention, is referred to as the 'traditionalist' approach by Fenwick (2000). Before the Human Rights Act 1998 came into force, there were indeed developments in the common law which protected rights. For instance, creative use was made of the law of tort (see e.g. *Entick v Carrington* (1765) 19 St Tr 1029 or *Kaye v Robertson* [1991] FSR 62) and of criminal law (see e.g. *Redmond-Bate v DPP* (1999) Crim LR 998 or *DPP v Jones* [1999] 2 All ER 257). These cases brought before the UK courts raise many of the classic issues of rights protection which are dealt with by the ECHR; for instance, the liberty of the subject, unwarranted intrusion by the State, or suppression of freedom of expression. However, care should be taken in applying case law from that period to interpret rights after 2 October 2000. The Convention rights have their own structure and logic which may be overlooked if it is assumed that the principles were there all along, and the Human Rights Act introduces new principles of interpretation.

4.2 Applying the Human Rights Act

Since the implementation of the Human Rights Act immigration decisions in the UK are subject to the rights contained in the Human Rights Act, which are derived from the ECHR. Other international human rights instruments may be used to interpret these rights. In a European law matter, any relevant human rights treaty to which states are parties should be respected (Treaty on European Union Article 6 ex F).

The Act sets out in Sch 1 the 12 Convention rights and the Protocols which the UK has ratified, and s 1 refers to these as 'Convention rights'. The key provisions of the HRA are ss 3 and 6. What follows here is not a general account of the Act, but guidance on the use of the Act and the ECHR as may be relevant in immigration and asylum law. It is apparent in courts and tribunals that the application and interpretation of human rights law is developing. Care and precision in using human rights concepts is important. When relying on case law of the ECHR it is useful to be aware of some of the principles guiding that law, and to know what its authority is in UK courts.

4.2.1 **ECHR principles**

The Court encourages the development of rights which are 'practical and effective' (*Artico v Italy* (1980) 3 EHRR 1), not just theoretical. This approach is also apparent in the HRA in the long title to the Act, which is said to be 'to give further effect to' the rights and freedoms of the European Convention.

Linked to this principle is the idea of the Convention as a living instrument (*Tyrer v UK* (1978) 2 EHRR 1 and *Loizidou v Turkey* (1995) 20 EHRR 99). In other words, its decisions are intended to be appropriate for the times and conditions in which they are made, and to adapt to developing understandings and changing opinions within the Council of Europe. Consistently with this concept, the Strasbourg Court does not operate the doctrine of precedent. Although the Court has an interest in developing coherent case law, and does use and often follow earlier decisions, it is not bound to do so. A clear example of how decisions are affected by the growth of knowledge in social and scientific spheres has arisen in the court's judgments in relation to transsexualism. This passage from *I v UK* (2003) 36 EHRR 53, which concerned violations of Articles 8 and 12 in relation to a transsexual, expresses these points.

54. While the Court is not formally bound to follow its previous judgments, it is in the interests of legal certainty, foreseeability and equality before the law that it should not depart, without good reason, from precedents laid down in previous cases (see, for example, *Chapman v United Kingdom* [GC], no 27238/95, ECHR 2001–I, § 70). However, since the Convention is first and foremost a system for the protection of human rights, the Court must have regard to the changing conditions within the respondent State and within Contracting States generally and respond, for example, to any evolving convergence as to the standards to be achieved…It is of crucial importance that the Convention is interpreted and applied in a manner which renders its rights practical and effective, not theoretical and illusory. A failure by the Court to maintain a dynamic and evolutive approach would indeed risk rendering it a bar to reform or improvement (see the above-cited *Stafford v United Kingdom* judgment, § 68). In the present context the Court has, on several occasions since 1986, signalled its consciousness of the serious problems facing transsexuals and stressed the importance of keeping the need for appropriate legal measures in this area under review…

55. The Court proposes therefore to look at the situation within and outside the Contracting State to assess 'in the light of present-day conditions' what is now the appropriate interpretation and application of the Convention (see the *Tyrer v. the United Kingdom* judgment of 25 April 1978, Series A no 26, § 31, and subsequent case-law).

Notable in the remainder of the judgment, as also in *Abdulaziz*, is the court's readiness to examine information from other disciplines in order to inform itself of the weight of the relevant scientific or social arguments.

The idea of the Convention as a living instrument should not be taken to imply that the Court changes with every wind that blows, or is open to political pressure. Many judgments use and stress another principle, namely that the terminology of the Convention is autonomous. This means that the Court gives a certain meaning, e.g. to the word 'criminal', as in *Malige v France* (1999) 28 EHRR 578 where penalty points on a driving licence were held to be a criminal sanction for Convention purposes. Governments are therefore not at liberty to impose upon the Court their own interpretation of such crucial phrases.

4.2.1.1 *Margin of appreciation*

An important Convention principle which does not apply in UK law, but which affects domestic application of ECHR case law, is the margin of appreciation. This principle does not derive from the nature of rights, but from the nature of the ECtHR as an international authority. The margin of appreciation is most classically defined in *Handyside v UK*.

 Key Case

Handyside v UK **(1979–80) 1 EHRR 737**

> By reason of their direct and continuous contact with the vital forces of their countries, state authorities are in principle in a better position than the international judge to give an opinion on the exact content of these requirements [for the protection of morals] as well as on the 'necessity' of a 'restriction' or 'penalty' intended to meet them '... it is for the national authorities to make the initial assessment of the reality of the pressing social need implied by the notion of "necessity" in this context. Consequently, Article 10.2 leaves to the Contracting States a margin of appreciation. This margin is given both the domestic legislator ("prescribed by law") and to the bodies, judicial amongst others, that are called upon to apply and interpret the laws in force'. (para 48)

This passage refers to principles which may restrict a qualified right, that is, a right which may be overridden in the public interest, and some of the terminology will be discussed again later. The reason for the margin of appreciation is clear, however. It is the closer contact which national authorities have with the matters in hand and the considerations which bear upon them. The margin of appreciation is by definition the deference of an international authority to a national authority. It therefore does not apply when there is no international authority in the situation.

For different reasons there may be a place for the national courts when deciding a human rights point to give weight to the views of the executive. However, to fall back too readily on the judgment of public authorities would undermine the purpose of the Act and the role which has been assigned to the judges by Parliament. This question is discussed in chapter 8, and some of the former debates about it have been laid to rest by *Huang and Kashmiri v SSHD* [2007] UKHL 11.

4.2.2 **Public authorities**

Section 6 makes it unlawful for public authorities to act in a way which is incompatible with a Convention right. An act includes a failure to act (s 6(6)). Section 6 includes 'core' public authorities (including courts and tribunals), whose actions are always regarded as public, and 'hybrid' authorities, who are regarded as public authorities under the Act in relation to public but not private functions (s 6(3) and (5)).

The most vexed questions have arisen where, as is increasingly the case, public functions are contracted out to private service providers. In the immigration context the identification of a public authority is rarely an issue. Immigration officers, entry clearance officers, and Home Office officials are undeniably public, and are regarded as 'core' public authorities. However, here too, contracting to commercial bodies is a growing practice, for instance, security firms running removal centres, escorts accompanying people being removed, or airline officials who prevent a passenger without a visa from travelling.

It seems that independent contractors running detention (now called 'removal') centres take on full responsibility for detainees both in common law (*Quaquah v Group 4 Securities Ltd* (No 2) The Times, June 27 2001) and under the Human Rights Act (*R (on the application of D and K) v SSHD* [2006] EWHC 980 (Admin)).

The Parliamentary Joint Committee on Human Rights, in its report on the meaning of 'public authority' in the Human Rights Act, concluded that a body functions as a public authority where there is an exercise of a 'function that has its origin in governmental responsibilities in such a way as to compel individuals to rely on that body for realisation of their Convention human rights' (JCHR report Seventh of 2003–04, The Meaning of Public Authority under the Human Rights Act HL Paper 39 HC 382 para 157). This principle was interpreted most recently in *YL v Birmingham City Council* [2007] UKHL 27, where the majority held that running a care home was not inherently a government function. Powerful dissenting judgments from Lord Bingham and Baroness Hale treated the care home as a public authority, on the basis that residents were receiving a service that was not otherwise available to them. *YL* may restrict the application of s 6 in more arguable cases, such as could arise on facts similar to *Farah v British Airways* The Independent, 18 January 2000. Here the appellants were prevented from boarding an aircraft by an airline relying on an immigration officer who advised that the documents were not valid. The decision not to carry the passengers was treated as a decision taken under the terms of the contract, and the commercial company acted as a buffer between the public authority (the immigration officer) and a person affected.

Section 6(3) excludes Parliament from the definition of 'public authority', so Parliament's actions in legislating or failing to legislate are not challengeable. The inclusion of courts and tribunals as public authorities means that courts and tribunals in their decision must uphold Convention rights. The combination of this and the interpretive obligation in s 3 means that where the law can be interpreted so as to uphold the applicant's rights, the court must do it.

4.2.3 Duty of interpretation

Section 3 creates a principle of interpretation which has far-reaching consequences. By s 3(1), so far as it is possible to do so, primary and subordinate legislation must be read and given effect in a way which is compatible with Convention rights. The phrase 'and given effect' makes it clear that the purpose is to uphold rights and echoes the principle of ECHR case law that human rights law should be practical and effective. The duty is to read statute and secondary legislation so as to protect rights whenever possible. This is a powerful principle, changing the normal rules of statutory interpretation. It may be compared with the purposive approach in European law, as applied, for instance, by the House of Lords in *Litster v Forth Dry Dock Engineering* [1990] 1 AC 546, and suggests that the courts must be ready to push statutory language as far as it will go in order to give it a meaning which would uphold the rights of the applicant.

This duty of interpretation overrides the duty to follow a superior court where the precedent predates the Act and would lead to a conflict with human rights. A case under the HRA can be heard in any court or tribunal, and this means that an Asylum and Immigration Tribunal is not bound by a pre-HRA interpretation of statute by the House of Lords. This was illustrated, albeit at a higher level in the court hierarchy, by the Court of Appeal's judgment in *Ghaidan v Godin-Mendoza* [2003] 2 WLR 478. The Court of Appeal was called upon to construe Sch 1 para 2 of the Rent Act 1977 compatibly with Convention rights. The authority on the interpretation of the paragraph was the House of Lords case, *Fitzpatrick v Sterling Housing Association Ltd* [2001] 1 AC 27, decided on the basis of pre-2000 law. The Court of Appeal in *Ghaidan*, using the s 3 duty of interpretation, ruled that the House of Lords' interpretation was not compatible with Convention rights. It was not bound by it and could interpret the statute differently.

In *R v A* (No 2) [2001] 2 WLR 1546 the House of Lords interpreted the Youth Justice and Criminal Evidence Act 1999 s 41 so as to permit the inclusion of evidence which was so relevant to the defence that to exclude it would endanger the fairness of the trial under Article 6. The section was quite clear and unambiguous, and the House of Lords' judgment involved a radical reading inserting words and in effect putting a gloss on the statute.

Immigration rules and statutes should therefore be interpreted so far as possible to uphold Convention rights, as illustrated in *R (on the application of Amirthanathan) v SSHD* [2003] EWHC 1107 (Admin), in relation to powers of detention. Despite this clear lead by the House of Lords, in *Radhika Sharma v ECO New Delhi* [2005] EWCA Civ 89 the Court of Appeal took a more conservative view of s 3, holding that it did not empower it to regard a natural parent who was unwilling to look after their child as being unable to do so. This meant that the child's adoption could not come within the immigration rules that would have enabled her to live with her adoptive parents. The court held that inability and unwillingness were 'quite distinct' and one could not be read so as to encompass the other, even to ensure respect for the appellant's family life.

The tribunal in *KP (India)* [2006] UKAIT 00093 proposed that the s 3 interpretive rule does not apply unless the immigration rule as expressed is inconsistent with a human right. This has a superficial appeal, as one might ask 'why would anyone need to interpret a rule to comply with human rights if it does not infringe them in the first place?' However, whether a rule infringes a right is itself a matter of interpretation and application. This approach therefore is arguably inconsistent with the accepted view that there need not be any ambiguity in the legislation for s 3 to apply, and with the wording of s 3 itself which is 'to give effect to' Convention rights. It means that, if the tribunal *interprets* the rule as not infringing human rights, there is no need to read it to protect the right. This includes where the tribunal judges that the interference with a qualified right is necessary and therefore lawful. By coming to this view they exclude the application of s 3. It remains to be seen whether this interpretation, followed in *AM v ECO Ethiopia* [2007] UKAIT 00058, will survive any challenge in the higher courts.

4.2.4 **Use of ECtHR case law in UK courts**

In human rights cases, HRA s 2 obliges courts and tribunals to 'take into account' the judgments and opinions of the European Court of Human Rights and the other Strasbourg decision-making bodies which operate the Convention. This raises the question of what weight the court or tribunal should give to the jurisprudence of the ECtHR. The UK courts are not bound by the Strasbourg court, and ECtHR judgments are not precedent setting, but it has been held that courts should follow ECtHR case law where there is, in the words of Lord Slynn, 'a clear and constant jurisprudence' on a particular matter (*R (Alconbury Developments Ltd) v Secretary of State for the Environment* [2001] 2 WLR 1389 at para 26). Indeed, in the same passage, Lord Slynn suggested that 'in the absence of some special circumstances' that would be the proper course of action. Singh J suggested in *Amirthanathan* that UK courts should be moving towards 'an autonomous human rights jurisdiction by reference to principles to be found animating the Convention rather than an over-rigid approach' (para 59). A less liberal approach by the UK courts would invite an application to Strasbourg, and should be carefully justified. This is not to say that ECtHR decisions are always radically rights-oriented, as they are not.

Reference has already been made to the doctrine of the margin of appreciation and its international character. Where UK courts take into account ECtHR case law, caution is needed to ensure that an international margin of appreciation is not imported into a UK decision.

The practice followed in this book is to use both ECtHR and UK cases when interpreting the Convention. In the course of discussing one topic we may move from ECtHR case law to UK case law and back again. The following points summarize the status of the decisions.

1. The ECtHR is not a precedent-setting court. Nevertheless, the Court does attempt to create a consistent jurisprudence, so ECtHR case law will give an indication of how the ECtHR might approach an issue. If a decision is old, and the subject matter is one in which there have been significant developments, then the decision may provide less reliable guidance as to how the court may approach a similar matter now.

2. Decisions of the ECtHR are not binding on UK courts. However, since 2 October 2000, where UK courts are deciding a question of Convention rights, they are obliged to take Convention jurisprudence into account. They must use the ECtHR case law as guide to interpretation of the Convention, and will follow a 'clear and constant' line of cases, but in suitable circumstances may differ from it.

3. Since 2 October 2000, UK courts have been called upon to interpret Convention rights directly for the purpose of the case before them. In doing so they become a source of authority on the interpretation of the ECHR as on any other question of law. A House of Lords or Court of Appeal decision on the meaning or application of the Convention therefore binds lower courts, whereas an ECtHR decision on the same point does not. In the Asylum and Immigration Tribunal therefore, a decision on a Convention right made by the House of Lords or Court of Appeal is binding; a decision made by the ECtHR must be taken into account.

4. Pronouncements by UK courts on the meaning of the Convention in the context of pre-Human Rights Act law are often treated as having persuasive value in the development of rights jurisprudence.

5. The exception to all this is EC law. The Treaty on European Union 1992 Article 6 (ex F) provided that the ECHR must be respected as a principle of EC law. Following this, EC law questions, whether in UK courts or elsewhere, must be decided compatibly with the Convention.

4.2.5 Declarations of incompatibility

Immigration provisions are subject to the unique power in the Human Rights Act to declare primary or secondary legislation incompatible with human rights. Although this does affect the continuing force of primary legislation, it creates a pressure on the government to consider amending it and report to Parliament on its reasoning. This power has been used in relation to the scheme for requiring the Secretary of State's consent to the marriage of foreign nationals, which was declared incompatible with Articles 12 and 14 (see *SSHD v Baiai and Trzcinska, Bigoku and Agolli and Tilki* [2007] EWCA Civ 478, and chapter 9). The Schedule to the 2004 Act which prevents the Secretary of State from considering the safety of a country to which it was proposed to remove someone was declared incompatible with Article 3 in *Nasseri v SSHD* [2007] EWHC 1548 (see chapter 12). The regime of indefinite detention imposed on foreign suspected terrorists by the Anti-terrorism, Crime and Security Act 2001 was declared incompatible with Article 14, and an improper use of immigration law (*A v SSHD* [2004] UKHL 56).

4.3 Scope of human rights claims

Immigration, by its nature, raises questions of the scope of the human rights jurisdiction. It does so in terms of those who can make a human rights claim, and where, geographically, liability for breaches of human rights begins and ends.

4.3.1 Who may make a human rights claim?

Anyone present in the jurisdiction may make a human rights claim. There is no requirement of lawful presence. Article 1 ECHR provides that the rights and freedoms of the Convention must be secured to everyone within the state's jurisdiction. This Article was not included in the HRA, but the statute contains no exclusions of people on grounds of their status, and anyone may apply who claims that their Convention rights have been violated, 'if he would be a victim for the purposes of Article 34 of the Convention if proceedings were brought in the ECtHR' (HRA s 7). This requires that the applicant be directly affected by the act or omission in question. The effect may be actual, as, for instance, in *Berrehab v Netherlands* (1988) 11 EHRR 322, where the applicant's right to have contact with his child was interfered with by the order to remove him from the Netherlands. Alternatively, the effect may be prospective, as, for instance, in *Campbell and Cosans v UK* (1982) 4 EHRR 293 where two children attended a school which permitted corporal punishment. They themselves had not been punished in this way, but by being at the school they were at risk of being so.

Appeals against immigration decisions on the basis that the decision infringes a human right are made on the ground that the decision, or a removal consequent upon it, 'is unlawful under s 6 of the Human Rights Act 1998...as being incompatible with the appellant's Convention rights' (Nationality, Immigration and Asylum Act 2002 s 84(1)). The substance of the human rights appeal proceeds just as if it were brought under the HRA, using the Convention rights, duties under ss 3 and 6, and so on. The main differences between s 84 and action under the HRA are that the appeal under the 2002 Act relates only to the immigration decisions listed in s 82, and that the appeal can only be brought by the person to whom the immigration decision is addressed.

In this respect s 84 draws the test of standing more narrowly than the HRA. The case of *SS Malaysia* [2004] Imm AR 153 was starred on a number of questions including the relevance of the interests of third parties. Departing from ECtHR judgments which considered the effect on all family members (*Boultif v Switzerland* (2001) 33 EHRR 50 and *Amrollahi v Denmark* Application no 00056811/00) and steering a course between earlier tribunal decisions, the tribunal held that the interests of third parties could only be taken into account as far as they impacted upon the appellant. It rejected the argument that if a decision defeated the human rights of third parties it would be 'not in accordance with the law', a ground of appeal under what was then Immigration and Asylum Act 1999 Sched 4 para 21. This followed an earlier line of reasoning represented by *Kehinde** 01/TH/02688, and appears to depart from *R (AC) v IAT, SSHD as interested party* [2003] EWHC 389 Admin. Tribunals have followed *SS Malaysia,* as they are bound to do, for instance in *HR Serbia and Montenegro* [2004] UKIAT 00088, noting that the rights of others are irrelevant 'save insofar as they relate to the human rights of the appellant'. In reality it may often be impossible to separate the family life of family members, and in some cases an attempt to do so would be 'hopelessly blinkered' (*R (on the application of Ahmadi)* [2005] EWCA Civ 1721, see chapter 9). Doubt has been cast on the tribunal's conclusion by the Court of Appeal in *AB (Jamaica)* [2007] EWCA Civ 1302 where, although the standing of family members was not argued before the court, they said:

In substance, albeit not in form, Mr Brown was a party to the proceedings. It was as much his marriage as the appellant's which was in jeopardy, and it was the impact of removal on him rather than on her which, given the lapse of years since the marriage, was now critical. From Strasbourg's point of view, his Convention rights were as fully engaged as hers...It cannot be permissible to give less than detailed and anxious consideration to the situation of a British citizen who has lived here all his life before it is held reasonable and proportionate to expect him to emigrate to a foreign country in order to keep his marriage intact. (para 20)

The question is now awaiting decision before the House of Lords in the case of *Betts v SSHD* [2005] EWCA Civ 828.

Where the human rights claim is made through judicial review, the test of standing is that of 'sufficient interest'. For an affected or at risk individual this is easily met. Neither s 7 nor the 2002 Act allow for human rights challenges by interested pressure groups. However, it is possible for public interest organizations to appear as intervenors in either appeals or judicial review, and since the implementation of the Human Rights Act there have been a number of immigration and refugee law cases in which this has been done. For instance in *R (on the application of Q) v SSHD* [2003] EWCA Civ 364, a challenge to withholding benefits from asylum seekers, both Liberty and the Joint Council for the Welfare of Immigrants were represented. The United Nations High Commissioner for Refugees sometimes intervenes in asylum cases of particular significance.

4.3.2 Immigration decisions

The appeal right in Nationality, Immigration and Asylum Act 2002 s 82 covers the majority of immigration decisions. The most significant exceptions are decisions to carry out a removal (removal directions, discussed in chapter 17) and to detain. In the event of an action or decision not covered by s 82, the decision-maker as a public authority is still bound by the Human Rights Act itself, but an alleged breach of a Convention right is not heard by the Asylum and Immigration Tribunal, but in any court or tribunal in which a Convention right arises (HRA s 7). In the case of a decision to detain, this would be a bail hearing. Removal directions may only be challenged by judicial review. By HRA s 8 each court in which a human rights matter is heard may only deliver the remedies that are normally within its jurisdiction. Therefore applications under the 2002 Act are limited to the remedies which the tribunal can normally award. It can, for instance, allow an appeal against refusal of leave to enter, but not grant damages.

4.3.3 Geographical scope – expulsions

Many human rights decisions in the immigration and asylum context are concerned with the effect of removing a person from the country, and this includes both the damage to their life here and what may happen to them abroad. As the consequence may be experienced outside the UK, expulsions engage the question of geographical scope.

The case of *Soering v UK* (1989) 11 EHRR 439 was the first to establish that, where a state expelled a person to face treatment in breach of a Convention article, the expelling state could be held to be in breach. This is not vicarious liability for the actions of the other state, but because the expulsion itself amounts to a breach. In *Soering* a German national challenged extradition to the US state of Virginia to face the death penalty on a charge of murdering his girlfriend's parents. The threat to his life could not be challenged because Article 2, the right to life, permits the death penalty and at that time the UK had not ratified Protocol 6 which outlaws it. However the ECtHR decided that expulsion to face the phenomenon of being on death row was a breach of Article 3 because of the inordinate delays and suspense, during which the condemned person might wait for years to know whether they would be killed or not. *Cruz Varas v Sweden* [1991] 14 EHRR 1 confirmed that expulsion itself may amount to a violation in the case of deportation as well as extradition. The principle is expressed in *Soering* as follows:

A decision by a contracting State to expel a fugitive may give rise to an issue under Article 3, and hence engage the responsibility of that State under the Convention, where substantial grounds have been shown for believing that the person concerned, if extradited, faces a real risk of being subjected to torture or inhuman or degrading treatment or punishment in the requesting country. The establishment of such responsibility inevitably involves an assessment of conditions in the requesting country against the standards of Article 3 of the Convention. Nonetheless, there is no question of adjudicating on or establishing the responsibility of the receiving country, whether under general international law, under the Convention, or otherwise. Insofar as any liability under the Convention is or maybe incurred, it is liability incurred by the extraditing Contracting State by reason of its having taken action which has as a direct consequence the exposure of an individual to proscribed treatment. (para 91)

This phenomenon is referred to loosely as 'extra-territorial' application of the Convention right. This is a convenient shorthand as the expulsion is a breach because of what is likely to happen elsewhere.

Soering and *Cruz Varas* put the application of Article 3 to expulsions beyond doubt. By extension of Article 3 it would be difficult rationally to exclude Article 2, and despite some case law to the contrary, this is now established (see account of Article 2 below). *Soering* itself seems to suggest there may be scope for extraterritorial application of Article 6. In *Bensaid v UK* (2001) 33 EHRR 205 the applicant failed in his challenge to removal on the ground of a feared breach of Articles 3 and 8, but the ECtHR considered his case on its merits, and found no obstacle to his arguing a feared breach of Article 8.

In the early days of the Human Rights Act, a number of cases, without deciding the point, assumed the possibility of extra-territorial application of qualified rights, that is, those which allow the state to interfere with the right when necessary for the protection of listed public interests. For instance, *Nhundu and Chiwera* 01TH00613 and *SSHD v Z, A v SSHD, M v SSHD* [2002] Imm AR 560 assumed that Article 8 could be breached by an expulsion as a result of conditions in the receiving country. The point was considered by Collins J in *Kacaj* [2002] Imm AR 213:

> We therefore see no reason to exclude the possible application of any relevant Article...in deportation cases, but it will be virtually impossible for an applicant to establish that control on immigration was disproportionate to any breach. (para 26)

The question of responsibility where breaches of qualified rights were feared abroad was settled by the House of Lords in *R v Special Adjudicator ex p Ullah and Do v SSHD*.

 **Key Case**

R v Special Adjudicator ex p Ullah and Do v SSHD [2004] UKHL 26

Both Mr Ullah and Ms Do feared infringement of their rights to freedom of religion (Article 9), and Mr Ullah additionally freedom of expression (Article 10) and freedom of association (Article 11) on return to their countries of origin. They had each claimed asylum as they feared persecution for their religious beliefs, but their asylum claims had failed. Mr Ullah was a citizen of Pakistan and a member of the Ahmadhiya, a minority faith. Ms Do was a Roman Catholic teacher from Vietnam.

The House of Lords held that:

- theoretically, a real risk of breach of *any* Convention right on return may make the expulsion a breach of the UK's obligations (overturning the CA that only Article 3 could be engaged in an extra-territorial case);
- such a feared breach would need to be flagrant, or in the case of a qualified right, amount to a fundamental denial of that right in order to engage the responsibility of the UK (departing from CA in which a breach of any other right would only be regarded if it amounted to a breach of Article 3);
- it is not the case that the Convention rights were not intended to interfere with the state's sovereign rights in relation to foreign nationals (refuting the CA's *obiter* comments in this respect);
- the expelling state cannot relieve itself of responsibility by saying the breach happens elsewhere. The action of expulsion takes place within the jurisdiction;

- *Soering* and *Cruz-Varas* clearly stated the law and may be followed. They are not exceptions.

On the facts, the appellants failed in their claims, but the points of principle are important. The third point above was the argument made for the UK government in *Abdulaziz* and which did not find favour with the ECtHR in that case. Indeed, 20 years of ECtHR case law since Abdulaziz had proceeded on the basis that immigration decisions are subject to human rights considerations. This is an argument that resurfaces in different forms. The reader may be able to see the link with arguments about deference and the margin of discretion (chapter 8). These are doctrines which tend to make rights connected with immigration non-justiciable.

In *R v SSHD ex p Bagdanavicius (FC) & another* [2005] UKHL 38 the House of Lords explained that the assessment of risk on return does not mean that the court is making a decision in law about that receiving country, which after all is not represented in the court. It only means there has to be an assessment of risk to the appellant (para 22).

Although the House of Lords held in *Ullah and Do* that expulsions may engage qualified rights as a result of anticipated treatment in the destination state, this is not a straightforward matter to assess. The appeals in *SSHD ex p Razgar* [2004] UKHL 27 concerned claims based on Articles 3 and 8, that the claimants would suffer deterioration in their mental health if returned to France or Germany. The House of Lords held that the right to respect for private life can be engaged by the foreseeable consequences for health or welfare of removal from the UK when removal does not violate Article 3, if the facts relied on by the appellant are sufficiently strong. The threshold is said to be a high one. Such a claim could not be successfully made simply by showing relative disadvantage in care between the sending and receiving state (para 9). It is settled law that removal can engage Article 8 because of the consequences for family or private life in the UK, and this is dealt with extensively below and in chapter 18.

Where the consequences of removal for family or private life are felt in the UK, the House of Lords called this a 'domestic' case. Where the consequences are feared abroad, they called it a 'foreign' case. The difference between these two is expressed by Baroness Hale:

42. ...In a domestic case the state must always act in a way which is compatible with the Convention rights. There is no threshold test related to the seriousness of the violation or the importance of the right involved. Foreign cases, on the other hand, represent an exception to the general rule that a state is only responsible for what goes on within its own territory or control...the Strasbourg court has not yet explored the test for imposing this obligation in any detail. But there clearly is some additional threshold test indicating the enormity of the violation to which the person is likely to be exposed if returned.

43. ...Lord Bingham also refers to a third, or hybrid category. Here 'the removal of a person from country A to country B may both violate his right to respect for private and family life in country A and also violate the same right by depriving him of family life or impeding his enjoyment of private life in country B'...On analysis, however, such cases remain domestic cases. There is no threshold test of enormity or humanitarian affront. But the right...protected by Article 8 is a qualified right, which may be interfered with if this is necessary to pursue a legitimate aim. What may happen in a foreign country is therefore relevant to the proportionality of the proposed expulsion.

Since *Razgar* there have been comments in the Court of Appeal that all expulsion cases are foreign cases (*SV v SSHD* [2005] EWCA Civ 1683 para 13) and even, in the tribunal, that a case was a foreign case because the appellant was not settled in the UK (*BK Serbia and Montenegro* [2005] UKIAT 00001). If this were so, the effect of the distinction would be to deny equal protection of fundamental rights to people present in the UK but without a secure immigration status. This position is not sustainable and is not consistent with the tenor of the House of Lords judgment in *Huang and Kashmiri* [2007] UKHL 11, though this is not precisely on the same point (see discussion on proportionality at 4.4.4.4 below). Guidance to Home Office caseworkers refers to 'domestic' and 'foreign' cases in the terms used in *Razgar*, and the distinction and its effects as delineated by Baroness Hale must be taken to represent the current state of the law.

The latest authority on the breach of qualified rights abroad is that of *EM (Lebanon) v SSHD*, now on appeal to the House of Lords.

 Key Case

EM (Lebanon) v SSHD [2006] EWCA Civ 1531

The appellant's asylum claim failed and she faced removal with her 10-year-old child to Lebanon. The accepted evidence was that if returned to that country she would lose custody of the child to her husband who had previously attempted to remove the child to Saudi Arabia and had subjected her to extreme violence. This was because the law would automatically give custody to the father if he did not approve the mother as custodian. It was unclear whether she would be given contact with the child or not. She claimed that removal would breach her right to respect for family life under Article 8.

In the Court of Appeal Carnwath LJ made a new distinction between a 'flagrant breach' of a right and its 'complete denial' (para 38). He thought that the parent/child relationship was the fundamental essence of family life, and that in *EM* the anticipated breach of the right to respect for that relationship would be 'flagrant' (para 39). However, because of the possibility of contact the denial of the right would not be complete (para 37) and thus the stringent standard to find a breach of a qualified right abroad was not reached. Bodey J agreed with this approach. Gage LJ used the two terms interchangeably and concluded there was not a breach. The court made the point that the best interests of the child were not paramount in an asylum case. Under the Refugee Qualification Directive (2004/83/EC) they now are, but this was not, before the Court of Appeal, an asylum case.

4.3.4 Geographical scope – entry decisions

The other main question concerning geographical scope is the application of human rights when the applicant is outside the UK. This is a trickier question in legal theory than in expulsion cases, though in practice it is often treated as much simpler.

The description of immigration control in chapter 7 shows that whether someone is outside the UK or not when they apply for leave to enter is in part a matter of factual accident. When an application for leave to enter is made in the UK, there is no doubt that the Human Rights Act applies. When the applicant is abroad, does their location make a difference? The usual immigration application made abroad is for entry clearance, though as chapter 7 shows, decisions on leave to enter may now be made anywhere in the world.

The Court of Appeal in *Farrakhan* (see later in relation to Article 10) came close to concluding whether human rights are engaged in entry decisions. They held that a qualified right was not engaged where its exercise was incidental and arose after entry, but that it was engaged in the case in hand because the Secretary of State had made the decision refusing entry partly *in order to* prevent his exercising freedom of expression. However, they did so having been content to accept the Secretary of State's concession that the fact that the appellant was outside the UK did not affect his right to a human rights appeal. This is the question which, having been left outstanding, now exercises the tribunals.

In actual fact, when entry clearance to join a family member is the UK is refused, Article 8 is frequently invoked, and the entry clearance officer usually defends the appeal on the merits of the case, rather than by saying that Article 8 does not apply. This is the simple practical aspect of the matter. The more difficult theoretical question is on what basis Article 8 is invoked. This matters:

- when reliance on Article 8 is challenged;
- in considering the rights of other family members;
- when other qualified rights are used;
- because of the export of immigration control (see chapters 1 and 7).

Refusal of entry clearance may be appealed on human rights grounds according to Nationality, Immigration and Asylum Act 2002 ss 82 and 84. However, the tribunal has suggested that this is a mistake by Parliament (*Rev Sun Myung Moon v ECO Seoul* [2005] UKIAT 00112 para 56). A number of tribunal decisions have suggested that human rights do not apply to entry clearance cases. *SS (Malaysia)* was starred on this issue and endorsed the earlier decision in *H (Somalia)* [2004] UKIAT 00027 that the protection of UK human rights law did not extend to those outside the territory of the UK, and that use of Article 8 in entry cases was by way of special extension, relying on the existence of family members in the UK. The argument against human rights applying to entry clearance cases is that these decisions are taken outside the jurisdiction. For ECHR purposes the jurisdiction is primarily territorial, but there are exceptions including the acts of a consular official (e.g. *Bankovic v Belgium* (2001) 11 BHRC 435). The question is whether entry clearance officers and their decisions come within this consular exception. The closest authority in terms of facts is *The Queen on the application of B v Secretary of State for Foreign and Commonwealth Affairs* [2004] EWCA Civ 1344 where the Court of Appeal considered a wealth of ECtHR authorities, none conclusive, on the question of whether the Convention applied to the actions of consular officials who gave temporary protection to asylum seekers in Australia. Being unable to reach a concluded view, the court was content to assume that the applicants were sufficiently within the jurisdiction of the UK.

Much of the growing case law on the jurisdictional reach of the ECHR outside the respondent state derives from conflict situations and does not translate directly to entry clearance. See, for instance, *Bankovic v Belgium* (2001) 11 BHRC 435 and *Issa v Turkey* (31821/96) 17 BHRC 473.

Most recently, the House of Lords in *Al-Skeini v SSHD* [2007] UKHL 26 held that the Human Rights Act could apply outside the UK where the principles of giving effect to Convention rights required that this was so, and within the limits of jurisdiction suggested by the principles of Article 1 ECHR. Accordingly, they held that the UK could be liable under the HRA for the death in UK military custody of Baha Mousa, though not the killing by British troops of Iraqi civilians in the streets. Lord Rodgers of Earlsferry said that legislation governing the conduct of public authorities should apply to them in the same way when they acted abroad as it did at home (para 53). This tends to support the argument that human rights under the Human Rights Act and the Nationality, Immigration and Asylum Act 2002 apply to entry clearance decisions in the same way as they would to an entry decision made at a UK port, but *Al-Skeini* concerns very different circumstances, so the matter is not explicitly resolved.

Meanwhile, in the ECtHR, in *Osman v UK* Application 12698/06 four teenage girls had been refused entry clearance to join their mother in the UK after suffering illnesses, very poor living conditions and displacement due to the conflict in Somalia. They applied to the ECtHR on the basis that the refusal of entry clearance breached their right to respect for family life under Article 8. The case ended in a friendly settlement after the UK government granted them entry clearance.

4.4 Convention rights

Not all the Convention rights will be examined in detail here. This section will concentrate on those rights which are most commonly encountered in the immigration and asylum contexts.

4.4.1 Article 3

4.4.1.1 *What 'treatment' is included*

This Article provides that:

No-one shall be subjected to torture or inhuman or degrading treatment or punishment.

In relation to persecution, Goodwin-Gill and Macadam say that it is 'a concept only too readily filled by the latest examples of one person's inhumanity to another, and little purpose is served by attempting to list all its known measures' (2007: 93–4). The same could be said of treatment that contravenes Article 3. Cross-reference may be made here to discussion of 'severe harm' in the refugee definition discussed in chapter 13, and no catalogue of violations is attempted in either chapter. Whether behaviour constitutes torture is rarely the issue in an expulsion case. More commonly the question is the degree of risk, whether the treatment can be justified (is the protection absolute?), and the parameters around contentious areas such as denial of welfare support or medical treatment. This is not to say that the definition of torture is generally agreed, as demonstrated by the current debate surrounding 'waterboarding' (see for instance http://en.wikipedia.org/wiki/Talk:Waterboarding), but treatment that falls short of torture will still be inhuman or degrading treatment and so breach Article 3.

Treatment must pass a certain threshold of severity in order to come within Article 3. The Convention moves with the times, and in *Selmouni v France* (1999) 29 EHRR 403 the ECtHR held that the interrogation techniques (hooding, exposure to noise, deprivation of food and drink, deprivation of sleep, and enforced standing against a wall) found to be degrading and inhuman in *Ireland v UK* (1978) 2 EHRR 25 would now be found to be torture. This is the case even if some local public opinion lags behind. In the case of *Tyrer v UK* birching a schoolboy on the Isle of Man was held to be a violation of Article 3, as this form of punishment, once considered acceptable, was now generally regarded as degrading. The Court's conclusion was not affected by evidence of belief by the public on the Isle of Man in the deterrent effect of such treatment. This arises from the absolute nature of the Article. The police force cannot, for instance, say that such treatment is necessary to extract a confession.

Whether treatment is degrading will depend on the circumstances of the individual. Adverse treatment on grounds of race may amount to degrading treatment if it is institutionalized, as in the *East African Asians cases* (1981) 3 EHRR 76. Here, the European Commission on Human Rights found that the refusal of entry to the UK to the British passport holders resident in Uganda, Tanzania, and Kenya (discussed in chapter 3) amounted to institutionalized racism. Such consistent adverse treatment of people on account of their race was degrading, and passed the threshold of severity to amount to a violation of Article 3.

A breach of Article 3 normally requires actual or threatened physical or psychological ill-treatment which is deliberately applied. There must be 'treatment'; an omission will not breach the Article. In *Q and M* [2003] EWCA Civ 364 there was argument as to what might constitute treatment. The Court of Appeal found:

> The imposition by the legislature of a regime which prohibits asylum seekers from working and further prohibits the grant to them, when they are destitute, of support amounts to positive action directed against asylum seekers and not to mere inaction. (para 57)

The denial of benefits was therefore 'treatment' for the purposes of Article 3, and this was endorsed by the House of Lords in *R v SSHD ex p Adam, Limbuela and Tesema* [2005] UKHL 66. If the asylum seeker has, by some other means, for instance friends or a charity, obtained shelter, sanitary facilities, and some money for food, the denial of benefit does not reach the threshold to be regarded as degrading (*R (on the application of S, D, T) v SSHD* [2003] EWHC 1951 (Admin)). The House of Lords' judgment in *Adam, Limbuela and Tesema* explores individual circumstances to assess whether the threshold for a breach of Article 3 has been reached: 'section 55 asylum-seekers...are not only forced to sleep rough but are not allowed to work to earn money and have no access to financial support by the state. The rough sleeping which they are forced to endure cannot be detached from the degradation and humiliation that results from the circumstances that give rise to it' (Lord Hope, para 60).

When Article 3 is applied to general living conditions it raises extremely difficult questions. In *N (Burundi)* [2003] UKIAT 00065 the claimant said that the ravages of civil war in her country were such that it would be inhuman to return her. However, the tribunal disagreed. The standards were general in that country and did not apply specially to her. This raises the question of whether human rights law can or should be used to equalize living standards, and which standards from the country of origin the Convention country is prepared to call acceptable.

4.4.1.2 *Inadequate medical treatment*

Where there is torture or other severe physical or psychological ill-treatment, there is little doubt that the treatment will cross the high threshold necessary to amount to a breach of Article 3. Other kinds of ill treatment are more controversial. The case of *D v UK* (1997) 24 EHRR 423 broke new ground in this respect, although it has generally been distinguished in subsequent cases where applicants have sought to rely on it. The Secretary of State sought to deport D after he had served a long prison sentence for supplying prohibited drugs. He was by this time in an advanced stage of AIDS. He was receiving terminal care in a hospice. The treatment he had been receiving had slowed down the progress of the disease and relieved his symptoms, and he was receiving support as he faced death. His life expectancy was short in any event, but if he was deported to St. Kitts the treatment upon which he depended would not be available at all, and he had no family or social network to support him. The end of his life would be marked by much greater suffering. The ECtHR held that to return him in these circumstances would breach Article 3.

In subsequent cases it has generally been difficult to show that an acceptable level of treatment would not be available in the destination country. In *Bensaid v UK* (2001) 33 EHRR 205 the applicant was suffering from schizophrenia, and argued both that the upheaval would aggravate his condition, and that suitable treatment would not be available in Algeria. He failed on the second point. There may be scope for arguments under Article 8 in relation to loss of medical care, as indicated in *Razgar* and discussed further below.

The leading case in relation to medical care is that of *N v SSHD*.

 Key Case

N v SSHD [2005] UKHL 31

N was an AIDS sufferer facing deportation to Uganda. In the UK where she had been living for five years her condition had stabilized on medication. This medication would not be available to her in Uganda. Her brothers and sisters had died of AIDS and her life expectancy would be reduced to a year or two. The House of Lords unanimously and carefully distinguished *D v UK*. It held that in *D* the removal was a breach of Article 3 because it would mean that his death, which was imminent, would take place in far more distressing circumstances. Here, death was not imminent, although their Lordships acknowledged there could be no real difference in humanitarian terms between removing someone to face imminent death and removing someone to face death within a year or two. The difference came in that the Convention could not be taken to have imposed upon the parties an obligation to provide medical treatment. Lord Brown identified *D* as concerning a negative obligation – not to deport D to 'an imminent, lonely and distressing end' (*N v SSHD* [2005] UKHL 31 para 93). *N*, he thought, concerned a positive obligation – to provide N with medical treatment. To allow N to remain but not give her medical care would not answer her needs.

All their Lordships expressed strong sympathy with N, and distaste for having to make this decision. Lord Brown came very close to suggesting that the Secretary of State should exercise discretion to let N stay (para 99). In the end, social policy considerations had to be overt in order to make sense of this case. Lord Nicholls and others acknowledged 'If the appellant were a special case I have no doubt that, in one way or another, the pressing humanitarian considerations of her case would prevail'. However, given the prevalence of AIDS in Africa in particular and the shortage of treatment, her case was 'far from unique' (para 9). Their Lordships saw the issue as being outside their capacity to resolve. The problem arose from 'Uganda's lack of medical resources compared with those available in the UK' (para 8) and the better answer than migration and human rights claims was, in the words of Lord Hope, 'for states to continue to concentrate their efforts on the steps which are currently being taken, with the assistance of the drugs companies, to make the necessary medical care universally and freely available' (para 53).

In terms of institutional competence or judicial restraint the message of this case is clear. It may, if one agrees with the decision, illustrate Gearty's point that 'sometimes it will be right for the judge to hesitate, to say – against his or her own moral intuitions – that bad though the case is it does not call for his or her intervention' (2004:6).

N applies to other health risks and conditions in the sense that there is a high threshold to be crossed to show that deprivation of medical treatment will breach Article 3. In *CA v SSHD* [2004] EWCA Civ 1165 the appellant was HIV positive, and the adjudicator found that she would not necessarily lack the requisite treatment on return to Ghana. However, her baby, who at the time of the hearing had not yet been born, would have little chance of staying well as he or she could not be breastfed, and dried formula milk would be mixed with unsafe water. There was a reasonable likelihood that the baby would die, therefore it was a breach of Article 3 to return the mother. Laws LJ, giving the leading judgment, said 'It seems to me obvious simply as a matter of common humanity that for a mother to witness the collapse of her new-born child's health and perhaps its death may be a kind of suffering far greater than might arise by the mother's confronting the self-same fate herself'. *JB Ghana* [2005] UKIAT 00077 was a pre-*N* decision concerning AIDS treatment. The tribunal held that if the appellant could not afford the treatment this was the same as it not being available at all. This point is now presumably subsumed within *N*.

An increasing number of cases are dealing with the question of suicide risk in the context of Articles 3 and 8; this arises in particular where the applicant has already made suicide attempts and there is a real risk that they will take their life if they are returned to their home country. In *J v SSHD* [2005] EWCA Civ 629 the Court of Appeal said that, in a case where suicide is anticipated on return, relevant questions for the court include whether there is a causal link between the removal and the risk of suicide, and whether the applicant's fear of ill-treatment is objectively well founded. An Article 3 claim could in principle succeed in a suicide case, but the threshold would be high because it is a 'foreign' case (i.e. the feared risk would materialize abroad) and higher still because the harm feared would not be directly caused by the authorities but as a result of an illness (following *D v UK* and *Bensaid v UK*). Finally, the decision-maker must assess 'whether the removing and/or the receiving state has effective mechanisms to reduce the risk of suicide' (para 31).

Where the risk arises in the UK when someone is told of their impending removal, the question still is whether there is a real risk of suicide. In *R (on the application of Kurtolli) v SSHD* [2003] EWHC 2744 (Admin) the Article 3 and 2 risks arose from the claimant's likely suicide or suicide attempt if removed. Whether the treatment in Germany would be adequate or even better than that in the UK was not the point. The claimant's mental state was such that notice of removal was in itself a danger to her. Her situation was analogous to that of Ms Soumahoro, one of the co-appellants in *Razgar*. In theory, a case of suicide risk might meet the threshold for Article 8 but not Article 3. Courts since *J* have stressed the importance in a case of suicide risk of considering all the questions that were set out in that case. See for instance *AJ (Liberia) v SSHD* [2006] EWCA Civ 1736 and *CN (Burundi) v SSHD* [2007] EWCA Civ 587, in both of which cases the Court of Appeal said that the high threshold set in *N* applies to suicide risk cases, though reiterating that a case could in principle succeed. In *R (on the application of Kurtaj) v SSHD* [2007] EWHC 221 (Admin) the claimant was entitled to make a fresh claim because of the deterioration of his already fragile mental health through his experiences in the asylum system, and the risk that he might now commit suicide if faced with return.

4.4.1.3 *Absolute right under challenge*

Article 3 confers an absolute right, the breach of which cannot be justified by any interest of the State. This is a settled principle of law, and the ECtHR confirmed in *Chahal v UK* (1996) 23 EHRR 413 that this means that even a person who may be a danger to national security cannot be expelled to face torture. This simple assertion, confirmed in *N v Finland* (2005) 43 EHRR 12, has now become the focal point of an international debate, in which states bent on defeating terrorism seek ways to circumvent the absolute nature of this prohibition.

In the UK, both the government and the Opposition have talked of withdrawing from the whole European Convention, and then re-ratifying without Article 3 (e.g. British Prime Minister on television's 'Frost Programme' on 26 January 2003). Legal opinion, unsurprisingly, was that 'it is strongly arguable that the ECHR does not permit a contracting state to use the power of denunciation ... as a device to secure a reservation which could not otherwise validly be made, and therefore the proposal floated by the Prime Minister would be invalid and unlawful' (29 January 2003, Blackstone Chambers, D. Pannick and S. Fatima, for Liberty). The absolute nature of the prohibition on returning someone to a risk of torture is challenged in a case awaiting hearing in the ECtHR, *Ramzy v Netherlands* Application No 25424/05. The case is typical of several which have been heard by the Special Immigration Appeals Commission in the UK. It concerns the proposed deportation to Algeria of an asylum-seeker who was suspected of involvement in an Islamic terrorist extremist group in the Netherlands, but has been acquitted of criminal charges. The British, Portuguese, Lithuanian and Slovak governments have been granted leave to intervene in the case, to argue that a mere risk of torture on return is not sufficient to prevent his deportation.

Ramzy illustrates one of the main difficulties for governments who wish to deport someone who is assessed by the Secretary of State to be a risk to national security. The alleged political involvements of the proposed deportee and the nature of the regime from which they have come may mean that there is a real risk of their being tortured on their return, therefore it is a breach of Article 3 to return them. However, without evidence to bring criminal charges in the UK there is no lawful way to keep such people out of circulation and obviate the risk they are thought to pose. A series of draconian measures has been attempted:

- Indefinite detention without trial – found unlawful by the House of Lords in *A v UK* [2004] UKHL 56;
- Control orders – many in force and accepted as lawful, but the most extreme conditions approximating to house arrest in solitary confinement found unlawful by the House of Lords in *SSHD v MB* [2007] UKHL 46;
- Deprivation of any protective status and associated civil rights (Criminal Justice and Immigration Bill 2007).

Meanwhile, there is a possibility (some would say the probability, e.g. C. Murray, speech at Chatham House, 8 November 2004) that evidence of the risk they are thought to pose to national security may have been obtained by torture. As evidence obtained by torture may be unreliable, some of the people upon whom these measures are imposed may be no risk at all. This is also the case because they often cannot test the evidence against them (see discussion of the Special Immigration Appeals Commission in chapter 8, and national security deportations in chapter 16).

As the government cannot actually withdraw from Article 3, it is attempting other measures. One is to intervene in *Ramzy*, above. Another is to obtain assurances from receiving governments that returnees would not be subject to torture. Memoranda of understanding that returnees will not be tortured have been signed with Jordan, Libya, and Lebanon. The reliability of these assurances in general has been seriously doubted (see Human Rights Watch 2005 and Amnesty International 2007). The position in law is that it is 'for the courts to determine the factual question of whether an individual faces a substantial risk of torture on his return, and in reaching that decision the courts will properly take into account the assurances given as part of all the relevant evidence, including evidence about the likelihood of those assurances being delivered in practice' (Counter-Terrorism Policy and Human Rights Joint Committee on Human Rights Third Report of sessions 2005–06 HL 75-I, HC 561-I para 145). The Court of Appeal in *MT (Algeria), RB (Algeria) and U(Algeria) v SSHD* [2007] EWCA Civ 808 gave an indication of some of the factors that would be taken into account in such an assessment:

- in the receiving country, a consistent pattern of gross, flagrant or mass violations of human rights or of systematic practice of torture
- the terms of the assurance – in *MT* the court considered it understandable and acceptable that this was 'couched in universally understood diplomatic language'
- monitoring – assurances would not be useful unless there were some system of checking whether they had been complied with. In this case the court considered that the refusal of Algeria to accept independent monitoring should be understood in the light of its sensitivity as a 'recently post-colonial state'. There were some mechanisms in place and these were accepted to be sufficient.

In *DD v SSHD, & AS v SSHD* Appeal nos. CS/42 and 50/2005, 27 April 2007, SIAC found that memoranda of understanding given by Libya could not be relied upon to prevent a real risk of torture on return. This was not because the assurances were given in bad faith, but because 'there is too much scope for changes to happen, for things to go wrong, and too little scope for a breach of Article 3 to be deterred or for acts which might lead to a breach of Article 3 to be remedied in time, essentially through effective monitoring' (para 428).

In *Othman aka Abu Qatada v SSHD* Appeal no. SC 15/2005 26 February 2007 SIAC found that there was not a significant degree of risk should Abu Qatada be returned to Jordan, and this conclusion was reinforced by the existence of the MOU. SIAC expected the MOU:

to have some influence on the way in which legal procedures pre-trial are carried out. The MOU and monitoring reinforce our conclusions about other risks, although we have not relied upon them as the crucial components which make what would otherwise be a real risk of a breach of Article 3 into something less. (para 490)

As to the problem of evidence which may have been obtained by torture, in *A and others v SSHD* [2005] UKHL 71 a committee of seven Law Lords unanimously rejected the Secretary of State's argument that evidence which might have been obtained by torture could, as a matter of law, be admitted before the Special Immigration Appeals Commission. Their uncompromising affirmation of the unacceptability of torture may, as Lord Brown said, 'spill over into other court proceedings designed to provide a judicial check on the exercise of other executive powers to place constraints of one sort or another on terrorist suspects in the interests of national security' (para 168).

The prohibition on the use of evidence obtained by torture was a principle going back many centuries, now buttressed by international agreements such as the ECHR, the Universal Declaration of Human Rights 1948, the International Covenant on Civil and Political Rights 1966, and the UN Convention Against Torture 1987. The International Criminal Tribunal for the Former Yugoslavia, in *Prosecutor v Furundzija* [1998] ICTY 3, 10 December 1998, even said that prohibition and prevention of torture: '... enjoys a higher rank in the international hierarchy than treaty law ... [and] ... has now become one of the most fundamental standards of the international community' (quoted by Lord Bingham, para 33).

In an interim report to the UN General Assembly on 1 September 2004, the UN Special Rapporteur on Torture criticized attempts by governments to circumvent the absolute nature of the prohibition on torture and other inhuman treatment on the ground of combating terrorism. A similar warning was issued by the Council of Europe's Committee for the Prevention of Torture in its 14th report on 21 September 2004.

The debate about extra-territorial liability in expulsion cases needs to be seen in the light of these developments, and of the recently uncovered practice of 'extraordinary rendition' – that is, transporting people to extra-territorial locations for interrogation 'in circumstances that make it more likely than not that the individual will be subjected to torture or cruel, inhuman or degrading treatment' (All Party Parliamentary Group on Extraordinary Rendition, December 2005). These locations include US bases and countries known for their record of torture (Amnesty International 2005:4). That the US was practising extraordinary rendition was confirmed by President Bush on 6 September 2006 (White House press release). Committees of the Council of Europe and the European Union continued to investigate allegations of European complicity in this practice, and the Council of Europe's Committee for the Prevention of Torture in its 17th report in September 2007 concluded: 'in the light of information now in the public domain, there can be little doubt that the interrogation techniques applied in the CIA-run facilities concerned have led to violations of the prohibition of torture and inhuman or degrading treatment'. A legal opinion prepared for the All Party Parliamentary Group was unequivocal that the UK's obligations in international law were independent of those of the US, and that such renditions engaged the international obligations of any state implicated (Crawford J. and Evans K., 9 December 2005).

The UK's Intelligence and Security Committee investigated questions of UK complicity, and found that the UK had not facilitated extraordinary renditions through the UK, but had co-operated in the removal of two men to Guantanamo Bay. An important finding of the ISC report was that expressions of concern by the UK did not materially affect US practice, and so assurances received that Diego Garcia was not being used for secret detention and questioning did not discharge the UK's obligation to investigate allegations of torture on its soil. The US and UK have not signed the UN's 2007 International Convention for the Protection of All Persons from Enforced Disappearance, though 57 countries have.

Extraordinary rendition provides evidence of the international climate in which decisions are made in the courts and tribunals about liability for extra-territorial effects of removal. Breaches of Article 3 may be committed even by 'friendly' states, and there is both an interest by governments in accepting assurances and not looking too closely, and pressure for openness and accountability.

4.4.1.4 Relationship with asylum claims

There is a substantial overlap between the treatment which might form the substance of an asylum claim and treatment which would breach Article 3. The majority of Article 3 claims are thus from people whose asylum claim has failed for a reason other than the severity of the treatment feared or the risk of its occurring. The case of *Kacaj* established that the standard of proof is the same for a refugee claim and for a human rights claim. The standard to be applied is to enquire whether there is a real risk of the feared treatment occurring. This was further explained by Sedley LJ in *Batayav v SSHD* [2003] EWCA Civ 1489: 'If a type of car has a defect which causes one vehicle in ten to crash, most people would say that it presents a real risk to anyone who drives it, albeit crashes are not generally or consistently happening' (para 38). The Administrative Court in *The Queen on the application of Kpangni* [2005] EWHC 881 (Admin) reiterated that the test of real risk as described in *Batayav* is the one that should be used.

Kacaj also established that the approach in the asylum case of *Horvath v SSHD* [2000] 3 WLR 370 to the question of state protection applies in Article 3 cases. In that case the Roma applicant had been subjected to attacks by skinheads, and the case in the House of Lords turned on whether the system of criminal law in Slovakia gave him adequate protection. It was held that where there is a system of criminal law which makes violent attacks punishable, and a reasonable willingness by the enforcement agencies to enforce that law, then the state is held to protect its citizens sufficiently. Therefore when treatment contrary to Article 3 is feared from people who are not part of the state machinery themselves, if there is such a system in place there will be no sustainable claim under Article 3. This was confirmed by the ECtHR in *HLR v France* (1997) 26 EHRR 29 in which a Colombian drug trafficker feared reprisals from drugs barons in Colombia. The Court said:

Owing to the absolute character of the right guaranteed, the Court does not rule out the possibility that Article 3 of the Convention (art 3) may also apply where the danger emanates from persons or groups of persons who are not public officials. However, it must be shown that the risk is real and that the authorities of the receiving State are not able to obviate the risk by providing appropriate protection. (para 40)

This was confirmed in the UK by the House of Lords in *Bagdanavicius*. The House went further and said (in the only reasoned judgment) that serious harm without a failure of State protection did not amount to inhuman or degrading treatment or punishment. Only the State was capable in law of inflicting these, and the prospect of a brutal attack by non-State agents where there was a reasonable system of protection did not constitute the treatment proscribed by Article 3 (para 24).

Scope may arise for an Article 3 claim where the asylum seeker is unable to prove that the ill-treatment they fear is for a reason laid down by the Refugee Convention (see chapter 13). The Jamaican case of *A v SSHD* [2003] EWCA Civ 175, discussed below, was one such, where violent reprisals were feared from a criminal gang. *AS (Appeals raising Articles 3 and 8) Iran* [2006] UKAIT 00037 also provided an example where the immigration judge found that the appellant feared punishment by lashes but not for a reason recognised by the Refugee Convention. This treatment would contravene Article 3.

Where an asylum claim has been turned down, but a claim is made under Article 3, there must be a reasoned decision on the Article 3 claim also. It is not enough for a decision-maker to dismiss an asylum claim and then dismiss the human rights claim without proper consideration (*I v SSHD* [2005] EWCA Civ 886).

4.4.2 **Article 2**

Article 2(1) provides that:

Everyone's right to life shall be protected by law. No-one shall be deprived of his life intentionally save in the execution of a sentence of a court following conviction of a crime for which this penalty is provided by law.

Article 2 does not outlaw the death sentence. This is done by Protocol 13, which the UK ratified on 10 October 2003. Protocol 13, unlike Protocol 6, outlaws the death penalty in all circumstances. The inclusion of Protocol 13 in the rights in Sch 1 to the Human Rights Act means that there are substantial constitutional problems in the way of any future government which might wish to re-introduce the death penalty, including in time of war.

Article 2(1) entails both that the State must take some positive steps to prevent life being taken and that the State must not itself take life.

4.4.2.1 *Positive obligation*

The positive duty to protect life is of a limited kind. In *Osman v UK* (2000) 29 EHRR 245 the police were aware that a schoolteacher who had developed an obsession with his pupil was harassing him. The European Court of Human Rights held that there was no breach of Article 2 in their failure to apprehend him and to prevent the killing which he committed, because there was no decisive stage at which the police knew or ought to have known that the lives of the applicant family were at real and immediate risk. The corollary of this is that if, in another case, there were such a decisive stage at which the risk was real and immediate then there could be a breach of Article 2. More generally, the court interpreted the duty of protection in Article 2 to mean that the state has a general duty to establish and maintain an effective system of criminal law to deter, detect, and punish offenders. Such a duty would be fulfilled by the maintenance of a police and criminal justice system such as that in the UK.

4.4.2.2 *Negative obligation*

The negative obligation not to take life is qualified by Article 2(2), which sets out possible defences the state may be able to maintain where death results accidentally from the use of force which is no more than absolutely necessary:

(a) in defence of any person from unlawful violence;

(b) in order to effect a lawful arrest or to prevent the escape of a person lawfully detained; and

(c) in action lawfully taken for the purpose of quelling a riot or insurrection.

The terms of this paragraph are strictly construed by the Court, and in determining whether the use of force was no more than absolutely necessary attention may be paid to whether adequate guidelines for the situation were in place and followed. This was demonstrated in the case of *McCann v UK* (1996) 21 EHRR 97 (the 'deaths on the

Rock' case) where the lack of training in shooting to wound rather than to kill was one of the reasons that the UK government was found in breach of Article 2 for the killing of IRA suspects in Gibraltar.

The negative aspect of the duty will generally have less relevance in the spheres of immigration and asylum, except where immigration enforcement involves policing functions. For instance, in 1993 a woman called Joy Gardner suffocated to death when she was bound and gagged by the police Alien Deportation Group. They were arresting her in order to deport her as an overstayer. Prosecution and complaints failed. What Article 2 may add to these existing legal routes is a further element of state responsibility. If the individuals were exonerated because sufficient justification was found for their actions at the time, given their training, responses, and state of knowledge, this does not exonerate the state from providing a level of training that would prevent such incidents from occurring. In the case of *McCann* the SAS officers were not trained to shoot to wound rather than kill. They were not held individually to blame but the state was in breach of Article 2. In the case of Joy Gardner, it seems that the officers were insufficiently aware of the effect of binding someone's head with 13 feet of surgical tape. This could suggest a similar level of state responsibility. The positive obligation also requires diligent and prompt investigation of a death at the hands of the state (*Kaya v Turkey* (1999) 28 EHRR 1).

4.4.2.3 *Article 2 and expulsions*

Article 2 is relevant in the case of threatened expulsion of someone from the UK to a risk of death. In general this refers to deliberate killing, and not to the circumstances in *N*. Earlier case law suggested that the risk of death must be 'near certain' in order to engage the responsibility of the expelling state, following a Commission decision, *Dehwari v Netherlands* (2001) 29 EHRR CD 74. The tribunal in *Hane* [2002] UKIAT 03945 used this standard. However, in *A v SSHD* [2003] the Court of Appeal applied the same standard to a risk of violation of Article 2 as to Article 3, namely that there was a 'real risk'. The risk to the appellant in that case came from gang members seeking revenge for her giving a name to the police of the person she thought killed her son. There was substantial other evidence of reprisals her family had already suffered and of the risk to her life should she return to Jamaica. Note here an example of the effect of the Human Rights Act on the doctrine of precedent. Prior to a decision of the Court of Appeal there was no binding authority on the level of risk to be proved where Article 2 was applied to an expulsion because of risk of death in the receiving state (so-called 'extra-territorial application'). The tribunal in *Hane* (for example) was obliged under HRA s 2 to take into account decisions of the Strasbourg bodies though not necessarily to follow them. They did not in fact quote *Dehwari,* but could have done, and accepted the principle from it as established. Since the UK Court of Appeal has decided the matter this is now binding on subsequent tribunals, and *Dehwari* ceases to have effect.

The case of *A* illustrates that it is immaterial whether the danger comes from the State or, as here, criminal gangs, if there is a real risk that the applicant will not be protected. This confirms the approach in *Kacaj,* referred to above, in relation to State responsibility.

4.4.2.4 *Death penalty*

If the danger to life comes from the State this may be by way of extra-judicial killing, or by the death penalty. The imposition of the death penalty raises different legal questions, which are changed and possibly simplified by the inclusion of Protocol 13 in the Human Rights Act. A minister in a Parliamentary written answer (WA 40 28 November 2001) confirmed that there would not be expulsions to face the death penalty.

The way in which the death penalty is carried out may involve an expelling state in a breach of Article 3. This is a small extension of the outcome of *Soering*, and is demonstrated in cases such as *Jabari v Turkey* [2001] INLR 136. Here, the applicant was granted refugee status by the UNHCR in Turkey, but because she had not made her application within five days, under Turkish law she was still vulnerable to expulsion from Turkey. There was a real risk that if returned to Iran she would face death by stoning for adultery. Returning her to face this was held to be a breach of Article 3.

4.4.3 **Article 6**

4.4.3.1 *Content of the right*

Article 6, the right to a fair hearing, is one of the most litigated Articles in the Convention. It sets out minimum requirements of a fair hearing which apply to the determination of 'civil rights and obligations' and criminal trials and provides further minimum rights for a person charged with a criminal offence, for instance to have information of the charge, facilities and time for preparing a defence, and so on.

In addition to the express rights set out, Article 6 also imports a general requirement of fairness into trials, which is open to interpretation by the court. It has been held to require access to a court (*Golder v UK* (1979–80) 1 EHRR 524), the right to put one's case on equal terms with one's opponent, which may, depending on the circumstances entail the right to legal representation and the right to participate effectively in proceedings (e.g. *Goddi v Italy* (1984) 6 EHRR 457).

4.4.3.2 *Defining a 'civil right'*

Where an immigration offence such as illegal entry is charged, then Article 6 applies as to any other criminal matter. However, the vast majority of immigration issues only come within the ambit of Article 6(1) if they are regarded as civil rights. The case law to date suggests that they are not so regarded. The dividing line between public and private is not clear, and the ECtHR does not necessarily take the same view as a domestic authority of what constitutes a private and what a public matter. For example, in *Salesi v Italy* (1993) 26 EHRR 187 the Court found that payment of a social security benefit falls within Article 6. In *Adams & Benn v UK* (1996) 23 EHRR 160 CD the Commission referred to personal, economic, or individual aspects as characteristic of a private law and thus a civil right. It could be argued that immigration matters have these as well as other characteristics. However, the Commission tended to focus on the administrative character of immigration matters, and thus deem them public and so not civil rights. In *Uppal v UK* (1979) 3 EHRR 391 the Commission found that decisions to deport were of an administrative nature and so not covered by Article 6(1). Extradition (*Farmakopoulous v Greece* (1990) 64 DR 52), nationality (*S v Switzerland* (1988) 59 DR 256) and entry for employment (*X v UK* 1977 9 DR 224) have all been found not to qualify as civil rights for Article 6. However, the matter was not settled by these decisions as they are all decisions of the Commission and not of the Court.

The case of *Maaouia v France* (2001) 33 EHRR 42 concerned the question of whether Article 6 applied to the rescission of an expulsion order against a foreign national. This was considered to be sufficiently important to warrant hearing by the full court.

 **Key Case**

Maaouia v France (2001) 33 EHRR 42

Mr Maaouia was unaware of a deportation order made against him as it was not served on him. The following year he went to the Nice Centre for Administrative Formalities to regularize his immigration status and was served with the deportation order. He refused to leave the country in compliance with the order, and was sentenced to one year in prison and ten years' exclusion from French territory. He appealed through the French system against his exclusion, but his appeals were finally dismissed in 1994 on the ground that he had not challenged the deportation order in the lower courts, though it was eventually quashed because it had not been served. Mr Maaouia then applied for rescission of the exclusion order, which clearly could not stand as the deportation order on which it was based no longer existed. Rescission is a remedy available on mainly humanitarian grounds. He continued to take steps to regularize his immigration status. Eventually in 1998 the exclusion order was rescinded and he obtained a residence permit.

Mr Maaouia claimed in the ECtHR that the four-year delay in rescinding the exclusion order was unreasonable and thus a breach of Article 6 as he had not had a fair hearing within a reasonable time in determination of his civil rights (6:1).

The Court, by a majority of 15 to 2, decided that Article 6:1 did not apply. Rescission of the exclusion order was not a criminal matter because the original merits of the criminal charges were not examined. The majority also thought that the exclusion order was not a penalty but an administrative measure particular to immigration control. It was also not 'civil' within the meaning of Article 6, for two principal reasons. The first was the view which the majority took of the existence and rationale of Protocol 7 Article 1, which provides procedural safeguards relating to the expulsion of aliens. They considered that the purpose of this Protocol was to fill a gap by making provision for the protection of aliens which had not previously existed. If there had been no previous protection then it must be the case that Article 6 did not apply to aliens faced with expulsion.

The Court's second main reason was that the Commission had previously expressed a consistent view that the rights of aliens faced with expulsion were not within Article 6. This reasoning is rather disappointing. Given that the matter was referred to a full court because of its importance and the lack of previous decisions of the Court, for the Court to follow the less authoritative earlier decisions rather than to look at the matter afresh seems something of a missed opportunity.

Personal and economic effects of rescission were not considered sufficient to bring the matter within Article 6. The Court said 'the fact that the exclusion order incidentally had major repercussions on the applicant's private and family life and on his prospects of employment cannot suffice to bring those proceedings within the scope of civil rights'.

There were powerful dissenting judgments from Judges Loucaides and Traja. They suggested that insufficient attention had been paid to the history of Article 6 and to Article 31 of the Vienna Convention on the Law of Treaties. This Article requires that if a term is capable of more than one interpretation, the meaning which enhances individual rights should be preferred. Their view of the history of Article 6 was that the phrase 'civil rights and obligations' was meant to catch all non-criminal matters, rather than to develop a new and specialized meaning. The result of limiting its application to private law matters is that the individual has less protection against the power of the State than against other individuals, which is 'absurd' and flouts the purpose of the Convention. Their view of Protocol 7 was that it was designed to furnish 'additional special protection' for people liable to be expelled. It refers to administrative safeguards rather than judicial safeguards, and it is the latter which are the realm of Article 6.

As the sole judgment on this matter of a full court, *Maaouia* is an important statement of the interpretation of Article 6 and reveals significant trends in judicial reasoning. In the UK *Maaouia* was applied in the starred tribunal case of *MNM v SSHD* [2000] INLR 576 and the non-applicability of Article 6 to immigration matters is treated as settled law. The majority of procedural issues which would affect a fair hearing in the immigration appeal tribunals are covered in the tribunal's procedure rules. However, its non-applicability to immigration procedure does not mean that it does not apply in related matters which may have a different claim to be called civil rights.

In the previous chapter we have already noted the case of *Harrison v SSHD* [2003] INLR 284 in which the court of Appeal held that the right to be recognized as a British citizen was not a civil right for Article 6 purposes. In *AM (Upgrade appeals: Article 6) Afghanistan* [2004] Imm AR 530 the tribunal held that an appeal by which a person with exceptional leave to remain could upgrade his status to that of refugee was not a 'civil right' and thus did not engage Article 6.

In the Court of Appeal in *A, X & Y v SSHD* [2002] EWCA Civ 1502, Woolf LJ thought that proceedings before the Special Immigration Appeals Commission were civil proceedings for the purposes of Article 6. In *SSHD v MB and AF* [2007] UKHL 46 the House of Lords was unanimous that proceedings challenging a control order under the Prevention of Terrorism Act 2005 were civil proceedings for the purposes of Article 6, and that a control order was not a criminal charge.

4.4.4 Article 8

Article 8 is discussed at length here because of its central relevance to immigration and asylum cases. Applications to enter to join family members and challenges to a removal or deportation which would break up a family are the substance of many cases in the courts and tribunals. Challenges based on Article 8 may also follow unsuccessful asylum claims where a person has built up a life in the UK while waiting for their case to be determined. The House of Lords in *Huang and Kashmiri* stated the 'core value' which Article 8 exists to protect:

Human beings are social animals. They depend on others. Their family, or extended family, is the group on which many people most heavily depend, socially, emotionally and often financially. There comes a point at which, for some, prolonged and unavoidable separation from this group seriously inhibits their ability to live full and fulfilling lives. (para 18)

This expresses the importance of the Article 8 right, which in immigration control may come into direct conflict with the exercise of state power. Thus, legal doctrine surrounding it has become highly developed, and its application raises all the difficult questions about proportionality and jurisdiction.

Article 8 paragraph 1 provides that 'Everyone shall have the right to respect for his private and family life, his home and correspondence'.

In an immigration context the issue is rarely of interference with home or correspondence. Interference with private or family life is usually the question. These are ECHR concepts which are given their meaning by the ECtHR. In accordance with HRA s 2 the UK courts are obliged to take account of these meanings. In applying Article 8.1, two questions arise. First, is there family or private life in this situation? Second, what does respect for it entail?

4.4.4.1 *Does private or family life exist?*

Private life
The concept of private life in Article 8 is a wide one. The ECtHR in *Niemietz v Germany* (1992) 16 EHRR 97 has said that it is not possible or desirable to define all the situations to which the concept of private life can apply. In *Marckx v Belgium* (1979) 2 EHRR 330 the Court identified the central purpose of Article 8 is to protect the individual from arbitrary interference by public authorities, and this principle may be used to help determine new situations which may come within the protection of Article 8. The range of circumstances which the Court has accepted as coming within Article 8 includes the right to have one's own body free from invasion or harm (as in e.g. *Costello-Roberts v UK* 19 EHRR 112 in which the issue, also raised under Article 3, was corporal punishment), and self-determination (*see Pretty v UK* (2002) 35 EHRR 1 where, although the court did not find in the applicant's favour, Article 8 was held to be engaged in the question of the applicant's desire to end her life in the way she chose). In *Niemietz*, private life was held to 'comprise to a certain degree the right to establish and develop relationships with other human beings'. This includes the most intimate relationships as in *Dudgeon v UK* (1981) 4 EHRR 149 and may include professional relationships, especially where these are not easily separated from the rest of life. The case of *Botta v Italy* (1998) 26 EHRR 241 is one of a number of cases endorsing the principle that private life includes physical and psychological integrity.

In the UK, in the deportation appeal of *B v SSHD* [2000] Imm AR 478, Sedley LJ held that private life could include the network of everyday contacts that made up the life of a Sicilian man who had lived in the UK since the age of seven. In *Razgar* the House of Lords held that the right to respect for private life can be engaged by the foreseeable consequences for health or welfare of removal from the UK, endorsing holistic concept of private life which extends 'to those features which are integral to a person's identity or ability to function socially as a person' (para 9). Following this, where a child with a specific language impairment would have to start all over again in a country where he had no functional ability to communicate in words, it could not be said that a claim under Article 8 was manifestly unfounded (*The Queen on the application of Jegatheeswaran v SSHD* [2005] EWHC 1131 (Admin)).

Despite the example of *B*, courts and tribunals in the UK have often declined to recognize that connections developed after years of residence in a place constitute a private life. Such recognition brings in the protection of Article 8 which the Secretary of State rarely concedes. However, despite many decisions to the contrary, there is a development of authority in this direction. For instance in *JN (Uganda) v SSHD* [2007] EWCA Civ 802 the appellant had lived a 'decent and industrious' life in the UK for 12 years. She was doing paid work, voluntary work, was deeply involved with her church and had a relationship with a man whom she had not married in case she was returned to Uganda (para 4). This was accepted as private life. This is in accordance with the approach in the ECtHR, as for instance in *Kaya v Germany* (Application no. 31753/02):

The Court notes, first, that the applicant was born in Germany, where he had legally resided, attended school and completed vocational training. It follows that the applicant's expulsion has to be considered as an interference with his right to respect for his private life guaranteed in paragraph 1 of Article 8.

Family life

Family life includes the society of close relatives. The ECtHR regards a 'lawful and genuine' marriage as amounting to family life, even if the couple have not yet been able to establish a home together (*Abdulaziz, Cabales and Balkandali v UK* and *Berrehab v Netherlands*). *J (Pakistan)* [2003] UKIAT 00167 illustrated that there must either be a valid marriage with a plan to cohabit, or a marriage which the parties believed, even if mistakenly, to be valid, with actual cohabitation. In this case (discussed further in chapter 9) the marriage had taken place by telephone and was not valid in the UK. The wife had gone to live with her mother-in-law, symbolizing the union, but, partly due to the sponsor's health, the husband and wife had not yet lived together. The tribunal held that there was no family life as required by Article 8.

Children are also regarded as having a relationship of family life with biological or adoptive parents, even if they do not live together, and the ECtHR has repeatedly held that in the absence of exceptional circumstances the parent–child relationship automatically gives rise to family life. In *Berrehab,* the parents were not married and no longer lived together. Nevertheless, the father had contact with the child four times a week for several hours at a time. The court found that family life between father and child had not been broken by the ending of the partnership between the parents. The Court of Appeal in *Singh v ECO New Delhi* [2004] EWCA Civ 1075 had to consider an application for entry clearance following an intra-family adoption which did not and never could meet the requirements of the immigration rules. The case had had a very protracted history, including a decision by the ECtHR that an application was admissible because the refusal to recognize adoptions carried out in India was prima facie discriminatory. The Court of Appeal followed the ECtHR's approach in *Lebbink v Netherlands* (Application no. 45582/99) para 36: 'The existence or non-existence of "family life" for the purposes of Article 8 is essentially a question of fact depending upon the real existence in practice of close personal ties'. It had no doubt that the substantial relationship between the child and adoptive parents amounted to family life. The fact that it did not meet the UK's stringent requirements in the immigration rules should not be allowed to impede the reality of genuine family life and entry clearance should be granted. The concept of family life must be understood in the context of the UK's multicultural society.

In *Soderback v Sweden* (2000) 29 EHRR 95 the relationship between the natural father and seven-year-old daughter was assumed to amount to family life where the parents had never been in a stable relationship and the contact between father and child was minimal for the first four years of her life and intermittent for the next four. This was a family law case, but the Immigration Appeal Tribunal has confirmed this approach to parent–child relationships, for instance in *Majji v SSHD* (01 TH 1352) where the father had had very little contact with his child.

Although the ECHR places a high value on biological fathering as the basis of the family tie, this was not the case where a child was born as a result of a sperm donation to a lesbian couple. Despite baby-sitting for seven months, the sperm donor was held by the Commission not to have established family life with the child (*G v Netherlands* (1993) 16 EHRR CD 38).

The anti-discrimination provisions of Article 14 mean that the marital status of the parents should not make any difference to the degree of respect accorded to the family under Article 8. The case of *Marckx v Belgium* expounded on this point: 'Article 8 makes no distinction between the legitimate and illegitimate family. Such distinction would not be consonant with the word "everyone" in Article 1 and this is confirmed by Article 14 with its prohibition...of discrimination grounded on birth'. It seems therefore that in order to comply with Article 8, immigration law should respect the relationship between parent and child, whatever the family's marital status and whether or not they are living together.

Somewhat in contradiction of these principles, Commission cases have not treated couples of the same sex in the same way as married couples. In the case of *Kerkhoven v Netherlands* Application no 15666/89, the Commission found that family life did not exist between unrelated cohabitees of the same sex, but that same-sex relationships amounted to private life and therefore still attracted the protection of Article 8. In the UK, following the Civil Partnership Act 2004 and the inclusion of registered partners in the immigration rules, it appears there is no justification for continuing to distinguish between couples on the basis of whether they are of the same or different sexes. In *Krasniqi v SSHD* [2006] EWCA Civ 391 there was no issue raised against respect for the same-sex relationship being for family life, though Sedley LJ said the characterization of same-sex relationships remained 'problematical'. In so saying he referred to *Secretary of State for Work and Pensions v M* [2006] UKHL 11, but the ambivalence which characterizes that case arises in part from the very different context of child support calculations.

Ascertaining whether a relationship constitutes family or private life may only be relevant as part of ascertaining what respect for it entails (see below). *JN (Uganda)* provides a helpful guide in this respect. As related above, the appellant had not married her partner for fear she would be removed to Uganda. The relationship thus constituted part of her private life. The Court held that the reasoning of the House of Lords in *Huang* concerning respect for family life applied equally to private life (para 16). It is suggested that the proper result is that there should be no penalty of lesser respect just because of the gender of the partner or even the legal status of the relationship. Rather, the reality of the situation should be considered. Less respect is required for a relationship with a recent and casual girl or boyfriend than for a cohabitation of 20 years.

It can be assumed that family life exists between brothers and sisters who are living together as children. However, in the case of adults the reality of the relationship will be relevant in determining whether there is family life. In *Moustaquim v Belgium* (1991) 13 EHRR 802 family life was held to exist between the applicant and his brothers and sisters and his parents. He was an adult no longer living with the family, but he maintained contact with them. Similarly in *Boughanemi v France* (1996) 22 EHRR 228, family life was engaged in a deportation which separated the applicant from his ten siblings who all lived in France. The Court of Appeal in *Senthuran v SSHD* [2004] EWCA Civ 950 confirmed that family life may exist between adult siblings where the requisite level of connection and dependency is present. The question depends on the facts of each case. In *Shevanova v Latvia* (Application no. 58822/00) the ECtHR declined to find there was family life between the applicant and her adult son, but held that this relationship still constituted part of her private life.

The evaluation of the level of contact between family members, as well as blood ties raises particular difficulties where adult children and parents are living in different countries. The UK case of *R v ECO ex p Abu-Gidary* CO 965 1999 concerned a challenge by way of judicial review to a repeated refusal of entry clearance as a visitor to a daughter who wanted to visit her ailing and elderly father. The case preceded the Human Rights Act, and Richards J did not need to come to a view as to whether the relationship between father and daughter in these circumstances amounted to family life. However, had he needed to decide the question, he 'would be reluctant to hold that the concept of family life under Article 8 does not include contact between a non-dependent and non-cohabiting daughter and her ailing father'. In this we can see that the definition of 'family life' is somewhat circumstantial as the father's illness was relevant. By way of contrast, in *E-Jannath v ECO Dhaka* [2002] UKIAT 02131 the tribunal did not recognize family life between an 18-year-old daughter and her father in the UK with whom she had had very little contact. She argued that family life arose simply from the relationship, following ECtHR case law such as *Berrehab*. The tribunal, however, pointed out that the Court in *Berrehab* had held that subsequent events could break the tie, and a long period in different countries with little contact had done that. This does not mean that relatives must live in the same country to enjoy family life, but just that there is 'an irreducible minimum' of actual and effective relationship (*Kugathas v SSHD* [2003] INLR 170 CA). In *Kugathas* the appellant was a man of 38 who had lived away from Sri Lanka for 17 years and had no family there. However, he had a mother, brother and sister in Germany and had lived with them before coming to the UK three years earlier. His sister had visited him and he had maintained contact by telephone. The Court of Appeal held there had been no family life with them since he left Germany. In *R (on application of Mthokozisi) v SSHD* [2004] EWHC 2964 (Admin) the court held that family life required more than the 'normal emotional ties' (following *Kugathas*) between a man of 21 and his foster parents. This seems somewhat harsh given the claimant's relative isolation in the UK. By way of contrast, see *MT (Zimbabwe) v SSHD* [2007] EWCA Civ 455, discussed further in chapter 18.

In terms of other blood relationships, although they did not directly arise in the case, in *Marckx v Belgium* the Court expressed the view that 'family life includes at least the ties between near relatives, for example grandparents and grandchildren'. This will, as the cases above demonstrate, depend on the quality of contact. In *Boyle v UK* (1994) 19 EHRR 179 family life was held to exist between an uncle and his nephew as the uncle was a father figure to his nephew, and there was substantial contact between them.

4.4.4.2 *What does 'respect for private or family life' entail?*

What a positive obligation of respect requires in the immigration context depends upon the situation. The implication of this are considered more fully in chapter 9, in the context of family settlement. In *Abdulaziz* no breach of Article 8 was found because the Court held that there was no lack of respect for the family life of the applicants. The immigration rules prevented them from bringing their husbands to the UK as of right, but the State was entitled to have an immigration policy which restricted the entry of non-nationals, and the applicants were considered to have been aware of the provisions of the rules when they entered into their marriages. Respect for the right does not prevent the State from establishing provisions which conflict with family life if such provisions maintain an appropriate balance between private and public interests. The Court in *Abdulaziz* found that respect does not necessarily entail enabling a family to establish themselves in the country of their choice. There were no significant obstacles, the Court said, to the applicants establishing family life in the home countries of their husbands.

The question of whether there are significant obstacles to the family living together outside the UK should not be elevated to a general principle which determines whether there has been a lack of respect for family life. This point was made by Pill LJ in *Husna Begum v ECO Dhaka* [2001] INLR 115. The question of whether the family could have lived together in Bangladesh was inappropriate as most of the family had legitimately gained entry to the UK under the rules. To in effect try to reverse history would punish the appellant (who had not gained entry) for their successful application and was not the right approach to her right to respect for her family life. The appellant's actual circumstances must be the basis of the decision.

Finally, just as the definition of 'family life' does not rely on cohabitation (*Berrehab*), so the respect accorded does not necessarily entail the opportunity of cohabitation, but rather of the level of contact appropriate to the relationship. So in *Abu-Gidary*, what would have been required was the capacity to visit, in *Husna Begum* what was required was the opportunity to live within the sphere of protection of the family. Respect for private life may not entail the opportunity of cohabitation at all.

In *ECO Dhaka v Shamim Box* [2002] UKIAT 02212 the tribunal held that the positive duty of respect is engaged by entry applications and the negative duty, to refrain from interference with family life, is engaged in removal and deportation. This received a tentative endorsement from the Court of Appeal in *Kugathas*. It also said, endorsing *Box* more wholeheartedly on this point, that 'the approach to Article 8 in the case of an entry decision is different from the approach in a removal case' (para 15). The 'underlying criteria', however, would be the same.

4.4.4.3 *Has there been an interference with the right?*

The next question in applying Article 8 is whether there has been an interference with the right to respect for private or family life. There is normally little doubt about the act of interference in the immigration context. It is likely to be a refusal of entry clearance or a decision to remove or deport. There is further discussion of removal and deportation as interferences in chapter 18. It has also been held that a requirement to move to another town pursuant to the policy of dispersing asylum seekers could be such an interference (*R (on the application of Blackwood) v SSHD* [2003] EWHC 98 TLR 10/2/03). The dispersal was held in that case to interfere with the claimant's psychological integrity and thus her private life.

A developing question is whether an insecure status is an interference with the Article 8 right. This could have repercussions in the UK in the future, given the increase in insecurity discussed in other chapters of this book. Insecurity as a result of an illegal status raises other issues, but a number of ECtHR decisions about Russians in Latvia are important in this respect. An example is *Sisojeva v Latvia* (Application no. 60654/00). The family had lived in Latvia for some 30 years. Mr Sisojev was a soldier in the Soviet army stationed in Latvia. His wife joined him and their child was born there. Following the break-up of the Soviet Union and Latvian independence in 1991, the family became stateless and there followed a series of conflicting administrative decisions about their rights to remain in Latvia and to be issued with Russian or Latvian passports. The European Court of Human Rights found that prolonged refusal to recognize a family's right to permanent residence in Latvia constituted an interference with their right to respect for their family life.

4.4.4.4 *Can the interference be justified?*

This is the main question in the majority of Article 8 cases. It is governed by Article 8.2 which, like the other qualified rights, has the following substantive requirements. The interference with the right, to be permitted, must be:

- in accordance with the law;
- in pursuit of a legitimate aim;

- necessary in a democratic society in the interests of that aim; and
- proportionate to the aim pursued.

Finally, the reasons given by the state must be relevant and sufficient (*Handyside v UK*). These are established principles of Convention case law, referred to in almost every ECtHR case decided using the qualified rights. According to the ECtHR in *Smith and Grady v UK* (1999) 29 EHRR 493, these principles 'lie at the heart of the Court's analysis of complaints under Article 8 of the Convention' (para 138). We shall consider each in turn.

In accordance with the law

This has the same meaning as 'prescribed by law', which is the wording used in the other qualified Articles and generally discussed in case law. It requires that the provision which interferes with the right not only complies with domestic law, but also that the law itself is accessible (*Silver v UK* (1983) 5 EHRR 347) and precise enough to enable an individual to regulate their conduct accordingly (*Sunday Times v UK* (1979) 2 EHRR 245). In immigration and asylum cases this requirement is very rarely an issue. The interference normally arises from the application of statute or rules, which easily meet these criteria. A rare case of an immigration provision not being 'in accordance with the law' was *KK (Jamaica)* [2004] UKIAT 00268 which concerned the concession that children under 12 only needed to show adequate accommodation with their parent in order to obtain settlement. The terms of the concession were held to be insufficiently precise as it was not clear whether it only applied to entry clearance cases, nor whether the applicant had to be informed that the concession applied to them.

In pursuit of a legitimate aim

This requirement is rarely the subject of case law, but in immigration cases it plays a significant role. The legitimate aims are listed in para 2 of the qualified Articles. They differ slightly as between the different qualified rights, and in the case of Article 8 are as follows:

National security, public safety or the economic well-being of the country, for the prevention of disorder or crime, for the protection of health or morals, or for the protection of the rights and freedoms of others.

This list of aims is said to be exhaustive. The Court in *Golder v UK* said that the words 'There shall be no interference...except such as...' left 'no room for the concept of implied limitations' (para 44). Article 18 provides that restrictions on Convention rights cannot be used for any purposes other than those prescribed. Indeed for this to be otherwise would subvert the purpose of the Convention, which is to control the situations in which governments can legitimately interfere with the rights of individuals. The aims listed are quite wide in their coverage, and it is not usually problematic for a government to bring their action within them. In relation to immigration control, Blake and Husain (*Immigration, Asylum and Human Rights* 2003:190) summarize the position as follows:

Immigration control has consistently been held by the European Court to relate to the preservation of the economic well-being of the country, the prevention of disorder or crime, the protection of health and morals, and the protection of the rights and freedoms of others. Exclusions and expulsions of illegal entrants are therefore likely to fall easily within a permissible competing interest under Article 8(2). It is important to note that immigration control is not of itself a valid end capable of justifying an interfering measure; it is rather the medium through which other legitimate aims are promoted.

The identification of the legitimate aim is a fundamental requirement for considering proportionality. Without identifying the legitimate aim there is nothing to which the interference must be proportionate. This was demonstrated in *Abdulaziz*, in which the government argued that the economic well-being of the country was preserved by having an immigration policy which limited access to the job market. Evidence was presented of unemployment rates. The ECtHR accepted the validity of the objective, but in the light of the evidence held that this did not justify sex discrimination.

In UK case law, for the first few years after the implementation of the Human Rights Act, the matter of legitimate aim was often neglected entirely or marked by substantial confusion. Commonly, immigration control itself was cited as a legitimate aim without further discussion. In *Ullah and Do* the Court of Appeal suggested that immigration control was a 'free-standing restriction on the Article 8 right' (para 44). However, this was not upheld by the House of Lords, and a practice of identifying the legitimate aim more accurately is developing. The importance of this was recognized in *CW (Jamaica)* [2005] UKIAT 00110 in which the adjudicator:

analysed some of the issues which were relevant to the prevention of crime, i.e. the nature and gravity of offending, but his conclusions on the risk of re-offending are not easy to discern. This may be because he focused on the wrong aim. It is difficult to be satisfied that the proportionality balance was weighed appropriately, according to law, if the wrong public interest was put into the scales. (para 26)

The reason that immigration control is not of itself a legitimate aim is illustrated in the case of *SSHD v Mobin Jagot* [2000] Imm AR 414. Article 8 was raised in *Mobin Jagot*, but it was not decided on that basis. Use was made of the policy document DP 069/99 in considering whether removal of a child was justified. The document allowed disruption to the child's family life if 'strong reasons' justified it. The Secretary of State argued that immigration control was just such a strong reason. However, the Court of Appeal pointed out that a breach of immigration control was the basis for invoking the policy. It was inherent in the policy that the person whose family life was under threat was in breach of immigration control. Therefore immigration control in itself could not amount to a 'strong reason'. Similarly, in a case decided on the basis of Article 8, if there were no attempts to enforce immigration control, there would be no interference with family life. To cite immigration control as a legitimate aim in an immigration case is circular and does not assist.

There must be a rational connection between the aim and the means by which it is pursued (*de Freitas v Permanent Secretary of Ministry of Agriculture, Fisheries, Lands and Housing* [1999] 1 AC 69). This means not just that the aim generally is a legitimate one, but that it can be served by interfering with individual rights in this particular case.

Following *Huang and Kashmiri* it is the court's task to investigate the connection between the aim and the measures employed, and to weigh up the competing considerations on each side and according appropriate weight to the judgment of a person with responsibility for a given subject matter and access to special sources of knowledge and advice (para 16). This is the question of whether the interference is necessary in a democratic society and proportionate *to the aim pursued*.

Necessity in a democratic society

The question of whether the interference is necessary in a democratic society was said by the ECtHR in *Smith and Grady* to be the core of rights protection. Necessity has been equated with serving a 'pressing social need' (*Sunday Times v UK*). There is a question as to the relationship of this requirement with that of proportionality. Is it the same thing in different words? The approach often used in the judgments of the ECtHR is to ask these questions: first, is it necessary to interfere with this person's rights in order to achieve a legitimate aim? If it is, is the *actual* interference proportionate to this aim? Finally, are the reasons advanced by the state relevant and sufficient to support that interference? For further discussion of this issue, see Fasti (2002). Sometimes the questions of proportionality and necessity seem to flow into each other. In *Miao v SSHD* [2006] EWCA Civ 75 Sedley LJ said that to treat the two issues separately is to overcomplicate the issue.

The question of necessity is considered in the context of a democratic society. The characteristics of a democratic society according to the ECtHR are tolerance, pluralism, broad-mindedness, and willingness to tolerate ideas that shock or offend (*Handyside v UK*). These qualities are derived from the context of freedom of expression cases, and have limited relevance to the immigration sphere. However, it is relevant that a democratic society is evidently not one in which all people think or behave in the same way. Necessity should be distinguished from reasonableness. The priority is given to the right, the interference permitted by paragraph 2 is the exception rather than the rule. This was explicitly stated in *Sunday Times v UK*, but in principle applies to all the qualified rights.

There was a significant development in the case of *ECO Mumbai v NH (India)* [2007] EWCA Civ 1330, in which the Court of Appeal endorsed the AIT's examination of the history of discriminatory legislation in deciding whether it was proportionate to refuse entry to an 18-year-old son of the sponsor. The AIT said:

> We regard this history and context as of the utmost relevance. We agree with the Appellants' representatives that the assessment of what is necessary in a democratic society in Article 8 terms should involve a consideration of all the circumstances including the previous history of any previous wrongful act and an understanding of how the convention rights have to be enforced. We accept the submission that '*in Strasbourg cases the Courts have looked at the history of development of legislation in assessing what is the right thing to do in the modern context when acknowledgements of past wrongful treatment are made*' (quoted in CA para 18)

The background to the case (discussed in chapter 3) was a 30-year history of legislation preventing British East African Asians from obtaining residence in the UK.

What is proportionality?

Proportionality is a relatively new concept in UK law, though it is established in some other countries and in the ECHR and in European law. A classic formulation of proportionality, consistent with the approach used in European law, may be found in *de Freitas,* which was a Privy Council case from Antigua and Barbuda. Here, Lord Clyde observed, at p. 80, that in determining whether a limitation on a right was arbitrary or excessive the court should ask itself:

> whether: (i) the legislative objective is sufficiently important to justify limiting a fundamental right; (ii) the measures designed to meet the legislative objective are rationally connected to it; and (iii) the means used to impair the right or freedom are no more than is necessary to accomplish the objective.

In the context of Convention rights, point (i) here overlaps with identifying the legitimate aim and the question of necessity in a democratic society. The second and third points are a useful guide in considering the question of whether an infringement of a right is proportionate to the aim pursued. Proportionality requires a rational connection between the interference and the aim pursued, and that the interference is no more than is necessary.

The *de Freitas* formulation was added to by the House of Lords in *Huang and Kashmiri*. They said that in addition to these points 'the need to balance the interests of society with those of individuals and groups' was something 'which should never be overlooked or discounted' (para 19). This gives a slight weighting to the interests of society as compared with the *de Freitas* formulation. In *de Freitas* the interests of society do not feature unless they are weighty enough to justify limiting a fundamental right. In *Huang* the interests of society do not need any further justification beyond being identified as the interests of society. Who identifies these and what kind of society they represent are questions left unasked. This statement of the need for balance between society and the individual is not new with *Huang*, and was said by the House of Lords in *Razgar* to be 'inherent in the whole of the Convention' (para 20).

Proportionality is very fact-specific. It is only possible to form a judgment about the infringement of an individual's rights in the light of all the circumstances of a particular case. Often in judgments one sees the phrase 'in all the circumstances'. In the context of proportionality these are not empty words but may actually be the nub of the issue. It may be justifiable policy in general to remove people who have entered the UK illegally, and still disproportionate in a particular case, given that person's situation. Where human rights are concerned, even within the context of a policy, the state must justify an infringement on the merits of the individual case. The question of proportionality involves a close examination of facts but it is not a factual question, it is a judgment based upon an investigation into facts. In *A and X v SSHD* Lord Bingham said: 'The European Court does not approach questions of proportionality as questions of pure fact...Nor should domestic courts do so' (para 44).

The nature of the proportionality exercise has been a vital and contentious question since the inception of the Human Rights Act. Some of these points concerning the jurisdiction of tribunals on appeal are dealt with in chapter 8 under the heading Human Rights Appeals. Many of the questions that have been debated have been settled by the judgment in *Huang*, and to the extent that *Huang* deals with issues, it is authoritative:

> The question for the appellate immigration authority is whether the refusal of leave to enter or remain, in circumstances where the life of the family cannot reasonably be expected to be enjoyed elsewhere, taking full account of all considerations weighing in favour of the refusal, prejudices the family life of the applicant in a manner sufficiently serious to amount to a breach of the fundamental right protected by article 8. If the answer to this question is affirmative, the refusal is unlawful and the authority must so decide. (*Huang* para 20)

The House of Lords rejects many of the doctrines which have complicated the issue. Determining proportionality, they say, 'is not, in principle, a hard task to define, however difficult the task is, in practice, to perform' (para 14).

It has proved in many immigration cases to be the nub of the responsibility given to the judges by Parliament in passing the Human Rights Act. It is also, of course, a requirement of primary decision-makers, and in an ideal world the immigration decisions of the Home Office would already be proportionate, pursuant to their duty under HRA s 6. The proportionality exercise is not a special one for the judges.

There is a substantial body of case law in the ECtHR applying the principle of proportionality in the expulsion of individuals with a settled family life. In the ECtHR such cases commonly concern the expulsion of people who have been found guilty of criminal offences, though they arise in other circumstances too, *Berrehab* discussed above in relation to family life being one such example. The many cases coming before UK courts and tribunals more often concern expulsion of those who have entered illegally and who no longer have any immigration or asylum law claim to stay. Typically there is no criminal involvement and the individual is not considered any threat to public order or safety. UK and ECtHR case law on these issues is discussed in more detail in chapter 18. It is difficult to make general statements about the ECtHR case law precisely because their judgments are strongly tied to the facts. A couple of examples show the court's approach to balancing individual and societal interests.

In *Nasri v France* (1996) 21 EHRR 458 the applicant had been involved in a gang rape, and some petty offences. He was deaf and mute, and the ECtHR held that to deport him would interfere with his right to respect for family and private life under Article 8(1). In *Yildiz v Austria* [2003] 2 FCR 182 the court took account of the fact that the applicant's traffic convictions not only were not particularly serious, but also were unlikely to pose a threat to public order.

The Strasbourg court tends to take a global approach to the situation, without extensive legal reasoning. For instance, in *Jakupovic v Austria* (2004)] 38 EHRR 27, which concerned the proposed expulsion of a teenager with a fairly minor criminal record to Bosnia, the Court said, 'very weighty reasons have to be put forward to justify the expulsion of a young person (16 years old), alone, to a country which has recently experienced a period of armed conflict with all its adverse effects on living conditions and with no evidence of close relatives living there' (para 29). We now consider some general factors that may have an impact on proportionality, not restricted to questions related to deportation or removal which are covered in chapter 18 or to jurisdiction and scope which are covered in chapter 8.

Delay

Delay in enforcement or in processing an application may have a major effect on the lives of applicants, and the appellant may accrue rights partly because of the time taken in dealing with their claim. *Shala v SSHD* [2003] EWCA Civ 233 established that delay is a relevant factor in the question of proportionality. Not only the effect of delay is relevant but also whether the appellant or the Home Office is responsible for it. In *Shala* delay by the Home Office affected the outcome as it meant that the application was not dealt with under an earlier policy that ethnic Albanians from Kosovo would generally be granted asylum. In *Oghenekaro* 00/TH/00682 the tribunal concluded deportation was not proportionate because the Home Office had not taken any enforcement action for eight years until the appellant herself took steps to try to regularize her position. It was disproportionate to support the Home Office's enforcement procedure at great cost to the appellant's family life when the Home Office itself had not taken steps promptly to remove her. A long stay in the UK may of course arise because of persistent evasion of immigration control. The Court of Appeal in *R (on the application of Ekinci) v SSHD* [2003] EWCA Civ 765 held that immigration history was a relevant factor in balancing an interference with private life against the public interest. However, in *ul-Haq v SSHD* [2002] UKIAT 04685 the tribunal held that despite a 'shocking immigration history', as the Home Office had taken no steps to enforce his departure until his wife was expecting their third baby, it would now be disproportionate to allow them to proceed. In *K (Russia)* [2004] UKIAT 00082 the tribunal held that the appellant should not benefit from the four-year delay by the Home Office because her claim was entirely false, and this was relevant to the question of proportionality. There is an implicit distinction here between an unsuccessful claim and one based on falsehood, but it would be rash to rely on such a distinction in a human rights appeal without clear proof (see *Khawaja*).

Sometimes delay takes a claim out of the ambit of a policy, but not because the policy itself changes. For instance, in *Mthokozisi* a delay of four years meant that the claimant did not have his claim decided while still a minor and thus lost the opportunity to apply for indefinite leave to remain, which would probably have been granted. The refusal of his claim was quashed.

The trend since *Shala* has been to distinguish it as turning on its own facts, and guidance has now been given in *HB (Ethiopia) v SSHD* [2006] EWCA Civ 1713. The main points of this are:

- where delay is relied on as a reason not to take enforcement action against a person, there is a distinction between someone who has a potential right under a policy and someone who has not;
- where a person has a potential right, in extreme cases of the system working so badly that it may be said to have broken down or be a national disgrace, it may be inequitable to take enforcement action;
- where there is no potential right under a policy, but only an Article 8 right, accrued perhaps through passage of time, delay in dealing with a previous asylum claim is relevant to proportionality, but must have very substantial effects to influence the outcome;
- the fact that the applicant through delay missed obtaining exceptional leave to remain (ELR) does not of itself determine an Article 8 claim. (ELR was a form of discretionary leave available until 2003.)

A striking case of delay is that of *R (on the application of N) v SSHD* [2003] TLR 7 March, in which atrocious delays and the service of a removal notice despite a policy not to return failed asylum seekers to Libya because of the risk of ill-treatment on return, resulted in an award of damages for breach of positive duties under Articles 3 and 8.

Near misses

The concept of 'near misses' developed in the uncertain period between *Huang* in the Court of Appeal and *Huang* in the House of Lords, when it looked as though only exceptional cases could succeed under Article 8. The underlying idea as it elaborates the concept of proportionality is that it is disproportionate to deny a person the benefit of immigration rules or policies if they come within the spirit of those rules or policies. The development of this after *Huang* (CA) was at least in part because that decision equated human rights with the immigration rules and said that only an exceptional case could succeed outside this structure. The human rights jurisdiction was reduced to rarities, and the doctrine of 'near misses' gave an opportunity for inclusion where it seemed just to do so. Since *Huang* in the House of Lords, the idea of 'near misses' remains as one way in which a decision may be seen as disproportionate. Guidance on the application of this idea is given fully by the tribunal in *KL (Article 8 – Lekstaka – delay – near misses) Serbia and Montenegro* [2007] UKAIT 00044. The appellant had fled Kosovo at the age of 16. Since then his parents had been killed there and he had lived with his uncle and aunt, who were refugees, and to whom he had become as a son. He would have come within a policy which would have granted him indefinite leave to remain if he had actually been their son. Likewise, if he had actually been their son he could have qualified for leave within the immigration rules.

The tribunal suggested appropriate considerations for such a case:

- How close are the appellant's circumstances to those covered by the policy or rule?
- Does the underlying purpose of those rules or policies also apply to the appellant?
- Is there an objective justification for not treating like alike?
- Has the appellant attempted to alert the Home Office to the justification for bringing them within the rule or policy?

On these considerations the tribunal thought that the appellant here should succeed.

Alternative application for entry clearance
It may be seen from the discussion of delay and of near misses that the proportionality exercise involves weighing up the proper functioning of immigration control and its impact on the claimant's life. A relevant consideration may be, whether they could or should regularize their situation by leaving and applying for entry clearance. Human rights cases will only arise where the claimant has no other claim to remain in the UK. Should they be asked to take a different route to a lawful status? Should the opportunity of this be taken into account by the tribunal? What if it is too difficult? Legally impossible? Too expensive? Carries other intolerable penalties such as loss of their employment?

The likely failure or legal impossibility of such an application might be thought to be a relevant factor, but the Court of Appeal in *R (Ekinci) v SSHD* [2003] EWCA Civ 765 held that it was not. This bites in cases such as *K (Russia)* [2004] UKAIT 00082 where the appellant's husband only had exceptional leave to remain which carried no right to be joined by a spouse. There was no application he could make within the rules. The tribunal held that the 'poor prospects' of success in an entry clearance application were irrelevant to whether refusal of leave was disproportionate.

Difficulties or dangers of travel to make an entry clearance application fall to be considered as part of the question of whether the decision is proportionate (*A v SSHD* [2006] EWCA Civ 1144, [2007] Imm AR1, in which the Court of Appeal speculated about possible routes to Northern Iraq). The Home Affairs Committee report on immigration control recommended:

In view of the serious difficulties caused to some applicants by the requirement to return home to apply for permission as a spouse, we recommend that where the Foreign Office advises against all travel to a particular country, applications for leave as a spouse or unmarried partner from nationals of that country who are already living in the UK should be decided in the UK with an interview. (Session 2005–06 Fifth Report para 300)

In *Mukarkar v SSHD* [2006] EWCA Civ 1045 the Court of Appeal explained that the above point in *Ekinci* was not a rule of law. It was common sense that likely failure of an entry clearance application could not determine an Article 8 claim in an applicant's favour. However, in *Mukarkar*, the appellant, who was a frail elderly man, would be unable to travel alone to make an entry clearance application, and no-one could reasonably be expected to go with him; these obstacles in the way of his application for entry clearance were relevant to the question of proportionality.

The latest authority on the relevance of an alternative entry clearance application is *SB (Bangladesh) v SSHD* [2007] EWCA Civ 28, which considers the question in detail. The applicant was the second wife of a man who had died since her arrival in the UK. She lived here with her two youngest children, but was refused indefinite leave to remain as she fell neither within the marriage rules nor the dependent relative rules. The tribunal considered the rules on entry clearance for access to a resident child, and took the view that such an application ought to succeed and therefore she ought to leave the UK to make it. The Court of Appeal held that, while the option of making an entry clearance application would be relevant to the enquiry into proportionality, it was inappropriate for the tribunal to anticipate the outcome of such an application and take into account its prospects of success or otherwise. This seems to leave the finding in *Mukarkar* undisturbed, as in Mr Mukarkar's case the issue was not the outcome of an entry clearance application but his limited opportunity of getting there to make it. Consistently, the Court of Appeal in *MM (Nigeria)* [2007] EWCA Civ 44 held that the adjudicator was not entitled to speculate that an entry clearance officer would be over-influenced by an unsuccessful settlement application and refuse future visit visas. The appellant had returned from many visits in the past, and the ECO ought properly to take that into account.

Finally there may be other serious consequences of leaving to make an entry clearance application. In *Miao v SSHD* the appellant was caring for his elderly refugee father who needed his constant care. The argument was made to the Court of Appeal that, as the appellant came within the refugee family reunion policy 'in every respect save his present location, it would be an unconscionable disruption of his family life to send him back to China simply so he could apply from the correct place, when the very interruption of that care might be fatal' (para 27). This was an argument which, the Court held, should have been considered by the immigration judge.

4.4.5 Other qualified rights

Article 10, which protects freedom of expression, is regarded as one of the most central Articles of the Convention. It protects freedom of expression in written or spoken words, action, and through any medium such as theatre, film, photography, or painting. A rare application to immigration law arose in *Farrakhan* [2002] 3 WLR 481 where it was held that refusal of entry to the Nation of Islam leader Louis Farrakhan for a speaking tour did not breach his right to freedom of expression. An important question was whether Article 10 was engaged at all prior to his entry to the country. The Secretary of State accepted that the fact that Mr Farrakhan 'was neither a citizen of a member state nor within the territory of a member state did not of itself preclude the application of the Convention' (para 34). The Court of Appeal, relying on the ECtHR cases of *Piermont v France* [1995] 20 EHRR 301, *Swami Omkarananda and Divine light Zentrum v Switzerland* (1997) 25 DR 105 and *Adams and Benn v UK* (1997) 88A DR 137, held that where an immigration decision was made with the purpose of preventing the exercise of Article 10 rights, then the Article is engaged. The basis for the *Farrakhan* decision in the immigration rules is discussed in chapter 7.

The Court of Appeal's decision in *Farrakhan* is not easy to understand. The ECtHR jurisprudence relied on concerned the application to immigration decisions of Article 10, but in these cases the applicant was in the Contracting State at the time of the decision. It seems that the Court of Appeal did not decide that Article 10 applied to decisions where the applicant is outside the country, because this is what was conceded. This was the conclusion, after argument, of the tribunal in *Rev Sun Myung Moon USA v ECO Seoul* [2005] UKIAT 00112 in which the application of Articles 9, 10, 11, and 14 to a refusal of entry fell directly for decision.

The situation therefore now seems to be that an immigration decision, such as deportation, may engage a qualified right such as Article 10 if the reason for exercising the immigration power is to prevent the exercise of that right. This would be, for instance, as in *Piermont v France,* where the detention of the applicant with a view to deportation prevented her from talking with the politicians who had invited her to speak. Without such a connection between the exercise of the immigration power and the right, the qualified right does not protect the applicant's stay in a country (*Agee v UK* (1976) 7 DR 164). This does no more than say that foreign nationals are protected by human rights law and immigration decisions are not exempt from it. Where an expulsion decision threatens a qualified right in the destination country, *Ullah and Do* is authority that in the case of a real risk of a fundamental breach, the qualified right may protect from the exclusion. Where an individual seeks to enter a country *in order to* exercise a qualified right, *Moon* suggests that they have no human rights appeal against refusal, aside from Article 8. However, the earlier discussion of the application of human rights to entry decisions shows that the question is not authoritatively concluded.

4.4.6 **Other derogable rights**

Article 12 provides that:

'Men and women of marriageable age have the right to marry and to found a family according to the national laws governing the exercise of this right.'

In *Abdulaziz, Cababales and Balkandali v UK* the right to marry and found a family was considered to encompass the right to live together, otherwise the notion of a family becomes rather meaningless. The Court in the same case, however, held that this did not include the right to live in the country of the applicant's choice, and so the right to live with one's family is regarded as subordinate to the State's right to regulate immigration, and cannot necessarily be used to support a family reunion application in an immigration context. It also cannot be used to establish a right of entry for a spouse married according to traditions regarded as unlawful in the UK, for instance, the marriage of a person under the age of 16. The Article expressly provides only the right to marry 'according to the national laws governing the exercise of this right'. This means according to the national laws of the country where Article 12 is or would be invoked, not the laws of the country where the marriage took place. In *SSHD v Baiai & Trzcinska, Bigoku & Agolli & Tilki* [2007] EWCA Civ 478, discussed in chapter 9, the UK government was found to be in breach of Article 12 through its requirement that foreign nationals obtain certificate of approval from the Home Office in order to marry, and the conditions placed upon that which made it almost impossible for some foreign nationals to marry.

Article 13 of the Convention provides a right to an effective remedy and is not included in the scope of the HRA. The government justified its omission by arguing that the Act itself was the guarantee of a remedy, but its omission may exclude the greater opportunity for judicial creativity which would have been generated by the right to a remedy.

Article 14 is potentially of wide application. The full text of Article 14 is:

The enjoyment of the rights and freedoms set forth in this Convention shall be secured without discrimination on any ground such as sex, race, colour, language, religion, political or other opinion, nationality or social origin, association with a national minority, birth or other status.

Article 14, as discussed above, was successfully used by the applicants in *Abdulaziz, Cabales and Balkandali v UK*. In that case the applicants succeeded in pleading sex discrimination in the application of Article 8 rights, even though no breach of Article 8 was found.

Article 14 guarantees non-discrimination in the delivery of the other Convention rights, but is not a free-standing right. In order to lodge a claim under Article 14 it is necessary that discrimination is alleged in some area that is within the ambit of one of the other Convention rights. For instance, in *Abdulaziz*, the applicants alleged that the immigration rules interfered with their Article 8 rights to family life and discriminated against them as women because it would have been easier for men to bring their spouses into the country. The Court found in their favour on the discrimination issue but not on the family life issue as it was not impossible for them to set up family life in another country. So, while UK immigration law treated men more favourably than women, it did not prevent people from establishing their family as they could do that elsewhere. It was necessary to claim under Article 14 that the Article 8 issue of the interference with family life was involved, but there did not need to have been a violation of Article 8 in order for the applicants to succeed under Article 14.

Discrimination for Article 14 entails a difference in treatment which is not based upon 'an objective and reasonable justification' and is not proportionate to the social objective of that difference in treatment. These principles were established in the *Belgian Linguistics case (No 2)* (1968) 1 EHRR 252. Although the wording of Article 14 makes no reference to any defences or justification, this potential defence is held to be inherent in the concept of discrimination, i.e. it is differential treatment which cannot be justified. The principles of discrimination and its justification are not fully developed in the law of the ECHR, but by analogy with cases in the European Court of Justice the defence must be strictly construed, and the justification must exist independently of any discriminatory reasoning (Case 170/84 *Bilka Kaufhaus GmbH v Weber von Hartz* [1986] ECR 1607).

In UK law a distinction is made between direct discrimination, which entails that one group is treated less favourably than another (e.g. men are paid more than women for the same work) and indirect discrimination, which entails that a requirement or condition is applied equally to all groups but has a disproportionate impact on one group (e.g. part-time workers have fewer rights, but more part-time workers are women, so women are indirectly discriminated against). Neither European law nor the law of the ECtHR expressly distinguishes between direct and indirect discrimination. In Article 14 arguments there is therefore no need to make this distinction.

One of the most significant decisions on Article 14 in recent times concerned not immigration, but why it was discriminatory to categorize an issue as one of immigration. The challenge by those detained under the powers of indefinite detention in the Anti-terrorism, Crime and Security Act 2001 was mounted partly on the basis that the statutory power was discriminatory as it allowed the detention of only foreign nationals (*A v SSHD* [2004] UKHL 56). The government's case was that the power was not discriminatory because these detainees could not be deported because they faced a real risk of treatment contrary to Article 3, and the relevant comparison was with non-UK nationals who could be deported. The House of Lords accepted the appellants' argument that the appropriate comparator for the purpose of assessing discrimination was a British suspected international terrorist. The difference in treatment between British and non-British suspects (i.e. the detention) had no bearing on the objective of defeating terrorism but was purely immigration or nationality related, an impermissible basis under Article 14. The Home Office's proposed comparator group were not the appropriate ones because they did not share the most relevant characteristics of the appellants, namely non-removability. British nationals did share that characteristic, and to say that they were not comparable because they had a right of abode whereas the appellants could not be removed, as did the Court of Appeal, was to accept the Secretary of State's treatment of the matter as an immigration issue, which it patently was not. The decision is discussed again in chapter 15.

The marriage provisions challenged in *SSHD v Baiai & Trzcinska, Bigoku & Agolli & Tilki* [2007] EWCA Civ 478 (see chapter 9) were also found to be in breach of Article 14 as they made an unwarranted exception for Church of England marriages.

In the actual immigration context, bringing immigration decisions within the ambit of the Race Relations Act 1976 has had significant ramifications. This is discussed in chapter 8.

Article 5 protects the right to liberty and security of person and is discussed in chapter 15. Immigration detention raises many human rights issues, as the practice of detaining asylum seekers is growing in the UK, and the changes in the law on deportation extend the detention of deportees. It is the Article from which the UK has derogated on a number of occasions. The first derogations were all in relation to overseas territories during their struggles for independence. Later, there was a derogation from Article 5 in relation to detention in Northern Ireland. This was withdrawn as part of the peace process. In 2001 there was the derogation discussed above in relation to 'international terrorists', also discussed further in chapter 15.

The UK government has no plans to sign Protocol 12 ECHR, which provides for a free-standing right not to be discriminated against in any action by a public authority and in delivery of 'rights set forth by law' (see their response to the Parliamentary Joint Committee on Human Rights report on the International Covenant on Economic Social and Cultural Rights, Session 2005–06 Eighth Report HC 850 HL paper 104).

4.5 Conclusion

In simple terms, human rights are a counterbalance to the exercise of executive power. Perhaps it is not surprising that the 'new human rights era', rather than simply shifting the balance, seems to have thrown existing tensions into sharper relief. The House of Lords decision in *Huang and Kashmiri* has brought the earlier wisdom of the House of Lords decision in *Daly* finally into immigration decision-making. This creates a more developed foundation for UK jurisprudence in Article 8 cases, but this is limited by a restrictive approach to the s 3 duty of interpretation in the tribunal. Protection against breaches of Article 3 after expulsion is becoming more limited in scope, reserved for clear risks of torture and lesser treatment of a similar kind that is inhuman or degrading. Article 3 is important in protecting basic rights for asylum seekers in the UK, but this safety net will be once again limited by provisions in the Criminal Justice and Immigration Bill (see chapters 8 and 14). The discriminatory impact of immigration provisions is increasingly being challenged, and Article 14 may have a stronger role to play, though it is limited by its reference to other Convention rights. The UK's human rights jurisdiction is developing, but not in a consistent direction.

QUESTIONS

1 How would you have decided the case of N?

2 Does it or should it make any difference to rights under Article 8 whether family life has been formed while waiting for an asylum claim to be processed or while spending time in the UK as, say, a student?

3 Is proportionality a question of law?

 online resource centre For guidance on answering questions, visit www.oxfordtextbooks.co.uk/orc/clayton3e.

FURTHER READING

All Party Parliamentary Group on Extraordinary Rendition, December 2005, *Briefing: Torture by Proxy: international law applicable to 'Extraordinary renditions'.*

Amnesty International (2007) *United Kingdom: Deportations to Algeria at all costs*, AI Index: EUR 45/001/2007.

Atrill, S. 'Keeping the executive in the picture: a reply to Professor Leigh' [2003] *Public Law* Spring pp. 41–51.

Clayton, G. (2006) 'Entry Clearance and Human Rights: Challenging the Boundaries of Jurisdiction' *Journal of Immigration, Asylum & Nationality Law* vol. 20, no.4, pp. 255–269.

Clayton, R. 'Regaining a Sense of Proportion: the Human Rights Act and the Proportionality Principle' [2001] *European Human Rights Law Review* 5, pp. 504–525.

—— 'Judicial deference and democratic dialogue: the legitimacy of judicial intervention under the Human Rights Act' [2004] *Public Law* 33–47.

Council of Europe (2007) European Committee for the Prevention of Torture and Inhuman or Degrading Treatment or Punishment CPT/Inf (2007)39.

Frost, T. (2006) *Legal Commentary on the use of Torture Evidence* http://www.campacc.org.uk/ Library/legal_commentary_torture_evidence_220106.pdf.

Gearty, C. (2004) *Principles of Human Rights Adjudication* (Oxford: OUP).

Gordon, R. 'Legitimate Aim: A Dimly Lit Road' [2002] *European Human Rights Law Review* 4, pp. 421–427.

Human Rights Watch (2005) Still at Risk: Diplomatic Assurances No Safeguard Against Torture.

Leigh, I. 'Taking Rights Proportionately: Judicial Review, the Human Rights Act and Strasbourg' [2002] *Public Law* pp. 265–287.

Lester, A. 'Universality versus Subsidiarity: a reply' [1998] *European Human Rights Law Review* 1, pp. 73–81.

—— 'The Art of the Possible: Interpreting Statutes under the Human Rights Act' [1998] *European Human Rights Law Review* 6, pp. 665–675.

Liddy, J. 'The Concept of Family Life under the ECHR' [1998] *European Human Rights Law Review* 1, pp. 15–25.

Mole, N. (2007) 'Asylum and the European Convention on Human Rights' AIRE Centre, Council of Europe.

Nash, S. and Furse, M. Regular Human Rights updates in the *New Law Journal*.

Ovey, C. 'The Margin of Appreciation and Article 8 of the Convention' *Human Rights Law Journal* vol. 19, no. 1, pp. 10–12.

Pannick, D. 'Principles of interpretation of Convention Rights under the Human Rights Act and the Discretionary Area of Judgment' [1998] *Public Law* Winter pp. 545–551.

Rogers, N. 'Immigration and the European Convention on Human Rights: are new principles emerging?' [2003] *European Human Rights Law Review* 1, pp. 53–64.

Shah, P. 'The Human Rights Act 1998 and immigration law' (2000) INLP vol. 14, no. 3, pp. 151–158.

Singh, R., Hunt, M., and Demetriou, M. 'Is there a role for the Margin of Appreciation in National Law after the Human Rights Act?' [1999] *European Human Rights Law Review* 1, pp. 15–22.

Steyn, Lord 'Deference – A Tangled Story' [2005] *Public Law* 346–359.

SECTION 2

European law and migration

5

....

The European context

SUMMARY

This chapter introduces the law and policy of the European Union concerning immigration and asylum. It is concerned with third country nationals who do not take primary benefit from the Union's free movement provisions. The focus of this policy on asylum deterrence is introduced as part of the context for UK law on asylum. 'Fortress Europe' is described in terms of stratification of rights according to nationality, and there is discussion of the rights of Turkish nationals and the UK's definition of British national for EU purposes. The chapter briefly charts the progress towards implementing the new immigration and asylum provisions deriving from the Treaty of Amsterdam. The UK's opt-in position is noted, as are its choices to date. Finally, there is an introduction to the EU dimension of human rights.

5.1 Introduction

The previous chapter mainly concerned the application of rights found in the European Convention on Human Rights, the most well-known treaty of the Council of Europe. This chapter concerns a different European system, that of the European Community and European Union. Both the Council of Europe and the European Community had their origins in the desire of states after the Second World War to avoid such a conflict ever occurring again. The European Community (EC) began as the European Economic Community (EEC), one of three associations of states which aimed to build close trading links in Europe. Economic interdependence was seen as a means to promote peaceful co-operation. The EEC became the EC, a supranational institution which has legal powers and a separate existence. It was established by the EC Treaty, also known as the Treaty of Rome. The EC Treaty contains the four freedoms upon which the Community is built, the free movement of goods, persons, services and capital, all of which serve the central purpose, stated in Article 14 EC (ex 7a) as the goal of establishing an area of freedom of movement 'without internal frontiers'.

The Treaty of Amsterdam 1997 extended the EC's competence in areas of social policy, the environment, public health, consumer protection, co-operation in policing and civil and criminal justice, and immigration and asylum. It had become apparent that market issues could not be seen in a vacuum. For instance, the employment of workers raises questions of their rights and health and safety; the establishment of businesses has an impact on the environment; the presence of transient nationals of other states has implications for policing, and so on.

The European Union (EU) is the political union of the member states of the EC, it encompasses a number of intergovernmental areas of co-operation as well as the institutions of the EC. It was established by the Treaty on European Union 1992 also known as the Treaty of Maastricht. The EU is developing a political vision which far exceeds in scope the economic idea of a free market and EU law is expanding to serve that goal. The creation by the Treaty on European Union of EU citizenship seems to prefigure a political union within which free movement derives from citizenship status rather than economic function. In May 2004 ten more states acceded to membership of the EU, and on 1 January 2007, Bulgaria and Romania also acceded to membership (Treaty signed 25 April 2005, OJ 2005 L 157).

The next stage of European unity was to be represented by the Treaty establishing a Constitution for Europe which consolidated all the treaties and advanced the political union of twenty-five states in Europe. However, the Constitution was rejected in referenda in France and the Netherlands in 2005. Some of the ideas of the Constitutional Treaty are now incorporated in a new Treaty, signed in Lisbon in December 2007, and to be called the Lisbon Treaty.

The UK's law on immigration and asylum is formed in the context of the UK's membership of the European Community and the European Union, and its influence both political and legal. At the present stage of development, the UK has not opted into many of the Treaty of Amsterdam implementing provisions concerning immigration, and while it is not impossible that at some point in the future, much of immigration law will be at least partly subject to European law, currently we are a long way from that position. However the UK has for the most part opted into the Common European Asylum System (CEAS), created through a series of directives, regulations and decisions, and the statutory and executive provisions of the UK's asylum system are increasingly not just politically influenced by European developments but subject to them in law. There is a vast body of writing on legal and political developments in Europe, both generally and as they affect immigration law. For a greater understanding, reference should be made to the selected bibliography at the end of this chapter. The accession of a further ten member states in May 2004 and two in 2007 has changed where the borders of Europe are drawn, with complex consequences both inside, outside and across the new border.

5.2 **Treaty of Amsterdam**

The first principle to grasp in coming to an understanding of the EU and its law and policy on migration is that it appears very differently depending on whether one is looking from inside or out. The origin of the EC in the idea of an internal market meant dismantling the barriers between member countries to the movement of persons, goods and services. On the other hand the development of the Union has been characterized by measures designed to restrict the entry to Europe of nationals of non-European countries: 'third country nationals'. The hardening of European immigration policies towards nationals of other countries has earned the EU the nickname 'Fortress Europe'. Until 1997 this took place through the gradual harmonization of the immigration policies of member states, and immigration and asylum were matters of intergovernmental co-operation. Now the Treaty of Amsterdam sets legal objectives to be attained by all the member states, these are developed in secondary legislation on immigration and asylum, and the European Court of Justice (ECJ) has competence to make decisions on these matters.

The Treaty of Amsterdam came into force on 1 May 1999 and inserted into the EC Treaty a new Title IV which governs immigration, asylum, and the issue of visas. The Title makes the dual purpose of EC law on migration very plain. Article 61(1)(a) says that the Council must adopt:

measures aimed at ensuring the free movement of persons in accordance with Article 14, in conjunction with directly related flanking measures with respect to external border controls.

In other words, member states must open their borders to each other and control their borders to those from outside. As the internal market developed, so, as Guild says, 'one member state's third country nationals become those of the whole unified territory' (in Guild and Harlow (eds) 2001:90). Member states would want to be assured that other member states were admitting third country nationals on similar terms to themselves. The stronger external border could be seen in part as a consequence of the more relaxed internal borders.

The required controls on external borders include 'standards and procedures' for external border checks and rules on visas, including a 'list of third countries whose nationals must be in possession of visas when crossing the external borders' (Article 62). The required asylum measures include minimum standards on a range of matters and, a particular concern of European states: 'criteria and mechanisms for determining which member state is responsible for considering an application for asylum submitted by a national of a third country in one of the member states' (Article 63(1)). Measures on immigration policy must include 'conditions of entry and residence' including for family reunion, and measures on 'illegal immigration and illegal residence'.

None of these provisions suggest what the standards or objectives of these measures should be. For instance, is the list of visa countries to be short, and thus permissive, or long, and thus restrictive? European law is interpreted in accordance with its purpose, and the purpose of Title IV is: 'In order to establish progressively an area of freedom, security and justice'.

The meaning of this phrase has been extensively debated (see, for instance, P. Boeles in Guild and Harlow (eds) 2001). In general terms the freedom referred to is the freedom to move within the Union, and security is safety from threats largely seen as external. This makes the question of 'and justice for whom?' an important one in the understanding of the Union objectives. On the whole, justice is understood as criminal justice. The purpose of Title IV, therefore, largely seems to be to replicate the strong external and relaxed internal controls which have already characterized the EU. There is only one requirement to promote the rights of third country nationals in Title IV, and that is that there must be provision for family reunion. The extent of this provision depends on secondary legislation.

Title IV allowed a period of five years after the entry into force of the Treaty of Amsterdam for the new measures to be adopted, which gave a deadline of 1 May 2004. There were exceptions to this deadline for provisions on the rights of legally resident third country nationals, conditions of entry and residence, and the promotion of balanced effort between member states in receiving refugees ('burden sharing').

5.3 **Migration into the EU – the Tampere Programme**

For the most part, the UK's law on immigration of third country nationals, aside from those seeking asylum, is not directly affected by the developing immigration law of the EU. The entry of TCN family members of EEA nationals is governed by the EC free movement provisions discussed in chapter 6. The development of EU immigration law is, however, part of the political and legal context in which UK immigration law is formed, and a brief account is given here of developments pursuant to the Treaty of Amsterdam. The UK is party to many of the provisions on asylum, and these are discussed in more detail where they affect the substantive law covered in later chapters.

Shortly after the Treaty of Amsterdam came into force, there was a meeting of the European Council at Tampere, devoted to the development of the 'area of freedom, security and justice'. It was a key opportunity to formulate some objectives for policy on migration. Four main principles emerged:

- partnership with countries of origin;
- moving towards a common European asylum system, which should in time lead towards a common asylum procedure and a uniform status for those granted asylum;
- fair treatment of third country nationals;
- more efficient management of migration flows.

5.3.1 **Tampere conclusions – partnership with countries of origin**

The Tampere conclusions set wide-ranging objectives in terms of partnership with countries of origin. The tone of the conclusions was liberal, although there was also scepticism as to whether this was form or substance (see, for instance, *Statewatch* vol. 9 no. 5). The Council recognized the need for a 'comprehensive approach to migration addressing political, human rights and development issues in countries and regions of origin and transit'. This would require 'combating poverty, improving living conditions and job opportunities, preventing conflicts and consolidating democratic states and ensuring respect for human rights, in particular rights of minorities, women and children' (Commission of the EC 2001 Conclusions para 11).

A High Level Working Group set up in 1998 was to continue its work to look at the causes of migration, including forced migration. The group's work was concentrated on six countries which were all perceived to produce large numbers of refugees, and action plans were adopted.

The main legislative result of the focus on partnerships with countries of origin has been to use the EU's political and economic power to conclude readmission agreements, the aim of which is to ensure that illegal entrants to the EU from these countries can be repatriated. Incentives for third countries to conclude such agreements with the EU include favourable trade terms and facilitating the grant of visas to their nationals. Readmission agreements have been entered into with a number of countries including Hong Kong, Sri Lanka, Macao, and Albania. Negotiations were completed during 2007 with countries which are notably candidate and prospective candidate countries for admission to the EU – Macedonia, Montenegro, Bosnia and Serbia – and are ongoing with Turkey. Other recently concluded agreements are noticeably with countries on the EU's new borders: Russia, Moldova and Ukraine. There are also negotiations ongoing with Pakistan, Morocco, Algeria and China. There are concerns in the creation of readmission agreements about 'guarantees of human rights in the accelerated readmission procedure and about respect for the status in international law of asylum seekers and stateless persons' (European Parliament debate 14 February 2007). The agreements generally require that the non-EU country agrees to accept people returned from the EU, even when they are not nationals of that country, or are stateless, if they have entered the EU irregularly through that country. Negotiations with Pakistan almost broke down on this issue, but, as with other negotiating partners, Pakistan's trade interests were too much at risk for Pakistan to pull out. Information given by the European Council of Refugees and Exiles (ECRAN) explains how important that risk is: 'The EU is Pakistan's largest trading partner, accounting for 28 per cent (EUR 3 billion) of its exports and 17 per cent (EUR 2 billion) of its imports in 2004' (ECRAN weekly update 19/3/2007). As the size and wealth of the EU grows, so its power grows in negotiations of this kind.

Even without formal readmission agreements, a third country's capacity and willingness to deal with irregular migration is a key factor in negotiations. For instance, in the case of Romania, the removal of a visa requirement for nationals of that country was delayed pending undertakings on irregular immigration and residence and repatriation. The first case brought under Title IV concerned the uncertain position in which this left Romanian nationals. Romania appeared on the list whose nationals do not require a visa for entry to an EU country, but whether this was in force depended on the view taken by the European Council of efforts by Romania to control irregular migration. An individual migrant's entry without a visa would thus be criminal or not depending on the European Council's view of the Romanian government's efforts (Case C–51/03 *Georgescu*).

Pressure on third countries to control the illegal migration of their nationals into the EU has direct effects also in those countries on the prospective immigrants. For instance, a crackdown by the Moroccan authorities included rounding up would-be illegal entrants to Europe and leaving them in the desert without food or water (Spijkerboer 2007:130, quoting Human Rights Watch and the Financial Times). Often, increased controls in target countries may mean that would-be migrants make longer and more hazardous journeys to avoid such controls. This is discussed below in relation to Frontex. The Commission's initiation of talks with Libya provoked a storm of protest in the light of evidence that Libya, which is not a signatory to the UN Refugee Convention, was forcibly returning even recognized refugees to their countries of origin (Italian Council for Refugees press release 4 October 2004). Italy itself summarily expelled to Libya about 1, 000 asylum seekers who had landed in the Sicilian island of Lampedusa, without consideration of their asylum applications. Ten NGOs filed a complaint with the President of the European Commission (*Statewatch* news online 25 January 2005), and the European Parliament passed a resolution stating that these expulsions were in breach of international obligations (Motion for resolutions on Lampedusa, vote 14 April 2005).

In September 2005 the Commission issued a further communication on integrating migration issues into relations with third countries (COM (2005) 390). A key focus is the economic role of money paid by migrant workers to families back home ('remittances', see chapter 2).

5.3.2 **Tampere conclusions – fair treatment of third country nationals**

The treatment of long-term resident third country nationals was one of the most liberal policy conclusions to come from the Tampere Council. Following Tampere the Commission proposed two Directives: one to enhance and consolidate the rights of long-term resident third country nationals, the second to give rights of entry and residence to their family members. In a number of respects the first draft Directives attempted to harmonize the rights of long-term residents with those of EU nationals. This could have heralded an equalization of rights within the Community based not on nationality but on residence, however, the provisions of the directives were much reduced during subsequent negotiations. It is still the case that lawful residence, not just nationality, became a basis for the acquisition of rights, but of a lesser kind. The watered down Family Reunion Directive 2003/86 EC was finally adopted on 22 September 2003, to be fully implemented by October 2005. The reduced nature of the rights given by the Directive drew criticism not only from non-governmental groups but also from the European Parliament which launched a legal action against the European Council on the grounds that the limitations imposed on family reunification for children were incompatible with the right to respect for family life and the principle of equality of treatment, as was the waiting period of up to three years for the issue of a residence permit (Case C–540/03 OJ 2004 C 47/35). The ECJ rejected this challenge (Case C-540/03 *European Parliament v European Council* ECR I-05769).

The Directive on the status of long-term residents (2003/109/EC) was finally agreed after refugees were removed from its ambit, and discretion restored to member states in a number of respects. Broadly speaking, the Directive gives to third country nationals who have been lawfully resident in Europe for five years security of status and the right to move to other member states on a limited number of grounds providing the destination state does not restrict the right. It was due to be implemented by January 2006. For an interesting discussion of this Directive, see Belaert-Suominen 2005. The Commission proposal concerning the entry of third country nationals for study or voluntary work has borne fruit in Directive 2004/114. Otherwise, development of the admission of third country nationals for work has proceeded slowly. There is a Directive on the admission of researchers (2005/71), and other proposals are under consideration, for instance on the admission of the highly skilled. More recently the question of residence rights for refugees has been revisited, and the Commission has published a proposal which is under discussion (COM (2007) 298 final).

5.4 **Hague Programme**

In November 2004 the member states approved a new five-year plan to further the creation of an area of 'freedom, security and justice'. The objectives of the Hague Programme include:

improvement of the common capability of the Union and its Member States to guarantee fundamental rights, minimum procedural safeguards and the access to justice, to provide protection in accordance with the Geneva Convention and other international treaties to persons in need, to regulate migration flows and to control the external borders of the Union, to fight organised cross-border crime and repress the threat of terrorism...development of a Common Asylum System...the approximation of law and the development of common policies.

The European Council's introduction to the programme reveals an emphasis on security 'in the light of terrorist attacks in the United States on 11 September 2001 and in Madrid on 11 March 2004', and exhorts member states to 'take full account of the security of the Union as a whole'.

Returning illegal migrants is prioritized in the Hague Programme, and a Directive on common policy on returns of those who have stayed illegally (COM (2005) 391 final) is before the European Parliament. It includes a radical new proposal for a re-entry ban that would be valid throughout the EU, reinforcing a European-wide approach to removals.

5.5 **UK's position**

In accordance with protocols appended to the Treaty of Amsterdam, the UK, Ireland, and Denmark have an anomalous position which enables them to remain outside the new immigration and asylum provisions unless they opt in. The UK has not yet opted in to any substantial provisions on legal migration or protection of third country nationals, although it would be fair to say that the UK's immigration provisions on admission of family members for those on short-term visas or for settlement are more generous than those in the ill-fated family reunion Directive (see chapter 9). The settlement rights of long-term resident third country nationals as set out in Directive 2003/109 are comparable with those in force in the UK. The major difference is that indefinite leave to remain in the UK does not entitle the holder to travel freely in the EU and, conversely, a beneficiary of third country national rights in Europe may not freely enter the UK. Ryan speculates that the desire to avoid granting such rights of entry is the reason that the UK did not opt into this directive (in Higgins and Hailbronner 2004:443). The UK has opted into many of the provisions concerning irregular migration, including: Directive 2001/40 on mutual recognition of expulsion decisions, Directive 2001/51 on carrier sanctions, a Framework decision on trafficking in persons (OJ 2002 L 203/1), a Directive and Framework Decision on facilitation of illegal entry and residence (OJ 2002 L 328) and Directive 2004/82 creating an obligation for carriers to communicate passenger data to immigration services. The UK has not opted into the majority of provisions on borders and visas, but has opted into the European common visa format (Reg 334/2002), and the format for residence permits (Reg 1030/2002).

Where the UK has not opted in there is not a consistent pattern as to whether the UK or EU provisions are the more generous, and the main reason given by the UK government for not opting in is to retain control and flexibility.

In terms of asylum policies, the UK is a key player, not swept unwillingly into European co-operation, but in the forefront of promoting deterrent measures. The Common European Asylum System and the UK's participation are discussed below.

5.6 Security – the Schengen Agreement

Before the Treaty of Amsterdam, co-operation in law and order and immigration was achieved by entering into agreements between states. Key among these was the Schengen Agreement 1985, and its implementing convention 1990, entered into by all the then member countries of the EU with the exception of the UK and Ireland, with the objective of achieving the gradual abolition of checks at common borders. The Schengen Agreement also declared an intention to reinforce cooperation between the customs and police authorities of the contracting states 'notably in combating crime, particularly illicit trafficking in narcotic drugs and arms, the unauthorized entry and residence of persons, customs and tax fraud and smuggling' (Article 9). To this end the Schengen Information System (SIS) was established, facilitating exchange of intelligence between the contracting states. The Treaty of Amsterdam brought the Schengen Agreement into the first pillar of the EC, i.e. into the Treaty, making it justiciable by the ECJ. The Schengen provisions are aimed at maintenance of external borders as well as dissolution of borders within the Community. The provisions of the Schengen *acquis* (i.e. the collection of authoritative documents) apply to third country nationals wherever the context so allows.

Under the Treaty of Amsterdam, the UK needs the consent of other Schengen states to opt into elements of the Schengen *acquis*. Council Decision 2000/365/EC determines in which Schengen provisions the UK participates, following its request to do so. Accordingly, there are limited provisions relating to border control which have effect in the UK. These concern security issues such as protection of personal data and the entry of individuals carrying narcotic drugs (Articles 75–76 and 126–127 of the Convention applying the Schengen Agreement). In Case C-77/05 *UK v Council* the UK argued that there are two categories of Schengen provisions – those which are directly part of the Schengen *acquis*, and those which build upon it – and that the UK has the power unilaterally to opt in to those provisions which build upon the Schengen *acquis*. The ECJ has held that this was a misinterpretation; there were not two categories of provision. As the UK did not participate in the burden of the Schengen system it could not unilaterally take the benefit.

The accession of 12 new member states to the EU necessitated a new information system (SIS II), but the opportunity is being taken to extend its use and capacities, and in particular to accommodate biometric data. The new system is now under construction. The SIS works on the basis of records (alerts) being created for five categories of people and for lost and stolen objects. Records suggest that Italy and Germany have been using the category of 'people to be refused entry to the Schengen area' to register all failed asylum seekers (*Statewatch* News Online April 2005: statewatch.org/news/). New categories of alert are being created for SIS II, widening the scope for creating records, and enabling greater data sharing, and this is not only for passport control. The Justice and Home Affairs ministers of the EU at a meeting in June 2003 agreed the addition of new categories of data and the possibility of access to that information being granted for other purposes, principally law enforcement. Development of SIS II is proceeding in accordance with the UK's proposal that law enforcement officers should have access to information that someone has been refused entry because they are believed to constitute a threat to public order, national security, or safety or there are grounds to believe they will commit a serious offence. Previously this information was only made available to immigration officers for the purposes of border control. The UK will participate in SIS II to the extent of criminal law and policing information, but not in relation to immigration information. The new SIS is accompanied by a new Visa Information System, but the UK has not yet opted into this. For a full discussion of the UK's role and of the progress, purposes and politics of SIS II, see the House of Lords European Union Committee Session 2006–07 Ninth Report HL paper 49.

5.7 **Frontex**

The major new development in Europe's control of its borders is the institution of Frontex, the European agency for the management of operational co-operation at the external borders of the European Union. This was established by Regulation 2007/2004 in October 2004, but the UK was excluded from discussions on the Frontex regulation, and it was this regulation and the creation of Frontex that the UK challenged in Case C-77/05 *UK v Council* (discussed above). Frontex has come into being at a time of rising concern about illegal entry on the southern borders of the EU, and in particular about deaths at sea. However, the actual role of Frontex in these situations is to ensure the integration of border forces between member states, and their cooperation with third countries, rather than to provide border guards. Having said this, two more developments followed hard on the heels of the creation of Frontex: a new emergency force came into being in 2007, the Rapid Border Intervention Team, known as RABITS, and Decision 574/2007/EC establishing a European Border Fund, to provide financial assistance 'to support the member states who bear, for the benefit of the Community, a lasting and heavy financial burden' (recital 4 to the Decision). As rapidly as RABITS are intended to act, so have questions arisen about their role and accountability. When RABITS act in conjunction with member state border guards, to whom are they accountable? RABITS came into being not long after the political spotlight turned onto new groups of illegal entrants arriving in the Canary Islands. Irregular migration on Europe's southern border generates two particular policy concerns: preventing unauthorized entry; and preventing deaths at sea. The irregular migrants who come by sea, while they may still be paying amounts beyond their means for the crossing, are also those who cannot afford forged papers for land or air border crossings. Spijkerboer argues that 'intensifying the EU's external borders has not decreased the number of irregular migrants, but, rather, has led irregular migrants to use alternative and increasingly dangerous routes' (2007: 127). Policy focus is on preventing unauthorised entry, with an assumption that saving life will follow. However, Spijkerboer suggests that, where authorities intensify their interception efforts, migrants will take more risks to avoid the more effective interception. This includes for instance taking much longer journeys, such as travelling south first to Senegal or Mauritania, or travelling in bad weather, and the practice of unloading potential migrants at sea without life jackets. This latter has resulted in people being mangled to death by propellers or drowning. Figures for deaths at the southern Spanish border (mainly in the Straits of Gibraltar) are as shown in the table.

Spijkerboer asks the question 'who is legally responsible for these fatalities?' The maintenance of a border force is a lawful activity. Except in any case of direct use of

Table 3 Deaths at the Spanish border

Deaths at Spanish border as recorded by:	2003	2004	2005
Spanish authorities	113	96	26
Press reports collected by www.unitedagainstracism.org	641	280	444

Compiled from information in Spijkerboer 2007

force, it could hardly be said that the individual border guards are responsible for the deaths of people who attempt to enter and die in the attempt. Yet policy decisions at EU level which purport to avoid these consequences seem to aggravate them.

To complete the account of border resource acronyms, Frontex maintains a Centralised Record of Available Technical Equipment, to help in the planning of operations. member states may check online to see what helicopters, vessels or planes are available; they do so by checking in the CRATE.

Although the UK was prevented from joining in Frontex by its non-participation in the Schengen Agreement, the UK government appears to be creating its own 'border guards', an occupation not formerly recognized in the UK. The UK Border Agency, whose creation is discussed in chapters 2 and 7, will inevitably enter into a working relationship of some kind with Frontex, and the activities of the European organization have been discussed here as a context for the creation of the UK's border force.

5.8 **Europe and asylum**

In absolute numbers, throughout the first years of the twenty-first century, the highest refugee populations in the world by far have been in Pakistan and Iran. Germany has come a close third. If the ratio of refugees to other inhabitants or to gross domestic product is measured, no country in the EU featured in the top ten refugee receiving countries in 2000 nor probably since (UNHCR). Nevertheless, globally, including in Europe, the number of refugees grew during the 1980s and 1990s. There was a dip from 2000 to 2003, then a gradual rise, and a sharp rise in global figures in 2006, accompanied by a decrease in Europe. The rise was attributable to 1.2 million people seeking refuge from Iraq in Syria and Jordan and a change in the method of counting in the USA. The drop in Europe was attributable to the naturalization of refugees in Serbia and a consolidation of Germany's statistics. Whatever the numbers, there is a widespread perception within Europe that asylum is a problem. The refugee determination process in Europe is centred on individuals proving their case in a legalistic framework according to the criteria in the 1951 UN Convention Relating to the Status of refugees. This has in part led to a popular perception that a successful applicant is a 'genuine' refugee and an unsuccessful one is a 'bogus' refugee. Some popular thinking also equates the unsuccessful asylum claimant with an 'economic migrant'. As the EU has not had a migration policy which enables economic entry, this motivation has not been regarded as legitimate.

Europe's more recent recognition of its need for labour has only very marginally penetrated asylum policy for fear that the asylum route will be used by economic migrants. There is a volume of research on causes and patterns of migration. Key findings are that:

- Repression and/or discrimination against minorities and/or ethnic conflict exists in all the main refugee-producing countries.
- Conflict seems to be a major cause of refugee movements.
- Poverty or underdevelopment may precipitate conflict but is not of itself apparently a cause of refugee movement.
- Where a country is undergoing rapid change or crisis, the motivations of individuals for leaving may be mixed – it is therefore difficult to distinguish between someone in need of protection (a Convention refugee) and someone seeking economic stability (an economic migrant).
- A reputation for democratic institutions, the rule of law, and developed social systems make Europe an attractive destination for people who decide to leave a situation of conflict and crisis.
- Existing personal, familial or other known links, knowledge of the language, and past colonial links are a strong influence on an individual's choice of a particular European country. (Castles, Crawley and Loughna 2003)

The above suggests that addressing the causes of forced migration requires addressing the causes of conflict, and that distinguishing between a Convention refugee and an economic migrant may not be simple. The main effort of EU policy however has been concentrated on prevention of illegal migration and the deterrence of asylum seekers. It may be argued that such measures 'make it more difficult for those who are genuinely in need of protection to seek asylum and at the same time have created a "migration industry" of smugglers, facilitators and traffickers' (Castles *et al* 2003:v). Asylum policy then must deal with controlling the smugglers and traffickers, and a further range of penal provisions has been introduced to this end.

The argument between Britain and France over the Red Cross camp at Sangatte may be seen in this light. It came to symbolize the supposed burden of asylum seekers in the context of European practice. Much of the public debate concerning the camp focused on the perceived differences between reception conditions and legal standards in the two countries. Despite the active role played by the UK in promoting common European asylum policy, the effort to remedy the problem of illegal entry to Britain from France did not concentrate on harmonization of standards, but rather on strengthening the border between the two countries. In the short to medium term it has produced a 'race to the bottom', that is, an endeavour by each country to be tougher than the other and therefore appear less desirable. There is a contradiction between this approach and creating a Common European Asylum System. Phuong makes the point that smugglers can capitalize on perceived differences, because legal controls between Britain and the rest of Europe exist. There would be no money to be made out of promising a route to the UK if the UK were part of the Schengen area (Phuong 2003).

The asylum provisions adopted under Title IV have completed the first stage of creating a Common European Asylum System and include the following provisions in force:

- Decisions to establish a European Refugee Fund, which concerns exceptional support for the costs of asylum. The second of such funds has been agreed.

- Regulation 2725/2000 on Eurodac, a Europe-wide fingerprint database for asylum seekers, and Regulation 407/2002 implementing it.
- Directive 2001/55 on temporary protection, limiting the obligations of states in the case of a mass exodus.
- Directive 2003/9, setting minimum reception conditions.
- 'Dublin II' Regulation 343/2003, making provision for the criteria for establishing which member state is responsible for an application. Regulation 1563/2003 gives the detailed rules.
- Directive 2004/83, giving the definition of a refugee or one who may obtain subsidiary protection, and the content of that protection ('the Qualification Directive').
- Directive 2005/85 on minimum standards on procedures for granting and withdrawing refugee status ('the Procedures Directive').

Council Regulation (EC) 2725/2000 [2000] OJ L316/1, concerning the implementation of the Eurodac system, was the first regulation made using Title IV, adopted on 11 December 2000. It institutes a system for collecting and identifying the fingerprints of all those who seek asylum in the member states which became operational on 15 January 2003. Fingerprints are retained for ten years in a Central Unit which can compare sets of prints against those in the database at the request of a member state. The aim is to be able to identify when an asylum seeker has already sought asylum somewhere else, thus giving effect to the central provision of the Dublin Convention (now Dublin II): that an asylum seeker must make their claim in the country through which they enter Europe. The Eurodac system was enlarged to include power to take fingerprints of third country nationals apprehended in connection with an irregular entry into Europe (Article 8). Therefore it would be possible to say of an asylum claimant in France that they previously entered Germany illegally. The fourth annual report, for 2006, shows that from a total of 165,958 asylum applications recorded in EURODAC in 2006 17 per cent were repeat applications (Annual report to the Council and the European Parliament on the activities of the EURODAC Central Unit in 2006, SEC (2007) 1184). 38.6 per cent of such applications were lodged in the same member state as the first application. The Eurodac system will be linked with the new system for biometric passport data (see chapter 7).

Legal provision concerning the minimum standards for dealing with asylum claims has taken longer to complete than the more explicitly deterrent and burden-sharing aspects of the Common European Asylum System. There are still outstanding issues concerning the procedures Directive (2005/85). Negotiations on a common list of safe countries of origin were shelved in order to complete the Directive as the list could not be agreed (see chapter 12 for further discussion). The European Parliament commenced a legal challenge to the constitutionality of compelling member states to abide by a common list of safe countries of origin, being countries from which member states would be obliged to consider an application as unfounded, thus removing the state's discretion and the individual's capacity for challenge. The Advocate General's opinion was that the option, written into the Directive, of compiling a list of safe countries of origin by majority voting, should be annulled as unconstitutional (*European Parliament v European Council* Case C-133/06). If there could not be a consensus on such an issue then member states could not be compelled to apply it. Here as elsewhere the debate on asylum provisions is dominated by the tension between, on the one hand, an attempt to tighten borders against asylum claims and, on the other hand, the need for protection of individual rights.

5.9 **UK implementation**

The UK has opted into all the provisions on asylum. This means that where asylum regulations are in force (for instance 'Dublin II'), the UK is bound by the regulation and must give effect to it (EC Treaty Article 249). Where directives are in force, the UK must adopt its own legal provisions which bring its law into compliance with the Directive by the date set for this purpose.

The Directive on reception conditions (2003/9/EC) was given legal force in the UK on 5 February 2005 by the Asylum Support (Amendment) Regulations 2005, SI 2005/11; the Asylum Seekers (Reception Conditions) Regulations 2005, SI 2005/7, and a new Part 11B of the immigration rules HC 395. SI 2005/7 provides for rudimentary minimum standards, for instance, in accommodating families to have regard to family unity and 'so far as...reasonably practicable' to accommodate families together (reg 3), and to take into account the needs of a vulnerable person, but not to assess for such needs (reg 4). SI 2005/11 deals mainly with discontinuation or suspension of asylum support. The new immigration rules deal mainly with obligations to give written information to asylum seekers. They also give the right to apply to the Secretary of State for permission to take up paid work if the asylum decision is still outstanding after one year. See Baldaccini 2005 for discussion.

The Directive on minimum standards for procedures in assessing an asylum claim (2005/85/EC) is discussed in the context of the asylum claim process in chapter 12, and the Directive concerned with the conditions for qualifying as a refugee (2004/83/EC) is discussed where that subject is treated in depth in chapter 13.

Dublin II (Regulation (EC) 343/2003), governing criteria and mechanisms for determining the member state responsible for examining an asylum application, is considered more fully in chapter 12 in the context of the development of so called 'safe third country provisions'.

The UK did not need to bring in further measures to ensure compliance with the Eurodac regulation as the power to collect fingerprints from asylum seekers had already been granted in the Immigration and Asylum Act 1999 s 141 (see chapter 7).

The Common European Asylum System is but one aspect of the strong external borders of Europe. The system of border control, both internal and external, rests upon a stratification of rights.

5.10 **Europeans in UK immigration law: shifting allegiances, freedom, and restriction**

The EU's political agreements and legal provisions produce a stratified system in which free movement rights, discussed in the next chapter, apply fully at the most privileged level and only in a limited way at the least privileged, whereas immigration and asylum provisions under Title IV apply not at all at the most privileged level but fully at the least. This stratification is largely dependent upon nationality. The EC's stratification of rights co-exists with member states' own system of immigration control, but as European law takes precedence where it applies, European membership has changed previous legal relationships.

In UK immigration law, European nationals are foreign nationals, as European countries are not and were not part of the British Empire or the Commonwealth. As we have seen, twentieth-century development of British immigration policy and law was formed with the Commonwealth in mind, and particularly the New Commonwealth. The development of immigration law has by and large meant the development of immigration control, and so those who were the target of that law have become the target of control. Thus, Commonwealth citizens, in the middle part of the twentieth century Britain's allies in the world, also from that time became subject to more stringent immigration control.

The second target group of policy, particularly in the last 25 years, has been asylum seekers, and the imposition of visa regimes has been used to deter travellers from countries which are considered to produce a high number of refugee claims. Some of the new members of the European Union are countries from which there have in the past been significant numbers of asylum claims, for instance the Czech Republic and the Slovak Republic. Asylum applications between EU member states are so rare as to be almost unknown. They would normally be unnecessary as a potential claimant may exercise rights of free movement, and the Qualification Directive does not provide for them. We can see, however, that the boundary between who is an asylum seeker and who is exercising European free movement rights is movable.

Since the Second World War European countries have been for the UK not only neighbours but also allies. European countries are not visa national countries, and could not be so because of the EC Treaty. In EC law EU citizens have freedom to come and go, and Commonwealth citizens, who before 1962 had the right of abode in the UK, are 'third country nationals'. This term also encompasses nationals of the main refugee-producing countries. However, while the aim of UK immigration law is immigration control, the aim of the EU Treaties and their implementing legislation is to promote freedom of movement within Europe.

5.11 European system of stratification of rights

Until recently, very broadly speaking, the EU's stratification was into three groups: EU nationals, nationals of countries with which the EC has association agreements, and third country nationals. Now there are changes in these groupings. First, there is differentiation within the category of 'favoured EC nationals' (a phrase occasionally used in case law). By the European Economic Area Agreement, and the Swiss Agreement, the specific free movement rights are extended to nationals of Iceland, Liechtenstein, Norway and Switzerland in addition to the member states of the EU. There is also a debate as to whether the establishment of European Union citizenship by the Treaty of Maastricht carries with it a general right to freedom of movement over and above specific rights under the primary and secondary legislation. If this were the case, nationals of Iceland, Liechtenstein, Norway, and Switzerland would not necessarily benefit as the agreements do not make them EU nationals. With the accession of ten new member states in 2004 and two in 2007, not all rights were automatically acquired on accession, but Malta and Cyprus were exempt from the derogations which old member states could apply to new member states in relation to freedom of movement. Therefore within the category of EU nationals there are some with more rights than others. The rights which accompany EU citizenship are discussed further in the next chapter. Secondly, the directive on third country nationals creates some rights at a European level on the basis of residence rather than nationality, though it did not go as far as recommended by the Opinion of the European Economic and Social Committee (EESC) on Access to European Union citizenship (OJ 2003 C 208/76) which proposed that European citizenship should be open to long-term resident third country nationals. The directives on TCNs entail that, in some instances, TCNs have more rights than some EU nationals. Finally, the common list of visa countries makes further differentiation between different groups of TCNs.

5.11.1 **The favoured group: EU nationals**

The most extensive rights in freedom of movement attach to EU nationals, and on the face of it those who qualify for this status are simply 'nationals of EU member states'. The member states upon entering into the Treaty on European Union declared that in cases of disputed nationality status the question should be settled solely by reference to the national law of the member state concerned. The jurisprudence of the Court has tended to follow this approach with the proviso that in making its determination the member state must have due regard to Community law. This proviso gives some jurisdiction to the ECJ on a question affecting entitlement under EC law.

In Case 21/74 *Airola v Commission* [1975] ECR 221 the question of the nationality of a female Commission staff member arose in the context of the application of the staff regulations relating to expatriation allowances. These would be paid to officials 'who are not and have never been nationals of the state in whose European territory the place where they are employed is situated'. The staff member in question was Belgian, but Italian law automatically naturalized her as Italian when she married an Italian man, thereby giving her dual nationality. Recognition of her Italian nationality would deprive her of the expatriation allowance. The application of the provision in the staff regulations would be discriminatory on grounds of sex, as men would not automatically acquire a new nationality on marriage. Combating sex discrimination is a principle of law of the European Community; the Court had jurisdiction on the interpretation of the regulation and was faced with a choice between upholding fundamental Community principles and respecting a State's view on nationality. It chose the former, and for the purpose of the staff regulations accepted the applicant's contention that it was necessary to define nationality 'as excluding nationality imposed by law on a female official upon her marriage with a national of another state when she has no possibility of renouncing it'.

The Court may also have a role when there is a difference in law between member states as to whether a person is a national of one of them. This arose in Case C–369/90 *Micheletti v Delegacion del Gobierno en Cantabria* [1992] ECR I–4329. Mr Micheletti had dual Italian and Argentinian nationality. He obtained recognition of his dental qualification in Spain, and went to live there from Argentina. The Spanish authorities, however, refused to grant him permanent residence as they did not recognize his Italian nationality and so would not grant him rights under European law. They followed a rule that where a person had nationality of more than one country, neither of which was Spain, then he would be regarded as a national of the country where he had last lived.

As in *Airola,* the ECJ set a limitation upon a member state's right to determine conditions of acquisition and loss of nationality. It was, they said, within the competence of each member state to define such conditions, but this competence 'must be exercised with due regard to Community law. Directive 73/148 (now 2004/38) provided that member states must admit Community nationals into their territory, merely upon production of a valid identity card or passport'. On producing his Italian passport Mr Micheletti should have been granted residence. It was not open to Spain to subject his Italian nationality to further scrutiny under their own domestic law, or to set a residence requirement in order to grant recognition.

5.11.1.1 *UK nationals for EU purposes*

A number of member states, including the UK, have made declarations, appended to the Maastricht Treaty, as to whom they regard as their nationals for EC purposes. The UK's Declaration ([1983] OJ C23/1) defines as nationals for EU purposes British citizens, British subjects with the right of abode in the UK, and British dependent territories citizens who acquire that citizenship from connection with Gibraltar. This appears to exclude Commonwealth citizens with right of abode in the UK, unless the Immigration Act 1971 definition of 'British citizens' can be implied into the declaration. Such people are treated by the Immigration Act 1971 as British citizens, indeed their right of abode in the UK is the same as that of a British citizen. However, it appears they do not obtain freedom of movement rights in the EU, even though they may well have lived in the UK all their lives, have the right to vote, and are in every other respect the equivalent in law of a British citizen (see comment by Dell'Olio 2002). The exclusion of British dependent territories citizens who are not from Gibraltar no longer has any significance: as British overseas territories citizens they now have become British citizens by virtue of the British Overseas Territories Act 2002. It may be noted that the Act did not give other European nationals the right to enter the British Overseas Territories (see Standing Committee D). Other categories of British national remain excluded, namely British overseas citizens, British nationals (overseas), and British subjects under the Act or British protected persons.

A challenge to this declaration and its exclusion of British overseas citizens arose before the ECJ in February 2001 in Case C–192/99 *R v Secretary of State for the Home Department ex p Manjit Kaur.* The case was an attempt to reverse the underprivileged immigration status of British overseas citizens, as discussed in chapter 3, and was important for the further reason that the applicant argued that fundamental rights were involved. The application to the British High Court was brought by Manjit Kaur, who was born in Kenya in 1949 of a family of Asian origin. She was at birth a citizen of the United Kingdom and Colonies. As such, she had a right of abode in the UK. After the immigration statutes of the 1960s she became subject to immigration control and after the commencement of the British Nationality Act 1981 in 1983, she became a British overseas citizen with no right of abode. In 1990 she claimed a right to enter and remain in the UK as an EU national, but her claim was denied on the basis of the UK's declaration defining UK nationals for EU purposes as excluding British overseas citizens.

Article 6(2) of the Treaty on European Union, as amended by the Treaty of Amsterdam, made fundamental rights a principle of Community law. Ms Kaur argued that her right of abode in the UK was a fundamental right, as recognized by Article 3, Protocol 4 of the European Convention on Human Rights which says that nationals shall not be deprived of the right to enter their country of nationality. The UK's failure to ratify this Protocol, at least in part because of a wish to avoid obligations to British overseas citizens, had no bearing on the decision in Ms Kaur's case, as under Article 6(2) the Convention is used as a source of principle for EU law rather than being directly applied. The ECJ, however, reaffirmed the pre-Maastricht principle that it was for member states, with due regard to Community law, to determine who would be their nationals and thus nationals of the Union. The court would therefore not interfere with Ms Kaur's status as determined by Britain. The High Court in *ex parte Zaunab Upadhey* 31 January 2000 (unreported) ILU vol. 3 no. 13 confirmed that a British protected person was also not a British national for EU purposes.

The British government's position on categories of British nationals is revealed in an amendment (Regulation 1932/2006) to the European Common Visa List regulation. The amendment adds to the list of those who require visas to enter the EU: BOTCs who do not have right of abode in the UK; BOCs; British Subjects who do not have rights of abode in the UK; and BPPs. It adds British Nationals (Overseas) to the list of those who do not require visas.

It is possible to summarize the current position on nationality in the following way. Although the determination of who is a national is primarily that of the State whose nationality is being claimed, this competence must be exercised within the principles of Community law; there is scope therefore for the Court to intervene. It is arguable that as the benefit of Community law and in particular of Union citizenship is dependent upon being a national of a member state, that deprivation of nationality is a matter of Community law as it operates to exclude a person from those benefits. However this has yet to be tested in the courts. Currently the definition of who may be a 'Union citizen', the prime category of privilege within the Union legal system, is largely in the hands of individual states.

5.11.2 Association agreements

These agreements with non-EU countries give rights to nationals of those countries to engage in economic activity in the EU. These are less than the rights available to EU nationals, but they provide a legal basis for workers. Each agreement provides for the establishment of a Council which has the responsibility for the development and implementation of the Agreement. Most of the countries which entered into these agreements have now become EU members, and their agreements with the EU operate as a minimum standard below which new rights on accession may not fall. The key exception is Turkey, which was the first country with which the EU entered into an agreement of this kind.

5.11.2.1 *EC–Turkey Agreement*

Many provisions of the EC–Turkey Agreement have direct effect, and Articles 12–14 provide that the contracting parties are to be guided by the relevant articles of the EC Treaty in progressively securing freedom of movement for workers, freedom of establishment, and provision of services. As in all the Association agreements there is not a right of entry as it is expected that a Turkish national will enter in accordance with the national law of the host country. However, once they have entered there is a principle of non-discrimination as between Turkish and EU nationals. Council Decision 1/80 Article 6 sets out the specific rights for a worker:

(i) after one year's legal employment, to renewal of the work permit to work for the same employer;

(ii) after three years' legal employment, to respond to an offer of employment from another employer; and

(iii) after four years' legal employment, to any paid employment of the worker's choice.

The meaning of 'a worker' under Decision 1/80 was considered by the ECJ in Case C-294/06 *Payir, Aykuz and Ozturk v SSHD*. Ms Payir came to the UK as an *au pair*, and applied for leave to remain to stay with the same employer. Her application was refused by the Secretary of State on the basis that the UK immigration rules applying to *au pairs* only permit two years' leave, and the Turkey Agreement did not apply because she was not a worker. The High Court, Court of Appeal and ECJ disagreed. She fulfilled the objectives conditions to come within the definition of worker in Decision 1/80, and the fact that her work was taken up with the motive of 'acquisition of cultural experience and deepening of linguistic knowledge' (Advocate General's opinion) could not affect her classification as a worker. There was no question of abuse of the rules, as suggested by governments intervening in the case. Her work was a genuine and effective economic activity, she was 'duly registered' as belonging to the UK labour force, as Article 6 required. There was no encroachment upon the competence of member states in regulating the entry of Turkish nationals, as the Secretary of State argued. This right only applied to a Turkish national who had been admitted pursuant to domestic law. In the same judgment the court held that these principles also applied to Mr Aykuz and Mr Ozturk, students who were working the full 20 hours per week permitted by their terms of leave.

Article 7 of Decision 1/80 provides that members of a Turkish worker's family who have been authorized by national law to join them may take up offers of work although they must first have three years of lawful residence. Children may enter education once one of their parents has been working for a period, and if they have been in vocational training in the host state are then free to enter employment, providing their parent has been legally employed for three years.

The Turkey Agreement has a protective effect which ensures that the movement is towards the integration of Turkish workers, not against it. This purposive approach also benefits family members, as demonstrated in Case C-325/05 *Derin v Landkreis Darmstadt-Dieburg*, where the ECJ held that a family member of a Turkish worker who had acquired the right to free access to employment would only lose the right of residence if his deportation was justified under the stringent test required for EU nationals (see chapter 6), or if he left the territory for a significant length of time without legitimate reason. This was so even though he was over 21 years of age, no longer dependent on his parents, living independently in the member state and not available to join the labour force for several years because he was in prison. He was not required, as the government had argued, to remain dependent on his parents in order to benefit from his rights as a family member. This was to the same effect as the earlier case of *Torun v Stadt Augsburg* Case C-502/04 ECR [2006] I-01563.

Some of the social issues affecting migrant workers and the importance of a purposive interpretation of rights under the EC–Turkey Agreement are illustrated in *Sedef v Freie und Hansestadt Hamburg*.

 **Key Case**

Case C-230/03 *Sedef v Freie und Hansestadt Hamburg* ECR [2006] I-00157

Mr Sedef was a Turkish national lawfully employed from 1977 to 1992 as a seaman on German ships. He obtained successive residence permits, restricted to employment in the merchant navy, and was actually working during that period for nearly nine years. Most of the times that he was not working were due to breaks between fixed-term contracts. During these breaks he either awaited the arrival of the ship on which he had his next contract, or went to Turkey to visit his family. In 1979 he had an accident on a ship, the effects of which entailed a number of surgical operations, and periods of incapacity for work. Eventually in 1992 he was pronounced unfit to work on ships on health grounds, though well enough for work on land that was not too physically strenuous. He was refused a residence permit to work on land on the grounds that he did not have four years of uninterrupted employment.

The ECJ found that the interruptions in Mr Sedef's employment were beyond his control, his absences did not call into question his integration into the work force, it was inappropriate to require him to have registered as a job seeker between contracts as he normally already held the next contract, and the German authorities had repeatedly issued residence permits and only refused when he applied to work on land. In these circumstances, and particularly though not crucially because his move to work on land was necessitated by his injury during work at sea, he should be regarded as having continuity of employment with legitimate breaks so as to benefit from the right to change employers.

Many, though not all, of the key ECJ cases concerning the EC–Turkey Agreement are on reference from courts in Germany. This is an example of how one may see patterns of migration behind the case law. Just as the UK invited workers from the Caribbean in the 1960s, so the German government in 1961 issued an invitation to Turkish workers to fill the labour shortages that arose after the Second World War. This established Germany as a key destination for Turkish migrant workers of succeeding decades: around a quarter of Germany's non-German registered population is Turkish.

The Standstill Clause

In Case C-37/98 *Savas* [2000] All ER (EC) 627 the ECJ held that the standstill provision in Article 41 of the Additional Protocol to the Agreement meant that the UK could not apply provisions on establishment to Turkish workers that were more restrictive than those which obtained at the time of the commencement of the Turkey Agreement. For the UK this was 1 January 1973 when the UK joined the EU. Immigration rules on self-employment were then more favourable to the individual than they are now. Consequently the old rules must be applied to Turkish workers.

The question of the scope of the standstill clause was considered by the ECJ in Case C-16/05 *Tum and Dari v SSHD*. The court held that unsuccessful Turkish asylum seekers were not debarred from benefiting from *Savas* and the standstill clause, which was a procedural limitation applying to decisions on entry just as much as any other decision.

The case was referred from the House of Lords to which it has yet to return, but the ECJ decision supports that of the Court of Appeal which held that the Secretary of State was wrong to apply current immigration rules to them and thus deny them leave.

Key Case

Case C-16/05 *The Queen (Tum and Dari) v SSHD*

Mr Tum and Mr Dari were Turkish nationals who entered the UK and made asylum applications. Pending the outcome of their asylum applications they were granted temporary admission, which is a provisional permission to be in the UK, and not the same as being granted entry. The asylum claims were unsuccessful, and decisions were made to remove them to European countries through which they had travelled, pursuant to the Dublin Convention. However, they were not actually removed, and made applications to enter the UK to set up in business. Although they were physically present, the applications had to be for leave to enter because they did not yet have this. By this time Mr Dari was running a successful pizza business.

The Secretary of State refused their applications on the grounds that the standstill clause did not apply to provisions on entry. Mr Tum and Mr Dari would not be able to comply with the more stringent requirements for setting up in business which applied at the date of their application, and it was fraudulent and thus an abuse of EC law for asylum seekers whose claim had failed to rely on the EC–Turkey Agreement and the standstill clause. Before the ECJ the Secretary of State also argued that it would undermine the competence of national authorities if the standstill clause applied to provisions on entry.

The ECJ preferred the interpretation put forward by Mr Tum and Mr Dari. The standstill clause did not grant a substantive right of entry and thus did not interfere with the state's right to control immigration. It was only a procedural limitation, preventing states from imposing any new obstacles after the entry into force of the EC–Turkey Agreement. It applied to provisions governing admission or entry. Community law could not be used for fraudulent purposes, but the national courts 'which gave rulings on the substance of these cases... expressly stated that Mr Tum and Mr Dari could not be accused of any fraud'. Additionally the protection of public interests such as order or security was not in issue. The fact that they had made unsuccessful asylum applications was irrelevant to their claim relying on the EC–Turkey Agreement.

Fraud exception to Tum and Dari

It was accepted by the ECJ and by the Court of Appeal that 'Community law cannot be relied upon for fraudulent or abusive ends' (ECJ para 64). In *Tum and Dari* itself the ECJ and UK courts held that merely making an asylum application which was unsuccessful did not amount to fraud or deception, and no fraud or deception was alleged in Mr Tum or Mr Dari's conduct. The scope of the fraud exception has been the subject of litigation in the High Court. In *R (on the application of Aksu) v SSHD* [2006] EWHC 1382 (Admin) the claimant made an unsuccessful asylum claim in Germany, but when he arrived in the UK denied that he had made any prior claim and claimed asylum again. In *R (on the application of Semsek) v SSHD* [2006] EWHC 1486 the adjudicator found that the claimant's asylum claim was based on untrue facts. In *Yilmaz v SSHD* [2005] EWHC 1068 the claimant attempted but failed to gain entry using false endorsements in his passport. *R (on the application of Taskale)* [2006] EWHC 712 (Admin) followed *Yilmaz* to find against the claimant who entered clandestinely in the back of a lorry. In all these cases the High Court found that the claimant came within the fraud exception. As the circumstances are very different in these cases there is a need for further clarification by the higher courts.

Limitation on Tum and Dari

The tribunal in the UK in *OY v ECO Nicosia* [2006] UKAIT 00028 held that the standstill clause could not be used to grant entry to the 19-year-old son of a Turkish worker who would have been able to enter under the rules applying on 1 January 1973. They distinguished *Tum and Dari* on the basis that that case referred to the standstill clause relating to freedom of establishment, whereas *OY* concerned the standstill clause in Decision 1/80 referring to 'access to employment'. Arguably at variance with principles of EC free movement law discussed in the next chapter, the tribunal held that being accompanied by one's family was not related to access to employment. Furthermore, the standstill clause could not govern conditions of entry. This last point will need to be reconsidered in the light of *Tum and Dari*.

5.11.2.2 *Other Association Agreements*

There were association agreements (the CEEC, Central and Eastern European Agreements) with Bulgaria, the Czech Republic, Estonia, Hungary, Lithuania, Poland, Romania, Slovakia, and Slovenia. These countries are now all Members of the EU. The CEEC agreements are relevant still for the new member states as a minimum standard for their rights to work in the old member states during the transition period (see below). The CEEC agreements are less far reaching than the agreement with Turkey. They set out some anti-discrimination provisions for employed workers, and rights of establishment (that is, to set up business) and provide services. The rights of establishment for Bulgarian and Romanian nationals are given effect in the UK in the Immigration Rules HC 395 paras 222 and 223, as amended.

A number of cases decided in late 2001 established principles on the effect of these agreements on the treatment of entry of nationals from these states. In C–63/99 *Gloszczuk* [2002] 2 All ER (EC), C–235/99 *Kondova* [2001] ECR I-6427, and C–257/99 *Barkoci and Malik* [2001] All ER (EC) 903, all referred from the UK, the ECJ held that the right of establishment has direct effect and so can be relied upon directly by individuals in national systems. The remaining aspects of these decisions are now of less importance: these concerned terms of entry, and nationals of former CEEC countries now have a right of entry as EU nationals, though their right to work is still curtailed.

There are less advantageous co-operation agreements with Algeria, Morocco and Tunisia, the so-called 'Maghreb agreements'. These provide for equality of treatment for employed workers only.

5.11.3 **New member states**

Under the Acts of Accession old member states have an option for the first two years after accession of new member states to continue to apply their national law, that means until 1 May 2006 for A8 countries, and 1 January 2009 for Bulgaria and Romania. There follows a three-year period during which old member states have agreed to introduce greater freedom of access to labour markets. See Table 6 in chapter 6 at 6.9. The transition period should then end (i.e. after five years), but an old member state which has not achieved full access to the labour markets for new member state workers may, in case of threatened or actual 'serious disturbances to its labour market', have a further two years in which to achieve full access. While full rights do not apply, the Association Agreements will continue to have effect and so, following *Kondova,* these same economic reasons cannot be used for refusing those entering as self-employed. The option to restrict access only applies to employment and does not apply at all to nationals of Malta and Cyprus. Full integration must be achieved after seven years.

The UK's scheme permitting Accession nationals to enter employment under certain conditions is discussed in chapters 6 and 11.

5.11.4 **Third country nationals**

Technically, third country nationals (TCNs) are nationals of non-EU countries. In practice we may regard them as nationals of non-EEA countries, as defined by the UK Immigration (European Economic Area) Regulations 2006, because nationals of Iceland, Liechtenstein, Norway and Switzerland have rights almost equivalent to EU citizens. The entry of TCNs is primarily governed by the national law of member states. EU law provisions set out some limitations upon what national law may specify. Note that the UK has not opted into any of these provisions, hence the brevity with which they are treated here.

First, there is a Common Visa List (Council Regulation EC 539/2001 as amended). The regulation lists those countries whose nationals require a visa to enter Europe and those whose nationals do not require a visa. Those who do not require a visa, e.g. nationals of USA, Japan, Singapore, may enter for up to three months without a visa. Nationals of countries on the visa list require visas for any purpose. The latest set of changes (Regulation 1932/2006) moves towards harmonization of the EU and UK visa lists, but the UK has still not opted into this provision as the European list includes a number of Commonwealth countries which the UK has not yet included on its own visa list, for instance Trinidad and Tobago and South Africa. The EU visa list is longer than the UK's, and note the changes in relation to British nationals mentioned above.

Secondly, as noted in 5.3.2 above, there is some secondary legislation governing entry and stay of TCNs for specific purposes.

Thirdly, the directives on resident TCNs and family reunion provide some rights for TCNs who are already resident.

Finally, nationals of third countries may be able to enter a European country by virtue of an EU freedom of movement provision by virtue of their connection with a European exercising free movement rights. For instance a third country national might enter if they were employed by a European business exercising its right of establishment in another member state, or if they were a family member of a European citizen who was moving between member states. Note that European free movement rights do not allow a third country national family member to enter Europe unless the European upon whose right they rely is exercising European treaty rights. For instance, the Cameroonian wife of a German business man may move to Italy with him when he sets up business there, but European law will not enable her to enter Germany from Cameroon in the first place. These rights are discussed more fully in the next chapter.

5.12 **Human rights in the EU**

The Treaty of Amsterdam gave the ECJ, in the course of exercising its normal powers under the Treaties, jurisdiction to examine the compatibility of actions of the institutions of the EU with fundamental rights. The source of these fundamental rights may be the legal traditions of the member states, the ECtHR, or other international treaties to which member states have contributed or to which they are parties (see e.g. Case 4/73 *Nold v Commission* [1974] ECR 491).

5.12.1 **Charter of Fundamental Rights**

In an initiative separate from the main Treaties, the new European Charter of Fundamental Rights (OJ 2000 C 3641) was formally adopted at the Council of Nice in December 2000. It recognizes a wide range of fundamental rights, but has a declaratory, nonbinding status. It may be used by the ECJ as a source of reference for the nature of rights which should be respected in the Union. The relationship between the Charter and the ECHR is not fully resolved. The two documents are intended to be compatible, though the scope of the Charter is wider. Concerning the relationship between the two documents, the Charter's Article 52(3) says:

In so far as this Charter contains rights which correspond to rights guaranteed by the Convention for the Protection of Human Rights and Fundamental Freedoms, the meaning and scope of those rights shall be the same as those laid down by the said Convention. This provision shall not prevent Union law providing more extensive protection.

There is a contradiction here, but a plausible interpretation is that the Charter may be interpreted so as to be more protective of rights than the ECHR, but not less, and the principle of consistent interpretation cannot be used to defeat rights granted in Union law. An interesting relevant example of where the Charter could extend protection is in Article 47(2), which extends the scope of the right to fair hearing to 'rights and freedoms guaranteed by the law of the Union'. This would include any rights arising from the immigration and asylum provisions under Title IV, which as we have seen in chapter 4, are excluded from the right to a fair hearing under the present case law of the ECHR.

Regulation 168/2007 establishes a new European Union Agency for Fundamental Rights. The objective of the Agency, based in Vienna, is to provide the relevant institutions and authorities of the Community and its member states when implementing Community law with **assistance and expertise relating to fundamental rights** in order to support them when they take measures or formulate courses of action within their respective spheres of competence to fully respect fundamental rights (see http:/fra.europa.eu/fra/index.php).

5.12.2 **Relationship of human rights and Community law**

The EU has not acquired a general human rights competence. In other words, it is not yet the case that the EU promotes human rights separately from Community law issues, but rather that it upholds human rights when these are potentially violated within the existing bounds of EU law. As the European Parliament's challenge to the Family Reunion Directive shows, this may include a direct challenge to secondary legislation even before it is applied.

The ECJ has on many occasions stated that fundamental human rights are a foundation of EC law, and is not a stranger to independent application of fundamental rights to the cases that come before it. For instance, in Case C–63/83 *R v Kirk* [1984] ECR 2689 the question was of the validity of the Sea Fish Order 1982 which prohibited fishing in UK waters by Danish fishing vessels. This, of course, is discriminatory. Council Regulation 170/83 Article 6(1) purported to allow member states to derogate from the non-discrimination principle in relation to sea fishing, and to do so retroactively. The ECJ held that this would amount to retroactive imposition of a penalty which was equivalent to a criminal penalty. The Court said at para 3:

> The principle that penal provisions may not have retroactive effect is one which is common to all the legal orders of the member states and is enshrined in article 7 of the European Convention for the Protection of Human Rights and Fundamental Freedoms as a fundamental right; it takes its place among the general principles of law whose observance is ensured by the Court of Justice.

Before the TEU Art F (now 6(2)) made fundamental rights a principle of EU law, the Court can be seen here employing a principle of fundamental rights by reference both to 'all the legal orders of the member states' and to the ECHR. Also before the TEU, in Case C–5/88 *Wachauf v Bundesamt für Ernährung und Forstwirtschaft* [1989] ECR 2609 the ECJ referred to general principles of fundamental rights as enshrined in numerous international instruments to which the member states were parties. Without naming any particular treaty or any particular right, the Court found that rules which, on the expiry of an agricultural lease, had the effect of depriving the tenant of the fruits of his labour, would breach such fundamental rights. The Court, at para 18, enunciated the following principle:

> The fundamental rights recognized by the Court are not absolute, but must be considered in relation to their social function. Consequently, restrictions may be imposed on the exercise of those rights, in particular in the context of a common organization of a market, provided that those restrictions in fact correspond to objectives of general interest pursued by the Community and do not constitute, with regard to the aim pursued, a disproportionate and intolerable interference, impairing the very substance of those rights.

The Court's first assertion here must be qualified as the ECHR, and in many cases criminal law, makes some rights absolute which in theory might be interfered with in the name of free movement of workers. The right to be free from slavery is an example of such a right. The principle of free movement of workers could not be advanced to promote for instance abusive domestic labour or sex-trafficking.

Having said this, the principle of balancing economic and fundamental rights appears so far to prevail in EC law. Case C–112/00 *Eugen Schmidberger, Internationale Transporte und Planzüge v Austria* [2003] 2 CMLR 34 broke new ground in this respect, for the first time weighing an interference with an EC right against the exercise of a fundamental right protected by the ECHR. A transport firm challenged the decision of the Austrian government to permit a demonstration by environmental protesters which blocked the Brenner highway, a major international route, for 30 hours. There had been forewarning and advertising of alternative routes. The Austrian government took its decision bearing in mind the protesters' right under Article 11 ECHR to demonstrate peacefully. The ECJ held that, although the Community law 'right to free movement of goods' was engaged, the State's decision to uphold the Article 11 right, given all the measures that were taken, was not disproportionate and did not infringe EC law.

The ECJ also found it was necessary to balance rights of freedom of establishment and rights of workers to organize and take industrial action in *Viking Line ABP v International Transport Workers' Federation and the Finnish Seamen's Union* (Case C-438/05). This was an instance of the phenomenon known rather unattractively in EU discourse as 'social dumping'. This refers to the practice of producing goods for export in a country with low standards of pay and protection for workers, thus making the exporter's costs artificially lower than those of its competitors in countries with higher standards, and giving an advantage in international trade at the expense of lower paid or less protected workers. The court held that industrial action by the union was a restriction on the freedom of establishment, but

that restriction may, in principle, be justified by an overriding reason of public interest, such as the protection of workers, provided that it is established that the restriction is suitable for ensuring the attainment of the legitimate objective pursued and does not go beyond what is necessary to achieve that objective.

For detailed discussion see Barnard C. 2007 (June 2007 update) at www.oup.com/uk/orc/bin/9780199298396/01student/updates.

The ECJ has sometimes of its own motion introduced an argument based on fundamental rights. In *Carpenter*, and *Gloszczuk* and *Kondova*, the first ECJ cases to refer to the right to respect for the family life of third country nationals, the Court said that any removal of the applicants would have to be carried out in accordance with Article 8, i.e. with due respect for their right to family life and only if necessary in a democratic society in the interests of a legitimate aim. The Court's approach in *Carpenter* suggests that mere regulation of immigration would not be sufficient to justify removal. The ECJ may draw upon 'the constitutional traditions common to the member states' as a source of principle or fundamental rights, and not only on the specific rights protected by the ECHR. In Case 36/02 *Omega Spielhallen und Automatenaufstellungs-GmbH v Oberburgermeisterin der Bundesstadt Bonn* ECR [2004] I 9609 the German public authority had prohibited the parts of Laserdrome activity which were 'playing at killing' or simulated homicide, in the interests of public order and the protection of human dignity. In upholding the prohibition the ECJ reiterated that fundamental rights play an integral part in Community law, and then said that Community law also 'strives to ensure respect for human dignity as a general principle of law'. This case is an unusual and interesting one in protecting human dignity as a fundamental principle.

Note the comparison with *Manjit Kaur*, where on a strong challenge to national sovereignty the ECJ did not uphold an argument based on fundamental rights. A less direct challenge to a state's authority on nationality issues succeeded in *Airola* where the fundamental human right in question, not to be subject to sex discrimination, derived from the original economic purposes of the Community.

5.12.3 Challenging EC primary legislation

Case C-540/03 *European Parliament v European Council* was a challenge to secondary legislation. What happens if the EC's own primary legislation appears to conflict with fundamental rights? In the normal course of things the ECJ does not have power to examine the validity of primary EC legislation, and human rights do not function in the EC as a constitutional standard which would give the ECJ any special jurisdiction in this respect. This limitation on the jurisdiction of the ECJ was revealed in *Matthews v UK* (1999) 28 EHRR 361. The case could not be heard in the ECJ but was considered by the European Court of Human Rights. The Court held the Members of the European Parliament, the UK, and the other member states to be in breach of the ECHR by entering into a decision and primary legislation which excluded the people of Gibraltar from voting in European Parliamentary elections. This breached their rights under Article 3 of Protocol 1 to the ECHR which guarantees free and fair elections. Primary legislation could not be challenged within the Community's own legal order. The ECtHR but not the ECJ could judge the matter.

5.13 Conclusion

This chapter has raised some of the policy issues which dominate immigration and asylum law in Europe, and the UK's negotiated opt-in arrangement to the provisions arising under Title IV of the Amsterdam Treaty. To date the UK has taken a leading part in discussions on asylum and has opted in to all provisions on that subject. It has also opted in to some of the increased security measures in the Schengen *acquis*, which now forms part of Community law. The Community as a whole has been slow to implement provisions creating rights for third country nationals, and the UK shows no inclination to opt into these. The European legal system provides a base for migration law that is purposive in its reasoning, and this provides part of the context for the development of UK migration law, not only politically and in terms of binding legal provisions, but also in terms of a different kind of thinking about law.

QUESTIONS

1 Why do you think the UK negotiated an opt-in arrangement to the Treaty of Amsterdam?
2 What are the benefits to the UK of opting in to the EU measures on asylum?
3 What do you think motivated the EC to enter into the Association Agreements?

 online resource centre For guidance on answering questions, visit www.oxfordtextbooks.co.uk/orc/clayton3e.

FURTHER READING

Baldaccini, A. (2005) 'Asylum support and EU obligations: implementation of the EU Reception Directive in the UK' *Journal of Immigration, Asylum & Nationality Law* vol.19, no.3, pp. 152–160.

Biondi, A. (2004) 'Free Trade, A Mountain Road and the Right to Protest: European Economic Freedoms and Fundamental Individual Rights' *European Human Rights Law Review* 1, pp. 51–61.

Boelaert-Suominen, S. (2005) 'Non-EU Nationals and Council Directive 2003/109 EC on Status of TCNs who are long-term resident: 5 paces forward and possibly 3 paces back' (2005) *Common Market Law Review* 42: 1011–1052.

Boeles, P. (2001) 'Freedom, Security and Justice for All', in Guild, E., and Harlow, C. (eds) *Implementing Amsterdam* (Oxford: Hart).

Castles, S., Crawley, H., Loughna, S. (2003) *States of Conflict: Causes and patterns of forced migration to the EU and policy responses* (London: IPPR).

Dale, G., and Cole, M. (1999) *The European Union and Migrant Labour* (Oxford: Berg).

Dell'Olio, F. (2002) 'The Redefinition of the Concept of Nationality in the UK: Between Historical Responsibility and Normative Challenge', *Politics*, vol. 22 issue 1, pp. 9–16.

European Commission (2004) Area of Freedom, Security and Justice: Assessment of the Tampere programme and future orientations, COM (2004) 4002, final, 2 June.

European Council on Refugees and Exiles (2004), *Broken Promises – Forgotten Principles: An ECRE Evaluation of the Development of EU minimum standards for Refugee Protection Tampere 1999* Brussels 2004.

Facenna, G. (2004) *'Eugen Schmidberger, Internationale Transporte und Planzüge v Austria*: Freedom of Expression and Assembly vs Free Movement of Goods' [2004] *European Human Rights Law Review* 1, pp. 73–80.

Guild, E. (2001) 'Primary Immigration: The Great Myths', in Guild, E., and Harlow, C. (eds) *Implementing Amsterdam* (Oxford: Hart).

—— (1999) 'Free movement of persons in Europe: the Amsterdam Treaty and its implications for the UK' *Immigration and Nationality Law and Practice* vol. 13, no. 4, pp. 128–132.

Guild, E., and Harlow, C. (eds) (2001) *Implementing Amsterdam: Immigration and Asylum Rights in EC Law* (Oxford: Hart).

Hailbronner, K. (1998) 'European Immigration and Asylum Law under the Amsterdam Treaty' *Common Market Law Review* 35: 1047–1067.

Hall, S. (1996) 'Loss of Union Citizenship in Breach of Fundamental Rights' *European Law Review* vol. 21, 129–143.

Higgins and Hailbronner, (2004) *Migration and Asylum Law and Policy in the EU* FIDE 2004, National reports, Cambridge: Cambridge University Press.

Langrish, S. (1998) 'The Treaty of Amsterdam: selected highlights' *European Law Review* (1998).

Lyasky, O. 'Complementing and Completing the CEAS: a legal analysis of the emerging extraterritorial elements of EU refugee protection policy' (2006) *European Law Review* vol. 31, 230–235.

Mitselegas, V. (2006) 'The Directive on the Reception of Asylum Seekers and its Implementation in the UK', *Journal of Immigration, Asylum & Nationality Law* vol. 20, no. 1, pp. 42–45.

O'Keeffe, D., and Twomey, P. (1999) *Legal Issues of the Amsterdam Treaty* (Oxford: Hart).

O'Leary, S. (1999) 'Putting Flesh on the Bones of European Union Citizenship' *European Law Review* vol. 24, no. 1, pp. 68–79.

Peers, S. (1998) 'Building Fortress Europe: The Development of EU Migration Law' *Common Market Law Review* (1998) 35(6) 1235–1272.

—— (2003) 'Key legislative developments on migration in the European Union' (2003) 5 *European Journal of Migration and Law* 107–141.

Phuong, C. (2003) 'Closing Sangatte: the legal implications of the asylum dispute between France and the UK' *Journal of Immigration, Asylum & Nationality Law* vol. 17, no. 3, pp. 157–169.

Rogers, N. (2006) 'Turkish Association Agreement Applications – A Myriad of Problems and Some Solutions' *Journal of Immigration, Asylum & Nationality Law* vol. 20, no.4, pp. 283–288.

Rollason, N. (2002) 'Free movement of persons: citizenship and the expanding European Union' *Journal of Immigration, Asylum & Nationality Law* vol. 16, no. 4, pp. 237–245.

Shah, P. (2002) 'Why some British nationals are not European Union Citizens' *Journal of Immigration, Asylum & Nationality Law* vol. 16, no. 2, pp. 82–96.

Stevens, D. (2004) *UK Asylum Law and Policy* (London: Sweet & Maxwell), Chapter 9.

—— (2005) 'Asylum Seekers in the New Europe: Time for a rethink?' in Shah, P. (ed.) *The Challenge of Asylum to Legal Systems* (London: Cavendish).

6

Freedom of movement for EU nationals

SUMMARY

This chapter gives an introduction to freedom of movement within the European Community. The focus is on rights of entry and residence, particularly for employed workers and their families. A brief account is given of schemes applicable to nationals of Accession States, and there is discussion of the public policy reasons for excluding rights.

6.1 Introduction

This chapter concerns the law of the European Community (EC) which governs the free movement of people within the European Union (EU). As such, it is principally about the movement of EU nationals, but it is also about the movement of non-EU nationals as governed by Community law, known in European law as third country nationals. TCNs may come within the ambit of Community law as a result of their connection with EU nationals, for instance as a spouse or employee. The chapter concentrates on the rights of EU nationals as workers to move within the EU. The rights of establishment and to provision of services are not covered, and for these, as for a fuller account of free movement generally, reference should be made to textbooks on EC law.

Knowledge of the system of EC law is useful but not essential to the reading of this chapter. For a full account of the law of freedom of movement reference should be made to textbooks devoted to EC law, as mentioned at the end of this chapter. This chapter follows a common practice of using the new number of Treaty Articles (after amendments and renumbering by the Treaty of Amsterdam) with the old number in brackets, e.g. 'Article 39 (ex 48)' so that the connection can be made with older cases and materials.

6.2 Sources of law

Free movement law is primarily contained in EC Treaty Articles and secondary legislation, and is given effect in UK law by statute and rules. In the unlikely or rare event of a European provision not being given effect by these mechanisms, the main relevant provisions are directly effective, and take precedence over any inconsistent national provision (Case 6/64 *Costa v ENEL* [1964] ECR 585). Although the doctrine of direct effect means that EU law takes effect where UK law fails to deliver an EU right, it does not prevent UK law from giving greater rights to EEA nationals than are contained in EU law.

Appeals against decisions made under the European provisions are made to the same appellate bodies as other UK immigration appeals (Immigration (European Economic Area) Regulations 2006, SI 2006/1003 part 6). This means that there are decisions of the Asylum and Immigration Tribunal and higher courts on European free movement issues. Providing the law is clear, domestic courts may rule upon it. Where it is not clear, under Article 234 (ex 177) EC Treaty any court or tribunal may refer a question to the European Court of Justice for a preliminary ruling, which will then return to the domestic court for application.

On 30 April 2006, Directive 2004/38/EC on the right of citizens of the Union and their families to move and reside freely within the territory of member states became binding on member states. This Directive replaced many of the earlier directives and regulations concerning entry and residence. It is known as the Citizens' Directive, and is now a major source of law which consolidates and enhances free movement rights. It builds on Commission Regulation 1251/70 concerning the right to remain after employment, and amends Council Regulation 1612/68 concerning eligibility for employment, equal treatment, and the rights of workers' families.

Section 7 of the Immigration Act 1988 implements in UK law the basic principle of free movement by providing that those who have an 'enforceable Community right' shall not require leave to enter under the Immigration Act 1971. This means that although they are technically subject to immigration control, within that system of control they have a right to enter to exercise their freedom of movement. This may be seen at any port of entry to the UK where there is a channel for EU citizens who are normally waved through on presentation of proof of right to travel. Those with an enforceable Community right are nationals of the European Economic Area (EEA), that is, EU countries, Iceland, Norway and Liechtenstein, and the UK regulations include Swiss nationals also (Immigration (European Economic Area) Regulations 2006, SI 2006/1003, reg 2(1)). The definition of EU nationals has already been discussed in chapter 5, to which reference should be made. Further Regulations apply the European freedom of movement provisions to workers from the 2004 Accession states and from Bulgaria and Romania, but with limiting provisions.

The detailed implementation in UK law is by the Immigration (European Economic Area) Regulations 2006, SI 2006/1003, intended to give effect to the Citizens' Directive, though whether they do so fully is a matter we shall consider.

6.3 Free movement of Union citizens

EC law is founded on the principle of the free movement of goods, persons, services and capital. Here we focus on the free movement of persons. This freedom has primarily developed in connection with economic activities, as an aspect of the Economic Community; but, as the political union develops, one of the questions is whether there is a right to freedom of movement aside from economic activity, and if so, who has it. The Treaty on European Union created EU citizenship, and in Article 18 EC Treaty (ex Article 8a) a right to move and reside freely within the territory of the member states. Although this right is advanced in argument in many cases in support of a right to free movement, the outcome often seems to be that the Article 18 right is read as a support to other rights. This question is discussed further below in relation to *Chen* and cases that followed it.

The objective of the Citizens' Directive is to develop Union citizenship as the 'fundamental status of nationals of the member states when they exercise their rights of free movement and residence' (preamble para 2). Here the Directive quotes the ECJ in Case C-184/99 *Grzelczyk v Centre Public D'Aide Sociale D'Ottignies-Louvain-La-Neuve* [2002] 1 CMLR 19 where the court's finding that a student residing in another member state could claim a benefit available to other residents in that state made a significant advance in developing the rights of EU nationals. We therefore begin with the rights of entry and residence of Union citizens, the term used in the Citizens' Directive. It may be recalled from chapter 5 that Union citizens are those who have the nationality of a member state.

The ECJ suggested, in both *Grzelczyk* and *Baumbast*, that Article 18 means that free movement is to be detached from the exercise of economic rights. We shall see as we examine the provisions of the Citizens' Directive the extent to which this is or is not becoming the case.

6.3.1 Union citizens' rights of entry and residence

The Citizens' Directive 2004/38 Article 5.1 provides that member states must allow Community nationals ('Union citizens') entry simply on production of such identity card or passport, and no entry visa requirement or similar may be imposed. Where a Union citizen or family member does not have the necessary travel documents, they must be given every opportunity to obtain them or have them brought before they are turned back at a border between member states (Article 5.4). On production of an identity document or passport and confirmation of employment a Community national must be issued with a residence permit (Article 8.3). The residence permit is proof of the existing entitlement to free movement rights, and so possession of such a permit cannot be required as a condition of exercising the rights (*Martinez Sala*). These provisions are implemented in the UK by reg 11 of the 2006 Regulations. There are also special provisions for temporary permits for seasonal workers, those on short-term temporary contracts, and frontier workers.

Member states must, 'acting in accordance with their laws', issue identity documents or passports to their own nationals (Article 4.3). A failure to issue a passport in the UK could be challenged as a breach of this Directive, which may only be permitted on the restricted grounds allowed by Article 27. This may be a more effective remedy than judicial review for an unreasonable exercise of the prerogative as in *R v Secretary of State for Foreign and Commonwealth Affairs ex p Everett* [1989] QB 811 though, unlike review of an exercise of the prerogative, it would be limited to the exercise of EU rights.

Having entered, any Union citizen and their family members have an initial right to reside for three months without any qualifying conditions (Article 6). After the first three months there is a further indefinite right of residence so long as qualifying conditions exist (Article 7). The conditions are that the person is a worker, self-employed, economically self-sufficient, a student with adequate sickness insurance, or the family member of any of these. How these conditions are met is discussed more fully below.

6.3.1.1 *Permanent residence*

Article 17(1)(b) of the Directive gives a right to remain to those who have ceased work through permanent incapacity, either through pensionable industrial disease or injury, or from having lived in the member state continuously for two years or more. This is implemented in the same terms in the UK Regulations, reg 5(3). Article 17(1)(a) gives the right to remain to workers who retire in a member state, having lived there for three years and worked there for one year, prior to retirement. Regulation 5(2) implements this in the UK. There is also a right of permanent residence for those who, after three years' continuous employment and residence in the host member state, obtain employment in another member state, but who return at least weekly to the first member state. Again this is implemented in the UK Regulations.

In addition to these particular situations, Article 16 gives a right of permanent residence to all Union citizens and their families after five years of continuous lawful residence. Provisions are made about breaks in continuity. There is an important and currently unresolved question concerning the interpretation of this right. There is a view that Article 16 refers to five years' residence in accordance with the Directive, in other words, exercising a right given by the Treaty or Directive for those five years.

This argument was made for the Secretary of State and accepted by the tribunal in *Chindamo v SSHD*. The tribunal drew on the preamble to the Directive, paragraph 17, which says that 'a right of permanent residence should be laid down for all Union citizens and their families who have resided in the host member state in compliance with the conditions laid down in this Directive'. The tribunal interpreted this to mean that the right to permanent residence which was given by the Directive must be in accordance with the Directive itself, and that the right was prospective, relying on residence accrued in accordance with a domestic legal provision implementing the Directive. In the UK, the 2006 Regulations (Sch 4 para 6) provide that residence under the 2000 Regulations counts as residence under the 2006 Regulations. This would mean that the UK Regulations were more generous than the Directive, allowing residence to be counted at the earliest from 2000, and thus operating retrospectively in the case of many EU citizens resident in the UK. This may still create difficulties in individual cases as *Chindamo* itself shows (discussed later).

A general difficulty is created in the case of this reading for Accession State nationals, who can only reside in accordance with the Directive from the dates that their home states acceded to the Treaty. The result of this is that the earliest date for A10 nationals to acquire permanent residence would be 1 May 2009, and for A2 nationals 1 January 2012. This view and its application to an Accession State national was confirmed by the tribunal in *GN* [2007] UKAIT 00073, in which a Hungarian student could not yet acquire permanent residence, despite having been in the UK since 1997, as Hungary did not accede to the EU until 2004. Although the tribunal accepted that GN had been residing lawfully in accordance with the 2000 Regulations, they rejected the appellant's argument that lawful residence in Article 16 referred to lawfulness within national law. It must refer to lawfulness within the Directive itself.

This reading of the Directive is implemented by UK Regulations which require residence 'in accordance with these Regulations' (reg 15(10(a)) but may not be correct in principle. It is strange that such a significant provision, substantially affecting rights, relies on a preamble rather than clear wording of the operative parts of the Directive. The view of the European Commission was given in a letter to Kingsley Napley solicitors dated 18 January 20007, disclosed in the *Chindamo* case:

'The Directive only requires for the acquisition of permanent residence that Union citizens have resided legally for a continuous period of five years in the host Member State. Since the Directive does not provide for the condition that the five-year residence has to be "on the basis of the

Directive" this notion should cover also those persons who have recently become Union citizens and have legally resided in the UK for five years. Otherwise such persons would have to wait for five years from the acquisition of citizenship of the Union which would be an additional condi-·tion not foreseen in the text'.

GN also relied on this letter, but to no avail.

The freedoms of the EC are generally to be construed broadly and not encumbered with unnecessary conditions and restrictions. This question awaits the decision of a higher court.

6.4 **Freedom of movement for workers**

Free movement of persons is set out in Article 3(c) EC Treaty as one of the four funda-mental freedoms of the EC. Consonant with the original purpose of the Treaty, the free movement of persons was linked to economic activity. However, even without consideration of Article 18, this is not limited to actually carrying out work, as the Community institutions, including the ECJ in interpreting Community law, take a liberal and purposive approach to the Community's legal provisions in order to make the free market effective. Case law and secondary legislation flesh out the content of the free movement right, but it begins with Article 39 (ex 48) of the EC Treaty, which reads as follows:

1. Freedom of movement of workers shall be secured within the Community.
2. Such freedom of movement shall entail the abolition of any discrimination based on nation-ality between workers of the Member States as regards employment, remuneration, and other conditions of work and employment.
3. It shall entail the right, subject to limitations justified on grounds of public policy, public security, or public health:
   (a) to accept offers of employment actually made;
   (b) to move freely within the territory of Member States for this purpose;
   (c) to stay in a Member State for the purpose of employment in accordance with the provi-sions governing the employment of nationals of that State laid down by law, regulation, or administrative action;
   (d) to remain in the territory of a Member State after having been employed in that State, subject to the conditions which shall be embodied in implementing regulations to be drawn up by the Commission.
4. The provisions of this Article shall not apply to employment in the public service.

Paragraph 1, setting out the objective of the Article, may be regarded as an agenda for the Court in its decisions and for the other Community bodies in making secondary legislation. Unlike UK legislation which usually prohibits a certain sort of activity, or sets out a power that may be exercised in defined circumstances, EC Treaty articles, which are the EC's primary legislation, are often phrased in terms of a purpose. The court's interpretive task is to promote that purpose within the framework of EC law.

In terms of achieving the purpose set out in para 1 of Article 39 (ex 48), the listed rights a, b, c, and d within para 3 may be regarded as the minimum content of the free-dom. Paragraph 2 expresses one of the key policies of the EU, the abolition of discrimi-nation based on nationality. Paragraph 4 on the other hand represents a concession to the sovereignty of states, permitting them, for national security or related purposes, to retain some posts specifically for their nationals. In a series of cases Article 39 has been held to be sufficiently clear, precise, and unconditional to be directly effective, see for instance Case 167/73 *Commission v French Republic* [1974] ECR 359. It may therefore be relied upon directly by a worker to protect their freedom of movement, which means it may be used as a basis for argument in national courts.

6.4.1 Personal scope – to whom Article 39 applies

The definition of who is a worker has been consistently held by the Court to be a matter of Community law, not domestic law, so member states cannot narrow the effect of Article 39 (ex 48) by using their own definition. In the Immigration (European Economic Area) Regulations 2006, SI 2006/003, reg 4(1), 'worker' means a worker within the meaning of Article 39 of the Treaty establishing the European Community.

6.4.1.1 *People in work*

The term 'worker' refers to someone who is or has been employed. The rights of self-employed people are dealt with separately by the provisions on the rights of establishment and provision of services. Case C-66/85 *Lawrie-Blum v Land Baden-Württemberg* [1986] ECR 2121 held that a worker in Community law was someone who, for a period of time, performs services under the direction of another in return for remuneration. In Case C-53/81 *Levin v Staatssecretaris van Justitie* [1982] ECR 1035 the ECJ considered whether there is a threshold of the amount of work that has to be done in order to qualify as a worker. A part-time worker had been refused a residence permit by the Dutch authorities on the grounds that she was not in gainful employment. The reason they gave was that she earned less than Dutch law regarded as a subsistence level of income, i.e. the minimum on which someone could live. The ECJ took account of the contribution low part-time wages can make to a family. The need to engage in such work was a real economic need. Concerning part-time work which paid less than subsistence wages, the ECJ said that it 'constitutes for a large number of persons an effective means of improving their living conditions'. Freedom of movement should not be restricted to full-time workers who were earning more than the minimum wage. However, there would have to be some lower limit on the amount of work which would qualify. The ECJ held that the Article guaranteed freedom of movement only for those 'who pursue or are desirous of pursuing an economic activity' and that that activity had to be 'genuine and effective'. It would exclude activities 'on such a small scale as to be marginal and ancillary'.

Case 139/85 *Kempf v Staatssecretaris van Justitie* [1986] ECR 1741 established that low paid work may be supplemented not only by the earnings of other family members, but also from other sources including public funds. In *Kempf* the applicant was a music teacher who taught 12 lessons per week and supplemented his income by a claim on public funds. The court held that:

It is irrelevant whether those supplementary means of subsistence are derived from property or from the employment of a member of his family, as was the case in *Levin*, or whether, as in this instance, they are obtained from financial assistance drawn from the public funds of the Member State in which he resides, provided that the effective and genuine nature of his work is established.

Remuneration is crucial to worker status, as found originally in *Lawrie-Blum*, however the remuneration need not be in the form of a wage. The economic nature of the work is

the key. In Case 344/87 *Bettray v Staatssecretarais van Justitite* [1989] ECR 1621 the applicant did not convince the ECJ that he was a worker as the work that he did was rehabili-
tative in purpose, and not economic. This was so even though he was paid a wage for
his work. The work was selected because of its suitability for him rather than he for the
work. However, in *Trojani v Centre public d'aide sociale de Bruxelles* Case C-456/02 the ECJ
held that a person who works for about 30 hours per week for a hostel under its direction, as part of a personal re-integration programme in return for benefits in kind and
in cash, could claim residence as a worker if the paid activity was real and genuine. It
would be for the national court to examine the facts to discover if this was the case.

The wage does not have to be the full rate for the job. In *Lawrie-Blum* the applicant
was regarded as a worker while working as trainee teacher. The wage was less than the
full rate for a qualified teacher but the court noted that a trainee was giving lessons to
pupils and thus providing a service of economic value to the school.

In Case 413/01 *Ninni-Orasche v Bundesminister für Wissenschaft, Verkehr und Kunst* the
ECJ held that the fact that the employment contract was for a fixed short term and
that she knew that in advance did not affect Ms Ninni-Orasche's claim to receive the
benefits of a worker. The question is an objective one as to whether the employment is
effective and genuine.

6.4.1.2 *People seeking work*

Article 39 itself does not mention people seeking work, but for the freedom of movement for workers to be fully meaningful it is necessary for that freedom to be extended
to those who have not yet secured a job offer in another European country but wish to
work there. The expectation that job-seekers will also benefit from freedom of movement provisions is implicit in Council regulation 1612/68 Article 5, which says:

A national of a Member State who seeks employment in the territory of another Member State
shall receive the same assistance there as that afforded by the employment offices in that State to
their own nationals seeking employment.

In Case 316/85 *Centre Public d'Aide Social de Courcelles v Lebon* [1987] ECR 2811 the ECJ
held that those who were seeking work should be entitled to equality of treatment
in access to employment under Article 39 and under Article 2 and 5 of Regulation
1612/68.

Case C-292/89 *R v Immigration Appeal Tribunal ex p Antonissen*, [1991] ECR I 745 considered more fully the position of unemployed job-seekers. Mr Antonissen, a Belgian
national, had entered the UK, but did not find work. The UK government proposed to
deport him following his conviction for drugs offences. Part of his challenge was to
the immigration rule then in force, para 143 of HC 169, which limited to six months
the stay of an EC national seeking work. The Court held that an EC national should be
allowed a reasonable period within which to become acquainted with the job opportunities available in the country to which they had moved, and that, in the context
of that case, six months was a reasonable period. However, at the end of that time the
person could still not be deported if they could show that they were genuinely seeking
work and had a chance of obtaining work. The UK 2006 Regulations expressly include
a job-seeker as a 'qualified person' i.e. a beneficiary of EC rights (reg 6).

In *Lebon* and *Antonissen* a job-seeker was not treated as a worker for all purposes. The
right to remain to seek work was simply a necessary corollary of Article 39, required to
give effect to the freedom of movement for workers, but not in itself giving entitlement

to all the rights which attach to a worker. In Case C-85/96 *Martinez Sala v Freistaat Bayern* [1998] ECR I 2691 the Court said that there was no single definition of 'worker' in Community law: 'it varies according to the area in which the definition is to be applied'. In the context of Article 39 (ex 48), 'a person who is genuinely seeking work must...be classified as a worker'.

6.4.1.3 *Unemployment after having been in work*

In the case of unemployment, as appears from *Antonissen* and *Martinez Sala* above, there is a distinction between retaining the status of worker in the context of social rights, and the status of worker giving a right to reside in a member state. The Citizens' Directive 2004/38 provides that the status of worker will be retained where s/he is temporarily unable to work because of illness or accident; s/he has been in employment for more than one year and is now involuntarily unemployed, registered and seeking work; s/he has been in employment for less than a year and is now involuntarily unemployed, though in this case the status may only be retained for a further six months, or s/he embarks on vocational training. If the unemployment was voluntary then the vocational training must be related to the previous employment (Directive 2004/38 Article 7(3)). This enacts the decision in Case C-39/86 *Lair v Universität Hannover* [1988] ECR 3161, and reg 6(2) of the UK Regulations implements these provisions precisely. The Citizens' Directive provides that where the worker becomes involuntarily unemployed during the first 12 months the status of worker is retained for a minimum of 6 months after that (Article 7(3)(c)). The UK Regulations implement this by requiring that after 6 months the worker retains the status if they can provide evidence of seeking employment in the UK and of a 'genuine chance of being engaged' (reg. 6(2)(b)(ii)). The Citizens' Directive protects a worker on the expiry of a short fixed-term contract, enacting an aspect of *Ninni-Orasche* (see 6.4.1.1 above). The UK Regulations make no such reference, but as the meaning of 'worker' in Article 39 is incorporated into the Regulations by reg. 4(1), the decision in *Ninni-Orasche* is also incorporated, and so a worker whose short fixed-term contract ends should still be regarded as a worker under reg. 6(2)(b).

In *RP (EEA Regs – worker – cessation)* [2006] UKAIT 00025 the appellant entered the UK in 1999, worked for four months, and was then unemployed for five years, except for one week in 2001. The tribunal held that he was a worker in 1999, and for some time thereafter. They were not convinced that he had been genuinely seeking work since then, and the week of employment in 2001 was 'marginal and ancillary'. Thus at some time before his application for an EEA residence document in 2004 he had lost he status of worker. He was thus no longer a qualified person under the EEA regulations.

6.4.2 **Material scope – the content of free movement rights for workers**

The underlying premise of European free movement law is that equality in conditions after arriving in another member state, such as rights to social benefits or access to employment, all support the freedom to move, though this book's focus on migration and constraints of space mean that the main emphasis is on rights of entry and residence.

To give a fuller picture we briefly touch here on some of the social rights. They derive from the Treaty's statement of principle and are expanded and interpreted in accordance with situations brought before the court, and new Directives.

Many employment contracts are of course with private employers. *Angonese v Cassa di Risparmio di Bolzano SpA* Case C-281/98 [2000] ECR I-4139 established beyond doubt that equality of treatment in Article 39 applies to collective agreements and contracts between individuals ('horizontal effect'). In that case the requirement to obtain a certificate of bilingualism issued only by the local authority in order to obtain employment at a bank was a discriminatory restriction contrary to the Article. The certificate would serve its purpose just as well if it was provided by a competent authority elsewhere.

6.4.2.1 *Entry and residence*

Article 39 (3) (ex 48(3)) provides the right to enter the territory of another member state and to reside there in order to take up an offer of employment. Directive 2004/38 ensures that there are not administrative obstacles to the exercise of this right, and the right of entry for workers is as described above for all Union citizens.

6.4.2.2 *Working conditions*

One of the fundamental principles of the Treaty is the abolition of discrimination between nationals of member states. Article 39(2) (ex 48(2)) requires the abolition of discrimination between workers of member states as regards 'employment, remuneration and other conditions of work and employment'. The provision has been held to apply to obvious working conditions such as the length and security of employment contracts, see for instance Case C-272/92 *Maria Chiara Spotti v Freistaat Bayern* [1993] ECR I-5185. It applies also to matters not within the direct province of the employer such as the refund of tax deductions. In Case C-175/88 *Biehl* [1990] ECR I-2779 these were held to be a matter affecting remuneration and so within the ambit of Article 39(2), even though the provision in question was a national tax rule rather than a condition of employment.

Regulation 1612/68 Article 7 which governs equality in relations to social and tax advantages may be interpreted to give effect to the right of non-discrimination in relation to working conditions. See for instance Case C-195/98 *Österreichischer Gewerschaftbund, Gewerkschaft Öffentlicher Dienst v Austria* [2000] ECR I-10497.

6.4.2.3 *Access to employment*

The most fundamental right relating to work is of course the opportunity to obtain a job in the first place. Article 39(3) (ex 48(3)) provides that the worker has the right to 'accept offers of employment actually made'. In addition to this, domestic legal systems must not put in place provisions which discriminate against other member state nationals in being able to obtain such an offer of employment (Article 39(2) (ex 48(2)). Regulation 1612/68 gives further effect to these Articles:

Any national of a Member State shall...have the right to take up an activity as an employed person, and to pursue such activity, within the territory of another Member State in accordance with the provisions laid down by law, regulation or administrative action governing the employment of nationals of that State. He shall, in particular, have the right to take up available employment in the territory of another Member State with the same priority as nationals of that State. (Article 1)

This prohibits indirectly discriminatory provisions i.e. those which apply both to foreign and home state nationals but which would deter other member state nationals, in addition to directly discriminatory provisions, i.e. those which discriminate between home and foreign workers. This is made explicit in Article 3 of the regulation which makes 'provisions laid down by law, regulation or administrative practices of a member state' of no effect if they

limit application for and offers of employment, or the right of foreign nationals to take up and pursue employment or subject these to conditions not applicable in respect of their own nationals; or
  though applicable irrespective of nationality, their exclusive or principal aim or effect is to keep nationals of other Member States away from the employment offered.

One of the best-known cases dealing with this principle, though in the application of Article 39 (ex 48) rather than the regulation, is the *Bosman* case from the world of football.

 Key Case

Case 415/93 *Union Royale Belge des Sociétés de Football Association v Bosman* [1995] ECR I-4921

Bosman was a goalkeeper with the Belgian team, RC Liege, who challenged the nationality rules which limited the number of foreign players a club could field in official matches. The ECJ ruled in his favour. The Court said that a limit on the matches in which a foreign player could appear obviously discouraged a club from employing them.

One of the arguments used by the Belgian Football Association was that the rules promoted cultural identity and thus were supported by Article 151(1) (ex 128(1)) which was one of the measures introduced by the TEU 'to contribute to the flowering of the cultures of the member states'. The TEU marked a move away from the strictly economic base of EC law and began the process of increasing the Community's competence in educational and cultural areas. The Court rejected this argument as applied to Bosman. It said that sport and culture should not be confused, and that the case concerned the freedom of professional sportspeople to move between member states. The *Bosman* decision was controversial, partly because it put players more in charge and partly because it meant that there was nothing to stop a football club from fielding a team which included no players from the home nation. UEFA has subsequently entered into an agreement to try to protect the number of locally trained players, but this agreement has also proved controversial. Intergovernmental discussions have not yet exempted sport from freedom of movement provisions, though the sporting bodies have promoted that view (see McAuley 2003). The Court has restated that sportspeople are protected by Article 39 (ex 48) in Case C-176/96 *Lehtonen v Federation Royale Belge des Societes de Basketball ASBL* [2001] 1 All ER (EC) 97, though accepting rules to ensure the regularity of sporting competitions, subject to a test of necessity.

  There are requirements for employment which may have a genuine cultural purpose which would be protected by the Treaty, even though they are discriminatory in their effect. One of the most obvious is language, and explicit provision is made for this in Article 3 of Regulation 1612/68. This article and its effect was considered in Case 379/87 *Groener v Minister for Education*. Groener was a Dutch national who had been working in Ireland as a part-time art teacher. After two years she applied for a full-time post and was recommended for the job. However, she was not appointed as she failed a test in Irish language. A level of Irish was required for all appointees even though the lessons would be given in English. Groener argued that as Irish would not be required for the lessons it could not be required, as provided in Article 3(1) of Reg 1612/68, 'by reason of the nature of the post to be filled'. However, the Court supported the lawfulness of the Irish government's policy which was that the use of Irish was being promoted in schools a means of expressing national culture and identity. The requirement was not disproportionate to this objective, and could be upheld within Article 3(1).

Even where a condition of employment explicitly or implicitly constitutes an obstacle to the free movement of workers, by for instance requiring prior experience in the host state, it may be lawful if it pursues a legitimate aim compatible with the Treaty, is justified by pressing reasons of public interest, and if application of the measure ensures achievement of that aim and does not go beyond what is necessary for that purpose. This has been illustrated in numerous cases in the ECJ, of which the following are but recent examples.

A preliminary ruling in Case C-40/05 *Kaj Lyyski v Umeå Universitet* concerned a scheme devised by the Swedish government to recruit and train people to remedy a shortage of qualified teachers. Requirements for entry to the scheme included that the candidates had to be employed in a Swedish school. This would discriminate against non-Swedish candidates. The ECJ accepted that the aim of the scheme was a legitimate one, and that it was more difficult to monitor practical training if it was taking place outside Sweden. However, as some colleges were exempting trainees from the practical part of the training, and as candidates could be allowed to carry out their training at a different school from the one where they were employed, it could not be said that current employment in a Swedish school was necessary to achieve the Swedish government's aim.

In *Kaj Lyyski* the employer imposed a requirement that indirectly affected applicants from other member states. In Case C-371/04 *Commission v Italy*, the member state directly refused to take into account experience gained in other member states when recruiting for the civil service, on the grounds that the recruitment process in other member states would be different from that in Italy. The ECJ held that this justification was insufficient. The aim of getting qualified people for the job was appropriate, but if someone was doing equivalent work in a different member state their experience was what counted and Italy could not discount that experience on the basis of how the person was employed.

6.4.2.4 *Social and tax advantages*

This provision of Article 7 of Reg 1612/68 is one of the major instruments in creating a legal basis for equality of social condition and opportunity. The social advantages covered by the Article are not confined to those arising from employment, as a result of Case 207/78 *Ministère Public v Even* [1979] ECR 2019. Even was a French national working in Belgium. He took early retirement, and his pension was reduced on the basis of the number of years early he had received the pension. This was the usual practice, but it did not apply to Belgian nationals who received a war service pension. Even received a French war service pension and so argued that his pension should not be subject to the early retirement reduction. Like nationality, war service is regarded as a quasi personal relationship between the individual and the State, and the Belgian provision was to give the country's own nationals 'an advantage by reason of the hardships suffered for that country'. Therefore, Mr Even lost his claim. However, the statement of principle made by the Court in the case has wider impact:

The advantages which this regulation extends to workers who are nationals of other Member States are all those which, whether or not linked to a contract of employment, are generally granted to national workers primarily because of their objective status as workers or by virtue of the mere fact of their residence on the national territory.

This principle has been built upon in succeeding cases. For example, Case 65/81 *Reina v Landeskreditbank Baden-Württemberg* [1982] ECR 33 demonstrates that this objective approach may prevent a national social policy from creating disadvantage for other member state nationals. In *Reina* an Italian couple living in Germany applied for a discretionary childbirth loan. The loan could only be granted where one member of the couple was German. It was means tested, and based on a policy of promoting population growth in Germany. The Landeskreditbank refused the Reinas' application, and defended their claim in the ECJ on the basis that the political objective meant that the loan was not a social right within the meaning of Article 7(2). The ECJ looked at the question from the point of view of the impact upon workers. The actual effect of denying the loan to non-German families was that families from other member states would be living with less material support than German families. This flew in the face of the purpose and the wording of Regulation 1612/68. Article 7(2) could include benefits granted on a discretionary basis, and the ECJ was not debarred from making decisions on social advantages which might have a political effect.

In Case 137/84 *Ministère Public v Mutsch* [1985] ECR 2681 the Court employed the *Even* formula to endorse the right of a Luxembourg national to use the German language in certain court proceedings, as Belgians were allowed to do. This social advantage had no connection with employment, and was unlikely to influence nationals of other member states in their desire or otherwise to travel to Belgium for work. However, the Court recognized that the ability to conduct court proceedings in their own language 'plays an important role in the integration of a migrant worker and his family into the host country, and thus in achieving the objective of free movement for workers'. It may be seen from this that the objective of the law relating to freedom of movement is not only to ensure equality in working conditions, but also to remove obstacles to the social integration of workers in pursuit of a vision of a European Community in which people are genuinely free to live wherever their occupation takes them.

The judgment in Case 249/83 *Hoeckx v Openbaar Centrum voor Maatschappelijk Welzijn Kalmthout* [1985] ECR 973 showed that Article 7(2) of Directive 1612/68 may be used to fill a gap left by another provision, in this case regulation 1408/71 on social security benefits. The minimum income allowance, the 'minimex' was granted to people who could show five years residence in Belgium, which the applicant could not as her residence in Belgium had been interspersed with periods in France. The Court found that the benefit was not one of those covered by Regulation 1408/71, but that it did constitute a social advantage in accordance with Article 7(2). Moreover, the residence condition discriminated against nationals of other member states in access to this social advantage. It did not apply to Belgian nationals, but even if did it would still be indirectly discriminatory as non-nationals would be less likely to be able to fulfil it.

6.4.2.5 *Social assistance*

However, Reg 1612/68 does not give open access for Union citizens to the welfare benefits systems of member states. Not all benefits of a host state are open to Union citizens who migrate there for work, and conversely migrants may, in moving, lose benefits that would have been payable in their home state. For full coverage of this subject reference should be made to EC law sources such as those listed at the end of this chapter. The following cases illustrate some of the main principles.

In *Lebon* the Court held that a work seeker did not qualify for equal social and tax advantages under Article 7 of Regulation 1612/68. The outcome was similar in *Collins* Case C-138/02 [2005] QB 145 although here the ECJ left open the possibility of a work seeker claiming social benefits. Mr Collins was in a similar position to Mr Antonissen, having come to the UK to seek work but not yet found it. Although he would have a right under Articles 1 to 6 of Reg 1612/68 to equal treatment in job opportunities, unlike Ms Martinez Sala, he had not made any economic contribution in the EU for 17 years. The Court held that his status as worker did not, for all purposes, remain intact for that period. It was relevant that his current search for work was unrelated to his casual employment 17 years earlier. He could not return to the UK and claim means-tested benefits. It was not irrational nor a breach of Article 39 for the UK to maintain a residence requirement, which he did not fulfil.

This is consistent on principle with the approach in Case C-184/99 *Grzelczyk v Centre Public D'Aide Sociale D'Ottignies-Louvain-La-Neuve* [2002] 1 CMLR 19 in which the denial of a student's claim for benefit was held to be discriminatory. The situation would have been different if he had arrived in Belgium and claimed straight away, but he was in his fourth year of study, had worked and supported himself so far, and thus had a claim to be accorded the benefits that a Belgian student would be able to obtain in this situation. This outcome resulted from weight placed on Article 18, and the Union citizen's right to reside in another state.

A number of cases on social security benefits concern frontier workers, that is people who work in one member state and are resident in another. In Case C-213/05 *Geven v Land Nordrhein-Westfalen* Ms Geven worked variable hours of between 3 and 14 hours per week in Germany, but lived in the Netherlands with her husband (who also worked in Germany) and her son. The ECJ upheld the refusal of the German child-raising allowance to Ms Geven, as it required a minimum of 15 hours' work per week. They accepted the German government's rationale for introducing the allowance: that it was to encourage the birth rate in Germany. Although Ms Geven's work was more than marginal and ancillary, so she was a worker for the purposes of Article 39, and although the child-raising allowance was a social advantage within Regulation 1612/68, the conditions for entitlement to it were rightly within the power of the member state, which had exercised them rationally in accordance with a legitimate policy. By way of contrast, on the same day (18 July 2007) the ECJ also decided Case C-212/05 *Hartmann v Freistaat Bayern*. Here again, a couple lived in Austria and one worked in Germany while the other cared for the child in Austria. Her claim for the child-raising allowance was endorsed by the court on the basis that the allowance was a social advantage acquired by her partner, and extended to her as a spouse. It looks as though Ms Geven's claim might have succeeded if she had claimed as her partner's dependant, but if so, this illustrates how EC law develops in accordance with principle, and the facts of each case extend or apply principle. The outcomes are not fact-dependent in quite the same way as UK case law.

In a different factual situation the ECJ held that the worker could claim a care allowance from the authorities in Austria, where he worked and paid taxes and national insurance. The care allowance was to support his disabled daughter who lived at home with him in Germany (Case C-286/03 *Hosse v Land Salzburg*). Entitlement may be lost to certain special non-contributory benefits relating to disability if the holder migrates to another member state. See for instance Case C-154/05 *J.J. Kersbergen-Lap, D. Dams-Schipper v Raad van Bestuur van het Uitvoeringsinstituut Werknemersverzekeringen*.

6.4.2.6 *Education*

Education is a social advantage which is the subject of specific provisions in secondary legislation. Article 7(3) of Regulation 1612/68 gives workers access to vocational schools and retraining on the same basis as national workers. As we have already seen, in the Citizens' Directive the status of worker is retained where training following work was either linked to the former occupation or was necessary re-training after the worker had become involuntarily unemployed.

The EC Treaty Articles 126 and 127 provide for the development of education and vocational training within the EU. Students have a specific right of residence for vocational education by virtue of Directive 2004/38 Article 7(1)(c) provided they can satisfy the relevant national authority: (a) that they have sufficient resources to avoid becoming a burden on the social assistance system of the host member state; (b) they are enrolled in a recognized educational establishment for the principal purpose of following a course of study and (c) they are covered by sickness insurance in respect of all risks in the host state. This does not give entitlement to the payment of maintenance grants by the host state (Article 24); however, *Grzelczyk*, above, established that social security payments may be available for students where they are to host state nationals.

By Article 12 of Reg 1612/68 children dependent on a worker have the same right of access to the education system of the host country as do nationals of that state.

6.5 Family members

The right to be accompanied by family members is one of the most significant and litigated rights accorded to workers, and we pay particular attention to it here because it generates migration rights for the families themselves. Directive 2004/38 replaces Reg 1612/68 in respect of family members' right of entry, residence and employment, and Articles 10 and 11 of the Regulation are accordingly repealed. Family members are 'qualifying persons' in the UK Regulations.

Rights are granted to members of Union citizens' families without reference to the nationality of those family members, and this is one of the ways in which a third country national may come directly within the ambit of EC law. As rights derive from the relationship with the Union citizen, the family member may be left vulnerable if that relationship is disrupted by for instance death, divorce or migration. The Citizens' Directive goes some way to enhance the rights of family members, though TCNs still have fewer rights than EEA nationals, and as we shall see, the UK Regulations may not fully implement the Directive.

6.5.1 Who is a family member?

Full rights under the 2004 Directive apply to the Union citizen's spouse, their registered partner if the *host* member state treats such partnerships as equivalent to marriage, children or grandchildren under 21, dependent children or grandchildren if over 21, parents or grandparents if they are dependent, in each case, on either partner. A registered partnership must be contracted in a member state. Prior to the Directive, the judgment in *Netherlands v Reed* [1986] ECR 1283 held that full rights applied to cohabitees to the extent that the host state treated such partnerships as equivalent to marriage, so the Directive is more limited in this respect. According to Article 3, member states must also facilitate the admission of other dependants of the Union citizen, including where health grounds strictly require personal care by them, and of an unregistered partner with whom the Union citizen has 'a durable relationship, duly attested'. This wider group of family members is called in the Directive 'beneficiaries'. In the UK regulations they are similarly defined, but called 'extended family members'.

In relation to all except partners and children under 21, rights only accrue where the family member is 'dependent' on the Union citizen. In Case 316/85 *Centre Public d'Aide Sociale de Courcelles v Lebon* [1987] ECR 2811, dependants were treated as those who were in actual fact dependent upon the worker. There was no need for an assessment of the reasons for the need for support, but simply of whether the worker is actually providing support for that person. In Case C-1/05 *Jia v Migrationsverket* the ECJ effectively endorsed more inquiry into the matter by holding that a family member was only dependent on a Community national if they *needed* the material support of the Community national to meet their essential needs in their State of origin. This test of necessity is closer to the UK's domestic immigration rules applying to dependent relatives, and is the current authority for interpretation of the Citizens' Directive.

Children are those who have been treated as children of the family, not only biological children. This is in keeping with the purpose of European secondary legislation and family life as defined by Article 8 of the European Convention on Human Rights, which takes account not only of biological relationships but also of the actuality of relationships. For instance in *Baumbast* the worker's stepchild benefited from Regulation 1612/68.

In Case C-370/90 *R v Immigration Appeal Tribunal and Surinder Singh ex p Secretary of State for the Home Department* [1992] ECR I-4265 a British national entered the UK with her Indian husband after they had both been living and working in Germany. If she had never left the UK she would have had to use UK law to bring her husband in. However, as she had exercised her Community right of freedom of movement by going to work in another EU country her husband had the right of entry with her under

Table 4 Family members of Union citizens

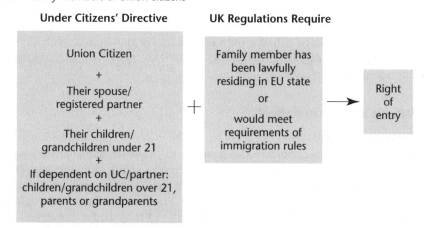

EU law. The general rule that an EU national who has lived and worked in another member state may rely on their EU right to be accompanied by their non-EU spouse when they return to their home country is known, following this case, as the rule in *Surinder Singh*. However, it is subject to qualification. In Case C-109/01 *SSHD v Akrich* the non-EEA spouse was the subject of a deportation order from the UK and as such had no right to reside in the UK. He and his British wife moved to Ireland and then sought to return to the UK some months later, claiming to exercise their Community rights. The ECJ held that in order to obtain a right of entry a non-EEA spouse must be lawfully resident in the country from which they move, though even in this situation the member state must have regard to the right to respect for family life under Article 8 ECHR when the couple seek to return. Mr Akrich could therefore not be refused entry without a proper consideration of the reasons for refusing him entry and the proportionality of so doing (see chapter 4). The court also held that the reasons for the couple's attempting to exercise treaty rights were irrelevant, providing the marriage was genuine.

On the other hand, in the UK tribunal, the UK national's exercise of her free movement rights without her spouse could not confer a right of residence on him. He had never left the UK since his illegal entry some 10 years earlier. The fact that his wife worked in Ireland for six months could not legitimize his stay. This was not the purpose of the right to be accompanied by one's spouse (*GC (China)* [2007] UKAIT 00056).

6.5.2 Family rights of entry and residence

Under Directive 2004/38 family members acquire rights in parallel with their Union citizen family member: to entry, to three months' residence without conditions (Article 6), to a longer period of residence while the Union citizen is a 'qualified person' i.e. a worker, self-employed, self-sufficient or a student (Article 7), and to permanent residence after five years' residence. Additionally the family member acquires rights to residence in the particular circumstances detailed below where their relationship with the Union citizen is severed. Exceptionally, family members may acquire rights to residence to make the right of the Union citizen effective (see discussion on *Chen* below).

The right to entry means that family members should be admitted on proof of their entitlement, i.e. of their identity and relationship. For third country nationals this includes a passport, though for EU nationals identity may be proved by a national identity card. The right of entry of a non-EU family member may be subject to a visa requirement, but it is disproportionate and therefore prohibited to send them back at the border for lack of a visa provided they are able to prove their identity and relationship and there is no evidence to suggest they present a risk to public policy, etc (Case C-459/99 *Mouvement Contre le Racisme, l'Antisemitisme et la Xenophobie Asbl (MRAX) v Belgium* [2002] 3 CMLR 25).

The UK Regulations on the issue of a family permit depart from the requirements of the Directive. Regulation 12 requires that the family member is either lawfully resident in another member state, or would meet the requirements of the UK immigration rules. This applies to all family members, whether a spouse, child, parent or other relative. This regulation relies on *Akrich*, in which the ECJ stated:

Regulation No 1612/68 covers only freedom of movement within the Community. It is silent as to the rights of a national of a non-Member State, who is the spouse of a citizen of the Union, in regard to access to the territory of the Community. (para 49)

The Citizens' Directive is similarly silent; however, the present position is governed by Case C-1/05 *Jia v Migrationsverket*, in which the ECJ has moved away from its statement in *Akrich*.

 Key Case

Case-C1/05 *Jia v Migrationsverket*

The family member was the Chinese mother-in-law of Ms Schallehn, who had German nationality and was self-employed in Sweden. Mrs Jia visited her son and daughter-in-law in Sweden and was in Sweden when she applied for a residence permit to remain there with them. The ECJ distinguished *Akrich*. The requirement that the TCN should be lawfully resident in the member state from which they sought to move could not be extended to Mrs Jia's situation where she was not coming from a member state at all. The ECJ held that 'Community law does not require member states to make the grant of a residence per-mits...subject to the condition that those family members have been residing lawfully in another member state' (para 33).

The UK Regulations would make Mrs Jia's initial entry subject to UK immigration con-trol because she was coming direct from China and not from another member state. The implication of *Jia*, even though the point does not directly arise, is that this would fall short of implementing the Citizens' Directive. The only requirement in the Directive is that the family member is 'joining or accompanying' the Union citizen (Article 7.1(d) and 7.2). There is no reference to where their journey began.

6.5.3 Extended family members

As mentioned above, the Directive provides that member states must facilitate the entry of extended family members in accordance with national law. These are defined to include:

- A partner in a provably durable relationship which has not been recognized in law.
- Another family member who is either dependent on the Union citizen, or lived as a member of their household, or 'on serious health grounds, strictly requires the personal care of the EEA national or their registered partner'.

The UK Regulations (reg 8) repeat this definition and add the category of a relative who would come within the UK's immigration rules for dependent family members. The UK Regulations implement the Directive by providing that extended family members *may* be issued with a family permit to join or accompany an EEA national if 'in all the circumstances, it appears to the ECO appropriate to issue' it. By comparison the ECO must issue a family permit for immediate family members.

The effect is that a married or registered civil partner may enter as of right, but an unregistered partner only does so as a discretion, subject also to application of *Netherlands v Reed*, above. Family members who would not come within the UK's immi-gration rules for dependent relatives (HC 395 para 317, see chapter 9), e.g. a cousin, would only be admitted on the ECO's discretion and if they had been dependent on

Table 5 Extended family members

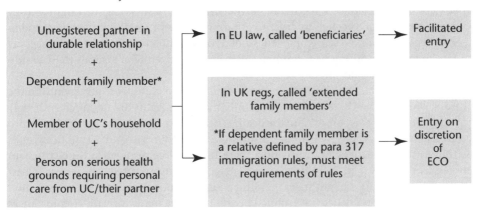

the Union citizen or a member of their household. Extended family members who *would* come within the UK's immigration rules (an adult sister, brother, uncle or aunt living alone in the most exceptional compassionate circumstances) are also subject to the discretion of the immigration officer. This also raises a question of priority between the parts of the Regulation. For instance, if an adult sister had been living with a couple who migrated to the UK using European free movement rights, would her claim to enter depend simply upon her having been a member of the Union citizen's household (reg 8(2)(a)) or upon meeting the immigration rules (reg 8(4))? In the latter case she would have to show she was (now) living alone in the most exceptional compassionate circumstances and was mainly financially dependent on the Union citizen.

The tribunal in *AK (Sri Lanka)* [2007] UKAIT 00074 relied on the requirement in Article 3.2 of the Citizens' Directive that the admission of extended family members be facilitated in accordance with national law. They held (upholding *AP and FP (Citizens' Directive Article 3(2); discretion; dependence) India* [2007] UKAIT 00048) that this referred to the substantive national law, and the facilitation was procedural, meaning that difficult hurdles should not be put in the way of such relatives. However, they rejected the argument for the appellant that as a relative who did not come within the terms of the Regulations (a cousin who had not been dependent on the Union citizen nor a member of her household) he gained a right of residence directly from the Directive. Article 3.2 did not, they thought, create rights of residence; it only defined who would benefit from the requirement to have their entry facilitated. Thus, the Secretary of State was permitted to apply the immigration rules, and a cousin's entry would be a matter of discretion.

6.5.4 Residence without the Union citizen

As mentioned earlier, family members may acquire or retain rights of residence in certain circumstances even if their relationship with the Union citizen comes to an end. In these cases there is an explicit difference in the Directive between family members who are not nationals of a member state and those who are. For family members who are nationals of a member state, their right of residence is not affected by the death or departure from the country of the Union citizen, nor by divorce, annulment of marriage or termination of registered partnership. This means that such right as they already have is not affected. In order to obtain permanent residence they must themselves become a worker, self-employed, student or self-sufficient, or once again become a family member joining or accompanying a Union citizen who satisfies these conditions (Articles 12.1 and 13.1).

Third country national family members are subject to additional requirements. In the case of death of the Union citizen the family member's rights are not affected if they lived as family for one year prior to the death. There is no provision for protecting a third country national where the Union citizen leaves the country. In the case of divorce, annulment and partnership termination, there are four circumstances in which the right of residence is retained: the marriage or registered partnership lasted three years, at least one of which was in the host state; the third country national has custody of the Union citizen's children; residence is warranted because of particularly difficult circumstances such as domestic violence; or the third country national partner has access rights to a minor child and the court has ruled that access must happen in the host state.

Third country national family members may only acquire permanent residence in these circumstances if they become workers, self-employed, self-sufficient or if they are members of a family 'already constituted in the host state' of a person who fulfils these conditions. This presumably means that a child of a marriage between a third country national and a Union citizen, who has not acquired an EU nationality, would acquire permanent residence after their parents' divorce if their TCN parent acquired it, say, by being a worker. However, if their TCN parent could not establish their own right to permanent residence, but remarried another EU national then the rights of both child and parent would depend on those of the new EU partner (Articles 12.2 and 13.2).

In the UK's 2006 Regulations, children at school of a qualified person (EU worker, self-employed, self-sufficient or student) who has died or left the UK retain rights of residence (reg. 10(3)) as do parents with custody of such a child (reg. 10(4)). Third country nationals retain residence under any of the conditions listed in the Directive for the ending of the relationship but only if they themselves are workers, self-employed or self-sufficient or they are still a family member of an EEA national in one of these categories (reg. 10(5)). This creates a substantial disadvantage for TCN family members in the Regulations as compared with the Directive. Additionally, if their EU partner dies they obtain a permanent right of residence if they lived with the qualified person immediately before their death and for the two years preceding, or the death was due to industrial accident or injury (reg. 15(e)). So, if a TCN spouse lived with their Community national spouse for two years and then that person dies, they acquire permanent residence. If a TCN spouse retains their right of residence due to having custody of a child and being self-employed, at the end of five years' residence (subject to points below) they acquire permanent residence.

A family member who retains the right to reside obtains permanent residence after five years' residence, as they would if their relationship had continued without disruption (reg. 15(1)(f)). The condition above concerning death of a partner under reg. 15(e) of the UK Regulations applies also to Community nationals. Strangely, no provision is made in the UK Regulations for EU national partners on the end of a relationship, except as the parents of children at school. They would of course have a right to work, and to acquire rights of residence as workers, and permanent residence after five years as a custodial parent or worker etc.

The failure in the UK Regulations to provide for the departure of the Union citizen is in line with court and tribunal decisions based on the earlier Regulations. In *Kungwegwe v SSHD* [2005] EWHC 1427 (Admin) Mrs Kungwengwe had lived lawfully in the UK from 1992 to 2004, and applied to be granted indefinite leave to remain in the UK on the basis of the long residence rules (see chapter 7), which required 10 years' lawful residence. Lawful residence was defined in the immigration rules as either exemption from immigration control or having leave to enter or remain. Mrs. Kungwengwe's marriage had broken down and her Portuguese husband's whereabouts were unknown. As she was unable to show that he was a qualifying person under the EEA Regulations she was unable to apply for indefinite leave to remain as his spouse. Wilkie J held that she was not lawfully resident for the purposes of the long residence rules as she was not exempt from immigration control, and did not have leave to enter or remain, because, as a holder of a residence permit and the spouse of an EEA national, she did not need it. In *DA (EEA – revocation of residence document)* [2006] UKAIT 00027 the tribunal held that where the EU spouse had left the UK the Secretary of State was entitled to revoke a residence document on the basis that the appellant was no longer the spouse of a qualifying person. This was because the qualifying person had ceased to qualify, having left the country. The 2006 Regulations make it clear that a residence document can be revoked where the holder has 'ceased to have a right to reside' under the Regulations.

The decision in Case C-267/83 *Diatta v Land Berlin* [1985] ECR 567 was that, while a couple are still married, the non-EU spouse retains their rights of residence whether or not they continue to live under the same roof. In the light of the UK Regulations it seems that this right is retained for an EU spouse, but only for a non-EU spouse if the Union citizen can be proved to be still exercising Treaty rights in the UK or if the relationship is legally ended and one of the conditions set out in reg. 10(5) applies.

6.5.5 *Chen* – the self-sufficient child

Case law has also developed a right to reside for TCN parents where their presence is necessary to give effect to the right of a Community national child, but this right is hedged about with many qualifications and conditions. In Case C-413/99 *Baumbast v SSHD* [2002] 3 CMLR 23, the court considered the situation of a German man who had been running a business in the UK, but when that failed, left his Colombian wife and children in the UK while he worked outside the EU. He considered the UK his family home. He was refused leave to remain in the UK on the basis that his German health insurance did not cover emergencies in the UK and that therefore he did not fulfil the requirements of Directive 90/364, the predecessor of Directive 2004/38 Article 7(1)(b). The ECJ held that the child of an EU national had a right to remain in education in the host state where their parents lived, and the fact that the EU national parent was now mainly working elsewhere would not affect that right. To hold otherwise would interfere with the mobility of workers within the EU. To make the child's right effective, Mrs Baumbast too must have a right to reside with the child. In addition, Article 18 confers directly effective rights of residence on all EU citizens. These may be curtailed, but only if conditions and restrictions are proportionate and authorized by Community law. Preventing Mr Baumbast from having a right to remain in the country where his wife and children lived, given that he supported them financially and there was nothing weighing against him apart from the terms of his health insurance, was strikingly disproportionate.

Zu and Chen v SSHD broke new ground in establishing the right to be accompanied by a parent.

Key Case

Zu and Chen v SSHD [2004] Imm AR 333

The claimants were a mother and her child. The mother and her husband were Chinese nationals who worked for a large chemical production company which exported to various parts of the world. In the course of the husband's work he frequently travelled to the EU including the UK. The couple wished to have a second child, which was against China's one child policy. They decided to have the child in Northern Ireland. The effect of Irish law at the time of *Chen* was that a child born on the island of Ireland acquired Irish nationality. The baby was an EU citizen and so had free movement rights within the EU. As she had adequate sickness insurance and sufficient resources, she had a right of residence for an indeterminate period of time under then Directive 90/36, now the Citizens' Directive (*Chen* para 78).

The mother and daughter sought to exercise this right in the UK. The mother was not the daughter's dependant, but she had a right to reside with the child in order to give effect to the child's right. The child was too young to live alone and her right of residence was otherwise meaningless. The conscious use by the couple of Community law was not an abuse because it did not distort the purpose and objectives of Community law, but rather 'took advantage of them by legitimate means to attain the objective which the Community provision sought to uphold; the child's right of residence' (para 122). This was so even though the necessary economic self-sufficiency derived entirely from the parents, the child being too young to provide this.

In the UK immigration rules, HC 395 paras 257C–E give effect to *Chen* by allowing a self-sufficient minor to live in the UK with their primary carer and other non-EEA national family members.

Following *Chen* a range of cases came to the tribunal and the Court of Appeal in which parents sought to establish a right to reside on the basis of *Chen*. The first distinction that became clear very quickly was that the judgment in *Chen* did not permit families to remain in the UK if they relied on benefits. In *RI* [2005] UKAIT 00125 the child's Ugandan mother could not establish a right to remain in the UK on the basis of her baby's Italian nationality as they were dependent on benefits. The baby's parents were not married, and so the father did not qualify as a family member under the EEA regulations. This is confirmed in the immigration rules defining a self-sufficient child.

More controversially, there is the question of whether the child's economic support may come from the parent's employment in the host member state. The Chens had sufficient income from their family business based in China, so the question did not arise for them. The UK immigration rules prevent the family income from coming from employment, whether or not the employment is lawful. This has also been the approach in the tribunal, confirmed in the Court of Appeal in *W (China) and X (China) v SSHD* [2006] EWCA Civ 1494, and arguments more fully explored in *ER and others (Ireland)* [2006] UKAIT 00096. In *W and X* the parents entered the UK illegally and made asylum claims that were rejected. They had no right to work, and their actual earnings from illegal working would be discounted as a resource for the child. In *ER* the mother was working legally on a work permit when the child was born. For her it was argued that this meant that she became an EU worker when her child with an EU nationality was born, and thus she had a right to work, so her work permit should have been renewed (which it was not) and her child had a right to reside which he was entitled to have supported by her work. The tribunal rejected this argument as circular. The rule on which *Chen* relies is that the child is already self-sufficient from resources that do not derive from the host country. That is the source of their EU right to reside (now in the Citizens' Directive Article 7). Then, in order to make that right effective, the parent is entitled to reside with them as a family member, not because they are providing the money, but because the child physically needs their care. *Chen* therefore does not support an argument that an EU national child can derive their support from their parent's paid work in the host state, even, on the current state of the case law, if that work is lawful. The clear result is that an EU national child may not live in the EU if their parents are not EU nationals unless the parents have sufficient wealth that originates outside the EU.

Even where one parent is an EU national, if they do not provide the financial support then the child will not have an independent right of residence. This, of course, would rarely arise as generally the EU parent will be present in the host state with the child and the child is then their dependant rather than having to establish an independent right. The question did arise, however, in *GM & AM (EU national establishing self-sufficiency)* [2006] UKAIT 00059. The couple met in the Republic of Congo, he being Congolese and she a French national. They had two children who were French nationals. When the child who was the appellant in this case was two and a half, her mother moved to France. Over a year later her father (the second appellant in this case) came to the UK and claimed asylum. The first appellant's mother then arranged for her to come to the UK to join her father. His asylum claim failed and he was prevented in UK law from working, although he had a genuine job offer. The appellants applied for residence documents on the basis of the daughter's EC right of freedom of movement, and that she would be self-sufficient if her father was allowed to work, which he would be as the family member of an EU national.

The circularity is apparent in the last sentence, and the claim failed, in part on similar reasoning to that in *W & X* (though predating it). Consider, however, if GM's mother had also moved to the UK and exercised her right as a French national to work, how different GM and AM's situation would have been. The right of residence of Union citizens contained in Article 18 was argued on the child's behalf, but the tribunal held, following *Ali v SSHD* [2006] EWCA Civ 484, that the Article 18 right of residence was subject to the conditions laid down in secondary legislation. As GM was not self-sufficient, Article 18 did not give a free-standing right that could be exercised over and above the requirement of self-sufficiency.

In *Ali v SSHD* [2006] EWCA Civ 484, Mr Ali, a Somali national whose asylum claim had failed, argued that he had an EU right of residence as one of his children was a Dutch national. It was not accepted either that he was married to the child's mother or that she was an EU worker as she could not be proved to have sought work or been in employment. The Court of Appeal rejected the contention that the child had a right of residence. He did not have the financial resources to be regarded as self-sufficient and Article 18 did not provide a freestanding right of residence over and above that, even to enable him to go to school. Compare *Baumbast* where the EU parent's status as a worker then gave the child a right to attend school even when the parent was absent.

6.5.6 **Article 18**

Arguments that Article 18 provides an independent right of residence have been unsuccessful. In *Chen* itself, the ECJ held that a child had a right to reside under Article 18 which she could exercise because she was economically self-sufficient, as required by secondary legislation. If she had not been able to fulfil the requirements of secondary legislation, Article 18 itself would not have provided an independent right. The Court treats Article 18 as something which implies a stronger interpretation of other rights; it indicates the direction in which interpretation should go where possible. In *GM & AM* the argument under Article 18 was rejected, and the tribunal rejected the idea that Article 18 itself should be widely construed and derogations from it narrowly construed, a principle that would be incontrovertible in the application of Treaty articles granting specific free movement rights. In fact, the tribunal went the opposite way, and held that, because GM could not bring herself within a narrow definition of self-sufficiency and thus within the secondary legislation, she could not benefit from Article 18. On the other hand, in Case C-408/03 *Commission v Belgium* ECR [2006] I-02647 the ECJ held that the state should take account of the income of a partner in determining self-sufficiency and not to do so was a breach of Article 18. Although the partner had no legal tie to the Union citizen, if the resources failed then they could be asked to leave. Refusing to recognize the financial contribution made by a partner was disproportionate.

6.5.7 **Article 8 ECHR**

In the cases above the whereabouts and activities of the Union citizen parent were crucial in practice to the European child's exercise of their rights.

In Case C-60/00 *Carpenter v SSHD*, however, the Union citizens' absences and the derivative nature of the family members' rights worked in their favour. Mr Carpenter was a UK national living in the UK from where he ran a business which involved a significant amount of travel to other member states, where most of his clients were based. Mrs Carpenter was a Philippine national who had overstayed her visitor's visa and married Mr Carpenter. She was refused leave to remain in the UK because of her irregular immigration status at the time of her marriage. She challenged the decision that she should return to the Philippines to apply for entry clearance and a residence permit on the basis that she had Community law rights. The fundamental question in the case is whether Community law rights were engaged at all. The ECJ concluded that they were. Mr Carpenter was exercising his rights under Article 49 (ex 59) to provide services in another member state. His capacity to do this was hindered if his wife had to return to the Philippines and so could not look after the children during his absences, and if she could not travel freely with him because she would not gain re-entry to the UK.

The ECJ placed great emphasis on the infringement of Article 8 ECHR which was entailed by separating Mr and Mrs Carpenter. Deportation was disproportionate as although she had infringed immigration law there was no other complaint against her. Therefore, Mr Carpenter's Article 49 rights were infringed by requiring his wife to leave the country. It may be seen here that Mrs Carpenter could have established no independent right to stay in the UK either under EU or national law. Her right derived from the nature of her husband's business.

6.5.8 Social and tax advantages

Citizens' Directive Article 24 provides that family members who obtain a right to remain are entitled to equality of treatment. An illustration of equal treatment in relation to social advantages is found in the case of Case 32/75 *Fiorini v SCNF*. Here an Italian woman and her children were resident in France. She was the widow of an Italian man who had worked in France and died in an industrial accident. During his life he had been entitled to a fare reduction card for large families, but when she claimed this after his death it was refused on the grounds that she was not French. She claimed discrimination in breach of what was then Article 7 of the EEC Treaty, now Article 12 (ex 6) and of Article 7(2) Reg 1612/68. This case predated *Even*, but the ECJ still took the view that the social advantages referred to in Article 7(2) did not have to arise from a contract of employment. The Article was intended to refer to all social and tax advantages. As the family had a right to remain in France after Mr Fiorini's death, pursuant to Regulation 1251/70, they also had a right to equal treatment in relation to these social advantages. Combining the effects of Article of Reg 1251/70 and Article 7(2) of Reg 1612/68 they were entitled to the fare reduction card as would be any French family in a comparable situation.

An important right for families established in Reg 1612/68 Article 11 and continued in Directive 2004/38 Article 23 is to 'take up any activity as an employed person throughout the territory of that same state'. Case C-10/05 *Mattern and Cikotic v Minstre du Travail at de l'Emploi* [2006] ECR I-03145 emphasised that the spouse's right to work is to work in the host state, not another member state. If the worker moves to another member state (unless for a short temporary period), the right of a third country national partner to remain in their job depends on Article 12, discussed above. An EU partner however would have the status of worker in their own right, providing they are engaging or can engage in meaningful economic activity.

As mentioned earlier, the worker's children's right to education is the same as that of host state nationals, and continues after their parent has ceased work. Entitlement to educational grants is now dealt with in the Citizens' Directive Article 24.2, and benefits families of workers, the self-employed and those with permanent residence.

6.5.9 Marriages of convenience

A spouse is held not to qualify as a spouse for the purpose of the Treaty or secondary legislation if the marriage is one of convenience. The ECJ judgment in *Akrich* is authority that the rights of family members do not apply where the marriage is one of convenience. By a non-binding resolution of 4 December 1997, the European Council defines a marriage of convenience as one entered into between an EU national or legally resident third country national and a third country national 'with the sole aim of circumventing the rules on entry and residence'. This is a much more stringent test than the old primary purpose rule in UK law. Evasion must be the *sole* aim of the marriage, rather than one motive among many. The resolution sets out a list of factors which may provide grounds for believing that the marriage is one of convenience. They include for instance that the parties do not live together after the marriage, that they do not speak a language understood by both, and they are inconsistent about details such as each other's nationality and job. These provisions are directed at obvious subversion of the rules, are more objective, and have not given rise to the invasions of privacy and voluminous case law that have accompanied national marriage rules.

6.6 Internal effect

In a number of cases applicants have sought to use rights granted by European law in situations which have not involved the crossing of national borders. The ECJ has held that these situations must be regarded as internal to member states and thus not involving freedom of movement. The doctrine of internal effect began with Case C-175/78 *R v Saunders* [1979] ECR 1129. Ms Saunders was a British national from Northern Ireland who was convicted of an offence in England and bound over to return to Northern Ireland and keep out of England and Wales for three years. The ECJ declined to interfere with this. They took the position that the state was entitled to impose restrictions within the member state upon its own nationals where this was done in the course of criminal law. This kind of restriction had no European law dimension, and the Court had no mandate to interfere.

A number of commentators have suggested that if borders within the EU are to be removed, the requirement of movement across borders in order to trigger family reunion rights is artificial. The artificiality was recognized by the Commission in early drafts of the Family Reunion Directive in proposing that discrimination between EU nationals who exercise their right of freedom of movement and those who do not should be abolished in respect of family reunion. This proposal did not survive to the final version of the directive, and discussions on the subject were finally abandoned and the Commission proposal withdrawn (COM (2004) 542 final 3). In *Carpenter v SSHD*, discussed above, the Court was invited by the UK government to find that the situation was purely internal as Mrs Carpenter did not cross EU borders. However they declined to do so. Likewise in *Surinder Singh*, the ECJ was invited to find that this was an internal situation – a national enforcing a Treaty right against her own government. However, the ECJ pointed out that EU nationals might be deterred from exercising their Treaty rights if they could not freely return to their home state with their spouses. Mrs Singh had exercised a Treaty right by working in Germany and so benefited from the rights accorded to an EU worker. Also in *Chen* the ECJ rejected the argument that the situation was purely internal. The fact that the child had not made use of freedom of movement did not, the court thought, make the situation entirely an internal one. Although she was exercising her right to live in the member state in which she was born (the UK), she was doing so as an Irish national.

6.7 Public service exceptions

The EC Treaty recognizes that some kinds of work may require a particular affiliation to the State, and where this is the case it may be legitimate for the state to restrict work to its own nationals. Accordingly, Article 39 (ex 48) includes an exception which provides that those who are employed in public service are exempt from the other provisions of the Article. This gives the state the right to discriminate on the basis of nationality in opportunities to be admitted to public service.

The question of what kind of work counts as public service is one of those issues, like the definition of a worker, which the ECJ regards as a matter of Community law, and thus within its provenance to determine. The definitions of member states will not be conclusive as this would give them power to define the terms of their own exemption, which would not be appropriate. Two approaches to the question have been identified, the 'institutional approach' and the 'functional approach'. The institutional approach would say that because a person is employed by a particular body, say, a national railway, this employment is defined as employment in the public service. The functional approach would look at what is entailed in the work and determine whether this should qualify as public service. The ECJ tends to prefer the latter approach, while member states have attempted to argue for the former.

In Case 149/79 *Commission v Belgium* the Court set out some characteristics which could bring employment within the definition of public service. First, the post presumes on the part of the employee and employer a 'special relationship of allegiance to the State.' Second, there is a reciprocity of rights and duties which form the foundation of the bond of nationality. Third, the post must involve the exercise of powers conferred by public law and duties designed to safeguard the general interests of the state.

The Commission has published guidance which suggests when the exception might apply. It includes certain functions within the armed services, police, judiciary, tax authorities, and certain public bodies engaged in preparing or mounting legal actions. It would generally not include nursing, teaching, and non-military research (1988 OJ C 72/2). This guidance is not legally binding.

When a non-national is actually employed in public service, the Article 39(4) exception cannot be used to treat them less favourably than national workers. The exemption allows states to restrict employment to their own nationals where special duties or allegiance are required, it does not give them freedom to discriminate against non-nationals where there are no such objections to employing them. This was illustrated in Case 195/98 *Österreicher Gewerkschaftbund, Gewerkschaft Öffentlicher Dienst v Austria* [2000] ECR I-10497. The case concerned the union's challenge to the practice of discounting periods of service spent in other member states when reckoning periods of service for the purposes of pay and promotion. Part of the government's defence was that the employment of teachers was employment in the public service and therefore exempt under Article 39(4). This argument was doomed as it was already settled law that teachers were not covered by the public service exception, but the court held in addition that non-recognition of earlier periods of service was not a matter connected with access to employment but to conditions of employment once in post. For this reason also the government could not claim the exemption under Article 39(4).

The exception in Articles 45 (ex 55) and 55 (ex 66) takes effect in relation to 'activities which in that state are connected, even occasionally, with the exercise of official authority'. In Case 2/74 *Reyners v Belgium* [1974] ECR 631 a Dutch lawyer had obtained his legal education in Belgium, but was refused admission to the Belgian bar on the grounds that he was not of Belgian nationality. The Court said that the extension of the exception to the whole profession was not permissible where activities connected with the exercise of official authority were separable from professional activity as a whole. The exercise of official authority in the legal profession was the exercise of judicial authority by judges, and not contact with the courts by advocates.

6.8 **Public policy exceptions**

The public policy exception to the freedoms we have been considering is the only basis for deportation of an EEA national, and should be compared with grounds for other foreign nationals, discussed in chapter 16. Substantial differences will be seen as the deportation of a European national is in every case an interference with their Treaty right to freedom of movement. Any ECHR rights are additional to this. Freedom of movement may be curtailed by refusal of entry or deportation on grounds of public policy, public security, or public health, known collectively as the 'public policy exception'. Directive 2004/38 replaces Directive 64/221 in implementing this exception, and enhances protection for the individual, as we shall see.

6.8.1 **Public health**

This may be dealt with briefly. Article 29 of the Directive says:

1. The only diseases justifying measures restricting freedom of movement shall be [those] with epidemic potential as defined by...the World Health Organisation and other infectious or contagious parasitic diseases if they are the subject of protective provisions applying to nationals of the host Member State.

2. Diseases occurring after three months from the date of arrival shall not constitute grounds for expulsion from the territory.

Article 29.1 represents a tighter policy than its predecessor, as Directive 64/221 listed specific diseases in addition to those listed by the World Health Organisation. Article 29.2 allows for some possibility of expulsion as opposed to refusal of entry; Directive 64/221 did not.

Medical examinations may only be required 'where there are serious indications that it is necessary' within the first three months after arrival. By way of comparison, UK immigration law may require a medical examination of any applicant for settlement.

6.8.2 **Public policy**

This is the more contentious and frequently used ground. It encompasses public security, which is not treated as a separate ground. There is no definition of public policy in the Directive or by the ECJ, but the court interprets the Directive restrictively in order not to interfere with the purposes of the Treaty.

Article 27.2 of the Directive provides:

Measures taken on grounds of public policy or public security shall comply with the principle of proportionality and shall be based exclusively on the personal conduct of the individual concerned. Previous criminal convictions shall not in themselves constitute grounds for the taking of such measures.

The requirement for proportionality is new in the 2004 Directive, the other wording being identical in the earlier Directive.

The first of the issues in Article 27.2, that of personal conduct, has been important in many cases. The requirement has been elaborated in uncompromising terms in the 2004 Directive, as follows:

The personal conduct of the individual concerned must represent a genuine, present and sufficiently serious threat affecting one of the fundamental interests of society. Justifications that are isolated from the particulars of the case or that rely on considerations of general prevention shall not be accepted.

To appreciate the radical nature of this paragraph comparison needs to be made with grounds for UK deportations discussed in chapter 16, where it will be seen that a general policy of deterrence is often accepted by the courts as justifying an individual deportation. This new element in Article 27.2 reinforces the social objectives of free movement law, showing that the power of the state in relation to the individual EU national is curbed by the Community.

Accordingly, it is clear if it was ever in doubt that one of the earliest and foundational decisions on the application of the public policy exception, would not be decided the same way today. Case 41/74 *Van Duyn v Home Office* [1974] ECR 1337, concerned whether association with an organization could amount to personal conduct. Ms Van Duyn was a member of the Church of Scientology and was refused leave to enter the UK to work for the Church because the UK government considered its activities to be socially harmful. The ECJ concluded that a decision of this kind was within the permissible range of discretion for a member state, and this was the case even if (as was the case here) the organization had not been made unlawful in that member state, and its nationals could participate in it without legal sanction. It would be an undesirable distortion of social policy to require a government to outlaw an activity so that it could prevent people from entering the country to take part in it. The Court would however expect to see some administrative measure taken against the activity. In the *Van Duyn* case a statement in Parliament sufficed for that. Arnull (1999) suggests that the political background of Britain's renegotiation of its terms of European membership may have encouraged the ECJ to be lenient to the UK in this case.

The judgment in *Adoui and Cornouaille* referred to above takes a different approach, and suggests a more likely approach if *Van Duyn* were heard again today. The ECJ would be concerned to see that effective measures were taken against nationals who engaged in the activity in question before regarding it as a suitable basis for excluding a non-national. In *Adoui and Cornouaille* the Belgian authorities were not permitted by the ECJ to derogate on grounds of public policy from the obligation to issue prostitutes with residence permits. Prostitution was not illegal in Belgium and there was not a strong enough policy reason to prevent non-nationals from engaging in an activity that was not prohibited for nationals.

EU nationals should not be deported as a sanction for administrative lapses or irregularities. In Case C-215/03 *Oulane* it was disproportionate to detain and deport a French national who did not produce proof of identity on two occasions when requested.

6.8.2.1 *Criminal convictions*

The most common basis for derogation on grounds of public policy is criminal conduct. The ECJ has reinforced on a number of occasions that previous convictions do not in themselves constitute grounds for exclusion or expulsion, although such convictions may be taken into account in determining whether someone should be deported on the grounds of public policy. The proper approach is identified in the leading case of *R v Bouchereau* Case 30/77 [1977] ECR 1999. Here the defendant, a French national working in the UK, was convicted for a second time of unlawful possession of drugs. The sentencing court wished to recommend that he be deported. Two questions were referred to the ECJ. First, was the recommendation for deportation a 'measure' in the terms of Directive 64/221 Article 3(1) ('measures taken on grounds of public policy or public security shall be based exclusively on the personal conduct of the individual concerned'). Second, if it was, in what circumstances could criminal convictions be taken into account in deciding to recommend deportation?

On the first question, the Court ruled that a recommendation for deportation was a 'measure' within Article 3. On the second, the Court ruled that 'the existence of previous criminal convictions can only be taken into account in so far as the circumstances which gave rise to that conviction are evidence of personal conduct constituting a present threat to the requirements of public policy'. Elaborating, the Court went on, 'recourse...to the concept of public policy presupposes...a genuine and sufficiently serious threat to the requirements of public policy affecting one of the fundamental interests of society'. However the court also issued a caveat that in sufficiently serious cases conduct alone would warrant deportation. Directive 2004/38 adopts these words from *Bouchereau*.

By way of illustration, the personal conduct of the applicant in Case 67/74 *Bonsignore v Oberstadtdirektor der Stadt Köln* [1975] ECR 297 could not be said to pose any threat to public policy affecting one of the fundamental interests of society. He was an Italian worker resident in Germany who purchased a gun. While he was handling the gun it went off and killed his younger brother. The incident was a tragic accident, and there was no reason to deprive Mr Bonsignore of his German residence on the grounds of public policy.

This requirement for exclusion to be based solely on the conduct of the individual leaves no scope for automatic expulsion connected to the commission of criminal offences. This must mean, as Macdonald suggests, that para 320(18) of the Immigration Rules HC 395 cannot be applied to EEA nationals as it provides that entry clearance or leave to enter the UK should normally be refused where the applicant has committed an offence punishable in the UK with imprisonment of 12 months or more. UK Borders Act 2007 ss 32–39, which introduce compulsory deportation for certain criminal convictions (see chapter 16), contain an exception for those protected by EC law so that deportation will not be automatic. However, this could not be otherwise. Legislation which made it 'possible to expel...citizens of the Union who have been convicted of an offence, without regard to the substantive and procedural safeguards provided by Directive 64/221' was held to be in violation of that Directive by the ECJ in *Commission v Netherlands* Case C-50/06. The wording of Directive 2004/38 is more explicit. This should mean that cases such as the challenge to the Netherlands and that of Case C-348/96 *Donatella Calfa* [1999] ECR I-0011 should no longer need to come before the ECJ. Here an Italian national was excluded from Greece under a rule which provided for exclusion in the case of certain offences. This rule was not based on the conduct of the individual as it was applied simply on the basis of the conviction.

6.8.2.2 *Weighing up the conduct*

We can usefully compare the EC public policy proviso with the UK law concept of a deportation being 'conducive to the public good'. Theoretically, the emphasis in both is not on what the individual has done in the past but on the effect on society of their continued presence. However, the Court of Appeal in *R v IAT ex p Al-Sabah* [1992] Imm AR 223 rejected an attempt to apply the European approach more widely than EEA nationals. The European law standard makes more demands on the state than the UK law standard, as the state's argument must be sufficient to outweigh the right of freedom of movement, within a system in which this freedom is the primary purpose, and the Court has repeatedly stated that this power of derogation must be interpreted restrictively.

In UK courts and tribunals the caveat in *Bouchereau*, permitting deportation when past conduct is sufficiently serious, has been applied in offences involving Class A drugs, for instance the case of *Marchon* [1993] Imm AR 384 in which a Portuguese doctor had been convicted of importing 4.5 kilos of heroin. The Court of Appeal found that this conduct by a doctor showed a disregard for the fundamental moral tenets of society. As such it would justify deportation following *Bouchereau* without any evidence of a likelihood of re-offending. This view has been regarded as 'unsound as a matter of Community law' by the tribunal in *MG and VC (EEA Regulations 2006; 'conducive' deportation; Ireland)* [2006] UKAIT 00053.

In cases where the proposed deportee has a family or private life in the UK, the disruption to this must be proportionate to the public interest pursued in accordance with Article 8 ECHR.

Judicial consideration of the deportation of the partner of an EU national may be found in *Machado v SSHD* [2005] EWCA Civ 597 where the Court of Appeal said that the tribunal's obligation was to stand back from the evidence and address the legal questions: 'does the appellant's conduct manifest a real and sufficiently serious threat to a fundamental interest of society, and if it does is it proportionate in all the circumstances to deport him?' His immigration history could come into the consideration of whether it was proportionate to deport him as it could be relevant to whether he would be likely to respect the law, and thus part of whether his presence presented a danger to public policy. Mr Machado married after a notice of intention to remove was served upon him, and his wife then took advantage of her entitlement to Irish nationality, thereby introducing EU rights. Following *Akrich*, his EC rights were valid in law, even if they had been obtained in order to rely upon them, and the Home Office dropped its contention that the marriage was one of convenience.

Directive 2004/38 Article 28 sets out counterbalancing personal factors which should always be considered. Equivalent to the widest possible interpretation of Article 8 ECHR, these include 'social and cultural integration into the host member state'.

6.8.2.3 *Protection for long-term residents*

Directive 2004/38 introduces new protections against expulsion where the individual has long residence in the host state. This means that there are now three tiers of protection against expulsion decisions, as follows:

- A decision against any Union citizen or their family member, only on grounds of public policy, public health or public security. Considerations as discussed above (Article 27.1).

- An expulsion decision against a Union citizen or their family member who has the right of permanent residence may only be taken on 'serious grounds of public policy or public security' (Article 28.2).

- An expulsion decision against a Union citizen who has resided for 10 years may only be taken on 'imperative grounds of public security' (Article 28.3(a)).

- An expulsion decision against a minor, unless expulsion is necessary for the best interests of the child, also may only be taken on 'imperative grounds of public security' (Article 28.3(b)).

It is clear that expelling an EU national is intended to be a rarity.

'Imperative grounds of public security' were interpreted in *MG and VC* [2006] UKAIT 00053 to mean something more than 'the ordinary risk to society arising from the commission of further offences by a convicted criminal' (para 34). The Home Office representative suggested that what was intended was the commission or suspicion of terrorist offences, but this, and its relationship with the widely defined terrorist offences in UK law, is yet to be tested.

The acquisition of enhanced protection against deportation was considered in *Chindamo v SSHD* Appeal no. IA/13107/2006. The tribunal's decision makes findings not only about the merits of the deportation decision, but also about the kinds of residence required to attain the protection of paragraphs 2 and 3 of Article 28.

Mr Chindamo had been in the UK since 1987, when he was aged six. In 1995 he killed headteacher Philip Lawrence, and was convicted of murder. He was sentenced to imprisonment, and due for release in January 2008. The Secretary of State proposed to deport him. As a Union citizen he could only be deported for public policy reasons, and automatically had the procedural and substantive protections associated with a deportation under Article 27.1. However, as he had lived in the UK since he was six years old, would he be able to benefit from additional protection through five or 10 years' residence?

To benefit from Article 28.2, he needed to establish that he had a right to permanent residence. It was argued for him that Article 16 which gives the right of permanent residence requires no more than five years' continuous lawful residence. However, as discussed at 6.3.1.1 above, the tribunal interpreted this to mean that only residence in accordance with the Directive itself would give the right to permanent residence. Residence under the 2000 Regulations counts towards residence under the 2006 Regulations (2006 Regs Sch 4 para 6). The tribunal held that this meant that residence from 2000 onwards counted towards the right to permanent residence. Mr Chindamo's right under the Directive to reside in the UK was as a family member, initially a child under 21. In August 2001 he became 21. As he was then in prison he could not be said to be in actual fact (*Lebon*) a dependant of his mother and so he was no longer residing in accordance with the Directive. Therefore, he had only resided for 20 months after 2000 in accordance with the Directive. Thus he had not acquired the right to permanent residence.

Chindamo Timeline

Illustrating tribunal's interpretation of Citizens' Directive and regulations on residence and deportation

1980 Learco Chindamo born in Italy

1987 Came to UK with his mother. As an EEA national she had right of entry, and he also as her child

1995 With a gang killed Philip Lawrence

1996 Imprisoned

2000 EEA Regulations came into force. Chindamo's residence then is by virtue of being a family member of a Union citizen – a child under 21

2001 Chindamo turned 21 years. Loses his right of residence under EEA Regulations as he is in prison and so not dependent on his mother (an alternative basis for the right of a family member over 21)

2006 Directive 2004/38 and UK 2006 Regulations come into force. Retrospectively, time from 2000 residing according to Directive could count towards five years' residence giving him greater protection against deportation

2007 Decision to deport him, and appeal. Tribunal decides only residence during 2000 and 2001 counts, but anyway his deportation does not satisfy the less demanding test. Secretary of State appeals

2008 Due for release from prison

The tribunal also interpreted the residence requirement for 10 years to include the reference to it in the Preamble, and thus to refer to someone who had 'availed themselves of the rights and freedoms conferred on them by the Treaty' (para 64). As Mr Chindamo had not done that after 2001, again he did not have the requisite 10 years' residence. Finally, they concluded that residence in prison did not count towards residence for the purposes of the Directive. The earlier case of *MG and VC* had held that it did, but without argument on this point. The tribunal in *Chindamo* relied on Halsbury's Laws: 'A mere place of compulsory and temporary detention such as a prison...is not sufficient' to establish residence.

All this being the case, Mr Chindamo's detention fell to be decided under the simple ground of public policy. The tribunal held that case law predating the Citizens' Directive, principally still the authority of *Bouchereau*, remained good law in this respect. Given the evidence that Mr Chindamo was unlikely to reoffend, they held that there were not reasons of public policy to deport him.

6.8.2.4 *Procedural rights*

Directive 2004/38 provides for a right to judicial procedures for all expulsion decisions. Furthermore, it provides that where an application is made for an interim order to suspend enforcement, with limited exceptions for repeat cases and where expulsion is based on 'imperative grounds of national security', no enforcement action may be taken until that application has been heard.

An important decision in terms of European law's impact on rights in UK law was C-357/98 *R v SSHD ex p Yiadom* [2000] ECR I-9265. Here the ECJ held that a decision refusing leave to enter after the applicant had been in the UK for seven months on temporary admission was in reality a decision to remove her, not a decision on entry. This would therefore attract a right under Article 9 Directive 64/221 to have an appeal before removal, which was not available to a non-European. As mentioned in chapter one, one of the sub-themes of immigration and asylum law in the UK at present is the creation of a kind of non-status; a condition of being present in body but not in law. Here the European Court of Justice takes a very realistic approach. It is not appropriate to give someone a temporary status in the country, then make a decision which means they must leave, but to label it a decision on entry rather than removal and so deprive them of appeal rights (compare *Khadir*, discussed in chapter 15).

6.9 **European enlargement and freedom of movement**

The fundamental status of Union citizen applies to nationals of states recently acceded to the EU. There is no status such as 'new union citizen' or anything of that sort. Nevertheless, the rights reserved to old member states to phase in their recognition of the rights of nationals of the states that acceded in 2004 and 2007 has the effect that nationals of the A8 (2004) and A2 (2007) do not have full rights of free movement as EU citizens.

Prior to their accession, the new member states had various levels of agreement giving some access to self-employment in the EU. However, despite the fact that some as a consequence may be quite established in old member states, as we have seen in 6.3.1.1 above, the requirement for residence to be 'according to the Directive' defers their right to permanent residence.

Their right to work is also in many cases deferred. Under the Act of Accession the old member states had an option to derogate from free movement provisions and to continue to apply their national law for two years after accession. There then followed a three-year period during which old member states agreed to introduce greater freedom of access to their labour markets, but could continue restrictions on notice to the Commission. The transition period was intended then to be complete (i.e. after five years), but an old member state which has not achieved full access to the labour markets for new member state workers may, in the case of threatened or actual 'serious disturbance to its labour market', have a further two years in which to achieve full access.

Ten countries became members of the EU on 1 May 2004, but no derogations are permitted in relation to Malta and Cyprus. The other countries which acceded on that day are known as the A8. They are: the Czech Republic, Estonia, Latvia, Lithuania,

Table 6 Accession state nationals' rights to work

YEAR	A8	Romania and Bulgaria
2004	Old MS may derogate. Pre-accession agreements provide minimum rights	National agreements
2006	Old MS should introduce greater freedom to work	National agreements
2007		Old MS may derogate. Pre-accession agreements provide minimum rights
2009	Restrictions lifted except for MS that has 'serious disturbances' to its labour market	Old MS should introduce greater freedom to work
2011	Free movement for work	
2012		Restrictions lifted except for MS that has 'serious disturbances' to its labour market
2014		Free movement for work

MS = member state

Hungary, Poland, Slovenia and the Slovak Republic. The permitted derogations only apply to employment, and are from Article 39 EC Treaty and Articles 1 to 6 of Regulation 1612/68, all of which govern free movement of workers. The UK, along with Ireland and Sweden, decided to offer access to workers from the A8 countries. The effect is that nationals of the A8 countries may enter the UK without needing a visa or leave to enter, and may benefit from rights to freedom of establishment as granted under the former CEEC agreements (see chapter 5). They may only enter paid employment by complying with the terms of the registration scheme. This entails registering with the Home Office within one month of obtaining employment (Accession (Immigration and Worker Registration) Regulations 2004, SI 2004/1219 as amended). Nationals of A8 countries who already have other existing rights in the UK, whether by virtue of a previous work permit, marriage to an EEA national, dual nationality, or for any other reason, retain those rights and do not become subject to the new registration system. There is no entitlement to welfare benefits.

Although the UK made it known that it would not derogate, the effect of the Regulations combined with the decision in *Zalewska* seem to mean that the UK has implemented its own system of entry for A8 workers. Some commentators doubt that this is compatible with EC law (see Mitsilegas).

The decision of the Court of Appeal in Northern Ireland in *Zalewska v Department for Social Development* [2007] NICA 17 concerned a Polish national who entered lawfully, registered and worked lawfully, but then did not register a change of employment. The Court held that as she did not comply with the requirements for registration under the Accession (Immigration and Worker Registration) Regulations 2004 SI 2004/1219 she was outside the labour market and thus not a worker for EU purposes so as to benefit from social advantages granted to workers, here, income support. In so deciding, the Court placed the UK's domestic law (the Regulations) above the EU right of residence that Ms Zalewska might have claimed under Article 18 or her rights to social advantages under Regulation 1612/68 reg. 7. On the face of it the decision is inconsistent with EC principles that regulatory mistakes or offences should not be allowed to have a fundamental effect on the exercise of freedom of movement. However, the Treaty of Accession permits derogation and the Court held that the derogation entitled the UK to impose its domestic scheme. Ms Zalewska has applied to the House of Lords for leave to appeal.

If *Zalewska* is correct, Accession workers are admitted to the UK under national law pursuant to a scheme which derogates from the EC law provisions on free movement for workers, so that although A8 workers are admitted, they are admitted under domestic rather than EC law. This exempts the state from being obliged to respect non-discrimination and other principles governing the entry to and for work of EU nationals, but allows those nationals to enter and work. It is evident that this creates a tier of less privileged EU workers.

If A8 workers are accorded a second-class set of rights and living conditions, A2 workers are given the third class. As with A8 workers, the EU Acts of Accession permitted member states to derogate from granting full rights to A2 workers in the years immediately following accession. The UK announced that it would not be opening its labour market to Bulgarian and Romanian nationals. In fact, some access is given, again subject to a registration scheme, but only to employment in listed categories (see chapter 11).

6.10 **Conclusion**

Directive 2004/38 represents a significant advance in developing rights of free movement. However, in the UK, the interpretation of the Directive by the Court of Appeal and in Regulations maintains a consistently restrictive approach. While, in theory, Article 18 provides a right of residence, in practice it is rarely given substantive effect.

QUESTIONS

1 Was the ECJ right to refuse entitlement to benefit to Mr Collins? Do you have any sympathy with the Commission's view that Article 18 requires that the mobility of citizens of the Union should not be impeded by being unable to claim benefits while they look for work? After all, Mr Collins would only have qualified for income-based job-seeker's allowance if he was genuinely seeking work.

2 Do you agree with the Court in *Akrich* that motivation is irrelevant when a couple relies on the rights arising from *Surinder Singh*?

3 The mother in *Chen* had no right of residence in the UK prior to the birth of her child. Is the case consistent with *Akrich*?

 online resource centre For guidance on answering questions, visit www.oxfordtextbooks.co.uk/orc/clayton3e.

FURTHER READING

Barnard, C. (2007) *The Substantive Law of the EU: The Four Freedoms* (2nd edn) (Oxford: Oxford University Press).

Carlier, J-Y (2005) 'Case Note on *Chen*', (2005) *Common Market Law Review* 42: 1121–31.

Craig, P. and de Burca, G. (2007) *EU Law: Text, Cases and Materials* (4th edn) (Oxford: Oxford University Press).

Currie, S. (2006) '"Free" movers? The post-accession experience of migrant workers in the UK' *European Law Review*, April, pp. 207–299.

Guild, E. (ed.) (1999) *The Legal Framework and Social Consequences of Free Movement of Persons in the European Union* (London: Kluwer Law International).

Handoll, J. (1988) 'Article 48(4) EEC and Non-National Access to Public Employment' *European Law Review* vol. 13, no. 4, 223–241.

Jacqueson, C. (2002) 'Union Citizenship and the Court of Justice: Something New under the Sun? Towards Social Citizenship' *European Law Review* vol. 27, no. 3, 260–281.

Journal of Immigration, Asylum & Nationality Law vol. 21 no. 3 is a special issue devoted to EC law, focusing on the implementation of the Citizens' Directive in the UK. All seven articles are relevant.

McAuley, D. (2003) 'Windows, Caps, Footballs, and the European Commission. Confused? You Will Be' *Competition Law Review* vol. 24, no. 8, 394–399.

McKee, R. (2007) 'Regulating the Directive? The AIT's Interpretation of the Family Members Provisions in the EEA Regulations' *Journal of Immigration, Asylum & Nationality Law* vol. 21, no.4, pp. 334–340.

Oosterom-Staples, H. (2005) 'Case note on *Collins*', (2005) *Common Market Law Review* 42: 205–233.

Peers, S. (2001) 'Dazed and Confused: Family Members' residence rights and the Court of Justice' *European Law Review* vol. 26, no. 1, 76–83.

Spaventa, E. (2005) 'Case note on *Akrich*', (2005) *Common Market Law Review* 42: 225–239.

Toner, H. (2001) 'Community law immigration rights, unmarried partnerships and the relationship between European Court of Human Rights jurisprudence and community law in the Court of Justice' *Web Journal of Current Legal Issues* [2001] 5 Web JCLI.

—— (2004) '*Chen* – judgment of the ECJ' *Journal of Immigration, Asylum & Nationality Law* vol. 18, no.4, pp. 265–266.

—— (2006) 'New Regulations Implementing Directive 2004/38' *Journal of Immigration, Asylum & Nationality Law* vol. 20, no. 3, pp. 158–178.

SECTION 3

The system of immigration control

7

.....

Crossing the border and leave to remain

SUMMARY

This chapter is concerned with the legal processes of crossing the border to enter the UK and the stages at which that can be encountered before and on arrival. The new extra-territorial powers of immigration officers and the increasing role of new technologies are discussed as characteristics of a more diffuse, intelligence-based and security-oriented system, embodied in the UK Border Agency. The chapter describes the role and powers of entry clearance officers and immigration officers in granting entry clearance and leave to enter, and considers the general grounds for refusal of leave or entry clearance. The Common Travel Area is introduced. Finally, there is discussion of the grant of leave, and of how the most secure immigration status of settlement may be achieved.

7.1 Introduction

The legal processes described in this chapter apply to all those who are subject to immigration control (Immigration Act 1971 s 3(1)). The law relating to the various categories of entry such as spouse, dependent child, work permit holder, is dealt with in the fourth part of this book and asylum claims in the fifth part. The provisions discussed in this chapter apply throughout, in other words, to those whose applications are discussed in part four, and, where relevant, to asylum seekers. The power to give or refuse leave to enter is the foundation of immigration control, and the study of these powers and of their interpretation by civil servants and judicial bodies tells us about the nature of immigration control and the way that it is changing.

7.1.1 Changing nature of immigration control

The development of immigration control from the Aliens Act 1905 up to the end of the twentieth century was increasingly complex in detail but quite simple in concept. Immigration control was the very visible exercise of sovereignty by an island nation. At the borders, whether sea or air, immigration officers determined whether a passenger needed leave to enter, and if so whether and on what terms to grant it. The exception to this was the Common Travel Area which expressed a recognition that the land border between Britain and Ireland required a more flexible approach, and, from 1969, entry clearance, which formalized a pre-entry stage of immigration control in British embassies and High Commissions abroad.

At the end of the twentieth and beginning of the twenty-first century this traditional model is dissolving. A key reason for this is membership of the European Union, as discussed in chapter 5. Although the UK has not yet opted into many immigration provisions made under the Treaty of Amsterdam, it is a full partner in the Common European Asylum System, and participates in security measures such as the Schengen information system and the Eurodac fingerprinting system. The UK's movement towards harmonization with the rest of Europe brings a dual preoccupation with freedom of movement on the one hand, and security on the other. Increasingly sophisticated international intelligence networks and communication media make this possible. Immigration control is becoming a matter of interception, policing, and international information exchange, not just granting leave by a stamp in a passport at a port of entry.

At the beginning of the twenty-first century the system is in transition. It still bears some of the features of geographical border control, but at the same time it bears features of a new and more dispersed system, which has statutory foundations in the Immigration and Asylum Act 1999. In the traditional model, immigration control is exercised principally at two points. One is the port of entry, administered by the immigration service, the other is an entry clearance post at an Embassy, High Commission, or diplomatic post overseas. In the emerging model, an integrated system considers visa applications and grants the effective leave abroad, having checked security details with immigration, police, taxation and security services in the UK. Passengers are vetted before embarking on a journey. The physical border, the point of arrival, becomes a place of checking and policing, of potential arrest and detention. The new UK Border Agency will carry out all these functions. Monitoring for immigration infringement becomes a function distributed through a range of practices and legal provisions to educational bodies, local authorities, other public bodies, commercial bodies, and even private individuals.

7.2 Scope of immigration control

7.2.1 Common Travel Area

7.2.1.1 *Common Travel Area – introduction*

Entry from another part of the Common Travel Area is an exception to the requirement for leave to enter. Agreements on absence of immigration controls between the UK and Ireland have existed in various forms since the founding of the Irish Free State in 1922. Although there were restrictions on travel during and for a short while after the Second World War, these were relaxed after an exchange of letters between the two governments in 1952 proposed a similar and mutually enforced immigration policy. This laid the foundation for the present day Common Travel Area (see Ryan 2001). The UK implemented this by repealing the requirement for aliens to obtain leave to land from Ireland (Aliens (No 2)) Order 1952, SI 1952/ 636. The arrangement for an absence of immigration control between the two countries and mutual assistance with enforcement included passing information between governments about the movement of aliens. In particular there was and still is a sharing of intelligence about those who appeared on the other country's list of undesirable aliens.

The present-day Common Travel Area consists of the United Kingdom of Great Britain and Northern Ireland, the Channel Islands, the Isle of Man, and the Republic of Ireland. It was established by Immigration Act 1971 s 1(3) which provides that journeys which are purely between any of these places (i.e. they do not start or end outside the CTA) are free of immigration control. This does not mean, however, that the whole of the immigration law of the CTA is entirely harmonized or that it is subject to the same laws. The UK, Islands, and Ireland remain different jurisdictions. Neither does it mean that no individual travelling is subject to any restriction, as there are exceptions to this freedom of movement. The effect of the CTA is to create an area somewhat similar to the Schengen system, in which there is mutual enforcement of each other's immigration laws but which does not facilitate entry to the area from outside.

7.2.1.2 *Common Travel Area – operation*

The Isle of Man and Channel Islands, while their inhabitants have British nationality, in theory have their own immigration laws. In reality, British immigration statutes are applied in the Islands with slight modifications. Because there is one nationality, Islanders are not subject to British immigration control, and vice versa. Immigration Act 1971 Sch 4 gives effect in the UK to the immigration laws of the Islands. The result is that limited leave granted in the UK or Islands has effect with the same limitations throughout the UK and Islands. Similarly, deportation orders made in the UK or Islands are given effect in each other's jurisdiction and illegal entry into one is illegal entry into the others.

Citizens of the Republic of Ireland on the other hand, are subject to British immigration control (and vice versa). The Common Travel Area means that British and Irish citizens may enter Ireland and Britain respectively without leave and without having to present a passport to establish their status, but like other EEA nationals they may be deported. There is an additional provision for the exclusion of Irish citizens if the Secretary of State personally directs that their exclusion is conducive to the public good (Immigration (Control of Entry through Republic of Ireland) Order 1972, SI 1972/1610 article 3(1)(b)(iv) and (2)).

The CTA effects mutual enforcement of immigration controls. An illegal entrant to Ireland for instance is not permitted by the CTA to enter Britain, and requires leave to do so. The UK and Ireland enforce each other's deportation orders, though not without question. The IDI Ch 9 s 2 para 3.4, June 2004, advises that an Irish deportation order is a relevant consideration, but an application for entry should still be considered on its merits. Visa nationals who do not, on entering another part of the CTA, have a valid visa for the UK, do not have this omission wiped out on entering the UK. They still need a visa. The Immigration (Control of Entry through Republic of Ireland) Order 1972, SI 1972/1610 article 3(1)(b) makes this plain in relation to entry through Ireland. The applicant in *R (on application of Alinta)* [2006] NIQB 61 lived in Northern Ireland but had overstayed his UK visa. On attempting to cross the border to the Republic of Ireland on a shopping trip he was detained, and in due course served with notice of removal signed by a UK immigration officer. He was escorted by security personnel back to Northern Ireland. He contended that he was not an overstayer as he was not in the UK at the time of the service of the notice, and he was not liable to removal as he had been brought back to the UK under the control of the law so his presence could not be unlawful. These ingenious arguments failed. According to Article 3 of the Order, as a person who had overstayed in the UK he needed fresh leave to re-enter. Without this he was an illegal entrant. The mutuality provisions mentioned above have the same effect in relation to the Islands. There are restrictions on some lawful travellers as well as those who are in breach of immigration law on entry.

SI 1972/1610 article 4 allows a limited stay in the UK for certain people entering through the Republic of Ireland. If someone's leave to remain in the UK has expired while they were in Ireland, the Order itself grants seven days' leave on return to the UK, unless they were a visitor on a short visa in which case it grants one month. If they have entered Ireland from outside the CTA they may only remain in the UK for three months and may not take paid work. The Court of Appeal in *Kaya v SSHD* [1991] Imm AR 572 confirmed that someone who exceeds this period is correctly treated as an overstayer. For more detail on the operation of the Common Travel Area, reference should be made to the IDIs and a practitioner work such as *Macdonald's Immigration and Nationality Law and Practice*.

7.2.2 Who is subject to immigration control?

The question of who is subject to immigration control has been answered more fully in the chapter on nationality and right of abode, but may be summarized as follows. British citizens and Commonwealth citizens with right of abode are not subject to immigration control (Immigration Act 1971 s 3(1)). The following groups are, strictly speaking, subject to immigration control but do not need leave to enter: nationals of the European Economic Area (Immigration Act 1988 s 7); air and sea crews making a lawful stop within s 8(1) of the 1971 Act; service people, diplomats, and their households; people arriving from another part of the Common Travel Area (1971 Act s 8); and prisoners brought to the UK to give evidence in drug-trafficking cases (Criminal Justice (International Co-operation) Act 1990 s 6). Certain representatives of governments and those benefiting from immunities conferred by Orders in Council referring to international tribunals and other international bodies are exempt from immigration control under the Immigration (Exemption from Control) Order 1972, SI 1972/1613, as amended. All other passengers need leave to enter. Visa nationals need entry clearance which must be obtained at an entry clearance post overseas. The list of visa national countries is appended to the Immigration Rules and is updated (usually lengthened) frequently. Since 13 November 2005 there is less difference between visa nationals and non-visa nationals as all non-EEA nationals need entry clearance for stays of more than six months, bringing the UK's visa provisions closer to those of the European common visa list.

Although asylum claimants need leave to enter, this cannot be granted until their asylum claim has been processed. This cannot be done at the port as the investigation is too complex, and by the nature of the claim cannot be done before arrival. Asylum claimants are therefore normally given a status called temporary admission pending determination of their claim (Immigration Act 1971 Sch 2 para 21); alternatively they may be detained. Detention and temporary admission are discussed in chapter 15.

For recognized refugees, the issue of a travel document pursuant to the obligation in the 1951 UN Convention Relating to the Status of Refugees was until recently all that was necessary. So, if a person was granted refugee status in Germany, they could present their travel document to enter the UK. However, from 11 February 2003 the UK suspended its participation in the 1959 Council of Europe Agreement on the Abolition of Visas for Refugees 'on public order and security grounds'. All holders of refugee travel documents now therefore require a visa before coming to the United Kingdom.

7.3 **Before entry – entry clearance**

Prior entry clearance was introduced by the Immigration Appeals Act 1969 for applications to join family members in the UK. This control was aimed at limiting entry from the New Commonwealth. It began with a written parliamentary answer in 1969, announcing a new system of entry certificates for Commonwealth men seeking entry to join wives and fiancées. This was rapidly followed by the requirement for an entry certificate for all dependent relatives in the Immigration Appeals Act 1969. Juss quotes contemporary criticism by the National Council for Civil Liberties of the 'last minute inclusion of yet another control – perhaps the most restrictive of all – the mandatory entry certificate' (1994:44). People required to apply for an entry certificate as opposed to a visa had in theory a right to enter. However, the application system created notorious delays, which in themselves operated as an illegitimate form of immigration control (*R v SSHD ex p Phansopkar* [1975] 3 WLR 322 CA). Once entry certificates were established, the entry clearance system grew from there. By the Immigration Act 1971 the basis for the present system was in place.

The expansion of the entry clearance system is a form of asylum deterrence which has been in use for longer than we sometimes think. For instance, anticipating Jewish refugees in 1938, the UK instituted a visa requirement for Austria and Germany (see Dummett and Nicol p. 157). The number of visa national countries, that is, those whose nationals require entry clearance for any purpose, is now around 103. To put that number in perspective, the United Nations currently recognizes 191 countries. Countries are added to the list when circumstances suggest that asylum claims from there will increase. For instance, during the three months of July to September 2002, a total of 2,105 Zimbabweans sought asylum in the United Kingdom, almost as many as in the whole of 2001. In November 2002 the Secretary of State announced that Zimbabwe would become a visa national country.

Entry clearance, strictly speaking, refers to entry certificates and visas, but now we refer to entry clearance as generally meaning a visa. An entry clearance application is the earliest point in time at which an intending immigrant might encounter UK immigration control. Where entry clearance is required it must be obtained before setting out for the UK (HC 395 para 28). As mentioned earlier, it is now mandatory for all non-EEA passengers coming to the UK for more than six months, and for nationals of visa national countries also for shorter stays. Those people for whom entry clearance is not mandatory may apply for entry clearance as a precaution (HC 395 para 24) to establish their eligibility for entry and so avoid the risk of being turned away at the port. This is all the more advisable since Immigration, Asylum and Nationality Act 2006 s 6 removed the right of appeal from those without entry clearance. The visa requirement does not apply to British nationals without a right of abode.

7.3.1 **Decisions on entry clearance**

Entry clearance applications are granted or refused by entry clearance officers (ECOs) based in 146 British posts abroad, that is, in Embassies, High Commissions, and Consulates. Entry clearance officers perform a vital function in the implementation of immigration control. Given this it is surprising both that entry clearance officers are not mentioned in any of the legislation, and that until the creation of the Joint Entry Clearance Unit in June 2000 they were answerable to the Foreign and Commonwealth Office rather than the Home Office. The defining reference to entry clearance officers in the immigration rules is in para 26, which says that where appropriate the term 'entry clearance officer' should be substituted for 'immigration officer'. The UK Visas website (ukvisas.gov.uk) gives ready access to the guidance notes for ECOs, called Diplomatic Service Procedures (DSPs).

The entry clearance system is undergoing a process of major change. Traditionally, applications for entry clearance were made in person, and the majority of applications were granted after a short discussion at a counter. Settlement applications entailed a lengthier interview. Problems with the entry clearance system mainly concerned

- delays in processing the application,
- cursory or poor quality consideration of the application,
- oppressive conduct and conditions of interview, and
- use of discrepancy system by ECOs.

Clearly the quality of decision-making by entry clearance officers is of primary importance. Delays are significant as people have sometimes waited years to visit relatives or join their spouse, missing deaths, weddings and funerals.

The interview for people seeking to join their family in the UK as a first experience of the UK immigration system has often been traumatic. The interview played a crucial role in determining the outcome of the application, but was affected by the conditions in which it was carried out. Entry clearance posts were not well distributed, though more have opened recently, so an applicant may have had a long and arduous journey to get to the interview. A research report by the UK Immigration Advisory Service described a common journey as follows:

The train journey from Sylhet to Dacca alone takes 13 hours, added to that, of course, the cumbersome boat, bus journey, including miles of walking to reach Sylhet town from the village. [Most wives were also] carrying an infant and other children of very young age through the long journey. (p. 11, as quoted by Juss, p. 73)

On arrival, an applicant, who would not have the resources to rest in a hotel before attending the interview, would be exhausted and not really fit for an important interview. Despite this, researchers reported that applicants would never answer in the negative the standard question asked by the ECO as to whether they were fatigued, nervous, or unwell. The reason was the fear that if they were unfit for interview on arrival the interview would be postponed for a long period (CRE p. 36).

The conduct of the interview could be oriented to catching people out rather than examining their application in the light of the immigration rules. ECOs used the 'discrepancy system', the practice of interviewing different members of the same family, then turning down claims to be related from people who differed in minor detail in their accounts of events or circumstances. Examples given by Juss include the colour of a sari worn by the wife at the wedding, the materials of which a house was built, the length of time the family had had their buffalo, and the names of a family member's barber and tailor (pp. 65–66). Because of the delays in the system the events in question could be years in the past, thereby increasing the likelihood of difference in memories in *bona fide* applicants.

Major studies in the early 1980s, later work for instance by Juss (1997), research conducted into the reinstated family visitor appeals, and the revised working holidaymaker scheme, all revealed concerns with the quality of entry clearance decisions. These were repeated in government-sponsored reviews – the annual review of the Entry Clearance Monitor, and reports in 2004 by the National Audit Office and FCO.

The Entry Clearance Monitor has encouraged the use of more objective measures of, for instance, whether a visitor has enough money for their visit. In student cases there is a rough tariff applied, and she has advocated the same be done for visitors using figures from the *Lonely Planet Guides* or *Rough Guides,* but this suggestion has been resisted. While, with good training and support and time to make considered judgments, there is nothing invidious in discretion as such, the reports of the Entry Clearance Monitor reveal that, in conditions where these elements are lacking, decisions may be made on a basis not permitted by the rules.

The Home Affairs Committee commented that the immigration rules are vague, allowing too much scope for inconsistency in decision-making. An additional pressure on ECOs is sheer numbers. The increased numbers of people requiring entry clearance are swelled by the increase in global travel generally.

7.3.2 Entry clearance as part of e-borders

Changes in processing entry clearance applications are coming from a number of directions. There are two principal forces. One is the introduction of the points-based system. This brings with it a routinization of decision-making which the government considers will reduce or eliminate mistakes. The government intends to achieve this by a tighter management of processes, as in the UK-based part of the system. The unit for managing entry clearance, UKvisas, has developed Operating Standards and Instructions which include ten minimum requirements, though only one deals with the substance of the decision. A Balanced Scorecard was introduced in 2007 to measure quality. This quantifies complaints, fraudulent applications, sick days, training days etc, but does not directly assess the quality of decisions. Modern processes moving towards dispensing with the interview are influenced by arguments that it is time-consuming, unnecessary, burdensome for the applicant and contributes to subjectivity. Sheer numbers now make routine interviewing unfeasible, and making initial entry clearance applications online is part of the government's managed migration plan. The Entry Clearance Monitor recommends that interviews are used 'where oral evidence is likely to tip the balance one way or the other' (September 2007 report, para 127). This chimes with the Operating Guidance, which recommends that interviews are focused on issues that need clarification, and anticipates that most applications will be resolved on the basis of the application form, biometric information and warnings index.

The introduction of compulsory fingerprinting for all entry clearance applicants is the second major instrument of change in the entry clearance system. Nationality, Immigration and Asylum Act 2002 s 126 granted power to require biometric information such as fingerprints with applications for entry clearance. Photographing and fingerprinting have rapidly become a routine part of any visa application (Cm 6472 para 51). The power is implemented in the Immigration (Provision of Physical Data) Regulations 2006, SI 2006/1743, which provide that, without fingerprints, an application may be treated as invalid. This method fits with the new integrated UK Borders Agency, making it easier to transfer to other parts of the border control operation unique information about applicants. The scanned fingerprints are checked against government records to identify if a prospective traveller has already been fingerprinted in the UK by the immigration authorities (UKVisas Annual Report 2006–07), or is on a watchlist or has made an asylum application (the Eurodac database – see chapter 5).

Fingerprints and photographs are evidence supporting an application. The way in which they are treated will be important in how the fairness of entry clearance processing develops from here on. The UKvisas Operating Standards and Instructions provide guidance to entry clearance officers on dealing with biometric information and checking the warnings index – i.e. the list of people for whom there is a security or police warning. However, this guidance is not publicly available. If, for instance, a check of biometric information showed a previous unsuccessful application that had not been disclosed by the applicant, the proper way to deal with this would be in accordance with para 321 of the rules, discussed below. It would be improper to refuse the application on the basis of a fingerprint record without relating it to a ground for refusal and obtaining further relevant information. Fingerprint records introduce a technological measure of genuineness. However, this does not dispense with the exercise of judgment by a human being, the entry clearance officer.

There may be a tendency, with the routinization of applications online and the collection of fingerprints, to make the entry clearance application into nothing more than a security check. This may be exacerbated by removal of rights of appeal from entry clearance decisions under Immigration, Asylum and Nationality Act 2006 s 4, as the lack of appeal right undermines the incentive to produce good decisions. This removal of appeal rights completes the bureaucratization of entry clearance. From the beginning of 2008, as each tranche of applications comes into the points-based system, so the right of appeal will be removed in relation to that kind of application. For instance, the first group is that of highly skilled applicants for work. Once these applications can be made in the points-based system, there will be no right of appeal against their refusal. They will be subject only to an internal administrative review.

7.3.3 Monitoring entry clearance applications

Informal interviews with powerful officials far away from the system of redress are a fertile ground for abuse of power and lack of transparency. The main method of redress is appeal but, where appeal rights have been removed, the government has appointed a monitor to oversee the quality of decisions. The first was appointed in 1993 when appeal rights were removed from visitors. The monitor has a brief to oversee the whole system, and so can report on the consistency of standards between different entry clearance posts. Although it is not a direct indicator of quality, there is concern when refusal rates vary as much as they do between posts: for instance, in 2006–07, 0.2 per cent in Canberra, and 52 per cent in Abuja. Global refusal rates have also risen steadily since the first monitor of the entry clearance system was appointed now reaching 19 per cent.

Under the new points-based system without entry clearance appeals, the Immigration, Asylum and Nationality Act 2006 s 4(2) allows the Secretary of State to set the terms upon which the monitor will report. The post has been made full-time and the monitor makes two reports a year. The Monitor cannot make recommendations in individual cases and her systemic recommendations are not enforceable, so it is doubtful whether this is adequate recompense for the loss of appeal rights. The Entry Clearance Monitor will be expected to work closely with the new inspectorate of the immigration system, being introduced as part of the current programme of reform (*Fair, effective, transparent and trusted: An independent and transparent assessment of immigration*, Home Office policy statement, March 2007).

Against this background, we now consider the legal effect of entry clearance once granted. The grounds upon which entry clearance may be refused are almost identical to reasons for refusal of leave to enter, and are discussed later in that context.

7.3.4 **Effect of entry clearance**

Entry clearance is called a 'visa' for visa nationals and an 'entry certificate' for others (HC 395 para 25). Each of these is a vignette which is stuck into the passport and so entry clearance is shown when the passport is shown.

Before the changes introduced by the Immigration and Asylum Act 1999, entry clearance and leave to enter were two distinct stages of the entry control process. Although possession of entry clearance made it highly likely that leave to enter would be granted, it was not in itself a grant of leave. That stage still had to be passed at the port of entry. The Immigration (Leave to Enter and Remain) Order 2000, SI 2000/1161 enabled entry clearance to have effect as leave to enter provided it meets the conditions in article 3. These are, that it specifies the purpose for which the holder wishes to enter the UK, and is endorsed with any conditions to which it is subject or a statement that it is to have effect as indefinite leave. In most cases now, therefore, entry clearance will function as leave to enter. Entry clearance granted before the effective date of this article, i.e. before 28 April 2000, will not have the effect of leave to enter as it will not comply with the conditions. Gradually, however, these old-style entry clearances will die out. The exception is for refugee travel documents. Entry clearance endorsed on these after 27 February 2004 does not have effect as leave to enter (Immigration (Leave to Enter and Remain) (Amendment) Order 2004, SI 2004/475).

As a consequence of this extended effect of entry clearance, the role of immigration officers at the port of entry has changed to more of a policing function, checking the validity of existing documents. Immigration Act 1971 Sch 2 para 2A says that, in the case of a passenger who arrives with leave, the powers of the immigration officer are to examine that person to ascertain whether any grounds exist to cancel that leave. However, there is no obligation to exercise these powers. The Diplomatic Service Procedures (DSP) for entry clearance officers described in the following terms the role of the immigration officer where the entrant holds entry clearance which functions as leave to enter:

The focus for the IO switches from examination to verifying the bearer's identity and the validity of the entry clearance/leave to enter and ensuring that there has been no change of circumstances since the entry clearance was issued. Under certain circumstances the IO has authority to refuse entry to anyone holding an entry clearance (paragraph 321 of the Rules). *(Entry Clearance* Ch 1 para 1, 9 May 2002)

Clearly, where the entrant holds leave to enter the legal focus of the immigration officer's examination must shift. However, as the grounds for refusing leave to enter to passengers with entry clearance were already limited before 2000 it may be doubted whether, in practice, the intensity of examination of such passengers has changed substantially. The key difference in law is that there is no longer any obligation to examine a person with entry clearance.

The grant of entry clearance which has effect as leave to enter has further practical implications in which, ironically, an individual's fate becomes once again a matter of the way in which administrative discretion is exercised. Leave to enter granted at the port of entry takes effect from the date of entry. If it is limited in time, say for a year, then the year will run from that date. Entry clearance which functions as leave to enter bears two dates, one when the entry clearance becomes effective, 'valid from . . .' and one which marks its expiry, 'valid until . . .'. The passenger may travel once the entry clearance/leave to enter is effective. The 2000 Order in article 4(3) states that the period of limited leave starts with the date on which the holder arrives in the UK. Entry clearance officers are advised to ask the passenger when they are planning to travel, and are permitted to make the entry clearance/leave to enter valid from a date up to three months after the date when they granted it (DSP Ch.1 1.3). If a person arrives before the 'valid from . . .' date the immigration officer on arrival has a discretion to cancel the entry clearance (HC 395 para 30C). This discretion must of course be exercised reasonably. So far so good. However, the period of limited leave ends on the expiry date of the entry clearance. If a person's departure is further delayed, although they travel while the entry clearance/leave to enter is valid, they may arrive with only a portion of their leave left. HC 395 para 31A permits a person who arrives with leave to enter to apply for a variation of that leave on arrival. This gives the immigration officer an opportunity to extend an initial period of leave to ensure that the passenger benefits from the full period of leave they were originally given. The IDI Feb 2002 Chapter 1 Section 4 Annex V advises the immigration officer to grant a short extension in such a situation. Paragraph 31A, however, states that the immigration officer is not obliged to consider any such application. An application for a short extension should not reasonably be refused, but this paragraph protects the immigration officer from having to deal with more complex applications for variation. The absence of an automatic extension of the 'valid until . . .' date seems to create unnecessary obstacles in the way of the applicant, and a risk that well-intentioned people will go through the ordeal of being treated as overstayers.

7.4 Development of the exported border

In the first decade of the twenty-first century a flow of new measures to export border control has been built upon the power in the Immigration (Leave to Enter and Remain) Order 2000, SI 2000/1161, to grant leave to enter outside the UK. The power to grant or refuse leave to enter from abroad was not only granted for convenience of some travellers, but also for deterrence of others, namely asylum seekers. The judgment of Simon Brown LJ in *European Roma Rights Centre and Others v Immigration Officer, Prague Airport and SSHD* [2003] 4 All ER 247 explains:

There are difficulties, however, of a political nature in imposing a visa regime on certain friendly states and so Parliament in 1999 authorized the Home Secretary to introduce in addition a scheme enabling the immigration rules to be operated extra-territorially rather than simply at UK ports of entry. Intending asylum seekers would in this way be refused leave to enter the UK by immigration officers operating abroad and so be unable to travel to the UK to claim asylum here. (para 2)

First we consider the Order itself, then the uses that have been made of it so far, illustrating its potential.

7.4.1 **Immigration (Leave to Enter and Remain) Order 2000, SI 2000/1161**

The Immigration (Leave to Enter and Remain) Order 2000, introduced above in the context of entry clearance, was made pursuant to a widely phrased power in Immigration and Asylum Act 1999 s 1 (which inserted a new section 3A into the Immigration Act 1971):

1. The Secretary of State may by order make further provision with respect to the giving, refusing or varying of leave to enter the United Kingdom.
2. An order under subsection (1) may, in particular, provide for–
    (a) leave to be given or refused before the person concerned arrives in the United Kingdom;
    (b) the form or manner in which leave may be given, refused or varied;
    (c) the imposition of conditions;
    (d) a person's leave not to lapse on his leaving the common travel area.

This was the first time since the 1971 Act that there had been a substantive change in the power to grant or refuse leave to enter. It should be noted that the power in s 3A is simply to 'make further provision with respect to the giving, refusing, or varying of leave to enter'. The specific powers which follow in subsection 2 are not necessarily an exhaustive account of how this power will be exercised.

The power granted to the Secretary of State by s 3A was first exercised in the Immigration (Leave to Enter and Remain) Order 2000, SI 2000/1161. By art 7 of that order, 'an immigration officer *whether or not in the United Kingdom*, may give or refuse a person leave to enter the United Kingdom *at any time before his departure for, or in the course of his journey to*, the United Kingdom' (emphases added). This means that neither the immigration officer nor the grant of leave are fixed to the port of entry any longer. Leave may be given before or during travel, and the immigration officer need not be based at the port. Article 8 provides that notice giving or refusing leave to enter, instead of being given in writing as required by s 4(1) of the 1971 Act, may be given by fax or e-mail, or, in the case

Table 7 Stages of immigration control – visitor from Sri Lanka

Example 1: visitor from Sri Lanka (visa national arriving by air)

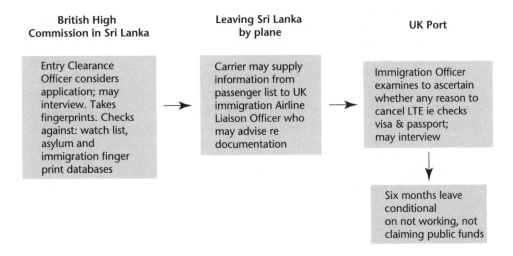

of visitors, orally including by telephone. Leave to enter may also be given to responsible third parties, not just to the passenger directly (art 9). This flexibility in the means of communicating a grant of leave to enter may have drawbacks if, for instance, a question of proof arises at a later date (see Luqmani, Randall, and Scannell 2000: 12). However, it was intended to be for the convenience of those regarded as 'low risk' passengers, for instance those on school trips or other organized tours. In these cases a passenger list may be presented and endorsed with leave to enter, even before setting out on the trip, and this is intended to minimize delay at the port of entry.

In addition to grant by entry clearance as discussed above, and advance clearance for groups of 'low risk' passengers, the power to grant or refuse leave to enter before travel is designed for schemes established abroad to deter unauthorized passengers and in particular asylum seekers.

7.4.2 Juxtaposed control

The first of these initiatives considered here is known as 'juxtaposed control'. This involves British immigration officers working at a port abroad alongside the immigration service of that country, sharing information and intelligence, and refusing to allow improperly documented passengers to board transport for Britain. The arrangement when fully implemented is a mutual one, enabling the immigration services of the other country to operate also in UK ports.

Juxtaposed controls have only been set up in Europe, and they may be seen as a form of European co-operation; alternatively, as a symptom of the need for a Common European Asylum System or as a failure of the attempt at harmonization to date (see Phuong 2003, discussed in chapter 5 and below). A main source of impetus for the establishment of juxtaposed controls was the furore surrounding the Red Cross refugee camp at Sangatte in northern France. There were daily illegal entries to the UK by asylum seekers waiting in the camp; and this, combined with the associated breaches of security, danger and injury to individuals, and delays to freight and other traffic, created a three-year dispute over causes and responsibilities between the two governments. Accordingly, the first juxtaposed controls were set up in 2002 in France, initially at the Eurotunnel site at Coquelles and the Eurostar stations at Paris Nord and Calais Fréthun. After the establishment of these controls and the closure of Sangatte at the end of 2002, there was a concern that other routes would then be used, so juxtaposed controls have now spread to Eurostar stations at Lille Europe and, in Belgium, the Gare du Midi, Ostend, and Zeebrugge. Controls on Channel Tunnel trains may all be made under powers granted by the Channel Tunnel Act 1987 and implemented in various orders. The Channel Tunnel (Miscellaneous Provisions) (Amendment) Order 2004, SI 2004/2589, for stopping trains from Belgium gives effect to an agreement between the British, French and Belgian governments and completes the move of UK immigration controls on Eurostar trains from London to continental Europe. The 2007 Order, SI 2007/2908, is the most recent, applying the Race Relations Act to immigration officers carrying out their functions in control zones. The Home Office announced in August 2007 that the number of illegal entrants in Kent had dropped by 88 per cent since 2002 as a result of these initiatives (Home Office press release 1/8/07).

The legal arrangements with France are contained in a Frontier Control Treaty 'concerning the implementation of frontier controls at the sea ports of both countries on the Channel and North Sea', Cm 5832, in force on 1 February 2004. The Treaty is given effect in UK law by the Nationality, Immigration and Asylum Act 2002 (Juxtaposed Controls) Order 2003, SI 2003/2818, made under the power in the Nationality, Immigration and Asylum Act 2002 s 141. This arrangement is constitutionally interesting, as s 141 allows an order to provide for 'a law' of England and Wales to have effect in a specified area outside the UK. The term 'a law' includes not only statutes and statutory instruments, but also case law and immigration rules.

The powers granted by the treaty include the designation of control zones, which are the areas of the port within which the authorities of the other country may exercise their powers. It gives operational control, including power to change the control zones if necessary, to the responsible authorities of the two countries. The powers which may be exercised there are 'all the laws and regulations of the Contracting Parties concerning immigration controls and the investigation of offences relating to immigration' (Article 2). The law and regulations of the destination state have the same effect in the state of departure as they would in their own state. So, the laws of the UK have effect in a French control zone as they would in the UK and should be applied 'in the same manner and with the same consequences' (Article 3). There are similar provisions in the Protocol on rail travel between Belgium, France and UK, given effect by SI 2004/2589.

Article 5 provides that the authorities of the destination state may 'arrest and hold for questioning' anyone who is subject to examination, including, but not limited to, those who are suspected of a breach of immigration law. As for the rights of those arrested and detained, the Crown Prosecution Service guidance on the Channel Tunnel says that PACE applies in some specified ways once jurisdiction is decided, but does not mention the Codes of Practice. The Nationality, Immigration and Asylum Act 2002 (Juxtaposed Controls) (Amendment) Order 2006, SI 2006/2908, extends the power to take fingerprints to someone who fails to provide a valid passport or equivalent on arrival in a control zone. The offences of absconding from detention, and obstructing a search (Immigration, Asylum and Nationality Act 2006 ss 40 and 41) are also extended to the control zone. By means of these incremental changes the control zones are increasingly treated as part of UK jurisdiction, and the network of border control is established more firmly outside the actual territory. New detection technology (NDT) may be used in control zones, but detection devices, applied to vehicles to detect human beings inside, have been reported as ineffective as they cannot distinguish between a human heartbeat and vibrations from ships and trains (www.telegraph.co.uk 6/8/06).

In its reply to concerns raised in the consultation process on juxtaposed controls the Home Office said that passengers would be able to contact their Embassy at any time, and 'those passengers refused entry who have a right of appeal from abroad will be served with a notice of refusal which will include information about the Refugee Legal Centre and Immigration Advisory Service' (Juxtaposed Control Implementation, Dover–Calais, Consultation Process Report, Response 1). This does not deal with the situation of someone who would have had a right of appeal in the UK, although the possibilities of this are extremely limited for the reason given below. It also does not take account of the possibility that judicial review might have been warranted, but without legal advice the detainee will be unlikely to be able to identify or pursue this option. Detention will be limited to 24 hours or, in exceptional circumstances, 48 hours.

The treaty and the whole system of juxtaposed controls are, on the face of it, aimed at preventing illegal entry. However, the broader context is the deterrence of asylum claims and the prevention of 'asylum shopping' in Europe, i.e. people seeking asylum in the state of their choice. This is particularly clear in Article 9 of the Frontier Control Treaty, which provides that if a person makes an asylum claim, or any other claim for protection which could be available in the state of departure, before the vessel in which they travel leaves the port, they must make that claim in the state of departure. This is the exception to the provision in the treaty that otherwise, once the state of arrival has commenced its enquiries, the state of departure has no further part to play. For this reason, a right of appeal in the UK is unlikely to arise. A person who asserts that their human rights would be breached by returning them to their home country would have a right of appeal in the UK if they were there, but if they make such a claim in France the application must be heard by the French authorities. The Protocol with Belgium does not refer to asylum claims, but says that the controls of the state of departure must normally be carried out before those of the state of arrival (Article 5).

The Orders made using powers in the Channel Tunnel Act 1987 only concern train travel and not port areas, although they do involve immigration officers being posted at railway stations abroad.

The Home Office commissioned research assessing the impact of asylum policies in Europe from 1990 to 2000 (Home Office Research Study 259) which found that it was difficult to attribute particular movements of asylum seekers to the adoption of particular policies. To the extent that it was possible, pre-entry and on-entry controls had perhaps the greatest impact on the number of asylum claims (p. 120). The researchers cited, for instance, visa regimes and pre-flight checks and noted these were most effective in combination with carrier sanctions (p. 25). A Home Office press release (172/2003, 23 June 2003) welcomed the publication of the research, saying that its finding of the effectiveness of pre-entry controls was an endorsement of the tight border controls being developed by the UK, and citing particularly juxtaposed controls. However, juxtaposed controls operate only at borders with EU member states and were not in place during the period of the research. The pre-entry controls discussed in the research take place in the country of origin. It is debatable whether juxtaposed controls may be placed in the same category. Phuong's work suggests that the Sangatte debacle,

Table 8 Stages of immigration control – student from Turkey

Example 2: Student from Turkey (visa national travelling overland)

British Embassy in Turkey	Calais	UK Port	
As example 1. → Travels overland	Juxtaposed controls. Immigration officer may exercise all powers as if in UK: examination: checks passport & visa; may interview to ascertain whether any reason to cancel LTE →	Immigration Officer. Examination as Calais, but may include checking biometric info electronically against national & European databases →	Time limited leave to study with restriction on working

paradoxically, demonstrates the need for the UK to join the Schengen area and open its borders to other member states (2003:168; see discussion in chapter 5).

In summary, juxtaposed controls are playing an increasing role in the UK's border management. On one viewing, they are an effective tool in deterring asylum claims, though no distinction is made between well-founded and other claims (RDS 259:120). From another viewpoint, they are a temporary local measure between Britain and its neighbours, indicating the failure of harmonization in Europe, and the need for it.

7.4.3 Airline liaison officers

The second kind of role taken abroad by immigration officers is as airline liaison officers (ALOs), to advise airlines on the validity of documents presented to them for travel to the UK. These immigration officers do not grant or refuse leave to enter, but advise airlines who may then refuse to allow the passenger to board. In 2001 about 2,500 passengers were prevented from travelling following such advice, rising to 50,803 in 2006 (HL 4304 25 June 2007). The liability of the officers for wrong advice is a matter of concern, given that there is no appeal against what is in formal terms advice to the airline rather than an immigration decision (see discussion of *Farah v British Airways & Home Office* TLR 26 January 2000, below). The main objective of these schemes is once again to limit asylum claims. Asylum seekers may often travel on false documents as this may be the only way to leave their country. If they are at risk they are not in a position while still in their own country to make an asylum claim. For obvious reasons, the effect on asylum seekers turned away from flights after such advice is unknown.

As part of implementing its five-year strategy *Controlling our borders: making migration work for Britain,* February 2005 Cm 6472, the government has been increasing the number of ALOs. The Independent Race Monitor in her report of July 2005 said that the intervention of ALOs had resulted in 'fewer refusals at UK terminals, which was in the interests of all parties' (2.11). She also commented that improved co-ordination between UK staff, UK Visas and airlines 'enabled a more strategic approach'. The UK

Table 8A UK Airline Liaison Officer Network

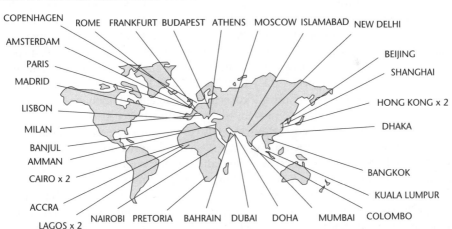

Reproduced with permission from 'Security in a Global Hub'

has opted into an EU Regulation establishing a network of immigration liaison officers who are stationed abroad and collect information on illegal activities connected with migration in order to help prevent illegal migration into the EU (Regulation 377/2004).

7.4.4 Passenger information

As part of developing the Schengen area, the UK has opted in to EC Directive 2004/82, binding from 5 September 2006. This entails that member states have systems requiring carriers to transmit passenger data to immigration authorities. The Immigration and Asylum Act 1999 amended the Immigration Act 1971 to require carriers to provide to immigration officers 'such information relating to the passengers carried, or expected to be carried...as may be specified' (Sch 2 para 27(2)). An additional power was inserted by the Asylum and Immigration (Treatment of Claimants etc) Act 2004 to require provision of 'a copy of all or part of a document that relates to the passenger'. The 2006 Act has amended these powers further, and added powers for the police to require passenger and freight information (ss 32 and 33). 'Controlling our Borders' says that passenger information will be provided electronically and will be checked against 'multi-agency watchlists' prior to boarding (Cm 6472 Annex 1). By these means, passenger information provided by carriers becomes part of the 'e-borders' scheme announced in the five-year strategy (Cm 6472).

7.4.5 Pre-clearance

Successive Home Secretaries have asserted that it would be desirable to pre-sift asylum claims abroad, and the third initiative discussed here is an example of an attempt to do this. The Home Office research discussed in connection with juxtaposed controls (RDS 259) suggests that this is the most effective way of limiting asylum claims, if any policy can be said to have an effect. The pre-clearance scheme at Prague in the Czech Republic was an experiment in this form of overseas activity of the British immigration service aimed at deterring unauthorized passengers from travelling, and targeting Roma asylum seekers. In this case, leave to enter was granted or refused before embarkation on a flight for the UK. In *European Roma Rights Centre (ERRC) v Immigration Officer at Prague Airport and SSHD* [2002] EWHC 1989 (Admin) the evidence of the Secretary of State confirmed that 'the Prague operation is not a pre-screening which is a prelude to a subsequent consideration of eligibility at a United Kingdom airport. Rather it takes the place of that consideration of that eligibility' (para 25). The judgments in the Court of Appeal [2003] 4 All ER 247 and House of Lords [2004] UKHL 55 confirmed what critics and the UK government had agreed upon, namely that the effect of such a scheme was to prevent asylum claims being made. The difference between the parties was whether this was lawful or not. This case was a dramatic illustration of the potential of the Immigration (Leave to Enter and Remain) Order 2000 to affect asylum claims. Where an asylum claim is made at a UK port of entry there is an obligation implied by the 1951 UN Convention Relating to the Status of Refugees to consider it. However, the courts in the *ERRC* case found there was no obligation to allow the claimant to reach the UK in order to make that claim. As discussed in chapter 8, the House of Lords found this scheme to be discriminatory on racial grounds and therefore unlawful.

The Prague scheme ran from 18 July 2001 to 26 February 2003. Following the Czech Republic's accession to the European Union in 2004 the scheme would have no basis.

Where such a pre-clearance system exists, a passenger has no option as to whether to use it. By contrast, HC 395 para 17A says that the immigration officer 'is not obliged to consider an application for leave to enter from a person outside the United Kingdom'. A passenger therefore cannot compel the immigration officer to afford them the convenience of an early decision, but the immigration officer can impose an early decision on the passenger, even if it means denying their access to asylum.

7.5 Trans-border controls – carriers' liability

A feature of current government policy is to extend the responsibility for immigration control to people in many walks of life. Liability placed on those who transport people and goods is not a new phenomenon, but until the 1980s it was relatively unimportant. Its use has expanded enormously in the UK since 1987 and it now represents a major plank in the government's policy to control asylum claims.

7.5.1 International context

Germany, Belgium, the USA, Canada, and Australia have all introduced measures imposing liability on carriers for the transport of passengers who either hide themselves and gain entry without being detected ('clandestine entrants') or who do not have the appropriate documents for travel, for instance their passport is forged or stolen or does not show the requisite entry clearance ('inadequately documented' passengers). Articles 26 and 27 of the Schengen Convention, which became part of EC law following the Treaty of Amsterdam, require the imposition of carrier sanctions by means of legislation, and the UK has been active in these measures.

7.5.2 Summary of legislative history

Under the Aliens Act 1905, a shipping company committed an offence punishable by a fine if a person subject to immigration control disembarked without leave to enter. If an immigrant who needed leave was admitted to the UK but expelled within six months, the Home Office could recover the cost of the return journey from the shipping company which had brought that passenger. Similar provisions persist to the present day in relation to removals. Immigration Act 1971 Sch 2 paras 26 and 27 set out various supplementary duties of shipping companies and airlines, which show how closely these commercial bodies are required to co-operate with the immigration service. For instance, if they carry passengers who require leave to enter, ships or aircraft may only call at designated ports of entry, and must ensure that passengers disembarking pass through designated control areas. Liability could be imposed without any implication of fault on the part of the carriers.

Although the risk of penalties gave an incentive to carriers to check the documentation of passengers and refuse passage where they had doubts as to someone's status, there was no statutory obligation to do so until the Immigration (Carriers' Liability) Act 1987. The Act imposed fines on airlines and shipowners or their agents of £1, 000 for each person carried by them who entered without a valid passport, and, where required, visa. This was increased to £2, 000 in 1991. This amount was per passenger, not per journey. Therefore, if 50 inadequately documented passengers were found on one ship, the fine imposed on the owner or agent would be £50,000, or, after 1991, £100,000. In 1993 the Asylum and Immigration Appeals Act 1993 s 12 added liability for carrying people who did not have the required transit visas. In 1998, legislation was introduced to include trains following the opening of the Channel Tunnel (Channel Tunnel (Carriers' Liability) Order 1998, SI 1998/1015).

In 1999 the Immigration and Asylum Act introduced liability for clandestine entrants as opposed to just passengers with improper documentation, and increased the scope of legislation to cover road transport. Later amending regulations have included rail freight (Carriers Liability (Clandestine Entrants) (Application to Rail Freight) Regulations 2001, SI 2001/280). These provisions represented an enormous extension of liability. Whereas a professional passenger carrier such as an airline would have in place procedure for checking documentation, the extension to clandestine entrants and road transport meant that other commercial organizations and individuals, who had no professional expertise in transporting passengers, could be held liable to a penalty for people who had hidden in their car or lorry. The Immigration (Carriers' Liability) Act 1987 was repealed. Current law is governed by the 1999 Act, as amended by Nationality, Immigration and Asylum Act 2002 Sch 8 and the Carriers' Liability Regulations 2002, SI 2002/2817, amending regulations and codes of practice. The major provisions are considered further in the next section.

7.5.3 The statutory scheme of carriers' liability

7.5.3.1 *Liability for clandestine entrants*
Section 32(5) of the 1999 Act imposed liability for clandestine entrants arriving in the UK on the owner or captain of the ship or aircraft, the owner, hirer or driver of another vehicle, including, if the vehicle is a detached trailer, its operator. Since amendment by the 2002 Act a penalty is imposed for each clandestine entrant, the maximum being £2,000 (Carriers' Liability Regulations 2002, SI 2002/2817, reg 3). In respect of each clandestine entrant a penalty may be collected from more than one responsible person. In this case there is a maximum aggregate penalty of £4, 000 per entrant (reg 3). If the driver is an employee of the vehicle's owner or hirer, the employer is jointly and severally liable for the penalty. The maximum applies to the passenger, not the carrier. So, up to £4, 000 may be paid by a number of different carriers for the one clandestine entrant, but if a carrier carries several clandestine entrants, the maximum penalty is £2, 000 per passenger.

The definition of 'clandestine entrant' in s 32(1) as amended is striking. There are two aspects to it, first of all the concealment. A person is a clandestine entrant if they arrive concealed in a vehicle, ship, rail freight wagon, or aircraft or pass or attempt to pass through immigration control concealed in a vehicle. Arrival includes in a control zone as prescribed for the purposes of juxtaposed control (Carriers' Liability (Amendment) Regulations 2004, SI 2004/244). The definition catches both a person who stowed away on a ship, but disembarks on foot, and someone who continues or attempts to continue through immigration control hidden in a vehicle. The second part of the definition is that the person evades, or attempts to evade, immigration control, or, which is more surprising, they claim, or indicate that they intend to claim, asylum in the UK. There can be no doubt that this provision catches a genuine asylum claimant. The penalty is on those who transport them rather than the clandestine entrants themselves, but of course the effect of this is to make carriers more wary of carrying clandestine entrants. There is a non-statutory scheme of refunding penalties paid for carrying inadequately documented travellers where the passenger ultimately succeeds in an asylum claim, but this does not apply when the passenger is granted humanitarian protection or discretionary leave (see *Charging Procedures – a Guide for Carriers*, Appendix B). A successful asylum claim might of course be years down the line and so of small comfort to the carrier.

There is a defence in s 34 to liability for the penalty if the carrier can show that they were acting under duress, or that they had an effective system for preventing the carriage of clandestine entrants, which was operated properly, and they did not know, and had no reasonable grounds for suspecting, that someone might be concealed.

In determining whether a system is effective, account will be taken of the code of practice for vehicles issued by the Secretary of State under s 32A. The code contains detailed provision for road haulage and other commercial vehicles concerning the sealing of containers and repeated inspections. It also contains provisions for buses and coaches concerning the locking of doors and inspections and even for private vehicles such as cars and caravans, making equivalent provision.

Following the extension of liability to rail freight operators by the Carriers' Liability (Clandestine Entrants) (Application to Rail Freight) Regulations 2001, SI 2001/280, a Code of Practice for securing rail freight has also been adopted, and a further code for rail freight shuttle wagons.

The carrier may serve a notice of objection to the penalty (Carriers' Liability Regulations 2002, SI 2002/2817) which the Secretary of State must consider. If the notice is upheld, the Secretary of State may sue to recover the amount of the penalty. Importantly, following the *Roth* case discussed below, the 2002 Act introduced a right of appeal to a court against the imposition of the penalty (1999 Act s 35A; *International Transport Roth GmbH and Other v SSHD* [2002] 3 WLR 344).

The penalty is backed up by the power in s 36(1) for a senior officer to detain vehicles pending payment of the charge, if 'there is a significant risk that the penalty will not be paid' and no satisfactory alternative security. This power was extended by the 2002 Act to detaining a vehicle while the matter is being considered (1999 Act s 36(2A) and (2B)). The court may order the release of a transporter if it considers that there is satisfactory security, or there is no significant risk that the penalty will not be paid or it considers that the penalty was not payable (s 37(3A) and (3B)). If the court does not order the release of the transporter and the penalty is not paid within 84 days, the transporter may be sold (s 37(4)).

7.5.3.2 *Improperly documented passengers*

Since the 2002 Act, liability for improperly documented passengers does not apply to bus, coach, and train operators but only to owners of ships or aircraft. The penalty is payable on demand to the Secretary of State like an 'on the spot' fine. Section 40(4) provides a defence if the carrier can show that the passenger embarked with the proper documentation. The *Charging Procedures – Guide for Carriers* sets out situations in which the penalty will be waived, including that the carrier acted on the advice of an airline liaison officer.

7.5.3.3 *Effect of scheme*

The new carrier provisions in the 1999 Act came into effect between 6 December 1999 and 18 September 2000. Simon Brown LJ, in the case of *International Transport Roth GmbH & Others* at para 10, described the effect as follows:

By June 2001, 988 penalty notices had been served in respect of 5,433 clandestine entrants. 249 vehicles had been detained, of which 190 were subsequently released on payment of the penalty or a substantial security. In some 25 per cent of cases where clandestine entrants were discovered, either no penalty notice was served or, following the carrier's notice of objection, the Secretary of State decided, under section 35(8), that the penalty was not payable. The average penalty payable is some £12, 000 (in respect, therefore, of six clandestine entrants). The bulk of the penalties are paid by companies, but some 10 per cent are paid by individuals including occasional car drivers. By October 2001 the value of the penalties paid or agreed to be paid was £2,432 million. In some cases instalment payments have been agreed, in the most extreme case at the rate of £40 per month for 12.5 years (£6,000).

In the *Roth* case, three of the appellants only discovered clandestine entrants when they were travelling up the motorway to London. They 'would never have been penalized had they not themselves alerted the police'.

The effect on small businesses of these penalties may be imagined, and the scheme generated an outcry. It was subject to a number of challenges.

7.5.3.4 *Redress for carriers*

When the system under the 1999 Act came into effect there was no appeal against the imposition of a penalty. In *R (Balbo B &C Auto Transport Internazional) v SSHD* [2001] 1WLR 1556 the Secretary of State had decided to uphold the penalty and in the absence of a right of appeal the claimants applied for judicial review of that decision. The Administrative Court held that judicial review was not appropriate, but when the Secretary of State began enforcement proceedings then liability could be challenged.

The claimants in *Roth* challenged the harshness of the scheme, demonstrated by the fixed penalty, by the carriers bearing the burden of establishing that they were not blameworthy and the lack of compensation for loss of business while a vehicle was detained, even if the carrier was determined not to be liable in the end. They suggested this was a disproportionate response to the problem of clandestine entrants. They challenged the lack of discretion and flexibility and the lack of provision for a fair hearing or a right of appeal, alleging under the Human Rights Act 1998 a breach of Article 6 and of Protocol 1, Article 1.

The specific procedural requirements of a fair trial in Article 6 apply only to a criminal matter, though the general principle of fairness applies also to the determination of civil rights and obligations. The requirements of fairness would therefore be greater if the proceedings were regarded as criminal. In the Act the charge levied is referred to as a 'civil penalty', there is no criminal charge and the penalty is recoverable as a civil debt. However, what a proceeding is called by the domestic authorities is not conclusive of whether it will be regarded as criminal or civil for the purposes of Article 6 ECHR. The Court of Appeal agreed (by a majority) with the carriers that the penalty scheme should be regarded as criminal, mainly because the carriers were in fact being punished, and the punishment meted out was severe.

It was a small step from this conclusion to decide that the scheme violated Article 6, though not necessarily for the reasons advanced by the carriers. Simon Brown LJ held: 'The hallowed principle that the punishment must fit the crime is irreconcilable with the notion of a substantial fixed penalty' (para 47). He accepted the claimants' characterization of the scheme as 'harsh', and this was his main reason for finding a breach of Article 6. In a similar vein, he concluded that the heavy burden on the carriers violated the principle of proportionality inherent in Protocol 1, Article 1, and that even if there was no violation of Article 6, then there was of this article.

Jonathan Parker LJ found the scheme incompatible with Article 6 for a different reason, namely that the Secretary of State had an exclusive role in determining liability, and the role of the courts was subsidiary. 'Accordingly, for the simple yet fundamental reason that the scheme makes the Secretary of State judge in his own cause, the scheme in my judgment is plainly incompatible with Article 6' (para 157).

Following the Court of Appeal's decision, a right of appeal was introduced and a flexible penalty.

The other main challenge to the penalty scheme by carriers has been that it breaches European law. This argument failed in *Roth* and in relation to the 1987 Act in the earlier case of *R v SSHD ex p Hoverspeed* [1999] INLR 591. It was alleged in *Hoverspeed* that the scheme restricted freedom to provide services, contrary to Article 49 EC (ex 59) and the free movement of EEA nationals and their families contrary to Immigration (European Economic Area) Regulations 1994 reg 3. The argument was lost on both counts. The administrative measures might be an inconvenience but not a restriction. If they were a restriction this was proportionate and justified in the interests of immigration control which was targeted at visa nationals, not EEA nationals. As carrier penalties were required by the Schengen Convention they were in principle endorsed by EC law.

7.5.3.5 *Redress for travellers*

While the carriers' liability scheme, particularly in relation to clandestine entrants, has clearly caused great problems for carriers, the scheme also carries particular hazards for potential passengers. The greatest hazard of the scheme is to an asylum seeker, who, by reason of their situation, may lack proper documents, and who is turned away from a flight, or discovered and removed from a lorry, perhaps directly into the hands of the authorities whose persecution they seek to escape. There has been considerable criticism of carrier penalties for the risks they may create for undocumented asylum seekers. There is also a potential problem for any traveller whose documents are not correctly understood.

This problem arose in *Farah v British Airways & Home Office* The Times 26 January 2000. In this case the Somali appellants had been prevented from embarking on a flight from Cairo to London. One had a passport. The other four appellants, all members of the same family, had declarations of identity documents issued by the British Embassy in Addis Ababa. The immigration liaison officer advised the airline that the passengers were incorrectly documented and should not be allowed to travel. As a consequence they were detained in Cairo airport for five days, then deported to Ethiopia. The Times report is of the Court of Appeal's judgment that the judge should not have struck out the part of the particulars of claim which claimed negligence. This was held to be an arguable matter which would turn on the particular facts and should be heard. The question of the duty of care here referred to the immigration officer who was working with the airline, and the standard of that duty is not yet ascertained. The question would need to be addressed again in relation to a decision of the airline staff.

The liability of airlines and of ALOs in this situation is as yet undetermined, though the *European Roma Rights Centre* case found that the Race Relations (Amendment) Act 2000 applied to decisions of immigration officers abroad (see discussion below).

The Council of Europe's Parliamentary Assembly considered the issue of sanctions against airlines in 1991 and commented:

Airline sanctions…undermine the basic principles of refugee protection and the rights of refugees to claim asylum, while placing a considerable legal, administrative and financial burden upon carriers and moving the responsibility away from the immigration officers.

Research on people illegally resident in the UK shows that different routes of entry are more likely to be taken by people of different nationalities. It would suggest that airline controls impact more on travellers from West and Sub-Saharan Africa, and carrier sanctions would bite more on travellers from Albania, Ukraine and Sri Lanka (Home Office 20/05 Chapter 4).

7.6 Immigration officers' powers on arrival

On arrival at a UK port, a passenger with or without entry clearance will encounter an immigration officer. By s 4(1) of the 1971 Act, immigration officers have specific statutory responsibility for giving or refusing leave to enter. Although this responsibility is no longer exclusive to them, as discussed below, in non-asylum cases leave to enter is still granted by immigration officers where it has not already been granted by way of entry clearance.

Until April 2000 leave to enter was only granted at the port of entry by means of a date stamp in the passport. For travellers receiving leave to enter at the port it may still be granted by this method, unless and until e-borders make that redundant. Leave to enter could, and still can, be refused on any of the grounds discussed below.

The extensive powers of immigration officers contained in Sch 2 of the 1971 Act are largely geared towards giving them the necessary scope of action in determining applications for leave to enter. Powers of examination, search, detention, and so on have all been granted and developed to lead ultimately to being able to make the decisive judgment – whether or not a person should have leave to enter the UK. Even the power to issue removal directions began as an administrative power to enforce a refusal of leave to enter.

The most widely applicable of the immigration officer's power is to examine any person arriving (Sch 2 para 2). This includes where entry clearance has been granted (Asylum and Immigration Act 2004 s 18) and even where leave to enter is not required, as Immigration Act 1971 s 1(1) provides that freedom to come and go, enjoyed for instance by British citizens, may be hindered 'to enable their right to be established'. Immigration Act 1971 Sch 2(1) provides that any person arriving may be examined to ascertain whether they need leave to enter, and para 4(2) requires such a person to produce 'either a valid passport with photograph or some other document satisfactorily establishing his identity and nationality or citizenship'. Therefore a British passport holder must show their passport to gain entry, even though they do not need leave to enter, and without such proof they may be refused entry (see also Immigration Act 1971 s 3(9) and HC 395 para 12). A 'valid' passport means a current one. The case of *Akewushola v Immigration Officer Heathrow* [2000] 2 All ER 148 CA established that an expired passport plus other proof of identity was not sufficient. Case C 378/97 *Wijsenbeek* [1999] I–6207 established that a European passenger could be required to

Table 9 Entry and arrival

Method of arrival and entry decision	Consequence for entry
At a port. No leave granted but allowed physically to remain pending further inquiries (probably on temporary admission –see chapter 15)	Has arrived but not entered
At a port. Leave granted or already held and not cancelled	Arrives on disembarking from ship or boat and enters lawfully when passes through immigration control
Not at a port. Crosses land border (Republic of Ireland to N. Ireland). Leave granted or already held and not cancelled	Arrives and enters lawfully on crossing border (see *R v Javaherifard and Miller* [2005] EWCA Crim 323)
Not at a port. Arrives by sea or air (e.g. on a remote beach). No leave	Arrives on disembarking. Enters at time of arrival, but not lawfully
Not at a port. Arrives by sea or air (e.g. private landing strip). Has leave.	Arrives on disembarking. Enters at time of arrival, lawfully.

prove their entitlement despite their right to free movement. However, in the case of EEA nationals a valid identity card is all that is necessary to establish the right to travel. In the case of other nationals, passports or refugee travel documents will be required.

The legal process called examination is at minimum a cursory inspection of a passport, and may go on from there (*Ogilvy v SSHD* [2007] EWHC 2301 (Admin)) to involve an interview or a series of interviews. These may be on different dates so that the whole examination may be spread over a considerable period of time. The examination also includes other investigations carried out by the immigration officer which may not involve the passenger directly (*Thirukumar* [1989] Imm AR 270). In between interviews the applicant may be in detention or released in the UK on a status known as temporary admission (Sch 2 para 21). Paragraph 4 imposes a duty on people who are undergoing examination to provide all information required for the examination including documentation. There is however no 'duty of utmost good faith' to disclose everything which might conceivably be relevant (*Khawaja* [1984] AC 74 HL). Documents so produced may be retained by the immigration officer until the examination is over (para 4(2A) and (4)). This power was extended by Immigration, Asylum and Nationality Act 2006 s 27 to allow retention of documents including a passport from arrival until the person 'is about to depart or be removed'. In other words, the passport can be retained throughout a person's stay in the UK. The immigration officer also has power to search the passenger and their luggage (para 3). Power are further extended by the UK Borders Act 2007 which provides that trained immigration officers may be 'designated', and these designated officers may detain a person suspected of a listed immigration offence (ss 1 and 2). This merges immigration and criminal policing functions.

Where a person arrives in the UK at a port, they are deemed not to have entered until they have passed through the designated area for immigration control (Immigration Act 1971 s 11). The repercussions of this are as shown in Table 9.

7.6.1 E-borders

There are a number of dimensions to the government's plan to establish 'e-borders'. In broad terms, this is the idea that personal details will be recorded and checked electronically and that this will become the paramount form of immigration control. The UK's e-borders system, once fully effective (perhaps 2018), will be one of the most intensive in the world (Statewatch). The integration of immigration control with security issues and the leading role of technology is expressed in the Prime Minister's 'Statement on Security' in Parliament on 25 July 2007:

Our first line of defence against terrorism is overseas at other countries' ports and airports where people embark on journeys to our country, and from where embassies issue visas.

As we have seen, the introduction of biometric information into the visa application process is the first step in the creation of e-borders. The Prime Minister goes on:

The way forward is electronic screening of all passengers...at ports and airports...The Home Secretary will enhance the existing E-borders programme to incorporate all passenger information.
    The second line of defence is at our borders where biometrics...are already in use.

So now we consider the changes taking place at passport control. E-borders apply to British and non-British nationals. The Council of the European Union has adopted a Regulation laying down new minimum security standards for European passports, including biometric fingerprint and facial data (2252/2004). This is part of the Schengen *acquis* which does not apply to the UK, but the UK has opted in to discussions about inserting biometric information into the uniform format visas. The UK's wish to achieve compatibility and common security systems with its European partners mean that the e-borders scheme will be designed to be compatible with documentation in other member states so far as possible.

Personal interviews are now used for first-time passport applications, at which identity is confirmed through biographical details, facial features are scanned and fingerprints taken (UK Passport Service Corporate and Business Plan 2005–2010). The information is recorded in a microchip which is read by an electronic reader at immigration control. Plans for reliance on e-passports may be undermined by the technology. The chips are only guaranteed for two years, despite the ten-year currency of passports. The front desk readers will only identify whether a passport photograph image matches the electronic image; more sophisticated readers which can detect changes in the chip will only be available in a back room at a second stage of checking. The readers will take eight seconds to scan a passport, rather longer than a cursory check by an immigration officer (National Audit Office report Session 2006–07 HC 152). Identity Cards Act 2006 s 38 allows orders to be made compelling disclosure of information from other government departments for the purposes of issuing a passport.

For non-British nationals the government plans to introduce a USA-style visa waiver programme, which will mean that visas will be required for all travellers unless their passports are machine-readable, in which case the visa requirement is waived. A voluntary iris recognition system is in place at nine airports including Heathrow, Gatwick and Birmingham. This is for frequent travellers, and promoted by the Home Office as a quicker way to get priority in immigration control. The iris recognition system is available to those with limited leave such as work permit holders and students as well as to British citizens. In return for the provision of biometric data, those registered with the scheme gain a privileged status in the e-borders system, with unhindered entry and exit.

The UK Borders Act 2007 introduces a requirement for all non-EEA nationals in the UK to obtain a biometric identification document, to be phased in over a number of years, beginning in 2008 (HC debs 5 Feb 2007: col 595).

7.6.2 **Extended powers in relation to terrorism**

Immigration officers have powers under Sch 7 to the Terrorism Act 2000 as amended to stop, detain, search, and question any person at an air or sea port for the purpose of determining whether that person appears to be concerned or to have been concerned in the 'commission, preparation or instigation of acts of terrorism' (s 40(1)(b)). A person at a port may have arrived in the UK from anywhere. There is a wider power in relation to journeys into Northern Ireland from the Republic of Ireland when a person may be stopped not only at the port, but also within the border area. This is defined as any place up to a mile from the border with the Republic, or, if the journey is by train, the first train stop in Northern Ireland (Sch 7 para 4). This places a limit on the freedom of movement given by the Common Travel Area, and consistently with current trends these constraints on movement are not immigration restrictions but are security restrictions entailing policing activity.

However, the 2000 Act contains no equivalent of the exclusion powers which were part of earlier anti-terrorism legislation. Under the Prevention of Terrorism (Temporary Provisions) Act 1989 and its predecessors, it was possible for individuals to be restricted to living in either Great Britain or Northern Ireland. These exclusion orders affecting British citizens did not appear in the 2000 Act, the omission being an aspect of the peace process in Northern Ireland.

Powers under the schedule do not require a basis of reasonable suspicion. They may be exercised 'for the purpose of determining whether' the person may have terrorist involvement, in other words, simply in order to find out. These powers are also given a wide scope by the broad definition of terrorism used in s 1 (discussed more fully in chapter 14). The exercise of these powers is subject to the usual administrative law restraints and to the Race Relations Act 1976 as amended, as discussed in chapter 8. However, this places the burden on the complainant to show that the powers were unlawfully exercised, rather than on the immigration officer to show that there was a reasonable basis for their actions.

In similar vein, an immigration officer may search a ship, aircraft, or anything on or which he reasonably believes to have been or be about to be on a ship or aircraft (e.g. a container) 'for the purpose of satisfying himself whether there are any persons he may wish to question under paragraph 2' (para 7).

The maximum period of detention for these powers to be exercised is nine hours (Sch 7 para 6), although the person may be detained for longer by the police if there are grounds for suspicion.

7.6.3 **The decision on leave to enter**

If satisfied that the passenger meets the requirements, the immigration officer (or in practice now often the entry clearance officer) may grant them leave to enter. This decision is subject to all the constraints of public law and to appeal, where available, on grounds listed in Nationality, Immigration and Asylum Act 2002 s 84. Since the amendment of s 89 by the 2006 Act there has been no appeal on arrival for a passenger who does not have entry clearance except on grounds of race discrimination, human rights or asylum claim. An immigration officer must act in accordance with the immigration rules and instructions given by the Secretary of State (Immigration

Act 1971 Sch 2 para 1(3)). There is fuller discussion of these legal constraints in the next chapter on appeals.

An immigration officer or entry clearance officer may grant leave to enter if satisfied that the passenger meets the requirements of the particular rules which apply to the kind of entry they want to achieve; that is, if they meet requirements for entry as a spouse, working holidaymaker, visitor, etc. The applicant is required to bring their application within the rules. This was illustrated in *Abid Hussain* v *ECO Islamabad* [1989] Imm AR 46 where the appellant failed because his answers were insufficiently clear for the entry clearance officer to be able to decide whether he was planning to visit the UK to marry his fiancée and then return to Pakistan, or whether he intended to settle with her in the UK.

7.6.4 **Refusal of leave to enter**

There are no general requirements for entry, but there are general grounds for refusal, which apply to leave to enter or entry clearance. The grounds for refusal in HC 395 para 320 are divided into those upon which leave to enter or entry clearance 'is to be refused' and those upon which leave to enter 'should normally be refused'. Before considering some of the grounds individually we shall consider their standing in administrative law.

The wording indicates that when a reason in the first group applies, refusal of leave is mandatory and when a reason in the second set applies, refusal is discretionary. However, although 'is to be refused' clearly implies an intention for refusals to be mandatory, the administrative law principle against fettering discretion does not permit prescription of a set of circumstances in which there must always be a refusal. The power to grant or refuse leave arises in statute, (s 4(1) Immigration Act 1971) and administrative provisions such as the immigration rules may not lawfully restrict the statutory power, though they may guide it. The principle against fettering discretion, or, it may be said, against having a rigid policy, arises from cases such as *R v Port of London Authority ex p Kynoch Ltd* [1919] 1 KB 176 and *British Oxygen Co Ltd v Minister of Technology* [1971] AC 610 in which it was held that an authority acted lawfully in having a policy as long as it was prepared to listen to someone who had something new to say which might justify dealing with them in a different way. This principle was applied to the immigration rules by the Court of Appeal in *Pearson* v *Immigration Appeal Tribunal*. Paragraph 5 of the immigration rules then in force, HC 80, provided that if the Department of Employment did not approve an extension of leave for work then the application 'should be refused'. The Court of Appeal said, at 225 that in making such a rule:

The Home Secretary did, in our opinion, make a rule as to how he would in future, as a matter of general policy, exercise his discretion, but not how he would exercise it in every case without considering the circumstances of a particular case and whether to make an exception to that policy.

The rule was therefore not a fetter on discretion and not *ultra vires*.

In *R(P) and R(Q)* v *SSHD* [2001] EWCA Civ 1151 the Court of Appeal held that the prison service was entitled to have a policy that when mothers were in prison, children should be separated from them at 18 months old. Human Rights Act 1998 (Article 8, the right to respect for family life) would not prevent such a policy from existing, but it would require that the application of the rule to the individual case should be examined. Article 8 therefore goes further than the existing administrative law rule in that it requires a decision-maker to show that infringement of the right to respect for family life caused by adherence to the policy was proportionate to the aim sought to be achieved. The result of this for the application of mandatory grounds for refusal is that they may be regarded as a legitimate statement of policy and therefore of what will normally happen, but that the immigration officer or entry clearance officer must be prepared to act outside the policy if individual circumstances warrant doing so. When a qualified Convention right is infringed by the refusal then the infringement must be proportionate to the public interest which the officer seeks to protect.

In the case of refusal of leave to enter or entry clearance the courts will not readily find that a Convention right is at stake. An indication as to the courts' approach is given by *SSHD v Farrakhan* [2002] Imm AR 447 CA. Louis Farrakhan, the controversial leader of the Muslim sect, The Nation of Islam, had been refused entry to the UK, the mandatory ground in paragraph 320 being that the Secretary of State personally directed that his exclusion was conducive to the public good. His application was as a visitor to conduct a week's speaking tour. The refusal was challenged by judicial review, contending, *inter alia*, that it breached his Article 10 right to freedom of expression. The Court of Appeal held that the Secretary of State's reason for excluding Farrakhan was a justifiable one relating to public order and a legitimate exercise of his statutory power to control immigration. It only incidentally affected Farrakhan's freedom of expression in that he would not be able to exercise that freedom in the territory from which he had been excluded. The decision to exclude was prior to the possibility of establishing any freedom of expression, which would only occur once the speaker was in the UK. This distinction does seem rather thin; nevertheless, the exclusion was upheld. In *Rev Sun Myung Moon v ECO Seoul* [2005] UKAIT 00112 the tribunal went further and held that human rights cannot be engaged in entry cases. This is not the view of the Entry Clearance Monitor (Report November 2007) and does not appear sustainable (see Clayton 2006).The reasoning in *Farrakhan* does not apply where the arrival itself constitutes the fulfilment of the right, as in a family reunion case where the right to respect for family life is recognized by the person being allowed to enter the UK. It is the geographical separation which caused the breach. These situations are discussed in chapters 4 and 9.

The existence of so-called mandatory reasons for refusal is not an unlawful fetter on discretion according to the principles of administrative law, because there exists a power to act outside the rules. This is acknowledged in the Immigration Directorate Instructions (IDI) Chapter 9 Section 2 para 1 June 2004, which says, referring to the mandatory grounds, '[I]n practice, however, entry clearance or leave to enter, as applicable, is *normally* refused on these grounds'. Guidance is provided in that section for 'occasions when refusal is *not* appropriate'.

7.6.4.1 *Immigration officer is satisfied*

A number of the reasons for refusal in paragraph 320 entail the immigration officer being satisfied that something is the case. This is a formula commonly encountered in statute and rules, and requires that the officer approaches the enquiry in a reasonable manner. *Secretary of State for Education v Tameside MBC* [1977] AC 1014 established that even though the statute said that the minister could exercise his powers if he was 'satisfied that' the local authority was acting unreasonably, this was not just a matter of his subjective judgment but of assembling all the relevant information and making a rational decision based on that evidence. He was required to act reasonably, and this requirement is implicit in any immigration rule using a similar phrase. *JC (China) v ECO Guangzhou* [2007] UKAIT 00027 confirmed that the burden of proof is on the Secretary of State on the balance of probabilities to prove any fact upon which a refusal under para 320 relies. The case also pointed out that the applicant must still be able to meet the requirements of the substantive rules in order to gain entry after a successful appeal on a para 320 ground.

7.6.4.2 *Reasons for refusal*

The first reason given in para 320 is that 'entry is sought for a purpose not covered by the rules'. As mentioned previously, the reason for entry must generally be brought within the categories provided for by the rules. However, the applicant is not a lawyer (usually) and the obligation on them is modified 'where there is an obvious link or connection' with another rule (*SZ (Applicable immigration rules) Bangladesh* [2007] UKAIT 00037). For instance in that case a child who could not gain entry as an adopted child could possibly have done so under another rule applying to children, and the decision-maker could have considered that without the applicant having to advance it.

Paragraph 320(1) gives the clearest example of when, although the rule might appear to mandate refusal, discretion could be exercised outside the rules. The application might be within the general scope of a category, for instance dependent relatives in exceptional compassionate circumstances (HC 395 para 317), but the particular applicant does not actually qualify because the family relationship to the sponsor is not one of those for which the rule provides. For instance, the applicant, although in exceptional compassionate circumstances, may be a nephew, which is a relationship not provided for in the rule. Refusal is possible under para 320(1), but so also is a grant of entry exceptionally outside the rules if the circumstances seem to the officer sufficiently compelling to make this an appropriate exercise of discretion.

The grounds in full are set out in Table 10.

7.6.4.3 *Grounds relating to public good*

There are three reasons for refusal relating to the public good. The mandatory reason in para 320(6) and the discretionary one in para 320(19) are similarly worded except that the mandatory one is a personal direction of the Secretary of State and the discretionary one is the decision of the immigration officer. Paragraph 320(18) referring to criminal convictions has an overlap with grounds of public good.

Personal directions such as that permitted by para 320(6) are not common, but are increasingly used when there is a perceived risk to national security. By their nature, they tend to be used when the individual has some degree of notoriety, or there is intelligence information suggesting risk. In *Farrakhan*, the Secretary of State had information that, because Mr Farrakhan had expressed anti-Semitic views, and because two members of the Nation of Islam had been arrested for public order offences outside the Stephen Lawrence Inquiry, his presence in the UK might give rise to disorder. As a personal decision of the Secretary of State, a decision under para 320(6) is not open to appeal (Nationality, Immigration and Asylum Act 2002 s 98). The Court of Appeal referred to this lack of appeal right as indicating that Parliament had taken the view that

Table 10 Grounds for refusal of leave to enter or entry clearance

Mandatory grounds	
Entry is sought for a purpose not covered by the rules	Prima facie, categories in rules are exhaustive
Currently subject to deportation order	Deportation order prevents entry during its currency – see chapter 15
Failure to produce a valid national passport or other document satisfactorily establishing nationality and identity	As discussed, this applied to everyone, even those with right of abode
In case of person intending to travel to another part of Common Travel Area, failure to satisfy immigration officer (IO) that passenger will be acceptable to immigration authorities there	Implementing the Common Travel Area
In case of visa national: failure to produce valid and current entry clearance for purpose for which entry is sought	Implementing visa regime
Secretary of State's personal direction that exclusion is conducive to public good	See discussion
Discretionary grounds	
For medical reasons, entry undesirable	See discussion
Failure to give IO information required for purpose of deciding whether leave to enter is needed and if so whether and on what terms it should be given	The IDI advises that this ground should be used only if the passenger continues not to provide the information so that it is impossible to proceed
Outside UK: failure to supply information, documents, medical report required by IO	Equivalent to the preceding ground for outside UK post 2000 applications
Failure by a returning resident to meet the requirements of para 18 of the rules	Discussed below
Presenting a passport of a government not recognized by the UK	IDI Dec 00 lists these as Turkish Republic of Northern Cyprus, Taiwan, and Palestine.
Failure to observe a time limit or condition attached to a previous grant of leave	Note this consequence of a breach of immigration law for future applications
Obtaining a previous leave to by deception	As above
Failure to satisfy IO that passenger will be able to return to another country	Though where this is because e.g. a passport may expire, limited leave may be given to avoid refusal (HC 395 para 21)
Refusal by sponsor to give undertaking	See chapter 9
Making false representation or material non-disclosure to obtain a work permit	Self-explanatory
In case of a child, failure to provide parent's consent to travel	Also self-explanatory
Refusal to undergo medical examination	See discussion
Criminal convictions	See discussion
IO believes exclusion is conducive to public good	See discussion

in this area of decision-making the courts should accord the Secretary of State's opinion a significant degree of deference. A personal direction under para 320(6) was used in the case of *Murungaru v SSHD, ECO Nairobi, British High Commissioner Nairobi* [2006] EWHC 2416 (Admin) in which the Secretary of State received information that the Kenyan MP and minister was engaging in activities concerned with corruption in Kenya during his medical visits to the UK. It was partly to show support for the Kenyan government that the Secretary of State acted quickly under para 320(6) to prevent his next visit.

The second ground for refusal on the basis that exclusion is conducive to the public good is that 'it seems right' 'from information available to the immigration officer'. The sub-paragraph gives some idea of the kind of information intended: 'if for example, in the light of the character, conduct or associations of the person seeking leave to enter it is undesirable to give him leave to enter'. The IDI elaborates, saying 'the immigration officer must specify what past or future action of the person makes his exclusion conducive to the public good. Vague generalisations...will not suffice' (Ch 9 s 2 para 21 June 2004). The case of *Ramanathan* v *Secretary of State for the Foreign and Commonwealth Office* [1999] Imm AR 97 gives an example of the kind of activities which might found refusal under this paragraph. Here the appellant was suspected of facilitating unlawful immigration. The appellant remained outside the UK and no criminal charges were brought, but suspicions expressed in communications between British High Commissions in Sri Lanka (his country of origin) and Singapore (his country of residence) were sufficient to support a refusal on this ground.

The information founding the decision might be prior information, such as a prohibition of a group of which the passenger is a member, for instance the ban on scientologists challenged in *Van Duyn*. It might be information gathered then and there at the port of entry, for instance if the passenger is found to be in possession of illegal drugs or quantities of pornography sufficient to suggest that they are intending to sell it rather than use it personally. The IDI suggests that, if the passenger is only carrying a small amount and has sufficient money to pay any likely fine, then entry should not be refused on this basis, although this is hard to reconcile with the current climate concerning offences by foreign nationals. Information disclosed by the examination of biometric data may give rise to refusals of entry clearance or leave to enter under this rule.

The phrase 'it seems right' in this sub-paragraph is another way of expressing a discretion. As elsewhere, this discretion must be exercised fairly and reasonably *(R v SSHD ex p Moon* [1996] COD 54, *Secretary of State for Education v Tameside MBC)*. 'Conducive to the public good' is also grounds for deportation, and arguably a person should not be excluded under this paragraph if they would not be considered liable for deportation, generally a more severe sanction, on the same facts. Paragraph 320(18) provides for the refusal of leave to enter or entry clearance on the basis of a criminal conviction 'save where the immigration officer is satisfied that admission would be justified for strong compassionate reasons'. The conviction must be for any offence which would be punishable in the UK by at least 12 months' imprisonment. It therefore includes all but the most trivial offences. The exclusion however is discretionary; discretion must be exercised fairly, and in a case where the right to respect for private or family life is interfered with by a refusal of leave, discretion must be exercised proportionately in accordance with Article 8. As 'strong compassionate reasons' often relate to private or family life, the arguments in pre-October 2000 case law about what would amount to 'strong compassionate reasons' are now largely superseded by human rights arguments and the requirement for proportionality.

The admission of the boxer Mike Tyson to the UK gave the occasion for the Divisional Court to consider the nature of the discretion given to the immigration officer in this sub-paragraph *(R v SSHD ex p Bindel* [2001] Imm AR 1). As Mike Tyson had been convicted of rape he would have been liable for exclusion under this sub-paragraph as rape carries a sentence of more than 12 months and in fact he had been sentenced to six years' imprisonment. Exercising his power to issue instructions to immigration officers, the Secretary of State directed that Mike Tyson should be admitted. A group called Justice for Women argued in judicial review proceedings that the Secretary of State was not entitled to give such an instruction, however, as we have seen (chapter 1), the Secretary of State is not bound by the rules and may direct immigration officers to act more generously towards an applicant. Sullivan J went further than this. He held that the discretion to admit Tyson was exerciseable within the rule, and the instruction by the Secretary of State was thus not inconsistent with the rule. There were reasons of public interest for admitting Tyson, such as the economic benefit that the boxing match would bring, the fact that tickets for the fight had already been sold, and business interests were depending on it. As Justice for Women argued, these are clearly not 'strong compassionate reasons', they are economic reasons. However, Sullivan J held that the reference to 'strong compassionate reasons' in the sub-paragraph was not an exhaustive description of the basis for exercising discretion, the sub-paragraph was a discretionary reason for refusing leave to enter, and this discretion could not be constrained. This seems to make the reference to compassionate reasons redundant. Macdonald refers to it as 'distressingly vague' (5th edn 2001, p. 84).

The Rehabilitation of Offenders Act 1974 applies to entry to the UK, so that a person should not be refused entry on the basis of a conviction which is 'spent' under the Act. Returning residents are not exempted from this sub-paragraph, so a settled person could be refused re-entry on the basis of a conviction (see below). In practice Article 8 rights are almost certain to be engaged in such a case, and a conviction would, it is suggested, have to be of a nature which was particularly threatening to the public interest in order to warrant exclusion of a settled person (but see *Ogilvy* below). Arguments about the rights of long-term residents to remain despite criminal convictions are considered more fully in the section on enforcement.

Travel bans
Increasingly there are international interests involved in restricting certain people from travelling between countries. These centre around the prevention of crime, particularly terrorist and drugs offences, and restriction of the movements of war criminals and national leaders upon whom groups of nations wish to bring pressure to bear. This latter power was given effect in UK law by s 8 of the Immigration and Asylum Act 1999, inserting a s 8B into the Immigration Act 1971. The section provides for a new category of 'excluded persons'. These are people named or referred to in a resolution of the United Nations Security Council or Council of the European Union which is designated for this purpose by an Order made by the Secretary of State. Since s 8B came into force the Secretary of State has made a number of Immigration (Designation of Travel Bans) Orders designating European resolutions concerning for instance former President Milosevic of Yugoslavia, and President Mugabe of Zimbabwe, and UN resolutions concerning Angola and Sierra Leone. The effect of these designations is, according to s 8B, that the excluded person 'must be refused' leave to enter or leave to remain in the UK. It is apparent that these resolutions and orders are targeted upon particular figures and will not often be encountered. Their significance lies not in the scope of their application, but in that they demonstrate the increase in concerted international

action on issues which are seen as relating to violations of human rights on a large scale, or to the spread of criminal activity.

7.6.4.4 Medical reasons

A person who intends to remain in the UK for more than six months should normally be referred to the medical inspector for a medical examination (HC 395 para 36). This applies to anyone who is coming to the UK to settle with family members. Referral to the medical inspector may also be made if the person seeking entry 'mentions health or medical treatment as a reason for his visit or appears not to be in good health' (para 36). An immigration officer may also refer a person for further medical examination after entry 'in the interests of public health' (Immigration Act 1971 Sch 2 para 7). This aspect of immigration control too is being exported. A new scheme implemented in 2007 requires applicants for more than six months' stay from Bangladesh, Ghana, Kenya, Pakistan, Sudan, Tanzania or Thailand to have a medical test for tuberculosis *before* making their entry clearance application.

Refusal to undergo a medical examination is a discretionary reason for refusal of leave to enter or entry clearance (para 320(17)) and so is failure to supply a medical report when an application is proceeding outside the UK (para 320(8A) and Immigration (Leave to Enter and Remain) Order 2000, SI 2000/1161, art 7(4)). The effect of this is that, when an immigration officer or ECO (HC 395 para 39) refers a person for a medical examination, that person is compelled to attend the medical examination if they want leave to enter. The IDI makes it clear that it is only in the most exceptional circumstances that a passenger who refuses to undergo a medical examination will be given leave to enter (Ch 9 s 2 para 19 June 2004). The content of the report too may be fatal to an application. If the medical inspector reports that 'for medical reasons it is undesirable to admit the person' this is a mandatory ground for refusal of entry clearance or leave to enter. There are broadly speaking two kinds of grounds upon which a medical inspector might come to such a view. These are, first, that the applicant suffers from a disease which is highly infectious or contagious and thus there is a risk to public health. There is a strong argument that refusal on these grounds should be restricted to those diseases which are listed as grounds for refusal in the case of EEA nationals as there seems to be no justification for treating non-Europeans less favourably than Europeans (see chapter 6). Note that people suffering from AIDS or who are HIV positive may not be refused admission on the grounds of this diagnosis alone (IDI Ch 1 s 8 para 2.5 Mar 2004). The second kind of ground for refusal for medical reasons would be the anticipated economic consequences of the applicant's ill health. There is provision to enter the UK for private medical treatment, and this is discussed in chapter 10. However, if a person in substantial need of medical treatment applied to enter as a spouse, for instance, there might be concerns that they would never be well enough to be financially self-supporting; alternatively there might be suspicion that National Health Service treatment was the real reason for entering the UK. These grounds reflect the same arguments against accepting immigrants which go back to the Aliens Act 1905 or even earlier, namely that people should not be admitted who appeared likely 'from disease or infirmity' (Aliens Act 1905 s 1) to become reliant on public funds. The March 2004 IDI perpetuates the inconsistency of earlier IDIs on this subject, as Ch 1 s 8 para 2.1 says that there could be refusal on this ground 'if the nature of the person's condition would interfere with his ability to support himself or his dependants'. Paragraph 2.2, on the other hand, says 'medical inspectors only certify that it is undesirable to admit a passenger to the UK when satisfied that a passenger's condition represents a significant risk to public health'. There must be doubt as to the lawfulness of a medical inspector certifying in the terms suggested in para 2.1, as this is an economic rather than a medical reason for refusal. It would, however, be possible for the immigration officer, not the medical inspector, to refuse on grounds of likely inability to maintain without recourse to public funds (see chapter 9), but only if there were genuine doubt about the passenger's being maintained. Where there are other sufficient sources of financial support, this reason for refusal could not be used. The National Health Service is not defined as 'public funds' for people entering to settle with family (HC 395 para 6 as amended) and so refusal on the grounds of likely demand on the National Health Service would not be lawful.

The medical inspector is a doctor employed by the Home Office to make reports on potential immigrants and asylum seekers (Immigration Act 1971 s 4(2) and Sch 2 para 1(2)) and medical officers attached to British posts abroad carry out examinations there. Trained as a doctor to make a diagnosis leading to treatment for the benefit of the patient, they are in this instance a servant of the Home Office required to screen the patient, not for the patient's benefit, but in order to implement immigration policy. Indeed, in para 320(7) there is something of a role reversal. The medical inspector, according to the wording of the rule, makes an immigration decision. The rule provides an exception to following the medical inspector's recommendation, when 'the Immigration Officer is satisfied that there are strong compassionate reasons justifying admission'. The medical inspector must not take their non-therapeutic role too far. The IDI stresses in Ch 1 s 8 para 2 that medical inspectors should not be asked to examine passengers to discover whether they have borne children or had sexual relations nor to X-ray them to determine their age. The prohibition in the IDI is worded more strictly here than is common, and this is because precisely these practices were carried out in the 1970s. The former refers to the virginity tests carried out on the claimed basis that a good Muslim or Hindu woman would not engage in sexual relations before marriage, nor would a respectable man of those faiths marry someone who had. Therefore genuine fiancées could be detected by their virginity. The ensuing scandal prompted the Commission for Racial Equality's investigation into immigration control and is not something that the Home Office would wish to repeat.

Tribunal decisions suggest that the medical inspector's opinion may not be challenged on its own merits, and that the immigration officer may only override it if, following the rule, there are 'strong compassionate circumstances' (*Al-Tuwaidji* v *Chief Immigration Officer Heathrow* [1974] Imm AR 34 followed in *Mohazeb* v *Immigration Officer Harwich* [1990] Imm AR 555). This illustrates a continuing difference between the mandatory and discretionary grounds, in that because the medical inspector's refusal is said to be mandatory there is no appeal on its merits but only the possibility of judicial review for failure to exercise the residual discretion. Indeed the now exclusive grounds for appeal in Nationality, Immigration and Asylum Act 2002 s 84 do not give scope for challenging the medical inspector's report on its merits (see chapter 8). There is arguably an unauthorised delegation of the immigration decision-making function to the medical inspector which seems to be less open to judicial review than the immigration officer's exercise of discretion.

This ground for refusal does not apply to people with settled status who, having travelled abroad, may not be refused re-entry on medical grounds.

7.6.4.5 *Exercise of discretion*

Following the so-called mandatory grounds for refusing leave to enter or entry clearance, para 320 sets out thirteen grounds on which leave to enter 'should normally be refused'. The discretion must be exercised fairly *(R V SSHD ex p Moon)* and based on evidence, taking into account relevant and excluding irrelevant factors (*Associated Provincial Picture Houses Ltd* v *Wednesbury Corporation* [1948] 1 KB 223). In *SSHD v Mowla and Patel* [1991] Imm AR 210 the Court of Appeal held that detriment to the applicants caused by the difference in rights of appeal accorded to those refused leave to enter, as compared with those refused a variation of leave in the UK, was not a factor which the immigration officer should take into account. Any such decision taken since 2 October 2000 must take into account any Convention rights affected by the decision and, where qualified rights are affected, any infringement of the right must be proportionate to the aim pursued.

Scope for the exercise of discretion is found particularly in sub-paras 11 and 12, which both concern previous breaches of immigration law. The previous breach in question need not have been during the most recent visit to the UK, according to *Ofoajoku* [1991] Imm AR 68. In this case a student had been refused leave to enter on the basis of previous breaches of immigration law even though in the intervening period he had had a further period of leave which had been granted without knowledge of the earlier breaches. The IAT held that this intervening leave did not wipe the slate clean, nor did it give rise to the legal doctrine of estoppel whereby the Secretary of State would be prevented from taking account of the earlier breaches. His discretion could not be limited in that way. The IDI makes it plain that refusal under sub-para 11 should not be used where previous breaches were trivial, and in a punitive way. It should be used where the passenger has shown that they have 'contrived in a *significant* way to frustrate the purpose of the rules'.

7.6.5 **Cancellation of leave to enter**

Leave to enter may be cancelled on arrival, or refused, even for a person who has prior entry clearance (HC 395 paras 321 and 321A). On the same grounds entry clearance may be revoked before travel (para 30A) but this is very rare. The effect of cancellation and of refusal is very similar, namely, at the port the passenger is not allowed to enter, although they may be admitted temporarily to pursue an appeal if they are among the dwindling few who still have a right of appeal that can be exercised in the UK. Cancellation does not have retrospective effect (*NM (Zimbabwe)* [2007] UKAIT 00002) so that, when the appellant in that case applied for a variation of leave before the cancellation decision, he had current leave which meant his leave was extended until his appeal was heard.

Leave to enter may be cancelled on the following grounds: (a) the leave or entry clearance was obtained by false representations; (b) the leave or entry clearance was obtained as a result of material facts not being disclosed; or (c) there has been a material change of circumstances since the leave or entry clearance was obtained. The tribunal in *BA (Nigeria)* [2006] UKAIT 00080 held that these grounds are mandatory.

7.6.5.1 *False representations and non-disclosure of material facts*

In *Akhtar* [1991] Imm AR 326 CA the Court of Appeal held that false representations were simply representations that were inaccurate, they did not necessarily have to be fraudulent. The effect of this is that the falsity does not have to be deliberate. In the case of cancellation of leave to enter, the rule requires that the applicant themselves must have made the false statement (para 321A(2)). In the case of refusal of leave to enter or revocation of entry clearance, the false representation may have been made by some-one else 'whether or not to the holder's knowledge'. The representations, whether oral or in writing, need only have been made in order to obtain entry clearance or leave to enter *(Akhtar)*. They need not have been decisive of the application. There is a question of degree here. An irrelevant representation, such as for instance that the bride wore a red dress, could not be said to being made in order to obtain entry clearance as nothing turned on it (or nothing should have turned on it – see the earlier discussion about the discrepancy system). However, in *Sukhjinder Kaur* [1998] Imm AR 1 CA, a representation that her husband was at a certain address, whereas he was in prison, was relevant and false and so resulted in a refusal of leave to enter even though entry clearance had been granted. His imprisonment if disclosed would not necessarily have been fatal to his wife's application for entry clearance; the factor about which the false representation is made does not have to be decisive of the application in order to deprive the applicant of leave to enter.

This is related to the second ground, and the materiality of facts not disclosed. Again for leave to enter to be cancelled the non-disclosure must have been by the applicant, though refusal of leave to enter and revocation of entry clearance can be based on non-disclosure by third parties. Facts are held to be material if they would have influenced the outcome of the application but similarly they need not be facts upon which the whole application would stand or fall. So in Sukhjinder Kaur's case, her failure to dis-close her husband's actual whereabouts was a material non-disclosure, even though she might still have been granted entry had the truth been known. The applicant, however, is not permitted to make that argument. They cannot oppose the cancellation of leave to enter on the basis that if the true facts had been known they would have gained entry anyway *(Bugdaycay* [1987] AC 514 HL).

7.6.5.2 *Change of circumstances*

A change of circumstances, in order to warrant refusal or cancellation of leave to enter, or revocation of entry clearance, must be so fundamental that it undermines the basis upon which the original application was made. In the case of a visitor who changes their itinerary or their sponsor, the change would not normally be regarded as funda-mental. It is in each case a question of fact and degree (*Immigration Officer Heathrow* v *Salmak* [1991] Imm AR 191). Changes in visitors' plans are discussed further in chapter 10. Each case under this rule turns upon its facts. In *Chakrabarty* 01/TH/1939 the tri-bunal found that considering the change of circumstances was a purely objective exer-cise, comparing the circumstances now with the circumstances at the time of the grant of entry clearance. It was not necessary to engage in speculation as to what decision the entry clearance officer would have reached if the present circumstances had been known then. The tribunal also confirmed that the onus is on the immigration officer to show that there has been a change of circumstances, and that as an adverse decision will deprive the individual of a benefit (i.e. leave to enter), the change of circumstances must be 'substantial and relevant'.

The rule can have harsh consequences, as in *Angur Begum* [1989] Imm AR 302, in which the Divisional Court held that there was a change of circumstances removing the basis for admission when the sponsoring father and husband of the applicants had died since the application was made.

7.6.5.3 *Further grounds for cancellation*

Where leave is in existence at the date of arrival, it may be cancelled under para 321A on additional grounds over and above those on which leave may be refused to a holder of an old-style entry clearance. These grounds are parallel to some of the reasons for refusal under para 320. They are the two public good grounds, both the Secretary of State's personal direction and the immigration officer's judgment and, save in relation to a settled person, medical grounds.

The public good grounds are discretionary as is clear from the wording of the rule: 'it seems right' (*CA v Immigration Officer Heathrow* [2004] UKIAT 00243). The medical grounds are different in that, although compassionate reasons may override the medical undesirability of entry, there is no necessary involvement of a medical officer in the decision. The rule (para 321A(3)) simply says 'where it is apparent for medical reasons', with no suggestion that this has to be apparent to anyone except the immigration officer. Additionally, while a person is still outside the UK, leave to enter may be cancelled for non-production of documents, information etc, in parallel with para 320(8A).

7.7 Leave to enter granted in the UK

As mentioned above, entry to the UK is a legal event which may or may not coincide with physical arrival. So a person may be living in the UK for a period of months or even years on temporary admission, but still not treated as having entered.

Referring back to s 4(1), it is apparent that in 1971 the statute contemplated a clear division of function between immigration officers and other Home Office civil servants. Immigration officers were to have the power to give or refuse leave to enter, and the Secretary of State, in practice the Immigration department, had power to give leave to remain or to vary leave. Decisions on leave to remain or varying leave are the 'in country' decisions, the decisions that are taken once a person is in the UK. These may be contrasted with the border control decisions allocated by s 4 to the immigration service. Decisions on asylum claims are made by the Home Office. The effect of this division of powers was that at the end of a claim for asylum, the papers related to the claim went back to the immigration service to grant or refuse leave to enter. This added to the administrative complexity of dealing with asylum cases and was nonsensical in the case of someone who had been living in the UK on temporary admission for perhaps years.

However, the power in Immigration Act 1971 s 3A includes the following:

The Secretary of State may, in such circumstances as may be prescribed in an order made by him, give or refuse leave to enter the United Kingdom. (s 3A(7))

In other words, the power previously reserved to the immigration service may now be exercised by the Secretary of State, to the extent that an order of the Secretary of State provides for this. The Immigration (Leave to Enter) Order 2001, SI 2001/2590, made under the power in s 3A, provides that the Secretary of State may give or refuse leave to enter to an asylum or human rights applicant.

The trend towards eroding the distinction between immigration officers and Secretary of State powers exercised by other Home Office civil servants has continued in the Nationality, Immigration and Asylum Act 2002. Section 62 envisages the power in Immigration Act 1971 s 3A being used to enable the Secretary of State to examine a person in order to decide whether to give leave to enter, to issue removal directions, to detain pending examination. In other words, all the powers formerly reserved to the immigration service are becoming Secretary of State powers also.

7.8 **The leave obtained**

In this section there is discussion of the possible kinds of leave that a person may have acquired as a consequence of passing through immigration control, and of the effects of such leave.

7.8.1 **Non-lapsing or continuing leave**

A further change made by the Immigration (Leave to Enter and Remain) Order 2000, SI 2000/1161 is the introduction of so-called 'non-lapsing' or 'continuing' leave. Before 30 July 2000, when article 13 of the 2000 Order was implemented the position was governed entirely by Immigration Act 1971 s 3(4), which provides: 'A person's leave to enter or remain in the United Kingdom shall lapse on his going to a country or territory outside the Common Travel Area...' There were a few exceptions to this rule, but in general what it meant was that people on limited leave, such as students, could go away from the UK for a weekend break, and be refused entry on their return.

From 30 July 2000, s 3(4) remains in force, but its effects are considerably modified. Article 13(2) of the 2000 Order provides that leave will not lapse on the holder's leaving the Common Travel Area if 'it was conferred by means of an entry clearance... or for a period exceeding six months'. The effect of this is that most people with limited leave will be able to come and go during the currency of that leave without fear of being refused entry on return. The reasons for cancellation of leave discussed in the last section of this chapter apply to a person returning who holds non-lapsing leave. The immigration officer is therefore entitled to examine them to discover whether any such reason applies (Immigration Act 1971 Sch 2 para 2A). *Ogilvy v SSHD* [2007] EWHC 2301 (Admin) was a decision with disturbing implications which confirmed that cancellation may apply to someone who has indefinite leave to remain. There was suspicion that the claimant was involved in criminal offences, and the court held that the Home Office acted lawfully in using this immigration power to hold his passport, suspend his leave and grant temporary admission while further criminal inquiries were conducted. The power was not limited to investigation of his current immigration status. Criminal offences might after all be a reason to cancel leave. This interpretation means that somebody may be deprived of leave to remain without any criminal charge being proved against them, and thus unable to work or claim benefits pending trial. This is the case whether or not they are ultimately convicted and even if they would not be liable to deportation.

The non-lapsing provisions do not apply to leave to enter as a visitor, but another provision has a very similar effect. Article 4 provides that a visit visa 'during its period of validity, shall have effect as leave to enter the United Kingdom on an unlimited number of occasions' for six months if the visa has at least six months of validity remaining, or its remaining period of validity if this is shorter. Visit visas may be granted for periods of up to five years, on the basis that any stay as a visitor is limited to six months, but permitting multiple entries during the five-year period. These visas are used particularly by business people. The leave to enter lapses on the visitor leaving the Common Travel Area (2000 Order art 13(2)) but on their return within the period of validity of the visa it operates as leave to enter again (art 13(2)). The Immigration (Leave to Enter and Remain) (Amendment) Order 2005, SI 2005/1159, makes an exception to this provision for visitors under an Approved Destination Status Agreement with China. These visas are normally for one entry unless endorsed for two.

The visitor who does not benefit from the 2000 Order is the non-visa national visitor who obtains leave to enter at the port which lapses on their departure (art 13(2)), but who does not possess a visa which can operate as leave to enter on their return. Therefore they must re-apply for leave to enter on arrival at the port on each occasion.

7.8.2 **24-hour rule**

The 24-hour rule is briefly discussed here as it gives a form of deemed leave to enter. It applies to people applying at the port for leave to enter for a limited period. This is now restricted to non-visa nationals wishing to enter as a visitor. After examination of the passenger is concluded, the immigration officer has 24 hours in which to give notice of their decision to the passenger. If the officer fails to do so, Immigration Act 1971 Sch 2 para 6(1) gives the passenger six months deemed leave with a prohibition on working. This is equivalent to the leave that a visitor would be granted routinely. The Immigration (Leave to Enter and Remain) Order 2000, SI 2000/1161 in effect nullifies the 24-hour rule where an examination has been adjourned for further enquiries or where there has been a further examination. Article 12 provides that

any notice giving or refusing leave to enter which is *on any date thereafter* sent by post to the applicant (or is communicated to him in such form or manner as is permitted by this Order) shall be regarded, for the purposes of this Act, as having been given within the period of 24 hours specified in paragraph 6(1) of Schedule 2. (emphasis added)

The words in brackets refer to the possibility of notice being given by fax or e-mail, as mentioned earlier. The words 'on any date thereafter' extend the 24-hour period and override an earlier body of case law. The 2006 Act gives power to make further provision about when an application is treated as being decided. The 24-hour rule applies to lawful applicants for leave, not those treated as illegal entrants on arrival.

7.8.3 **Limited leave to enter**

Leave to enter may be for an indefinite or a limited period of time. Most leave is limited, and may be subject to conditions (Immigration Act 1971 s 3(1)(c)). The conditions may be:

- restricting or prohibiting employment,
- requiring the holder to maintain themselves and any dependants without recourse to public funds,
- requiring the holder to register with the police
- reporting to an immigration officer or the Secretary of State, and
- about residence.

The last two conditions were added by UK Borders Act 2007 s 16 as part of the government's intention to keep track of people, particularly asylum seekers and unaccompanied children seeking asylum. There were objections (e.g. from Liberty, see Public Bill Committee 1 March 2007 col 121) about the width of the condition about residence. There is no limit on the face of the condition as to *what* can be specified about residence, so it could in theory be used like house arrest. A proposal to insert a test of necessity and explicit human rights protection in the clause was defeated. No other conditions are possible. If and when the time limit is lifted on the holder's stay in the UK, any conditions will also be lifted, as indefinite leave may not be subject to conditions (s 3(3)).

If the holder of limited leave does not intend to leave the country on the expiry of the leave, an application to extend or vary the terms of leave must be made before it expires, otherwise the person becomes an overstayer and is liable to removal (Immigration Act 1999 s 10).

7.8.4 Indefinite leave to enter

For a minority of entrants to the UK, leave to enter is indefinite. This is the case for adult dependent family members coming for settlement. When leave is indefinite there may be no further contact with the Home Office and there is no further stage to pass through in terms of immigration status. For such a person leave to enter and leave to remain are one and the same. A person with indefinite leave to remain has full access to the National Health Service and may freely change employment as no conditions may be attached to indefinite leave (Immigration Act 1971 s 3(3)(a)). As no conditions may be attached it might appear that such a person will also have full access to the welfare benefits system. However, in most cases adult dependent relatives will only gain indefinite leave straight away if their sponsor has signed an undertaking to support them for a fixed period of perhaps five years. During this period no claim for welfare benefits may be made by them or on their behalf. Residence without immigration restriction is one of the qualifications to apply for naturalization as a British citizen (British Nationality Act 1981 Sch 1 paras 1 and 3), and so a person who gains indefinite leave straight away may begin to count time towards qualifying to naturalize as British if they so wish.

7.8.4.1 *Returning residents*

A person with indefinite leave has no immigration restrictions on their stay in the UK, but they are still subject to immigration control in that if they leave the country they may be examined by an immigration officer on their return and refused entry on limited grounds. Prior to the Immigration (Leave to Enter and Remain) Order 2000, SI 2000/1161, the position of such people was governed by the so-called returning resident rules, found in HC 395 paras 18–20. These rules were based on the fact that indefinite leave lapsed when the holder left the UK, but enabled the holder to be readmitted provided they had not been absent for more than two years, that when they last entered they had indefinite leave, that they now returned for settlement and that they did not leave the UK with the assistance of public funds (i.e. using a government repatriation scheme). These rules are still in existence, but must now be read together with SI 2000/1161. The effect of the 2000 Order is that leave does not lapse during an absence of less than two years. So a person with indefinite leave who returns within two years no longer has to re-apply for leave. The effect of the change removes the basis for confusion and distressing refusals of leave to enter provided the person returns within two years. The continuing existence of the requirement to prove that they had indefinite leave when they last left and that they now enter for settlement does not really make sense in the light of the fact that they have no application to make at the port. They may only be examined at the port to see if the leave should be cancelled, for the reasons discussed in the earlier section on this subject. Rather bizarrely, following the 2000 Order, the returning residents' rules seem to place a greater burden on a person with indefinite leave than is placed on a person with limited leave.

After two years, even so-called non-lapsing leave actually lapses (Immigration (Leave to Enter and Remain) Order 2000, SI 2000/1161 article 13(4)). Outside the two-year period re-entry is a matter of discretion, but if the only factor preventing return is that the person has been away too long, they should be admitted if, for example, they have lived in the UK for most of their life (HC 395 para 19). This is a wide discretion, and the example of when it should be exercised is no more than an indication of a basis for exercising it. Reference may be made to the IDIs for more examples. Visa nationals returning after more than two years will need a new entry clearance.

Returning residents may be refused readmission on grounds under para 320, in the limited situations where these are relevant, but not on medical grounds. Refusal is possible on grounds of exclusion being conducive to the public good, and para 320 (9) gives the basis for refusal of leave where the requirements of para 18 are not met.

7.8.4.2 *New limits on indefinite leave*

The security of indefinite leave to remain is somewhat undermined by the new power in Nationality, Immigration and Asylum Act 2002 s 76, discussed in chapter 1. Under this section the Secretary of State may revoke a person's indefinite leave to enter or remain if the person is liable to deportation but 'cannot be deported for legal reasons'. In a similar vein, under s 76(2) indefinite leave can be revoked if it was obtained by deception but the person cannot be removed for legal or practical reasons. A person whose leave is revoked will not be able to work or claim benefits and therefore will have no basis for economic support unless they are detained or work illegally. Their children will not be British, and depending on the laws of their country of nationality may be born stateless. They will have no right to be joined by other members of their family. This raises the prospect of a new group of people forced into destitution. There is no exemption in the section for children. Section 76 does not require that national security is in issue and the application of this section may raise issues under Human Rights Act arts 3, 8, and 14. It is implemented in the immigration rules paras 276A to 276E. Those with indefinite leave but not with British nationality do not have a right to the protection of the state nor a formal obligation of allegiance (see *Al-Rawi*).

Section 76 may be cross-referenced with the designation power in the Criminal Justice and Immigration Bill, see chapters 1, 8 and 16.

7.8.5 **Grant of leave to remain**

Most people who obtain leave to enter the UK initially obtain limited rather than indefinite leave. This may later be made indefinite on an application made to do so. It does not happen automatically. For instance a partner will obtain an initial two-year period of leave. At the end of that time they must apply to the Home Office, who, if requirements of the rules continue to be met, will lift the time restriction together with any conditions lifted and grant indefinite leave to remain (paras 287 and 295G).

Leave to remain for a person already in the UK is granted by the Secretary of State under the power in Immigration Act 1971 s 4(1). The power includes giving further limited leave to remain, either by way of extending the existing leave or by varying it to a different immigration category, or giving indefinite leave to remain. Where limited leave is extended or varied the Secretary of State may also vary or continue any conditions attaching to the earlier leave (Immigration Act 1971 s 3(3) and HC 395 para 31).

7.8.6 **No-switching rules**

Some categories of entry do not lead to indefinite leave. For instance, the immigration rules concerning leave as a student do not make any provision for indefinite leave to be granted. If therefore a person who is in the UK as a student wants to make the UK their permanent home, they must change the category of the immigration rules under which they are staying. They may then encounter the 'no-switching' rules, which restrict the categories between which such changes may be made. These restrictions are mainly apparent from the immigration rules. However, there are certain changes which, although not provided for or even prohibited by the rules, are permitted either exceptionally or as a matter of policy ascertainable through the IDIs. Permissible switching is now generally very limited. Until 2003, all categories could change to spouse, though not fiancé(e). Rule changes following the 2002 White Paper *Secure Borders, Safe Haven,* Cm 5387 now prevent visitors from staying in the UK for marriage (see HC 395 para 284(i)). Some provisions for visitors and students are covered in chapters 10 and 11. For full details of current permitted and prohibited switches, reference should be made to the immigration rules and the latest edition of JCWI Immigration, Nationality and Refugee Law Handbook, which provides a useful chart. Where the change of category is permitted, under the terms of the Immigration Act 1971, there must be an application for a variation of leave.

7.8.7 **Variation of leave**

The power to vary leave is granted to the Secretary of State by Immigration Act 1971 s 4(1). This is in accordance with the traditional division of function discussed earlier according to which the Secretary of State grants variation of leave and leave to remain whereas the immigration officer grants leave to enter. It may be recalled that the new Immigration Act 1971 s 3A enables the Secretary of State to 'make further provision with respect to the giving, refusing or varying of leave'. Two changes have been introduced using this power with respect to variation of leave. The power to vary remains with the Secretary of State, but the Immigration (Leave to Enter and Remain) Order 2000, SI 2000/1161 article 13(6) extends the scope of that power by providing that it may be exercised while the holder of leave is outside the UK. This is introduced into the rules in para 33A.

The other new power concerning variation is one we have already noted, the power of an immigration officer to vary leave of someone who already has leave when they enter. This power is exercised on behalf of the Secretary of State (HC 395 para 31A), and so is not given to immigration officers in their own right. It is a corollary of the power to grant leave outside the UK as entry may be precisely the occasion when variation of existing leave is needed. Section 3C of the Immigration Act 1971 provides a statutory extension of leave where an application for variation of leave is made within the currency of existing leave. It is quite likely that, for reasons outside the control of the applicant, such as Home Office delays, existing leave may expire before the application for variation is decided. This would result in an injustice if a person were then treated as an overstayer simply because their application had not been heard. Section 3C extends the existing leave, on the existing conditions if any, until the decision has been taken.

7.9 **Settlement**

The terms 'settlement' and 'settled' are used widely in immigration law, and it is important to grasp their meaning. Settled status must be distinguished from right of abode, indefinite leave to remain, and ordinary residence. 'Settled' is a term of art, defined by statute. 'Settlement', despite its wide colloquial use, is not.

The Immigration Act 1971 s 33(2)A defines a person who is 'settled' as subject to no immigration restrictions on length of stay and ordinarily resident in the UK. These two components of the definition are both important. Someone who has no immigration restrictions on their length of stay may be in that position either because they have indefinite leave to remain or because they have right of abode. Right of abode, it may be recalled from the chapter on nationality, is the right to come and go 'without let or hindrance' (Immigration Act 1971 s 1) and is held only by British citizens and the relatively few Commonwealth citizens with right of abode. Settlement includes indefinite leave to remain but carries the additional requirement of ordinary residence.

The meaning of the term 'ordinary residence' was considered by the House of Lords in *Shah v Barnet London Borough Council* [1983] 2 AC 309, not an immigration but an education case, concerning a student's entitlement to a grant, which also, under statute, depended upon 'ordinary residence'. The House of Lords held that it was possible to have more than one ordinary residence. The country of ordinary residence was the person's home, chosen as part of a settled way of life for the time being. It could be of long or short duration and did not imply permanence. The reason for being present was irrelevant providing it was voluntary, and immigration status had no bearing on the matter, providing the person was not in breach of immigration law. This meant that someone with limited leave could be ordinarily resident. In the context of defining 'settled status' it means that there is no need to prove that the person intends to be in the UK for the rest of their life. The case of *Chugtai*, [1995] IAR 559 developed *Shah* in holding that a person could be ordinarily resident in two countries at the same time. In *AB Bangladesh* [2004] UKIAT 00314 the tribunal held that this could include where the appellant intended to spend six months of each year in each country. He could therefore be said to be coming to the UK 'for settlement'.

The point in *Shah* about illegality was *obiter*, as none of the students in that case were present illegally. This was taken up by the House of Lords in *Mark v Mark* [2005] UKHL 42 who considered that whether illegal presence in immigration law affected ordinary residence would depend upon the context. Where a statute requiring ordinary residence confers a benefit from the state then it might be relevant to require lawful presence. However, where, as in *Mark*, it was only relevant to the question of which jurisdiction governs divorce proceedings, then legality of residence was not relevant. This decision, while being careful and restricted in its scope to the civil matters in hand, also offers a welcome counter to the trend of excluding foreign nationals without immigration status from the usual benefits of the law.

Colloquially, it is often said that when a person obtains indefinite leave to remain they 'get settlement', as for instance when a work permit holder has lived in the UK and obtains indefinite leave to remain, or a spouse whose restrictions are lifted after their probationary period. The words 'settlement' and 'indefinite leave to remain' are often used interchangeably and for practical purposes this is quite valid. However the two are not exactly the same. Though settled status may be acquired at a particular date, it may not be. It is not awarded by the Secretary of State explicitly, and the term 'settlement' will not be found in the immigration rules. It is a description of a state of affairs rather than an immigration status awarded.

Although the word 'settlement' is not used in the immigration rules, the word 'settled' is. It is necessary to be able to identify when a person is settled as important rights accrue to someone with settled status. Children born in the UK to a settled person will be British (British Nationality Act 1981 s 1), and in the immigration rules a settled person is qualified to sponsor a partner or relative to come to the UK (HC 395, e.g. paras 281, 317).

In practical terms, settlement and indefinite leave to remain are virtually coterminous. As we have seen, a person with indefinite leave to remain who stays away from the UK for more than two years may lose that leave. Therefore an ordinary residence requirement is implied in retaining indefinite leave to remain. The practical result is that it equates to being settled. Although it is technically accurate to refer to a British citizen ordinarily resident in the UK as 'settled', these entitlements are of greater real significance to people who are not British. In general, therefore, the word 'settled' is used to refer to people who have indefinite leave to remain and are ordinarily resident in the UK.

Settled status in this usual sense does not carry full rights of citizenship. A settled person can be deported on the ground that deportation is conducive to the public good (Immigration Act s 3(5)(a)) and does not have the right to vote or stand for Parliament. In these respects as well as the possible loss of status after two years' absence, settled status is less secure than right of abode.

7.9.1 Acquiring settled status

From 2 April 2007, provisions introduced in 2005 for nationality now apply to indefinite leave to remain, as all applicants must pass a test on Life in the UK or an English test for Speakers of other Languages (ESOL) which includes citizenship materials. Where people's English language is at ESOL level 3 or above, they take the Life the UK test. Where it is not, they must attend an English course which includes citizenship materials and then take the English test. EEA nationals are exempt from this requirement, but must comply with it if they apply for British nationality. There are also exemptions for medical conditions and those under 18 or over 66. The tests must be taken by any non-exempt person who is applying for indefinite leave, on any basis. If the applicant has not passed the test by the time their existing leave expires, they can be granted an extension for this purpose.

As suggested above, settled status may be acquired after a period laid down in rules relating to particular categories of entrant. So, for instance, a spouse may obtain settlement after two years, and people on some temporary kinds of leave such as work permit employment may apply for indefinite leave after five years' residence.

UK practice was to grant immediate settlement to people on acquisition of refugee status, but since 31 August 2005 a grant of five years has been normal practice. Either refugee status, humanitarian protection or discretionary leave, the two kinds of leave given for human rights protection, may lead to settlement, refugee status and HP after five years and DL after six, but only if a continuing need for protection is shown.

There are other concessions entailing grant of settlement, for instance a British overseas citizen may be granted settlement after seven years of lawful residence. The final and important provisions relating to grant of settlement are those based on long residence.

7.9.1.1 *Long residence*

It is appropriate that people who have been living for a long time in a country should have some security of residence, when they have not otherwise obtained a secure immigration status. This principle was given effect in the UK by a concession, which in April 2003 became part of the immigration rules. The residence requirement in both the rule and the concession is ten years' or more continuous lawful residence or 14 years' or more continuous residence of any legality. The concession gave effect to Article 3(3) European Convention on Establishment, which the UK ratified on 14 October 1969, and which provides that nationals of any contracting party who have been lawfully residing for more than ten years in the territory of another party may only be expelled for reasons of national security or for particularly serious reasons relating to public order, public health, or morality. The IDI Dec 2000 Chapter 18 pointed out that the concession extended this provision in three respects:

- to include all foreign nationals, not just contracting states;
- to grant indefinite leave rather than simply refrain from removing such a person; and
- to allow those who have been in the UK illegally to benefit also.

It could be misleading to set this provision in the context of the Convention article if it implies that once a person has ten years' lawful residence that they will be safe from expulsion. This is not the case. What it does is to give some security of immigration status to people whose status is insecure. It does not give immunity from deportation or removal. Cases considered in the chapter on deportation make this abundantly clear, for instance the appellant in *B v SSHD* [2000] Imm AR 478 was a settled resident who had lived in the UK for 35 of his 42 years before a deportation order was made, the respondent in *Dinc* [1999] Imm AR 380 had indefinite leave to remain and had been resident for 13 years.

The long residence provisions provide a presumption for the grant of indefinite leave, thus giving peace of mind to someone who has been unsure about their future.

The presumption has been weakened in the rule which replaced the concession which, instead of requiring strong countervailing factors to refuse leave after long residence, says that indefinite leave may be granted if 'having regard to the public interest there are no reasons why it would be undesirable'. The words 'should normally' have been removed. The rule also introduces consideration of the individual circumstances and this may have the effect of weakening the presumption (para 276B(ii)).

Short absences of up to six months will not break continuity if the person has leave when they are abroad. Sometimes longer ones also will be accepted as part of the period of residence, depending on the intention shown. The approach is similar to that for establishing ordinary residence as set out in *Shah* v *Barnet London Borough Council*. Similarly, short breaks in legality, as where, for instance, an application was filed late, but then granted, will not break continuity. In *Kungwengwe* v *SSHD* [2005] EWHC 1427 (Admin) Wilkie J did not accept that residence pursuant to a residence permit issued under EEA regulations amounted to lawful residence for the purposes of this rule, although the guidance in the IDI May 2007 provides that there is discretion to count this residence (2.2.3).

The 14-year rule enables overstayers, people in breach of condition and illegal entrants to declare themselves to the Home Office and obtain a status which enables lawful working, an application to be joined by relatives, entitlement to welfare benefits, and so on. However, they cannot count time after enforcement proceedings have been commenced against them (HC 395 para 276B(i)(b)). The way this works was illustrated in the case of *R* v *SSHD ex p Ofori* [1994] Imm AR 581. Here, the applicant had six years' leave, then overstayed for five. He then applied for indefinite leave to remain but was refused. At the date of decision he had been in the UK for 12 years. A decision was made to deport him and he appealed. At the (unsuccessful) end of the appeal process he had been in the UK for 14 years. He applied again for indefinite leave to remain, relying on the long residence concession. The High Court supported the Secretary of State's decision that he could not rely on time spent during the appeal process towards his 14 years.

There was a practice, now abandoned, of serving notice of intention to deport 'on the file', i.e. where a person could not be traced, the notice was issued but left to lie on the file. There are still people in relation to whom this was done at some point in the past. *Popatia* [2001] Imm AR 46 establishes that this does not count as service for the purpose of the long residence provisions and service on the file does not commence enforcement proceedings.

7.10 Conclusion

This chapter has considered some of the legal provisions relating to crossing the UK's borders and obtaining an immigration status here. The border itself is described as an increasingly distributed, intelligence-led and security-focused system, rather than permission to cross a border which is granted at the geographical boundary. There has been some discussion of the way in which discretion is exercised within this system, as despite the complex of rules and policies, the judgment of officials is still at the heart of immigration control. Reference has been made to the deeper penetration of immigration control into the everyday business of life, not just for those who have traditionally regarded that as their job, but also, potentially, for any of us. The widening scope of control is accompanied by its transformation into a technologically driven policing and deterrence system. The dominance of executive discretion in immigration law has been problematic, and difficult for the individual to challenge, but a machine reading which tells the operative that the passenger is denied entry cannot be argued with. Issues of technological reliability and data protection will enter into immigration law. It is debatable which is more transparent as befits a democracy.

QUESTIONS

1 How do you think the Immigration (Leave to Enter and Remain) Order 2000 changes the substance and nature of immigration control?

2 What would you consider to be appropriate medical grounds for refusal of leave to enter and who do you think should make that decision? How does your idea compare with the present law?

3 What do you think are the reasons for limiting the categories of leave to and from which a person can switch?

 For guidance on answering questions, visit www.oxfordtextbooks.co.uk/orc/clayton3e.

FURTHER READING

Commission for Racial Equality (1985) *Immigration Control Procedures: Report of a Formal Investigation* (London: Commission for Racial Equality), Chapter 3.

Guild, E. (2000) 'Entry into the UK: the changing nature of national borders' (2000) INLP vol. 14, no. 4, pp. 227–238.

JCWI (2006) *Immigration, Nationality and Refugee Law Handbook*, 6th edn. (London: JCWI).

Juss, S. (1997) *Discretion and Deviation in the Administration of Immigration Control* (London: Sweet & Maxwell).

Luqmani, J., Randall, C., and Scammell, R. (2000) 'Recent Developments in Immigration Law' *Legal Action* July 2000, 11–17.

Reports of the Entry Clearance Monitor 2000–2006.

Ryan, B. (2001) 'The Common Travel Area between Britain and Ireland' *Modern Law Review* vol. 64 November 2001, pp. 855–874.

Shah, R. (2007) 'Language test for Permanent Residents' *Journal of Immigration, Nationality & Asylum Law* vol. 21, no. 1, pp. 26–27.

Sondhi, R. (1987) 'Divided Families: British Immigration Control in the Indian Subcontinent' (London: Runnymede Trust).

Statewatch bulletin: 'UK: e-Borders plan to tackle "threats"' vol. 15 no. 3/4.

Wray, H. (2006) 'Guiding the gatekeepers :entry clearance for settlement on the Indian sub-continent' *Journal of Immigration, Asylum & Nationality Law* vol. 20, no. 2, pp. 112–129.

8

Challenging decisions: appeals and judicial review

SUMMARY

This chapter describes the structure of the appeals process, the grounds of appeal, and some of the significant uses of judicial review in the immigration and asylum field. Particular points concerning asylum appeals are reserved for chapter 12. The chapter ends with a section on those who represent immigrants and asylum seekers and the regulation of their services.

8.1 Introduction

Immigration law is unlike, say, criminal or tort law in that the possible grounds for appeal are set out in statute. This means that appeal rights are vulnerable to further legislation. Obtaining or retaining a right of appeal has in itself become a major source of litigation. The more technical aspects of law relating to appeals are outside the scope of this book, and for this reference should be made to practitioner works such as Macdonald or the JCWI Handbook.

The first part of this chapter describes the structure of the appeals system and then we discuss the principles of law which are the grounds for appealing immigration decisions.

8.2 Asylum and Immigration Tribunal

The Asylum and Immigration (Treatment of Claimants etc) Act 2004 abolished the previous two-tier system of immigration appeals, which had been in place since 1969 for Commonwealth citizens and since 1973 for all immigrants. The two-tier system was of an initial appeal to an adjudicator, with a second appeal from that decision to an Immigration Appeal Tribunal (IAT). The Nationality, Immigration and Asylum Act 2002 restricted appeal to the IAT to grounds of error of law only. The 2004 Act instituted a new, single-tier, Asylum and Immigration Tribunal (AIT), with effect from 4 April 2005. Members of the AIT are called Immigration Judges, and adjudicators and legally qualified members of the IAT transferred immediately to this role and title (2004 Act Sch 2 paras 27 and 28). Non-legally qualified members of the IAT became non-legally qualified members of the AIT (para 28).

Immigration judges may sit in panels of one, two, or three. A practice direction issued by the President of the tribunal gives guidance on the composition of panels for different kinds of cases (consolidated 30 April 2007: www.ait.gov.uk). The tribunal is headed by a President, and there is a structure under his direction of two Deputy Presidents, Senior Immigration Judges, who have judicial management and legal responsibilities, Designated Immigration Judges, who support teams of about ten Immigration Judges, and finally Immigration Judges.

The proceedings of the tribunal are governed by the Asylum and Immigration Tribunal (Procedure) Rules 2005, SI 2005/230. The overriding objective of the rules provides a principle by which they can be interpreted and which may guide discretionary decisions. In the 2003 Procedure Rules the overriding objective was to 'secure the just, timely and effective disposal of appeals and applications'. This was changed in the 2005 Rules to handling proceedings 'as fairly, quickly and efficiently as possible' (r 4), suggesting that expediency may take precedence over fairness. The UNHCR had recommended that the rule be 'amended to reflect more clearly the emphasis that should be given to the fundamental concern of correctly identifying those who are in need of international protection' (UNHCR December 2004 para 2). While speed and efficiency are generally desirable for all concerned, the main purpose of a refugee determination and appeal procedure is to make accurate decisions about those in need of protection and not to put claimants at risk.

The rules allow short time limits for appealing (ten days, or five for someone who is in detention: r 7). This can create severe problems in a situation where legal advice is hard to come by, public funding for cases equally scarce (see later section on representation), and the appellant's first language may well not be English. They contain features which cast doubt on the perceived impartiality of the system and its capacity to protect those in danger. In *FP (Iran) and MB (Libya) v SSHD* [2007] EWCA Civ 13, rule 19(1) read with rule 56(2) of the Asylum and Immigration Procedure Rules 2005 allowed an appeal to go ahead in the absence of the appellant when his former solicitors had closed down and failed to inform the Asylum and Immigration Tribunal of their clients' new address. This went to 'the very essence' of the right to be heard and was unlawful. The rule was amended and now allows for a hearing not to go ahead in a party's absence if the tribunal is aware that there could be good reasons not to do so.

In asylum cases, the tribunal's determination is served on the Home Office who must then serve it on the appellant (r 23(4) and (5)), though in non-asylum cases it is served by the tribunal on both parties within ten days (r 22). Notice of appeal must be filed by the appellant on the AIT, who must then serve it on the Home Office 'as soon as reasonably practicable' (r 12). This is intended to prevent the delays which used to ensue after the appellant had lodged their appeal with the Home Office and then had to wait for lengthy periods before the Home Office informed the tribunal (see McKee 2005:99). However it also opens up the possibility that the Home Office, having no notice of the appeal, may arrest, detain and even remove the appellant before the appeal is heard.

Initial appeals to the AIT are rehearings of the whole case, and the tribunal may 'consider evidence about any matter which it thinks relevant to the substance of the decision' (Nationality, Immigration and Asylum Act 2002 s 85(4)). See *EA (s 85(4) explained) Nigeria* [2007] Imm AR 487 discussed in chapter 10, for a rather harsh result if what constitutes 'the decision' is narrowly construed. In entry clearance and certificate of entitlement cases, i.e. those where the applicant is outside the UK, evidence is limited to matters arising before the date of the decision (s 85(5)). The tribunal may adopt an inquisitorial style, asking questions of the Home Office representative and the applicant, but the proceedings are in most respects adversarial in nature.

The burden of proof is on the appellant, and the standard of proof in immigration cases is the balance of probabilities (confirmed in *ECO Dhaka* v *Shamim Box* [2002] UKIAT 02212). There is an ongoing debate as to whether this standard is properly applied, and this is a question the reader might bear in mind in reading tribunal cases. It is to be hoped that examples of contrary practice as extreme as this one identified by Juss (1997 Chapter 4) will not often be found. In *Walayat Begum* v *Visa Officer Islamabad TH/13561/75* the tribunal had before it the passport of the appellant's first wife, whom he claimed had died. The passport was endorsed: 'The holder of this passport has died. Passport has been cancelled and returned'. There was other evidence also. The tribunal held 'There is no really direct or solid evidence that Manzoor Begum has died' (1997:129).

The Nationality, Immigration and Asylum Act 2002 has simplified the statutory basis for immigration appeals, although the procedures have become ever more complex. Sections 82 and 84 of the Act set out the decisions against which appeals may be brought and the grounds upon which appeals may be made. The appealable decisions are all the major decisions made in relation to a person's stay in the UK. These include refusal of leave to enter, refusal of entry clearance (though this will apply to few cases once s 4 of the 2006 Act is implemented), refusal to vary leave, a decision to remove, and a decision to deport. Appealable decisions do not include the issue of removal directions, i.e. the actual implementation of the decision to remove (see chapter 18).

Despite the retention of the term 'tribunal', from the appellant's point of view the tier of appeal that has disappeared is the second tier. The changes to the appeals structure are in the later stages. If an appellant loses at the AIT, i.e. the first appeal stage, what happens then? The 2004 Act changes the system of onward appeals.

8.2.1 **Challenging decisions of the AIT**

The system of challenging the AIT's decision is quite complex, and some commentators have doubted whether the single-tier system is actually simpler or more streamlined (Shaw 2005; McKee 2005). The route for challenge depends on the composition of the panel at first hearing. If there were three legally qualified members and the appeal is dismissed, the appellant may apply to the AIT for permission to appeal to the Court of Appeal, on a point of law only. If the AIT refuses permission, an application may be made to the Court of Appeal.

If fewer than three legally qualified members heard the first appeal, the appellant can apply to the High Court for a reconsideration order, which compels the tribunal to look at the case again on the basis that it has made an error of law. The application for a reconsideration order is made on paper only, i.e. there is no hearing. On receiving an application for a reconsideration order, the High Court can of its own motion refer a question of law of importance to the Court of Appeal. This may not be initiated by the parties. The reviewing court may direct the tribunal to reconsider its decision '*if it thinks* the tribunal may have made an error of law' (Nationality, Immigration and Asylum Act 2002 s 103A: emphasis added). This suggests a low threshold.

For an extended transitional period, applications for a reconsideration order are considered first of all by a member of the AIT. This is described as a filter mechanism (e.g. Shaw 2005: 92). The tribunal member decides whether the tribunal should reconsider the initial decision, and their decision is sent to the parties. The parties then have the option to renew the application for reconsideration, and if it is renewed, the application goes to the High Court, as mentioned above.

At the reconsideration hearing the tribunal must first of all decide whether there has been an error of law. If it decides there has, then it must go on to hear the case again and make fresh findings. After a reconsideration hearing there is an opportunity to appeal to the Court of Appeal, with permission, on a point of law.

It is not always easy to distinguish between an error of fact and an error of law, though one will give the right to challenge an immigration judge's decision whereas the other will not.

In *E v SSHD and R v SSHD* [2004] EWCA Civ 49 there was a delay of some months between the hearing and the tribunal decisions being promulgated. During that period, human rights reports were produced on the country to which the appellants would be sent. These reports significantly affected the factual basis on which the decisions had been made. The Court of Appeal held that the IAT could have reviewed its decision. They made the further important statement that:

It was time to accept that a mistake of fact giving rise to unfairness was a separate head of challenge in an appeal on a point of law, at least in those statutory contexts where the parties shared an interest in cooperating to achieve the correct result. Asylum law was such an area. For a finding of unfairness there must have been a mistake as to an existing fact, including a mistake as to the availability of evidence on a particular matter. The fact or evidence must have been 'established' in the sense that it was uncontentious and objectively verifiable. The appellant must not have been responsible for the mistake and the mistake must have played a material part in the tribunal's reasoning.

This issue is also discussed in chapter 12.

Changes to the appeals structure in recent years have consistently aimed to reduce the availability of appeals and of judicial review. However, the fundamental importance of the matter to an asylum claimant means that it is often necessary to challenge the limits of the system. In *R on the application of AM (Cameroon) v AIT* [2007] EWCA Civ 131 the immigration judge had refused to allow evidence to be given by telephone link to Cameroon, and to adjourn the case to enable the appellant, who was ill, to attend. He invited her representatives to judicially review his decisions if they wanted to persist in their challenge. The case went ahead without the evidence. As it went to a reconsideration, where it was turned down, it was not clear whether it was still possible to judicially review the refusal of evidence and adjournment. The Court of Appeal held that in an exceptional situation, given the importance of the matters in hand, it must still be possible to challenge such interlocutory decisions by judicial review.

For discussion of the nature and work of the tribunal, please refer back to chapter 1.

8.3 Special Immigration Appeals Commission

There is a separate system for appeals involving national security. This used to be a secret procedure before a panel of advisers, known as the 'Three Wise Men', but the conduct of these proceedings was very restricted. The panel was required to make the case against the person known to them as far as they considered national security would allow, but there was no obligation to disclose evidence or identify witnesses. The individual could make representations to the panel, but had no right to legal representation, and per-haps most strangely of all, no right to see the decision in their case.

Article 5(4) ECHR requires that someone who is detained should have the right to challenge their detention in a court. The applicant in the case of *Chahal* v *UK* (1997) 23 EHRR 413 was detained for several years following a decision to deport him on national security grounds. The ECtHR held that there was a violation of Article 5(4) of the Convention in that there was no provision for him to challenge his detention before a court as the 'Three Wise Men' procedure could not be called a court. The ECtHR recognized that there may be a necessity for national security matters to be heard in a private forum as disclosure of some issues to the public could cause harm to national security. Nevertheless, some countries, Canada for example, had devised procedures which gave more protection to the rights of the individual while still taking account of the state's need for security. The procedure was also found to breach Article 13 of the Convention, as the panel of special advisers did not provide an effective safeguard for Mr Chahal against removal from the UK to a place where he could suffer torture or inhuman or degrading treatment or punishment in breach of Article 3.

In response to the judgment of the ECtHR the UK replaced the 'Three Wise Men' with the Special Immigration Appeals Commission (SIAC), set up by the Special Immigration Appeals Commission Act 1997(SIACA). The Commission must consist of one member who has held (or holds) high judicial office, one member who either is or has been a legally qualified member of the AIT and a third member who would normally be some-one with experience of national security matters (SIACA 1997 Sch 1). The Commission has power to exclude anybody from a hearing, including the appellant and their rep-resentative if the Commission accepts a submission from the Secretary of State that it is necessary to rely on 'closed' material – that is, material which it would be against the public interest to disclose, even to the appellant. If the Commission decides to hold a closed hearing, the interests of the appellant are represented by a Special Advocate, appointed by the Attorney General (or in Scotland the Lord Advocate) for that purpose. The Special Advocate is not at liberty to discuss those proceedings with the appellant. This procedure is intended to comply with Article 5 ECHR, while still providing some protection for government concerns about national security.

8.3.1 Jurisdiction

The jurisdiction of the SIAC is to hear appeals against immigration-related decisions involving national security, usually exclusion, refusal of entry as an asylum seeker, deportation or appeals against deprivation of nationality (see chapters 3 and 16). In the Anti-terrorism, Crime and Security Act 2001 the Commission had jurisdiction in relation to the indefinite detention of foreign nationals. This jurisdiction lapsed in March 2005 after the Law Lords had declared the detentions unlawful (*A v SSHD* [2004] UKHL 56: see chapter 15) and the statutory powers were repealed. The Commission can hear appeals on the same grounds as those which may be raised in the AIT (1997 Act s 2(2)(e), as substituted by 2002 Act Sch 7 para 20). The Commission has similar powers to those of the tribunal on appeals, in that it must allow the appeal if it considers that the decision appealed is not in accordance with the law or the immigration rules, or that a discretion should have been exercised differently (SIACA 1997 s 2(3)(b), as substituted by 2002 Act Sch 7 para 20). In *SSHD v Rehman* [2001] 3 WLR 877, the first case to come before SIAC, the House of Lords agreed with the Court of Appeal and the Commission that its role was to review the merits of the case in full, which could include reviewing the Secretary of State's findings of fact. The political deportation appeals heard by SIAC are discussed fully in chapter 16. The standard of proof of allegations against the appellant is the civil one, even though in content and implications for an unsuccessful appellant the proceedings have much in common with criminal cases. The House of Lords in *A and others v SSHD* [2005] UKHL 71 held that SIAC could not admit evidence which could have been obtained by torture (see chapter 4 for full discussion).

8.3.2 **Review of SIAC**

The extension of SIAC's role to hearing appeals against detention under the 2001 Act was thought by some to push its procedures beyond what they could deliver in the way of the elements of fairness. The Constitutional Affairs Committee conducted an inquiry into the workings of SIAC and identified a number of important reservations with respect to the work of the Special Advocates.

The Special Advocate sees the evidence and is required to make representations and conduct cross-examination upon it, but without instructions as they are not permitted to discuss any closed material with the appellant. They lack the resource of an ordinary legal team to conduct a defence, and have no access to expert opinion or research assistants to help them to interpret intelligence information on which they have no expertise. They cannot call witnesses, and have no capacity to interview any. If they have already acted in a case in which they have seen closed material which has relevance to other cases, they may not act in the later cases. Alternatively, they would have to deal with a later case without seeing the appellant at all. This tends to mean they are always dealing with issues for the first time, exacerbating their lack of capacity to challenge government evidence, produced with the whole panoply of state security and intelligence resources. Even if evidence in closed material shows that the case in the open material is flawed, they may not deal with this in an open hearing or take further instructions on inconsistencies (Constitutional Affairs Committee Seventh Report 2004–05, and Rick Scannell, address at ILPA: One Hundred Years of Immigration Law, 7 November 2005). The Constitutional Affairs Committee recommended that these issues be addressed.

In 2007, SIAC's procedure rules were amended. One function of the new rules is to specify in more detail how SIAC should deal with applications to use closed material (Special Immigration Appeals Commission (Procedure) (Amendment) Rules 2007 SI 2007/1285).

Similar issues arise in cases of control orders under the Prevention of Terrorism Act 2005 as, here too, closed material and special advocates are used. The House of Lords in *SSHD v MB and AF* [2007] UKHL 46, considering the lawfulness of three control orders, held that the system of using special advocates was capable of giving a fair process. However, in order for this to be the case, sometimes great efforts would need to be made to summarize and give the gist of evidence to ensure that the appellant knew the substance of the case against them. This was a crucial requirement of a fair hearing, and a person subject to a control order who was not able to instruct their advocate about the case against them was at a 'grave disadvantage'.

We now move from the appeals system to the content of appeals.

8.4 Grounds of appeal to Asylum and Immigration Tribunal

The grounds of appeal are set out in Nationality, Immigration and Asylum Act 2002 s 84, and are as follows:

(a) that the decision is not in accordance with the immigration rules;

(b) that the decision is unlawful by virtue of Race Relations Act 1976 s 19B;

(c) that the decision is unlawful under Human Rights Act s 6...as being incompatible with the appellant's Convention rights;

(d) that the appellant is an EEA national or a member of the family of an EEA national and the decision breaches the appellant's rights under the Community Treaties;

(e) that the decision is otherwise not in accordance with the law;

(f) that the person taking the decision should have exercised differently a discretion conferred by immigration rules;

(g) that removal of the appellant in consequence of the immigration decision would breach the UK's obligations under the Refugee Convention or...Human Rights Act s 6.

Section 86 provides that the tribunal must allow the appeal 'in so far as it thinks that' one of the above is the case. This largely repeats an earlier provision found both in the Immigration and Asylum Act 1999 (Sch 4 para 21) and in the Immigration Act 1971 (s 19).

Breach of the Refugee Convention forms the subject of the chapters on asylum law. European Community rights are explored in chapter 6, though note that breach of such a right is a ground for an immigration appeal within the UK system. The other grounds are discussed here. The substance of rights under the Human Rights Act is also discussed in chapter 4.

8.4.1 Not in accordance with the immigration rules

The effect of s 86 and its predecessors is to give binding force to the immigration rules. Immigration officers, Home Office officials, and entry clearance officers are bound to act in accordance with the rules in the sense that if they do not their decisions are appealable. This means that at the appeal stage, if the tribunal considers that requirements for entry are met, the appeal must be allowed and entry granted. Although the applicant, as we saw in chapter 1, cannot at the beginning insist on obtaining entry if they consider they meet the requirements, at the stage of appeal, the rules have the force of law.

The status of the immigration rules (discussed in chapter 1) has implications for appeals, as illustrated in *MO (Nigeria)* [2007] UKAIT 00057, one of many cases arising out of the changes to the rules for postgraduate doctors to complete their training in the UK.

Key Case

MO (Nigeria) [2007] UKAIT 00057

MO came to the UK in 2005 as a postgraduate doctor and completed two clinical attachments in order to progress with her necessary training. In January 2006 she received confirmation that her basic surgical training was regarded as 'acceptable' by the UK's Postgraduate Medical Education and Training Board. She applied for leave to remain as a postgraduate doctor. On 3 April 2006 there was a 'radical restructuring' (*MO* para 1) of the immigration rules relating to medical graduates, including that only a UK medical degree would now suffice as a basis for leave. MO's application was refused on 26 April. She appealed on the basis that the rules applied to her should be those in force at the time of her application, in accordance with which she would have obtained leave to remain. The tribunal held that the immigration rules, even though they had the force of law for appeals, represented policy, and the Secretary of State was free to change them and to implement start dates as a matter of policy and without transitional provisions. The applicable rules were held to be those at the time of the decision.

This result in *MO* would be different if the immigration rules were or had the status of delegated legislation. An application would normally be decided under legislation in force at the time of the application, though sometimes statutory instruments are made with retrospective effect. An applicant for leave to remain in the UK, according to the thinking behind *MO*, applies for the Secretary of State to exercise their statutory power to grant leave in accordance with rules and guidance then in force. Given the unpredictability that this introduces into the system, and the JCHR disquiet at the government's claim to be able to change the rules at will (Session 2006–07 Twentieth Report para 53), this issue is surely destined to go further.

8.4.2 Race discrimination as a ground of appeal

The changes to the immigration rules on international medical graduates, which affected MO, had a major impact on doctors of Indian origin. A challenge to the changes made by the British Association of Physicians of Indian Origin (BAPIO) is considered below and in chapter 11. Here we consider race discrimination in an immigration decision as a ground of appeal under the Nationality, Immigration and Asylum Act 2002 s 84(1)(b).

In *SK India* [2006] UKAIT 00067 the tribunal gave general guidance on making race discrimination claims in the tribunal. They said that the usual principles of discrimination law apply, so that it is necessary to identify a comparator who would be better treated than the appellant, and where indirect discrimination is alleged then statistics may be used to show differential impact of a rule or policy. Where this is done, the populations chosen must be comparable. In that case the appellant presented information that some entry clearance posts, including New Delhi, had a much lower rate of granting working holidaymaker applications than others, for instance in Canada and Australia. This could not establish discrimination without information on other characteristics of the applicants.

An appeal on race discrimination grounds is unlike other appeals because the grounds refer to how the decision was taken, and success on that point may not in itself be enough to decide the claim in the appellant's favour (see Quayum and Chatwin 2004:97). For instance, in *CS (Race discrimination; proper approach) Jamaica* [2006] UKAIT 00004 the entry clearance officer made sweeping generalizations about Jamaican men, which the adjudicator accepted must have influenced the refusal of entry clearance. However, for separate reasons she found that without this discrimination the requirements for entry clearance would still not have been fulfilled, and the tribunal agreed that the finding of race discrimination did not necessarily vitiate the refusal if there were other objective grounds. This was a simpler decision than in *SK India* as direct discrimination of this kind does not require statistical evidence.

Where an appeal on the merits is allowed, it is still necessary for the tribunal to make a finding on the race discrimination issue (Nationality, Immigration and Asylum Act 2002 s 86(2)(a)). The Race Relations (Amendment) Act 2000 brought immigration officers, entry clearance officers and other Home Office officials within the ambit of the Race Relations Act 1976. Consequently, over and above a race discrimination appeal there may be a claim in the county court for damages for injury to feelings arising out of the same facts (Quayum and Chatwin p. 98). Generally, if entry clearance is granted while an appeal is pending, the appeal is treated as abandoned (2002 Act s 104). This could mean that race discrimination would then be without a remedy – 'a particularly unfortunate consequence of the abandonment provisions' (*VE Nigeria* [2005] UKIAT 00057 para 21). The Immigration, Asylum and Nationality Act 2006 now prevents the appeal from being treated as abandoned where it was brought on race discrimination grounds so that the appellant may still claim damages in the county court.

Section 57A of the Race Relations Act 1976 provides that no claim for damages can be made in the county court if, *inter alia*, the challenge to the allegedly discriminatory act 'could be raised in proceedings on an appeal which is pending' in the immigration tribunal. The Court of Appeal in *Emunefe v SSHD* [2005] EWCA Civ 1002 held, approving *R (on the application of Bibi) v IAT* [2005] EWHC 386 (Admin), that s 57A does not oust the jurisdiction of the county court if for any reason the matter has not been determined.

Race discrimination may also found a human rights appeal under Article 14 where the discrimination occurs in the ambit of another Convention right. Therefore, where for instance it is claimed that an alleged breach of an Article 8 right affected one racial group more severely or even exclusively, a complaint of discrimination may be made under Article 14. Race discrimination was found in itself to be capable of amounting to a breach of Article 3 in the *East African Asians Case* (1973) 3 EHRR 76, it being a 'special affront to human dignity' to single out a group of people for differential treatment on racial grounds. This does not mean that in all circumstances race discrimination can be regarded as a free-standing breach of Article 3. The level of severity to cross the threshold for Article 3 would have to be met in each case.

8.4.3 Human Rights Appeals

Entry clearance officers (though see discussion on scope in chapter 4), immigration officers, and officials in the Home Office are all public authorities for the purposes of Human Rights Act 1998 s 6, and therefore bound not to act in breach of a person's Convention rights. This obligation is confirmed in HC 395 para 2, and a breach of it is the basis for an appeal against an immigration decision under s 84.

Determining a human rights appeal is not an exercise of discretion (*AG and others (Policies; executive discretions; Tribunal's power Kosovo)* [2007] UKAIT 00082), it is a judgment on whether a decision is lawful. Therefore if the decision is overturned on appeal the tribunal's judgment must be implemented if there is no further appeal. It is not something which needs to return to the Secretary of State for further consideration, as an exercise of discretion might sometimes do.

The human rights appeal introduced into the appeals jurisdiction the concepts and principles of human rights law and the European Court of Human Rights. In the case of the qualified rights this also entails taking into account countervailing public interests. So, for instance, the right to respect for family life may be outweighed by the need for the prevention of disorder or crime. This entails appeal bodies evaluating the impact of social policy upon an individual and the necessity or otherwise of that. These questions have traditionally been the preserve of the executive, and especially in the area of immigration where, as we have seen, the government makes special claims for control. Human rights appeals have made immigration cases an even more politicized field than before.

The substance and scope of the protected rights is discussed in chapter 4. Here we briefly consider the constitutional challenges about the nature and scope of the human rights appeal itself in the context of three dominant legal issues.

8.4.3.1 *The jurisdiction of appeal bodies in human rights cases*

From the early days of the Human Rights Act onwards there were two strands of case law that proceeded side by side without a binding judicial authority either way. One strand said that, in immigration human rights appeals, the tribunal had no jurisdiction to substitute its judgment for that of the Secretary of State, unless the decision was irrational. The Secretary of State was the primary decision-maker for immigration matters and the court had no jurisdiction to re-assess the merits of the issue. This strand began with the judicial review case of *R (Mahmood) v SSHD* [2001] 1 WLR 840 whose principles, which arguably were inappropriate even for judicial review, were adopted by tribunals as an authority in Article 8 cases. This line of authority reached its high water mark in *Edore v SSHD* [2003] 3 All ER 1265, the first Court of Appeal authority actually on the issue, where the court said that the tribunal could not overturn the decision of the primary decision-maker unless it was irrational.

The other strand said that an appeal on a human rights issue is an appeal which examines whether the original decision was lawful or not, and as a matter of law, the courts were not only able but bound to consider the merits of the case for themselves, in accordance with their duty under Human Rights Act s 6. This was pronounced in one of the first authoritative tribunal decisions after the commencement of the Human Rights Act, *Nhundu and Chiwera* 01TH00613. It was the implication of the House of Lords' decision in *R (on the application of Daly) v SSHD* [2001] 2 WLR 1622, but it did not thrive until the authoritative pronouncement of the House of Lords in *Huang and Kashmiri*.

 Key Case

Huang and Kashmiri [2007] UKHL 11

Mrs Huang was about 60 years old. She had been staying with her daughter, son-in-law and their child in the UK. She was estranged from her husband. She applied to stay in the UK so that she could live with her daughter and son-in-law, but she did not come within the requirements of the immigration rules. She appealed on the basis that to compel her return to China would breach her right to respect for family life under Article 8.

Mr Kashmiri came to the UK at the age of 20. His father already had leave to remain as a refugee, together with his wife and younger sons. Mr Kashmiri's own asylum claim failed, and at the age of 20 he was held not to qualify as his father's dependant, so leave was refused. He also appealed on Article 8 grounds.

Both appellants' cases fell outside the immigration rules but both had family reasons for wanting to be in the UK.

The House of Lords, in relation to the question of jurisdiction, held:

the task of the appellate immigration authority, on an appeal on a Convention ground against a decision of the primary official decision-maker refusing leave to enter or remain in this country, is to decide whether the challenged decision is unlawful as incompatible with a Convention right or compatible and so lawful. It is not a secondary, reviewing, function dependent on establishing that the primary decision-maker misdirected himself or acted irrationally or was guilty of procedural impropriety. The appellate immigration authority must decide for itself whether the impugned decision is lawful and, if not, but only if not, reverse it. (para 11)

Earlier authorities to the contrary are now displaced. This question is a vital one, as without this jurisdiction there is no effective appeal and thus no effective protection for human rights.

8.4.3.2 *Margin of discretion in statutory human rights appeals?*

Various doctrines have been argued to set the boundaries and define the difference between the roles of the judiciary and the executive in human rights cases. A doctrine sometimes known as the 'margin of discretion' and sometimes as 'deference' has been used in the context of judicial review. Attrill suggests the principled basis for it is found in four factors:

- decision-makers should be accountable to a democratic body;
- a decision-maker may have more expertise in the relevant matter;
- the primary decision-maker will have evaluated the facts;
- the allocation of a kind of decision to a particular decision-maker is the will of Parliament (e.g. the Home Secretary is entrusted by Parliament with immigration control), and to undermine that would interfere with the will of Parliament (Attrill 2003).

One might also say that Parliament has made the judiciary the guardian of rights through the Human Rights Act, a matter in which it, as the traditional arbiter of justice, also has expertise (see *Huang v SSHD* [2005] EWCA Civ 105 para 55). That the judiciary is not answerable to Parliament for its decisions is in itself a constitutional safeguard, rather than being somehow anti-democratic, because they are not elected, and a 'cardinal feature of the modern democratic state, a cornerstone of the rule of law itself' (*A v SSHD* [2004] UKHL 56 para 42).

Lack of expertise is perhaps the most common reason used by the judiciary for deferring to the executive. A common example is in judging risk to national security (e.g. *Rehman v SSHD* [2001] 3 WLR 877 HL). However, as Lord Steyn said in *Daly*, 'in law, context is everything', and this reason falls down where the judiciary is as well placed as the executive to judge the matter. This was endorsed by Laws LJ in *International Transport Roth GmbH v SSHD* [2002] EWCA Civ 158, seeing the distinction between branches of government in terms both of constitutional responsibility and expertise (paras 83–87). The separation of powers requires both independence in the branches of government and the power to check and balance each other. Lord Hoffmann considers that the margin of discretion is a rule of law contained in the doctrine of separation of powers and should not be referred to as 'deference' because of its 'overtones of servility' (*R (on the application of ProLife Alliance) v BBC* [2003] UKHL 23).

Others see the discretion as that of the court in determining when it is appropriate not to intervene (e.g. Lester 2004:265). This makes it a voluntary practice of restraint, exercised on the basis of the courts' respect for the constitutional functions of other branches of government, not something that can be demanded because of the subject matter (Steyn 2005). This chimes with the views of R. Clayton who points out that 'routine decision-making by civil servants' should not be elevated to a constitutionally protected act just because a minister somewhere up the chain of command was put in post by an elected government (2004:40). Lord Bingham in *A v SSHD* [2004] UKHL 56 adopts the idea of 'relative institutional competence', rather than suggesting that one branch of government gives way to the other (para 29).

These principles have often been applied and argued in immigration and human rights appeals, but it may be apparent that they have no place in them. When they are used, it is to justify that the court should accord special weight to the view of the Secretary of State, who is charged by statute with responsibility for immigration control.

The House of Lords in *Huang and Kashmiri v SSHD* [2007] UKHL 11 said that the court would weigh in the balance factors such as the Home Secretary's judgment that a particular person presented a threat, or that there was a need to deter others from breaking the law, but that

> The giving of weight to factors such as these is not, in our opinion, aptly described as deference: it is performance of the ordinary judicial task of weighing up the competing considerations on each side and according appropriate weight to the judgment of a person with responsibility for a given subject matter and access to special sources of knowledge and advice. (para 16)

Refining elements of this judgment process with concepts such as 'due deference, discretionary areas of judgment...and so on' they regarded as 'a tendency...to complicate and mystify what is not, in principle, a hard task to define, however difficult the task is, in practice, to perform' (para 14).

The application of the margin of discretion or deference to immigration appeals has in theory been laid to rest by this judgment.

8.4.3.3 *Human rights, the immigration rules and the mistaken doctrine of exceptionality*

On the question of the jurisdiction of tribunals in human rights appeals the House of Lords in *Huang and Kashmiri* confirmed the Court of Appeal's judgment, but on this question of the rules and exceptionality they overturned it. The Court of Appeal in *Huang* had propounded these two interlinked doctrines which were taken up rapidly and elaborated in the tribunals and which led, as acknowledged by the Court of Appeal in *AG (Eritrea) v SSHD* [2007] EWCA Civ 801, to something 'going wrong'.

The first was the novel proposition that 'the Rules have themselves struck the balance between the public interest and the private right' (para 57). The Court suggested that the immigration rules had the democratic authority of having been subject to parliamentary scrutiny, and as such the tribunals should defer to the provisions in the rules. Therefore if a case failed under the rules, the judiciary would not normally have authority to overturn that decision. The House of Lords rejected this view, saying that the immigration rules are 'not the product of active debate in Parliament, where non-nationals seeking leave to enter or remain are not in any event represented'. Furthermore, the statutory right of appeal on human rights grounds which was enacted by Parliament is based on the supposition that 'an applicant may fail to qualify under the Rules and yet may have a valid claim by virtue of Article 8' (para 17). The equation of the immigration rules with human rights standards, which was in any event short-lived, falls with the House of Lords judgment.

The second point, however, does not lie down so easily. Equating a proper balance of interests with the immigration rules, the Court of Appeal went on to say that cases which can be shown to succeed on the basis of human rights would therefore be exceptional. Immigration judges had jurisdiction to decide whether an infringement with a protected right was proportionate, as required by human rights law, but only in exceptional cases. They based this proposition not only on the view they took of the immigration rules, but also on dicta of Lord Bingham in *Razgar v SSHD* [2004] UKHL 27:

Decisions taken pursuant to the lawful operation of immigration control will be proportionate in all save a small minority of exceptional cases, identifiable only on a case by case basis. (para 20)

This Court of Appeal decision in *Huang* created a flood of cases in which litigants and the tribunal searched for or denied the existence of 'exceptional' features in order to establish or refute a human rights claim. Rapidly there arose 'the test of exceptionality', downgrading human rights protection into a search for the unusual. The tribunal in *WK (Palestinian Territories)* [2006] UKAIT 00070 took this a step further by proposing a *threshold* of exceptionality, basing this on dicta of Lord Buxton in *ZT v SSHD* [2005] EWCA Civ 1421. Even without this authority, some immigration judges were in effect applying a threshold of exceptionality, and this was what was 'going wrong' according to the Court of Appeal in *AG (Eritrea)* where the tribunal had overturned a well-reasoned first instance appeal decision by looking for the individual's whole circumstances to be exceptional.

The House of Lords in *Huang and Kashmiri* resolved the question of what Lord Bingham meant in *Razgar*:

He was there expressing an expectation, shared with the Immigration Appeal Tribunal, that the number of claimants not covered by the Rules and supplementary directions but entitled to succeed under Article 8 would be a very small minority. That is still his expectation. But he was not purporting to lay down a legal test. (para 20)

Exceptionality is a prediction, not a precondition. The House of Lords' judgment in *Huang* does away with a test of exceptionality, but it is not so clear what meaning can be given to the expectation that not many cases will succeed. Some judgments after *Huang and Kashmiri* have interpreted this in a way that tends to perpetuate exceptionality as a test. The Court of Appeal judgment in *AG (Eritrea)* was given in order to clarify *Huang* in this respect. They said:

While its practical effect is likely to be that removal is only exceptionally found to be disproportionate, it sets no formal test of exceptionality and raises no hurdles beyond those contained in the article itself. (para 25)

It is doubtful whether tribunals can or should give any practical effect to an expectation, which is more appropriate for comment by those who keep statistics of outcomes, and there is continuing controversy over its meaning. It is suggested here that the House of Lords was saying no more than that, if the law functions as it should, then it should not often get it wrong.

The House of Lords' interpretation of Lord Bingham's comments in *Razgar* left out of account the origin of his prediction, which was the case of *Kacaj*. *Kacaj*, like *Razgar*, concerned a 'foreign' case in the terms of *Ullah and Do* (see chapter 4), i.e. a case in which the effects of the infringement of the right would be experienced outside the UK. These cases, according to *Razgar* and *Ullah and Do*, involve a higher threshold of risk and of breach in order to succeed. Therefore, it follows that very few will. It was in this context that Lord Bingham expressed his expectation. Sadly, the courts have lost sight of this crucial factor which must have influenced Lord Bingham's view.

Reference may be made to articles at the end of this chapter to pursue this important question further.

8.4.4 Not in accordance with the law

The ground that the decision is not in accordance with the law has played an important part in the development of immigration appeals. Where the decision is said not to comply with statute or common law, this ground may be used. It is also a ground for appeal where a decision is not in accordance with a policy or concession. It may be recalled (from chapter 1) that a basis for entry may be contained in policies and concessions outside the immigration rules, and that failure to apply a published policy could result in the decision being quashed in judicial review proceedings (*R v SSHD ex p Amankwah* [1994] Imm AR 240). However, judicial review as a remedy is limited in that it only compels the decision-maker to take the decision again properly. It is expensive, and subject to strict time limits and the hurdle of the permission stage. In the case of *Abdi v SSHD* [1996] Imm AR 148, the Court of Appeal decided that a failure to take into account a published policy was contrary to established principles of administrative law, and therefore not 'in accordance with the law' as required by Immigration Act 1971 s 19, the relevant section then in force. The decision would therefore be subject to appeal. This was a major breakthrough for immigration appeals as it made failure to implement a policy appealable. This ground of appeal is retained in the 2002 Act, but its effect is limited by the exclusive prescription of appealable decisions in s 82. Where a concession directly affects an appealable decision, such as leave to enter, then it is appealable under s 84(1)(e). Where it does not, for instance, a procedural waiver concerning the application process as applied to Kosovan families in 2000, then there is no appeal, only judicial review. Macdonald puts it that there is still room for argument that a decision is not in accordance with the law where 'the *purpose* of the stay is recognized by the rules, although waiver of part of the rule's requirement, or an extension of its application, is sought in accordance with Home Office policy' (2005:1196).

It is still not always clear what is not in accordance with a policy. The wording of many of the IDIs is loose, and certainly cannot be construed like a statute (see for instance *JJ and SS (student: regular attendance: which course?) Gambia* [2007] UKAIT 00050, discussed in chapter 10). Failure to apply a policy is the basis of challenge, and this does not always mean that the appellant will gain the benefit of it; the policy itself may well suggest otherwise. For instance, the policy that a family with children who have been in the UK for seven years will not normally be removed also provides that they may be, depending on the family's immigration history (e.g. *Baig v SSHD* [2005] EWCA Civ 1246).

Where a policy conflicts with a rule of general law, it is not binding. The Court of Appeal in *Ishtiaq v SSHD* [2007] EWCA Civ 86 held that they could not be bound by the IDI to refuse to accept evidence of domestic violence that was not in a list which purported to be exclusive. Where policy in the published instructions conflicts with the immigration rules the situation is complicated. Immigration Act 1971 Sch 2 para 1(3) provides that immigration officers must act in accordance with the law and the rules and instructions given to them by the Secretary of State, provided these are not inconsistent with the rules. However, the purpose of instructions is often to supplement or supersede the rules. This purpose could not be achieved if officers refused to obey instructions where they were inconsistent with the rules. The rules on the other hand have a superior authority in law to policy.

A case in point is the IDI July 2004 Ch 4 s 5 para 2.3, providing that leave to enter the UK on an initial work permit for training may be given for five years. For some considerable time before amendment, para 117 of the rules said that the limit was three years. If in a suitable case an immigration officer refused to consider granting leave for five years, their decision would be open to judicial review for failure to take into account the published policy (e.g. *R v SSHD ex p Khan* [1985] 1 All ER 40). This is an example of where failure to follow the policy would not be appealable following the 2002 Act, as the decision would not be an appealable immigration decision under s 82, just a grant of a shorter period of leave than anticipated. In avoiding judicial review the immigration officer must flout the rules.

As the statutory power to give leave to enter is not made subject to the immigration rules, there is a residual power based on s 4 to make decisions which are more favourable towards the applicant than the rules permit. As Vincenzi (1992) discusses, this does not do away with the problem of Sch 2 para 1(3). It results in a complete contradiction.

Where the proper result on applying the policy is ascertainable from the facts before the court, an appeal court itself may apply the Secretary of State's policy and decide the issue (*AB (Jamaica) v SSHD* [2007] EWCA Civ 1302). Where this is not possible, the court or tribunal may send the case back to the Secretary of State to take the decision in accordance with the policy (see, further, Glossop 2007).

The tribunal in *AA and others v SSHD* [2008] UKAIT 00003 took it as settled law that the tribunal's jurisdiction to hear an appeal that a decision was not in accordance with the law included jurisdiction to hear an argument that there was a breach of a legitimate expectation. They said that *Abdi* was the authority that at least some public law challenges are within the jurisdiction of the tribunal, and cited tribunal cases which pursued an argument based on legitimate expectation. Given the breadth of the other grounds in s 82 – human rights, race discrimination, and so on, all relying on statutes other than the immigration acts – it was inconceivable that the jurisdiction under s 84(1)(e) should be restricted to decisions under the Immigration Acts. Furthermore, 'the tribunal's jurisdiction lies within the heart of public law adjudication' (para 50). This case was discussed at length in chapter 2 as an example of executive control of policy. Similar issues arise below in discussion of judicial review.

8.4.5 **Exercise of discretion**

The power to allow an appeal if the tribunal considers that a discretion should have been exercised differently appears to be a wide power, but its scope is probably diminishing as the number of discretions in the rules diminishes. Where there has been an exercise of discretion, the tribunal can decide that it should have been exercised differently and substitute its own decision. The power to deport has been a key example of this but, as discussed in chapter 16, the discretion in that power is vanishing.

The appeal body's power is also limited by Nationality, Immigration and Asylum Act 2002 s 86(6), which replicates earlier similar provisions. The subsection says that a refusal to depart from the rules is not to be regarded as an exercise of discretion. This means that where, for instance, leave has been refused in accordance with the rules, an applicant cannot appeal on the grounds that they asked for discretion to be exercised outside the rules but were refused. The only appeal in this situation would be that the decision was not in accordance with the law if a relevant policy had not been applied.

8.5 **Judicial review**

Because appeal rights in immigration and asylum matters have been so frequently curtailed, and their scope limited, judicial review has been and continues to be a very important recourse for those who are subject to the immigration and asylum law system. Immigration decisions are subject to judicial review in accordance with usual public law principles, including since 2 October 2000 on the basis that they infringe Convention rights. In accordance with the normal rules of judicial review, any relevant appeal rights must first be exhausted (e.g. *Cinnamond v British Airports Authority* [1980] 2 All ER 368).

A number of principles of administrative law have been established in immigration cases. Examples include: the court's power to examine the factual basis of a decision-maker's exercise of power where this is necessary to see that the decision-maker has jurisdiction (*Khawaja v Secretary of State for the Home Department* [1983] AC 74 concerning illegal entry); the publication of an express promise or undertaking will lead to a legitimate expectation of its being honoured (*Attorney General for Hong Kong v Ng Yuen Shiu* [1983] 2 AC 629, also concerning the treatment of illegal entrants); the right to reasons for a decision (*R v Secretary of State for the Home Department ex p Fayed* [1998] 1 All ER 228, CA, a challenge to refusal of British nationality); and the obligation to hear both sides of a case which affects fundamental rights, even where strict rules of natural justice do not apply (*R v Secretary of State for the Home Department ex p Moon* (1996) 8 Admin LR 477, concerning the issue of entry clearance).

Refusal of permission to appeal may also be subject to judicial review, and often judicial review is the only way to restrain an impending removal if all appeal rights have been exhausted, or would be of no avail once the person is removed. Ascertaining the correct proceedings is not a straightforward matter, and for fuller discussion reference should be made to practitioner works on this issue. The Court of Appeal in *SSHD v R (on the application of Lim and another)* [2007] EWCA Civ 773 held that the claimants could not have recourse to judicial review to prevent their removal where they had a right of appeal, even though the appeal was only from outside the UK. This was the case even though Mr Lim, a work permit holder, was detained with removal directions set for the following day for the minor immigration infraction of being thought to be working at a different restaurant from the one for which he had permission, though in the same town and owned by the same employer. The Court of Appeal, while judging detention and removal a 'colossal overreaction', found that the appeal mechanism was the correct one, except in cases where the facts showed there was no jurisdiction to remove.

In principle, all the usual grounds of judicial review apply, but there are some which have particular relevance. A full account of public law challenges, even in the immigration and asylum law field, is beyond the scope of this book. Here we concentrate on some key cases and particular grounds in relation to which important issues have been litigated.

8.5.1 Natural justice or fairness

Administrative law recognizes a distinction between a judicial function and an administrative function. A judicial function is one which decides between competing arguments on the basis of evidence, and determines an outcome which will be decisive of rights or entitlements (e.g. *Ridge* v *Baldwin* [1964] AC 40), for example, imposing a criminal sentence or granting compensation. An administrative function is to process an application or otherwise follow a procedure according to the rules and principles governing that action. This may include the use of discretion where the rules permit. So, for instance, issuing a driving licence is an administrative matter. While administrative decisions must be made fairly and in accordance with relevant procedures, a judicial decision must be made in accordance with the principles of natural justice, giving both sides a fair hearing and acting without bias. Sometimes fairness and natural justice are equated, for instance in *Lloyd* v *McMahon* [1987] AC 625.

There is not always a clear distinction between administrative and judicial decisions, and it may be readily apparent that it is not easy to determine whether immigration decisions are administrative or judicial. They have qualities of each. In *Re HK* [1967] QB 617, Lord Parker CJ held that in making inquiries to ascertain the age of a child seeking to enter the UK the immigration officer should act fairly, 'only to that limited extent do the so-called rules of natural justice apply, which in a case such as this is merely a duty to act fairly'. The role of immigration officers in deciding applications was considered in *R* v *SSHD ex p Mughal* [1973] 3 All ER 796 not to be a judicial but an administrative one. The same goes for entry clearance officers and Home Office officials. Strictly, this means they are not bound by the rules of natural justice, but they are bound to act fairly. This means making all proper enquiries to obtain all relevant facts of the case, but not necessarily notifying the applicant of further information which confirmed the immigration officer's view, and so not necessarily giving the applicant an opportunity to reply to every point as would be the case in a criminal trial. However, in *R* v *SSHD ex p Moon* The Times, 8 December 1995 the Divisional Court held that in dealing with an application for entry clearance the entry clearance officer should give the applicant an opportunity to deal with objections to their application.

The distinction between fairness and natural justice can be pressed too far. The Court of Appeal in *R* v *SSHD ex p Thirukumar* [1989] Imm AR 270 held that asylum decisions were of such importance that only the highest levels of fairness would be sufficient, and this includes providing a copy to the applicant of their answers at previous interviews. The Court of Appeal in *R (Dirshe)* v *SSHD* [2005] EWCA Civ 421 held that, where the applicant had no public funding either for a representative or for their own interpreter, the overall fairness of the process required that the applicant be able to tape record the asylum interview, although there is not necessarily a principle of equality of arms, as there would be between private litigants.

The current state of case law is that Article 6, the Human Rights Act provision on fair hearings, does not apply in immigration matters (see discussion on *Maaouia v France* in chapter 4). Currently, therefore, the Human Rights Act does not make up any difference in standards between the principle of fairness in administrative law and a fair trial under Article 6. However, as Lord Steyn said in *R v SSHD ex p Anufrijeva*, 'the Convention is not an exhaustive statement of fundamental rights under our system of law' (para 27) and fundamental principles may still be found and applied. In *Anufrijeva* the appellant's asylum claim had been turned down but she was not informed. Shortly after that, the welfare benefits she had received as an asylum seeker (90 per cent of the usual income support rate) were stopped as her asylum claim was no longer current, but she was not given a reason. She argued that the asylum decision could not be treated as effective because she had not been notified. Her case was not isolated as this practice was part of Home Office policy at the time. Lord Steyn said:

> The arguments for the Home Secretary ignore fundamental principles of our law. Notice of a decision is required before it can have the character of a determination with legal effect because the individual concerned must be in a position to challenge the decision in the courts if he or she wishes to do so. This is not a technical rule. It is simply an application of the right of access to justice. That is a fundamental and constitutional principle of our legal system. (para 26)

He referred to the view that an uncommunicated administrative decision could bind an individual as 'an astonishingly unjust proposition' (para 30). Where the individual is excluded not from an administrative but a judicial process, as we saw in *FP (Iran)*, there may be a breach of natural justice.

In conclusion, even though full rules of natural justice entailing equality of arms may not yet be applicable in immigration and asylum cases, a high degree of fairness and openness is required, consistent with the importance of the matters at stake and fundamental principles of access to justice and the rule of law.

8.5.2 Unfairness amounting to an abuse of power

This head of judicial review has recently been the subject of significant developments, centred on two cases, *R (S and others) v SSHD* [2006] EWCA Civ 1157 and *Rashid v SSHD* [2005] EWCA Civ 744.

 Key Case

Rashid v SSHD [2005] EWCA Civ 744

Mr Rashid was an Iraqi Kurd who sought asylum in the UK in December 2001. At that time there was a Home Office policy that people who had a well-founded fear in other parts of Iraq would not be forcibly returned on the basis they could find safety in the Kurdish Autonomous Zone (KAZ). The policy was based on the stance of the Kurdish authorities who, because of a lack of infrastructure and resources after the 1991 Gulf War, were not able to admit people who had been living in other parts of Iraq. The policy was not applied to Mr Rashid and his asylum claim was refused within a week on the basis he could relocate in the KAZ.

Six months later, in correspondence, the Home Office reiterated the refusal. A year later, on appeal to the adjudicator, relocation to the KAZ was fully argued by the Home Office Presenting Officer. The policy was still in force. The Home Office resisted an application for leave to appeal, then unsuccessfully opposed an application for permission for judicial review on the same point. Until late February 2003, the argument was maintained. There were two other applicants in a situation legally identical to Mr Rashid, M and A. By letter of 6 March 2003, A's legal representatives were told that the Secretary of State was not, 'as a matter of policy...relying on the availability of internal relocation' to the KAZ and that A would be granted refugee status. On 12 March 2003, Mr Rashid's solicitors wrote to the Treasury solicitors asking that he too be granted refugee status, as the Home Office had already accepted that his case was on the same point. On 21 March 2003, it was announced that, because of the military action in Iraq, decision-making on Iraqi nationals had been suspended. The suspension lasted until June 2003. The Home Office agreed in March to reconsider Mr Rashid's case, but did not do so until January 2004, by which time, they said, he could return, and he was refused refugee status.

The judicial review on Mr Rashid's behalf successfully claimed that he had a legitimate expectation that the policy would be applied to him, and that the repeated failure to do so was 'conspicuous unfairness amounting to an abuse of power'. In earlier cases this has been described as something 'illogical' or 'immoral'(*R v Inland Revenue Commissioners, ex parte Unilever plc* [1996] STC 681), or, as counsel for Mr Rashid said, something which 'leaps off the page'. Other factors which induced the court to find in his favour were the lack of consistency with M and A, 'the persistence of the conduct, and lack of explanation for it' (para 36), particularly in a country which at the time was in the focus of the Secretary of State's attention, Iraq being a source of the one of the highest numbers of refugees.

A number of attempts to follow *Rashid* have failed in cases where delay in making a decision has meant that a different policy has been applied to the applicant than would have been if the decision had been made more promptly. In *Rashid* there was no initial delay in making a decision, but rather a number of points over a 16-month period in which decisions and representations *were* made about his case, but always on the wrong basis. There was then a delay in applying the policy to him once it was acknowledged that it should be (March 2003 to January 2004), but this was only another in a catalogue not of periods of inaction, as is often the case, but of actual errors.

Rashid was followed successfully, if success is an appropriate word, where once again, three Iraqi Kurds had been refused asylum on the basis they could relocate in the KAZ, in ignorance of the same policy (*A, H and AH v SSHD* [2006] EWHC 526 (Admin)). Collins J found that this was conspicuous unfairness amounting to an abuse of power. As in *Rashid*, only a finding of such extreme unfairness could warrant going against the *Ravichandran* principle, which entails that asylum decisions are to be made on the situation as it stands at the time of the hearing. Application of that principle would mean that if it is safe at the time of the hearing the claimants would be expected to return.

The case of *R (S and others) v SSHD* was a high-profile one for all the wrong reasons. It was discussed in chapter 2 as an example of the misrepresentation in the media which sometimes distorts public debate on immigration and asylum cases.

 **Key Case**

R (S and others) v SSHD [2006] EWCA Civ 1157

The case was the application for judicial review by a group of people from Afghanistan who in February 2000 hijacked an aeroplane in order to enter the UK. They were convicted of criminal offences. Then their convictions were set aside by the Court of Appeal because the jury had not been directed properly on the issue of duress but by this time they had served their prison sentences.

They opposed the Taleban government, and belonged to a group four of whom had been detained. Not long after this, the dead body of one was returned bearing marks of torture. They devised the plan to hijack an aircraft as a means of escape. Their asylum claim was turned down. In an unusual step, a panel of adjudicators was convened to hear their appeal. The panel generally believed their accounts, but held that they were debarred from refugee status because of their action in hijacking the aircraft. There were mitigating circumstances certainly, but there would also have been alternatives. However, they did face a real risk of treatment contrary to Article 3 if they returned, so they succeeded on human rights grounds. Under the policy then in force they should have been granted six months' discretionary leave, which would be reviewed and was renewable. Instead, they were kept on temporary admission with the consequence that they could not work or claim benefits.

This situation went on for a year, after which the Secretary of State inserted into the policy a caveat that leave would not be granted when 'Ministers decide, in view of all the circumstances of the case, that it is inappropriate to grant any leave and instead place or keep the person on temporary admission'.

After a further period of time and sustained pressure by the claimants' solicitors the Secretary of State wrote to say that he had decided not to grant the claimants' discretionary leave but to keep them on temporary admission.

This inserted clause may readily be recognized as a claim of arbitrary power. There is a policy, but the Minister decides when it will and will not apply. In the High Court, Sullivan J said:

the policy does not give any, or any effective, protection against arbitrary interference by Ministers…It is a paradigm of an unfettered administrative discretion to depart from a published policy whenever the Minister thinks it appropriate to do so. It therefore leaves them 'vulnerable to interference by [ministers] acting on any personal whim, caprice, malice, predilection, or purpose other than that for which the power was conferred.' (para 113, referring to Lord Bingham in *R (Gillan) v Commissioner of Police for the Metropolis* [2006] 2 WLR 537)

Sullivan J found the failure to grant discretionary leave and the insertion into the policy unlawful and, on appeal by the Secretary of State, the Court of Appeal agreed. It was not open to the Secretary of State to extend those who could be subject to temporary admission without the sanction of Parliament. Temporary admission is allowed by statute only where a person would otherwise be detained. This was not the case here.

To summarize, there were two errors made by the Secretary of State. Once the appeal body had decided that the claimants' human rights claim succeeded, there should have been no significant delay in the grant of discretionary leave. Although the leave is called discretionary, there is a clear policy which applied without question in the situation, and there were no further factors for the Secretary of State to consider. Nothing more than practical reasons for delay was warranted.

The second error was the change in policy. The Secretary of State *is* entitled to change his policy. The mistake here was

- To change it as a substitute for implementing it
- To claim untrammelled power by the change
- To claim a new power to grant a status awarded by statute without consulting Parliament.

If for instance the change had been to grant three months' leave instead of six, the case would have been somewhat different, although a legitimate expectation would still have had to be considered.

The Secretary of State is dealing with defeat in *S v SSHD* by legislation. In the Criminal Justice and Immigration Bill 2007 currently going through Parliament there is a power to take away the right to any kind of leave for someone in the position of these appellants, and keep them on temporary admission with residence conditions and electronic tagging.

8.5.3 Legitimate expectation

Policy is designed to provide a degree of predictability and transparency in the exercise of executive power, and consistent treatment between comparable individuals. The public law doctrine of legitimate expectation may be invoked where an applicant is deprived of the benefit of a policy which should have been applied to them, and it is now settled that, in cases where the policy applies specifically to the individual and they have relied upon it to their significant detriment, there can be substantive as well as procedural expectation (*R v North and East Devon HA ex p Coughlan* [2001] QB 213, *Nadarajah and Abdi v SSHD* [2005] EWCA Civ 1363). If an individual comes within the terms of a policy they can expect to be treated in accordance with it (e.g. *R v SSHD ex p Khan* [1985] 1 All ER 40).

As has been apparent already in relation to the immigration rules (*MO (Nigeria)*), the timing of a decision is crucial. Many claimants have sought to argue that delay in deciding their claim has deprived them of the benefit of a policy that was in force at the date of their application and which would have applied if their application had been decided with reasonable promptness. This issue is discussed in chapter 4 in relation to proportionality of interfering with an Article 8 right.

The question of changing policy was dealt with directly in judicial review in *R (on the application of Rechachi, Kalobo, Fodil, Yusuf)* [2006] EWHC 3513 (Admin). In 2005 the Home Office changed its practice of giving recognized refugees indefinite leave to remain, and replaced it with a routine grant of five years' leave. Mr Rechachi's situation may be given as the example which raised the issues in their most acute form. He claimed asylum in 2002, submitted medical evidence in 2003, and his claim was finally refused in April 2005. His appeal was heard in May 2005, decided in June, and the decision promulgated in July. The policy change took effect on 30 August 2005. On 20 December 2005, after much chasing by his solicitors, he received five years' leave to remain.

The High Court held that:

- There can be no challenge to the Secretary of State's right in principle to change his policy;
- Refugee status is recognized, not granted;

- Nevertheless the formal grant of leave to remain which is consequent on refugee status confers the entitlement to remain;

- Five years' leave is an adequate discharge of the obligation under the Refugee Convention;

- The Secretary of State in changing his policy specifically decided that the five-year period would apply to leave granted as a consequence of an appeal which succeeded before 30 August 2005. This was to avoid inconsistency and for administrative convenience (*Rechachi* para 44). The Secretary of State was entitled to make policy of this kind and on this basis. The application of the policy to these claimants was intentional and not an oversight.

These conclusions only left open the question of whether the delay in each case was unreasonable. The court held it was not, though only just in the case of Mr Rechachi.

Similar issues arose with the legitimate expectation of applicants under the Highly Skilled Migrants' Programme, that they would be dealt with according to the scheme in force at the date of their original application as opposed to their application to extend. An appeal in the tribunal, dealing with this issue, is discussed at length in chapter 2 (*AA v SSHD*).

Rechachi deals with a deliberate change of policy which still discharged the obligation to which it was addressed. This is not the same as ignoring the policy or treating it as though it had no content. In *R (on the application of Tozlukaya) v SSHD* [2006] EWCA Civ 379 the family came within the scope of policy DP5/96, as amended by statement in Parliament on 24 February 1999. This was that where children had spent seven years in the UK the family would not normally be removed, though other factors would be taken into account which might displace that presumption. The Secretary of State denied the family the benefit of the policy on the basis that each decision must be taken on its own merits, a basis for decision-making which denied any substance to the policy at all. Evidence for the Home Office was that caseworkers did not have access to the statement in Parliament, or an approved summary of the policy. The Court of Appeal held that 'all this is contrary to the basic principles of good administration' (para 89). There was a legitimate expectation that the policy would be applied.

In *Tozlukaya* there is a purported application of the policy, but in such a diluted version as to be meaningless. The case also discloses a variation on a theme in *Rashid*. Caseworkers know a policy exists but are not provided with the information to enable them to apply it properly.

Knowledge of relevant policies was an issue in *Rashid* not only for caseworkers but also for Mr Rashid. It was argued that he could not have a legitimate expectation of the policy applying if he did not know about it. However, his legitimate expectation is that decisions will be taken in accordance with relevant polices, i.e. according to law. The Court of Appeal built on earlier principles (e.g. in *R v SSHD ex p Ahmed and Patel* [1998] INLR 570) by holding that the legitimate expectation applied even though he was not aware of the policy:

Whether the claimant knows of the policy is not in the present context relevant. It would be grossly unfair if the court's ability to intervene depended at all upon whether the particular claimant had or had not heard of a policy, especially one unknown to relevant Home Office officials. (para 25)

8.5.4 **Fettering discretion**

There is a complex relationship in public law between policy and discretion. Policy is not binding, like statute, it is a guide to the exercise of discretion. To protect against arbitrariness, the person who comes within it may expect the benefit of it, but if a decision has been properly considered and the policy applied, the individual may still be excluded from benefiting by the terms of the policy itself. Another relevant principle is that discretion is to be exercised, and when a decision-maker fails to do this, there may be an unlawful fetter.

The claimant in *SSHD v R (S)* [2007] EWCA Civ 546 alleged a conspicuous unfairness, amounting to abuse of power, following *Rashid*, but the court saw it differently.

 **Key Case**

SSHD v R (S) **[2007] EWCA Civ 546**

The claimant had entered the UK as an asylum seeker from Afghanistan in 1999 at the same time as his cousin. The cousin's application was dealt with, but R's was not. If R's application had been dealt with during the first couple of years of his stay he would have received the benefit of a policy which would have entailed his being granted ILR. The first substantive response from the Home Office to R came in 2002 and informed him that applications made prior to 2001 had been put on hold. The reason for this, not given to him at the time, was the government's desire to meet targets for dealing with later applications, as set in a Public Service Agreement.

The Court of Appeal said: 'All other considerations, including fairness and consistency in the treatment of individual applicants, were ignored in order to meet the target' (para 19). The claimant and those in this position were 'sacrificed so that it could be said that the government was meeting a target' (para 18, the CA adopting the 'suspicion' of the court below).

Delay alone could not found a case of 'conspicuous unfairness amounting to abuse'. Unlike *Rashid*, this was not a decision made in ignorance of a policy that should have been applied. It was rather a failure or even refusal to make decisions, which Carnwath LJ identified as a 'textbook case' of fettering discretion, contrary to an established principle of public law (para 50). The exercise of discretion requires that individual cases are treated individually, and in accordance with any relevant policy.

8.5.5 **Failure to consult**

The challenge of delegated legislation on the basis of procedural unfairness is an established heading of challenge in judicial review. Verifiable procedures for making immigration rules consist only of the negative resolution procedure in Parliament. Procedures for making immigration or asylum policy do not seem to involve any public formality. One ground of alleged procedural unfairness is a failure to consult, and this was alleged in *R (on the application of BAPIO Action Ltd) v SSHD and Department of Health* [2007] EWCA Civ 1139. The facts of this case are given in chapter 11.

BAPIO Action did not dispute that the Secretary of State could lawfully change the immigration rules in a way that was disadvantageous to its members, but claimed that the government should have consulted first. The court found there was no duty to consult. Although BAPIO's members had an interest in a benefit (training opportunities and employment in the UK) which could found a legitimate expectation of consultation, there was no duty to consult, and he would only be obliged to do so if fairness required it. The Court of Appeal found that this was not something the courts could imply. There were too many unknown factors such as who should be consulted, and upon what questions exactly, and how, and should anyone be excluded, and so on. Thus no duty to consult could be implied in this case.

The other executive act challenged in the *BAPIO* case was the guidance issue by the Department of Health to NHS employers that international medical graduates with limited leave should only be offered a vacant training post if the resident labour market criterion was satisfied. That criterion is used in issuing work permits and means that there is provably no suitable EEA applicant for the post in question. Here the Court of Appeal judgment is brief and uncompromising. The Court said that the Crown has a statutory obligation (in Immigration Act 1971 s 3) to obtain the approval of Parliament for principles by which it intends to regulate admission to the UK. No such approval had been obtained in this case. The Department of Health had even given evidence to the effect that discussions with the Home Office to achieve the restriction had broken down, as the Home Office considered that a fundamental change in the immigration rules would be required (para 60). So the Department of Health went ahead anyway. If the Home Secretary had issued such guidance it would not have been lawful. It could be no more lawful for being issued by the Department of Health (para 54). This seems to be a case of simple illegality.

8.6 Race discrimination

We have already briefly discussed race discrimination as a ground of appeal against an immigration decision. This section considers further provisions applying to the Borders and Immigration Agency as a public body, in particular where a whole policy or scheme is racially discriminatory. Paragraph 2 of the HC 395 requires immigration officers, entry clearance officers, and Home Office staff to carry out their duties 'without regard to the race, colour or religion of persons seeking to enter or remain in the UK'. As mentioned earlier, the immigration service, Home Office, and entry clearance officers are bound by the Race Relations Act 1976, following the implementation of the Race Relations (Amendment) Act 2000 on 2 April 2001. The Act was passed after the McPherson Inquiry into the death of Stephen Lawrence, and the public disquiet that followed at the fact that the police were not bound by the Race Relations Act. As a consequence all public bodies are now brought within the Act's provisions, both as regards the obligation not to discriminate on racial grounds, and to have a positive policy to promote racial equality. For the purposes of the Act racial grounds are grounds of 'colour, race, nationality or ethnic or national origins' (Race Relations Act 1976 s 3).

Race Relations Act 1976 s 19B(1) provides:

It is unlawful for a public authority in carrying out any functions of the authority to do any act which constitutes discrimination

This application of the Race Relations Act to immigration matters brings with it a duty to carry out a racial equality impact assessment of policy changes. The changes to entry provisions for overseas doctors were one such example, where the members of the British Association for Physicians of Indian Origin (BAPIO) would be adversely affected. In their challenge for failure to consult them, they also challenged the failure to carry out a racial equality impact assessment. An assessment was carried out after the event, and so although the court agreed with their challenge in principle, no remedy was ordered (*R (on the application of BAPIO Action Ltd and Yousaf) v SSHD and Secretary of State for Health* [2007] EWHC 199 (Admin).

8.6.1 Ministerial authorizations

Immigration and asylum matters are subject to exceptions under the Race Relations Act. The exceptions are so far as permitted by ministerial authorizations under Race Relations Act 1976 s 19D, and allow decisions to be taken on grounds of nationality or ethnic or national origin, but not on grounds of race or colour. Nationality decisions are no longer part of this exception following their removal from s 19D by Nationality, Immigration and Asylum Act 2002 s 6.

The first authorization was made on 27 March 2001. There have been regular reviews and further authorizations since that time, and the accumulated set of powers now in force may be grouped as follows:

Powers to discriminate in immigration decision-making, pursuant to authorization of 12 February 2004

Where a person is subject to examination under Immigration Act 1971 Sch 2 an immigration officer may

   (a) subject the person to a more rigorous examination than others in the same circumstances;

   (b) subject the person to further examination to ascertain if existing leave should be cancelled, request production of documents, search for and seize them, grant temporary admission;

   (c) detain the person pending examination;

   (d) decline to give notice of grant or refusal of leave to enter by fax or e-mail as is permitted by SI 2000/1161;

   (e) impose a condition or restriction on temporary admission.

These powers may be exercised on the basis of a person's nationality where the minister is satisfied that:

   (a) specific intelligence suggests that a significant number of person of that nationality have breached or will attempt to breach the immigration laws, or

   (b) there is statistical evidence showing that in the preceding month the total number of adverse decisions or breaches of the immigration laws by persons of that nationality exceeded 50 in total and 5 for every 1,000 admitted persons of that nationality, or that there is an emerging trend of breaches.

A person may also be refused leave to enter, or documents or information may be requested from them or priority may be given to setting removal directions.

The power to subject a person to more rigorous examination than others in the same circumstances has no other basis in law, though the rest are existing powers under the Immigration Act 1971. Since July 2003 statistics are collected monthly so that, in order to comply with the decision of the High Court in the *Tamil Information Centre* case (see below), they may be made in accordance with latest information and under the minister's personal direction.

Narrower authorizations are made from time to time, for instance on 16 January 2006 for more rigorous examination of applications from Zimbabweans for indefinite leave to remain, made on the grounds of UK ancestry. The authorization was to last for a six-month period and was based on evidence of fraudulent applications made before 25 October 2004. In 2004 additional examination was authorized of nationals of Somalia, Turkey, Iran, Iraq, and Sudan, the five nationalities which statistics showed would be most likely to be subject to return to a third country (see chapter 12).

Prioritizing asylum claims

Asylum claims may be given priority for consideration if the asylum seeker comes from a country from which a large number of 'unfounded' applications are made or which raise similar issues under the Refugee Convention. The implication here is that the application is judged not to merit or require extensive examination (authorization 27 March 2001). The fast-track schemes discussed in chapter 12 are authorized by this power.

Language analysis

Following disputes about nationality in individual cases, from time to time there are authorizations which provide that asylum applicants from certain countries may be required to submit to language analysis testing. The most recent of these, relating to Eritrea and Somalia, provided that refusal may be taken into account in assessing credibility.

Permission to work

The authorizations also provide for some positive discrimination to give permission to work when the rules would not normally allow this to

(a) participants in the British Universities North America Club Programme; and
(b) participants in the Japan Youth Exchange Scheme
(c) participants in the UK-China Graduates Work Programme.

Authorisations were also used in the scheme for sectors-based work permits, discussed in chapter 11.

Data transfer

An authorization in March 2006 allowed transfer of an asylum seeker's fingerprint data to another country if they were of a nationality considered to be among those most frequently claiming asylum in more than one country.

The lawfulness of the first authorization was tested in *R (Tamil Information Centre) v SSHD* TLR 30/10/2002. As the actions permitted by the authorizations are acts of discrimination which would otherwise be unlawful, on principle they should be construed narrowly. This conclusion is supported by the principle that the Race Relations Act 1976 should be construed purposively so as to enable and not defeat its object

(*Jones v Tower Boot Co* (1997) ICR 254 and *Anyanwu v South Bank Student Union* [2003] All ER (D) 285 Nov, followed in the *Tamil Information Centre* case). Section 19D which gives the power to make the authorization says explicitly that the permitted discrimination may be carried out only by a Minister of the Crown acting personally, or in accordance with 'a requirement imposed or express authorization given with respect to a particular case or class of case by a Minister of the Crown acting personally' (s 19D(3)(a)).

The authorizations allow discrimination on the basis of intelligence information that 'there is statistical evidence showing a pattern or trend of breach of the immigration laws by persons of that nationality'. There was no requirement to maintain statistics of any particular type, nor for anyone other than the immigration officer to take a view on the meaning of them. Forbes J found for the claimant in holding that these terms of the authorization 'delegated the essential task of actually identifying and defining any such case or class of case entirely to the decision-making of immigration officials, and what is more, by reference to their standards and/or thresholds rather than his own' (at para 19). Forbes J held the statute required that the minister personally made the actual decision. A licence to discriminate should be strictly controlled, and this the authorization did not do as it left too much in the hands of immigration officers. The amended authorization, as has already been noted, requires that the minister is satisfied that the statistics show the basis as claimed. Comparing the permitted basis with the requirements to show indirect discrimination, as discussed in *SK India* above, it appears that the requirements for a licence to discriminate are less onerous.

Finally, a Race Monitor was appointed, in accordance with Race Relations Act 1976 s 29E, to monitor the likely effect of the authorizations and their operation. A constant theme of her annual reports has been that basing selection on previous adverse decisions means that passengers of the identified nationalities are less likely to be given the benefit of the doubt, and so more likely to receive a refusal, and thus the authorization can be self-fulfilling (Annual Report 2004–05 paras 2.31–2.35).

The immigration service has often been charged with acting in a discriminatory fashion. The Race Monitor in her report of 2005–06 concluded that the authorizations were on balance more useful than otherwise, as the self-fulfilling stereotyping would probably have happened anyway (para 8.1). As illustrated by the *Tamil Information Centre* case, the authorizations may open up the possibility of challenge and judicial consideration and promote monitoring.

The Race Monitor has also commented on the difficulty in practice of maintaining the vital distinction between selecting for more intensive procedures on the basis of nationality and making a greater number of negative decisions on that basis (e.g. 2005–06 report 2.18). The authorizations permit discrimination in procedure, not outcome.

Discrimination without an authorization is unlawful, nevertheless not only individual discriminatory decisions but also discriminatory polices persist. The *ERRC* case below is an example. Another policy subject to a current legal challenge is in relation to granting unaccompanied asylum-seeking children discretionary leave to the age of 17.5 (APU notice 3/2007). This is subject to an exception in the case of children from certain countries, who are to be given 12 months' leave only (Asylum Policy: Application of Non-Suspensive Appeal process to asylum seeking children). There is no ministerial authorization for this (ILPA mailing 07.11.27, Colin Yeo).

8.6.2 **Where a whole immigration scheme is racially discriminatory**

The *Roma Rights* case was a challenge to a pre-clearance scheme (see chapter 7).

 Key Case

European Roma Rights Centre and other v Immigration Officer, Prague Airport and SSHD
[2004] UKHL 55

This case entailed immigration officers stationed at Prague Airport refusing leave to enter to passengers before they could board the plane. The scheme was located in Prague because there was a high number of asylum claims refused from the Czech Republic and the scheme was to deter claims that were considered to be not well founded. The great majority of claims were made by people of Roma ethnicity, and they generally failed because the applicant was considered to be experiencing discrimination rather than persecution, or the treatment they feared was not at the hands of the state (*Horvath v SSHD* [2000] 3 All ER 577 HL). Perhaps surprisingly, the Secretary of State did not use an authorization under s 19D to operate the scheme, but rather said that it was not discriminatory at all. When it was challenged, the Court of Appeal found that although Roma were selected for more intensive questioning and were more likely to be refused passage, they were not refused as Roma, but as potential asylum claimants. This fine distinction was explained by Simon Brown LJ saying that the higher refusal rate for Roma was not because they were being stereotyped, but because 'they are less well placed to persuade the immigration officer that they are not lying in order to seek asylum' (para 86).

The House of Lords looked at the matter quite differently. Baroness Hale gave the leading judgment on the issue of discrimination:

The Roma were being treated more sceptically than the non-Roma. There was a good reason for this. How did the immigration officers know to treat them more sceptically? Because they were Roma. That is acting on racial grounds. If a person acts on racial grounds, the reason why he does so is irrelevant. (para 82)

As Baroness Hale pointed out, direct discrimination cannot, in law, be justified, and this was direct discrimination.

There was in existence an authorization under s 19D which permitted more intensive examination of Roma. Although the Secretary of State decided it had no application in this case and did not rely on it, Baroness Hale found that it was not irrelevant.

The combination of the objective of the whole Prague operation and a very recent ministerial authorization of discrimination against Roma was, it is suggested, to create such a high risk that the Prague officers would consciously or unconsciously treat Roma less favourably than others that very specific instructions were needed to counteract this. (para 89)

This is very similar to the point made by the Independent Race Monitor. Authorisations, while intended to limit discrimination to particular cases, may in themselves contribute to an atmosphere of discrimination which needs to be positively countered. 'It is worth remembering that good equal opportunities practice may not come naturally' (Baroness Hale, para 90).

The Prague scheme was found to be discriminatory in its operation, contrary to Race Relations Act 1976 s 1, and a declaration made to that effect.

Some of the difficulties in litigating on race discrimination grounds in immigration matters are illustrated by the *BAPIO* case. There could be no doubt that Indian doctors would be adversely affected by the changes to the rules for international medical graduates. Their standing to bring the action, and to challenge the failure to consult them, depended on precisely this. The Indian doctors were going to be badly affected, but if they had been consulted they could have made some input that might have mitigated the impact upon them. A Racial Equality Impact Assessment would have forced the government to consider these questions openly. Why was the challenge not made on the grounds that the rule changes were discriminatory? The probable reason is that there would be no chance of winning an argument that in effect challenges the basis of immigration control. The change to the rules limited training posts to graduates of UK medical schools. The government can lawfully favour its own nationals in the matter of entry to the UK to gain access to employment and training, and some would say they are obliged to do so.

8.7 Representation

In such a complex and powerful system, effective, knowledgeable and affordable representation is essential. Procedural points are often essential to the outcome of an immigration case, and many issues can only be tested on judicial review, which is a virtually impossible task for an unrepresented applicant. The importance of the matter to the individual also may often mean that representation is highly desirable.

Organizations of experienced representatives also have an important role in commenting on the almost continuous flow of legislation and policy-making and in responding to consultations. In fact they are in a better position than most to assist government to see the implications of their proposals. This has political significance also as immigration and, to a greater extent, asylum are fields in which political battles are fought with legal tools. However, immigration and asylum law are unusual branches of legal work in that until recent reforms it was possible for unqualified people to represent clients both in dealings with the Home Office and at adjudicator hearings and tribunals. In addition, prior to 1 January 2000 no legal aid was available for representation.

The combination of lack of public funding and the freedom given to unqualified and unregulated advisers gave scope for unscrupulous individuals to set themselves up as immigration practitioners and charge high fees for work of dubious quality and sometimes of no value at all. It would be wrong to suggest that poor practice was the preserve of the unqualified. It was also the case that, due perhaps partly to the absence of immigration law from most legal professional training, bad work for high prices was done by legal professionals. Added to this was the vulnerability of immigration and asylum clients due to the profound importance to them of the matter, the scarcity of sound knowledge of the subject, and the possibility that they may not be fluent in English.

A regulatory system was set up to control so-called 'unscrupulous immigration advisers', but the terms of the regulatory system have been contentious.

8.7.1 **Regulatory system**

Part V of the Immigration and Asylum Act 1999 provided the first statutory controls of the provision of immigration advice and representation by prohibiting such work from being done by an unqualified person (s 84(1)). A qualified person is, broadly speaking, an authorized member of a legal professional body (the Law Society, Institute of Legal Executives, or General Council of the Bar), or someone registered with the newly created Immigration Services Commissioner. Voluntary organizations such as citizens' advice bureaux, and other publicly funded organizations providing immigration advice are exempt from the requirement for individual workers to be registered, but the organization must comply with the requirements of the scheme. It is possible for independent organizations, rather than applying for their own exemption, to undertake all of their immigration work under the supervision of a solicitor, providing the supervision is active (Law Society Gazette vol. 99, no. 33, p. 16). To provide immigration advice outside these provisions is an imprisonable offence under s 91.

The Immigration Services Commissioner's role is (s 83) to promote good practice in immigration advice and representation and to maintain a register of qualified advisers (s 85). Their powers and duties include preparing a code setting standards of conduct which applies to registered individuals and exempt bodies, i.e. all except legal professionals and government employees (Sch 5). The Commissioner's Rules and Codes of Standards allow for registration at a number of different levels, depending on the scope and level of competence of the organization or registered individual. This does not include representation in immigration offences as these are a branch of criminal law. The 2004 Act amended and increased the OISC's powers, introducing a power of entry and search of premises and seizure of documents including a power to seize materials that are subject to legal privilege (s 38). The 1999 Act also makes provision, in s 87, for an Immigration Services Tribunal which may hear complaints from those aggrieved by a decision of the Commissioner, or disciplinary matters referred by the Commissioner. Non-practising barristers must apply for regulation with the Office of the Immigration Services Commissioner (OISC news April 2002).

As mentioned earlier, bad work was done by legal professionals as well as by unqualified people. There was a lobby for all immigration advisers to be liable for individual registration, but the government's policy in the 1999 Act was to allow the professional bodies to regulate themselves. Both the Law Society and the Bar Council set up voluntary panel and accreditation schemes, but the greater impact on legal professionals is from compulsory accreditation for publicly funded work. This was instituted by the Law Society and Legal Services Commission together.

The provisions of the scheme are complex (see 'Immigration accreditation scheme explained' Everett, K. and Arnold, N. (2004) *Legal Action* June, pp. 10–12). Since 1 April 2005 all advisers must be accredited. In early 2004 the allowable amount of public funding for each asylum case was radically reduced, as was legal aid firms' capacity to authorize their own expenditure (see for instance 'Asylum advisers face axe' The Guardian 11 October 2004, 'Open and shut case' Law Gazette 10 February 2005). Further waves of legal aid reductions have followed. There is evidence that the regulatory system, combined with legal aid restrictions, is having a devastating effect on the availability of legal advice.

QUESTIONS

1 Is it appropriate to limit an appeal on the merits of the case to one tier? Consider the arguments for and against this proposal.

2 Is it appropriate to use discrimination on the grounds of nationality in making immigration or asylum decisions? What about ethnic group? How does this differ from making decisions on the basis of colour?

3 Who should decide whether legal advisers are abusing the system?

 For guidance on answering questions, visit www.oxfordtextbooks.co.uk/orc/clayton3e.

FURTHER READING

Buck, T. (2006) 'Precedent in Tribunals and the Development of Principles' *Civil Justice Quarterly* no.25 October pp. 458–484.

Clayton, G. (2007) 'Prediction or precondition? The House of Lords Judgment in *Huang and Kashmiri*', *Journal of Immigration, Asylum & Nationality Law* vol. 21, no. 4, pp. 311–323.

Coussey, M. (2004, 2005 and 2006) Annual *Reports of the Independent Race Monitor.*

Dummett, A. (2001) Ministerial Statements – the immigration exception in the Race Relations (Amendment) Act 2000, ILPA.

McKee, R. (2005) 'Highlights of the 2005 Procedure rules', *Journal of Immigration, Asylum & Nationality Law* vol. 19, no. 2, pp. 98–108.

Mitchell, H. (2005) 'The *Roma* case in the House of Lords and the question of the 2001 authorisation', *Journal of Immigration, Asylum & Nationality Law* vol. 19, no. 1, pp. 34–38.

Office of the Immigration Services Commissioner – codes and standards, press releases, annual reports (www.oisc.org.uk).

Paraskeva, J. (2003) 'Keeping up standards' *Law Society Gazette* vol. 100, no. 16, p. 16.

—— (2003) 'Protecting legal aid' *Law Society Gazette* vol. 100, no. 23, p. 20.

Quayum, M. and Chatwin, M. (2004) 'For whites only? Does the working holidaymaker scheme still discriminate?' *Journal of Immigration, Asylum & Nationality Law* vol. 18, no. 2, pp. 94–99.

Shaw, M. (2005) 'The Asylum and Immigration tribunal', *Journal of Immigration, Asylum & Nationality Law* vol. 19, no. 2, pp. 86–97.

Thomas, R. (2005) 'Evaluating tribunal adjudication: administrative justice and asylum appeals', *Legal Studies* 25(3) pp. 462–498.

Vaughan, A. 'The tribunal's new role in Article 8 statutory appeals' *Journal of Immigration, Asylum & Nationality Law* vol. 21, no. 2, pp. 129–136.

SECTION 4

Entry to the UK

9

Family life

SUMMARY

This chapter deals with the subject of joining family members in the UK. The emphasis is on applications related to marriage, that is, applications to join a married partner in this country, to come to the UK in order to marry, or to be with a partner in an established relationship akin to marriage. The rules are considered as they affect joining people settled in the UK, then briefly those with limited leave, and finally refugees and asylum seekers. The rules relating to adult family members are considered, and there is discussion of some issues raised by the rules relating to children. The chapter sets these issues of family settlement in the context of the human rights they represent and the political controversies that these policies have generated.

9.1 The politics of family life

Much contention surrounds family settlement applications as a result of differences and perceived differences between the practices of immigrant and host communities. Jackson comments that marriage has 'attracted the most controversial immigration rules' (Jackson, *Immigration Law and Practice* 1996:395). Marriage and child-rearing practices, concepts of the family, and family duties are all raised by family settlement applications. The law governing marriage-related applications has been created in a climate of suspicion, and as we shall see, this has affected the content of the immigration rules. In the area of marriage in particular, the rules reveal an overriding concern with preventing abuse of the system. The marriage issue has, as Bevan puts it, 'offered an opportunity to vent a gamut of powerful and well rehearsed emotions' (Bevan 1986:253). These emotions have not been dominated by a concern for human rights. Specifically in the marriage rules, the concerns reflected are for the economic independence of the migrant, the 'genuineness' of the marriage, the compatibility of the relationship with the practices of the dominant culture and, latterly, abuse not only of the system of entry for marriage but also of those who suffer as a consequence.

A former President of the Immigration Appeal Tribunal has commented that the provisions directed towards the abuse of the system 'have an effect on the system of arranged marriages among the Asian communities' (Pearl, 1986:24), but the effect is not accidental. The infamous primary purpose rule, one of the main ways that this was achieved, is discussed in more detail in the context of the marriage rules below. The 2002 White Paper, *Secure Borders, Safe Haven* (Cm 5387), whose subtitle was *Integration with Diversity in Modern Britain,* said this: 'a marital partnership should be formed of only one man and only one woman – we do not recognize polygamous households' (para 7.2). In the same White Paper the government advised young people from British Asian families to think about marrying someone who lived in the UK.

The Asylum and Immigration (Treatment of Claimants etc) Act 2004 introduced a requirement for all non-EEA nationals to have permission of the Secretary of State to marry, unless their visa already implied that permission (e.g. they entered as a fiancé(e)), or they were settled. These dramatic inroads into the right to marry drew declarations of incompatibility from the courts in respect of both Article 12 (right to marry) and Article 14 (non-discrimination) (*SSHD v Baiai and Trzcinska, Bigoku and Agolli and Tilki* [2007] EWCA Civ 478, discussed further below).

Apparently undaunted by the prospect of further challenges under Articles 12 and 14, in December 2007 the government produced two consultation papers governing the entry of married partners. One proposes a pre-entry English language test for prospective marriage partners. This introduces labour market considerations into the marriage rules, even though partners are not required to work, and takes no account of the difficulty for many people of acquiring such language ability. The other proposes a series of measures said to be addressed to the problem of forced marriages. These include raising the minimum age for sponsors and marriage partners from abroad to 21, and requiring a declaration before travel of an intention to marry while abroad as a condition of sponsoring the spouse to return.

Cultural differences concerning marriage and family are apparent in the case law. The decision in *J (Pakistan)* [2003] UKIAT 00167, discussed at 9.3.8.1 below, reveals a concept of marriage underlying the rules which does not accord the same importance to the family dimension as did the parties in that case. The tribunal gave short shrift to the idea that they should respect the Muslim perspective on the matter. See also discussion of *AB Bangladesh* [2004] UKIAT 00314 at 9.3.6.1 below, where a monogamous view appears to affect the interpretation of the rules. Recent developments on the question of financial support to enable a marriage partner to enter the UK have moved in the direction of promoting the nuclear family model of financially 'independent' couples (see discussion and *MW (Liberia)* [2007] EWCA Civ 1376 below).

9.1.1 Same-sex couples

Discrimination and cultural assumptions operate in immigration law also in the realm of sexuality. Until 13 October 1997 there was no immigration provision for same-sex couples. At that time a concession was granted as part of the programme of the new Labour government, but it contained a requirement that the couple show four years' cohabitation. Where, by definition, one partner is settled in the UK and the other is not, this presented obvious obstacles. The concession was amended on 17 June 1999 to reduce the period of cohabitation to two years, and became a rule on 2 October 2000 (HC 395 para 295A). This rule continued until 5 December 2005 when the Civil Partnership Act came into force.

The appellant in *LD (Article 14; same sex relationships) Brazil* [2006] UKAIT 00075 applied on 2 March 2005 for leave outside the rules. He was in a gay relationship which had lasted for less than two years, but his leave was running out. The Civil Partnership Act had received Royal Assent but was not in force. If he had been in a relationship with a woman he would have been able to marry her during the currency of his leave and so apply for further leave to remain, but in a same-sex relationship he did not have that choice. He argued that the existence of the Civil Partnership Act confirmed that the existing scheme was discriminatory so it should not be applied to him. The tribunal followed *Secretary of State for Work and Pensions v M* [2006] UKHL 11, which also concerned the interim period between the Civil Partnership Act gaining Royal Assent and coming into force. The House of Lords held that the time required to implement legislation was a democratic necessity which justified the discrimination. The tribunal came to the same conclusion in *LD*. Although the consequences for him were severe, as he would have to leave the country until he could apply to re-enter to marry his partner, it was not discrimination contrary to Article 14 to refuse to grant him leave outside the rules. It was reasonable to have a start date for legislation.

9.1.2 Marriages of convenience

In the Immigration and Asylum Act 1999 the search for ways to counter alleged abuse of the marriage rules has turned to the work of marriage registrars. Section 24 replaced the former discretion of registrars with a duty to report to the Secretary of State any marriage which they have reasonable grounds for suspecting will be a 'sham marriage' (see Cohen 2003). This duty arises if the suspicion is formed before, during, or immediately after the marriage or civil partnership, or (though it is difficult to imagine how reasonable suspicion could be founded upon documentation) upon receiving notice of the intended marriage. A 'sham marriage' is defined in s 24(5) as one which is entered into by a person 'who is neither a British Citizen nor a national of an EEA state other than the UK... for the purpose of avoiding the effect of one or more provisions of the UK immigration law or rules'. This could indicate that immigration must be the sole purpose of the marriage for the registrar to form such a suspicion. This interpretation is to be preferred, but it is also possible to read it as meaning that immigration avoidance is one among a number of purposes, which would make this provision more wide ranging than the former primary purpose rule.

These powers are additional to the AITOCA regime, which includes a requirement for foreign nationals to give notice of marriage to a specified registry office. AITOCA s 20 provides that the whole of the Marriage Act takes effect in relation to the marriage of a foreign national subject to the AITOCA requirements. This is a powerful instance of immigration law affecting civil authorities. The section does not authorize the registrar to refuse to perform the marriage, which must in any subsequent legal action be treated as lawful and valid unless declared otherwise in proceedings under Family Law Act 1986 s 55. That power is reserved for the Secretary of State in the AITOC provisions.

In parliamentary debate in the House of Lords the Minister for the Home Office revealed that numbers of reports by registrars had doubled after the 1999 Act provisions came into force, but less than 5 per cent of these reports resulted in arrests, and only about one-third of arrests resulted in criminal charges being brought. The number of convictions secured is not mentioned. In addition, an unspecified number of people were removed from the UK.

9.2 Legal context

It is perhaps surprising that there is no enshrined right in law for a British resident to be joined in the UK by their married partner. This is not to say that entry for a married partner cannot be achieved through the legal system, as of course it can and frequently is. However, the married partner from abroad must fulfil certain requirements laid down in the immigration rules.

The implications of this are, first, whether the married partner gets leave to enter depends upon the judgment of an entry clearance officer as to whether they fulfil the requirements of the rules. Secondly, although an unsuccessful applicant can appeal, the appellant is the person from abroad whose case is conducted in reality at appeal stage by the sponsor in Britain. Thirdly, the requirements for entry are contained in the immigration rules, not in any Act of Parliament. As we have already seen, the immigration rules are made by a minister after, usually, the most cursory scrutiny by Parliament. The requirements concerning marriage change approximately every two or three years and their content is therefore neither stable nor secured by democratic scrutiny and may change without notice to the applicant. Also, there is very little statutory requirement as to the content of the immigration rules, and such as there is (Immigration Act 1971 s 1(4)) does not include a requirement that rules be made for the entry of married partners. In reality it is unthinkable that rules would be made which did not make such provision, but the lack of statutory grounding makes it easier for them to be restricted and attenuated.

Under the Human Rights Act 1998 it is not open to an individual to sue directly for the omission to provide an enshrined right to be joined by their married partner, as this is an omission of the legislature and as such immune from action under s 6 (3)(b).

Where a British citizen has lived and worked in another EU country, they may re enter the UK with their non-European married partner, the married partner under certain circumstances entering as of right (see chapter 6).

Although the application is made by the person who needs leave under immigration law to be with their family member, the requirements they have to fulfil and the kind of leave they can obtain are conditioned by the status of the person that they are joining. So, although the law concerns those applicants, this chapter may also be viewed from the other perspective, as an account of the levels of respect accorded to the family life of people with different kinds of immigration status in the UK. We begin with the rights of settled people, including British citizens, then consider those with limited leave, and finally refugees and asylum seekers. Before any of these, we look at the right itself.

9.2.1 Right to respect for family life

The right to respect for private and family life is a universally recognized fundamental human right. It is included in the Universal Declaration of Human Rights 1948 (UDHR) and the International Covenant on Civil and Political Rights 1966 (ICCPR), both of which forbid arbitrary and unlawful interference with family life. The International Covenant on Economic, Social and Cultural Rights 1966 says, in Article 12, that 'the widest possible protection and assistance should be accorded to the family, which is the natural and fundamental group unit of society'. In domestic law, the Human Rights Act 1998 provides remedies for a breach of Article 8, the right to respect for private and family life. The breach of Article 8 gives grounds for appealing against an immigration decision including a refusal of entry clearance or leave to remain (Nationality, Immigration and Asylum Act 2002 s 84(1)(c)).

The scope and application of Article 8 (Human Rights Act 1998 Sch 1) is discussed fully in chapter 4. In this chapter we consider how the obligation to respect family life is manifested or otherwise in the law concerning entry of family members.

The Article provides:

1. Everyone has the right to respect for his private and family life, his home and his correspondence.

2. There shall be no interference by a public authority with the exercise of this right except such as is in accordance with the law and is necessary in a democratic society in the interests of national security, public safety, or the economic well-being of the country, for the prevention of disorder or crime, for the protection of health or morals, or for the protection of the rights and freedoms of others.

The application of a family member to enter the UK engages the positive obligation in Article 8 to 'respect' private and family life. While the other qualified Articles use the formula 'everyone has the right to freedom' whether of religion, expression, or assembly, Article 8 does not say that everyone has the freedom to have a family life, but that everyone has the right to 'respect for' their private or family life. This has two implications. First, Article 8 does not provide a right to establish a family life. To the extent that this is covered in the Convention it is dealt with in Article 12, the right to marry and found a family according to the laws of the host state. The tribunal in *ECO Lagos v Imoh* [2002] UKIAT 01967 held that Article 8 could not be used to enable a four-year-old girl to move to the UK to live with her aunt whom she had only visited once. The minimal prior contact meant that this would be to establish family life, not to respect family life which already existed.

Second, this wording implies a positive obligation on the part of the state to respect existing private and family life (*Marckx v Belgium*). It should be recalled in this context (see chapter 4) that when a couple are married they are regarded as having family life even where they have not yet lived together, so an application to join one's spouse engages the right to respect for family life. If the family was established before the first member migrated to the UK, then there is an established family and an obligation of respect. Although this may not outweigh immigration control in a particular case, it provides an important starting point. This principle was used by the ECtHR in *Sen v Netherlands* (2003) 36 EHRR 7 where the ECtHR found that the right to respect for family life was violated where the Netherlands refused entry to a 13-year-old girl who had been left behind in Turkey by her parents at the age of three. The court referred to the fact that the family was established before the separation. This principle has not been often identified or relied on in UK case law, but an amendment to the UK immigration rules demonstrates an implicit acceptance that established families should not have to cross major obstacles: from 1 April 2003 the non-British married partner of a couple who have been established outside the UK for four years may gain immediate settlement once leave is granted (HC 538). This provision is discussed below.

9.2.1.1 *What respect requires*

The courts sometimes say that respect does not necessarily require cohabitation, because family life is lived in different ways in different relationships (see discussion of the differences between private and family life in chapter 4, and family visits in chapter 10). For some relationships, just being able to visit is appropriate to maintain family life. Each situation needs to be considered on its own facts.

In *R (on the application of Fawad and Zia Ahmadi)* [2005] EWCA Civ 1721 Zia had been granted refugee status from Afghanistan. His brother Fawad arrived later in the UK and was refused. Zia suffered from a severe form of schizophrenia. There was some evidence that Fawad could provide effective support to Zia, such that his symptoms would be more manageable. Fawad claimed that respect for his family life entailed being given the chance to do that. The Court of Appeal held that this claim should be examined. The Secretary of State had certified that it was 'clearly unfounded' (see chapter 12) but the court disagreed.

In *MS (Ivory Coast)* [2007] EWCA Civ 133 the appellant had no hope of being able to live with her children. She had served a prison sentence for offences of violence to them, and they now lived with their father. She had lost her right to contact with them, and was seeking to regain this through the courts. She had no right of residence in the UK apart from temporary admission, as her asylum claim and appeals had all failed. The Secretary of State had a usual practice of not removing people who had contact applications pending in a UK court, and if she had a contact order in her favour she could apply under the immigration rules for leave to enter to exercise it. Despite this practice, the Secretary of State had on previous occasions issued removal directions against her and detained her. During the tribunal proceedings the Secretary of State agreed not to remove MS until her contact application was resolved. However, she remained on temporary admission. The AIT thought that was sufficient. The Court of Appeal held that she was entitled to a decision as to whether it would be a breach of Article 8 to remove her. If it would be a breach then she was entitled to the discretionary leave that would normally be awarded. The right to respect for family life could encompass being able to be present in the country to pursue a contact application. The case has been appealed by the Secretary of State to the House of Lords.

9.2.1.2 *Obstacles or special reasons*

The ECtHR in *Abdulaziz* said that there were no obstacles to establishing family life elsewhere or 'special reasons why that could not be expected of them' *(Abdulaziz* para 68). More recent cases on refusal of admission weigh the factors which indicate whether the family could live together elsewhere and regard this as an important question but not necessarily crucial (see, for instance, *Gul* v *Switzerland* (1996) 22 EHRR 93, *Ahmut* v *Netherlands* (1996) 24 EHRR 62, and *Sen* v *Netherlands* (2003) 36 EHRR 7). Without necessarily determining the precise weight to be attached to the matter, tribunals also consider whether there are obstacles to establishing family life in another country. For example, in the case of *Hussein* v *ECO Nairobi* [2002] UKIAT 01408 the appellant was a refugee from Somalia, living in Kenya. He applied to join his wife who was also a refugee from Somalia. She had six children by his deceased brother, and he had married her according to tradition. The tribunal found that there were obstacles to the establishment of family life in Kenya. Somalia was clearly not an option. The children had been in the UK for some years, and it would be 'unduly harsh' (borrowing a phrase from refugee law) to expect the children to relocate to Kenya. The proper approach now is referred to in *Huang and Kashmiri* as a question of whether 'the life of the family cannot reasonably be expected to be enjoyed elsewhere' (para 20). This question is discussed in the context of removal in chapter 18.

If there is a failure to respect family life, the question moves on to whether such an interference is necessary in a democratic society for a reason permitted in Article 8.2. These tests have been discussed fully in chapter 4.

9.2.1.3 *Article 8 and cultural diversity*

The Human Rights Act and ECHR do not include a free-standing right to cultural identity such as is found for instance in the Canadian Charter of Rights and Freedoms 1982. The jurisprudence of the Court has developed a little in the area of using Article 8 to protect an individual's right to respect for their identity. For example the Court accepted that an application could be made by transsexuals, objecting to the forced disclosure of their birth gender (e.g. *Sheffield & Horsham v UK* (1998) 27 EHRR 163 and *I v UK* (2003) 36 EHRR 53). The matter of self-definition in something as fundamental as gender was held to be within the ambit of Article 8. In *Chapman v UK* (2001) 33 EHRR 18 the Court accepted that the occupation of caravans by gypsies was an integral part of their ethnic identity. Although the applications were lost because the Court found that the state's interests in Article 8.2 prevailed, nevertheless, ethnic identity was a matter which could be considered as an aspect of private life under Article 8.

Paragraph 2 of the qualified rights permits interference with the rights if it is necessary in a democratic society. The Court in the leading case of *Lingens v Austria* (1986) 8 EHRR 407 emphasized that 'in a democratic society' there must be space for ideas which 'disturb, shock or offend'. This case was brought under Article 10, the right to freedom of expression, and cultural practices which might come within the ambit of Article 8 and which might 'disturb, shock or offend' are regarded differently from ideas.

The role of immigration law as it affects diversity in a pluralist democracy arises frequently in case law, though more often implicitly than explicitly.

In *Abdulaziz* the ECtHR found 'persuasive social reasons' for treating more favourably people whose link with a country stemmed from birth. Differential impact therefore, even when intentional, will not always be a breach of Convention rights, but it must be proportionate to a legitimate aim in order to comply with Article 14. Again, the crucial context is the democratic society, an idea which itself contains the problem, implying both pluralism *and* the rule of the majority.

9.3 Immigration rules for married partners

From 5 December 2005, when the Civil Partnership Act 2004 came into effect, same-sex couples have been able to register their relationship as a union under law. Immigration rules on married partners have been amended to include civil partners, and the rules are the same for the two groups so far as the content allows. The term 'married partner' is used here to include both groups.

Anyone who is subject to immigration control (i.e. is not an EEA national and does not have right of abode) who wants to come to the UK as the married partner of someone settled here, must obtain prior entry clearance. This is so even if they do not come from a visa national country. The requirements are set out in para 281 of the current immigration rules, and since the implementation of the Immigration (Leave to Enter and Remain) Order 2000, SI 2000/1161, entry clearance obtained as a married partner will operate also as leave to enter providing its duration and any conditions are endorsed on it.

Most of the requirements to obtain leave as a married partner are the same whether the applicant is applying for entry clearance from abroad or is already in the UK in another capacity. Therefore, case law on a leave to remain case may sometimes be used to illustrate the same point applying to leave to enter.

9.3.1 Present and settled sponsor

The first requirement is that 'the applicant is married to a person present and settled in the UK or who is on the same occasion being admitted for settlement'. This person is referred to as the 'sponsor'. Mole *(Immigration: Family Entry and Settlement* 1987:xxiv) defines the sponsor as a:

UK relative who confers eligibility to enter the UK on an overseas national, or
　UK relative or friend who assumes financial responsibility for an overseas national.

At present we are referring to the UK married partner as the first of these alternatives, a sponsor who confers eligibility for entry.

Paragraph 281(i)(a) says that the sponsor must be 'present and settled or on the same occasion being admitted for settlement'. As discussed in chapter 7, a 'settled' person includes both a person who has acquired indefinite leave to remain under immigration law, and one who has right of abode. Settled immigrants, Commonwealth citizens with right of abode, and British citizens therefore all qualify as sponsors, providing they are ordinarily resident in the UK (Immigration Act 1971 s 33(2)(A)). Note that under 281(i)(a) the requirement of ordinary residence or admission at the same time for settlement applies to British citizens just as to others. This flows from the definition of settlement and was confirmed in *Zarda Begum* [1983] Imm AR 175, the tribunal taking the view that the rule was intended to provide a basis for an applicant to join a partner ordinarily resident in the UK, not to be installed here while their partner lived elsewhere. This does not prevent a settled person, including a British citizen, from having a home in the UK where their partner lives, and another outside the UK, providing they can be said to be ordinarily resident in their UK home.

The time when the sponsor must be physically present or entering is not specified in the rules. While most requirements must be fulfilled at the time of the decision, in this case physical presence would be impractical and arbitrary, as the sponsor has no idea when the decision will be made and there is no reason why they should be in the UK at that date. The most practically workable timing is the date when the applicant married partner will be entering the UK, and this interpretation of the rule was confirmed in *Angur Begum* v *Secretary of State for the Home Dept* [1990] Imm AR 1.

At the time of the application, so long as the sponsoring partner is ordinarily resident in the UK with a right to return, then the condition is met *(Mokbul Bibi* (4954) INLP vol. 2(2) 1987: 50). This was confirmed in *Rourke v ECO Pretoria* [2002] UKIAT 05666, in which the sponsor was regarded as present and settled although he had been living and working abroad since 1992. This gives the opportunity for the sponsor to accompany the applicant to the entry clearance interview, but ECOs are advised as a general rule to see sponsors separately from applicants if at all, both to check for inconsistencies and to protect reluctant applicants (DSP 8.13).

Since October 2000 para 281 of the rules has deemed a member of the forces, diplomat, or staff member of the British Council or Department for International Development to be present and settled in the UK for the purpose of the married partner rules.

An alternative basis from 1 April 2003 is that the applicant is the married partner of a person with right of abode or indefinite leave to remain in the UK who has been living abroad with that person as their married partner for at least four years. This would apply to the married partner of a British citizen and someone who has lived in the UK for most of their life, as in accordance with the returning residents' rules (paras 18 and 19: see chapter 7), a person with indefinite leave who stays outside the UK for more than two years will have to reapply for settlement unless they have lived in the UK for most of their life. The married partner rules therefore now in this sub-paragraph distinguish between the married partners of settled immigrants and the married partners of British citizens or others with right of abode, in effect, though not on their face. The new rule does not enable a man who has lived in the UK for 40 years to gain immediate settlement for his wife of 20 years' standing from Bangladesh, but it does enable a British man who has worked abroad for 10 years to bring his wife of five years' standing back with him to gain immediate settlement.

Married partners may still be admitted together for settlement under para 281(i)(a). This is most likely when one of them has a right of abode, as in *Rourke,* but the difference where they do not have four years of marriage behind them is that the applicant partner will only get two years' leave initially, instead of immediate settlement.

9.3.2 That the parties have met

The second requirement, that the parties have met, would rarely have any impact for applications based on a marriage which has taken place, as in almost every case the couple will have met at the marriage ceremony, if not before. It is possible in the Muslim tradition for a marriage to take place by proxy, providing there is an offer and acceptance before witnesses (e.g. as in the case of *Akhtar 2166*). However, this is extremely rare. The provision may be in issue in applications by fiancé(e)s, to whom this requirement also applies. The impact of this provision is on fiancé(e)s entering very traditional arranged marriages, and while it is increasingly the norm that engaged couples will meet, it may not always be the case. The guidance to ECOs (DSP 13.11) states that relationships developed over the internet will not fulfil the requirement to have met. It entails a face-to-face meeting.

The requirement that the parties have met was introduced into the rules at the end of 1979, as part of the programme of the new Conservative government. It was one of a number of proposed changes which were so far-reaching that the rules (HC 394) were debated in the House of Commons. The introduction of these rules marked an important stage in the development of immigration law in the UK. The opposition accused the government of equating marriages of convenience with arranged marriages. Alex Lyon MP went on: 'it is intended to hit the genuine arranged marriages of Asian girls, whether or not they were born in this country' (HC (14 November 1979) col 1336). The Home Secretary in his response did not deny that this was the case, but revealed another objective for the rule:

I remember the Hon. Member for Ealing, Southall telling me that in the future it will increasingly be the practice that Asian girls in this country will wish to marry Asian boys in this country. I should have thought that was a position that we should encourage.

This position re-emerged 23 years later in the White Paper *Secure Borders, Safe Haven* (Cm 5387) in which the Home Secretary was more prescriptive than his predecessor:

We also believe that there is a discussion to be had within those communities that continue the practice of arranged marriages as to whether more of these could be undertaken within the settled community here. (para 32)

Here, immigration policy is used to encourage adoption of the practices of the host community and to discourage immigration which occurs for reasons which reinforce the distinctive characteristics of the immigrant community. The contrast with the present day is more in terms of process than content. In 1979, the controversial nature of these rules was recognized by the fact that they were introduced by a White Paper. More recently, even a statute which interfered with fundamental rights (the AITOCA regime) was not introduced by a White Paper.

HC 394 was challenged in *Abdulaziz, Cabales and Balkandali*, but the European Court of Human Rights found that the requirement for the parties to have met was not racially discriminatory under Article 14 of the Convention. It considered that the changes in the rules were mainly to limit primary immigration in order to protect the labour market at a time of high unemployment, and that this fell within the legitimate aim of 'protecting the economic well-being of the country' (Art 8.2). The greater impact on people from the New Commonwealth and Pakistan (which at that time was not in the Commonwealth) was because it was from there that the greater number of applicants came. The requirement for the parties to have met was directed towards preventing abuse of this system. The government's argument concerning the economic well-being of the country related to conditions prevailing at the time of that case, but the persistence of these rules at a time of labour shortage has not been subjected to legal challenge.

So much for the rationale and origins of the requirement that the couple should have met. Where there has not been a recent meeting the requirement is fulfilled by meeting the test in *Meharban* v *ECO Islamabad* [1989] Imm AR 57. In that case the sponsor and her fianc had played together as children, but she could not recall what he looked like, nor any of his other characteristics. His application for entry clearance was refused. The tribunal laid down guidance that there was no need for the parties to have met each other in the context of marriage or marriage arrangements, provided they had an appreciation of each other in sense of appearance or personality. In this case they did not, as neither seemed to have any knowledge of the other. In *Hashmi* (4975) the families found a way to satisfy both the immigration rules and their religious tradition. The fianc and his parents stayed for a few days at the same house as the sponsor and her mother. This was arranged in order to comply with the rule, but because of religious tradition they did not speak to each other. The tribunal accepted that there had been a 'meeting' within the rule.

9.3.3 Maintenance

The requirement in para 281 is that 'the parties will be able to maintain themselves and any dependants adequately without recourse to public funds'. This means that their financial position is sufficiently strong that they will not need to claim from a list of state benefits. In *Konstatinov v Netherlands* Application no. 16351/03 the ECtHR said that there was no objection in principle to rules such as these which require a minimum level of income sufficient to meet the basic costs of subsistence of family members (para 50). Interestingly, they refer to a rule which requires this of a 'settled alien' who wishes to have their family join them. In the UK rules there is no distinction between the rules which apply to settled foreign nationals and settled British Citizens and is debatable whether any such distinction would be right in principle. Paragraph 6 of the rules defines 'public funds', and the list has gradually become longer since

1985 when 'public funds' were first specifically identified. They now include virtually all means-tested and disability benefits apart from emergency provision. Public funds are not limited to cash benefits but include housing. Housing provided under home-lessness provisions was included from 1985, but from April 1996 Part II housing was included, i.e. council housing provided to people on the waiting list. National Health Service treatment and state education are not classified as public funds. The anticipation that a married partner will make use of the National Health Service therefore has no bearing on meeting this requirement of the rules, although where they are in a serious and chronic state of ill health, this may have other repercussions as discussed in chapter 7.

Until 2 October 2000, there was a thorny legal issue as to what constituted recourse to public funds. The problem was this: where a family had saved money from benefits to support the incoming family member, or would continue to live on their existing benefits without making an extra claim or receiving any increase on that person's arrival, could the incoming person be said to be having recourse to public funds? The matter was resolved by the October 2000 rule changes, inserting paragraph 6A, as follows:

For the purpose of these Rules, a person is not to be regarded as having (or potentially having) recourse to public funds merely because he is (or will be) reliant in whole or in part on public funds provided to his sponsor, unless, as a result of his presence in the United Kingdom, the sponsor is (or would be) entitled to increased or additional public funds.

9.3.3.1 Adequacy

The rules require that the parties can maintain themselves 'adequately'. There is potential unfairness or even discrimination here if the rules are interpreted so as to exclude married partners of people with low incomes. According to established authority this cannot mean that their standard of living may be allowed to fall below the minimum considered acceptable in general in the UK. Adequacy is an objective standard (*KA (Pakistan)* [2006] UKAIT 00065 para 6).

In determining adequacy, the tribunal considers that the income support figures offer a 'helpful yardstick', as set out in *Uvovo* 00/TH/01450 in the following way:

3. Income support is what would be provided for the family if they were British residents of the United Kingdom with no other resources: it is not suggested in the rules that family members seeking immigration should be better maintained than those who are already here; and the government can hardly say that the level of support it provides for its destitute citizens is not adequate. What the recipient or holder of the funds spends money on is his own business. We would in general take the view that if the appellant can show a level of income at the income support level or higher, that will be enough.

4. It is, however, essential to maintain comparability. Income Support carries entitlement to a number of other benefits and, in particular, a family on Income Support will be able to obtain Housing Benefit. The appropriate comparison is therefore between the Income Support level on the one hand and the family income net of accommodation costs on the other. (There are other Benefits to which Income Support is a 'gateway', such as free school meals and free prescriptions. These are not always to be ignored, particularly where those seeking entry are of school age or have some medical condition.) It follows that, although we should be slow to enquire into the Sponsor's spending habits, we need to be satisfied that, at the date of decision, his income after paying his rent was sufficient to maintain himself and his wife.

This approach was confirmed more recently in *KA (Pakistan)*. *Choudhury v ECO Dhaka* [2002] UKIAT 00239 reiterated that income support is a starting point, and allowance must be made for other benefits to which a couple on income support would be entitled.

The couple do not need to prove that they will have enough money to support themselves indefinitely. In the case of *Ishtiaq Ali* (11568) the tribunal commented:

to require some certainty that the parties to the marriage will at all times in the future be able to support and accommodate themselves would make it virtually impossible for a young couple with modest means to meet the requirements of the rule.

In *Shakila Kauser* (17428) INLP vol. 13(2), p. 78, the tribunal considered there was no need to look further ahead than six months after the appellant's arrival to ascertain whether the couple could maintain themselves adequately. This approach is commonly taken also at the point of applying for indefinite leave at the end of the probationary period and is confirmed in subsequent case law (see, for instance, *Adesegun v ECO Lahore* [2002] UKIAT 02132).

9.3.3.2 *Disabled sponsor*

This approach does not solve all the problems which arise where the sponsor is disabled. In this case the sponsor receives higher benefits than income support, but these are paid because of the sponsor's greater needs. There is no general rule in such cases. In *Shabir v ECO Islamabad* 01/TH/2897 the sponsor, who was severely disabled, received £115.20 per week, 'substantially in excess' of £80, which was the figure deemed necessary for two people living together according to income support rules. The tribunal said that the mere fact that her income was more than the income support level was not enough; they must consider whether all the disability living allowance would be used up by the sponsor's own needs. She had in fact been saving from her benefits. Her main disability was limited mobility. It was a matter for her how she used the extra money which was paid to deal with this. On the facts, there would be enough to maintain her husband as well.

In *ECO Islamabad v Nazia Bi* [2002] UKIAT 05214 on similar figures it was held that maintenance would not be adequate. The tribunal considered that the sponsor's needs would absorb all the benefits and noted that there was nothing to spare in the family finances generally – accordingly, entry clearance was refused. There was substantial evidence that the sponsor, who suffered from paranoid schizophrenia, would have been much better with his wife present and he might well have stabilized sufficiently in order to be able to work. However, this consideration does not feature in the rules. The Immigration Advisory Service commentator on *Nazia Bi* noted that there had been a number of Home Office policy reviews in which there had been a promise to consider a relaxation of the rules for disabled sponsors, but nothing had ever come of this. This was still the case five years later when the tribunal in *MK (adequacy of maintenance – disabled sponsor) Somalia* [2007] UKAIT 00028 suggested a presumption that disability benefits are required for the needs of the disabled sponsor, and not available to support their spouse. This approach was also used by the tribunal in *AM* (see below). It must be apparent that these cases are not simple to judge, involving the complex matter of assessing needs, which in itself can scarcely be done without attributing value to different areas of life. Does respect for family life under Article 8 entail allowing a person to choose to give up some of their mobility for the society of their marriage partner?

9.3.3.3 *Third party support*

One of the outstanding questions concerning maintenance is whether a couple must support themselves from their own resources or whether they may rely on support from a friend or relative to meet the requirements of the rule. A supplementary issue is whether, if so-called third party support is allowed, it may be long-term or not.

The issues involved in this question will be examined by means of a case study: *AM (3rd party support not permitted r 281(v))* [2007] UKAIT 00058.

 Key Case

AM (3rd party support not permitted r 281(v)) **[2007] UKAIT 00058**

The husband and wife were of advanced age, had suffered physically and psychologically because of war, and had been separated for many years. Neither was well. The appellant lived with his son in Ethiopia where the sponsor, now a British citizen, had no right of residence, so the couple could not live together there. The sponsor lived in the UK on benefits including disability living allowance, which the tribunal ruled was not adequate to maintain her husband as well as herself on the same reasoning as in the cases discussed above. The appellant received regular and substantial payments from his cousin and daughter. He would otherwise be in very reduced circumstances and anyway lived in poor accommodation. The daughter had a well paid job in London and no other dependants and was prepared to maintain him indefinitely, including if he came to the UK to join his wife, her mother.

The rules say that 'the parties' must be able to 'maintain themselves and any dependants adequately without recourse to public funds'. One line of case law takes this to mean the couple must be 'self-sufficient and self-sustaining' (*Zabeda Begum* (16677)). The implication is of resources earned by employment or self-employment or, presumably, investment or property, including inherited wealth.

The tribunal in *AM* said that 'self-sufficiency' was the natural meaning of the rule, and that the daughter's maintenance should therefore not be taken into account. The tribunal took the view that third party support is not contemplated by the rules because it is not mentioned, and because the natural meaning of the words is self-sufficiency. This is an authoritative ruling from the President of the tribunal, though a panel of two rather than three sat in the case and it is not starred. There is no authority of the higher courts precisely on this point, although there is a recent Court of Appeal case on the equivalent rule for children.

 Key Case

MW (Liberia) **[2007] EWCA Civ 1397**

MW was born in Liberia in 1994. Her mother fled the war, taking her and her brother. MW's mother left the two children in the care of a family friend in Ivory Coast and came to the UK, where she was granted exceptional leave to remain. She enrolled as a student, was in receipt of benefits, and friends in the church gave regular money every week which she sent to look after MW. Her friends were willing to maintain this level of support to enable MW to come to the UK. MW's brother had gone missing.

The rules for maintenance of children are more explicit than for spouses, though there is still room for interpretation. They say that the children must be maintained 'by the parent or relative' that they are coming to the UK to join (para 297(v)). The appellant argued that maintenance sent and organized in this way by the parent was maintenance 'by' the parent. The Court of Appeal held that it was not. The parent was a channel for the money, not the provider of it.

The rule on child maintenance was changed in October 2000 to require the maintenance to be 'by' the parent. The change, according to the ECO in *AA Bangladesh* [2005] UKAIT 00105, was for reasons of child protection, and was intended to overturn the previous ruling in *Arman Ali*:

> If a rich relation or a benefactor is willing and able to maintain a family in this country so that there is no need to have recourse to public funds, I see no reason in principle why that family should be kept apart. The purpose of the rules is quite clearly met and the natural meaning of the language used is consistent with the construction I have espoused. (at 147)

Collins J in *Arman Ali* held that a rule which prevented reliance on public funds was consistent with Article 8 as being an interference necessary 'for the economic well-being of the country' (Art 8.2). A rule requiring nuclear family self-sufficiency has no such legitimate aim.

MW (Liberia) must in future be relied on in children's cases in preference to *Arman Ali*. Where does this leave third party support for spouses? As argued for MW, permitting third party support 'reflects changing ideas of family life in a pluralist society where wider communities or extended families support each other in various ways' (para 11). This argument did not persuade the court, but there are powerful arguments of this kind in favour of third party support for spouses, and no equivalent to the child protection argument to weigh against it.

In *Amjad Mahmood v ECO Islamabad* [2002] UKIAT 01819, the tribunal spoke in strong terms about a repeated refusal of entry clearance to a husband where there was adequate short-term third party support. The adjudicator considered that the couple should be financially self-sufficient, and this was held by this tribunal to be wrong in law, following *Arman Ali*. The tribunal requested that the decision be sent to the Chief Adjudicator, the Immigration and Nationality Department and Visa offices to reinforce that families should not unnecessarily be kept apart by refusals of adequate maintenance.

Neither the tribunal nor the court seems to have examined the coherence of the distinction between money from a relative or church and money from an employer. The permissible limits of what the couple's 'own' resources have not been tested. In *MW (Liberia)* the court accepted it 'might' be different in the case of a deed of covenant or a court order for maintenance, but as that was not directly before the court they could not decide upon those possibilities. The argument that the purpose of the rule is to avoid reliance on public funds did not feature in *MW*, but this point would still need to be answered in a case of third party maintenance for a married partner, where the practical effect of such maintenance was to enable them to be independent of public funds.

9.3.4 Accommodation

In addition to financial maintenance para 281 requires that 'there will be adequate accommodation for the parties and any dependants without recourse to public funds in accommodation which they own or occupy exclusively'. This requirement contains a number of elements which may be considered in turn.

The base line is a standard represented by the case of *Mushtaq* (9342), that accommodation would be 'adequate' as long as occupation of it would not be an offence. This means that it is not statutorily overcrowded according to the standard laid down by the Housing Act 1985 s 326. Reports from independent Environmental Health Officers are often prepared to establish that standards are met, however the tribunal in *Thompson v ECO Kingston* (17926) observed that this is not always necessary, in particular because the standard of proof is the civil standard. Compliance with statutory housing standards is therefore to be proved on the balance of probabilities. Where it had proved impossible to gain access to the flat in which the sponsor had lived at the time of the decision, the tribunal were prepared to say that they found it highly unlikely that main living rooms in a local authority flat would measure less than 10 by 11 feet. On the balance of probabilities, therefore, the overcrowding standard was satisfied.

On the other hand, compliance with the overcrowding standard does not in all cases automatically mean that the accommodation is adequate. In [2004] UKIAT 00006 *S(Pakistan)* ILU vol. 7, no. 5 the tribunal held that a small terraced house, although it would not be statutorily overcrowded, was not adequate for two adult couples and four small children. There were three bedrooms and a through living room from which the stairs went up.

HC 395 para 6A applies equally in the case of accommodation. Consequently the provision of accommodation without recourse to public funds simply means without additional recourse. In *Rahman* (14257) INLP (1997) vol. 11(4), p. 135 a husband was applying to join his wife in the UK. She lived in her parents' house and was not working. The housing costs were met by housing benefit. The tribunal held that the question it had to consider was whether there would be any additional claim as a consequence of his arrival. As there would not, his appeal was allowed on the accommodation issue.

The accommodation must be owned or occupied exclusively by the parties. Ownership may be of any form of legal interest in land, freehold or leasehold. Occupation must be by virtue of some legal right to occupy, but this can be as a licensee or a lodger. Exclusive occupation need be of no more than a bedroom *(Saghir Ahmed 8260).*

The requirement for the couple to own or occupy exclusively was introduced into the immigration rules in 1994. At the time of its introduction there was concern that it would discriminate against people living as an extended family. A letter written in October 1994 by Nicholas Baker MP, Minister of State for the Home Office, to Giles Shaw MP gave the interpretation of the rule which was approved by the tribunal in *Saghir Ahmed:*

Arrangements whereby the applicant joins his or her married partner in an established household with other residents are...acceptable providing...the applicant and their married partner have at least a small unit of accommodation e.g. a bedroom for their exclusive use.

In this area of immigration law there are relatively few cases at appeal court level, and tribunal decisions are not binding on each other. Add to this that officers on the ground may not always be aware of decisions of appellate bodies, and the situation is ripe for inconsistency and confusion. At approximately the same time as *Saghir Ahmed* another tribunal decision, that of *Shahida Kauser* (8025), held that the accommodation for exclusive use must be an independent unit. Later cases have tended to follow *Saghir Ahmed,* and the Minister's letter makes it clear that this is the better authority. However, as late as 1998, in the case of *Parkar v ECO Bombay* (17948), the case got as far as the tribunal because the adjudicator had found that it was necessary to show exclusive occupation of all parts of the house. The tribunal accepted that this argument was 'simply wrong'. It is characteristic of immigration law that a principle of interpretation of the rules is settled and now practically incontrovertible, without a decision of a higher court. In case of doubt, the principle in *Abdi* (see chapter 7) could be used to adduce the minister's letter as settling the meaning of the rule.

9.3.5 Time when requirements must be met

Clearly, when accommodation *is* an independent unit, it is unlikely to be empty and waiting for the applicant at the date of the application. This is all the more the case because of the long waiting time which many applicants experience. *Prima facie,* the date when the accommodation must be available is the date of the decision, but this has been mitigated in practice by an approach typified in *ECO Islamabad v Younis* (17469), approving:

the question as to whether the accommodation could be made adequate within a reasonable time of that decision. A reasonable time has been held by the tribunal in other cases to be six months.

A subject of ongoing contention has been whether, if an application was refused, but accommodation or maintenance later became available, evidence of this could be admitted in an appeal. Following the Court of Appeal judgment in *R v IAT ex p Kotecha* [1982] Imm AR 88 account could be taken of arrangements which were positively and reasonably foreseeable at the time of the decision. The current position is given by the Nationality, Immigration and Asylum Act 2002 s 85 which provides that evidence available up to the date of the hearing should be considered in all immigration and asylum appeals except refusal of entry clearance or certificate of entitlement (s 85(5)). In these cases the adjudicator 'may consider only the circumstances appertaining at the time of the decision to refuse'. The reviewer in ILU vol. 8, no. 5 suggests that this grammatical error should be corrected by reading the section as 'circumstances obtaining', i.e. in existence at the time of the decision to refuse. Therefore evidence which arose after the date of the decision will not be admissible except to the extent that it sheds light on the situation at the date of the decision. This does not allow for evidence of events that were reasonably foreseeable. This interpretation was confirmed in a starred decision, *DR Morocco* [2005] UKIAT 00038 where intense correspondence between a couple after refusal of entry clearance was admissible evidence that at the date of the refusal they did in fact have an intention to live permanently together.

The same principle was apparent in *Hashim v ECO Karachi* [2002] UKIAT 00928 in which the sponsor was awarded a significant backdated increase in benefit by the Social Security Appeal Tribunal after the ECO's decision but before the hearing before the adjudicator. This made his income indisputably adequate. The adjudicator felt unable to take account of this increase because the ECO could not have had it in contemplation at the time of the decision. The tribunal held that this was the wrong approach. The decision of the SSAT meant that the sponsor at the time of the decision had a legal entitlement to the increased income, therefore it should be taken into account on appeal.

The effect is to exclude post-decision facts, with the above exception where light is shed on the state of affairs at the time of the decision, in appeals where the appellant is outside the UK, such as refusal of entry to a married partner. This is in keeping with a policy underlying recent immigration legislation of relating entitlements to the perceived level of a person's connection with the UK. It does not apply to a refusal of indefinite leave to remain to a married partner at the end of their probationary period.

The tribunal in *SA Pakistan* [2006] UKAIT 00018 held that the exclusion of post-decision facts applied even where the appeal was on human rights grounds. Here the wife's application to enter was refused on the basis that the marriage was void in UK law. She had later had a child, and the couple pursued their appeal on human rights grounds because of the birth of the child. The tribunal held that, as the child was not even conceived at the time of the decision, his presence could not be taken into account, even to substantiate a human rights appeal.

9.3.6 Intention to live permanently with each other

When Alex Lyon said in the House of Commons that there were other provisions which were intended to prevent marriages of convenience, one of those he may have had in mind was the requirement to show the intention to live permanently together.

9.3.6.1 *Conflicting commitments*

A couple may intend to live permanently together even though present circumstances prevent them from cohabiting. In *Kumar* (17779) INLP vol. 13(3) p. 109 (1999) the wife stayed with her parents during the week as her stepmother needed her care and attention. The couple were together at weekends and made every effort to see each other when they could. This arrangement was accepted by the tribunal not to conflict with an intention to live permanently together. In the case of *Janat Bi* (16929) the couple had been together for the first 11 years of their marriage, and then apart for most of the following 40, because of the wife's family commitments. Their intention to live together was not questioned. In *Barlas* TH/ 03975/2000 there were four years of separation before the appellant applied to come to the UK. The tribunal did not regard this as preventing intention to live together being established, particularly in the context of an arranged marriage.

Not only family commitments but also working patterns may interfere with cohabitation. Immigration and appellate authorities need to take into account the demands of the global economy, including particularly employers' demands for workers to be mobile. For instance, in *Niksarli* (21663) (INLP vol. 14, no. 2, p. 110) the wife had to stay in Glasgow where she had a job and medical treatment while her husband had to go to London to find work. Shift patterns too may affect actual cohabitation without rupturing the intention to live together. In *Satnam Singh* (19068) INLP vol. 13(2) (1999) p. 78 a man who was seeking indefinite leave to remain after his first 12 months was refused because he had not been sleeping with his wife. She and her parents lived above a shop. The appellant was working night shifts. In order to have a better chance of sleeping during the day, instead of joining his wife he slept next door in a friend's flat. The tribunal allowed his appeal, saying that the couple's intention to live permanently together had 'nothing to do with sleeping in the same bedroom every night'. Restricted actual cohabitation in the past or present therefore will not jeopardize the intention to live together, provided the reasons are compelling. On the other hand, where a sponsor had at the time of the marriage committed an offence which resulted in his receiving a nine-year prison sentence, the tribunal held that no intention to live together could be formed. When the application was made he was in prison. An intention was more than a wish *(Shabbana Bibi v ECO Islamabad* [2002] UKIAT 06623).

In *AB Bangladesh* [2004] UKIAT 00314 ILU vol. 8, no. 2 the tribunal held that the appellant's intention to live six months of each year with his British wife and the other six months with his wife in Bangladesh could not amount to an intention to live permanently together. The appellant argued that not recognizing his obligations to divide his time between his two wives amounted to religious discrimination contrary to Article 14. However, the tribunal disagreed, holding that so far as it had evidence, the Quran did not require cohabitation of equal time with each wife, only that each be treated equally.

9.3.6.2 *Relationship difficulties*

A troubled period in the marriage is not fatal to an intention to live together. In *Bryan* (14694) INLP vol 11(3) (1997) immigration officers apparently caught the sponsor on a bad day. When they called he expressed his doubts about the appellant, thought she might be having a relationship with another man, that the marriage was just being used to enable her to stay in the UK, and so on. She was not interviewed. The tribunal allowed her appeal, saying that the whole intention to live together did not turn upon the credibility of what was said or done on a particular day, but rather on the position 'in the light of the whole evidence relating to cohabitation and living together since the marriage took place'.

The level of investigation in which a tribunal may engage in deciding this question is illustrated in the case of *Noisaen* (18213) heard in April 1999. Here, the tribunal considered the couple's behaviour during a period of separation, the extent and quality of the contact they had in that time, and speculated about the emotional states and motivations of the sponsor. The marriage of this couple, some two years after it was entered into, was subjected to a scrutiny as to its viability which most couples would hope to avoid, and which is reminiscent of the family court. Fortunately for the appellant the tribunal took a humane approach and endorsed the view advanced by the appellant's representative that 'relationships are…complex and unique in nature and the weight of the evidence in this case suggests that the intentions are genuine'.

9.3.6.3 *Primary purpose, intention to live together, and credibility*

This level of scrutiny of a relationship with a view to establishing the intention to live together would have been almost unknown before 5 June 1997. On that date the new Labour government, in accordance with its manifesto commitment, abolished (by HC (26)) the infamous 'primary purpose' rule. This rule required the couple to prove that 'the marriage was not entered into primarily to gain admission to the UK' (HC 395 para 281 before amendment). A moment's thought will reveal that there are many reasons for getting married and that these vary between individuals, between cultures, between social groups, and at different stages of life. An examination of them is probably a subject more fit for psychology than law. Where the intended married partner lives may be a factor entering into the decision.

Applicants were faced with the impossible task of proving a negative, that any motivation in relation to where the sponsor lived was *not the* primary one. In order to show that entry to the UK was not the primary purpose, a couple was expected to show evidence of 'intervening devotion'. This required production of letters, and evidence of telephone calls and visits. In an arranged marriage the intentions of the families would be relevant *(R v IAT ex p Hoque and Singh* [1988] Imm AR 216). Investigation of primary purpose was marked by intensive and intrusive questioning. As the matter in issue was so subjective, great weight was placed by entry clearance officers on their findings as to the credibility of the applicant. A key method of determining credibility was the so called 'discrepancy system', in which different family members would be asked questions which might have little bearing on the central matter in hand, but if their answers differed, this would be used to cast doubt upon their credibility in relation to the central issue, the marriage, and its purpose. The assumptions of entry clearance officers about traditional (and therefore predictable and credible) practices in effect meant that the correct civil standard of proof could not be applied (as demonstrated by Juss 1997). It is hardly surprising that Macdonald refers to the 'primary purpose' rule as one which 'generated more anger and anguish than perhaps any of the other Immigration Rules' (1995:343).

Disturbingly, since the abolition of the 'primary purpose' rule the discrepancy approach has sometimes been applied to showing intention to live together. In *ECO Islamabad v Nasir Mahmood* [2002] UKIAT 01034 the adjudicator and tribunal both disapproved this approach as it did not focus on the central question of intention. Even if the parties had been less than frank, this did not mean that they did not intend to live together as husband and wife. This conclusion on credibility is similar to the approach used in asylum cases and is regarded as correct. Even if some matters are not as stated, the question is whether this affects the core of the claim. The same approach was taken in *Anju Malik v ECO New Delhi* [2002] UKIAT 00738. Here the point was made that discrepancies do not have the same significance in an arranged marriage as in a love match. This point was also made in the case of *Sabar Gul v ECO Islamabad* TH/5118/99 and in *Choudhuryv ECO Dhaka* [2002] UKIAT 00239. In both these cases the adjudicator had looked for evidence of personal knowledge of each other's circumstances which should not be expected where the marriage had been arranged and the parties had little prior direct knowledge of each other.

When the primary purpose rule was current, intention to live together was hardly ever regarded as a free-standing factor. It was treated, along with 'intervening devotion', as evidence towards establishing the primary purpose. For instance, in the case of *Kari Shahjad Miah v ECO Dhaka* [2002] UKIAT 02533 the original refusals were on the basis of primary purpose, maintenance, and accommodation. Intention to live together was not raised. In a later refusal of the same married partner it became a ground. A development which may be seen in the case of *Noisaen* and a number of others, *Chowdhury* (16080), *Hanif* (17561) both INLP vol. 12, (4), p. 146 (1998) and *Iqbal* (17293) in June 1999, is to make credibility again a central issue. An examination of credibility as it relates to intention should be confined to whether the surrounding circumstances and the whole context suggest that the intention exists. For instance, whether they actually have a house they intend to live in together, as in *Chowdhury*, rather than, as the ECO had done in that case, inquiries about what conversations they had had about the house. Where the application is for entry clearance the parties' statements and practical plans, such as the existence of accommodation, are probably the limit of necessary enquiry. The parties' motives for living together permanently are not a relevant matter. The investigation of 'intervening devotion' should have lapsed together with the requirement it was used to prove, that of primary purpose. It is not relevant to the intention to live together which may be formed, as was said in *Hoque and Singh,* 'after only a short acquaintance'. This comment by the Court of Appeal referred to the context of arranged marriages, which were most often the target of this rule. The same however might be said of a whirlwind romance in the western tradition. By examining motivation, decision makers open the way to limited conceptions of what is a valid motivation. As McKee points out (1999:5) 'money can be a more durable bond than romance in holding a marriage together, but there persists a notion that a marriage cannot be genuine if it does not fit into the Western convention of being entered into for love rather than money'.

Even within a single culture views of a valid motivation will vary. For instance, the Home Office has written to advisers, saying that sexual relations are not an essential component of a genuine marriage. At the same time too much sexual enthusiasm may also fall foul of what is considered a proper motivation for living together. McKee (1999:4) discusses a case in which there was fairly clear arrangement that the young woman would gain material advantages and the older man considerable sexual gratification. Both parties had an obvious motivation to live together permanently, but the adjudicator disapproved of it and upheld the refusal of entry clearance on the issue of intention to live together.

Aside from illustrating the futility and irrelevance of the search for a proper motivation there is a further point of importance in this case, which is that it would have failed the 'primary purpose' test, although the intention to live together is present. The point was made explicitly in the case of *Canas* (20557) INLP vol. 13(3) (1999) p. 109 that there can be intention to live together even when the primary purpose is to live in the UK. In such a case, entry clearance should be allowed. In *Alaezihe v ECO Dublin* [2002] UKIAT 01168 the tribunal overturned the adjudicator's decision because he had placed too much reliance on the appellant's adverse immigration history, from which he had gleaned an intention to come to the UK. This however was not the question. The appropriate question was, given that the parties were married, whether they had the intention to live together permanently.

9.3.7 The marriage is subsisting

In *GA ('subsisting' marriage) Ghana* [2006] UKAIT 00046 the tribunal treated the requirement for the marriage to be subsisting as a separate requirement from its legal validity and from intention to live together. A subsisting marriage, they said, is one which has some real substance in terms of relationship. This couple had lived apart for 20 years, so the substance of the relationship was in doubt. It was a legal tie, but not subsisting. This was a starred decision and the ruling is therefore binding on subsequent tribunals, overturning the earlier view in *BK* [2005] UKAIT 00174 that 'subsisting' only meant the marriage was current in law.

9.3.8 Legal issues concerning marriage and divorce

The final issue in relation to establishing marriage applications is the validity of the marriage, contained in the rules simply by the phrase in para 281 'is married'. This entails that the marriage be valid according to law and meet the requirements of the Immigration Rules. The validity of the marriage is adjudged at the date of the marriage. It is established by showing that both parties had the legal capacity to marry and that the celebration took place in accordance with appropriate formalities. The second of these requirements is the more straightforward to apply in law, although there may be practical difficulties in obtaining evidence. If the marriage is properly conducted according to the law of the country in which it is celebrated, its formal validity is accepted in English law. This means that in a country where same-sex marriage is recognized, a properly conducted same-sex marriage will be recognized for immigration purposes. In *S.H. v K.H.* [2005] CSIH 70 the Scottish Court of Session held that going through the formality of a civil marriage did not constitute a marriage where the couple did not intend to take each other as husband and wife at that time. After the marriage they had continued to live separate lives, and the apparent plan was that they would enter a religious marriage at a later date once the sponsor's education was completed. In the meantime the husband gained entry on the basis of the marriage. However, the religious ceremony did not take place, and the husband became involved in an affair with a third party. The court held that the lack of an intention *at the time of the ceremony* to live as husband and wife from that time on invalidated the marriage. See Shah P for comment on this case.

The country in which the marriage is celebrated is usually where both parties are physically present. The only exception may be where the marriage is conducted by telephone. The guidance to ECOs DSP 13.10 says that in countries where marriage consists of an offer by a man accepted by a woman, a telephonic marriage is celebrated in the country where the woman is. Therefore where the wife is resident in the UK and the offer made from overseas, the marriage is considered as having been celebrated in the UK and so not valid in UK law.

This does not mean that if the husband were in the UK the marriage would be recognized, as although it may accord with the formalities of the country where it was celebrated, it may still fall foul of the rules on domicile (see below).

Aside from such rare situations, a marriage certificate is normally enough to prove formal validity. In *Babul* (16466) it was held that where a marriage certificate is produced which provides *prima facie* proof of a valid marriage, the party asserting that the marriage is not valid has the burden of proof to a high standard. If a finding is made that the marriage is not valid, this only has a direct effect for immigration purposes. There would need to be a separate declaration under the Family Law Act 1986 to affect the marriage for any purpose other than immigration.

The issues which have a greater effect on the recognition of marriages in the UK are the questions of the legal capacity to enter into the marriage in question and the recognition of previous divorces.

9.3.8.1 *Capacity*

The capacity to marry is determined for each individual separately, and is governed by the law of the country which is their domicile. *Halsbury's Laws* (vol. 8(1) para 680) explains domicile in this way:

A person is domiciled in that country in which he [sic] either has or is deemed by law to have his permanent home. Every individual is regarded as belonging, at every stage in his life, to some community consisting of all persons domiciled in a particular country...Although a person may have no permanent home, the law requires him to have a domicile.

Domicile differs from ordinary residence, in that a person may have more than one ordinary residence but not more than one domicile. Domicile may also differ from nationality and the personal civil law which applies to an individual is the law of their domicile. Domicile of origin is acquired at birth and is the domicile of the father for a child born inside marriage, of the mother for a child born outside marriage. *Cramer v Cramer* [1986] Fam Law 333 CA confirms an old rule that there is a strong presumption in favour of retaining one's domicile of origin. A domicile of choice is acquired by residence in a country where one intends to stay permanently. This intention must be proved by objective criteria. Statements of intention will not suffice. The House of Lords in *Mark v Mark* [2005] UKHL 42 held that if a person's presence is illegal in immigration law, this does not affect their domicile. The House of Lords made the distinction between a status which would give some benefit against the state, when illegality ought not to benefit an individual, and domicile, which is a private law matter and a question of fact. Domicile does not give an advantage against the state, but simply determines which legal system will govern private law matters, in this case, divorce proceedings.

The burden of proving that the domicile of origin has been lost rests on the person making this assertion. If they do not succeed in discharging the burden of proof, the domicile remains the domicile of origin.

To say that the law of a person's domicile governs their capacity to marry means that conditions for entering into a marriage, such as age and existing marital status, are according to that country's law. In *J (Pakistan)* [2003] UKIAT 00167 it was conceded that a telephonic marriage where the man was present and domiciled in the UK was not valid as the law of the UK governed his personal capacity to marry and does not recognize telephonic marriages. The claim under Article 8 also failed. The tribunal considered it settled law that an invalid marriage followed by a period of cohabitation may amount to family life attracting the protection of Article 8. Here, however, the sponsor was seriously disabled and could not travel to Pakistan. His mother did so, and his new wife went to live with his parents in Pakistan for three weeks. This, said the tribunal was 'of symbolic significance and reflects the fact that both the families regarded the couple as married' (para 4). However, this practice was not accepted by the Home Office, adjudicator or tribunal as establishing family life.

The law of the UK requires that a person must be 16 years old and not married to anyone else in order to enter into a valid marriage. Although married partners need to be over 16 in order for the marriage to be valid, the age at which someone may sponsor their married partner was raised in 2002 to 18, and at which someone may enter as a married partner in 2004, also to 18 (HC 395 para 277). These changes were introduced as part of the government's programme to prevent forced marriage (see e.g. Home Office press release 330/2004). The government's stated intention was to allow young people more time to mature and be able to resist family pressure to enter into a marriage they don't want. Of course, it does not actually prevent the marriage, which can take place at whatever age is allowed by law in the country where the marriage is celebrated. It only means that a married partner cannot enter the UK until they are 18, and a young person taken abroad to marry against their will cannot sponsor their married partner to come to the UK until they themselves are 18. In the February 2005 White Paper Cm 6472 the government announced its willingness to rise the age further to 21 'if necessary' (para 38), and in December 2007 produced proposals to do just that.

9.3.8.2 *Polygamy*

Where a polygamous marriage has been validly entered into in another country, English law does not recognize it as valid where one party to the marriage is domiciled in the UK (Matrimonial Causes Act 1973 s 11(d)). *Hussain v Hussain* [1982] 3 All ER 369 CA found that this applied to the marriages of British women to men domiciled in countries that permitted polygamy and celebrated in that country, as they were potentially polygamous. The Private International Law (Miscellaneous Provisions) Act 1995 s 5 simplified the application of s 11(d) by providing that it only applies to *actually* polygamous marriages. The effect of this is that where the practical reality of the marriage is that it is monogamous it will be treated as such by UK law, wherever it is celebrated.

Where a marriage is in fact polygamous, if one of the parties is domiciled in the UK the marriage is void under s 11(d). If neither party is domiciled in the UK the validity of the polygamous marriage is recognized if it was recognized in the country where the parties are domiciled. However, para 278 of the immigration rules prevents entry clearance from being granted to a wife where another wife of the same man has, since her marriage to him, visited the UK or been granted entry clearance or a certificate of entitlement. The rule is wider than Immigration Act 1988 s 2(2) which first removed rights of entry from second wives. The Act provided that women who had the right of abode by virtue of their marriage to a British citizen would not be able to exercise that right where there was another wife alive who had been to the UK since the marriage or had been granted entry clearance or a certificate of entitlement. Paragraph 278 applies whether or not the second wife has a right of abode. In *R v IAT ex p Hasna Begum* [1995] Imm AR 249 an earlier identical rule was challenged on the basis that it was ultra vires the 1988 Act. The challenge failed. Tucker J did not find any problem in the rules being wider than the Act, and rejected the idea that the 1988 Act was the source of the power to make the rules. This must be right, as the source of the power remains the principal Act, the 1971 Act. Also, rights of abode were statutory and could only be taken away by statute, whereas conditions of entry are set by the rules and can be changed by them.

These provisions illustrate the point made at the beginning of this chapter, that immigration law does not focus on the right of the settled person to be joined by their family, but on the status and circumstances of the proposed entrants. The passage of the 1988 Act caused a storm of criticism as the statutory rights of women abroad were taken away. The rules and case law exhibit a mixture of perspectives on the rights of women in these situations. In the unpublished case of *Bibi v UK* 19628/92, 29 June 1992, the European Commission on Human Rights endorsed the UK's prohibition on entry of a second wife, partly on the basis of the legitimate aim of 'the protection of rights of others', namely the first wives.

Many rule changes of October 2000 eliminated distinctions on the face of the rules, in anticipation of challenges of discrimination under the Human Rights Act. Paragraph 278 was then amended to apply to both sexes.

9.3.8.3 *Recognition of divorce*

Because the UK does not recognize polygamy for people domiciled in the UK and does not permit entry of further married partners, no entry clearance will be granted where an earlier divorce is not recognized as the person will be regarded as still married to the previous married partner. The law in relation to recognition of divorces obtained in other countries is set out in Family Law Act 1986 ss 44–54. A divorce obtained in a foreign jurisdiction will be recognized if it complies with the legal requirements of the country in which it was obtained, if it was obtained by proceedings, and provided either party was habitually resident, domiciled in or a national of the country in which it was obtained (Family Law Act 1986 s 46(1)). The majority of divorces obtained abroad are therefore recognized.

In an immigration context issues may sometimes arise as to the recognition of Islamic talaq divorce. Talaq pronounced in the UK will not be regarded as valid in the UK as within the jurisdiction divorce may only be granted by a civil court (see, for instance, *ECO Islamabad v Tanzeela Imran* [2002] UKIAT 07383). Talaq pronounced in an Islamic country is recognized in the UK if it is obtained by means of proceedings, or, if obtained without proceedings, neither party was habitually resident in the UK for one year before the divorce (Family Law Act 1986 s 46(2)). In an immigration case, however, usually one party has been resident in the UK, and so a divorce without proceedings is generally not recognized. Talaq may be validly obtained in Azad Kashmir without proceedings. Here, a 'bare' talaq, whereby a husband obtains dissolution of the marriage by making repeated declaration of divorce in the presence of witnesses, is recognized. Although this is permitted under Sharia (religious) law, the civil system of most countries imposes an additional requirement of legal proceedings. In Pakistan generally the Muslim Family Law Ordinance of 1961 requires proceedings, but this does not have force in Azad Kashmir. A requirement of the Muslim Family Law Ordinance is registration of the talaq with the Union Council. The divorce then becomes effective in Pakistani civil law after a period allowed for reconciliation. A talaq so registered will then be recognized in UK law but not otherwise (for a dispute on evidence of this see *Niaz Parveen* v *ECO Islamabad* 01/BH/0061). This should be distinguished from the situation in *Naseem Akhtar* (15412) INLP vol. 12(1) (1998), p. 30 where there had been ancillary proceedings carried out after the divorce. These could not convert a bare talaq into a talaq by proceedings.

The tribunal in *Baig v ECO Islamabad* [2002] UKIAT 04229 gave a starred decision in which it laid down guidance as to the proper approach to be taken to ascertaining whether a divorce was obtained by proceedings. In so doing the tribunal made an important distinction between tradition and proceedings. The talaq in question in this case was not a bare talaq, but a talaq al-hasan, which entailed formal declarations of divorce at monthly intervals. The appellant argued that this was by way of proceedings as it entailed more ritual and process than a bare talaq. The tribunal said, however, that talaq al-hasan

> lacks any formality other than the ritual performance. It lacks the invocation or assistance of any organ of the state. It does not even require an organ of the state to act as a registrar or recorder of what has happened. (para 39)

Accordingly, it was regarded as a purely personal act and not a divorce obtained by proceedings. The tribunal's decision to give the case a starred status was no doubt influenced by a perception of its particular contemporary relevance, which arose from a trend in Pakistan towards recognition of a bare talaq as fully effective. This trend had been noted in argument for the appellant as a reason to recognize the talaq al-husan. The tribunal gave this argument a rather startling twist. If Pakistan developed the recognition of divorce without proceedings this would not influence English law. Rather, the opposite would be the case, and English law would become reluctant to recognize Pakistani divorces. In this rather forceful response it is possible to see a significant underlying debate about increasing Islamic influence in civil matters and the limits and possibilities of pluralism.

If a person is not free to marry another, their application to enter as a married partner cannot be treated as an application to enter as a fiancé(e) and granted on that basis *(ECO Islamabad v Mohammad Rafiq Khan* 01/TH 2798 and *ECO Islamabad v Shakeel* [2002]

UKIAT 00605). These cases were distinguished from the earlier authority of *Ach-Charki* [1991] Imm AR 162 as in that case the parties had been free to marry by the time of the tribunal hearing.

These questions of the recognition of marriage and divorce have consequences for the recognition of the legitimacy of children born to those marriages and consequently their entitlement to come to the UK. This will be the final subject considered in this section.

9.3.8.4 *Legitimacy*

Where a marriage is valid at the time of a child's conception, the child is legitimate wherever the marriage was celebrated. So the child born in Bangladesh of a couple domiciled in Bangladesh and married according to the laws of that country is legitimate, including when the marriage is polygamous (see, e.g. *Taslima Begum v ECO Dhaka* [2002] UKIAT 06644 where the father was a British citizen and as a consequence of that, his children acquired British citizenship by descent and so a right of abode in the UK (see chapter 3)).

Where a marriage is considered void in English law, the children of that marriage are not regarded as legitimate unless, at the time of their conception, one of their parents believed that the marriage was valid (Legitimacy Act 1976 s 1). In *Azad v ECO Dhaka* [2001] Imm AR 318 the Court of Appeal held that this must mean a belief in its validity in English law. In that case the father, who was domiciled in the UK, was aware that his marriage was not recognized, but there was no evidence as to the state of mind of the mother. Therefore it was held that there was no evidence of a 'belief' as that was a positive state of mind, not just an absence of belief in the marriage's invalidity. The effect for children born after 4 April 1988 was mitigated by the introduction of a presumption of a belief in the validity of the marriage. This may be displaced if lack of belief is proved (Family Law Reform Act 1987 s 28). This was the argument advanced by counsel for the appellant in *Azad* and is surely a more satisfactory situation. The result of *Azad* is to require people to hold positive beliefs about legal provisions in another country, not something to which most people would naturally pay attention.

The effect of the provisions above is that where a man is domiciled in the UK, his children by second or subsequent marriages are not regarded as legitimate and so are not British citizens by descent and have no right of abode in the UK. This has the perverse consequence that a man who intends to make the UK his permanent home may not, as of right, bring in his children by later marriages, whereas one who intends to return to his country of origin may do so. This effect is mitigated by the amendment to the Legitimacy Act, and all minors now benefit from this presumption.

The Nationality, Immigration and Asylum Act 2002 s 9 makes a further welcome reform in this area, inserting into the British Nationality Act 1981 a new s 50(9)A which provides that a child's father includes 'the husband, at the time of the child's birth, of the woman who gives birth to the child'. This means that nationality law moves into conformity with family law, treating such a child as a child of the family, even if it turns out that the child actually has a different natural father. When this section comes into force it will remove the stigma for children such as Taslima Begum in the case of that name, who could not obtain entry to the UK when her siblings could, as DNA tests showed she was not her father's daughter.

9.3.9 **English language**

Depending on the outcome of the consultation paper issued in December 2007, it may be that a level of English language becomes a requirement for entry as a married partner.

9.3.10 **Limited leave to enter**

If all the above conditions are met, a married partner is given leave to enter the UK for two years (HC 395 para 282). As this is a period of limited leave it may be subject to conditions, and since 8 November 1996 it is routinely subject to the condition not to have recourse to public funds. Breach of a condition is a criminal offence and potentially a basis for removal. However, a policy statement by the Home Office made in a letter from David Waddington MP to Max Madden MP states: 'We would not use this power if a person had become dependent on public funds for a short time through no fault of his own'. Although this statement was made in December 1985 in relation to complying with the requirements for entry rather than as a condition, in practice it is also followed where the condition is attached.

Additionally, the Social Security (Persons from Abroad) Miscellaneous Amendment Regulations 1996 removed entitlement to non-contributory benefits from people with limited leave, such as married partners in their first two years.

A married partner who gains leave to enter on the basis of the newer four-year marriage rule in HC 538 (see 9.3.1 above) does not have a probationary period, but if they satisfy all the above rules, they gain immediate settlement.

9.3.11 **Indefinite leave to remain**

Shortly before the end of the two-year period, the married partner may apply for indefinite leave to remain if they continue to meet all the requirements of the rules (para 287). This is another reason why any reliance on public funds during the first two years must be short term, otherwise this reliance would undermine their case for meeting the maintenance and accommodation requirement for indefinite leave, unless there was a dramatic change in circumstances.

Once indefinite leave is granted the married partner from abroad is free to claim benefits in their own right. They are free of immigration restrictions on their stay, and may come and go freely, subject to the requirements of para 18 of the rules (see chapter 7). Note that having indefinite leave to remain is not the same as citizenship. After three years of residence as a married partner they may apply to become a British citizen (British Nationality Act 1981 s 6 and Sch 1, amended by Civil Partnership Act 2004 Sch 27 para 72) but until they acquire that citizenship the married partner with indefinite leave may, if they fall foul of the criminal law, be recommended by a court for deportation (Immigration Act 1971 s 3(5)) and may not vote unless they are a commonwealth citizen (Representation of the People Act 1983). See chapters 3 and 7 on naturalization and settlement.

9.3.12 **Leave to remain as a married partner**

As mentioned earlier, a person with limited leave under some other categories of the immigration rules may apply to stay after the end of that leave as a married partner (para 284). The White Paper *Secure Borders, Safe Haven* (Cm 5387) expressed doubts about the genuineness of marriages entered into by people who had been in the UK for less than six months (para 7.11). Consequent rule changes ended the possibility of extending leave to stay as a married partner for those granted six months' leave or less. This affects visitors, student visitors and prospective students (though not actual students). The rule was amended again in August 2003 because the original wording did not take account of the fact that visitors actually get six months and one day, as their leave expires on the same date of the month. e.g. the visa lasts from 6 March to 6 September, and not 5 September (*FB (HC 395 para 284 'six months') Bangladesh* [2006] UKAIT 00030).

Rules as to accommodation and maintenance, the marriage and so on apply as for an application for entry clearance. In addition, a person applying for leave to remain as a married partner must not have remained in breach of immigration laws. Where a person who is an illegal entrant, or has overstayed, has married in the UK and wishes to stay, their application may be considered in accordance with Article 8 and Home Office Policy document DP 3/96 (see chapter 18). Since the introduction of the certificates of approval regime under AITOCA, a person in this position will have difficulty obtaining permission to marry in the first place.

An applicant for an extension of stay as a married partner will be granted for two years in the first instance, placing them on a similar footing to a married partner who comes directly from abroad (para 285). Immigration Act 1971 s 3(1)(c) also applies, giving a power to impose a condition that there be no recourse to public funds during the probationary period.

The grant of indefinite leave after an initial two years, whether following leave to enter or leave to remain, is expressed to be a discretion. In practice indefinite leave will be granted where the conditions are met. The discretion however gives scope to grant a further extension where there may be some doubt about the fulfilment of conditions, instead of refusing the application. This may now be used where the married partner does not pass, by the time their leave expires, the language test introduced in April 2007.

9.3.13 **Domestic violence and bereavement**

On the basis of the rules above an incoming married partner would have no claim to remain where the marriage broke down in the first two years or their partner died. This has caused particular anguish to those bereaved and to women who were subject to violence from their husband in the probationary period. The latter group could safely neither stay in their marriage nor leave it, particularly if return to their country of origin might be financially or socially impossible. Paragraphs 287(b) and 289A of the immigration rules provide for leave to remain to be granted in these circumstances under certain conditions.

Under the domestic violence rule, applications have been refused where the marriage broke down due to violence after the probationary period expired but before an application had been determined for indefinite leave to remain. The tribunal in *IN (domestic violence IDI policy)* [2007] UKAIT 00024 held that the domestic violence rule could not be used to remedy overstaying. While the IDI lays down particular kinds of evidence required to prove domestic violence, that cannot be taken to limit the discretion implicit in the rule to admit whatever evidence the decision-maker thinks fit (*Ishtiaq v SSHD* [2007] EWCA Civ 86).

No allowance seems to be made in these cases for the likelihood that a person whose marriage is moving towards breakdown through violence may well lose track of the requirement to apply in time for indefinite leave, or indeed may well be ambivalent about doing so. The resultant delay will mean, following the case law, that they are treated like any other overstayer.

9.4 Unmarried couples

While the law may refuse to ratify a relationship, there are also human rights issues involved in denying family life to couples who, for whatever reason, are not married. The admission of unmarried partners did not obtain a stable place in the immigration rules until 2 October 2000. The previous rule was abolished in 1985, and unmarried partners since then had been considered only under concessions. April 2003 rule changes abolished the requirement for a legal obstacle to marriage. By changing the probationary period for married partners to two years the government achieved greater parity between the married and the unmarried. The current rules provide that an unmarried couple, whether same or different sexes, must show that any previous marriage or comparable relationship has broken down, they must have lived together for two years before applying for entry, and that they are not so closely related that the law would prevent their marriage. Where they have lived together for four years the applicant partner will be able to gain immediate settlement as married partners do.

The IDI March 2006 Ch 8 s 7 Annex Z para 2 concedes 'short breaks apart for up to six months would be acceptable for good reason, such as work commitments or looking after a relative', providing it was clear that the relationship continued throughout the period. Visiting often will not amount to cohabitation, but the cohabitation does not have to have been in one country, and there does not need to be an established joint home if they have, for instance, been living alternately at each other's separate homes.

Other requirements for unmarried partners such as the present and settled sponsor, accommodation and maintenance, are as for married couples and are interpreted in the same way.

The relationship is protected by Article 8 ECHR. In *Marckx* v *Belgium* (1979) 2 EHRR 330 the ECtHR held that there should be no discrimination between the married and unmarried in relation to the status of their children.

9.5 Fiancé(e)s

Finally, it is possible for an individual who is not yet married but engaged to be married to a settled person to apply for entry clearance as a fiancé(e). The requirements are set out in para 290 of the rules. They are as for a married partner except that they refer to the situation after the marriage, and in place of an existing valid marriage is the requirement that the fiancé(e) is seeking leave to enter *for* marriage or civil partnership with a settled person.

Partly because of the waiting time involved between application and decision, it may happen that the ceremony takes place after the application but before the decision has been made. In this case, if the entry clearance officer is informed, the application will proceed as a married partner application. If the marriage takes place after a fiancé(e)'s application has been refused but before an appeal has been heard, how it is treated may depend on how far the appeal has proceeded. When an appeal is lodged the entry clearance officer would normally review the case when they receive the grounds of appeal. If they have received notice of the marriage by then, they may choose to treat this as a fresh application for entry clearance for a married partner. The case can then be reconsidered on this basis. Otherwise, the fact of the marriage will be relevant at the appeal hearing to the intention of the parties.

If a fiancé(e) application succeeds, leave is granted to enter the UK for a period of six months, during which time the ceremony must take place, and there is a prohibition on working (para 291). Leave is also conditional on not having recourse to public funds. If the marriage does not take place during the six-month period a further extension 'for an appropriate period' (para 294) may be granted to enable the marriage to take place, provided the Home Office is satisfied that there is good cause for the delay, there is satisfactory evidence that the marriage will take place at an early date, and all the other conditions for leave to enter continue to be met (para 293).

9.6 Other adult relatives

9.6.1 Admissible relatives

Other adult relatives may be admitted for settlement if they qualify under para 317 of the rules. The relationship by which their admissibility is determined is their relationship to the sponsor. Those relatives admissible are limited to:

(i) widowed parents or grandparents aged 65 or over;

(ii) parents or grandparents travelling together at least one of whom is 65 or over;

(iii) a parent or grandparent aged 65 or over who has remarried or entered into a second civil partnership but cannot look to the married partner or children of the second relationship for financial support; and

(iv) a parent or grandparent under the age of 65, or son, daughter, sister, brother, uncle, or aunt over the age of 18 if living alone in the most exceptional compassionate circumstances and mainly dependent financially on relatives settled in the UK.

Other relatives may be considered outside the rules, but only where there is a close emotional bond and very strong compassionate circumstances. In *KP (para 317 mothers-in-law) India* [2006] UKAIT 00093 the appellant's initial application to join her son had been turned down on the basis that she was not financially dependent on him and that she had other relatives in India to turn to. During the currency of her appeal he died, and she pursued the application as one to join her daughter-in-law. The tribunal held that the distinction between mothers and mothers-in-law was not discrimination in the terms of Article 14, but a legitimate distinction that could be made as a matter of policy. Accordingly, there was no breach of human rights and thus no need to invoke

Human Rights Act s 3 to interpret the rule. The particular relationship was not strong enough, they thought, to warrant grant of leave outside the rules.

The tribunal in *AM*, discussed above in relation to third party support, relied on the reasoning in *KP* in concluding that the Human Rights Act was not engaged. Like *KP*, *AM* revealed a tragic limitation to para 317. The appellant in *AM* was 73 years old and financially dependent on his daughter in the UK. Could he therefore apply to come to the UK under para 317 as he was not permitted to join his wife? The tribunal raised this possibility only to dismiss it. He did not come within para 317(i) because he was not a widower. So if the wife he could not live with were to die, he could come to the UK as his daughter's dependant. As an alternative, could he come within the last part of para 317? No, because he was not living alone, he was living with his son. He could have qualified to come with his wife if she were not already here. It is difficult to see how this interpretation of the rules gives effect to the right to respect for the family life of this couple. The tribunal held that the rules were not required to be read using Human Rights Act s 3 to give effect to rights because they did not interfere with them (see for comment Clayton, ILD Spring 2008).

9.6.2 Financial dependency

Parents and grandparents over 65 must be 'financially wholly or mainly dependent' on the sponsor. Those applying on the basis of the most compassionate circumstances need only show that they are financially wholly or mainly dependent on relatives settled in the UK, not necessarily the sponsor. This gives some scope for responsibility for financial support to be shared and still come within the rules.

Case law has established that the dependency must be a necessary one, on the basis that 'the question of dependency has to be construed in the context of immigration control. The question of genuineness runs through all the immigration regulations...dependants have to show their genuine need' (*Chavda* v *ECO Bombay* [1978] Imm AR 40). This further requirement not only places another hurdle for applicants to cross, but also introduces a judgment as to what is necessary, and this brings decision-makers once again into the arena of making judgments about matters which may vary between cultures.

This was illustrated in the case which established the test of 'necessary dependence', *Zaman* v *ECO Lahore* [1973] Imm AR 71. Here, an elderly farmer and his wife were refused entry clearance to join their son in the UK. They were financially dependent upon him because Mr Zaman gave the modest income from the farms to his sons who were still resident in Pakistan, in accordance with custom. The tribunal held that their dependence was not necessary. This case contrasts with *ECO New Delhi* v *Malhan* [1978] Imm AR 209. In this case the familial duty described perhaps came nearer to the tribunal's idea of family responsibilities. The appellant's eldest son had voluntarily taken over her main support. He had done this out of a desire to fulfil his moral obligations. The tribunal held that she was entitled to look to him for support. She should not be compelled to look to 'more distant' relatives (her brother and father).

The question also arises: what steps to maximize income is it reasonable to expect the applicant to take? In *Chavda* itself the appeals of the widow and her daughter were allowed. It was accepted that she was not in a position to compel her three sons who lived with her to work, so from her point of view the dependency on her eldest son in the UK was a necessary and not a contrived one. Where the sons could clearly get work this might have been different, as in *Hasan* v *ECO Bombay* [1976] Imm AR 28. In *Piara Singh* (19579) INLP vol. 13 (3) (1999), p. 107 elderly parents had a spare room which they kept for visits by family members. It was held by the majority of the tribunal that they should not be expected to let this out in order to reduce their financial dependency on the sponsor.

In *Bibi v ECO Dhaka* [2000] Imm AR 385 the Court of Appeal confirmed that financial dependency may be in the form of money or money's worth. If someone had their need for accommodation, clothing, food, and other necessities provided in kind, they were financially dependent on the person who made this provision for them. In this case the appellant lived with her son and daughter-in-law and their children, and was applying to join another son in the UK who sent money regularly to the family. The money was used mainly for the children's education. The Court of Appeal found that the true situation was that the family had some dependency on the proposed sponsor, but the appellant was dependent on the family she lived with, not on her son in the UK. The principle therefore is that the applicant must be directly financially dependent on the sponsor. This was confirmed in *VS (para 317(iii) no 3rd party support)* [2007] UKAIT 00069. Here the sponsor, who was severely disabled, sent a regular £100 per month to the appellant, but it was provided by a distant relative who gave evidence that he was willing and able to continue this support into the future. The tribunal held that the sponsor was just a conduit for the relative's money, and that the appellant was not financially dependent on him. The tribunal purports to apply the House of Lords' decision in *Huang and Kashmiri*, but shows that that case has not laid to rest the range of approaches that existed before it by saying 'Although the concept of a legal test of exceptionality has been rejected, the approach to Article 8 cases will be as before' (para 30). This is a far cry from case such as *Arman Ali* and *Amjad Mahmood*, in which the judiciary were concerned to emphasize that families should not be kept apart unnecessarily.

If a relative comes to the UK for a visit and then applies under para 317, they must be able to prove that they were dependent on the sponsor before they came to the UK. So held the tribunal in *MB (para 317: in-country application) Bangladesh* [2007] Imm AR 389. This decision makes plain the underlying spirit and purpose of para 317. It is not a means by which people settled in the UK may make arrangements for the care of their elderly relatives within the family, and in this respect a first-generation immigrant settled family does not have the choice of a 'granny annexe' in the same way that families do whose parents live in the UK. The rule depends on material and physical need. It is more like a safety net than a positive support to family life.

9.6.3 No close relatives to turn to

A further requirement of the rules is that the applicant must be without close relatives in their own country to whom they can turn for financial support. A leading judgment on the meaning of 'close relatives to turn to' was given by Dillon LJ in the Court of Appeal in the case of *R v IAT ex p Swaran Singh* [1987] 1 WLR 1394. He read the phrase 'as importing "to turn to in case of need" – any sort of need which may afflict elderly parents'. He gave examples of illness or accident and said that the rule was one of 'broad humanity'. It should be so regarded in the future even though in some cases it had not been in the past. Family relationships should be borne in mind, and where relatives are hostile or unwilling to help they are clearly not relatives to turn to. However, while

Swaran Singh continues to be an authority that the rule is one of broad humanity, the need referred to in this part of the rule is no longer 'any sort of need which may afflict elderly parents'. HC 395 changed the rule so that it is financial support which is in issue, here as in the previous part of the rule.

In a more recent case the tribunal has found that the issue of dependency and no close relative to turn to are 'two sides of the same coin'. Where a person was found to be dependent as of necessity on the sponsor, this would normally mean that there was no other close relative to whom they could turn *(Parekh* (14016) INLP vol. 11 (2) (1997), p. 73).

The case of *ECO Islamabad v Rehmat Bi* (16074) March 1998 Legal Action provides useful guidance on identifying financial dependency and whether there is a another close relative the applicant can turn to. It suggests that both requirements should be assessed by starting with the needs of the applicant. In *Rehmat Bi* the applicant's needs were for repairs to her house, frequent contact with her son, medical treatment, and assistance with her mobility. Her son funded the repairs, the cost of telephone calls between them and his own air fares and arranged the medical treatment. When he was there he gave her the practical assistance which she needed to get around. He had also paid for his father's funeral. She was emotionally dependent on him. In *R v IAT ex p Bastiampillai* [1983] 2 All ER 844 the court had held that where there was emotional dependency, this might tip the balance to show that dependency existed. In *Rehmat Bi,* the tribunal took the approach that where meeting needs could be done by financial outlay, as here, the applicant was probably dependent as of necessity on the person who met the expense, and this could include meeting emotional needs such as for contact with her son.

The IDI Chapter 8 s 6 para 3.2 says that where applicants are over 65, detailed inquiries are not usually necessary, though sponsorship must be assured. Annex V advises that applications should not be refused from married couples solely on the grounds that they have each other to turn to. 'Account should be taken of the age and health of the applicants as well as the ability of other relatives to visit them regularly'.

9.6.4 Living alone in the most exceptional compassionate circumstances

This part of the rule provides the only possibility for entry for adult relatives who are under 65. 'Living alone in the most exceptional compassionate circumstances' is a further condition which must be met in addition to the others. Being financially dependent on a relative in the UK and having no other close relatives to turn to are not regarded as exceptional compassionate circumstances in themselves *(Nessa* (16391) INLP vol. 13(2) (1999), p. 75). This means that families may be kept apart because there is nothing exceptional that would unite them. Indeed the whole of paragraph 317 to a lesser degree creates an obstacle to the enjoyment of family life. However, the Court of Appeal has held that it is not a breach of Article 8 for the government 'to confine the circumstances in which dependent relatives of persons living in the United Kingdom are permitted indefinite leave to enter in the way that they have done in paragraph 317' *(Husna Begum* para 12).

Living alone does not always require that there is literally no other person in the home, but that anyone who is there is not able to meet the needs of the applicant. Severe mental or physical disabilities without the necessary care being available will normally be regarded as the most exceptional compassionate circumstances (e.g. *Visa*

Officer Islamabad v Sindhu [1978] Imm AR 147). In *EK v ECO Colombo* [2006] EWCA Civ 926 the appellant could not be said to be living alone on the basis that her mother, with whom she had always lived, was now in the UK. She was 23 and lived with her father's two sisters who 'were not treating her unkindly or harshly' (para 22). The compassionate circumstances may have arisen since the applicant's arrival in the UK, if they have been here for instance on a visit. This was found to be the case in *Alyha Begum* (17162) INLP vol. 13 (3) (1999), p. 107 where in the applicant's absence her brothers in law had been taking away her possessions, and she would be isolated if she returned.

A former version of the rule made specific provision for widowed mothers. This one does not. In the case of *Akhtar Bi v ECO Islamabad* 01/BH/0002 the appellant was in this position, her sons and daughter having moved to the UK. The chair of the tribunal did not consider that she met the requirements of the rule because her situation was like that of any widowed mother whose children have left, and therefore while her sadness was very understandable her situation was not exceptional. The other two members of the tribunal found that her situation was exceptional because owing to a combination of circumstances she had had at least one of her children with her for most of her life until a few months before this application. She therefore faced living alone for the first time at the age of 57.

There are broadly two approaches taken to this rule. One is following *Swaran Singh* referred to above, construing the rule as one of 'broad humanity' and which therefore should not be interpreted in a strict and literal way. The other, referred to in a later Court of Appeal case, *Zohra Begum* [1994] Imm AR 381, requires that each word should be given its full value. The chairman in *Akhtar Bi* could be regarded as following the latter approach, and the other two members the former. It was argued unsuccessfully in *Sayania v IAT and SSHD* CO/ 3136/2000 that Article 8 required the broad approach. It may be that *KC v SSHD* [2007] EWCA Civ 327 tips the balance towards the broad approach. The court there found it difficult to imagine what 'living alone' might add to 'the most exceptional compassionate circumstances'. They declined the Secretary of State's request to give guidance as there was no evidence of the purpose of the rule, and they suggested that the rule be amended to make its purpose clearer.

There are difficulties about how the financial support of the sponsor is considered to affect the applicant's situation. The Court of Appeal in *Zohra Begum* held that the rule should not be interpreted as if the sponsor's contribution was not there. On the other hand, the tribunal in *Nessa Bibi v ECO Dhaka* (21162A) may have gone too far in regarding the applicant's sound financial circumstances provided by the sponsor as an indication that she was not living in exceptional compassionate circumstances.

Like widowed mothers, unmarried daughters under 21 also were specifically included in a former version of the rule, and like widowed mothers, their applications must now show that they are living alone in the most exceptional compassionate circumstances. In *Husna Begum* the Court of Appeal found in favour of a woman of 22, all of whose immediate family were now in the UK apart from her brother who had entry clearance to travel. Evidence suggested that as a young single woman in rural Bangladesh she would be isolated and at risk. This could not be generalized to all women in this position, as each case must be decided on its facts. In *Sayania* a young woman left alone in India did not succeed in the High Court in quashing the refusal of leave to appeal to the tribunal. Burnton J did not think that Article 8 assisted or that her lonely position could bring her within the rule. The IDI Chapter 8 s 6 is to a similar effect, saying that the situation of such a woman may be taken into account, but does not of itself bring her within the rule.

9.6.5 **Terms of stay for a successful relative**

Entry clearance for dependent relatives will function as leave to enter and remain indefinitely providing the entry clearance is endorsed that it is to have that effect (Immigration (Leave to Enter and Remain) Order 2000, SI 2000/1161). There is no probationary period.

Maintenance and accommodation requirements are similar to those for married partners, and must be met in order for the application to succeed. Despite the apparent scope in the rules for sharing responsibility, in practice the sponsor will be placed in a position of liability for the relative's support, and *VS* adopts a similar approach to *AM*, holding that third party support is not acceptable. Paragraph 35 of the rules gives power to immigration authorities to require the sponsor to sign an undertaking that they will be responsible for their relative's maintenance. The effect of this is to disbar the sponsored relative from any claim to key means-tested benefits for five years from the date of admission to the UK. The benefits affected are income support, income-based jobseeker's allowance, housing benefit, and council tax benefit (Social Security (Persons from Abroad) Miscellaneous Amendment Regulations 1996). If the relative does make a claim, the Social Security Administration Act 1992 and the Social Security Administration (Northern Ireland) Act 1992 empower the paying authorities to recover any income support from the person who gave the undertaking. Refusal by the sponsor to give an undertaking is a discretionary ground for refusal of entry clearance under para 320.

An undertaking is a formal document. In *Ahmed* v *Secretary of State for Work and Pensions* [2005] EWCA Civ 535 the Court of Appeal held that a statement by the sponsor that he was 'able and willing' to maintain and accommodate his uncle was a statement of his then circumstances designed to show to the entry clearance officer that the requirements for granting entry clearance were met. These words did not amount to an undertaking, which was a solemn promise for the future. Formal undertakings often also stated liabilities which could be incurred for breach, though this was not essential. The sponsor's uncle therefore was not debarred from a claim for backdated benefit on the grounds of being a person who had leave to enter the UK 'as a result of a maintenance undertaking' (Immigration and Asylum Act 1999 s 115).

9.7 **Children**

9.7.1 **Introduction**

The UK's reservation to the UN Convention on the Rights of the Child (CRC) exempts the UK from the Convention in relation to immigration matters. This has been criticized by the Children's Commissioner and human rights bodies, and the Joint Parliamentary Committee for Human Rights points out that 'of the 192 signatories to the CRC...only the UK has entered a general reservation to the application of the Convention to children who are subject to immigration control...We do not accept that the CRC undermines immigration controls' (Tenth report 2006–07 para 180). On 31 January 2008 the government announced its intention to consult on the possibility of withdrawing the reservation.

This announcement came together with a Code of Practice for Border and Immigration Agency dealings with children. The need for this was noted by the 'Home Affairs Committee in its 2005–06 report, the BIA up to now appearing to be the only government department that does not have specific policies for dealing with applications by children' (Stanley 2006). This is not, of course, because children do not migrate. Children may migrate with their families, but may move countries as a result of other family arrangements which may be for their benefit or abusive. They may seek asylum on their own. Migration is a situation in which children are particularly powerless and vulnerable. As the tribunal said in *OM (Children: settlement – cross border movement) Jamaica* [2005] UKAIT 00177, 'Cross border movement of minor children is of the utmost importance...it is implicit in the law and the immigration rules...that it is in the public interest...to ensure that...such cross-border movement only takes place with scrupulous adherence to the relevant law'.

The migration of children involves domestic and private international law provisions concerning abduction, custody, and adoption as well as complex nationality rules.

The UK's immigration law on children is only a small part of the picture which cannot effectively be considered in isolation. This is an area of increasing complexity now warranting specialist texts (see, for instance, Coker, Finch, and Stanley 2002). This section is therefore limited in its aim and scope. It aims to explain some of the particular immigration rules relating to children in a way that illustrates the relationship between what might be broadly categorized as a 'family law approach' and an 'immigration law approach'.

What is meant by a 'family law approach' here is one which pays attention to the quality of relationships and in particular the welfare of the child. The welfare principle found in Children Act 1989 s 1 and in Adoption and Children Act 2002 s 1 says that, when the court is making any decision about the upbringing of a child, 'the child's welfare shall be the court's paramount consideration'. What is meant here by an 'immigration law approach' is one which focuses on control of entry to the UK. The Court of Appeal in *In re S (Children) (Abduction: Asylum Appeal)* [2003] Imm AR 52 drew attention to the need for co-ordination between the family courts and the immigration authorities including tribunals. Such co-ordination may be difficult to achieve when the underlying purposes are not always consistent with each other. Neither are they always in direct conflict.

Clearly, whether a child is permitted to move to a different country, which may entail living with different relatives, or being adopted, a decision is being made about the upbringing of the child. However, the place of the welfare principle in immigration law is precarious. It does not appear in the immigration rules, and the judgment of the Court of Appeal is that the welfare of the child is not paramount in immigration matters *(R v SSHD ex p Gangadeen* [1998] Imm AR 106). Although not to overstate the case, it is a primary consideration which must inform decisions, and must be balanced against other interests *(R v SSHD ex p Ahmed and Patel* [1999] Imm AR 22).

The High Court decision in *R v SSHD ex p Mobin Jagot* [2000] INLR 501 reveals that different outcomes may be indicated by these two approaches. Mobin had spent most of his childhood in the UK with his grandparents, and had never had an easy relationship with his parents in Malawi. When his other grandmother was terminally ill he was sent to Malawi to visit her and, at the age of 12, was refused entry on his return. He appealed the refusal and as this appeal took place in the UK, it was in practice not only in order to obtain leave but also against removal. The policy guidance DP069/99 required 'strong reasons' to justify removal of a child who had spent a substantial and formative part of his life in the UK. The Home Office advanced the possibility of family life with his parents as such a strong reason. It pointed out that his parents were wealthy enough to look after him. Moses J ordered the Secretary of State to reconsider.

The Secretary of State's refusal letter is quoted extensively in the judgment of Moses J. It places importance on the fact that Mobin had just spent four months with his parents. The fact that this was not his own choice but was a family duty and that he had run up a £1, 000 phone bill to his grandparents reveals how he felt about being there. However, what we are loosely calling the immigration approach is more concerned with financial viability. There is a pervasive concern with financial support and non-reliance on public funds. Evidence that a person has done something is evidence that they can do it. It is therefore a viable alternative to entry to the UK, eligibility for which has to be proved. In a family law context it is unthinkable that the wishes and experiences of a competent 12-year-old would not be given a significant place in the decision. Also, in terms of his care arrangements there would be a bias in favour of the status quo if the status quo was working well.

'...It must also be ensured that the welfare of the child is a primary concern so that such movement is shown to be in the best interests of the child'. This statement from *OM (Children: settlement – cross border movement) Jamaica* [2005] UKAIT 00177 shows child protection-oriented thinking in an immigration case. The tribunal supported the requirement for proof of the child's father's inability to care for her and the mother's right to do so, without which they were not prepared to allow her application to remain. The girl had arrived in the UK on a visit to her mother and step-father. The application for leave to remain was supported by letters from the appellant herself (aged 10), her mother and paternal grandmother, to the effect that her father was mentally ill, treated her badly and was unable to care for her. However, there was no other evidence of this or of his consent to the application. There was thus no evidence of compelling family reasons making her exclusion from the UK undesirable. Without such evidence, there was no basis to admit her. The tribunal's judgment goes further, suggesting that, in the case of an application by a child for settlement, there should be engagement of the social services department and a check of the new carers' names on child protection registers. 'This...is to be seen as a general policy requirement that assists in ensuring the protection of the child...in question, not least in the light of the recent findings of the enquiry into the death of Victoria Climbié' (para 44).

OM was distinguished in *FO & ors (children: settlement – OM distinguished) Nigeria* [2006] UKAIT 00089 where the application was made from the country of origin and the sponsoring parent met the requirements of the rules. The general policy statements in *OM* were obiter, and should not be followed in that case where the application for entry clearance enabled fuller consideration of the application from the outset.

As a matter of legal precedent, *OM* has not established a rule of law. Nevertheless it raises important issues concerning the migration and protection of children. The fact that the approach advised in *OM* is not commonplace is partly because immigration law relating to children is geared to family situations in which all parties are consenting, and partly because it is, obviously, geared to entry to the UK. The majority of protection-oriented law that has effect in the UK concerning cross-border movement of children concerns their removal from the UK, not their movement into it.

The rules relating to entry of children will not be considered in detail here. Principles of accommodation and maintenance are already familiar, and when children enter to join both parents, whether or not travelling with a parent, the only additional requirement is that the child is 'not leading an independent life, is unmarried and has not formed an independent family unit' (para 297(iii)). The reason for such a rule is to avoid entry of more than one household. The rule change of October 2000 preventing third party accommodation for children did not prevent the arrangement in *ECO Lagos* v *Sokoya* 00/TH002272 where teenage sisters were to be accommodated in their father's flat. He had retained the tenancy when he moved to live with his new wife precisely for the purpose of accommodating his daughters.

Adequate accommodation was given an unusually extended meaning by the Court of Appeal in *M & A v ECO* [2003] EWCA Civ 263. Other children of the same parents had been taken into care, and one had died as a result of serious abuse. The court had no remit to consider welfare within the rules where children apply to join their own parents. This gap in the protection capacity of the rules was filled by the tribunal's creative decision that the accommodation was not adequate because the children would not be safe there.

Sometimes a child who is under 18 when their application is refused passes the age of 18 before their appeal is heard. The effect of that birthday may depend on whether the child is in the UK applying for leave to remain, or is outside applying to enter. In the case of an application for leave to remain, according to Nationality, Immigration and Asylum Act 2002 s 85(4) the tribunal may take into account matters arising after the date of the original decision, and so may take into account the child attaining 18, meaning that a young person of over 18 could then be refused leave to remain. This interpretation was confirmed in *SO (Nigeria)* [2007] EWCA Civ 76. In entry clearance cases, according to s 85(5) the tribunal may only take into account the facts at the date of the decision. If a child becomes 18 during the Home Office decision-making process, whether they apply in the UK or abroad, the IDI makes allowances, so a child's application should not be turned down in the first place because of delays in the Home Office.

There are special rules which apply when the child is only joining one parent or relative.

9.7.2 **Sole responsibility**

When the other parent of the child is still living, it must be shown that the parent the child seeks to join has 'sole responsibility' for them (HC 396 para 297(i)(c)). In many cases it is, of course, highly unlikely that in practical terms the parent in question will have had sole care, and they will certainly not have done where the child has been living with someone else and is now joining the parent in the UK. Why have such a rule? The rationale for it is only to grant entry to a child if they can be regarded as the responsibility of a person in the UK. This immigration rule underscores a parental obligation, but does not support admission of a child if someone else could be considered responsible for them. The focus is on the role and obligation of the parent as a determinant of where a child should live. This is not an emphasis which would be familiar in family law, although sole responsibility may be identified by an order made by a family court. If there is a residence order in favour of the UK parent, this is regarded as a strong indicator that they have sole responsibility in immigration terms. Some custody orders obtained overseas are similarly regarded (IDI Aug 2003 Ch 8 Annex M para 4.4).

The sole responsibility rule does not give separated parents and children the power of choice over where the child should live. An example given in the IDI makes this apparent:

Two foreign nationals living abroad have a child, then separate. One parent comes to the United Kingdom and obtains settlement. The child remains with the parent abroad for several years, then at the age of 13+ wishes to join the parent in the United Kingdom to take advantage of the educational system. There is no reason why the child should not remain with the parent who lives abroad. In this case the parent who lives in the United Kingdom would not be considered to have sole responsibility. (Annex M para 4.1)

The suggested motivation here implies abuse of the rule; however, in terms of the sole responsibility rule, the outcome would be no different if the child and custodial parent had started to argue and the family thought it was time for a change in the interests of the child.

The Court of Appeal in the case of *Nmaju v IAT* [2001] INLR 26 held that there were two points of principle in determining sole responsibility. One is the quality of control which will amount to sole responsibility, the other is for what period of time that control must be exercised. In the IDI's example given above, the child was left in the care of a parent. Where the child is left in the care of other relatives, then there may still be a conclusion that the UK resident parent does not have sole responsibility even though this may mean that no one does. The quality of control which will give rise to a finding of sole responsibility requires retention of ultimate responsibility for the child. The Court of Appeal acknowledged that when someone else is in fact looking after them, they will have day-to-day care. This does not affect the question of responsibility. Action taken by the caring relatives may be taken 'under the direction' of the responsible parent. A decision for instance as to which school the child should attend would involve a parent who had sole responsibility. The parent would be expected to show a continuous interest in the child's welfare and upbringing.

Where there are two parents actually involved, the tribunal in the case of *Zahir* 00/TH/02262 held that sole responsibility is still capable of arising, for instance, if one parent's role was clearly subsidiary, though it was not so on the facts in that case. *TD Yemen* [2006] UKAIT 00049 gives a helpful review of the authorities on this issue and an advised approach to sole responsibility cases:

i) The question of sole responsibility for a child's upbringing is a factual one.

ii) 'Responsibility' may be undertaken by individuals other than a child's parents and may be shared. The issue of sole responsibility is not just a matter between the parents.

iii) If both parents are involved in the upbringing of the child, it will be exceptional that one of them will have sole responsibility.

iv) If it is said that one is not involved, one of the indicators will be that they have abandoned or abdicated their responsibility.

v) If day-to-day responsibility (or decision-making) is shared with others (such as relatives or friends) that does not prevent the parent having sole responsibility within the meaning of the Rules.

vi) The test is whether the parent has continuing control and direction of the child's upbringing including making all the important decisions in the child's life. If not, responsibility is shared and not 'sole'.

In *TD* the child had lived with his mother in Yemen and been brought up by her. His father phoned him every week and was entirely responsible for his financial support. He took part in major decisions, though there had been few of these. The tribunal concluded that responsibility was shared, not sole. They referred to the underlying purpose of para 297 as 'to effect family unity'. This, they thought, would be undermined if the sole responsibility provision was interpreted in a way that allowed a child to move to a parent who was not actually solely responsible for the child (para 48).

The other issue in *Nmaju* is that of the period of time for which sole responsibility must be assumed. In that case, three children were left in the care of their father who, in September 1996, said that he was too old to look after them any longer and left them in the care of a maid. In November of that year their application to join their mother was refused on the basis that if she had had sole responsibility it was only for two months and that was too short a period of time. The reality of the situation at the time of the entry clearance decision was that the mother had sole responsibility. This was sufficient to meet the requirements of the rule, even though it had only been for two months. *TD Yemen* confirms this result.

According to para 6 of the rules a parent includes a step-parent, an adoptive parent, and an unmarried father, if paternity is accepted or proved. If the child turns out, as in *ECO Accra v Attafuah* [2002] UKIAT 05922, after DNA testing not to be the father's natural child, it seems there is no provision parallel to that in nationality law to treat the child as the child of that person.

9.7.3 Exclusion undesirable

The welfare of the child takes greater priority under the next sub-paragraph of the rule, 'that there are serious and compelling family or other considerations which make exclusion of the child undesirable'. This is not a question of whether it would on balance be better for the child to move to the UK. For instance in *Dawson v ECO Accra* 01/TH/1358 the tribunal in refusing the appeal on this ground noted that there was no evidence of mistreatment of the appellant or of his mother or stepfather according him a lack of respect. It is possible using this part of the rule to enter to join a relative other than a parent. The IDI Ch 8 Annex M para 1 Aug 2003 emphasizes that this basis for entry is only to be used when parents or relatives in the child's own country are *unable* to care for him or her. The IDI states that the family circumstances which make exclusion undesirable may relate to the sponsor, but only if the sponsor is a parent. This appears to be an attempt to avoid children being brought in as carers for other relatives in need. Although the 'exclusion undesirable' rule is aimed at the welfare of the child, the child is still not the centre of the proceedings. Their interests are not independently examined and represented. As the tribunal has said, the rules are aimed at family unity, which is a broad brush measure of the interests of vulnerable individuals within the family.

Case law on the 'exclusion undesirable' rules has suggested that it is only if the living conditions in the child's country of origin are intolerable that the situation in the UK should be considered. However, this is now thought to be too harsh. It is not a question of comparing the two to find out which is better, but if for instance as in *Rudolph* [1984] Imm AR 84 a father is incapable of caring for a child, that of itself could make exclusion undesirable.

The same case noted that the rule is intended to unite families not divide them. Some overall view must be taken therefore, including such factors as the willingness and availability of the overseas adult to look after the child; the living conditions available for them; the greater vulnerability of small children, and the need for family unity (*Hardward* 00/TH/01522). In *Hardward* itself there is still an emphasis on conditions abroad as a starting point, even in that case where the appellant was already in the UK and applying to vary leave. The appellant lost because although there were compelling family reasons why she should stay in the UK, it was not convincingly shown that her father in Jamaica was unable to care for her.

The case of *Hardward* predated the implementation of the Human Rights Act by a few months. The application under the 'exclusion undesirable' rule was turned down, but the tribunal considered whether, given the imminence of the Human Rights Act, it should make a recommendation using Article 8. The tribunal suggested that para 298(i) of the rules was incompatible with the Human Rights Act:

> ...the onus of justifying that interference under Art 8(2) shifts to the immigration authorities. That is in clear contrast with the wording of the rule set out at paragraph 298(i) which places the burden throughout on the appellant to justify why her exclusion would be undesirable, (para 19)

This argument seems to have much force.

9.7.4 Adoption

Inter-country adoption is a growing and complex subject, combining immigration and family law. This brief coverage just raises some of the issues associated with it. It is necessary to distinguish between adoption of a non-British child in the UK, and adoption overseas with the intention or consequence that the child moves to the UK.

9.7.4.1 *Adoption in the UK*

The adoption of a non-British child in the UK by a British citizen confers British nationality immediately upon the making of the adoption order (British Nationality Act 1981 s 1(5)). In the case of *In re B (a minor (AP)* [1999] 2 AC 136 the House of Lords established new principles for immigration considerations in the adoption of children in the UK.

 Key Case

In re B (a minor (AP)* [1999] 2 AC 136

B had visited the UK with her mother. She attended school in Leeds while they stayed with her grandparents, and appeared to be thriving, so her mother left her there when she returned to Jamaica. B and her grandparents applied for exceptional leave for B to stay in the UK as it appeared to be in her best interests, all the more as her father in Jamaica had now died, and her mother and sister were living in very reduced circumstances. Her application was turned down. They were advised that the only way that B could stay in the UK would be for her grandparents to adopt her. Her mother gave consent to this arrangement, but the Home Secretary intervened to oppose the adoption. He also made it clear that if just a residence order were made in favour of the grandparents, he would still seek to deport B. As Lord Hoffmann says in his judgment at 140:

> Ms B had only two years of minority left. And although the benefits to her from being able to spend those two important years living with her grandparents and

going to school in Leeds were plain and obvious, it would not ordinarily be necessary for her to be adopted. Were it not for her precarious immigration status, she could simply have stayed with her grandparents or, if the situation needed to be formally regulated, the court could have made a residence order under the Children Act 1989. But the Home Office made it clear that if the court merely made a residence order, it would nevertheless order her deportation. Thus the acquisition of British citizenship by adoption was an essential element in securing her the advantages of living with her grandparents and continuing at her school.

The Court of Appeal had accepted the Home Office's proposition that 'the court should ignore benefits which would result solely from [a] change in immigration status when determining whether the child's welfare calls for adoption' (at 141). As the acquisition of right of abode was the main benefit, it discharged the adoption order. The House of Lords considered that this interpretation flouted the terms of the Adoption Act, which required the judge to 'have regard to "all the circumstances" and to treat the welfare of the child "throughout his childhood" as the first consideration'. It was impossible to ignore the immigration benefits of the adoption. Lord Hoffmann continues with a passage (at 141) which has great significance for adoptions, and arguably for other cases concerning children:

No doubt the views of the Home Office on immigration policy were also a circumstance which the court was entitled to take into account, although it is not easy to see what weight they could be given. Parliament has not provided, as I suppose it might have done, that the adoption of a non-British child should require the consent of the Home Secretary. On the contrary, it has provided that the making of an adoption order automatically takes the child out of the reach of the Home Secretary's powers of immigration control. The decision whether to make such an order is entirely one for the judge in accordance with the provisions of section 6. In cases in which it appears to the judge that adoption would confer real benefits upon the child during its childhood, it is very unlikely that general considerations of 'maintaining an effective and consistent immigration policy' could justify the refusal of an order. The two kinds of consideration are hardly commensurable so as to be capable of being weighed in the balance against each other.

Adoption decisions *are* subject to the welfare principle and do not suffer from the reservation to the UN Convention on the Rights of the Child. The presence of an immigration dimension to the adoption decision does not mean that the reservation can be invoked to the child's detriment.

9.7.4.2 *Adoption outside the UK*

A child adopted outside the UK may enter the UK for settlement if the requirements of HC 395 para 310 are met. Note that in this case the adoption does not automatically confer British citizenship. Here it is a question of whether the adoption has taken place in circumstances which mean that it will be recognized. Policy considerations have been to prevent adoption being used as a means of circumventing immigration control and to protect children from abuse. Before March 2003 in order to meet the requirements of the rules the adoption had to be 'in accordance with a decision taken by the competent administrative authority or court' in his country of origin or residence. This rule still applies where the adoption was by legal order, however the rules now also make provision for *de facto* adoptions.

'Administrative' does not mean necessarily part of the civil administration, it just means an authority other than a court and therefore a properly licensed religious body is included *(Tarinder Kaur* 01/BH/0048). However, following a rule change on 18 September 2001 (Cmnd 5253) the adoption will only be recognized if it has taken place in one of the countries recognized by the Adoption (Designation of Overseas Adoption) Order 1973, SI 1973/19. The adoption of Tarinder Kaur would therefore not now be recognized as India is not included in the 1973 order. Many countries have developed their adoption proceedings since 1973, and it is surprising that such an outdated provision should become mandatory in 2001. Furthermore, the Hague Convention on the Protection of Children and Co-operation in Respect of Inter-Country Adoptions 1993 is moving towards a different system of international recognition of adoption orders, and adoptions under the Hague Convention are also provided for under the immigration rules paras 316 D–F.

Recognition of the country's adoption process is not enough to bring the child within the requirements of the rule. Paragraph 310 requires that at the time of the adoption both of the adoptive parents were resident together abroad or that either or both were settled in the UK. In addition it lays down requirements of the adoption, namely that the adopted child has the same rights and obligations as any other child of the marriage; that the child was adopted due to the inability of others to care for them; that there is a genuine transfer of parental responsibility to the adoptive parents; that the child has lost or broken ties with their family of origin, and that the adoption is not one of convenience to facilitate admission to the UK. These requirements are more stringent than those for an adoption order in the UK which would not necessarily require that the child was adopted 'due to the inability of others to care for them' nor that the child has lost or broken ties with their family of origin. Indeed it is no longer thought good practice in family law to insist upon a child severing contact with their family of origin. In *Boadi* v *ECO Ghana* [2002] UKIAT 01323 the tribunal took account of this in its interpretation of the rule, holding that severing ties with a family of origin did not mean severing emotional ties, but just that the adoption was not an arrangement which could be seen as reversible. A different view of the rules had been taken in the case of *Kamande v ECO Nairobi* [2002] UKIAT 06129 a few months earlier in which the tribunal refused to recognize the adoption for the purposes of the rules because although responsibility had been transferred, the appellant still retained a strong emotional relationship with his grandparents who had brought him up. It was their aging which had prompted his adoption by his aunt in Britain, and the approach here carries echoes of the 'sole responsibility' rules, in not giving recognition to the family's choices.

When an adoption is arranged within the family, for instance the adoption of a niece or nephew where a couple is infertile, it does not fulfil the latter two requirements of the rules. *In H (A Minor) (Adoption: Non-Patrial), Re* [1997] 1 WLR 791 the Secretary of State, as in *Re B,* intervened in an adoption case, applying to overturn the adoption of a child who entered the UK for a family wedding and was adopted by the relatives he came to join. It was a genuine adoption, and the Court of Appeal declined to overturn it simply because the motivation arose from their infertility. In *J (A Minor) (Adoption: Non-Patrial), Re,* [1998] 1 FLR 225 the Court of Appeal in a comparable case again refused the Secretary of State's application to overturn the adoption order. Although there might be an element of deception in the child's entry, as it seemed that the intention to enter for adoption was present at the beginning, this did not mean the adoption itself was a sham. The Court of Appeal distinguished between deception used to gain entry to achieve a genuine adoption and deception as to the nature of the adoption itself. The Court expressed a view that while the adoption rules were so restrictive the Secretary of State was not well placed to argue that they should not be circumvented by genuine applicants (see Macdonald 2001:455).

These cases would not have been helped by the rule change concerning de facto adoptions, as these adoptions must have taken place prior to entry. The adoptive parents and child must have been living together for a year before the application. If the child cannot gain entry or stay under the adoption rules an alternative is to apply using the rule that exclusion is undesirable. In effect in these two cases, the Court of Appeal declined to apply the immigration rules although their wording was plain, as to do so would conflict with the best interests of the child, which is the prime consideration in adoption proceedings.

These two cases preceded the Human Rights Act. Two Court of Appeal cases since commencement of the Human Rights Act reveal two very different approaches. In *Radhika Sharma v ECO New Delhi* [2005] EWCA Civ 89 the Court of Appeal adopted a strict interpretation of the requirement of HC 395 para 310(ix) that the adoption was due to the inability of the original parents to care for the child. They held that inability did not include unwillingness, as in the present case where the appellant's parents did not want a girl, were not willing to care for her and arranged for her adoption by her aunt and uncle who were eager to have a girl. The Court considered Human Rights Act 1998 s 3 which requires that the rule be interpreted so as to uphold Convention rights as far as possible, but it was not possible, they thought, to construe 'unable' so as to include 'unwilling', and rejected the appellant's invitation to take the more proactive approach to statutory interpretation suggested by the House of Lords in *Ghaidan v Godin-Mendoza* [2004] 3 WLR 113. The entry of the girl under 'exclusion undesirable' rule was also rejected.

The decision in *Radhika Sharma* does not refer to the earlier Court of Appeal case of *Singh v ECO New Delhi* [2004] EWCA Civ 1075 in which the court had to consider an application for entry clearance following an intra-family adoption which did not and never could meet the requirements of the immigration rules because the child had not severed ties with his family of origin. Indeed, he was being cared for well by his parents pending being able to join his adopted parents, his aunt and uncle, with whom he had a strong relationship and who cared for him deeply. His birth parents had three children, but his aunt and uncle had one daughter and were not able to have more children. The adoption was carried out according to a Sikh ceremony. The case had had a very protracted history, including a decision by the ECtHR that an application was admissible because the refusal to recognize adoptions carried out in India was *prima facie* discriminatory. The Court of Appeal heard and decided an application purely upon Article 8 grounds (see chapter 4). It had no doubt that the substantial relationship between the child and adoptive parents amounted to family life. The fact that it did not meet the UK's stringent requirements in the immigration rules should not be allowed to impede the reality of genuine family life and entry clearance should be granted.

Singh did not decide anything about the validity of the restrictions on adoption in the immigration rules. The court simply rejected a 'rigid and formulaic approach' (para 33) which would require adherence to legal form at the expense of looking at the human reality of an individual situation. The tribunal decision in *SK India* [2006] UKAIT 00068 held that the non-recognition of Indian adoptions was not a matter that the immigration tribunal could or should overrule, as adoptions had a wider significance than immigration and there were other effects to be reckoned with. The UK was entitled to require certain formalities of an adoption. This approach was endorsed in *MN India* [2007] UKAIT 00015, where the tribunal rejected an argument that the rules were discriminatory. See Chowhury 2007 for discussion of the issues and a critique of these decisions.

There are other regulations also governing adoption of children abroad. The Adoptions with a Foreign Element Regulations 2005, SI 2005/392, as amended, lay down an extensive system of regulation and approval for adoptive parents. However, they only apply to adoptions under the Hague Convention, adoptions of a foreign child in the UK, or adoptions abroad effected less than six months before the child enters the UK, and so not all those that are permitted in the immigration rules. The Children and Adoption Act 2006 also provides for special restrictions on adopting children from abroad where there is a suspicion of harm to children.

None of these rules protects British children of a non-British parent who is to be deported. It might be thought that such a thing would not happen, because after all the British child has a right to abode and therefore protection from deportation. However, the work of Sawyer shows that such children are often treated as adjuncts of their parents, and deported regardless of their right of abode (see chapter 3 reading list).

9.7.5 Evidence

The issue of credibility which we have encountered so often has been raised particularly in relation to two issues concerning children – their age, and whether they are 'related as claimed'. The extensive questioning and interviewing, village visits, excessive reliance on the discrepancy approach, and distressing refusals of genuine applicants have to a large extent been swept away by the advent of DNA testing. This is not infallible and is limited in what it can prove. Nevertheless, DNA evidence can rarely be effectively disputed and the scope for all the other evidence about relationships is much reduced.

9.8 Family life for those with limited leave

The preceding material in this chapter has dealt with applications to join people settled in the UK. People entering for a limited time, for instance for work or study, have the right to bring their immediate family with them. Establishing a new family while they are here may be less straightforward.

Partners and children of most groups of people who can obtain limited leave under the immigration rules may also obtain leave to enter, with the same restrictions as their partner or parent. This does not apply to visitors, seasonal workers, or those on the sectors-based scheme, and the partners of working holidaymakers may only enter if they too are working holidaymakers, and their children only if they are under five.

All the same conditions for partners and children must be met as for entry with a view to settlement, and the person must intend to leave at the end of the permitted period. Leave to enter is subject to a prohibition on claiming public funds. Partners of students are usually permitted to take employment where the student is admitted for 12 months or more. Partners of all other groups are usually permitted to take employment. There is no right for people with limited leave to be joined by family members other than their partner and children.

The children of people with limited leave who are born in the UK will not be British, as their parents are not settled.

9.8.1 Restricting the right to marry

One of the most restrictive provisions concerning marriage and immigration has its main impact on those with limited leave, or no leave to be in the UK, including recognized refugees. The regime introduced under Asylum and Immigration (Treatment of Claimants etc) Act 2004 ss 19–25 interferes with the actual right to marry, by requiring that any non-EEA national who is not settled in the UK (Immigration (Procedure for Marriage) Regulations 2005 SI 2005/15 reg 6) or does not have entry clearance specifically for marriage (2004 Act ss 19(3)(a), 21(3)(a), 23(3)(a)) must obtain the consent of the Secretary of State before marrying and pay for a certificate of approval (reg 8). If both parties need consent, each must obtain (and pay for) a certificate of approval.

The Parliamentary Joint Committee on Human Rights considered that the scheme was likely to 'be incompatible with the right to marry because it introduces restrictions on that right for a wide class of people which are disproportionate to the legitimate aim of preventing sham marriages and which may impair the very essence of the right' (JCHR Session 2003–04 Fourteenth Report para 68). The Registration of Marriages (Amendment) Regulations 2005, SI 2005/155 prescribe 76 registry offices at which people subject to immigration control must give notice of marriage, in person, with their partner, though the marriage itself need not take place there. Because the provisions apply only to marriages performed by registrars, there is in effect an exemption for Church of England marriages; the provisions therefore discriminate unjustifiably on grounds of religion or belief, and on grounds of nationality. These provisions apply to non-visa nationals. So, for instance, a visitor from New Zealand, who decides to celebrate their marriage in the UK, must make that decision before they enter the UK so that they can obtain a marriage visit visa. Otherwise, the registrar must decline to accept notice of their marriage.

Once the 2005 regulations were introduced there were many instances of distress caused by them. The Churches Commission for Racial Justice found that people had entered into non-Christian religious marriages, then been denied a certificate of approval of their registry office marriage, but not been notified of this. They were detained by an immigration officer waiting at the registry office for that marriage ceremony (Response by the Churches' Commission for Racial Justice to the UK government's document: *Controlling Our Borders: Making Migration Work for Britain. Five-year strategy for asylum and immigration*). Legal challenge was inevitable.

 Key Case

SSHD v Baiai and Trzcinska, Bigoku and Agolli and Tilki **[2007] EWCA Civ 478**

Mr Baiai was an Algerian national who had entered the UK illegally. He was in a relationship with Ms Trzcinska, a Polish national living and working legally in the UK. Their applications for certificates of approval (COAs) were rejected.

Mr Bigoku was an ethnic Albanian from Kosovo, Ms Agolli was also an ethnic Albanian from Serbia, both were nationals of the former republic of Yugoslavia. Both were given exceptional leave to remain. Mr Bigoku's leave had expired before he applied to marry Agolli. Her leave was current. Their applications for COAs were refused after six months delay.

Ms Tilki was a Turkish national who also had discretionary leave which had expired. The man she wished to marry and by whom she was pregnant was a Turkish national with indefinite leave to remain. Her COA application was refused.

The High Court in *R (Baiai, Bigoku & Tilki) v SSHD* [2006] EWHC 823 (Admin) held that the interference with the Article 12 right to marry was disproportionate, and there was unjustified discrimination infringing Article 14 on grounds of religion and nationality. The scheme was unlawful because it:

(i) regards all marriages by someone who requires a COA as automatically actually or potentially marriages of convenience;

(ii) discriminates irrationally in favour of Anglican marriages;

(iii) fails to take account of evidence, if available, that a particular marriage is not a sham;

(iv) makes their immigration status the only factor affecting whether a non-EEA national can marry in this country;

(v) does not allow representations by people affected by the scheme.

There was not a sufficiently rational connection between the measures introduced and the legitimate aim of preventing marriages of convenience. The measures were too broad, interfering with the right to marry of all foreign nationals, regardless of their intention. The court granted a declaration of incompatibility under Human Rights Act s 4 in relation to the regulations and the statute, and this was upheld by the Court of Appeal (*SSHD v Baiai and Trzcinska, Bigoku and Agolli and Tilki* [2007] EWCA Civ 478). As set out by the IDIs, the guidance on granting a certificate of approval created a system of even more draconian controls than the statute. The guidance required that the applicant had extant leave of at least three months. This did not cater for the plans of, for instance, a student who planned to marry at the end of their student leave, and could invalidate plans that were within the law when made. The guidance included setting the fee.

This guidance was also held to be unlawful by the High Court and Court of Appeal. Following the High Court judgment, the guidance was amended to say that applications could be considered on the basis of more individual details in cases where there was less than three months' leave. Amazingly, the discriminatory fee has risen from £135 to £295. The additional information requested is very similar to that which the applicant will also provide in their leave to remain or visa application (there is a £500 visa fee for proposed marriage settlement from abroad), but perhaps it is money well spent to ensure safe transit of information within the Home Office.

Asylum seekers fell outside the scheme, as originally written, as the majority have no leave. They were catered for as 'exceptional', requiring 'compassionate circumstances' to be shown as to why they should not return to their home country and marry there or apply for entry clearance as a married partner. The reasons for this in the case of asylum seekers do not need spelling out and are not, of course, exceptional. Following the Court of Appeal judgment the guidance was amended again to say that applications from those without permission to be in the UK would also be considered in the light of more detailed personal information, but that enforcement action could be considered at the same time. This allows the applications of asylum seekers to be treated on the same basis as those with short periods of leave, but with the threat of enforcement for those who have exhausted all legal procedures.

After the damaging Court of Appeal decision the government announced that they would be applying for leave to appeal to the House of Lords. The amended guidance, dated June 2007, is a stop-gap pending that application. However, it remains current at the beginning of 2008.

9.9 Refugees and asylum seekers

The prospects of maintaining or establishing family life for those seeking asylum in the UK are bleak unless they have arrived with their family.

Once a person has obtained refugee status, or a grant of humanitarian protection after 30 August 2005, they have a right to be joined by a partner and children whom they left behind in their country of origin. However, the right only accrues once refugee status or humanitarian protection has been granted. It may take years before a claim is dealt with, and then the most likely outcome is refusal. In 2006, only 10 per cent of initial decisions resulted in a grant of asylum and 9 per cent in other forms of leave. Although current Home Office targets aim to decide asylum claims quickly, the reality for many claimants is still a long drawn-out process. Then, any appeal may take further years, and again the outcome is uncertain. Once the legal process is over and has failed, the asylum claimant may well be unwilling or unable to return to their country of origin. Many people spend years of their lives in the UK, often at an age when they would be likely to make relationships and have children. Life cannot go on hold, though sacrifices are often made. The appellant in *MT (Zimbabwe)* [2007] EWCA Civ 455, for instance, would not live with or marry her partner for fear of the effect on him if she was removed to Zimbabwe. The appellant in *A v SSHD* [2007] Imm AR 1, although his asylum claim had failed, was living a full family life and had become, like his wife, an approved foster carer.

The minority who are awarded refugee status or humanitarian protection must meet the same conditions in the immigration rules for admission of their immediate family as non-refugee settled sponsors, except for the maintenance and accommodation requirements. Hathaway explains that 'the drafters of the Refugee Convention assumed that the family members of a refugee would benefit from the protection of the Refugee Convention, even if not themselves able to show a "well-founded fear of being persecuted"' (2005:541). The Refugee Qualification Directive 2004/83/EC Article 23.1 says: 'Member states shall ensure that family unity can be maintained', though this only refers to the spouse, unmarried partner and minor children. The definition of family members in the rules and directive is thus more restrictive than the concept of family life in the ECtHR (see Lambert 2006). Other family members who formed part of the household unit in the refugee's country of origin have been considered in the UK on a concessionary basis which is currently under review.

The right to family reunion for refugees in the UK also now needs to be seen in the light of the limited leave given to refugees since 30 August 2005. Before that date, refugee status resulted in indefinite leave to remain. Now a refugee is given five years' leave, which is renewed in the light of conditions in their country of origin. Their family members are given limited leave, to run for the same period as the refugee. This policy contributes to instability and uncertainty for refugee families. The demoralizing effects of separation must be weighed against the upheaval and uncertainty for children and partners.

For a refugee who does not leave a partner and children behind, but who forms a relationship while waiting in the UK for the determination of their claim, the situation is at least as problematic, even though for the time being they have the company of their partner and any children. Whoever their partner is, they will be unable to marry without a certificate of approval. Their application for this will be considered under provisional guidance issued after the Court of Appeal decision in *Baiai* discussed above. This gives no guide as to the criteria for grant or refusal of a certificate and appears likely to generate expedition of their asylum claim and a probable refusal. If their asylum claim has already failed they are unlikely to obtain permission to marry.

If their partner has some security of status in the UK, and there is a substantial delay in dealing with their asylum claim, even if their asylum claim fails they will be able to argue against their removal on the basis of Article 8, though there is no guarantee this argument will succeed. They will be unable to avail themselves of Home Office policy not to remove people who have been married for two years at the date of enforcement action (DP 3/96, see chapter 18) if they have not been permitted to marry.

The rules leave an extraordinary lacuna that operates against a refugee who marries in the UK. In order to qualify for refugee family reunion under para 352 of the immigration rules, the partner and children of a refugee must have been part of their family before they made their asylum claim (para 352A). A partner whom they met in the UK will not usually fulfil this condition. So, although a person granted refugee status who marries a settled person can hope to gain indefinite leave under the immigration rules, if they marry someone without a secure immigration status (even supposing both parties can get a certificate of approval for such marriage) they are not able by virtue of their refugee status to act as sponsor for their spouse. As they will have five years' leave rather than indefinite leave they will not qualify as a sponsor under the marriage rules for settled people (para 284). As their marriage post-dates their asylum claim, they cannot qualify as a sponsor under the refugee rules (para 352A). The rationale for the restriction in para 352A was explained in *Chikwamba v SSHD* [2005] EWCA Civ 1779 as being to discourage opportunistic marriages and encourage the family left abroad to apply for entry clearance. However, as *Chikwamba* itself shows, the rule catches genuine as well as opportunistic relationships, and in fact offers no way to distinguish between them.

 Key Case

Chikwamba v SSHD [2005] EWCA Civ 1779

Ms Chikwamba married in the UK while awaiting the hearing of her appeal against refusal of her asylum claim (note that if the facts were repeated now she would be unlikely to get a certificate of approval). She was from Zimbabwe and married a Zimbabwean man she had known since childhood who was in the UK as a recognized refugee. Her application to stay as his wife was turned down under para 352A, as the marriage had taken place after her husband left Zimbabwe to seek asylum. There was a policy in force at that time of not returning failed asylum seekers to Zimbabwe as it was not deemed safe to do so, and by the time of the appeal the couple had a small baby. Despite these circumstances, the Court of Appeal upheld the tribunal's decision that it was not disproportionate to expect Ms Chikwamba to return to Zimbabwe and apply for entry clearance.

Ms Chikwamba is appealing to the House of Lords.

The Refugee Convention requires that refugees are integrated into the host society and given the benefit of social goods that are available to others, but the immigration rules do not seem to allow for recognized refugees to sponsor a married partner, even one who already has limited leave under the immigration rules.

9.9.1 Family amnesty policy

On 24 October 2003 the government announced that indefinite leave would be granted to families, that is, adults with at least one dependent child, who had sought asylum in the UK before 2 October 2000 and who had been in the UK for at least three years. The rationale for the policy was to cut the cost of welfare support for claims that had not been dealt with, to reduce the administrative burden of outstanding claims, to prevent families becoming long-term asylum claimants as each member of the family claimed in turn, to avoid having to deal with the difficult situation of removing families, and to prevent disruption to the lives of children (*AL (Serbia) v SSHD* [2006] EWCA Civ 1619 paras 22–28). The appellant in *AL (Serbia)* had arrived in the UK as a child, and if he had come with a parent, he would have benefited from the family amnesty policy. However, as a lone child he could not. The Court of Appeal held that this was not discriminatory. The court rejected the argument that there was a relevant comparison to be made between those who sought asylum as unaccompanied children before 2 October 2000 and children who sought asylum with their parents before that date. The policy was intended to benefit families, not children.

The Refugee Qualification Directive requires that refugee decisions are taken in the best interests of the child, which is a significant change in the UK's law applying to refugee children. However, there was no reliance on the directive in *AL (Serbia)* and it could be argued that it did not apply as the amnesty policy was not a grant of refugee status. The appellant has appealed to the House of Lords.

9.10 Conclusion

The rules on family settlement still carry the real burden of policy on integration and diversity. The continuing proposals for change and the reasons given for these changes indicate that they continue to be instruments of social policy.

In comparison with the 1960s and 1970s, the law relating to family settlement is now relatively transparent. The IDIs and guidance to ECOs are published, concessions are increasingly integrated into the rules; even the initial entry clearance interview is more controlled, as the reports of the Entry Clearance Monitor, while not referring to family applications, cast some public light into initial decision-making (see chapter 7).

This greater transparency combined with the albeit limited effect of Article 8, is no more than is necessary and appropriate, given that in matters of family settlement the decisions which are made have a fundamental effect on the welfare and happiness of the individuals concerned.

QUESTIONS

1 What is the immigration purpose which is sought to be achieved by the probationary period for partners? Is this something which should be regulated by immigration control or by families and family law?

2 Why is there no probationary period for other adult relatives?

3 Draft your own immigration rule for the admission of children, taking into account the policy priorities you would consider most important. How does this compare with the existing rules?

 online resource centre For guidance on answering questions, visit www.oxfordtextbooks.co.uk/orc/clayton3e.

FURTHER READING

Chowdhury, Z. (2007) 'Recognition of foreign adoption: The immigration rules and English conflict of laws,' *Immigration Law Digest* vol. 13, no. 2, Summer, pp. 10–16.

Clayton, G. (2008) 'Section 3 of the Human Rights Act and the Immigration Rules' *Immigration Law Digest* vol. 14, no. 1, Spring, pp. 7–13.

Coker, J., Finch, N., and Stanley, A. (2002) *Putting Children First* (London Action Group).

Finch, N. (2007) 'Family and Immigration Cases: Implications for practice' *Family Law* no. 37 August pp. 716–720.

James, C. '50 years of family immigration: Changes in British legislation for partner and family immigration: 1955–2005' *Journal of Immigration, Asylum & Nationality Law* vol. 20, no. 1, pp. 21–36.

Jones, A. (2002) 'A Family Life and the Pursuit of Immigration Controls', in Cohen, S., Humphries, B., and Mynott, E. (eds) *From Immigration Controls to Welfare Controls* (London: Routledge).

McKee, R. (1999) 'Primary purpose by the back door? A critical look at "intention to live together"' *Immigration and Nationality Law and Practice* (1999) vol. 13, no. 1, pp. 3–5.

Menski, W. (2007) 'Dodgy Asians or Dodgy Laws? The Story of H' *Journal of Immigration, Asylum & Nationality Law* vol. 21, no.4, pp. 284–294.

Mole, N. (1987) *Immigration: Family Entry and Settlement* (Bristol: Jordan & Sons).

Pearl, D. (1986) *Family Law and the Immigrant Communities* (Bristol: Jordan & Sons).

Pearl, D. & Menski, W. (1998) *Muslim Family Law* 3rd edn. (London: Sweet & Maxwell).

Rogers, N. (2003) 'Immigration and the ECHR: are new principles emerging?' *European Human Rights Law Review* 1, pp. 53–64.

Sachdeva, S. (1993) *The Primary Purpose Rule in British Immigration Law* (Stoke on Trent: Trentham).

Shah, P. (2002) 'Children of Polygamous Marriage: an Inappropriate Response' *Immigration and Nationality Law and Practice* (2002) vol. 16, no. 2, pp. 110–112.

Shah, P.(2006) 'Registering Marriage in Shifting Sands' *Journal of Immigration, Asylum & Nationality Law* vol. 20, no. 1, pp. 37–41.

Sondhi, R. (1987) *Divided Families British Immigration Control in the Indian Subcontinent* (London: Runnymede Trust).

Stanley, A. (2006) 'Children First, Migrants Second' *Legal Action* March pp. 7–8.

Wray, H. (2006) 'An Ideal Husband? Marriages of Convenience, Moral Gate-Keeping and Immigration to the UK' *European Journal of Migration and Law* vol. 8 pp. 303–320.

10

Entry for temporary purposes

SUMMARY

Most entry to the UK is for a temporary purpose. This chapter considers the law relating to temporary purposes aside from employment. The law concerning visitors is discussed and the application of the rules and importance of appeal rights is noted in the context of respect for family life as required by Article 8 Human Rights Act. The rules concerning students are discussed and their connection with the employment market. The theme of credibility is seen to run through the application of the rules in both these categories. Finally, there is a brief outline of the rules relating to au pairs and working holidaymakers.

10.1 Visitors

The majority of passengers arriving in the UK do so not for settlement but for temporary purposes, and the most common reason for temporary entry is as a visitor.

Around 100 million people each year travel to or through the UK. The vast majority of these are visitors, i.e. people who are coming for a brief period for reasons such as business, tourism, or visiting family, and who do not intend to stay for settled purposes. Despite the steady increase in the numbers of visa national countries, it is still the case that the great majority of visitors to the UK do not require entry clearance. Many come from the European Economic Area, and EEA nationals do not even require leave to enter for a visit. They also come from countries such as the USA, Canada, Japan, New Zealand, and Australia, whose nationals require leave to enter but not visas. In 2006 there were 104.8 million arrivals from outside the Common Travel Area, 92 million of whom were EEA nationals (Control of Immigration: Statistics UK 2006, Cm 7197). Non-EEA visitors in that year numbered 7.4 million. Of these, almost 6 million were non-visa nationals.

The law relating to visitors is not much concerned with that majority. Non-visa nationals, for instance Japanese tourists, may obtain leave to enter on arrival, and only in a very rare case will there be refusal or any legal issue arising. The law relating to visitors is concerned with essentially the same issues as much of the rest of immigration law. It is concerned with deterring illegal entry, overstaying and asylum claims; it operates on the basis of discretionary judgments challengeable by limited appeal rights. It affects the family lives particularly of settled people from the Asian subcontinent, and in operation lays emphasis on the credibility of the applicant. Of course there are more matters involved in visitor applications than these. However, these familiar themes are clearly present.

The visa regime itself, as we have already seen (chapter 7) is designed to prevent illegal entry and deter asylum claims. No more will be said about this here. The right of appeal against refusal of entry clearance for visitors was removed by the Asylum and Immigration Appeals Act 1993. This meant that the only possibility of challenging refusal of entry clearance was by judicial review. As we have already noted, judicial review is concerned not with the merits of the decision but with the decision-making process. Usually in the case of refusal of a visa, this is the question of whether the entry clearance officer's decision was unreasonable, and it is rarely possible to show that this was the case (see, for instance, *R v SSHD ex p Kurumoorthy* [1998] Imm AR 401 or *R v ECO Accra ex p Aidoo* [1999] Imm AR 221). One effect of a lack of appeal right is that much of what happens is, as it were, off the record. There are few recent tribunal cases, and given the limitations of judicial review, there is a relatively small body of law on the application of the rules.

The Immigration and Asylum Act 1999 ss 59 and 60 reinstated a right of appeal for family visitors after protests at its abolition, in particular in relation to the effect on settled families from the Asian subcontinent. The Report of the Independent Entry Clearance Monitor gives global statistics on entry clearance. These statistics reveal that the refusal rate for South Asia is consistently higher than the average refusal rate. In 2002–3 and 2003–4 the refusal rate for the West Indies and Atlantic leapt up to also well over the average. Because of Commonwealth links, giving rise to a greater number of settled people in the UK with family in South Asia and the West Indies, the impact on these settled families of a high entry clearance refusal rate from these parts of the world is significant. Refusal can affect attendance for instance at weddings and funerals and other aspects of family life that human rights issues are most likely to arise in relation to visitor applications. Policies on refusal may also give rise to race discrimination issues.

To summarize, visitors form by far the greatest number of UK arrivals. Most do not require prior entry clearance, but of those that do, the highest number of refusals takes place in South Asia, thus affecting settled communities in the UK. The right of appeal against these refusals was withdrawn from 1993 to 1999, leaving only the unsatisfactory remedy of judicial review. The law in this area is much concerned with credibility. The effect on settled communities raises human rights issues.

In December 2007, as part of its ongoing programme of reform, the government issued a consultation paper on radical changes to the visitor rules. Instead of the single category of visa as used at present, it proposed four main visitor categories: tourist, business, short-term student (already implemented – see below), and sponsored family visitor. Suggestions for the tourist visa include reducing the time given to three months and making more use of the group travel scheme at present only available to Chinese nationals, the 'Approved Destination Status'. A family visit sponsor would take on some responsibility for their visitor complying with the immigration rules. The proposals are referred to as they relate to the provisions discussed in this chapter.

10.1.1 Requirements of the rules

10.1.1.1 *Purpose of visit*

A person who wants to enter the UK as a visitor must meet the requirements laid down in the immigration rules, HC 395 Part 2. Paragraph 41 deals with visits in general, and there are other specialized rules dealing with visits for private medical treatment, to visit a child at school, as part of a tourist group from China, to marry, in transit to another destination, as a student visitor or as a child. These groups are not discussed in detail in this chapter, but the rules are fairly self-explanatory. There are also some concessions outside the rules, set out in the IDIs, for instance for academic visitors.

Certain activities are prohibited for visitors, but currently the visa is a generic one and it is not required that the visitor spends their time in a particular way. Paragraph 41 requires that the visit must not be for the purpose of:

(a) taking employment in the UK;

(b) producing goods or providing services in the UK, including selling goods or services direct to members of the public; or

(c) undertaking a course of study.

The visit may therefore be for any purpose which does not contravene these requirements, provided the individual is not excluded for a general reason under para 320 (see chapter 7). Common purposes for a short stay are holidays, family visits, or to transact business. Transacting business includes a number of temporary purposes where the visitor is employed elsewhere, for instance lorry drivers delivering goods, people installing equipment, giving advice or lectures. Some of these may be separated into smaller categories following the December 2007 consultation. The reason must not be one which is covered by other immigration rules. In *Gusakov* (11672) the applicant was planning to stay with a family to improve her English and help look after their children. The ECO refused the application on the basis that in substance she was coming as an *au pair,* but as a Russian citizen she fell outside the *au pair* scheme and therefore she was neither a visitor nor an *au pair* and could not be granted entry. The IAT held that as a matter of law there are few restrictions on what a visitor can do. The authorities could not prevent her spending her time as a visitor in looking after children or improving her English. What the visitor intends to do with their time is not crucial in the case of a family visit (*W (Ghana)* [2004] UKIAT 00005 ILU vol. 7 no. 3).

10.1.1.2 *Duration of visit*

The visitor must state the period of time that they intend to stay and this must not exceed six months. There is no automatic entitlement to six months' leave if a lesser period would be sufficient to fulfil the purposes of the journey (para 42), for instance a business meeting on a fixed date would only need a short period of leave. In practice six months' leave should usually be given even when less would satisfy the purpose (Feb 2006 IDI Ch 2 s 1 para 2.3). An exception is for holders of Refugee Convention travel documents issued by a signatory to the Council of Europe Agreement of 1959 on the Abolition of Visas for Refugees. In 2003 the UK suspended its recognition of these travel documents, which means a refugee visitor now needs a visa. Three months entry is advised, and following the current consultation it seems that this may become the norm also for other travellers.

A visitor who has been given less than six months and continues to satisfy the requirements of para 41 may apply before the expiry of their leave for a further period up to the maximum, although the IDI Annex A advises that the original reasons for granting short leave should be obtained from the immigration service, and consideration given to whether these still apply.

Where an application for an extension is made which would take the visitor beyond the six months, the Home Office should not refuse the application outright but consider granting leave up to the maximum as mentioned above. For instance in *Wong* (11979) the appellant stayed for five months as a visitor, then the full two years available as a working holidaymaker (see below), then applied for a further three months as a visitor. The Home Office responded that 'any further extension' would lead to a stay of more than six months as a visitor. The IAT held that the Home Office could have considered granting a shorter period, i.e. something up to a month, which would have meant that the appellant would not exceed six months' leave as a visitor.

The IDI advises in para 4 of Annex A that 'there is no restriction on the number of visits a person may make to the UK, nor any requirement that a specified time must elapse between successive visits'. The frequency of visits however is something that will be considered in the light of the purpose of the visits, and may affect the view taken of the visitor's credibility. The IDI gives guidance that a visitor should not normally spend more than six out of any 12 months in the UK, although there will be legitimate exceptions such as for private medical treatment.

10.1.1.3 *Maintenance and accommodation*

Evidence of the visitor's financial status is required to assess their capacity to maintain themselves during their stay, as another requirement under para 41 is that there must be no recourse to public funds.

While some assurance about the applicant's financial circumstances is necessary, the purpose is only to show that the applicant has the capacity to maintain themselves and return. This does not require their finances to be a model of clarity according to the tribunal case of *Osibamowo* (12116). The assessment of this requirement involves an examination not only of the means of the visitor but also, where applicable, of the means of those who will support them.

One of the contentious issues in visitor applications arises from the application of this part of the rule. The problem is illustrated by the case of *Hussain* (10037) in which the ECO refused entry clearance on the basis that the trip expenditure was out of all proportion to the applicant's income. The ECO doubted whether a proportionate benefit would be obtained from the visit. The IAT found that the satisfaction of seeing family was quite sufficient reason for the trip and the expenditure involved. The visit did not need to be a demonstrably wise financial move. However the appellant still lost in this case because he could not show that he could afford the airfare home. There was a similar approach in *Kaur* v *ECO New Delhi* [2002] UKIAT 05692 in which the tribunal said that the emotional value of the trip might well mean that the visitor would pay more than strict economics might dictate. However, in *Iskola* (11334) it was held relevant that one year's income from the applicant's business was equivalent to the price of the air tickets. The IAT held that the refusal of entry clearance was justified. The difficulty here is that the difference in standard of living and income between the applicant's home country and the UK may make it very difficult for the applicant to show that the trip is financially viable. This is not really because of this part of the rule taken alone, but because of the way it interacts with the requirement to show intention to leave.

10.1.1.4 *Intention to leave*

As with other temporary purposes, a key requirement of the visitor rules is proof of the intention to leave at the end of the period permitted. Like the other requirements this is something which the applicant is required to prove, but only on a civil standard of the balance of probabilities. In order to meet this standard of proof the applicant will need to adduce circumstantial evidence from which the immigration officer will make a judgment. Evidence from the sponsor may help to build a picture of the applicant's intention (*DM* [2005] UKIAT 130 ILU vol. 8 no. 19). They will consider matters such as what incentive the applicant has to return, e.g. whether they have family and work commitments in their home country. In *Aye* (10100) the tribunal said that an apparent lack of incentive to return should not of itself be treated as a reason to refuse. This is clearly right in principle, otherwise the less engaged and committed a person's life, the less chance they would have to expand their horizons by travel. However, lack of incentive could, the tribunal said, be taken into account as part of all the circumstances which would be used to develop a full picture of the applicant's intentions. The IDI Ch 2 s 1 Annex A para 1 Feb 2006 illustrates the difficulty of proving this intention:

the fact that a passenger... may be able to produce a return ticket (and other supporting evidence) does not guarantee that he intends to abide by his conditions of stay of that his intention to leave at the end of his visit is genuine.

The immigration officer or ECO in considering incentive to return may take into account the economic circumstances in the applicant's home country by comparison with those in the UK. There are many cases in which this reasoning is demonstrated, (see *Ashfaq Ahmad* v *ECO Islamabad* [2002] UKIAT 03891 below in the context of intention to work). Such considerations are fraught with the potential for stereo-typing and discrimination. In *R v ECO ex p Abu-Gidary* CO 965 1999 the argument was advanced for the applicant that the ECO's reasoning in this respect, if taken too far, could result in no young single women from developing or poor countries being able to obtain entry clearance as visitors. The applicant for entry clearance, who was the daughter of the applicant for this judicial review, had made numerous unsuccessful applications before. The case was heard before the commencement of the Human Rights Act 1998 and Race Relations (Amendment) Act 2000, so arguments could not be relied upon from those statutes. However, it was argued in the context of irrationality that the application of the requirement of strong financial circumstances amounted to indirect discrimination as fewer people of the applicant's racial group would be able to comply with it. The potential visitor was a recent university graduate who on her earlier applications had not had a job, but at the time of her most recent application did have a job to return to. In a country riven by conflict and offering very limited opportunities for independence for women, this was a considerable achievement, but the ECO did not regard it as an incentive to return, describing her income from the job as 'modest'. The view of the High Court was more sympathetic. That approach is also found in tribunal decisions such as *Ogunkola* v *ECO Lagos* [2002] UKIAT 02238 in which the tribunal endorsed the view that 'if lack of economic incentive to return to the country of origin were sufficient to found a refusal of a visit application, then no person living overseas whose standard of living was lower than that prevailing in the UK could ever come on holiday here, or visit relatives settled here. That is not the law' (para 7).

Government scepticism about the intention of visitors to return home is illustrated by the proposal in the 2002 White Paper *Secure Borders, Safe Haven* (Cm 5387) to prevent switching from visitor to spouse status. The White Paper says:

In 1999, 76 per cent of those granted leave to remain on the basis of marriage had been admitted to the UK for another purpose and 50 per cent of those who switched into the marriage category did so within six months of entry. As it seems unlikely that such a large percentage of this number would develop permanent relationships within such a short period of time, the indication is that many of these persons had intended to marry all along but had not obtained leave to enter on this basis and had therefore lied about their intentions to the entry clearance officer. Alternatively, they may have entered a bogus marriage to obtain leave to remain after arrival. (para 7.11)

This leaves out of account that the entrant may have lied about their reason for entry, not because they did not intend to marry their partner, but because they did, and would prefer to be in the country with them than to wait abroad. They may also have more confidence in their capacity to deal with the Home Office and any problems in the application while in the UK. This points up a central issue concerning credibility to which we shall return, that deception or mistakes about one matter do not necessarily demonstrate bad faith about the substance of the application. This reasoning by the Home Office also leaves out of account, in the case of visitors, the effect of six months limited leave on a new relationship. A person who has entered as a *bona fide* visitor and formed a relationship in that time has a difficult choice to make.

As an additional requirement to the intention to leave, the visitor must also show that they can meet the cost of the return or onward journey, the basis of the refusal in *Hussain*. This may be simply proved by the purchase of a return ticket. The cost of return, duration of the visit, and adequate maintenance and accommodation are more easily proved than intention to leave.

10.1.1.5 *Intention to work*

Paragraph 41 requires proof of a negative, that the visitor does not intend to take employment in the UK. This is not necessarily proved by evidence that they can be maintained and accommodated. In *Ashfaq Ahmad v ECO Islamabad* the tribunal found that the sponsor could maintain and accommodate the visitor, and in fact this had never been in dispute. However, the sponsor could not control the actions of the visitor. While the sponsor may genuinely intend only a family visit, the visitor, as a free adult, may make other choices, such as working during their stay. The sponsor cannot prevent this and so the application for entry clearance could be refused on the basis of the incentive which the visitor would have to work, based on a view of his financial circumstances.

The tribunal in *Mistry* v *ECO Bombay* [2002] UKIAT 07500 put the matter rather starkly as follows: 'It comes down to the question of whether someone making a modest living in India must inevitably be regarded as too much prey to the temptations of doing much better here, at least in cash terms, to be regarded as a genuine short-term visitor' (para 7). The implied answer here is 'no', but the discriminatory potential of such a blanket judgment would be very clear.

10.1.2 **Credibility**

The immigration rules do not contain a further heading, 'credibility', but this issue lies behind all the requirements we have discussed above. Annex A to the IDI Ch 2 s 1 Feb 2006 does begin with a section headed 'Credibility' which advises officers to investigate the background to applications if they have doubts. The Annex says that the proposed purpose of the visit 'must bear some reasonable relationship to [the visitor's] financial means and his family, social, and economic background. Previous immigration history and evidence of a pattern of family migration, both here and abroad, are also matters to be taken into account'.

The issue of credibility therefore also brings in other factors which are not included in the rules. The practice of taking family migration history into account was approved in the two judicial review cases cited earlier, *Aidoo* and *Kurumoorthy.* Both held that family members' migration histories were a relevant matter to the exercise of discretion. In the case of *Aidoo,* the sponsor and applicant's half-brother had overstayed and there was suspicion that the applicant might do the same. In *Kurumoorthy* the ECO thought that the applicants, who were a couple, might consider following the wife's sister's example. She, however, had done nothing unlawful. She had come on a visit to her children and had applied while in the UK for indefinite leave to remain, which was granted. However, in *Gurgur* v *ECO Istanbul* [2002] UKIAT 024626 the tribunal found that a history of lawful migration in a family should not be used to prevent the appellant from visiting her children and grandchildren in the UK.

In relation to the maintenance and accommodation requirement, as the above cases show, there can be a difference of opinion about the use and adequacy of funds. The effect is that all too easily the examination can become a trial of credibility. In a close examination of a subjective state such as intention, credibility is clearly relevant. However, it is easy for credibility to become elevated out of its rightful place and be treated as the overriding factor. At worst, the process then resembles a criminal trial where, if a witness's credibility can be attacked, the whole of their evidence can be undermined. Time and time again, the tribunal has stated that the issue of credibility should not be so used. Where there are discrepancies in evidence which do not go to the question in issue, these should not be held against the applicant. A clear case of the misuse of the discrepancy approach in the context of visitor applications is that of *Singh* (10139). The applicant was a 40-year-old married man in India who had applied to visit his brother in the UK. There was a discrepancy between him and his brother on the ages of the brother's children and on whether the brother paid maintenance to his former wife. The tribunal held that these were not matters of which he would necessarily have an accurate knowledge, and a negative assessment of his credibility based on such discrepancies was unreasonable. There were other more relevant factors which supported his credibility, for instance that he had visited before and had left before his allotted time. These should have been given more weight.

10.1.3 **Entry clearance**

The requirements set out in paragraph 41 apply to all visitors. Where they are met the applicant may be granted leave to enter at the port. Where entry clearance has been obtained beforehand the enquiry into these matters will have been completed before arrival and the entry clearance will function as leave to enter (Immigration (Leave to Enter and Remain) Order 2000, SI 2000/1161: see chapter 7). The rules concerning visitors do not require that a visitor obtains entry clearance. However, a person who comes from a visa national country must obtain entry clearance for any purpose, including a visit. Visa national countries include a number of Commonwealth countries, so the belief which is sometimes held, that Commonwealth citizens may visit their UK relatives without prior entry clearance, is a false one. It depends on the Commonwealth country from which they come. For instance, Australian nationals have no such restriction; Indian nationals do.

The rate of refusal of leave to enter at the port to visitors from some non-visa national countries (notably in the Caribbean) is higher than for visitors from other countries.

It can therefore be advisable for nationals of those countries to obtain entry clearance, and the rules permit though they do not strictly require it (para 23A). Even before the Immigration (Leave to Enter and Remain) Order 2000, SI 2000/1161, entry clearance would ease the traveller's passage through immigration control and help to avoid wasted airfares and the distress of refusal at the port. There is a further advantage of applying for entry clearance where the visit is to a close family member, which is that refusal may attract a right of appeal. There is no appeal against refusal of leave to enter without entry clearance (Nationality, Immigration and Asylum Act 2002 s 89(2)).

10.1.4 Family visit appeals

As mentioned above, the Immigration and Asylum Act 1999 reinstated a right of appeal against refusal of entry clearance for visits to family members. This right is now contained in Nationality, Immigration and Asylum Act 2002 s 90, and a family member is defined in Immigration Appeals (Family Visitor) Regulations 2003, SI 2003/513, reg 2(2) as the applicant's

(a) son, daughter, grandparent, grandchild, uncle, aunt, nephew, niece or first cousin;

(b) own or their spouse's parent, brother or sister;

(c) own or their son or daughter's spouse;

(d) step-parent, step-child or step-brother or sister;

(e) and any person with whom they have lived as a member of an unmarried couple for at least two of the three years before the application for entry clearance was made.

There appears to have been concern in government at reintroducing a right of appeal outright, and the reintroduction was accompanied by a review, to examine aspects of the working of the system, and a fee charged to appellants. The fee was the subject of a good deal of public outcry. It was to be refunded if the appellant won their case. The fees were seen to be a disincentive to use the system, a right of appeal being as it were given with one hand and taken away with the other. The charge for appeals (in addition to visa fees) had not been made before in the immigration system, and was seen disproportionately to affect black and Asian people. The fee was reduced, and finally abolished, with effect from 15 May 2002 (SI 1147/2002), however, the reason given was the inconvenience of administering it, and research was inconclusive as to whether it deterred people from appealing (see Gelsthorpe, Thomas, Howard, and Crawley 2004).

This research showed that oral appeals were far more successful than those which were decided on the papers only, having a success rate of 73 per cent compared with 38 per cent. Appellants were often unaware what the choice of these two kinds of appeal meant. In the government's five-year strategy published in February 2005 there is a proposal to end oral appeals, and the December 2007 consultation paper asks whether the appeal right should be 'revisited'.

10.1.5 Family visits and Article 8

It may be recalled from chapter 4 that what respect for family life requires, or what constitutes an interference with family life, depends to some extent on the particular relationship. In a sense, the very specification of family members in regulations gives rise to questions under Article 8. The list has been criticized as being insufficiently comprehensive, as concepts and experiences of the family differ widely (see Review of Family Visitor Appeals, June 2003).

The case of *RK (purpose of family visit)* [2006] UKAIT 00045 raised issues of this kind, although arguments were not made under Article 8.

 Key Case

RK (purpose of family visit) [2006] UKAIT 00045

The appellant and her husband (A) planned to visit their family in the UK, and to stay with A's niece, primarily because the niece's son had had a brain tumour and been very ill. On reconsideration A's appeal was allowed. Although he had stated his purpose as to visit L, who was his grand-nephew, he was going to stay with his niece and her husband. This was within the rules. However, a spouse's niece is not within the rules so the Home Office maintained its challenge to the appellant's being given leave. After being refused, the appellant pointed out that she had mentioned her sister-in-law (who *is* designated in the regulations) in her application form and that she would be visiting her too. Indeed, it was unthinkable that the couple would travel to the UK to visit the sick grand-nephew, stay with his parents (A's niece and her husband), and not visit A's sister, who was also elderly and unwell.

The tribunal held that the purpose of a family visit must be to visit the designated relative. Incidental visits to designated relatives did not make the visit a family visit. This decision makes no reference to the effect on family life of not recognizing that, in the normal way of things, the husband and wife would travel together.

In *GB (family visitor – half-brother included)* [2007] UKAIT 00063 the appellant had been refused a visa to visit her half-brother, and refused an appeal on the basis that this was not a family visit. The tribunal noted that step-brothers and step-sisters were included in the regulations but have no blood tie. It would therefore be an 'absurd anomaly' if step-siblings had a right of appeal but half-siblings did not, the blood tie making the relationship closer. Half-brothers must be included in the reference to 'brothers' in the regulations (and the same would apply to half-sisters).

As we have seen, Article 8 cannot be used to *establish* family life if it does not already exist. We noted this in the case of *ECO Lagos v Imoh* [2002] UKIAT 01967 in which an application was made for a four-year-old girl to join her aunt in the UK as a dependant. The application was doomed to fail because the aunt was not settled. However, the tribunal found that there was no family life in this case but rather an attempt to create one. It said: 'Article 8 requires that there is as a matter of fact family life in existence and the mere payment of money for the care of a child and one visit to see that child, is not capable of creating a family life' (para 5 of the judgment).

One might ask, though, whether Winsome Imoh would have been refused entry clearance just to visit her aunt rather than to join her as a dependant, and if so, whether she could have challenged this successfully using Article 8. The case of *Praengsamrit v ECO Bangkok* [2002] UKIAT 02791 may be considered by way of comparison. In this case an aunt applied to visit her niece, and was turned down on the basis that there had been insufficient contact between the two of them. Article 8 was not argued, but the Vice President of the tribunal held that:

There is no need to prove contact as an expression of devotion which one might expect between husband and wife. They are relations whose family life goes back over the period of the niece's life. That sort of relationship does not to my mind require to be demonstrated by evidence of frequent contact. It is of the essence of family life that the bond is there to be renewed as and when the occasion arises when members of a family are separated by considerable distances as in this case.

This must be a familiar idea to anyone with relatives who live at a distance from them. It suggests that the better way for the courts to approach Article 8 cases is not to consider whether family life exists, but rather what respect for family life requires in this instance. As discussed in chapter 4, this will vary from one situation to another. It may not require a government to respect the choice of residence of a married couple who could live elsewhere, but it is difficult to see how it would not require at least the possibility of contact between family members. In *Ramsew v ECO Georgetown* 01/TH/2505 the tribunal confirmed that family visit cases do normally engage family life. On the other hand, in *Hussain and Noor v ECO Islamabad* (01/TH/2746) the tribunal held that family life was not interfered with by refusing a visit. It could be carried on by other means, for instance letters and phone calls. See the comment in ILU vol. 6, no. 19, p. 16 that the lack of personal contact affects the *quality* of family life. The approach in *Ramsew* is implicitly endorsed in *Ashrif v ECO Islamabad* 01/TH/3465 in which the tribunal held that there did not have to be a particular reason for the visit at a particular time. 'The whole point of family visits is that the existence of the family ties of themselves will normally furnish the reason for the visit' (para 14).

The current consultation raises the question of whether family sponsors should be required to give financial security for their visitor's compliance with the rules.

10.1.6 **Change of circumstances**

As we have seen in chapter 7, where there is a fundamental change of circumstances after the grant of entry clearance, this may justify cancellation of leave to enter (HC 395 para 321A). In the context of visitor cases the question may arise whether a change in the purpose of the visit is fundamental enough to justify such cancellation or refusal.

In *Dapaah* (11823) the principle established in *Eusebio* (4739) was reiterated, namely that the question of the effect of a change of circumstances is a question of fact and degree, particularly when the applicant is seeking entry under the same rule as the one under which they obtained entry clearance. In a visitor case a change of sponsor does not warrant cancellation of leave to enter. However, leave to enter may be refused or cancelled even when the change of circumstances does not take the journey outside the visitor rules. In *Hiemo v Immigration Officer Heathrow* (10892) the appellant's original application had been to visit his sister. On arrival at Heathrow he sought instead 20 days to attend a training course at the Church of Scientology in East Grinstead. His sister had gone to Germany. The tribunal held that the change of circumstances was fundamental and the refusal was justified. While his current proposed purpose would fall within the visitor category, the change did not have to take the application out of the category to warrant refusal of leave to enter.

10.1.7 **Particular purposes**

10.1.7.1 *Carers*

Applications from people wanting leave to enter to care for a sick friend or relative in the UK may be refused on the basis that this is outside the rules; however IDI Jun/01 Chapter 17 s 2 para 2 advises that where the care will be for a short time, entry for this purpose may be considered under the normal visitor rules. This was illustrated by *Mahid v ECO Dhaka* [2002] UKIAT 00935 where the applicant sought to enter to care for his severely disabled cousin. The cousin, I, had previously been cared for by his father, mother and brother. However, his father had become ill, his brother had started a university course and his mother was unable to lift I alone. The Social Services Department had offered a system of carers, but the family preferred to have I cared for by the family. It was clear that the need was long term, although the application was made for six months leave as a visitor, it was said on a respite basis.

The case is one of those referred to in chapter 4 in which the tribunal misidentified the legitimate aim, citing 'the prevention of disorder or crime' (para 10). On the issue of proportionality the tribunal said: 'it is not proportionate to expect those duties to be taken over by one young man travelling all the way from Bangladesh' (para 12). Unfortunately for Mr Mahid and his cousin, this is a misuse of the concept of proportionality. The tribunal seems to have lost sight of the fact that it is harm done by the interference, i.e. the refusal of entry clearance, which must be proportionate to the legitimate aim pursued by the ECO. Whether the family decision is proportionate to their circumstances and resources is not an Article 8 question. In *R (Fawad and Zia Ahmadi) v SSHD* [2005] EWCA Civ 1721 the Court of Appeal held that an Article 8 claim of a brother to remain to look after his younger brother was not bound to fail and thus should be considered.

Family visitors caring for children have sometimes been challenged on the basis that this is acting as a childminder and so contravenes the requirement not to take employment. As a result of a combination of case law and the IDIs the position on this is now relatively clear. Visitors may not be paid for childcare. Beyond this, the tribunal in *Jumawan* (9385) states the principle as follows. If the essence of the application is to take over domestic responsibilities to enable another family member to obtain gainful employment then it may be justified to refuse entry clearance. This is a task which could be undertaken by a third party employed for the purpose. However, merely because a person intends to occupy some or all of their visit in the care of their grandchildren, which could be done by an employee, it does not follow that domestic employment is the applicant's object. Leave to enter as a visitor may still be granted.

The IDI July 2005 Ch 2 s 1 Annex B para 7 says that it is acceptable for visitors to act as temporary childminders where, in addition to the points made above, the visitor is a close relative of the parent (e.g. parent, sibling, in-law), neither parent is able to supervise daytime care of the child, and neither parent has an immigration status leading to settlement.

10.1.7.2 *Private medical treatment*

It is not permissible to come to the UK for the purpose of receiving National Health Service treatment. A person who is here as a visitor also may not take advantage of the National Health Service unless there is an emergency and they belong to one of a limited list of countries set out in Annex F to IDI Dec/01 Ch 2. Entry for private medical treatment is a special category in the rules, and a visitor for private medical treatment does not automatically need to show that their visit is for a fixed period of less than six months and that they will leave at the end of that period. Instead, the duration of the visit is linked to the duration of proposed treatment.

A medical visitor must meet all the rules for a general visitor, as per para 41. The maintenance and accommodation requirement will entail showing that all the costs of treatment can be met. They must show they intend to leave the UK at the end of their treatment, and if they have a communicable disease they must satisfy the medical inspector that there is no danger to public health from their entry to the UK.

The immigration service may require evidence of the nature of the illness and treatment, of the arrangements for treatment including frequency duration and cost, and availability of funds to meet those costs (para 51 and IDI Dec/01 Ch 2 Annex F). Evidence should come from a registered medical practitioner who holds a consultant post. The treatment must be shown to be finite, but the decision-maker should take a reasonable view of this, relating it to the condition which is being treated. The tribunal in *LB (medical treatment of finite duration)* [2005] UKAIT 00175 held that this may be for years in a suitable case. The limit is the duration of the treatment, and though this must be finite it need not be short. Extensions will not be given for treatment from a GP or alternative health practitioner, although initial leave to enter may be granted for this purpose.

10.1.8 Switching immigration categories

For a visitor, opportunities to stay under a different immigration rule have almost vanished. The only exceptions now seem to be in rare family cases where a change of circumstances makes a return to their country of origin inappropriate for a child or older dependent relative, and they would fulfil the requirements of Part 8 of the rules, as discussed in chapter 9. This does not debar an application outside the rules in suitable cases, for instance an emergency in the family requiring the visitor to stay as a carer (see IDI Ch 17 s.2 June 2001).

10.2 Students

There is a centuries-old tradition of travel to other countries in pursuit of learning and education. As a former imperial power, Britain has played a significant role as host to students seeking opportunities which could not be provided in their country of origin, and entry as a student is the commonest short-term immigration reason after visitors. In 2006, the latest year for which figures are available, 309,000 non-EEA students were admitted. This figure is around the middle of the range for the last decade. Students are not only from the Commonwealth but also from many other nations as well. In fact a British education has been a significant way in which British influence has been maintained and extended in the world, as well as providing developmental and economic benefits for those who obtain their education in the UK.

Therefore in terms of government policy the entry of foreign students involves not only the practices of the immigration service but also the education system, cultural exchange, foreign relations, finance, and, potentially, employment and industrial or vocational training. The purpose of the student's entry is learning, and, probably, obtaining a qualification. The course of attendance at the educational institution is the bare minimum which the student desires and the government must grant to make the entry meaningful. Around this other variables, such as how much the student is charged for their course, whether they or their spouse are allowed to work, whether they are allowed to stay after their course, for how long and for what purposes, may be changed from time to time in accordance with policy objectives. These may not have to do only with education but also with economic conditions, with needs in the UK employment market, and political debates about race or the welfare system.

Very broadly, from the Commonwealth Immigrants Act 1962 up to the end of the twentieth century, the rules relating to students changed from being brief and welcoming to increasing complexity and restriction. In June 1999 the government launched the Prime Minister's Initiative (PMI) to welcome international students, addressed particularly to those who intended to train for occupations in which the UK government perceived a need to recruit and retain workers. The removal of the requirement to show intention to leave for graduates and medical students, with effect from 17 October 2001, was a significant step in this direction. A summary of the PMI is given in the student IDI. While the IDIs often have the appearance of practical guidance, and cases discussed below and in chapter 8 reiterate that this is their purpose, they have to date been presented in legal terms as policy, and the inclusion of the PMI reinforces this. Despite this policy change towards welcoming students, the details of the rules and their interpretation by tribunals subsequently became more restrictive once again, and the sudden and radical limitations introduced for postgraduate medical students from 2006 are a deliberate attempt to reduce the number of overseas medical students in the UK (see below and next chapter). Phase 2 of the PMI was launched on 18 April 2006 as a marketing campaign, targeting international students particularly in identified priority countries. Although the government's PMI 2 targets for overseas students are set out in a general way in the IDI, there is no indication as to how this should affect individual immigration decisions. The limited information available on how students will be affected by the five-tier system of managed migration suggests there will be a polarization between different kinds of students, with more control and bureaucracy overall, and the application of a points system. All these developments are discussed in the course of considering the rules below.

The current rules governing the entry of students are extensive and detailed. They are found in paragraphs 57–87F of the Immigration Rules, para 57 setting out the basic requirements for entry. In addition to general rules applying to most student applicants they cater expressly for particular categories of student such as student nurses as well as particular purposes such as resitting examinations, writing up theses, or being a student union sabbatical officer.

The rules are designed to address four areas of government concern: genuineness or bona fides of the student's intention, genuineness of the educational institution, financial independence of the student, and control of access to employment.

10.2.1 **Type of educational institution**

Vetting of the educational institution has become simpler since the introduction of the Department for Education and Skills' Register of Education and Training Providers. Now a student will only obtain leave to enter if the institution at which they intend to study is listed on this register.

Such institutions are either:

(a) a publicly funded institution of further or higher education; or

(b) a *bona fide* private education institution which maintains satisfactory records of enrolment and attendance; or

(c) an independent fee paying school outside the maintained sector.

The case of *Syed Tareq Ali v ECO Dacca* [2002] UKIAT 02541 suggested that the adjudicator had power to go behind the decision of the Secretary of State that the college was not *bona fide*. Although the requirement that the college is bona fide remains in the rules, since the introduction of compulsory DfES registration, presumably registration will be regarded as conclusive and this criterion not applied on an individual basis. The only challenge then would be the college's challenge by judicial review of a refusal to register them.

Falling foul of an unregistered college is not necessarily easy to remedy. In *EA (s 85(4) explained) Nigeria* [2007] Imm AR 487 the claimant had leave to remain to study at London Metropolitan University. He did not continue his studies there but instead transferred to Anfell College and applied for leave to remain to do this. The college was unregistered, and closed before the decision was made. Accordingly, leave was refused. By the time of his appeal hearing the claimant had a place at another college, but the tribunal held that the rule permitting evidence that accrued up to the date of the hearing only applied to evidence that referred to the decision that was made, not another decision. So the claimant could not now obtain leave to remain as a student at the new college because that was not the application which was the subject of the appeal. The tribunal was not an extension of the decision-making process. The logic of this decision is cogent enough, and the claimant would probably have been better advised to make yet another application rather than pursue his appeal, but it is also the kind of decision which illustrates that the system is not made easy for the lay person to negotiate.

Rule changes in September 2007 introduced a requirement for all educational institutions to maintain satisfactory records of enrolment and attendance and produce those to the BIA on request. This is a step towards the greater involvement of sponsors in the immigration process as part of the new five-tier system.

There is no general age requirement in the student rules, and they include entry to the UK to attend an independent school. Paragraph 57(iii) of the rules says that children under 16 can qualify as students, but only 'if they are enrolled at an independent fee-paying school on a full-time course of studies which meets the requirements of the Education Act' and is registered with the Department of Education and Employment.

The first part of the requirement, that of acceptance for the course, is simply established by objective evidence such as an acceptance letter from the educational establishment.

10.2.2 **Full-time course**

Paragraph 57(ii) of the rules prescribes the kind of course for which a student may obtain leave. It must be either:

(a) a recognized full-time degree course; or

(b) a weekday full-time course involving attendance at a single institution for a minimum of 15 hours' organized daytime study per week of a single subject or directly related subjects; or

(c) a full-time course of study at an independent fee-paying school.

Where the course is a full-time degree course, nothing further needs to be shown about the number of hours attendance required. In the case of other full-time courses at private institutions, 15 hours of organized daytime study is required. Guidance defines 'daytime' study more specifically by excluding weekend study and evening classes which start after 6 p.m. Study at the Open University will qualify for entry for certain postgraduate work only (DSP 12.8, August 2007 IDI).

The requirement that the course is full-time is intended to exclude people whose main occupation in the UK is not study but paid work. This not only relates to the question of genuineness but also the protection of the domestic labour market as a preoccupation in immigration policy. The rules on students working during their studies (considered below) and the rules on switching from student leave to other kinds of leave may be seen to vary in accordance with economic and social policies and labour market fluctuations. As part of the PMI, these rules were considerably relaxed. However, the switching rules tightened again in 2007.

10.2.3 Ability to follow the course

The question of whether the student is able to follow the course will have already been assessed by the educational institution, and it is unlikely that entry clearance officers will be equipped to improve on that judgment. As a requirement of the rules, it is not a primary assessment of the student's ability. It is in the immigration rules as being relevant to genuineness, and entry clearance officers should not attempt to go behind the academic judgment of the educational institution. In particular a superficial assessment of English language ability may be misleading and unwise. The DSP advises that adequate English needs to be demonstrated 'in general terms' and where the educational institution offers prior teaching in English or has set an entry standard that the applicant has met, this should be enough. However, in *ECO Islamabad v Asif* [2002] UKIAT 07454, the tribunal held that the ECO was entitled to differ from the University. The applicant's English at the time of arrival was not strong, but he had a place on a ten-week language course preceding his degree course. The ECO was not convinced that he would be able to start a degree course in English even after the language course, and the tribunal held that he was entitled to come to that view. In *DC* [2005] UKIAT 00011 the tribunal held that the applicant's choice to be interviewed by the ECO in her native language should not be regarded as evidence of lack of capacity to pursue a course in English unless she had been warned that that inference could be drawn.

The entry clearance officer may, in order to satisfy themselves that the student is able to follow the course, consider the student's existing educational record and qualifications. The DSP advise that these enquiries are made in the context of the appropriateness of the course for this person and how it fits in with their life plans. General statements about their country's aspirations or development will not suffice. This is also relevant in applying the rule on intention to study and leave at the end of studies.

10.2.4 Intention to study and to leave at end of studies

The intention to study is in a sense, although central, absorbed by the proof of all the other requirements. If the student has been accepted on a qualifying course at a *bona fide* institution, can support themselves and intends to leave at the end of their studies, it would be perverse to make an issue of whether they intended in fact to be a student unless there is clear evidence which raises doubt about this.

The intention to leave at the end has been in the past a more litigated issue because it relates directly to perceived abuse of the rule in order to stay in the UK. Doubt about a student's intention to leave at the end has been a major factor underlying decisions on student leave. Enquiries may cover the cost of studies, the availability of suitable courses in the passenger's country of residence and whether the proposed study is reasonable for a person of his family, social and economic background. This can be assessed by weighing the material benefit to the applicant, including enhanced job opportunities, against the cost of the course.

In October 2001, to attract graduates as workers to the UK, the requirement to show intention to leave was suspended for students applying to undertake a recognized degree course or equivalent (a recognized degree is defined in para 6 of the rules). The requirement remains in the rules, but the IDI advises that it should be disregarded for degree course applicants with an unconditional offer or a conditional offer they have accepted, including where the offer is conditional on successfully completing foundation or English language courses. The change applies also to student nurses, doctors, and dentists. The indications are that the new five-tier system will include a similar provision. This policy change removes this requirement from a large number of student applicants. The paragraphs that follow therefore refer only to non-medical students applying for non-degree courses.

In deciding whether there is cause for doubting that the student intends to leave at the end of their studies, decision-makers should avoid relying on evidence which is purely circumstantial. For instance in the case of *Bourchak* (17209) the adjudicator had concluded that the applicant was unlikely to leave the UK at the conclusion of his studies because soon after his entry clearance interview he started a course at a university in Algeria and because he was nearing the age for military service. The tribunal accepted that the clearest evidence of his intentions, which are after all a state of mind, was to be found in the answers of the appellant at interview. His stated intention had not been challenged by the interviewer and so there was no evidence for doubting it. This decision and the terms of the IDI follow older reported tribunal decisions such as *ECO New Delhi v Bhambra* [1973] Imm AR 14 where it was held that '[g]rounds for doubting the genuineness of an applicant's intentions must be based on some evidence (as opposed to suspicion)'.

The factors referred to in the IDI have been endorsed by case law as relevant to the question of intention to return, and cases have turned on points such as the cost of the course in relation to the family budget, the job opportunities which would be opened to the applicant by the course, etc. The consideration of such factors is a highly value-laden matter. The reported adjudicator's decision in *Islam v ECO Dacca* [1974] Imm AR 83 famously refused to confine anticipated benefit from the course to economic benefit. He said, 'There is still some truth, though hard to discern in these material times, in the Victorian belief that to be a crossing sweeper with a BA degree is better than to be a crossing sweeper without a BA degree. Knowledge for the sake of knowledge is a benefit, whatever way one looks at it'. Furthermore, there was no basis in the rules for confining the applicant's future expectations to his home country. Although at that time the rules were not intended to lead to settlement in the UK, there might be many other countries in which he could flourish.

In *Goffar and Dey v ECO Dacca* [1975] Imm AR 142, the appeals failed partly because the applicants could not show that they had made enquiries about computing opportunities in Bangladesh. This does not mean that the adjudicator was wrong in *Islam*. It is not necessary that job opportunities be available to the student in their home country, but rather that failing to enquire about such opportunities may cast doubt on the student's genuineness. This will particularly be the case where the cost of the course is great in terms of the applicant's family income.

Factors such as whether the applicant has a family or job to go back to are not listed in the DSP as relevant, and cases such as *Seinn Mya Aye* (10100) have established that an incentive to return is not required. Enquiries of this sort may easily turn into looking for such an incentive.

The question of the availability of similar courses in the applicant's home country is material, but is a difficult one to assess as it goes to the heart of the reasons to travel for study. In *DC* [2005] UKIAT 00011 the applicant wished to study for a diploma in health and social care. There might, as a matter of fact, be a course of this kind in the Philippines, but the tribunal accepted that there was need for investigation of the applicant's contention that a British course would carry more weight. This in turn would be relevant to her future job opportunities in the Philippines, a crucial matter in assessing her intention to return at the end of studies. The DSP now refer to the need for the ECO to take into account the worldwide prestige of a degree and/or qualification from the UK, that 'studying in the UK is aspirational and does not always result in a mathematical return on the cash investment', and all the other advantages of studying in the UK (DSP 12.9.1).

10.2.4.1 *End of studies*

The intention which must be shown is to leave at the end of the student's studies. This is not necessarily the end of the course for which they now apply. It may be that there will be a natural progression to further studies, and it is only at the end of such further studies that the student is expected to leave. Paragraph 57 (v) says 'intends to leave the UK at the end of his studies', and case law has consistently interpreted this to mean at the end of all proposed studies, not the present course. For instance, in *X v ECO Karachi* (18688) the appellant intended initially to undertake a course at the City Business College, London, which would last for six to eight months. There would then be a succession of follow-up courses available to him, and he might stay for up to two years before returning to be part of the sponsor's business operations in Pakistan. The tribunal held that the adjudicator had been wrong to require evidence of intention to leave at the end of the first course.

In the five-tier system, students will be expected to have a certification of sponsorship entitling them to study a particular course at a particular institution. Arrangements for extending or changing this have not been published at the time of writing.

10.2.4.2 *Wish or intention*

In the guidance concerning applications after entry the IDI says that a 'student who expresses the wish to remain in the UK beyond his studies should not be refused without the opportunity to clarify his intentions'. This conforms with the earlier trend of case law in which a distinction has been made between a wish and an intention. This question arose because sometimes applicants seem to have been penalized for their own honesty. In the context of a visitor appeal the tribunal in *ECO Hong Kong v Lai* [1974] Imm AR 98 found that the respondent and his family members whom he wanted to visit in the UK would like him to be able to settle there some day, but appreciated that at the present time he did not have a basis for such a settlement. Therefore there was no intention other than to leave at the end of the allotted period, even though the idea of staying was desirable. This raises particular problems for students who would like to work in the UK but at the time of making an application for leave to enter as a student are not in a position to formulate any such intention. The IDI encourages immigration officers not to find an intention to stay when there is in reality only a wish. Now, of course, in the case of degree or medical students, such a wish would be unproblematic as there is no need to prove an intention to leave.

An uncertain or conditional intention to leave the country at the end of studies should not necessarily be detrimental to an application. So held the tribunal in *Sivasubramaniam* (13174) where the appellant stated that he intended to leave the country when his studies were completed 'provided it was safe to do so given the uncertain situation in Sri Lanka and particularly in view of an incident of shooting of certain members of his family and the destruction of his home'. His recognition that he might not be able to return to Sri Lanka immediately on the completion of his studies was simply a recognition of the reality of the situation. The tribunal said that he was if anything 'too honest in merely expressing recognition of his inability to forecast the future'. How and whether this policy will survive the five-tier system is also unknown.

10.2.5 Meeting costs

The rule which directly addresses the requirement of financial independence is para 57(vii), that the student:

is able to meet the costs of his course and accommodation and the maintenance of himself and any dependants without taking employment or engaging in business or having recourse to public funds.

Despite this explicit wording, para 58 provides that leave may be given 'with a condition *restricting* his freedom of employment' (emphasis added) not *prohibiting* employment. For a prospective student a prohibition on working may be given (see later).

The difference between a prohibition and a restriction is significant. A prohibition means that any work done will amount to a breach of condition with the resulting possible penalty of removal (Immigration and Asylum Act 1999 s 10) or criminal prosecution (Immigration Act 1971 s 24). A restriction permits work within limitations.

The nature of the standard restriction on work has changed significantly since the PMI in 1999. It is no longer necessary to obtain the permission of the Department of Employment before obtaining work. Students may now take up to 20 hours' work per week in term-time, and are free to work as many hours as they wish during vacations. Students are also entitled to use Job Centres to look for jobs and apply for them, which they were previously not permitted to do. They may take internships of three months or less with an employer or prospective employer and carry out work placements in limited circumstances.

There are still some restrictions on the type of work that may be done. They may not engage in business, self-employment, or provide services as a professional sportsperson or entertainer, nor 'pursue a career' by filling a full-time permanent vacancy (IDI Aug 2007 Ch.3 Section 3.18.1). In relation to business or self-employment, the case of *Strasburger* v *SSHD* [1978] Imm AR 165 still has force. The appellant was in something of a cleft stick. She was an art student who wanted to stay in the UK as a self-employed artist. She had sold some paintings during her time as a student. In order to remain in self-employment she had to show that she could maintain herself. Unfortunately from that point of view, her earnings were considered insufficient. If they had been sufficient, there would have been a risk of her breaching her conditions as a student. As it was, the tribunal held that sale by an art student of their artwork was not a breach of conditions. Although this was decided under HC 82, it is applicable to the present as a guide to permitted self-employment as a student.

The relaxation of the restrictions on students working during their studies is a reflection not only of reduced anxiety about protecting jobs but also of government desire to attract overseas students who pay higher fees than home students, and who may contribute ultimately to the skilled labour force. Of course the option of working makes study more economically viable, although for the most part students are not allowed to refer to prospective earnings in proving that they will be able to support themselves. The only exception is that an entry clearance officer may take into account earnings from part-time work if the student will be studying at a further education college or university and has guaranteed work at the same institution (IDI Aug 2007 Ch. 3 section 3.17.4).

Paragraph *77* allows the spouses and children of students to work providing the student they are accompanying has been granted leave for 12 months or more. Prior to October 2000 the rule said that 'Employment is to be prohibited except where the period of leave being granted is 12 months or more'. It now reads 'Employment may be permitted where the period of leave being granted is or was 12 months or more'. This more positive wording suggests that this permission is the norm which spouses and children of students could expect. Again, such earnings may not be shown prospectively as a source of maintenance for the family, but if the spouse is already in employment then their earnings may be taken into account (3.15.4). In reality the spouse's earnings may be used to support the student and their family once they have arrived.

To obtain entry, aside from the allowable earnings, common sources of income upon which students may rely are: sponsorship from a private individual such as a relative, sponsorship from a government department or employer, savings and grants (including from UK sources). The IDI also points out that students may be charged low fees or reduced fees or even have their fees waived altogether, and all of these arrangements are acceptable for the immigration purpose of showing that the cost of tuition can be met.

10.2.6 **Extensions of stay**

Students may be given leave for the duration of their course, or for a shorter period. Paragraph 58 says 'an appropriate period depending on the length of his course of study and his means'. The IDI suggests that students should be given leave for the period of the course 'unless there is doubt about them which makes a shorter landing preferable'.

A student may therefore need to extend their stay as a student, either because the leave originally granted was not as long as their course, or because they want to continue with further studies. Applications for extensions will be considered under para 60 of the rules which contains the following requirements.

First, the applicant must have been admitted to the UK with a valid entry clearance as a student or leave in one of the few categories from which switching to student status is permitted (see 10.2.11 below). This applies also to the dependants of students who may have engaged in studies themselves while in the UK with leave as the dependant of a student. The end of their partner or parent's leave will interrupt their studies as they will have to leave the UK and obtain entry clearance to return as a student. Family members of students are not included in the categories from which switching to student status is permitted. A letter of the Home Office IND to an International Student Adviser at Sheffield University stated on 14 December 2000 that this was not a suitable case for a concession. The visa national, who was writing up her PhD, would need to leave the country to obtain entry clearance to return and complete it, as her husband's student leave would expire before she had finished her writing up. Rules introduced on 20 September 2000 to enable extensions of stay for writing up a thesis (Cm 4851, inserting para 69J) would not avail her as she did not originally have student leave in her own right. Despite many rule changes since this instance was brought to the Home Office's attention, the situation remains unchanged.

Second, the applicant must meet all the requirements for student leave and be enrolled on a full-time course of study which meets the requirements for admission as a student.

Third, the applicant must show satisfactory evidence of regular attendance and progress on the current or a previous course. Much of the case law concerns this issue. What a university regards as an acceptable level of attendance to pass the course, the Home Office may not regard as satisfactory. In *WR (student: 'regular attendance', maximum period)* [2005] UKAIT 00170 the Home Office rejected 40 per cent attendance as satisfactory. However, a better attendance at later courses was accepted, taking a global view, by the tribunal. This approach was rejected in *JJ and SS (student: regular attendance: which course?) Gambia* [2007] UKAIT 00050 which held that satisfactory attendance must be on the course for which leave was given.

The question of satisfactory progress is a fraught one as a student may not do well in one course, change to another to which they are more suited and then do better, or they may be struggling, but still getting through on the maximum number of re-sits allowed by the university. Are these circumstances 'satisfactory' in immigration terms? The main question behind the immigration enquiry into these matters is whether the student is genuinely in the UK to pursue studies or is using the study route as a front for other activities, perhaps more lucrative ones. It should not be an enhanced academic selection process.

The question of passing exams after re-sits is dealt with by the tribunal in *SM (paragraph 60(v): 'passing' and 'relevant')* [2007] UKAIT 00068. The rule specifically requires progress to be shown by passing all relevant examinations (para 60(v)). This case points out that the rules provide for extending leave to re-sit exams, so it is not required for immigration purposes that a candidate passes on the first attempt. In *SM* itself, the student had not passed re-sits through extenuating circumstances. The first immigration judge held that this was still satisfactory progress overall, but the tribunal on reconsideration disagreed. The exams had not been passed, the rules allowed no discretion on that matter, and any discretion would have to be exercised outside the rules. The IDI gives some further guidance on how effort with limited success will be regarded.

Where there are doubts as to progress but attendance is satisfactory and all other requirements are met, leave may be granted but with a warning that failure to produce evidence of satisfactory progress could result in a refusal to grant a further extension of stay in that capacity (IDI August 2007 Ch.3 section 3.16.3). In *KL (student: IDI 'warning' about progress)* [2007] UKAIT 00005 the tribunal held that this wording did not give rise to a legitimate expectation of a warning, nor did it mean that the student could be given an extension with a warning if progress was not satisfactory. *JJ and SS* made the same point in relation to warnings about attendance. *ML (student: 'satisfactory progress', Zhou explained)* [2007] UKAIT 00061 follows the same approach as *JJ and SS*, in that later and better progress on other courses was not held to satisfy the requirements of the rule, as progress had to be in relation to the course for which the appellant was given leave. A meritorious applicant could argue for leave to be extended outside the rules. This approach to attendance and progress seems to be more tightly controlled in the tribunal, mirroring the tighter control by sponsoring educational establishments that will be required under the five-tier system (see McKee 2007).

Fourth, the applicant must not, as a result of extension of stay, spend more than two years on short courses at lower than degree level (i.e. courses of less than one year's duration, or longer courses broken off before completion). The intention of this rule is made clear in the sub-heading relating to it in IDI Ch 3 Section 3 para 19 August 2007: 'Short Courses – Perpetual Students'. The paragraph says that the rule is not intended to affect those 'with a clear study plan showing a logical progression from one course to another'. However, it advises that enquiries should be made where a student has 'enrolled on a new course which bears no relation to previous studies' or 'there is any reason to suspect that a student is making his studies an excuse for remaining in the UK for some other purpose'. The limit of two years refers to two years of immigration leave, not necessarily to 24 months spent in study. There may be breaks, but if at the end of the two years the student has spent 20 months in study and four not, this does not give them four months' further leave. The period has come to an end (*WR (student: 'regular attendance', maximum period)* [2005] UKAIT 00170). A course of exactly one year is not a short course (*KM (definition of short course)* [2006] UKAIT 00014).

Finally, official sponsorship must not have come to an end, or if an official sponsor is for some reason unable to continue the sponsorship then they must have given written consent for studies to continue supported by other sponsorship which the student must demonstrate is adequate.

The burden of proof that these requirements are met is on the applicant. There is therefore no legitimate expectation that an extension will be granted simply because circumstances have not changed. Each application for leave to remain in the UK was a free-standing and independent application to be considered afresh. So held the Court of Appeal in *Adegoke v SSHD*, 97/1720/4 22 July 1998.

Where student leave has expired but there is sufficient evidence of the student's place on the next course, the Home Office may give an extension of leave to tide the student over between courses.

There are special provisions in the rules for extensions of stay for re-sitting examinations (paras 69A–F), writing up a thesis (69G–L) and serving as a student union sabbatical officer (87A–F). All these provisions follow the principles of the main student rules, e.g. the time allowed for each purpose is limited, restrictions on working continue, and so on.

It has previously been held that poor attendance on a course does not automatically deprive a student of student leave. In *R (on the application of Zhou) v SSHD* [2003] EWCA Civ 51 the Court of Appeal held that the attempt to remove the applicant as in breach of his conditions of stay was misconceived. He had stopped attending college, and had been working, but only within the limits allowed by his student leave. The Home Office contended that he was no longer a student, but this was wrong. If they believed his studies had come to an end they should have curtailed his leave under the immigration rules, which would then have given him the right of appeal. As it was he had been detained pending removal, for which there was no lawful authority. This situation must be distinguished from a failure to show satisfactory attendance or progress so as to obtain an extension of student leave as in *KL* and *ML* discussed above. *Zhou* was relied upon unsuccessfully by the student in *ML*. Although the distinction is a valid one, it may be that, in the growing climate of integrating immigration control with student progression, the ratio in *Zhou* will be subject to erosion, particularly if attending a nominated institution becomes a condition of leave. Currently, as a Court of Appeal decision, it remains good law. In line with *Zhou*, if a student who has lapsed in their studies leaves the country, their student leave may be cancelled if they attempt to return (*B (Nigeria)* [2004] UKIAT 00055).

10.2.7 Student nurses

There are special provisions in the rules for student nurses, found in para 64 of the rules. Some of the requirements are equivalent to those for other students, namely having been accepted on the course, the accommodation and maintenance requirement, the ability and intention to study, the intention to leave at the end of studies, the requirement not to engage in business or employment except in connection with the course.

The kind of course for which they must be accepted and the nature of the educational institution are naturally different, and rather intriguingly, the rules include a requirement that acceptance on the course must not have been obtained by misrepresentation. Following the October 2001 policy change, student nurses no longer need to show that they intend to leave at the end of their studies as they may be eligible for work permit employment. Although the requirement to intend to leave remains in the rules, the IDI confirms that it should not form part of the entry clearance considerations (Ch 3 5.2.1 March 2006).

10.2.8 Postgraduate doctors and dentists

Paragraphs 70–75 of the rules set out specific provisions for these two groups. Graduates of UK medical schools may take limited periods of employment prior to registration with the General Medical Council, i.e. the usual period that intending doctors must work as a postgraduate trainee on what is now the Foundation Programme before they are fully qualified. The applicant must intend to leave the UK at the end of training unless they obtain work permit employment, a clinical attachment, or they qualify to remain on programmes discussed in the next chapter for highly skilled migrants or those who are self-employed. These rules are substantially more restrictive than they were before 2006, in particular the requirement to graduate from a UK medical school, which excludes the majority of doctors from abroad. This rule change and Department of Health guidance on the eligibility of doctors for the Highly Skilled Migrants Programme were the subject of the *BAPIO Action* litigation discussed in the next chapter.

10.2.9 **Prospective students**

Paragraphs 82–87 of the rules deal with applications to enter as a prospective student. This kind of entry gives the opportunity for someone who wants to study in the UK but does not yet have arrangements finalized to come to the UK before those arrangements are completed. This is one of the few immigration categories from which a person can change to ordinary student or student nurse status.

In order to obtain leave to enter for this purpose an applicant must show:

(i) that they have a genuine and realistic intention of undertaking, within six months of their date of entry, a course of study which would meet the requirements for extension of stay as a student or student nurse; and

(ii) that they intend to leave the UK at the end of their studies or on the expiry of leave as a prospective student if the arrangements do not come to fruition; and

(iii) that they are able without working or recourse to public funds to meet the costs of study, accommodation and maintenance of themselves and their dependants both during the initial period of leave and during their studies.

Note that this group is given a prohibition on working, not a restriction. This can and should be lifted once student leave is given, and the usual restriction imposed. However, during the initial period of leave, which will be a maximum of six months, the student must support themselves from their own resources without taking paid work.

The rules relating to prospective students are the only ones in the student rules which retains the words 'genuine and realistic', a key phrase in earlier case law. There is no indication in the consultation on the five-tier scheme of whether this category will survive.

10.2.10 **Entry clearance**

Since September 2007 all nationalities require entry clearance to enter as a student or prospective student (HC 395 paras 57(viii) and 82(iv)). Following implementation of Immigration, Asylum and Nationality Act 2006 s 4 there will be no appeal against refusal of entry clearance, despite opposition to this proposal from University Vice-Chancellors. It may seem to conflict with the government's policy of issuing a warm welcome to overseas students. The Immigration Advisory Service reported in 2005 (press release 23 February) that they won a high proportion of student appeals, reaching 75 per cent.

10.2.11 **Switching status**

The temporary nature of student leave has previously been fiercely guarded by successive governments to prevent student leave from being used as a path to settlement. In addition to the focus on proving intention to leave at the end of studies, this has also been done by limiting the immigration categories to which a person can switch at the end of their studies.

The rules prevent switching to other temporary categories such as *au pair* (para 92) or working holidaymaker (para 98 which permitted extension as a working holidaymaker was deleted on 7 February 2005), although students who can continue to support themselves and want to sightsee may stay as a visitor for a maximum of six months. Students may stay as Commonwealth citizens with UK-born grandparents seeking employment (para 189), or as a child, dependent relative or partner of a settled person (Part 8 of the rules generally).

The area of most contention and change is that of students staying for work. In accordance with the policy changes reflecting the government's recognition of the need for skilled workers, and the removal of the requirement for degree level and medical students to show intention to leave at the end of studies, an option has been introduced for graduates, student nurses and post-graduate doctors and dentists, to stay for work-permit employment.

The work permit scheme is discussed in chapter 11. Transferring from student to work permit status has in the past been very difficult, in part because it was necessary to leave the UK to make the application for a work permit. This requirement has now been relaxed for graduates. A practice endorsed by the IDIs became a rule on 18 September 2002 by the insertion of a new para 131A in the rules. This allows an extension of stay for employment where the applicant has had leave as a student, has completed the degree course, meets the conditions for work permit employment, holds a work permit and has the written consent of their official sponsor if any. Similar arrangements are indicated for the five-tier system. Equivalent provisions for nurses, doctors and dentists are contained in para 131B.

The Training and Work Experience Scheme was introduced to allow people to do work based training for a professional or specialist qualification, a graduate training programme or to undertake work experience, and switching into this scheme is possible for students (para 119). As with work permits, the employer must make the application to Work Permits (UK) for permission to employ the person in that capacity.

The other side of the coin is the capacity to switch *into* student status. Visitors are no longer allowed to switch into student status, even if they come in the new category, created in September 2007, of 'student visitor' (paras 56K–M). People with student visitor leave may study on short courses but must leave at the end of six months. Prospective students and those on a number of student-related kinds of leave such as to re-sit exams, or as a student union officer or various graduate schemes, may switch into student status, but this is no longer an option for people with leave in other immigration categories.

Note that an application to switch status is an application for a variation of leave which may be refused if the general grounds of refusal apply in HC 395 para 322. There have been a number of cases of refusal of variation of leave to become a student on the basis of para 322(7), namely, a failure to honour a declaration or undertaking as to the intended duration or purpose of the previous leave. In relation to that paragraph the tribunal in *Tekere* 01TH00174 said that an undertaking or declaration was a formal matter, not just a statement of present intentions. It implies a promise, or something more than a mere statement. *Ahmed* v *Secretary of State for Work and Pensions* [2005] EWCA Civ 535 was to a similar effect. A visitor stating their intention to leave is not making a declaration or giving an undertaking. This was followed by the tribunal in *Rwabeta* 01TH01960. It must be so, otherwise para 322(7) could be used to prevent any switch from a temporary category.

10.3 *Au pairs*

There follows a brief treatment of another temporary category of entry, that of *au pairs*. This is given for the sake of completeness, and for more detail reference should be made to practitioner works such as Macdonald or the *JCWI Handbook*.

The relevant immigration rules are paras 88–94. *Au pairs* come to the UK to live for a time with an English speaking family for the purpose of learning English, and to help in the home for a maximum of five hours per day (para 88). They are to receive appropriate time for study, a reasonable allowance, and two free days per week. This is not regarded as an employment relationship, and the description of the *au pair* scheme as given in para 88 is an immigration requirement for entry to the UK; it is not a contract which the *au pair* can enforce once they have entered the UK.

The *au pair* scheme only applies to people between 17 and 27, unmarried, without dependants, who are nationals of the nine countries listed in para 89. This list has shrunk as the European Union has grown, as the *au pair* scheme traditionally applied to Europeans but is unnecessary for those with EC free movement rights. It now consists only of Andorra, Bosnia-Herzegovina, Croatia, The Faroes, Greenland, Macedonia, Monaco, San Marino and Turkey. The *au pair* must not intend to stay in the UK as an *au pair* for more than two years, must intend to leave the UK at the end of their stay as an *au pair,* and be able to maintain and accommodate themselves without recourse to public funds. All these requirements are found in para 89.

In Case C-294/06, *The Queen on the application of Ezgi Payir* the ECJ confirmed the view of Stanley Burnton J in the High Court that *au pairs* come within the definition of 'workers' for the purposes of Article 6 of Decision 1/80 of the Council of the Association between the EU and Turkey. Therefore a Turkish *au pair* may take advantage of rights given, whereby after a year's legal employment she could apply for further leave to remain to work for the same employer, and after three years of lawful residence she could change employers. The two-year limitation was unlawful in relation to Turkish workers.

10.4 **Working holidaymakers**

Finally, this chapter takes a brief look at entry as a 'working holidaymaker'. A number of countries have schemes like this which enable young people to travel and work. The standard visitor visa allowing a maximum stay of six months does not enable an extended experience of another country and its life, but the working holidaymaker scheme gives a greater opportunity by allowing a stay of two years, which can be funded at least in part by paid work.

The details of the scheme are found in HC 395 paras 95–103 (but without 98–100, which have been deleted) and are expanded upon in the IDI Ch 4 s 2, particularly Annex C.

In order to qualify as a working holidaymaker the applicant must be a 'national or citizen of a country listed in Appendix 3, or a British Overseas Citizen; a British Overseas Territories Citizen; or a British National (Overseas)' (para 95). Appendix 3 lists Commonwealth countries with the exception of Lesotho. They must be between the ages of 17 and 30, unmarried (unless their spouse qualifies under the same rule and applies to come too), have no child who would be more than five years old at the end of their stay, intend to leave at the end of the working holiday, be able to pay their fare to leave, be able to maintain and accommodate themselves without recourse to public funds, and intend

only to take employment incidental to a holiday, and not to engage in business, or to provide services as a professional sportsperson, and in any event not to work for more than 12 months during his stay. (para 95)

It is not necessary for the applicant to have a sponsor in the UK, although a sponsor is one way of proving that there will be no reliance on public funds. Alternatively, such proof can come from savings, realistic work plans and so on.

All this builds up the picture of a young person who has not settled down, and in fact earlier versions of the immigration rules provided explicitly that the scheme was for an extended holiday before settling down.

In 2002 the Home Office carried out a consultation to consider reform of the scheme. Figures it had produced showed that in 2000, 96 per cent of applicants were from New Zealand, Australia, Canada, and South Africa, in other words, there were few applicants, and even fewer successful applicants, from New Commonwealth countries. In *Pancholi v ECO Bombay* [2002] UKIAT 04170 the greater ease of applicants from wealthier countries in fulfilling the rules was noted by the adjudicator. Equally important, in the particular case the tribunal was careful to point out that the Indian applicant did fit the requirements of the rules. The rules could be applied in a non-discriminatory way providing the decision-maker did not look for the stereotypical Australian traveller. Clearly there were problems in new Commonwealth nationals getting access to the scheme, but whether, noting the advice of the tribunal in *Pancholi*, the problem lay in the rules or their application was another question.

During the consultation, the discriminatory effect of the scheme was reported on by respondents, and the Home Office suggested that there was abuse of the scheme by people working full-time during their stay. The consultation resulted in rule changes which removed the restriction on the kind of work a holidaymaker could do. The age limit was raised to the present 30, the reference to work being 'incidental' was removed, and replaced by a requirement that the entrant intends to 'take employment as an integral part of a working holiday' (para 95(vi)). The intention appeared to be to address the discriminatory effect of the scheme by allowing more freedom to work, at the same time tackling abuse by legalizing what working holidaymakers were said to be actually doing. The requirement to have no commitments which would require a regular income was also removed (Cm 5949) and changes made to enable a working holidaymaker to stay in the UK for work permit employment in certain circumstances (HC 395 para 131D).

In the course of the consultation the government considered but rejected the idea of extending the nationalities involved, considering that the other changes would be sufficient to widen the scheme's availability. These should be seen in the context of endeavouring to control entry to the UK and prevent illegal working while at the same time widening legal entry for work.

After the 2003 changes, some posts experienced a significant increase in applications. Comparing regional figures for 2002–3 and 2003–4, applications in Equatorial Africa and South East Asia rose by around 400 per cent and in South Asia by more than three times this figure. Refusal rates fell in all these regions, perhaps reflecting that the rules were easier to comply with. However, they were still high, particularly in South

Asia (62.6 per cent) and Equatorial Africa (33 per cent). Quayum and Chatwin (2004) report that after these rule changes, ECOs in some posts were still applying (a) the old rules and/or (b) the old attitudes. There was not the rate of successful applications from poorer Commonwealth countries that might have been expected if the rule changes had really removed the discrimination in the system. Compare the refusal rates for Australia and the South Pacific, fairly steady between these two years at 0.2 and 0.3 per cent. Interesting too, in comparing rich and poor countries of origin are the refusal rates with the Southern Africa region: Pretoria 7.7 per cent, Harare 37.4 per cent (2003–4).

On 8 April 2005 the government suspended applications in Malaysia, Sri Lanka, Botswana, Namibia, and Nigeria (The Times 9 April 2005). On 8 February 2005 the rules changed again to limit work to one year of the applicant's two-year stay and partially restore the restrictions on the kinds of work a holidaymaker might do by once again prohibiting engagement in business or professional sport. The capacity to change to work permit employment was limited to shortage occupations. These changes apparently reinstated those parts of the rules one might imagine would most affect applicants from poorer countries. On 15 June 2005 the specification was reinstated that entry clearance is for two years, as it has been since 1994. This appeared to have been omitted in error in the earlier changes (letter IND to Camden Community Law Centre 14 July 2005).

The restoration of the limits on work was explained by the Home Office in the same letter by concerns that 'the scheme might have come to be regarded as an avenue for entry for the purposes of economic migration, and that its cultural exchange ethos might be undermined'. At the same time the scheme is becoming subject to bilateral agreements which include provision for the UK to suspend its operation at any particular diplomatic post where the rise in applications exceeds the average rise in applications overall and affects the working capacity of the post.

The net result of the consultation, the finding of discrimination against poorer applicants and abuse of the system by successful applicants, the subsequent changes and their reversal, seems to be to slightly tighten the system against abuse by specifying 50 per cent working time in the rules (though this is still unenforceable unless a condition is attached to leave), to support the UK's need for workers by gearing work permits to shortage occupations (see chapter 11), but to leave the discriminatory aspects unaffected.

An attempt to prove discrimination failed in *SK India* [2006] UKAIT 00067. The case gives some insight into the decision-making process.

 Key Case

SK India [2006] UKAIT 00067

The appellant planned to visit the UK for two years on a working holiday and had a job offer through his brother who lived in the UK. The details of the job were unclear. The offer of accommodation was of a house owned by the appellant's brother which was already rented out to other tenants. The appellant's plans for his UK trip were unformed, but the impression that comes through the case is that he was keen to have the opportunity that the scheme allowed for two years in the UK. His application was refused on the basis that the ECO did not find him credible and so did not believe that he would return to India at the end of the two-year period. The appellant appealed on the rules and on race discrimination grounds.

Clearly, evidence in this case was thin, and so the question in law is what the ECO believed on balance of probabilities about the appellant's intentions. The claim of race discrimination was based on the ECO's assertion that the appellant would have little to return to in India. It is clear that the concreteness of plans is geared to the question of credibility. The discrimination claim failed as the tribunal rejected the reference to India as direct race discrimination, and the statistical differences between refusals in different entry clearance posts was not sufficient to establish that comparable groups had been treated in a discriminatory way (see chapter 8).

In *AK (WHM – maximum 12 months work) Bangladesh* [2007] UKAIT 00064 it seems that the tribunal was revisiting *Pancholi*, though no reference was made to this case. The appellant was a national of Bangladesh, planning to come to the UK for two years as a working holidaymaker, and with an offer of part-time employment of 15 hours per week throughout his stay. The appellant said: 'I only intend to work part-time so I will get money to cover my expenses and will not be a burden on anyone. I will not work full-time because I wish to benefit from my working holiday by seeing sights, meeting new people and tasting the UK culture and lifestyle' (*AK* para 6). He would be staying with a family member, the arrangements for which were accepted by the adjudicator, and would also be visiting his cousin, sister and family.

The tribunal held that an applicant could not work for more than 12 months in total, even if the work was part-time. The fact that he intended to work throughout his stay in their view prevented the work being incidental to the holiday. In so deciding, the tribunal drew upon the reasoning in *AG (Working holidaymaker: 'incidental') India* [2007] UKAIT 00033. Here, the tribunal held that, where an applicant who only intended to stay for 12 months intended to work for 12 months, such work would not be incidental. It was clear from the wording of the rule that the 12-month limit was a qualification of the basic criterion, which was that the work was incidental. This did not entitle a holiday maker to work for 12 months regardless of other factors, and whether work was incidental to a holiday would depend on the facts of each case.

In *AK* the tribunal adopted this reasoning to hold that the work could not be incidental because the appellant's intention was to work throughout the time.

These cases raise questions about the purpose of the rules. In *Pancholi* the purpose of the rule was given, quoting from the earlier case of *Malik* (01/TH/02564):

The purpose of the rule is to enable young Commonwealth citizens to come to the United Kingdom for a holiday, which they can finance by taking employment from time to time, part-time or full-time in the United Kingdom. Employment is permitted only if it is incidental to the holiday. The essence of the rule is holiday. It does not provide the opportunity to take employment independent of holiday. We agree that holiday can mean different things to different people and in construing the word 'holiday', one must bear cultural values and sensitivities in mind. We do not disagree with the proposition that the word 'holiday' should be given a broad meaning so as to include spending time with relatives. Sightseeing is not essential to a holiday but time out or rest is.

The tribunal relied on this to refute the cultural stereotype to which the adjudicator referred, and which required sightseeing as a major part of a holiday. The tribunal said, in *Pancholi*:

Even if the Appellant were to work sixteen hours a week for the whole of the two years, this would be considerably less than half of what is normally regarded as a full working week and less than half of the time available to him. The fact that the Appellant has pre-planned his employment in this detail does not…mean that he has placed greater emphasis on work rather than 'holiday'. (para 20)

Table 11 Changes to the working holidaymaker rules

Requirements of immigration rules	Pre August 2003	August 2003 to February 2005	February 2005 to date
Commonwealth or British national	Yes	Yes	Yes
Age limit	17 to 27	17 to 30	17 to 30
Absence of financial commitments at home	Yes	No	No
Can pay for onward or return journey	Yes	Yes	Yes
Unmarried or married to another WHM	Yes	Yes	Yes
Maintain and accommodate without public funds	Yes	Yes	Yes
Restrictions on kind of work	Yes	No	Yes
Work to holiday must be	Incidental	Integral	Incidental
No dependent children	Yes	Yes	Yes
12 month limit on work	In guidance	In guidance	In rules
No previous WHM leave	Yes	Yes	Yes
Tribunal allows part-time work for whole period of stay	Yes	No new decision on this point	No

The tribunal in *AK* went in the opposite direction on comparable facts. However, they did not take a purposive approach to construing the rules, as did the tribunal in *Pancholi*, but rather what it called its 'ordinary meaning': 'There can be no doubt it seems to us that the primary requirement is that the employment will be incidental to the holiday and that any period of employment will not exceed 12 months in total'. The 12-month requirement was not in the rules at the time of *Pancholi*, but was a rule of guidance applied by entry clearance officers.

The changes in the working holidaymaker provisions are summarized in Table 11.

It is worthwhile to consider from this summary whether the changes that have been sustained from this period of consultation and change have alleviated discrimination or not.

10.5 Conclusion

The temporary purposes reviewed in this chapter facilitate travel, and cultural exchange and learning especially for young people. By and large, they do not fit the image of what is considered to be 'immigration' and, indeed, the *Black's Law Dictionary* definition regards immigration as entry to a country 'for the purpose of permanent residence'. Nevertheless, as we have seen, immigration law and immigration control are concerned with regulating these movements, which are the very essence of what travel (as opposed to immigration) is all about for many people. The earlier dominant concerns with avoiding people gaining settlement and access to the UK labour market is breaking down now that the UK is going through another period of need for workers. It is entry specifically for work, therefore, that we shall move on to consider in the next chapter.

QUESTIONS

1 Is the existence of family life for the purposes of Article 8 dependent on the legal context in which it arises?

2 The Department for Education and Skills encourages universities to recruit overseas students. The Court of Appeal in *Asif* said that the ECO could refuse leave to a student on the basis of his English language ability. Who should decide whether a student is able to follow a course of study?

3 How would you have redrafted the working holidaymaker scheme?

 For guidance on answering questions, visit www.oxfordtextbooks.co.uk/orc/clayton3e.

FURTHER READING

Dunstan, R. (2003) 'Family visitor visa applications: an analysis of entry clearance officer decision-making in 2002' *Immigration and Nationality Law and Practice* vol. 17, no. 3, 170–178.

Dunstan, R. (2004) 'Family visitor visas: ECO decision-making 2000–2003', *Immigration, Asylum and Nationality Law* vol. 18, no. 2, pp. 100–105.

Gelsthorpe, V., Thomas, R., Howard, D., Crawley, H. (2004) 'Family visitor appeals: an examination of the decision to appeal and differential success rates by appeal type' *Immigration, Asylum and Nationality Law* vol. 18, no. 3, pp. 167–185.

Gillespie, J. (1994) 'The new immigration rules: visitors and students' *Immigration, Asylum and Nationality Law* vol. 8, no. 4, pp. 126–128.

McKee, R. (2007) 'Tightening up? "Managed migration" may manage to make migration more messy' *Immigration Law Digest* vol. 13 no. 2 Summer 2007 pp. 7–9.

Quayum, M. and Chatwin, M. (2004) 'For Whites only? Does the working holidaymaker scheme still discriminate?' *Journal of Immigration, Asylum & Nationality Law* vol. 18, no. 2, pp. 94–99.

UKCOSA Manual (2008) (London: Butterworths).

11

··

Entry for work and business

SUMMARY

This chapter deals with the law relating to entry for work. It gives a brief history of the development of this branch of immigration law, then considers the operation of the work permit system and the rules for non-work permit employment. There is commentary on the imminent development of the points-based system.

11.1 **Introduction**

In the previous two chapters we have seen that the immigration rules restrict or prohibit paid work for people who enter the UK for other temporary reasons. Entry for the purpose of work is only permitted in accordance with the particular schemes and rules governing work. Leave to enter for work is always for a limited period initially, although such leave may lead eventually to settlement. Working in the UK is a right for EU nationals, though limited in the case of nationals of newer member states; often a necessity for those who seek settlement; permitted for some categories of entrant; prohibited for others, and for those whose skills or money the UK seeks to attract, it is a lawful and positively encouraged means of entry. In modern day conditions the distinctions between these groups are breaking down. Castles regards the merging of work and settlement as an inevitable process. The natural pattern of migration which he describes is that as spouses arrive and children are born, foreign workers lose their mobility (Cohen, R. (ed.) 1995). However, the trend of present UK policy seems to be to try to reverse this process and keep categories more separate.

This chapter concerns the entry of workers as workers. There are a number of specific ways in which a person may lawfully work in the UK. First, they may be someone who does not need permission or further permission to work. Second, they may qualify under the Workers' Registration Scheme. Third, they may be eligible for a work permit. Fourth, they may come to the UK to do work which is expressly provided for by the immigration rules and Immigration Directorate Instructions, so-called non-work permit employment. Fifth, they may qualify as self-employed business people under the immigration rules. Finally, they may come within one of the special schemes for people with certain qualities, characteristics, or assets. We shall deal with each of these possibilities in turn.

First, we shall look at the history and development of the law, then at the current legal provisions in that light.

11.2 A brief history of entry to the UK to work and the development of the work permit scheme

Work permits began in 1916 as a form of permission to work which was issued only to foreign nationals, i.e. non-Commonwealth citizens including Europeans. Work permits were issued for certain kinds of skilled work, but Dummett and Nicol comment that the purpose of the scheme in these early times was 'not very clear' (*Subjects, Citizens, Aliens and Others*, 1990:111). Only a relatively small number of foreign nationals came to work in the UK and the scheme was in part a carryover from the wartime practice of monitoring the presence of 'aliens'. It may be recalled that at this time Commonwealth citizens were British subjects and had, in theory, an unfettered right to enter the UK, though few actually did so.

After the Second World War there was active recruitment to fill Britain's labour needs. Thousands of work permits were issued following very specific recruitment drives, e.g. of Italian men for coalmining. In 1945 the government instituted the European Voluntary Workers' Scheme (EVWS) which for six years recruited Europeans from the refugee camps for three-year contracts in jobs assigned by the Ministry of Labour. They were to be single people without dependants; they initially obtained no settlement rights and were not treated as full citizens. Alien workers could be directed towards specific occupations as a condition of entry whereas British subjects could not. Paul's work reveals a mixed and changing agenda in relation to these European workers. Crudely summarized, this consisted initially of explicit short-term recruitment to fill labour shortages, then, after initial successes, government began to think in terms of 'the benefits that come from the assimilation of virile, active and industrious people into our stock' (Paul 1997:84). The expectation shifted towards selected European migrants learning English, marrying British citizens, integrating, and solving the labour problem. The Ministry of Labour maintained the right to deport those who ' "through ineptitude or general low mental capacity" or "undesirable character" proved useless' and to refuse entry to disabled refugees or married women with children (Paul 1997:79). The welcome was conditional, and strongly controlling, but national resources were devoted to making it work. In its crudest form the recruitment of foreign workers may be seen as like the operation of a valve, opened when the nation needs certain kinds of workers, and closed when it does not. Bevan, writing in 1986, paints this kind of picture (e.g. p. 278). While it may be seen that even today the form of the work permit scheme is based on national need, allowing recruitment for the skills and jobs which the resident work force cannot supply, there are also rights for the worker to be joined by their family and to apply for settlement in due course. The EVWS and other work permit schemes for Europeans after the Second World War illustrate the valve model with a double agenda. The new workers were selected initially for their usefulness to the labour market and their returnability, being aliens, and therefore entirely subject to immigration control. Quickly, however, they were selected for their assimilability, being white and European.

Low pay and local resentment often accompany the employment of foreign workers, and this may have been a factor contributing towards the shortness of the life of the EVWS scheme. Dummett and Nicol (1990:176) refer to trade union opposition, for instance that of the National Union of Mineworkers, to Poles and Italians being employed in the mines. Another factor may have been that European workers were no longer needed as Commonwealth citizens were filling the vacancies. As described in chapter 1, Commonwealth servicepeople, who had fought or otherwise served Britain during the Second World War, returned to make a living and a future in the UK. During the 1950s, Commonwealth citizens were actively recruited by major employers such as London Transport, and the British Hotels and Restaurants Association, with inducements such as the payment of fares to the UK. Much of this work was low paid. As with the EVWS, public opinion ranged between regarding the new workers as saviours of the nation or as taking the jobs of British workers. Paul suggests that in government the welcome was not even ambivalent towards the 492 British subjects who arrived from the West Indies on the *Empire Windrush,* in 1948: 'The colonials were met and housed to avoid "disorder and with the determination that this was to be a once-only affair' (Paul p. 118). The linkage made between labour market issues and race is covered in chapter 1, and the reader is referred to that chapter for fuller discussion.

During this period, then, there were two systems of entry for work operating alongside one another. For foreign nationals the work permit system continued. Public attention, however, was focused not on the entry of foreign nationals but of Commonwealth citizens, who entered by virtue of their right as British subjects, but did so at this time because of the labour shortage and accompanying recruitment campaigns.

In 1962 vouchers were introduced for Commonwealth citizens. Category A vouchers were for Commonwealth citizens with specific jobs to go to; Category B were issued by British High Commissions overseas to Commonwealth citizens with recognized skills or qualifications considered to be in short supply; Category C was open, but issued on a 'first come first served' basis, with a priority for war service. Work vouchers, unlike work permits, carried a right to immediate settlement. However, prior to the scheme, Commonwealth citizens would have been able to settle anyway, and the voucher scheme limited their right to do so. Commentators note that even from its beginning it was a process which subjected Commonwealth citizens to the UK's market needs, and for which their settlement was a necessary concession (see, for instance, *Worlds Apart: women under immigration and nationality law* (ed. Bhabha, Klug and Shutter) WING (1985) and Holmes, *John Bull's Island: Immigration and British Society* (1988)).

The 1965 White Paper restricted entry further by abolishing Category C vouchers and limiting the rest to 8, 500. The Immigration Act 1971 completed the process by bringing foreign nationals and Commonwealth citizens within the same work permit scheme. Work vouchers were abolished altogether. The remaining workrelated advantages of being a Commonwealth citizen were lost, with the exception of the non-permit basis for entry mentioned below for Commonwealth citizens with a UK born grandparent. On the same date as the 1971 Act came into force, the UK became a member of the European Communities, giving European nationals the right to travel to the UK for work.

In 1979 the work permit scheme was reviewed. This was a time of high unemployment, and the result of the review was to tighten the conditions for obtaining a work permit, so that these only became available for workers with a high degree of professional skill, qualifications, or experience. In 1989 economic circumstances were different, and a further review had a rather different outcome. Devine and Barrett-Brown note that 'there was sustained economic growth with an increasing demand for highly skilled labour, an increase in internationalization in the way business was operating and substantial inward investment by foreign companies' (2001). The Department of Employment was then responsible for the work permit scheme. In the light of these economic conditions its traditional policy of protecting the resident labour force needed some modification to support the development of an enterprise economy. For instance, this required certain applications to be processed more quickly and with fewer demands on employers where they were clearly furthering business growth and investment. The 1989 review therefore resulted in the development of a two-tier system within the work permit scheme. Tier 1 was for applications which would be processed with less investigation. This two-tier system remains in place today and its current criteria will be examined shortly.

In the twenty-first century the conditions of the labour market are different again and the terms of the debate also different. A research report for the Home Office, *International Migration and the UK: Recent Patterns and Trends*, summarized the issues as being 'the contribution labour migration can make to alleviating the possible impacts of demographic change; a need to compete in a global skills market to remain economically competitive; and a need to recruit overseas workers to meet specific labour shortages' (Dobson, Koser, Mclaughlan and Salt 2001). The first of these three issues, that of Europe's ageing population, was also discussed in the United Nations report of 2000, Replacement Migration. Projections of the numbers of migrant workers that would be needed to sustain European economies briefly became headline news. There was an announcement of change of policy by Minister for Immigration, Barbara Roche, who declared that there would be a new route of primary immigration for people with the skills Britain needed (The Independent 21 July 2000). The labour migration survey casts doubt on these projections, and additionally points out that migrant workers also age, so migration is not a complete answer to the problems of an ageing population. Nevertheless, it has a part to play, and all three factors obtained a place in forming government policy as evidenced in the 2002 White Paper *Secure Borders, Safe Haven* (Cm 5387). This White Paper was significant in indicating, for the first time since the 1960s, that there might be a positive role for new primary immigration, 'managed migration' to meet the need for workers: 'if we are able to harness the vitality, energy and skills of migrants, we can stimulate economic growth and job creation' (para 3.5).

Globalization and the dominance of information technology are also changing the picture very rapidly. Transnational companies need to place their own skilled workers in countries where they choose to site their operations, increased industrialization in developing countries creates needs for training and travel, ease of travel and transport opens opportunities for workers and for education which in turn changes expectations. For instance, in 1992 the European Union sponsored schemes which allowed approximately 86, 000 students to study in other European countries. A decade earlier there was almost no exchange of this kind (Findlay in Cohen, R. (ed.) 1995).

The work permit scheme was opened up to a significant degree by a review carried out in 2000 and 2001. Qualifications of eligible workers were reduced, occupations in which there were shortages were included in the faster procedure of Tier 1 and switching employers within the UK became easier. From its inception, the work permit system had been administered by the government department concerned with employment, by a unit now called Work Permits (UK), formerly the Overseas Labour Service. In June 2001 Work Permits (UK) was transferred from the Department of Education and Employment to the Home Office. A Statement of Changes to the Immigration Rules changed the name of the Department in the rules but no other changes were made to the rules or the legal basis for the issue of work permits. In conjunction with this change the powers of Work Permits (UK) were expanded by enabling them to grant work permit extensions and in-country applications, without the applicant needing to correspond separately with the immigration department. This was also in the interests of speed and streamlining for employers who already have someone available to do the work they need. BIA are therefore only involved when the application is made (as most are) from outside the UK. This attempt to make the system more responsive to the needs of business seems, simply from the figures, to have worked. The number of extensions almost doubled in 2004 as compared with 2000.

The 2002 White Paper Cm 5387 recognized shortages of workers in the UK in the most and least skilled sectors of work, and proposed opening up more lawful routes for economic migration. A general intention to move to the UK to improve one's stand-ard of living by working has not been and still is not a lawful basis for entry unless the application comes within allowable categories. The White Paper concept of 'man-aged migration' was implemented not in the Nationality, Immigration and Asylum Act 2002 but in schemes and rules outside statute. For instance, like other industrial-ized nations (see Mclaughlan and Salt 2002), the UK introduced a new Highly Skilled Migrants Programme (HSMP), aimed at the most skilled, which may lead to settlement. Significantly for later developments, both the HSMP and the new innovator scheme were based on a points system, common in other Commonwealth countries but not previously used in the UK. Expansion of the working holidaymakers scheme was also proposed as discussed in the previous chapter, and of the Seasonal Agricultural Workers Scheme (SAWS) considered below. In May 2003 a new sectors-based scheme was intro-duced which extended the work permit scheme from its traditional base in professional work to fill needs in the food-processing and hotel and catering industries (Cm 5829).

The fact that many asylum seekers are highly skilled and professional people have led some commentators to make the link between the UK's labour shortage and skilled asylum seekers present here but unable to work. See, for instance, the *Immigration, Nationality and Refugee Handbook* (JCWI 2002:421). However, governments have been reluctant to legitimize contributions by asylum seekers to the labour market. On 24 October 2003, the then Home Secretary, David Blunkett, announced that 15,000 families whose asylum claims had been outstanding for more than three years would be considered for settlement and work in the UK. This was to 'clear the decks' before tougher measures were proposed (press release 295/2003). On 13 November 2003 entry clearance was made compulsory for all work permit holders who were coming to the UK for more than six months, effectively sealing off the possibility of asylum seekers obtaining work permits.

On 1 May 2004, ten new member states acceded to the European Union. The UK, unlike most of its European partners, granted nationals of the new member states an immediate right to work, provided that they register under the Workers' Registration Scheme. Regular Accession Monitoring Reports detail the range of occupations in which Accession State nationals are engaged. They include work as bus, lorry and coach drivers, care workers, teachers, researchers and classroom assistants, dental practition-ers (including hygienists and dental nurses), GPs, hospital doctors, nurses and special-ists. The main immediate impact on the UK's labour market was felt in agriculture and fishing, in which employment grew sharply (Portes and French 2005).

At the same time, quotas were established in the Seasonal Agricultural Workers Scheme, and then reduced, and quotas were reduced also in the newly created Sectors

Based Scheme. As already described in the last chapter, criteria for the working holidaymaker scheme were tightened again very soon after having been relaxed. The positive tone towards economic migration which emerged in the 2002 White Paper did not seem to be sustained. In April 2004 the government announced a ' "top to bottom review" of managed migration routes to assess the extent to which they were subject to abuse or otherwise open to improvement' (*Selective Admission* para 4.8). The results were a number of measures tightening immigration control, not limited to the economic categories which were the broadly understood scope of the term 'managed migration'.

In February 2005 the publication of the White Paper *Controlling our Borders: Making migration work for Britain* (Cm 6472) announced the introduction of a tiered points system encompassing all immigration for work or study, privileging the most skilled both in terms of entry and settlement. In July a consultation document was published, entitled 'Selective Admission', in which the criteria were uncompromisingly economic. After the closure of the consultation period, the new managed migration scheme was published in March 2006 as Cm 6741, *A Points-based System: Making Migration work for Britain*. The structure of the scheme remains as in the consultation paper. Entry is based on points for attributes and points for control factors. The attributes relate to the migrant's particular contributions towards the labour market, such as their income, qualifications etc. Some will be treated as essential and some will simply contribute towards the overall score. For instance, an undergraduate degree might be essential for some kinds of work, and the level of existing income might simply add points. Control factors relate to whether the individual will leave at the end of their work or study period. The proposed control factors for which points will be awarded are: certificate of sponsorship (except for Tier 1), funds, previous compliance with immigration conditions, and for some categories, English language ability. The certificate of sponsorship and funds will be requirements, while the other two will be factors for which points will be awarded but which are not necessary for a positive decision (except for Tiers 1 and 2, where English language is a requirement).

Tier 1 was described in the consultation paper as for 'the most highly skilled individuals and people with large sums of money to invest' (para 6.6). Points will be awarded for youth, English language ability, high earnings and recognized qualifications. It incorporates the existing Highly Skilled Migrant Programme. Tier 2 is for 'skilled individuals with a job offer from a UK employer'. Tiers 1 and 2 may lead to settlement. Tier 3 is entitled 'low skilled workers'. Existing schemes for 'low-skilled work' will be phased out. Initially, the government said that there would be a new, quota-based scheme set up only for countries with which there are approved arrangements for return of migrants, but already this has been abandoned, and low-skilled work is only available to Romanian and Bulgarian workers. The Command Paper points out that there are other migrants lawfully present who often take up low-skilled work, but do not need further immigration clearance to do so, for instance working holidaymakers and students and their partners. The distinction between Tiers 1 and 2 and so-called low-skilled work is drawn in a way that does not recognize some skills or specialisms. While in Tier 1 or 2 the applicant has to be a person specially suited for the job, in Tier 3, people are treated by the scheme as interchangeable. Some restaurant owners disagree: 'most east Europeans wouldn't know a thing about the spices we use or the way we prepare dishes'. Language would be a barrier too (Enam Ali, Guild of Bangladeshi Restaurateurs, The Guardian 30 January 3006). Tier 4 is for students; Tier 5 encompasses two disparate groups: those on 'youth mobility' schemes, which is intended to amalgamate the present *au pair* and working holidaymaker schemes, and 'temporary workers'.

All except Tier 1 will need a sponsor. A significant feature of the new scheme is that sponsors will be drawn further into the system of immigration control, being required to report on whether the migrant is engaged in the occupation for which they came. Sponsors too will be rated (A or B), and rewarded for approved levels of compliance and monitoring with greater freedom in their sponsorship decisions. Initial applications will be made online abroad by the proposed worker, who will be able to get an indication of the likely success or otherwise of their application by filling in an online question-naire. Sponsors will be expected to collaborate with prospective workers at this stage to assist their application. Universities will also be expected to monitor overseas students' attendance and performance, though most do not have any system for distinguishing between absence from classes as a result of sickness, boredom or simple default. Sponsors may include the largest corporation, as well as the smallest local business.

A disturbing and radical aspect of the proposed scheme is that applications will be made online and at entry clearance posts abroad and there will be no appeal against refusal. The Immigration Law Practitioners Association says that the current work per-mit scheme: 'is probably the most efficient and effective employment related scheme in the world. It is employer-led and accessible. Work permit applications are processed by teams of highly trained caseworkers' (response to consultation, November 2005). Decision-making in the entry clearance scheme on the other hand, as we have seen, is still of questionable quality (chapter 7). 'Selective Admission' was published at the same time as the government proposed in the Immigration, Asylum and Nationality Bill 2005 to remove the right of appeal from entry clearance decisions. The minister's jus-tification in Parliament was that decision-making in the new system would be robust and on the basis of objective, accessible criteria (HC Debs July 5 2005).

The proposed scheme does not appear to include self-employed business people, and some existing categories of entry such as domestic workers are not included. There is a profound contradiction between the avowed intention to serve the economic needs of Britain, and the transformation of entry for work into a non-responsive, routinized immigration decision. The proposals pay scant regard to factors such as the capacity of a worker to have their family with them, change into different employment or settle. They seem to be based on a view that economic advantage is to be calculated in terms of money and labour during working hours, turning the clock back to the early days of the European Volunteer Worker scheme. Indeed an interesting parallel emerges from BBC news coverage of working conditions for eastern Europeans working for one major agricultural employer in the east of England:

The workers sleep in bunk dorms but also have entertainment facilities, free English lessons twice a week and barbecues and a sports pitch for summer nights. On days off, there are coaches to tourist attractions such as Oxford or Alton Towers. ('A foreign corner of an English field' 11 October 2004)

Compare this list of requests from the Ukrainian representatives of European Volunteer Workers in 1948: observance of more national holidays, more organized sports within the hostels, more native-language books in the library, more English lessons and a Ukrainian edition of the BBC show 'Workers' Playtime' (Paul p. 88). The phrasing clearly indicates that these facilities (apart from 'Workers' Playtime' in Ukrainian) were already being provided.

As discussed earlier, Paul compared this with the more grudging reaction to black British subjects who entered to work in the 1940s and 1950s. In 2005 government reaction to new Commonwealth take-up in the working holidaymaker scheme was to tighten the conditions again (see previous chapter) and when Bangladeshi restaurateurs moved swiftly to take up the opportunity to recruit workers in the new sectors-based scheme was to close the catering and hospitality sector. Simplistic comparisons may be unwise. Nevertheless the overall impression of the policy underlying the new scheme was that it was based on a vision of an open door for people who are already highly skilled, highly paid, and fluent in English; a monitored scheme for people from eastern Europe to fit in with labour demands, overlapping with a highly controlled scheme for people to do low-paid work, probably also from eastern Europe; cultural exchange including study for people who are financially independent, and immigration control for the rest.

Following the publication of the new scheme in 2006 the options for foreign medical graduates to complete their training and obtain work in the UK were dramatically reduced. This rule change and the litigation which followed are described more fully below. As commented upon by Stanley Burnton J in the High Court, the majority of doctors adversely affected by these changes were from the Indian sub-continent, but the racial impact of these changes was neglected until the last minute (see the *BAPIO* case below). The Highly Skilled Migrants Programme was amended without notice in November 2006 to remove the credit given for experience and increase the credit given for earnings in the UK, applying these criteria to extensions of leave for those already in the UK, and undermining at a stroke the expectations of tens of thousands of people who had already migrated to the UK and made the undertaking required by the scheme to make the UK their permanent home. A key reason given by the government was that many were not in highly paid employment as the scheme envisaged, but were working as, inter alia, taxi drivers (letter of Minister of State to JCHR 18 May 2007). This action was confirmed as lawful in *AA and others (Pakistan)* [2008] UKAIT 00003. The possible relevance of racial discrimination to the situation was not only disregarded, but in effect those who may have been discriminated against were subjected to the further distress of termination of their leave and deportation if they refused to go. A further likely effect of the emphasis on earnings rather than experience was to make it more difficult for women to qualify. Thus, very mixed messages were given during 2006 to highly skilled migrants in the UK or those who were considering applying for entry.

Tier 1 and the sponsorship register are planned to come into effect in the first quarter of 2008; Tiers 2 and 5 in the third quarter of 2008, and Tier 4 in 2009. Given the current state of flux in relation to immigration for work, the present schemes are described here more in principle than in detail so that the reader may appreciate the position under the current law, and also the nature of the changes as they occur.

11.3 Needing no permission to work

There are various people who may enter the UK to work without needing any kind of permission from the immigration authorities. These are:

(a) British citizens, including those from the Overseas Territories, as they have right of abode (British Overseas Territories Act 2002 and Immigration Act 1971 s 1);

(b) Irish citizens, who are exempted from immigration control in the Common Travel Area (Immigration Act 1971 s 1(3) and see chapter 7);

(c) EEA nationals, as they have a right to freedom of movement for the purpose of work under the EC Treaties, though limited for A8 and A2 nationals (see below and chapter 6);

(d) Commonwealth citizens with a right of abode in the UK (see chapter 3);

(e) People who have indefinite leave to remain in the UK (see chapter 7), in other words, are settled;

(f) People with entry clearance in the form of a certificate of entitlement (see chapter 7); and

(g) People who are on their 'probationary period' as a married or unmarried partner (HC 395 paras 282 and 295B).

In addition to those who need no permission to work there are three groups of people who may be granted permission to work, after which the Home Office exercises no further control over the kind of work that they do. These are, first, people who have been granted refugee status; second, those students who are covered by the general consent discussed in chapter 10, which permits them to work without restriction in the vacation and up to 20 hours per week in term-time, and their dependants; third, Commonwealth citizens with UK ancestry. This last is a special category in the immigration rules, HC 395 paras 186–193, which provide that a Commonwealth citizen aged 17 or over who can prove that one of their grandparents was born in the UK, that they intend to seek work in the UK, and can maintain and accommodate themselves and any dependants without recourse to public funds may be granted entry clearance and subsequently leave to enter for five years in this capacity. The capacity and intention to work is all that the applicant needs to prove, they do not have to have a particular job to come to. This kind of leave may lead to settlement, though numbers of people seeking and obtaining such settlement are low, at about 4, 000 each year. Providing that the general terms of entry have been kept, so that the person has in fact been working, it is not necessary to show that employment has been continuous. Using its power to discriminate on the basis of information (see chapter 8), the Home Office suspended applications from Zimbabweans in 2004, having formed a view that they were abusing the scheme. In November 2005 applications were resumed (Home Office press release 21 November 2005). The Command Paper gives no indication of the future of this scheme under the five-tier system.

11.4 Workers' Registration Scheme

As described in chapter 6, nationals of countries that acceded to the EU in 2004 and 2007 have restricted access to the labour market. They must apply through a Workers' Registration Scheme. The full details of this are now available in English and in the languages of the A8 countries on the BIA website.

Workers and employers both have seen the registration system as onerous, and so not always complied. One problem of non-compliance is that it opens the worker to exploitation by employers operating outside the system. Such employers may not pay tax and national insurance, which then means that the worker may not receive benefits to which they are entitled and may have no redress in case of unlawful dismissal, failure to pay a minimum wage, breaches of health and safety provisions, and so on. The effects of poor working conditions are compounded by the fact that new member state nationals do not have access to means-tested social benefits. Keith Puttick describes how the lack of access to the welfare system and often to housing creates serious problems of poverty and disadvantage for this new group of migrants. For illustration of an alternative, see Puttick's comparison with Sweden's attempt to avoid creating second-class working conditions for A8 nationals.

The sectors-based scheme is now only open to Bulgarian and Romanian nationals. Otherwise, access to work for Bulgarian and Romanian nationals is only to employment in listed categories. These are work permit employment and various specified occupations including *au pairs*, domestic workers, postgraduate doctors and dentists, teachers, nurses and ministers of religion.

11.5 Work permit employment

11.5.1 Nature of work permit scheme

The work permit scheme will be subject to reorganization in 2008 under the points-based system. This section describes the scheme as it stands in 2007. The kinds of criteria and in many cases the actual criteria are unlikely to change a great deal under the new system. What will change is the legal process. This will have repercussions for applicants who wish to challenge decisions and perhaps constitutionally, in that decision-making may be dispersed in a new way. The work permit system is already interesting constitutionally, and unique in immigration law, in that work permit decisions, although vital to obtaining leave to enter, are taken outside the IND.

Until 2001 the work permit scheme was governed by two separate government departments, reflecting the governmental interests in both immigration and employment. The operation of the scheme is discretionary and decisions are based on policy rather than legal rules.

Leave to enter for work permit employment is needed, and this is granted under the immigration rules (paras 128–130) by immigration officers or entry clearance officers. However, the role of the Immigration and Nationality Directorate in reality has been secondary to the role of Work Permits (UK) as the influential decision is the one to grant the work permit. This is the sole province of Work Permits (UK). Following the creation of the Border and Immigration Agency in April 2007, Work Permits (UK) as a separate name will be phased out in due course.

The maintenance of this separate aspect of decision-making has certain repercussions. Bevan wrote that decisions as to whether work permits should be issued, in what numbers and for what occupations were taken by a government department whose decisions were 'unsupervised and surrounded by secrecy' (1986:280). The fluctuating nature of the labour market and of policies as to how it should be served means that the policy on dealing with certain kinds of work permit applications changes frequently. The conditions of eligibility for work permits are not found in the immigration rules but in guidance notes issued with work permit application forms and other notes and statements, which are accessible on the website of Work Permits (UK) (working-intheUK.gov.uk). Bevan's assessment would therefore be only partly true today as the criteria are more publicly available than 20 years ago. However, their discretionary and non-statutory basis means that they are open both to change without formalities and to variations to suit economic policy. The way that criteria will be applied is therefore largely unregulated and is accessible mainly to specialists who maintain contact with decision-makers. This flexible and policy-based nature of the work permit scheme has been able to grow up easily outside the IND structure, but bringing Work Permits (UK) within the Home Office has not changed these characteristics as they derive not only from the involvement of a separate government department but also from the scheme's economic role and purpose.

The legal basis for the scheme is unique. Neither the immigration rules nor the immigration statutes refer to the making of work permit decisions, but only to the existence of work permits. The decision to issue a work permit, although now made within the Home Office, is not a Secretary of State decision within the Immigration Acts. McLaughlan and Salt make the intriguing suggestion that the power to issue work permits comes from 'the Crown Prerogative within the context of the Immigration Act 1971' (2002:136). However, this may be doubted, as even before the House of Lords decision *Council of Civil Service Unions v Minister for the Civil Service* [1985] AC 374 HL which established that an exercise of the prerogative was subject to judicial review, work permit decisions were treated as judicially reviewable (see, for instance, *Pearson v IAT* [1978] Imm AR 212, CA). Furthermore, the issue of work permits does not find a place in established accounts of the prerogative, and the Court of Appeal in *R v SSHD ex p Northumbria Police Authority* [1988] 1 All ER 556 cautions against using the prerogative as a legal basis for government action in the absence of any specific authority. In *R v Secretary of State for Education and Employment and SSHD ex p Shu Sang Li* [1999] Imm AR 367 Dyson J describes the scheme as 'operated on behalf of the Secretary of State for Education and Employment' and 'not a statutory scheme' but one which 'sets out the policy adopted by the Secretary of State in relation to work permits.' *Macdonald's Immigration Law and Practice* describes the work permit scheme as 'a manifestation of policy similar to Home Office concessions outside the Immigration Rules' (2001:370). The conclusion seems to be that the issue of work permits is indeed a manifestation of policy, just that, without any further legal basis. Scarcely anyone would want to challenge the existence of the power, which is of benefit to all concerned. The question of its nature is relevant to challenging decisions, as discussed below.

11.5.2 Challenging work permit decisions

As decisions to issue or refuse work permits are not subject to the immigration rules nor are they an exercise of the Secretary of State's discretion outside the rules, they are not appealable within the immigration appeals system. All that may be appealed to the immigration appellate authorities is the immigration decision to refuse leave to enter or remain when a work permit or extension of a work permit has been refused. However, such an appeal is unlikely to succeed as lack of a work permit is a valid reason for refusal of leave (by Nationality, Immigration and Asylum Act 2002 s 88 a work permit is an 'immigration document', the lack of which may found an unappealable refusal of leave). The effect of this is that the 'real' decision, the one which actually determines whether the prospective worker will gain entry, is the work permit decision and this is subject only to a limited right of internal appeal within Work Permits (UK). The lack of appeal to any judicial body is a further illustration of the nature of the work permit scheme as an expression of economic policy which is not, like other immigration decisions, treated as a matter affecting the exercise of fundamental rights. Once Immigration and Asylum Act 2006 s 4 is in force, there will also be no appeal against refusal of entry clearance.

A failure to issue a work permit may be challenged by judicial review, but the highly discretionary nature of the scheme means that a challenge is unlikely to succeed (see, for instance, *ex p Li*).

As the effective decision is the work permit decision, and leave will not be given under para 129 without a work permit, the Secretary of State or immigration service could be argued, in administrative law terms, to be unlawfully delegating or fettering their discretion. Variations on this argument were made in a number of early cases, but did not succeed. In the case of *Munasinghe v SSHD* [1975] Imm AR 79 the tribunal held that it was within the power of the Home Secretary to provide, in rules made under Immigration Act 1971 s 3(2), for consultation with the Department of Employment, and this is so even though the Department of Employment is not assigned any responsibility directly by the Act itself. In *Lim Chow Tom v SSHD* [1975] Imm AR 137 the argument of unlawful delegation was made, relying on the case of H. *Lavender & Sons Ltd v Minister of Housing and Local Government* [1970] 3 All ER 871 in which the minister was found to have unlawfully delegated planning powers because he held himself bound by the decision of another minister (Agriculture, Fisheries and Food) in relation to a planning application. However, the tribunal did not accept this argument as they considered *Lavender* distinguishable on the basis that under the immigration rules the Home Secretary was required in certain cases to refer applications to the Department of Employment. This distinction is not entirely clear, and is even less clear when the tribunal expand on their reasoning, saying: 'if the Department of Employment (against whose decision there is no appeal within the Immigration Rules) is not prepared to approve the proposed employment the respondent [i.e. the Home Secretary] has no discretion in the matter'. It is indeed difficult to see the difference between this formulation of the position and a minister fettering their own discretion. A similar conclusion was reached in *Chulvi v SSHD* [1976] Imm AR 133 in which the tribunal found that the Home Secretary had discretion in relation to leave to enter but that that discretion 'should not be exercised contrary to the principle... that the granting of permission to take a particular employment is essentially a matter for the Department of Employment'. The case law was reviewed by the Court of Appeal in *Pearson* which came to the same conclusion. The immigration rule then in force was held to be a guideline which indicated how the Home Secretary would 'as a matter of general policy, exercise his discretion' but there would still be room for making an exception. The Secretary of State retained the final decision on entry, as reinforced by the High Court decision in *R (on the application of Thapa) v SSHD* [2004] EWHC 3083 (Admin) in which Bennett J held that the issue of a work permit did not give rise to a legitimate expectation that the claimant would be given leave to remain in the UK.

It follows from what has been said above that there is a limited number of appeal cases in this area of immigration law. Judicial review of refusal of a work permit is available, but success is unlikely, and Macdonald suggests that employers may be reluctant to pursue refusals in the courts (2001:372). Indeed it is evidently more cost-efficient for them to employ someone else rather than hold a post open and fight for a work permit for a particular individual. The prospective worker of course is the real loser, and they may well be outside the country with little prospect of launching successful litigation, especially if the employer is not keeping the post open for them. Whether these issues will remain live under the new five-tier system will depend upon what level of transparency is achieved. The new system seems to envisage that all applications will be made by the entrant rather than the employer. This will not bring them much closer to a remedy, though a system of internal review is proposed, as at present within Work Permits (UK).

Not being governed to a significant extent by accessible and binding rules of law, work permits are an area of practice in which the publication of Immigration Directorate Instructions (IDIs) and guidance notes is of crucial importance. In this chapter we shall rely on those of the IDIs which have been published and on the guidance notes available on the Work Permits (UK) web site. Paragraph numbers are not given for the guidance notes, because although the substance does not change greatly, minor changes are introduced every few months and the paragraph numbers change accordingly. However, a very full contents list makes it easy to find particular subjects.

11.5.3 Structure of work permit scheme

The work permit scheme may be divided into three categories: first, business and commercial; secondly, sportspeople and entertainers, these two groups forming together the main work permit scheme; and, thirdly, the training and work experience scheme (TWES). It is the business and commercial scheme which is divided into the current Tier 1 and Tier 2. The application for a work permit is made by the prospective employer and must be an application for a named person to do a specific job. The application for entry to the UK under the immigration rules is then made by the employee, under HC 395 para 128, as a holder of a valid work permit. Working in the work permit employment specified is then a condition of leave to enter. Under Immigration and Asylum Act 1999 s 10 a person who breaches that condition may be removed. However, a change of location for the same employer would more usually be dealt with by negotiation and amendment, and application may also be made to change employer. See *SSHD v R (on the application of Lim)* [2007] EWCA Civ 773, discussed in chapter 8, for an example of judicial process when this informal route was not followed.

11.5.3.1 *Business and commercial*

Qualification level
The work permit scheme has become geared to facilitating the entry of skilled and qualified people. For an employer to obtain a work permit, the post for which they are recruiting must require certain minimum qualifications. Additionally, for a work permit to be issued the particular applicant who has been appointed must show that they meet these qualifications and are thus a suitable person for the job. The minimum qualifications are:

(a) a UK equivalent degree level qualification; or

(b) a Higher National Diploma level qualification which is relevant to the post on offer; or

(c) a Higher National Diploma (HND) level qualification which is not relevant to the post, plus one year of relevant work experience; or

(d) three years of experience using specialist skills acquired through doing the type of job for which the permit is sought. This should be at National or Scottish Vocational Qualification (N/SVQ) level 3 or above.

These qualification requirements are easier to fulfil than those which applied before the 2000–1 review when experience was required in addition to a degree and HNDs were not regarded as relevant qualifications. N/SVQ level 3 experience would be for instance as a suitably qualified paramedic, dental nurse or veterinary nurses. Experience gained through working illegally in the UK will not be taken into account.

No suitably qualified resident worker
The idea that the job cannot be filled by the resident work force has historically been fundamental to the work permit scheme. 'Resident' means someone who is an EEA national or has settled status in the UK within the meaning given by s 33 Immigration Act 1971. As an EEA national has a right under the EC Treaty Article 39 (ex 48) to enter the UK for work, there is no necessity for a work permit in their case, though A8 and A2 nationals are subject to a Workers' Registration Scheme, as mentioned earlier. A settled person by definition (s 33) has no restrictions on their stay in the UK which includes no restriction on their working. The inclusion of EEA national in the definition illustrates that policy on the protection of the workforce is now a Europe-wide matter, not just a national one. This requirement will be used in Tiers 2 and 3 of the five-tier programme.

It is for the employer to show that they have attempted to recruit a resident worker but that no suitable person is available. Extensive evidence is required of recruitment methods and the reasons why a suitably qualified resident worker was not employed, nor one who with training could do the job. Copies of advertisements must be sent to Work Permits (UK) and these must give all details of the post including salary and experience required. They must also show that the post was advertised in the most suitable media, Europe-wide, for that job.

Since the 1989 review which divided the work permit scheme into two tiers, the requirement to show there is no suitably experienced and qualified resident worker does not need to be met in relation to posts coming within Tier 1, and since the 2000 review, increasing numbers of posts have been brought into that exempt category.

Where the advertising requirements do apply, the relaxation of qualification criteria discussed above does not necessarily help the employer to obtain a worker through the work permit scheme. The intention of relaxing qualification criteria was to help recruitment to meet the labour shortage. However, there is a paradoxical effect in that if the requirements for the post are easier to fulfil, it may be harder for an employer to show that they cannot fill the vacancy from the resident labour force.

Tier 1 of the Work Permit Scheme
The recognition of a skills shortage in the UK and the increasing demand of globalized business for mobility and flexibility have led to greater numbers of work permit applications being designated as falling into Tier 1, which is speedier and less onerous for the employer. Applications for business and commercial permits falling into this tier are not required to give such extensive detail of the proposed employee's qualifications and experience, and do not have to demonstrate that it has not been possible to recruit from the resident labour market by sending details of recruitment methods and advertising. Applications falling into Tier 1 include intra company transfers and board level posts.

Applications for work permits to effect intra company transfers enable transnational companies to transfer skilled employees within the company to work in the UK. For the company to qualify the British and overseas companies must be part of a group of companies controlled by the same parent or holding company or one company must own the other. The post must need an established employee who has essential company knowledge and experience. For the individual to qualify, they must have at least six months' experience working for the overseas company. Board level posts are at senior board level where the individual has a personal daily input into directing the company at strategic level and substantial board level experience.

The growing transnational quality of the business world creates a different need for mobile workers from the traditional purpose of the work permit scheme. It is not simply that the national economy lacks particular skills or workers and looks elsewhere to recruit them, but for large companies national boundaries have less meaning. The work permit system has adapted to this working environment. Findlay identifies a new group of migrant workers which he calls 'skilled transients', that is, 'highly skilled persons moving internationally on relatively short-term assignments before returning to their place of origin or transferring to another international location' (Cohen:1995).

Tier 1 also includes new posts that are essential to an inward investment project which brings jobs and money to the UK. This is for investment by overseas companies, not individuals. Individual investors and people intending to set up their own businesses may obtain entry clearance in their own right under special categories of the immigration rules (HC 395 paras 201 and 224) and do not come within the work permit scheme. The rules for individuals setting up in business however are far more onerous. In order for posts to qualify under Tier 1 the investment in this category must be a minimum of £250, 000.

The remaining category of Tier 1 applications is that of occupations in which there is deemed to be a shortage of suitably skilled and qualified people. Shortages are identified by meetings with governing bodies of the industries concerned. Occupations are divided into categories, which at July 2007 were engineering, health care and 'other' consisting at that time of teachers and vets. Within each category the shortage occupations are listed. The lists are available at workingintheUK.gov.uk. By their nature, the lists change regularly. The kinds of occupations included in the shortage category were considerably expanded in the 2000–1 review. This seems to be an unambiguous extension of the reach of the work permit scheme and this is where the expansion of the minimum qualifications has a significant effect. Here there is both no advertising requirement and unlike the categories which are for the benefit of transnational companies, the individual recruited does not need to have an existing relationship with the employer. The intention is clearly to help recruit nonresidents to obtain skilled jobs which are not sufficiently filled by resident workers. Occupations are not included in this category just because the skills, knowledge, or experience that they require are rare. If, although unusual, there are enough people to fill the need, then there is no shortage and the occupation will not be listed.

Skills shortages have been identified in collaboration with the Sector Skills Development Agency, and mainly with direct input from employer bodies about their labour shortages. As part of the points-based system the government initially proposed a Skills Advisory Board to fulfil this role. However, the structural changes in 2007 resulted instead in the Migration Advisory Committee, which has a broader remit. It is a smaller body, made up of academics and experts in broader labour market issues. The aim is that this body does not represent the narrower sectional interests of particular employer groups, but takes a wider perspective on labour market needs. The minutes of their meetings can be read at www.bia.homeoffice.gov.uk/sitecontent/documents/aboutus/workingwithus/mac/minutes. The new committee's stakeholders to be regularly consulted include the major employment-related organizations such as the Confederation of British Industry (CBI) and the Trades Union Congress (TUC).

Other criteria

Apart from the establishment of qualifications, and either fulfilling the advertising requirements or showing that the application comes within Tier 1 as described above, there are a number of other criteria applying to both Tier 1 and Tier 2 applications. These are set out in the guidance notes. In summary, the employer must be British-based, and the employee must be employed by that British-based employer. This may sound too obvious to be worth mentioning, but the distinction is between employment by a British employer and a temporary transfer from an overseas subsidiary or a secondment from overseas. Where the situation is really one of temporary transfer or secondment then it is more appropriate to retain the overseas contract of employment. Note that the General Agreement on Trade in Services (GATS) allows employees of overseas companies to work in the UK when their employer has contracted to perform work in the UK, and a GATS work permit may be issued accordingly (see www.working-intheuk.gov.uk). The vacancy must also be a genuine one which existed before the work permit application as the work permit scheme is geared to meeting existing economic need, not to creating jobs for particular individuals.

In general, an employee would work at the employer's place of business. However, it may also be that an employee works at the address not of the business but of its clients. In this case the employer must be providing a service at the client's address, not just sending personnel, otherwise there is no true distinction between an employer and an agency.

As we have seen, employing foreign workers on lower pay and worse conditions than resident workers has, in addition to the simple injustice, has caused a great deal of opposition to those foreign workers. It is a condition of the grant of a work permit that the pay and conditions of employment must be at least equal to those normally given to a resident worker doing similar work. In particular they must meet all relevant UK legislation including by payment of the national minimum wage, compliance with the Working Time Regulations (1998), SI 1833/1998 as amended, payment of Class 1 National Insurance contributions and PAYE income tax and the employer must also comply with any relevant licensing requirements.

This is welcome, but historically the worst practices probably occurred outside the work permit scheme, and this is still the case. Whereas the scandals of the 1960s were seen in the long hours and low pay of for instance the Pakistani workers in northern towns and cities, the most acute problem of exploited foreign workers identified now by the government is to be found in illegal working. The issue of illegal working is discussed later in this chapter.

Finally, the potential employee must not have a controlling or significant interest in the British-based company. This is identified as a shareholding of more than 10 per cent. This was raised in the 2000–1 review from the previous rough figure of 5 per cent, but seems inconsistent with the 49 per cent shareholding allowed to a sole representative (see below). As in that case, the intention here is to ensure that the prospective entrant is an employee, not self-employed or an owner of the company.

11.5.3.2 *Sportspeople and entertainers*

Work permits for sportspeople and entertainers are part of the main work permit scheme. The basic principles relating to sportspeople and entertainers are not very different from those in the business and commercial section. The principle of not employing a person where a resident worker could have done the work is the same, as are the requirements for illustrating that all efforts have been made to employ a resident worker. However, the emphasis on the qualities of the person for whom the permit is obtained is rather different. Instead of showing that there is a need which is not being met, the emphasis is more on showing the unique contribution that can be made by the person or group in question, though this is a question of emphasis rather than absolute difference.

A separate set of guidance notes is available at workingintheuk.gov.uk. Sportspeople will be those who are 'internationally established at the highest level in their sport, and whose employment will make a significant contribution to the development of that particular sport in this country at the highest level'. Entertainers are 'people who have performed at the highest level and have established a reputation in their profession; and people/groups who are engaged to perform or do work which only they can do'. Entertainers may apply as individuals; they may also apply as groups if they are a unit company, which is 'a large group of entertainers who have performed together in their own country and have toured overseas as part of an established production before entering the UK'. For instance, an orchestra will be a unit company, a pop group will not. Members of a pop group would thus have to apply individually. Cultural artists are defined as 'people who are skilled in foreign arts that are rare or unavailable in this country and can make a contribution to the arts, cultural relations and cultural awareness'. Finally, technical or support people may enter in this category if they have proven technical or other specialist skills, and their 'work is directly related to the employment of an entertainer, cultural artist, sportsperson or a dramatic production'.

Where someone makes a unique contribution because of their particular skill or creativity the question of available resident workers becomes irrelevant. The government has agreed with the governing bodies of various sports that individuals with a certain level of international standing will be granted work permits without the need to show that no resident worker is available. In the case of men's football, for example, a player must have played for his country for 75 per cent of its competitive 'A' team matches and the player's country must be 70th or above in the official FIFA world rankings for the relevant period. For established entertainers or cultural artists there is no need to consider whether a resident worker could do the job. If Madonna is touring, fans do not want to see someone else instead. There is also a list of festivals to which artists may travel to appear without a permit. The list for 1 May 2007 to 30 April 2008 was of over forty festivals including, for instance, the Edinburgh International Festival and Glastonbury. The proposal in the March 2006 Command Paper was to include festivals in Tier 5 of the points-based scheme, and to require performers to obtain a business visit visa. After an outcry in Scotland over the effect on the Edinburgh Festival (e.g. Work permits 'threat to Fringe', Scotsman.com 3 March 2007) this is being reconsidered.

11.5.3.3 *Duration of work permits*

As part of the 2000–1 review, from 1 November 2000 the duration of work permits is longer and more flexible. They may be issued for any period up to 60 months, depending on the job. For entertainers and sportspeople who come for an event, the duration of the permit is limited to the time that is needed for the engagement to be completed.

For both business and sports or entertainment purposes it is possible to apply for a multiple entry permit which allows workers based overseas to enter for short periods on a regular basis rather than applying for a new work permit every time they want to come to the UK. Multiple entry permits are issued for a minimum of six months and a maximum of two years (HC 395 paras 199A and B, inserted by Cm 5597). After five years of work and residence the work permit holder may apply for settlement (HC 395 para 134). As is usual for settlement applications, the grant of settlement is a discretionary matter (*Parviz Saddati* (11564)), though of course the discretion must be exercised fairly and rationally. The Home Office's Immigration Statistics show that numbers of those who obtained settlement on this basis remained quite steady from 1996 to 2002. Then figures nearly doubled in 2003 and again in 2004, they rose to an all-time high of 25,470 in 2005, then dropped sharply in 2006 to 11,270, which was below the 2004 level. In 2005 and 2006 the total number of people who settled for employment related reasons was 63,015 and 31,830 respectively.

11.5.3.4 *Switching into work permit employment*

The work permits scheme is designed for a British employer to bring in a specific employee from abroad. This raises the question, what if they want to employ someone who is already in the UK but who cannot legally work without a work permit?

If the worker is already in other work permit employment in the UK, since 2000 the prospective new employer does not have to show that no resident worker is available, providing the new role is of the same kind as their original work permit employment. Where the worker changes the kind of job they do, whether within the same employer or for a new employer, a recruitment search will have to be carried out to satisfy Work Permits (UK) that no resident worker is available.

The immigration rules used not to make any provision for switching into work permit employment for a person who was already in the UK in another immigration capacity. As the rules were silent on the point there was a discretion to allow an extension of stay for this purpose, and the use of this discretion developed in accordance with the policy of retaining graduates in the UK. IDI Chapter 5 Annex C Aug/01 para 3 explained that the discretion was primarily to facilitate the employment of graduates in shortage occupations, 'to minimise disruption to UK businesses that have urgent need of a particular person with specific knowledge and skills' and 'to support inward investment'. The concession was used in respect of student nurses, postgraduate doctors and dentists as well as other graduates, and Commonwealth holidaymakers. In accordance with the 2002 White Paper proposal (Cm 5387 para 3.14), the rules now make explicit provision for these and other highly skilled groups to stay for work permit employment (HC 395 para 131).

11.5.3.5 *Entry as a work permit holder*

So far in this part of this chapter we have been looking at the policy and guidance issued by Work Permits (UK) which indicate when a work permit will be granted. The decision to give leave to enter for work permit employment is a separate one taken by immigration officers and is governed by the immigration rules paragraphs 128–130. The first three requirements set out in para 128 will almost invariably be met if a work permit has been issued. These are that the applicant:

(i) holds a valid work permit;

(ii) is not of an age which puts him outside the limits for employment; and

(iii) is capable of undertaking the employment specified in the work permit.

Additionally the rule requires that the applicant does not intend to take employment except as specified in the work permit, is able to maintain and accommodate themselves and dependants adequately without recourse to public funds, and in the case of a work permit which is valid for 12 months or less, intends to leave the UK at the end of the approved employment. On 13th November 2003, rule change HC 1224 introduced a requirement for all work permit holders to have entry clearance unless their permit is for less than six months or they are a British national. Until this rule change it seemed that immigration requirements did not in practice add much in the way of hurdles to overcome for most work permit applicants, and there seemed to be a trend towards a more perfunctory role for immigration officers in work permit cases. At this early stage before the points-based system comes into effect, it carries signs of both an increase in immigration control involvement in decisions on entry for work, because of that decision formally being moved to entry clearance posts, and a decrease, in that the enhanced role of sponsors and the online application checking for applicants suggests a more commercial and private law arrangement.

11.5.4 **Training and Work Experience Scheme (TWES)**

The significance of TWES is reduced since the 2000 amendments to the work permit scheme as many of the people who would formerly have been admitted under TWES will now come within the main scheme. As in the main scheme, since 13 November 2003 entry clearance is required for all TWES trainees unless their permit is for less than six months or they are a British national (HC 395 para 116(vii) inserted by HC 1224).

As the name implies, the purpose is to enable individuals to gain skills and experience through work-based learning, which builds on their previous education and training and which they intend to use on their return overseas. TWES permits are issued either for work-based training leading to a professional or specialist qualification or for a period of work experience. TWES trainees must be employed by the employer who made the application in accordance with the full standards of pay and conditions which would apply to a resident on training or work experience. However, unlike the main work permit scheme the role of a TWES entrant, either for training or work experience, must be supernumerary, i.e. extra to the employer's normal staffing. This is to avoid the TWES scheme being used to take the place of permanent jobs.

Training must be completed in the shortest possible time, so Work Permits (UK) will expect a TWES trainee normally to take examinations at the first possible sitting. Permits for training will be issued for the expected period of the training to obtain the desired qualification (HC 395 para 117) and former time limits no longer appear in the rules, although a normal maximum of five years appears in the TWES guidance.

The minimum entry level qualification for TWES is N/SVQ level 3 or equivalent, but the person may also need to have relevant work experience to enable them to benefit from the programme. The qualification to which the training leads should be a professional or specialist qualification which requires an NVQ level 3 for entry to training. Work experience must be managerial or at least NVQ level 3 or equivalent.

TWES permits are not issued for sports and entertainment or multiple entry.

11.5.4.1 *Switching into and out of TWES*

The only immigration status which enables the holder to switch into TWES is that of student (HC 395 para 119(i)). A student may obtain a TWES work permit to stay in the UK as a TWES trainee after the end of their studies if all the other requirements of the rule are met. A person in the UK in any other immigration capacity must leave the country in order to apply for TWES. It is possible for a TWES permit holder, with consent of the Home Office, to transfer between employers to do the same kind of training or experience, but only for the balance of time left on their original leave to enter or remain.

A TWES permit holder may not switch directly into work permit employment. In order to obtain a permit on the main work permit scheme they must have been out of the country for 12 months if they had a TWES permit for up to 12 months, or 24 months if they had a TWES permit for longer than 12 months. This buttresses the purpose of TWES, which is that the trainee will return to their home country to use their experience or qualifications, and this should be borne in mind at the application stage as TWES is not a route to settlement.

The Command Paper does not indicate how this scheme would fare under the five-tier system.

11.5.5 **Doctors and the *BAPIO* case**

Over a period of around 20 years, the terms on which overseas medical graduates may complete their medical training or work in the UK have been changed many times. A short history of the rule changes may be read in the judgment of Stanley Burnton J in *R (on the application of BAPIO Action Ltd and Yousaf) v SSHD and Secretary of State for Health* [2007] EWHC 199 (Admin).

 Key Case

R (on the application of BAPIO Action Ltd and Yousaf) v SSHD and Secretary of State for Health **[2007] EWHC 199 (Admin)**

Until 2006, the principal means of entry for a medical graduate was through Permit Free Training, which enabled an International Medical Graduate (IMG) to complete their medical training in the UK and then return to their home country. In April 2006, rule changes were introduced so that only a graduate of a UK medical school could benefit from Permit Free Training. The crucial background information is that four new medical schools had opened in the UK, and UK medical graduates had increased by 56 per cent. The need for medical graduates from abroad had reduced. Alongside the rule changes, the Department of Health issued guidance that removed the points that had been awarded for doctors to obtain leave to remain on the Highly Skilled Migrants Programme. The employment of doctors was brought within the work permit scheme, but subject to a resident labour market test. There were transitional arrangements, nevertheless there was a severe impact on the lives of many doctors. The situation of the second claimant in the High Court challenge, Dr Imran Yousaf, was described as follows:

> He obtained his primary medical qualification in Pakistan. He then worked there as a junior doctor for 2 years. He came to the UK in 2004 with the intention of continuing his postgraduate medical training. He took and passed part 1 of the PLAB in Pakistan, and then came here and took and passed part 2. The fees for the PLAB tests together with the costs of a visa and of travel to the UK amount to a very considerable commitment for someone from Pakistan. However, he had not succeeded in obtaining a

post before the change in the Immigration Rules was announced in March 2006. As a result, he had incurred substantial debts during his period here. He could no longer remain under PFT (permit free training). The transitional arrangements did not apply to him. He would not have been able to obtain a position under the HSMP. He said that if he had known that PFT was under threat, he would not have come to the UK or remained here. (para 32)

Tragically, Dr Yousaf took his life three weeks before judgment was given in the High Court.

The challenge by the British Association of Physicians of Indian Origin (BAPIO) related to the failure to consult them about the rule change and the Department of Health guidance. This challenge was lost as there was no statutory obligation to consult, no previous established practice of consultation (cp. *Council for Civil Service Unions v Minister for the Civil Service* [1985] AC 374 (the GCHQ case), and BAPIO were unable to establish that fairness required it. The High Court did find that the failure to carry out a Racial Equality Impact Assessment was unlawful, but as an assessment had later been carried out the rules were not quashed on that basis. The Court of Appeal found that associated guidance by the Department of Health was unlawful ([2007] EWCA Civ 1139, see chapter 8).

The legal basis for the challenge is discussed in chapter 8.

11.5.6 Sectors-based scheme

This scheme was introduced in 2003 to meet shortages of workers in the hotel and catering and food processing businesses (mainly meat and fish). The shortages were in occupations which would not meet the usual requirements of the work permit scheme. A quota of permits was issued; the first tranche on 30 May 2003 included 7, 500 set aside for workers from EU accession countries. This was made possible by a ministerial authorization of discrimination under the Race Relations Act 1976 (see chapter 8).

The distinction between immigration and work permit decisions became painfully apparent. In Bangladesh in particular, there was a rush to apply for permits. On 15 June 2004, the government announced, as an interim measure prior to the introduction of country-specific quotas, a limit on the number of SBS permits that may be issued to a single nationality (per Keith Best, IAS Chief Executive, 11 October 2004, Curry Life Round Table Conference). The quota for Bangladeshi applications had already been reached in the hospitality sector so this sector was soon afterwards suspended for Bangladeshi nationals. However, 89 per cent of the prospective workers were refused entry clearance. The employers had paid £153 for the work permit, but the application of immigration criteria, particularly the requirement to show intention to leave at the end of 12 months, demolished most of the applications. Bangladeshi restaurant owners ended feeling aggrieved that their expectations had been unfairly raised (per Keith Best as above). The entire quota for the hospitality sector was suspended in June 2005. During the same period the quota for accession state nationals was not filled (see Annual Report of Independent Race Monitor 2003–04).

The Sectors-Based Scheme is now (since 1 January 2008) limited to Romanian and Bulgarian nationals aged between 18 and 30. In key respects the scheme is like the rest of the work permit scheme, as the employer must show that there is no resident worker available to fill the job, and so on (HC 395 paras 131I–K). The occupations listed are in the fish and meat industry and mushroom growing. They include fish filleters and packers, animal gut removers, meat bone breakers, slaughterers and trimmers.

11.6 Specified occupations – non-work permit employment

Non-work permit employment for groups and occupations specified in the immigration rules gives the third basis upon which a person may lawfully work in the UK. All need entry clearance, with the exception of seasonal agricultural workers who need a Home Office work card issued by an approved scheme operator. Importantly at the present time, until the implementation of the 2006 Act, these groups all have a relevant and substantive right of appeal, unlike work permit applicants. The rules in each case require that the person will be able to maintain and accommodate themselves without recourse to public funds, and that the person does not intend to take employment except within the terms of that particular rule. In the case of all except teaching exchanges and seasonal agricultural workers the applicant must intend to work full-time. In chapter 10 we considered the rules for *au pairs* and working holidaymakers. These are also special categories of entry for work purposes under the rules, and were separated out because they have historically more in common with students and visitors.

For details of the particular categories and requirements to be met under these sets of rules, reference should be made to the rules themselves and a practitioner work such as *Macdonald's Immigration Law and Practice*. Here we are concerned to pick out common threads, issues of principle, and to identify the part played in immigration control by these specific categories. For the most part the occupations listed entail certain ties to the country from which the worker comes, which cannot be replicated by a resident of the UK. There is no competition with the resident work force for permanent jobs as the posts are, nor the most part, essentially international. For instance, employees of overseas governments (paras 160–168) or broadcasters (paras 136–143) cannot effectively be replaced by UK residents. The category of ministers of religion does not neatly fit this description, and that of seasonal agricultural workers does not fit it at all. However, these groups have different roles to play in the development of immigration policy, as discussed below.

11.6.1 Ministers of religion

While most religious groups may be satisfactorily served by resident ministers, for faith communities who are in a minority in the UK it may be more difficult to find fully trained ministers. These immigration rules enable minority faiths to recruit fully trained ministers from abroad. The category also recognizes the international character of most religious organizations and enables exchanges between religious communities. In order to apply as either a minister, a missionary, or a member of a religious order, an individual must have relevant training and/or experience (para 170(i)). A sponsoring organization is required, and it is necessary to show an intention to work full-time in the proposed role (HC 395 para 170(ii)). The criteria for dealing with applications are elaborated in considerable detail in the Immigration Directorate Instructions. Notes are given in Chapter 5 Annexes Q, R, T, and U on recognized religious organizations and both core and ancillary duties to be expected of a minister. By way of contrast with this present elaborate system of rules and guidance, at the beginning of the era of control of workers entering the UK, ministers of religion, missionaries, and members of religious orders were one of the few categories of employee who were exempt from the work voucher scheme (Commonwealth Immigrants Act 1962, Instructions to Immigration Officers, Cmnd 1716 para 21).

Following the 2002 White Paper *Secure Borders, Safe Haven* agenda of 'integration with diversity in modern Britain', it is now possible to switch into the category of minister so that a theological student who has been studying in the UK is able to continue as a minister after their studies. The same rule change in 2004 introduced an English language requirement for ministers. The need for this requirement was located in the disturbances in northern towns in summer 2001 in relation to which the White Paper put forward the view that religious leaders needed to be able to communicate effectively with leaders of other faiths (para 3.31). There is a parallel here with the language and citizenship provisions on nationality in the subsequent statute (Nationality, Immigration and Asylum Act 2002: see chapter 3).

11.6.2 Seasonal agricultural workers

Migration for seasonal agricultural work is an old practice. In the UK, Irish workers in particular have for centuries come to work when picking and harvesting were needed and returned to Ireland at the end of the season. Also in the east of England in particular, workers from many European countries have entered for a few months each year to do seasonal work. In 1990 this practice was regulated in the immigration rules by the seasonal agricultural workers scheme (SAWS). This was a clear-cut modern example of recruitment which was highly controlled to meet the economic need of the country. It was essentially a short-term programme. Workers were only given leave to stay for six months in the year, with no option to bring their families or to settle. The scheme was aimed at full-time students (para 104(i)) who worked for authorized operators (para 104(ii)), and filled a need for agricultural work which fluctuates over different times of the year. The government's proposals in the points-based system to phase out temporary schemes for entry for work met with strong opposition from the agricultural sector. Rogaly (2006), citing other studies earlier in the year, notes:

Firstly, the preference for migrant workers was much stronger in agriculture, secondly, only in agriculture did employers unequivocally see migrant workers as 'crucial' to their businesses, and thirdly agricultural employers were the most hostile to the phasing out of temporary migration schemes under the British government's new points-based system. (p.4)

Rogaly describes how pressure from supermarkets to deliver standardized, high-quality goods to tight timescales put pressure on agricultural producers which resulted in higher recruitment of migrant labour and reliance upon migrant workers. Resident workers were not perceived as able to fulfil the industry's requirements, being regarded as unreliable, unwilling to work the long hours necessary, slow and therefore expensive in piece work because the minimum wage would in any event have to be paid, and not able or willing to maintain quality standards. Respondents in Rogaly's study prefer eastern European students keen to earn money to British industrial workers laid off as a result of the closure of mines and factories. Rogaly notes in this context the greater vulnerability of migrant workers, and the phenomenon of employment by licensed gangmasters, described below.

After the government set and then increased quotas of SAWS workers from Accession States, from 1 January 2008 the SAWS scheme is restricted to Bulgarian and Romanian workers. It is no longer restricted to students, though workers must be aged between 18 and 30, and accommodated by their employer.

11.6.3 Sole representatives

Because of the wide potential of the category of sole representative a short account will be given here of its requirements. This category, rather than being directed towards a specialized employment market allows an overseas firm to set up branches or subsidiaries in the UK. The purpose of the sole representative's entry must be to set up such a branch or subsidiary. They must have been recruited and taken on outside the UK by a firm which has its headquarters and principal place of business outside the UK and which has no branch, subsidiary, or other representative in the UK (HC 395 para 144). The parent company must be a genuine commercial enterprise and the decision on this will take into account the length of time that the company has been established, its turnover, profitability, number of employees etc. The sole representative also must be a senior employee with full authority to take operational decisions by establishing and operating a registered branch or wholly owned subsidiary of the overseas firm (HC 395 para 144). It is expected that the applicant will be someone who has been employed by the parent company for some time and holds a senior position with them.

In order to show that the business is not transferring its operations to the UK, the sole representative must not be a majority (i.e. more than 49 per cent) shareholder in the firm which employs them (HC 395 para 144(iv)). If two representatives of the same firm come to the UK they cannot both be admitted in this non-work permit category. One may be treated as a sole representative, and after that person has entered they may make an application for a work permit for the other.

If a branch or subsidiary is established within the two years' leave initially allowed to the sole representative (HC 395 para 145) then a further three years' stay may be granted in that capacity (para 148). As for other work categories, five years in total is required to apply for settlement. The case of *Trivedi* 00/ TH/1059 INLP vol. 14, no. 3, p. 176 confirms that if a sole representative then applies for settlement in their capacity as sole representative, it is not necessary for the branch or subsidiary to have been established for the whole of the time they have been there. In other words, they could establish the branch in their second year and still qualify to apply for indefinite leave to remain at the end of five years in the UK.

11.6.4 Resident domestic workers

The entry of domestic workers in private households has been included in the immigration rules since 18 September 2002 by Cm 5597, replacing the former concession. This concession was introduced in 1980 when the Department of Employment stopped issuing work permits for unskilled workers. It operated in an anomalous way, as it was based on a fiction, the fiction apparently being derived from the dependence of the domestic worker on their employer, and their lack of a separate legal basis for entry. The concession enabled domestic workers already employed by those entering the UK for instance as visitors or business entrants to come to the UK with their employer. The fiction was that the domestic worker (i.e. a cook, a nanny, a chauffeur, etc.) obtained entry clearance as a visitor, which of course prohibited paid work. The reality was they were entering for paid work, but domestic work with a named employer. The arrangement was described as a concession because this was work for which a work permit would normally be required, but was unavailable. Entry clearance was therefore granted on a basis which meant that the employee was unable to change their employer after arriving in the UK as their entry clearance prohibited paid work. The worker was in a catch-22, because if they argued that this restriction should not apply because they were not really a visitor but a worker, their terms of work were held to be restricted to the one employer. The appellant in *Mendoza v SSHD* [1992] Imm AR 122 attempted to argue that she had obtained entry as one of a category, namely, that of domestic servants employed by wealthy non-UK residents. This argument failed, the tribunal relying on the argument that without the concession a work permit would be required, and this would prevent a change of employer.

This feudal situation was changed in 1998 when the terms of the concession were altered to permit employees who had suffered abuse or exploitation to change employer. In the new rules in force from 18 September 2002 the requirement to stay with the same employer went, as did the limitation of entry to those whose duties exceeded standards laid down in the International Standard Classification of Occupations. The employer is obliged to set out the terms of employment and undertake to maintain and accommodate the employee (para 159A).

The IDI contains other protection against abuse, requiring that the employee should initially be interviewed separately, and both parties given written information on the legal obligations contained in the employer/employee relationship. However, the IDI also states that entry may not be refused on the basis that the employer refuses to provide an assurance that they will pay the national minimum wage (para 3.3).

The new points-based system contains no provision for domestic workers. The Immigration Law Practitioners Association briefing on the Command Paper (March 2006) reveals that officials working on the points-based system have stated that domestic workers will be given a maximum of six months' leave which cannot be extended. Then their employer will be expected to recruit a replacement worker from the EEA. The Joint Council for the Welfare of Immigrants comments that many non-EEA migrant domestic workers 'undertake caring tasks which cannot be switched off at the end of six months because their ability to function effectively in post is based on relationships with member of their employer's family such as children. It is also not clear where they are supposed to return to since many do not come from their countries of origin but from third countries', presumably the residence of their employer (JCWI 2006). The points-based system appears to turn the clock back and open the door again to exploitation and to migrant domestic workers going 'underground'.

11.7 **Establishing a business**

Part 6 of the immigration rules is devoted to leave to enter or remain for people seeking to set up in business. It includes also provision to enter or remain as an investor, and incorporates relevant provisions of the EC Association Agreements with Bulgaria and Romania, for whose nationals these rules operate as a minimum standard for self-employment, as the free movement rights granted so far only relate to employment.

No particular kind of business is contemplated, and the form of the business may be as a sole trader ('trading' here does not imply buying and selling, it refers to anyone who is in business on their own), a partnership or a company (para 200).

In relation to setting up a business as in many other areas, the early immigration rules were rather open and flexible. For instance, Cmnd 1716, the instructions to immigration officers which accompanied the Commonwealth Immigrants Act 1962, stated that

[s]elf-employed people and persons seeking to set up business on their own account should be admitted freely unless it seems unlikely that they will make a sufficient living and may therefore need to seek employment for which a voucher would ordinarily be necessary or to have recourse to public funds. (para 23)

This broad approach to assessing self-employed or business applications has now been replaced with very detailed rules requiring minimum investment, creation of employment and so on. The pre-1973 rules, however, are preserved in the case of Turkish nationals because of the ruling of the European Court of Justice in the case of *R v SSHD ex p Savas* [2000] 1 WLR 1828. The court applied the standstill clause in Article 41 of the Additional Protocol to the EC–Turkey Association Agreement, which provided that EU countries should not, after the date of the agreement, introduce new obstacles to Turkish nationals setting up in business in EU countries. HC 510, in force on 1 January 1973, therefore provides the relevant rules for Turkish nationals, and these give more favourable conditions, for instance allowing switching into self-employment from visitor status. A range of highly skilled migrant workers may switch into the business category if they meet the requirements (see HC 395 para 206), but in general visitors may not.

A distinguishing feature of business applications is that this category is intended for owners of businesses and may not be used for an employee as this would be to subvert the work permit system. The business need not be a new business, as the applicant may take over or join an existing business. It is essential, whether the business is a new or existing one, that the applicant has a minimum of £200,000 of their own money to invest in the business, and that the business needs this investment (para 201). This must be money held in their own name over which they have control and which they will invest in the UK business. It must be new money, not already in the business, and fully available for that purpose, so not tied up for instance in a house. The minimum investment requirement does not apply to nationals of Romania and Bulgaria (para 222).

As Macdonald points out, the question is not whether the applicant can demonstrate that the UK economy needs their services. The question of market forces and feasibility is not irrelevant as it has a bearing on profitability (2005:556), but the main question is whether this business can be demonstrated to need £200,000 worth of investment. If very little investment is needed then the application will not succeed. Despite the very open wording of para 200, this requirement influences the kind of business that can be set up or joined by nationals of countries outside the EEA. For instance, starting or joining a business as a window cleaner or street trader would be unlikely to require an investment of £200,000.

The remaining requirements of the rule, though onerous, are generally addressed to the same issues namely, ensuring that the person will be financially self-sufficient and ensuring that the application is not a disguised application for employment. Additionally, to demonstrate the economic benefit of the business the applicant will be required to show that two new jobs will be created (para 201).

11.7.1 **Writers, composers, and artists**

Writers, composers, and artists are a special category of business applicant for whom the requirements of the immigration rules are not nearly so extensive. There is no minimum investment, job creation requirement, etc. It is simply necessary that they are established in their work, both in the sense of having had their work published, performed, or exhibited and in the sense of being able to support themselves and any dependants from their own resources without working except as a writer, composer, or artist. This opens up the possibility of using other resources than just the current proceeds of their work, providing they do no other work (see paras 232–239).

There are some rather bizarre distinctions between those who may apply under these rules and those who must apply for a work permit as an entertainer. For instance, television and radio scriptwriters need a work permit but playwrights may apply as writers under para 232 of the rules. The creators of some artistic installations using the human body would need to decide whether to define themselves as sculptors or dancers, as sculptors may apply under para 232 whereas dancers are treated as entertainers and so must apply for work permits. Finally, composers come within the rules, but musicians do not, which puts a singer/songwriter in an interesting position. In Macdonald's discussion of this he suggests that such a person entering under para 232 as a composer would face difficulties if they sing as they are working outside their self-employment, singing being regarded as employment. However, only a well-known singer may obtain a work permit, thus making it difficult for new entertainers to enter the UK. He suggests that composers may conduct their work, but not perform otherwise without the permission of Work Permits (UK) (2005:561).

11.7.2 **Investors**

Since 1994 there have been provisions in the immigration rules to enter the UK as an investor. An investor must have at least £1 million of their own money, of which they intend to invest not less than £750, 000 in the UK 'by way of UK Government Bonds, share capital or loan capital in active and trading UK registered companies' (HC 395 para 224(ii)). The investor must also intend to make the UK their main home and be able to support themselves and dependants without recourse to public funds – a rather extraordinary requirement as of course the possessor of such wealth would not qualify for any means-tested benefit. They must also be able to support themselves without taking employment, as again this would circumvent the work permit scheme. Leave may be granted for 12 months in the first instance, extendable to five years, and entry in this capacity may lead to settlement.

11.8 Special schemes

The rules governing entry for business are geared to the creation of jobs and investment in the UK and to attracting business people with significant financial assets. Skilled and creative people may not of course be wealthy, and the new twenty-first century objective to attract skilled people to the UK required some flexibility so that talent as well as wealth would be a basis for admission. Five new schemes have been devised since 2000: the innovators scheme; the Highly Skilled Migrants Programme; the Science and Engineering Graduates Scheme; the International Graduate Scheme; and the Fresh Talent: Working in Scotland Scheme. The first two schemes are still highly selective, but at least initially reduced the standard of wealth required for entry. Maclaughlan and Salt (2002) concluded that the UK had moved 'faster and further' than any other developed country except Australia and Canada in terms of the range of specific schemes to attract the highly skilled.

11.8.1 Innovators

The innovator scheme is for people with new and creative business ideas, and is aimed at science and technology generally, and e-commerce in particular. The objective is to facilitate the setting up of such businesses, but without the requirement for minimum capital laid down by the rules for other business entrants. There must be enough money available to finance the business for the first six months after arrival in the UK, but this may be provided by a third party and need not be the innovator's own money. Like other business applications, the proposal must be one which will create two full-time jobs in the UK. The innovator must own at least 5 per cent of the shares in their company, which must be registered in the UK, and they must be able to support and accommodate themselves and any dependants without working outside the business until it is able to provide an income. If these criteria are met, the application will be assessed on a points system in which there are scores for work and business experience, proven entrepreneurial ability, educational qualifications (again there is an emphasis on science and technology), a realistic business plan, job creation potential, the new and creative aspects of the proposal, how much will be spent on research and development, and personal references. It will be apparent that this is not a scheme to help start inexperienced people in business. The Home Office said that the aim was to attract people who would bring 'exceptional economic benefit' to the UK. The details of the scheme are not in the immigration rules, but on the site currently of Work Permits (UK), which sets out the evidence an applicant must submit.

11.8.2 Highly Skilled Migrants Programme

The 2002 White Paper said that the aim of the HSMP was to attract 'high human capital individuals, who have the qualifications and skills required by UK businesses to compete in the global marketplace' (para 3.18). Both the innovator scheme and the HSMP can lead to settlement.

The HSMP is also run on a points system. In this scheme, points are allocated for educational qualifications, work experience, past earnings and youth. Fitness for the programme is separately assessed by Work Permits (UK), and is not a matter for the entry clearance officer. The great benefit of the scheme from a migrant's point of view is that qualification is on the basis of the points awarded, and there is no requirement to have a job to come to. Migrants were given 12 months' leave initially, extendable by a further three years if they could show that they had taken all reasonable steps to become lawfully economically active. They were required to sign an undertaking that they would make the UK their permanent home, and after four years could expect settlement. The scheme was trialled and amended, but in all versions of the scheme up to 2006, points were allocated for exceptional achievement in the applicant's chosen field, and for their past experience. Changes made in November 2006 with little warning introduced a new English test, points for UK experience, abolished points for exceptional achievement, other prior experience and having a skilled partner, and increased points for youth, qualifications and earnings.

These changes applied to extension applications as well as applications for entry. Having taken all reasonable steps to become lawfully economically active was no longer enough to qualify for an extension. Beynon (2007) explains the impact of awarding points for UK experience but not for previous work experience and achievements: 'employers will not consider them for the high earning jobs favoured under the new points system because of their short-term initial visas and lack of UK work experience'. As a consequence, entrants were obliged to take other work in the hope that, once in employment, their capacity would be recognized. Now, because they had not yet earned highly in the UK, such applicants would be faced with having to return to their home country. The changes were announced to take place the following day, and there were limited transitional arrangements. The changes favoured men, who were more likely to have entered the job market and earned more at a younger age.

In a rare instance of a report specifically on the immigration rules, the Parliamentary Joint Human Rights Committee reported on this rule change. The government accepted that the changes affected the right to respect for private and family life under Article 8 ECHR, but said they were in accordance with the law because migrants were aware that they would be subject to further enquiries before leave was extended, and the government could not commit itself to not changing the content of those requirements as they had a power to change the rules without notice at any time. The aim was a legitimate one because as some highly skilled migrants were in low-skilled work the aim of the scheme was not met, and the government was entitled to interfere with Article 8 rights in the interests of the economic well-being of the country. The legitimacy of this reason was accepted, but the immediate change which affected individuals retrospectively was, according to the Committee, 'the essence of arbitrariness'. Many people had, in the course of emigrating permanently to the UK as the scheme required, entered into financial arrangements, given up secure jobs, their partners and children were established in new jobs and schools, and so on. The Committee considered that the changes were not only not in accordance with the law but also disproportionate.

These findings were barely referred to in a tribunal case challenging the application of the changes to three individuals. In *AA and others v SSHD* [2008] UKAIT 00003 the tribunal's findings coincide with the government's argument to the JCHR, related above, except that they did not accept that in each case the decision to refuse leave to remain under the scheme affected the right to respect for private or family life. This case was discussed more fully in chapter 2.

11.8.3 **New graduates**

The SEGS, International Graduate Scheme and Fresh Talent schemes are all directed to new graduates. The Fresh Talent: Working in Scotland scheme enables graduates of Scottish higher education to receive 24 months' leave within which to obtain work permit employment, set up a business which would qualify for leave under the immigration rules, or obtain a place as a highly skilled migrant or innovator. The graduate schemes give 12 months' leave to those who have graduated within the last 12 months, within which to obtain further leave, as for the Fresh Talent scheme. Graduates on all schemes must be able to maintain and accommodate themselves without recourse to public funds.

11.9 **Illegal working**

In the immigration context 'illegal working' means the employment of people who are subject to immigration control and do not have one of the lawful bases for work which have been discussed in this chapter. This aspect of unlawfulness however often goes hand in hand with other unlawful practices by the employer such as low pay, breach of health and safety regulations, failure to pay income tax and national insurance contributions, and so on. The last mentioned are almost inevitable as the worker needs to be left out of official records or they may be traced. In effect they also have no remedy against unfair dismissal.

The International Convention on the Rights of Migrant Workers was adopted by the General Assembly of the United Nations in December 1990. It sets out requirements, for instance, of provision of essential information on their status in languages that migrant workers will understand, and requirements for basic social provision. The Convention makes the link between migration and human rights, which as we have seen is missing in the European Convention on Human Rights and many other earlier human rights instruments. It recognizes the many reasons why people migrate and work in another country, and aims to support conditions of respect and protection of rights for those who do. The UK, along with most other countries that are destinations for workers, has not signed the Convention. The 37 signatories to date are predominantly countries from which people migrate to work, but calls are mounting for its ratification, including from the Global Commission on International Migration.

Sanctions against employers for employing those not entitled to work are an aspect of the spread of immigration control into wider society, involving companies and private individuals in monitoring immigration status. In his evidence to the Home Affairs Committee on 7 November 2007, the Minister of State for Borders and Immigration was at pains to point out that employers are responsible for checking employees' documents (HC 123 (i)). His insistence to the Committee that this was the responsibility of employers and not of BIA confirms the impression that ministers are interested in spreading actual responsibility for 'managing migration' to the wider society.

It is a moot point to what extent these sanctions are effective to prevent the abuses just described, and to what extent they deter employers from offering work to people who they think might involve them in complex obligations and the risk of penalties. Portes and French reported that early indications were that the Accession Workers'

Registration Scheme appears to have reduced illegal working (2005:15). Asylum and Immigration Act 1996 s 8 created an offence of employing a person subject to immigration control who is not permitted by their terms of stay to work in the UK or who does not have valid leave to be in the UK. The offence is one of strict liability, that is, it is simply to employ the person who does not have permission to work. There were very few prosecutions under the 1996 Act. This section is repealed by the Immigration, Asylum and Nationality Act 2006 and replaced by a similar offence but which importantly requires knowledge of the employee's immigration status or at least that it prohibits them from working (s 21). The 2006 Act also institutes a system of civil penalties for employing someone who does not have permission to work (s 15). Here, no knowledge of status is required. The penalty system provides an opportunity to object, and to appeal. There is a statutory defence for the employer, which is that they complied with a list of prescribed actions, including requesting sight of specified documents relating to the employee in question, taking all reasonable steps to check their validity, keeping them safely (Immigration (Restrictions on Employment) Order 2007 SI 2007/3290). The specified documents include some which are acceptable only in combination, for instance a birth certificate together with notice of national insurance number.

When the 1996 Act offence was introduced, concern was expressed by employers at this responsibility, and by representatives of immigrants and minority ethnic groups that the section would give rise to increased racial discrimination. A predicted scenario was that employers would be reluctant to employ people if they thought that there might be an immigration issue involved, especially as the fine for the offence was £5,000. This kind of decision would be more likely to be made in relation to a minority ethnic applicant. A code of practice for employers on how to avoid race discrimination while complying with the Act, issued under s 23 of the 2006 Act, is in force from 29 February 2008, together with regulations instituting the new penalty scheme (Immigration (Restrictions on Employment) Order 2007 SI 2007/3290).

The Nationality, Immigration and Asylum Act 2002 empowers the Secretary of State to make orders concerning the production and retention of documentation by employers. For instance, by s 134 the Secretary of State may require an employer to supply information about an employee whom the Secretary of State reasonably suspects of having committed an offence under the Immigration Act 1971, such as illegal entry or obtaining leave by deception or of having committed fraud in relation to asylum support. The information must be related to the employee's earnings or history of employment or be required in order to establish where the employee is (s 134(2)). Under s 137 it is an offence to fail to supply the information without reasonable excuse. It may happen that information provided by an employer for instance about earnings shows an offence committed by the employer, such as failure to deduct national insurance or tax. Section 139 provides that information provided pursuant to a request under s 134 may not be used as evidence in criminal proceedings. This is consistent with the ECtHR's interpretation of Article 6 in the case of *Saunders* v *UK* (1997) 23 EHRR 313 in which the Court held that it was a breach of Article 6 to use information gathered under compulsion against the defendants in the Guinness trial. These provisions are unaffected by the 2006 Act.

It is a criminal offence to employ a worker from the new EU member states if they are not authorized to work for the employer, that is, registered or in the process of registration (Accession (Immigration and Workers Registration) Regulations 2004, SI 2004/1219 as amended).

Trafficking is briefly discussed in chapter 14, in the context of criminalizing activities connected with immigration.

11.10 Conclusion and the future

The broad welcome to economic migration combined with greater specificity in terms of the UK's needs, which appeared to be heralded by the 2002 White Paper, is vanishing already. Policy is repeating old patterns rather than breaking the mould. Comparison between government response to take-up of opportunities by east Europeans on the one hand, and Bangladeshis and new Commonwealth working holiday makers on the other, is reminiscent of the years after the Second World War. At that time too Britain had a labour shortage, though at that time it was the Commonwealth citizens who had a right to come and the Europeans did not.

At the same time, the system of entry for work may be on the threshold of the greatest change since its beginnings. There are fears that the result will be to surrender the current responsive, speedy and employer-led process and to submit decisions on entry for work to officials whose training and working environment is geared to a culture of gate-keeping. The work-related schemes currently operated by entry clearance officers have been the subject of the first race discrimination claims under the rights of appeal instituted on that basis, but the new scheme makes no proposal for guarding against this bias.

The tiered system itself has not been disclosed in detail, but early indications that the most qualified and wealthy are welcome to come and stay should be balanced against the 2006 changes to the work and training opportunities for overseas medical graduates and the Highly Skilled Migrants Programme. These changes show immigration control as a rather crude instrument of economic control, which in these cases reinforces inequality rather than countering it.

QUESTIONS

1 What are the objections to allowing asylum seekers to obtain work permit employment in the UK? Do these arguments apply to allowing them to work while their claim is being decided?

2 Describe what you see as the advantages of the new tiered system.

3 What is the justification for special categories of non-work permit employment?

 online resource centre For guidance on answering questions, visit www.oxfordtextbooks.co.uk/orc/clayton3e.

FURTHER READING

Andonian, B. (2002) 'Desirable Aliens' *Solicitors Journal* vol. 146, no. 9, pp. 218–219.

Beynon, R. (2007) 'Highly Skilled, No Longer Wanted' Catalyst, 22 January.

Castles, S. (2000) *Ethnicity and Globalisation: from migrant worker to transnational citizen* (London: Sage).

Cohen, S. (2000) 'Never mind the racism…feel the quality' *Immigration and Nationality Law and Practice* vol. 14, no. 4, pp. 223–226.

Devine, L. and Barrett-Brown, S. (2001) 'The Work Permit Scheme – an analysis of its origin and scope' *Journal of Immigration, Asylum and Nationality Law* vol. 15, no. 2, pp. 92–101.

Devine, L. (2007) 'Is the new Highly Skilled Migrant Programme "fit for purpose"? If not, the Government's Proposed Points Based Immigration System is Fundamentally Flawed' *Journal of Immigration, Asylum & Nationality Law* vol. 21, no. 2.

Dobson, J., Koser, K., Maclaughlan, G. Salt, J. (2001) *International Migration and the United Kingdom: Recent patterns and trends*, RDS Occasional Paper no. 75.

Gillespie, J. (2000) 'Review of work permits' *Journal of Immigration, Asylum & Nationality Law* vol. 14, no. 2, pp. 75–76.

Home Office (2006), 'A Points-Based System: Making Migration Work for Britain'.

Joint Committee on Human Rights, 'Highly Skilled Migrants: Changes to the Immigration Rules' Session 2006–07 Twentieth Report HL Paper 173, HC 993.

Joint Council for the Welfare of Immigrants (2003) *The Politics of Managed Migration* JCWI Bulletin. Autumn Issue.

Joshi, S. (2002) 'Immigration Controls and Class', in Cohen, S., Humphries, B., and Mynott, E. (eds) *From Immigration Controls to Welfare Controls* (London: Routledge).

McLaughlan, G. and Salt, J. (2002) *Migration Policies Towards Highly Skilled Foreign Workers* (London: Migration Research Unit, University College London).

Momsen, J. H. (ed.) (1999) *Gender, Migration and Domestic Service* (London: Routledge).

Paul, K. (1997) *Whitewashing Britain: Race and Citizenship in the Postwar era* (New York: Cornell), Chapters 3, 4 and 5.

Portes J. and French S. (2005) *The impact of free movement of workers from central and eastern Europe on the UK labour market: early evidence* DWP Working paper no. 18.

Puttick, K. (2006) 'Welcoming the new Arrivals? Reception, Integration and Employment of A8, Bulgarian and Romanian Migrants' *Journal of Immigration, Asylum & Nationality Law* vol. 20, no.4, pp. 238–254.

Rogaly, B. (2006) 'Intensification of Work-Place regimes in British Agriculture: the Role of Migrant Workers', Sussex Migration Working Paper no. 36 (University of Sussex, Sussex Centre for Migration Research).

Stalker, P. (2000) *Workers Without Frontiers: The impact of globalization on international migration* (Geneva: Lynne Reiner/ILO).

SECTION 5

The asylum claim

12

The asylum process and appeals

SUMMARY

This chapter describes the asylum process from application through to cessation of refugee status, including the use of fast-track systems of decision-making and the New Asylum Model. It discusses the problems of fairness and evidence that have arisen in the asylum process including the concept of credibility and the safe third country and country of origin provisions which may prevent a claim or appeal from being heard at all.

12.1 The nature of an asylum claim

Millions of people face persecution worldwide. This is often on account of their political or religious beliefs, their race or nationality, or another fundamental quality such as their gender or sexuality. The purpose of refugee law is to protect people in this position. In the UK, whilst someone is applying for this protection, they are called an 'asylum seeker'. The asylum process and appeals system are the stages that an asylum seeker goes through in order to establish their claim to refugee status. Asylum or refugee status is unique in the legal and political order, and we begin this chapter with examining some of its particular characteristics.

12.1.1 Asylum and migration

The distinction between seeking asylum and other reasons for migration is a modern one. It is a distinction which is imposed in present-day law, politics and administration. In the experience of migrants, however, the distinction is not necessarily clear cut, and in earlier times, no such distinction was made even in law. Stevens (in Nicholson and Twomey 1998) says:

There is evidence to suggest that England was acting as a country of refuge from as early as the 13th century. Until the late 18th century, however, the word 'refugee' had not become a generic term; rather, individuals fleeing from persecution or oppression were viewed, alongside other foreigners, as 'aliens' with nothing to distinguish the normal migrant from those with cause to escape their countries of origin.

In Shah's discussion of the consequences of the Africanization polices pursued by Kenya, Tanzania, and Uganda in the 1960s he makes the point that those Asian citizens of the UK and Colonies who were forced to leave East Africa were in a practical sense refugees (2000:77). The focus at the time was on Britain's obligations to its nationals, but the phenomenon of flight from serious discrimination is in reality a search for asylum. As we have seen in chapters 1 and 3, the situation was dealt with by way of immigration restrictions. However, the Africanization policies which forced them out may be compared with the Serbianization policies which forced those of Albanian descent to leave Kosovo in search of asylum in the 1990s and who were treated as asylum seekers in the UK. The policies were characterized by favouring Africans (or Serbs) over Asians (or Albanians) in matters such as employment, business, and public office.

The House of Commons Home Affairs Committee noted:

> The difficulty of distinguishing between economic and non-economic causes of migration is compounded by the fact that the two categories may frequently overlap. Some refugees are undoubtedly motivated solely by the impossibility of continuing to live without persecution in their own countries. Some may be fleeing persecution in their homeland and be seeking a better job and income than is available there. Some may be primarily seeking to improve their economic position which is limited by the political or economic instability in their country of origin. Yet others will have identified the asylum system as a means of gaining access to the economic prosperity and welfare systems of Western Europe. (Session 2003–04 Second Report, *Asylum Applications*, HC 218 para 42)

Whether a person gets refugee status is as much a matter of whether they fit the legal definition as it is to with the personal circumstances which led to their claim for asylum. It may be for instance that someone has been severely tortured in detention but, if that is not on account of one of the reasons provided for in the definition of a refugee, they will not be granted refugee status. In the UK legal system, asylum claims are dealt with in the same government department as border control (the BIA). However, unlike for instance applications to visit a relative or study in the UK, there is no direct route to making an asylum claim without breaking immigration law in at least some respect. Asylum seekers fit into the immigration legal structure mainly as people who are subject to immigration enforcement, and so the integration of asylum and immigration law facilitates the detention and removal of asylum seekers rather than protecting them.

This emphasis is shared in the EU:

> We are concerned that EU member states and institutions are placing far greater emphasis on practical cooperation in border control than on refugee protection. Recent events in those EU states bordering the Mediterranean highlight the need to address the pressures faced by their asylum services and reception capacities.

(Joint Refugee Council, Scottish Refugee Council and Welsh Refugee Council submission: House of Commons Home Affairs Committee inquiry on EU issues, September 2006).

12.1.2 The legal concept of asylum

The legal concept of asylum is nowhere near as old as the practice of seeking it. Dummett and Nicol (1990:143) say that 'the granting of asylum to refugees is as old as the concept of sovereign states'. The legal idea was originally conceived as a matter between states, not, as we tend to see it now, as a matter of an individual's claim for protection from a particular country. This original idea still has importance in the development of asylum law.

A national has the right to expect protection from their government. One way of looking at refugee status would be to say that it arises when that relationship has broken down to the extent that the state is not giving protection. Traditionally, the right involved in asylum is said to be the right of the state to grant asylum, not the right of the asylum seeker to receive it (see, for instance, Grahl-Madsen, *The Status of Refugees in International Law* (1972). The state owes its nationals a duty of protection, and nationals owe a duty of allegiance, but the state cannot insist on its nationals being returned to its territory (except in legally controlled extradition proceedings); another state can assert the right to give them asylum. The Universal Declaration of Human Rights 1948 Article 14 recognizes the right to 'seek and enjoy' asylum, but this is not a right to *be granted* asylum. Indeed, Shah (2000:61) recounts how at the stage of negotiating the terms of the Declaration a British amendment removed the words 'to be granted', substituting 'enjoy'. This means to be able to benefit from the status once it is granted, but not to be granted it. In the European Union this is now changed by the Refugee Qualification Directive, which does give a right to asylum to those who qualify for it. The Directive is discussed below in the context of claims in the UK.

12.1.3 Refugee Convention

The 1951 Refugee Convention sets out the internationally agreed definition of who is a refugee and standards for treatment of refugees and is the legal basis for refugee claims. The Refugee Convention was originally drafted to deal with the displacement of people as a result of the Second World War. It restricted the definition of refugees to those whose fear of persecution arose from events occurring in Europe before 1 January 1951. The Protocol of 1967 removed the time restriction and promoted a gradual removal of the geographical restriction but the refugee definition was not changed. The definition is derived from the needs and negotiations of the time, and its central requirement for a fear of persecution arises from the treatment of political dissidents in what were then the Communist countries of Eastern Europe and the Soviet Union. The main present day causes of refugee movements are not the escape of political dissidents from persecution, but armed conflict, large-scale human rights abuses and natural disaster. Thus, refugee recognition through the 1951 Convention is only a small part of the international phenomenon of people seeking refuge. Flight from war and natural disaster were not in the mind of the drafters of the Refugee Convention. Its terms do not lend themselves easily to these situations, and the vast majority of uprooted people in the world do not apply for legal status through the Refugee Convention.

The UNHCR is the body given the task, worldwide, of protecting all refugees and addressing the issues which give rise to refugee movements. People who have fled intolerable conditions but not used the Convention are referred to as *de facto* refugees, a much larger group than Convention, called *de jure,* refugees. In 2004 around half of the refugee population under UNHCR care was granted protection under the Convention, some were granted protection under other international instruments, and the majority were granted refugee status on a group basis. In Europe however the majority (76 per cent) were granted status on the basis of an individual determination process, and it is this process and the law governing it that we are studying.

Different jurisdictions have developed the law of the Convention in somewhat different ways. In the European Union it is intended that there will be consistency of meaning through the Qualification Directive. Prefiguring this, in the context of returning asylum seekers to other European countries on the grounds that it was safe to do so, the House of Lords in *Adan v SSHD* [2001] 1 All ER 593 affirmed the view that the Convention should be given a consistent interpretation among the contracting states in order to provide an effective system of refugee protection. This overruled the previous Court of Appeal decisions in *Kerrouche* v *SSHD* [1997] Imm AR 610 and *Iyadurai v SSHD* [1998] Imm AR 470, both of which had decided, in a similar context, that there was a range of permissible meanings. The meaning of the Convention is, they decided, an autonomous meaning, in accordance with the purposes of the Convention, and cannot differ as between states. The greater accessibility of the case law of other jurisdictions now makes the objective of consistency more attainable and knowledge of the case law of other jurisdictions is essential to a full understanding.

In the European Union the Refugee Qualification Directive 2004/83 now governs the interpretation of the Convention in member states and has been implemented in the UK by the Refugee or Person in Need of International Protection (Qualification) Regulations 2006 SI 2006/2525 and changes to the immigration rules. The Qualification Directive gives an EU-wide interpretation of all the aspects of the definition of a refugee. It became binding on states on 10 October 2006 and applies to all asylum claims in a member state after that date. The Directive however does not perfectly implement the Convention. What will happen when there is a difference between them? There is no authoritative ruling on this question yet. Where the Refugee Convention and its case law appear more generous than the Qualification Directive, it may be that the Convention will be regarded as the authority. Symes suggests this is the case on the basis of Preamble 3 to the Directive: 'The Refugee Convention provides the cornerstone of refugee protection'. Lambert suggests this may be the case on the basis of the EC treaty which provides for the primacy of treaty agreements entered into before conflicting European ones where these agreements are between member states and third countries (article 307 EC). This would apply to the Refugee Convention. Whether an individual can invoke that principle to rely on any greater protection given by the Refugee Convention is untested and uncertain (see Lambert 2006).

Where the Directive is more favourable to refugees than the Refugee Convention and its case law, because it represents an agreed minimum standard then it is binding. The Directive appears to give member states latitude to operate more favourable standards than the minimum it sets, though this too is open to interpretation (see Lambert).

There are calls from a number of quarters for the Convention to be amended, but these come from opposing viewpoints. Some would like to see the Convention widened to include more contemporary forms of refugee movement, and situations that are at present difficult to bring within the Convention, such as the oppression of women and the abuse of children. Others would prefer to narrow the definition and so reduce the numbers of refugees that states can be obliged to take. Therefore while the Convention definition is a product of its time, a redraft would be the product of the present time, in which refugee movements are a more contentious issue internationally than they were at the time of the original Convention.

The UNHCR Handbook is a major aid to interpretation of the Refugee Convention. Its use was endorsed by the House of Lords in *T v SSHD* [1996] 2All ER 865 and it will be referred to frequently throughout this chapter.

12.1.3.1 *Non-refoulement*

The obligation which is central to the whole scheme of refugee protection is that of *non-refoulement*:

No Contracting State shall expel or return (*refouler*) a refugee in any manner whatsoever to the frontiers of territories where his life or freedom would be threatened on account of his race, religion, nationality, membership of a particular social group or political opinion.

By Article 33, whether or not a state has an obligation to grant refugee status, it does have an obligation not to return someone on its soil to persecution. *Refoulement* can happen directly, by putting someone on a plane to their home country, or more controversially it is said that it may be done indirectly, by making their life so miserable and impossible that the better choice is to return and risk persecution. In this latter respect some of the UK's legal provisions denying welfare support to asylum seekers have attracted adverse comment (see, for instance, Harvey in Twomey and Nicolson 1998). The obligation of *non-refoulement* applies to people seeking refugee status as well as those who are granted it, as the status is declaratory, in other words, to be granted refugee status means to have it recognized that one is a refugee, rather than to be made a refugee (Goodwin-Gill 1996:141). This means that someone who is successful in their asylum claim has been a refugee since entering the country in which they are seeking protection.

Arguably, Article 33 is limited to those already on the territory of the contracting state. This limitation on Article 33 has meant that states have been free to develop policies which prevent asylum seekers from ever reaching their territory in the first place. We have seen in chapter 7 how visa rules, airline liaison schemes, juxtaposed controls, and carrier sanctions operate with this effect (see also, for instance, Blake in Twomey and Nicholson 1998), and the development of criminal sanctions is discussed in chapter 14. This territorial view of Article 33 is not universally shared. Goodwin-Gill, for instance, espouses the view that the Convention has extraterritorial effect (1996:141 *et seq*). He describes the actions of the US in intercepting refugees on board ships from Haiti and returning them to Haiti as a breach of the obligation, despite the Supreme Court ruling permitting the practice in *Sale, Acting Commissioner, INS v Haitian Centers Council* 113 S Ct 2549 (1993).

It is clear that the Refugee Convention does not apply to people who are still in their country of origin (*R v Immigration Officer at Prague Airport ex p European Roma Rights Centre* [2004] UKHL 55) and does apply once the asylum seeker reaches the territory of a destination state. These points however do not address the situation in the *Sale* case, i.e. when the asylum seekers are in transit. This question has had life and death importance in relation to allowing boats to land. The most well-known example in recent times was the refusal of the Australian government to allow landing to the Norwegian ship the *Tampa,* which had rescued hundreds of asylum seekers from drowning. Despite international criticism and partially successful constitutional challenges in the Australian courts, the Refugee Convention did not avail the travellers. Head cites the lack of extraterritorial reach as a failure of the Convention (2004:22), and see Willhelm for an account of Australia's legal response.

12.1.4 **Political nature of asylum**

The grant of asylum might seem to imply criticism of the state of origin, as recognized by the Court of Appeal in *Krotov v SSHD* [2004] EWCA Civ 69: 'it is in the very nature of adjudication upon asylum issues that the tribunals or courts concerned with them are, for the purposes of surrogate protection underlying the 1951 Convention, obliged to examine and adjudicate upon events internal to another state' (para 42). Accepting that someone has a well-founded fear of being persecuted in their country of origin is an acknowledgement that the host state is offering protection where the country of origin has failed to do so. This is a humanitarian act, and thus should not be construed as a hostile action. As Dummett and Nicol say, quoting Lauterpacht: 'An enemy of his government is not an enemy of mankind' (1990:144). Unfortunately, sometimes an asylum claim which fails *may* be treated as a hostile act, not one committed by the government in the state where the claim was made, but by the asylum seeker themselves. There is therefore sometimes a risk that people whose asylum claim has failed may face persecution on returning to their country of origin for having made a claim. The question then is whether the failed asylum claim can give rise to a claim for asylum in itself (see e.g. *BK (DRC CG)* [2007] UKAIT 00098 discussed in the next chapter).

It follows from Lauterpacht's principle not only that a home state must allow an asylum claim to be made and to be successful without taking revenge, but also that governments should not band together against the asylum seeker. Lauterpacht also says that the international community is not one of mutual insurance for the maintenance of established governments and that treason is not an international crime. In other words, governments should not focus on supporting each other to refuse asylum claims, and ideally they would support each other to recognize the rights of asylum seekers. However, in today's political climate, countries increasingly work together in the interests of national security and the fight against terrorism, and an individual asylum seeker's interests may be prejudiced by this focus. Legal principle is developing in this direction. For instance, the definition of 'national security' used in the House of Lords judgment in *Rehman v SSHD* [2001] 3 WLR 877 asserts that a threat to the security of one nation is a threat to all. This theme is explored more in chapter 14 in the context of exclusion from asylum and membership of organizations proscribed as terrorist.

Despite the humanitarian principles, there is no doubt that the grant of asylum is intimately connected with politics at all levels. Macdonald makes no bones about this:

The recognition rate for refugees has less to do with merits than with politics. Thus between 1989 and 1998 Canada granted refugee status to over 80% of applicants from Sri Lanka, France to 74%, and the UK to 1%: Refugee Council response to the Home Secretary's Lisbon Proposals, January 2001. (2001:468 n 2)

Not only the outcome but also the conduct of refugee cases is subject to political considerations. For example, at the outbreak of war with Iraq at the beginning of 2003, the hearing of Iraqi asylum appeals was suspended by the Immigration Appellate Authority, initially for six weeks. At a legal level, it is possible to see reasons for this as it could be difficult to assess the risk of persecution to an individual when the country to which they would be returned is in chaos. At a political level, to grant asylum to those individuals at that stage could be seen to undermine confidence in the outcome of the war. The Home Office often announces suspension of removals to a country at a time of civil disturbance. This was done for instance in the case of Sierra Leone. However, in the Iraqi cases the suspension was not only of the Home Office's own executive action but was of the judicial process, and at the request of one party to the proceedings, the Home Office.

12.1.5 Legal nature of the refugee claim in the UK

The system for claiming asylum has become integrated into the legal systems of signatory states and has become a branch of law in its own right. In the UK the choice was made at an early stage to give this responsibility to the Home Office, the same government department that deals with immigration, rather than an independent body. Although the same government department is often involved in immigration and asylum, in some countries such as Canada and New Zealand, there is a separate status determination process with an appeal against refusal of refugee status. This is not the case in the UK, where, as noted earlier, the trend is rather for asylum decisions to become increasingly intertwined with the immigration system.

This increasing incorporation of asylum into the immigration system has tended to bring the border control mentality into the grant of asylum. As the Joint Refugee Councils' submission to the Home Affairs Committee said, 'the immigration controls introduced by the UK and other EU states are a blunt instrument that do not distinguish between those fleeing persecution and irregular migrants seeking to enter a country for other purposes'. Once this merging has taken place, it appears less controversial to make extensive use of detention and other draconian control measures, such as the removal of welfare support, because dealing with asylum claims is seen as part of managing migration and policing a frontier (see, for instance, Kostakopoulou and Thomas 2004 and Cornelisse 2004).

12.1.5.1 *Jurisdiction and appeal rights*

The Aliens Act 1905 gave the courts jurisdiction over the question of whether a person's circumstances would give grounds for exemption from deportation where political asylum could be claimed. However, when the 1905 Act was repealed and replaced by the Aliens Restriction Act 1914 and 1919, the exemption for refugees disappeared. Refugee status was a matter for the Secretary of State (*Bugdaycay* [1987] AC 514), not an independent body and not the appeals authority.

Immigration statutes continued to omit any provision for refugees until the Asylum and Immigration Appeals Act 1993 provided that a claim for asylum was a claim that it would be contrary to the UK's obligations under the Refugee Convention for the claimant to be removed from the UK. This refers to the *non-refoulement* obligation under Article 33, and gave a statutory meaning to an asylum claim. However, although there is a process to make an application for asylum, when it is refused there is no appeal against refusal of asylum as such, but rather against the associated immigration decision. So for instance, a person may appeal against refusal of leave to enter the UK or a decision that they are to be removed from the UK (Nationality, Immigration and Asylum Act 2002 s 82) *on the ground that* 'the removal of the appellant in consequence of the immigration decision would breach the UK's obligations under the Refugee Convention' (2002 Act s 84).

This means that the tribunal hearing an appeal can only say that leave to enter *should* be granted, or that the appellant *should not* be removed. They cannot grant refugee status as 'that is a status conferred on the basis of criteria prescribed in an international treaty and should not be conferred if those criteria are not at the time of the decision satisfied' (*SSHD v R (Bakhtear Rashid)* [2005] EWCA Civ 744 para 37). In a successful case it is the Home Office that sends the letter out granting asylum after the tribunal office has sent the decision and reasons for allowing the appeal. In practice, if an appeal is allowed and the Secretary of State does not go on to appeal to a higher court, the grant of asylum will follow shortly after the determination and reasons as a matter of course. There is no escaping the fact that, in substance, the judicial body determines the asylum claim: 'in asylum cases the appellate structure...is to be regarded as an extension of the decision-making process' (*Ravichandran v SSHD* [1996] Imm AR 97 at p.112). The procedures and principles by which asylum claims are decided are set out in the immigration rules paras 327–352 and in the Asylum Policy Instructions (APIs), disclosed on the Home Office website. The procedure should now be in conformity with the Procedures Directive, which takes precedence over any inconsistent domestic provision.

12.1.5.2 *Refugee Qualification Directive*

The content of the refugee definition is set out in the Refugee or Person in Need of International Protection (Qualification) Regulations 2006, SI 2006/2525, which implement into domestic law the EC Qualification Directive 2004/83/EC. These legislative provisions, which give statutory guidance for interpreting the Convention, guide decision-making by the Home Office and courts in the asylum process and have led to a major overhaul of the immigration rules, which now set out in unprecedented detail the criteria for granting asylum or humanitarian protection in the UK. The immigration rules state that asylum claims will be decided in accordance with the Refugee Convention (para 328) and that asylum will be granted if the claimant is found to be a refugee in accordance with the regulations (para 334).

Asylum law, which until recently was based solely on the Refugee Convention, general immigration rules and case law, has now been placed on a legislative footing and the courts will have to follow the regulations which implement the Directive. Where there are gaps in the rules or regulations, the Directive is directly effective and can be drawn upon to fill the gaps (e.g. in *AD* [2007] UKAIT 00065 the Directive's definition of 'family member' was relied upon as there was not one in the immigration rules). Commentators have argued that the impact of the Directive and new rules and regulations may make arguing appeals easier, given the clearly stipulated definitions of refugee status and subsidiary protection (see Symes, 2006 – full extract below). Lambert argues that the UK will have to raise its standards in some areas but possibly lower it in others. One of the key innovations brought by the Directive is that it makes the best interests of a child a primary consideration in implementing social rights for refugees (Article 20.5), and recital 12 says that the best interests of the child should be a primary consideration in implementing the whole Directive. This does not appear in the UK regulations, and the extensive new policies relating to asylum-seeking children issued on 31 January 2008 may be an effort to show compliance with the principle of the Directive. As mentioned in chapter 9, the UK is at the same time consulting on withdrawing its reservation to the UN Convention on the Rights of the Child in relation to immigration matters. As the Directive is now directly effective where implementation is defective, one way or another the best interests of the child will need to achieve greater prominence in UK refugee law. We will discuss elements of the Directive as they arise in the course of examining the refugee definition in the next chapter.

The direct relationship between the Refugee Convention and domestic law may still have some relevance, in the event of a provision of the Refugee Convention not covered by the Qualification Directive. The presumption is that Parliament intends to legislate compatibly with Treaty provisions, subject to displacement by express contrary indication.

Current authority as represented by *R (on the application of Pepushi)* v *Crown Prosecution Service* [2004] EWHC 798 (Admin) follows this usual principle. Here the statute clearly conflicts with the Refugee Convention, and it was held that the statute prevails, even though this defeats part of the protection of the Convention (see chapter 14). The disturbing implication of this is that Parliament can legislate its way out of international obligations, though not in matters covered by the Qualification Directive. In relation to delegated legislation the position is different. Although not yet challenged in the courts, the conclusion of the Parliamentary Joint Committee on Human Rights was that delegated legislation which conflicted with the Convention and made under a statutory power that purported to give effect to the Convention was ultra vires (see chapter 14 re Specification of Particularly Serious Crimes Order 2004, SI 2004/1910).

12.1.6 Asylum and human rights

Arguments under the European Convention on Human Rights, as enacted in the Human Rights Act, run alongside an asylum appeal and must be put forward at the same time as the grounds of appeal against a refusal of asylum by completing a form called a 'one stop notice'. This one-stop appeals system means that asylum seekers have one hearing at which their asylum and human rights claims are heard.

The Qualification Directive deals with some of the human rights protected under the ECHR as well as the Refugee Convention. Arguments that an asylum seeker will face treatment contrary to Article 3 ECHR, or Article 2 the right to life, will become submissions that they merit 'subsidiary protection' under the Directive. The conditions for subsidiary protection appear in Article 15 of the Directive, and are that the individual is at risk of a violation of Article 3 ECHR, namely torture or inhuman or degrading treatment or punishment, or the death penalty or execution, or a 'serious and individual' threat to their life as a result of 'indiscriminate violence in international or internal armed conflict' in their home country. The protection given is more limited than that to a refugee, but it is the first time that this kind of human rights protection has been collectively recognized by European states. Subsidiary protection does not cover other human rights claims such as a breach of Article 8 through separation from one's family by a threatened removal. These rights will still be governed by the safety net of the Human Rights Act.

Following the Qualification Directive, asylum and human rights cases will involve consideration of at least three broad grounds (Symes 2006):

- First, that the Appellant deserves refugee status under the Directive.
- Secondly, that they merit subsidiary protection.
- Thirdly, other human rights issues which could prevent their removal from the UK albeit not falling with the Directive's confines (e.g. Article 8).

Detailed provisions on granting humanitarian protection are now found in the amended immigration rules (rules 339C–H).

12.2 Process of making an asylum application

The outline of the process of making an asylum application will be described in this section in order to give the context for the legal issues that arise. Making an asylum claim is, in practice, a difficult thing to do within the law. Even before deterrent provisions were as fully developed as they are now, the predicament was described by Schiemann J in the case of *Yassine v SSHD* [1990] Imm AR 354 at 359:

The effect of the Carriers' Liability Act 1987 coupled with the Secretary of State's action in the present case is to pose substantial obstacles in the path of refugees wishing to come to this country. This is because:

1. Visa nationals require a passport before coming here;

2. You [sic] cannot get a visa on the basis of being a refugee in a country where you are being persecuted because at that stage you [sic] are usually not outside the country of nationality and thus do not fall within the definition of refugee and there is no provision for such situation in the immigration rules;

3. By reason of the 1987 Act carriers are disinclined to carry those without visas.

The Asylum and Immigration (Treatment of Claimants etc) Act 2004 has introduced further obstacles which will be discussed later in this chapter and in chapter 14.

Asylum applications may be made at the port of entry or at a later stage after legal or illegal entry. The latter are known as 'in-country' applications. Since March 2007 all new asylum claims are considered under the 'New Asylum Model' (NAM) introduced in the government's five-year plan in February 2005. In this model, the first interview is a screening interview which does not deal with the substance of the claim, but determines which route the claim is to follow. The NAM involves five routes, or 'segments', which determine: the speed at which the claim is processed; how the asylum seeker can obtain legal advice; the type of accommodation where they are required to live; how and where they are to remain in contact with the BIA; and whether they are subject to electronic monitoring. At the screening interview the applicant is required to produce their identity documents, particularly their passport, which will be retained for the duration of the claim. As discussed in chapter 14, coming to the interview without a passport may be an offence. They will have fingerprints and photographs taken and be given an application registration card (ARC) which holds biometric details, a prototype of the government's identity cards for all. A decision is taken on whether to detain the applicant or admit them on temporary admission (see chapter 15). Applicants from countries deemed safe or whose claims can be decided quickly may be detained immediately in Harmondsworth Removal Centre or Oakington Reception Centre and subjected to the 'fast-track' procedure (see below).

The five segments of the NAM are shown in the table below.

Table 12 New asylum model

Segment	Definition
1. Third country	People who the Home Office believes have, or could have, applied for asylum in a third country and are thus deemed ineligible for asylum in the UK. Some of these people are detained whilst others are not.
2. Minors	Unaccompanied minors and children in families who apply in their own right. Separated children may require a social services assessment to confirm their age and if they are accepted as a minor they are accommodated by social services. Until a social services age assessment determines that an age disputed young person should be dealt with as an adult their case will be processed through this segment, although they may be provided with support as an adult during this time.
	Case Owners dealing with cases in this segment have been specially trained to deal with children.

Table 12 *continued*

Segment	Definition
3. Potential non-suspensive appeal (NSA)	Nationals from one of the countries designated as generally 'safe'. Cases are considered on their merits but may be certified as clearly unfounded in which case the right of appeal has to be exercised from outside the UK. Individual asylum claims may also be certified clearly unfounded and attract only the NSA right. Some people in this segment are detained whilst others are not.
4. Detained fast track	Any asylum claim, whatever the nationality or country of origin of the claimant, may be fast tracked where it appears, after screening to be one that may be decided quickly.
5. General casework	Cases that do not come into any of the other categories. Some may be detained.

Reproduced with permission from the Refugee Council, *New Asylum Model* August 2007, showing the NAM as at that date (minor amendments made)

The objective of the NAM is speed. Each segment is allocated a tight timetable:

Table 13 NAM processing by type of case (in working days)

Segment	Screened	First Reporting to Case Owner	Asylum Interview	Decision served	Appeal	Removal
Third Country	1	Not processed as asylum claims				
Minors	1	10	25	35	35–115	N/A
NSA detained	1	1	3	10	Post removal	
NSA non-detained	1	2	5	11	Post removal	
Detained fast track	1	1	2–3	3–4	9–10	After 10
All other cases	1	3	8–12	30	30–100	After 100

Reproduced with permission from the Refugee Council, *New Asylum Model* August 2007. These details were correct at that date but, with the rapidly developing programme, could be subject to change. In particular, the January 2008 changes suggest that minors may be removed.

In the NAM, each asylum claim is allocated to a 'case owner', who sees the claimant through from arrival to refugee status or removal. The consideration and completion of the claim is speeded up by abandoning, in most cases, the former written application process, made by a SEF (Statement of Evidence Form). The substance of the asylum claim is explained by the claimant at interview with their case owner. Where, as in the majority of cases, the application is refused, the applicant receives what is known as a 'reasons for refusal' letter. These are discussed below in relation to the quality of decision-making. Asylum interviews require specific discussion.

12.2.1 Asylum interviews

The asylum interview gives the body of information upon which the claim will be decided. Until the NAM, and still in cases not decided under the NAM, the interview was preceded by a written statement (the SEF) which could be clarified at interview. Under the NAM this is no longer the case, and the claim depends upon the interview and any supporting evidence.

The UNHCR Handbook says,

While the burden of proof in principle rests on the applicant, the duty to ascertain and evaluate all the relevant facts is shared between the applicant and the examiner. (para 196)

The Qualification Directive echoes this approach:

Member States may consider it the duty of the applicant to submit as soon as possible all elements needed to substantiate the application for international protection. In cooperation with the applicant it is the duty of the Member State to assess the relevant elements of the application. (Article 4)

The UK accordingly does consider this the duty of the applicant, and sets out in the immigration rules in general terms the matters which the Secretary of State must take into account in determining the claim (para 339J).

The API on interviewing says that

The purpose of the asylum interview is to establish the facts of an asylum claim. Whilst an asylum claimant might have submitted information to the Home Office previously, the asylum interview will be the principal opportunity for a claimant to set out their claim and for the caseworker to examine any details they consider necessary. (para 2.2)

Thus, the interview should not be an adversarial process, but rather a collaborative investigation. Numerous inquiries into the asylum process have nevertheless commented on the poor and combative quality of asylum interviewing. For instance, Amnesty International records a perception by Home Office caseworkers of the interview as an opportunity to obtain material to attack the applicant's credibility by noting inconsistencies between the interview and the SEF and storing them up for a later refusal letter rather than putting the inconsistency to the applicant then and there (2004:20). The current APIs are a model of good practice in this respect, advising that any such discrepancies 'are thoroughly probed at interview', but it is clear from repeated studies of decision-making that the high standard of the APIs is not necessarily maintained in practice. Interviewers have also been criticized for chaotic questioning, not dealing with the relevant issues, appearing adversarial and intimidating, and not dealing sympathetically or appropriately with those who have suffered trauma such as rape or torture (e.g. Asylum Aid 1999, Amnesty International 2004). The Home Office's plan in conjunction with implementation of the NAM is that all case owners will be more fully trained and accredited. Obviously, it is crucial for the success of this new system that the quality of asylum interviewing improves. Unfortunately, the NAM has been started with a very tight timetable for implementation, so training of case owners will in many cases take place more than a year after the NAM began.

From 1 April 2004 it is no longer possible in most cases for an applicant for asylum to have public funding for a representative to be present at their asylum interview. The Court of Appeal in *R (Dirshe) v SSHD* [2005] EWCA Civ 421 held that in these circumstances, where the applicant had no public funding either for a representative or for their own interpreter, the overall fairness of the process required that the applicant be able to tape record the asylum interview, so that there is some record of it independently of that kept by the Home Office. The earlier case of *Mapah v SSHD* [2003] EWHC 306 (Admin) went in the opposite direction, but this was when legal aid was available for a representative to attend.

Dirshe has been interpreted in the API as an obligation to record the interview 'on request by the claimant'. Applicants may request an interpreter or interviewer of their gender, but this is of little use if they do not have advice about this before interview. Not only is publicly funded legal advice rarely available for asylum interviews but, as discussed in chapter 8, is now generally in very short supply. Immigration Law Update reports that the Home Office acted rapidly upon the requirement to tape interviews, but the Legal Services Commission has been less willing to fund the time for lawyers to listen to the tapes (vol. 8, no. 11, p. 28).

12.2.2 Quality of initial decision-making

The initial decision on an asylum claim is crucial for a number of reasons:

- Most obviously, it concerns matters of fundamental human rights, and affects the physical safety, the material and psychological well-being of the applicant
- As a public law decision of a governmental body it is an exercise of power and uniquely disposes of the matter in question (unlike say a private commercial transaction in which if a greengrocer puts up their prices the customer can decide not to buy or go somewhere else)
- It is increasingly difficult for the applicant to obtain legal representation to appeal a wrong decision as sources of advice are few and far between, and in the NAM in particular, timescales are very tight
- Asylum law and procedure is demanding and complex, and an unrepresented appellant has little chance of succeeding
- If the applicant can obtain legal advice, the work and public expense of undoing a wrong decision can be considerable, causing a burden on the legal system
- The asylum decision is an implementation of an international protection treaty. The decision-maker has a responsibility to implement this so as to maintain the standards and principles of that international scheme.

The actual quality of asylum decision-making has by no means matched its importance. Criticism of the process has been sustained from a variety of sources. Since 1995 eleven major reports from governmental and non-governmental organisations have been published which are highly critical of the asylum decision-making process. They are listed in the reading at the end of this chapter. The reports on quality focused broadly on three areas: the interview, the reasons for refusal letter, and information about asylum seekers' country of origin. This last subject is treated separately below at 12.7.3.

Asylum Aid drew attention to 'unfair and arbitrary methods' as 'the norm' and found that 'many people with valid reasons for seeking the UK's protection were refused asylum on the basis of cursory and careless examination and fundamental misunderstandings of the situations of refugees' (1999:1). Across all the reports, concerns are found in common, including:

- medical evidence corroborating horrific abuse was dismissed or misunderstood;
- proof was required to an excessively high standard (see below and chapter 13 for the asylum standard of proof);
- minor ambiguities or discrepancies were used to discredit the applicants, even when these had no bearing on the basis of the asylum claim;
- insensitivity in interviewing about serious trauma, particularly torture and rape;

- ignoring evidence relating to an individual;
- but also turning down claims on the basis that country-wide human rights reports documented abuses but did not refer to the applicant personally;
- unreasonable assertions about individual credibility;
- inappropriate use of standard paragraphs in reasons for refusal letters;
- making findings at odds with the evidence.

The reports contain dozens of examples. Just one which illustrates some of the points above is that of an asylum seeker who had over a hundred burn marks on his back, and bruises where he had been held down. The reasons for refusal letter opined: 'Taking into account your appalling lack of credibility the Secretary of State considers that in fact these wounds were inflicted at your request in an attempt to strengthen your claim' (Asylum Aid 1999:19).

Asylum Aid (1999), the Medical Foundation and the Constitutional Affairs Committee considered that there had been an improvement in the quality of interviewing and decision-making over the time upon which they were able to comment. However, serious concerns remained. The Home Office's written guidance had improved greatly, so that the Medical Foundation in 2004 was able to say that the APIs were on the whole good. Crucially, though, the APIs were not necessarily followed, and it was clear that monitoring and research had to continue along with a programme of measures to generate better quality decisions.

One, albeit contested, indicator of the quality of initial decision-making is the number and outcome of appeals. The Home Affairs Committee noted:

> Over the past ten years there has been a steep rise in initial-level appeals...from 2, 440 determined in 1994 to 64, 405 determined in 2002. This has been accompanied by a significant rise in the proportion of appeals which are successful, from 4% in 1994 to 22% in 2002. (Second Report 2003–4 HC 218 para 122)

The Committee took this as an indication that 'there are still grounds for concern about the poor quality of much initial decision-making by immigration officers and caseworkers' (para 143). The government took the view that the way to deal with an increase in the number of appeals was to cut down the right of appeal. Thus, in the Asylum and Immigration (Treatment of Claimants etc) Bill which became the 2004 Act they proposed reducing the appeals system to one tier. When asked to report on the Bill the Home Affairs Committee took this view of the problem and the solution:

> The real flaws in the system appear to be at the stage of initial decision-making, not that of appeal. We recommend that the implementation of the new asylum appeals system should be *contingent* on a significant improvement in initial decision-making having been demonstrated. In particular, the relevant sections of the Act should not be brought into force until the statistics show a clear reduction in the number of successful appeals at the first tie, adjudication level. (First Report 2003–4 HC 109, para 43)

The Committee repeated this view in its report on asylum applications (HC 218 para 143) and the Constitutional Affairs committee supported the recommendation (HC 211 recommendation 5). The remit of the Constitutional Affairs Committee's second report was to consider the effects of the 2002 Act and whether it had improved efficiency savings and improved the quality of the appeal process. Ostensibly, neither this nor the Home Affairs Committee in its first report was concerned with the asylum application process. However, the conclusion of both was that the problem did not lie in the arena of appeals and the matters addressed by the legislation. The real problem lay in the quality of initial decisions. The Home Affairs Committee recommended that there should be 'greater "front-loading" of the applications system, that is, putting greater resources into achieving fair and sustainable decisions at an early stage' (HC 218 para 144). It recommended more good-quality legal advice and interpretation at an early stage, recruitment of more caseworkers with specialist knowledge of asylum seekers' countries of origin and review of the 'overall calibre and training' of those who take initial decisions (para 144).

Even as recently as 2005 the report of the Independent Race Monitor says:

I reviewed samples of initial decisions and concluded that there was evidence of inappropriate decision-making. In some instances, caseworkers disbelieved claimants who told 'similar stories' about events, assuming they must have learned the details from others. Several refusal decisions were based on caseworkers' assumptions about what should have occurred, or on small discrepancies and inconsistencies in accounts of events, giving the impression that there was a tendency to disbelieve, and whatever the applicant's experience, some grounds for refusal would be found. (para 18)

The House of Commons Committee of Public Accounts recommended that IND find out why appeals are upheld, particularly among nationalities for which the highest rates of appeals are allowed (recommendation 7).

The government responded to the Constitutional Affairs Committee that they did not accept that the quality of initial decision-making was poor (Cm paper 6236) and the single-tier proposal was not only retained but swiftly implemented. Numbers of appeals have now dropped again, but the successful percentage remains the same. 16,145 appeals determined in 2006, of which 23 per cent were allowed.

Sometimes case law reveals a lack of training or information within the decision-making process. For example, from October 2000 there was a policy in force that asylum seekers should not be refused asylum on the ground that they could relocate in the Kurdish Autonomous Area (KAA), having travelled through government-controlled Iraq. This was on the ground that travel through this route would not be safe for a failed asylum seeker. Mr Rashid was refused asylum during the currency of this policy, on the ground that he could relocate to the KAA. He did not know of the policy. Nor apparently did any caseworker or lawyer for the Home Office at any of the six decision-making points in his claim and appeal, though it was well known to some others. The Court of Appeal held that this was unfairness amounting to an abuse of power (*SSHD* v *R (Bakhtear Rashid)* [2005] EWCA Civ 744).

Since 2004 the UNHCR has been working with the Home Office to achieve an improvement in the quality of decision-making. Their observations and recommendations focus on improving assessment of credibility in asylum claims. They emphasize the need to concentrate on the facts at the initial decision stage, and warn against disbelieving the asylum seeker before the claim has been properly assessed. This remains a challenge, they say, 'for a significant number of NAM decision makers' (UNHCR 2006). The Refugee Council made a study after six months of the NAM being in operation for all initial claims. The results suggested that there was some positive experience, also that several aspects were not working as intended, including that the case owner was not able to see all claimants personally due to workload (Research Report January 2008). They suggest that the NAM has not brought about any significant change in the underlying 'culture of disbelief' (New Asylum Model August 2007).

12.2.3 **Non-compliance refusals**

Paragraph 339M of the immigration rules allows the Secretary of State to refuse an asylum or human rights claim where there is 'failure, without reasonable explanation, to make a prompt and full disclosure of material facts, either orally or in writing, or otherwise to assist the Secretary of State in establishing the facts of the case'. This includes failure to report for fingerprinting, or to complete an asylum questionnaire (the SEF), comply with a request to attend an interview or report to an Immigration Officer for examination.

In *Haddad* (00HX00926) the tribunal held that refusal must not be for non-compliance alone. The rules require, as we have seen, that applications must be determined in accordance with the Refugee Convention. Therefore even in a case of non-compliance, whatever evidence is available about the claim, even if it is in the form of brief notes taken by the immigration officer on arrival, must be considered (API on non-compliance). See Macdonald (2005:784–785) for further discussion of the law surrounding these refusals.

Although the position following *Haddad* is that a refusal may not be issued on the grounds of non-compliance alone, it is clearly unsatisfactory that a matter of perhaps life and death should be determined without an interview, or even on the basis of just a few notes. There is room for speculation as to what difference, if any, it would make if Article 6 ECHR were applied to refugee claims. Article 6 requires a fair and public hearing in the determination of civil rights and obligations. As there is no civil right to asylum, Article 6 could only apply, if at all, to the right to have a claim assessed. The determination of whether this has happened in a sense only occurs at an appeal hearing. Perhaps the application of Article 6 would open the decision-making process to greater scrutiny at the tribunal. See also the Court of Appeal's discussion of fairness in *R (on the application of the Refugee Legal Centre) v SSHD* [2004] EWCA Civ 1481, discussed below.

12.3 **Fast-track procedures**

The Home Office is placing more and more emphasis on speeding up claims and getting asylum cases dealt with as quickly as possible. Even before the NAM, from 2000 onwards there have been increasing initiatives in fast-track decision-making.

The Joint Committee on Human Rights, in its Report on Treatment of Asylum Seekers, explains as follows:

Detained fast track processes currently operate at three centres: Harmondsworth, Yarl's Wood and Oakington. The fast track process at Harmondsworth and Yarl's Wood is a key part of the IND's New Asylum Model, and the Home Office Five Year Strategy sets out plans to process up to 30% of new cases using detained fast track. IND states that the process is geared to claimants being detained pending a quick decision on their asylum claims, and that the average timescale from making a claim to removal is one month, including any appeal.

The route associated with Oakington is used for those asylum seekers who come from countries that are designated safe by statutory instrument, based on the Secretary of State's belief that there is 'in general' or relating to a particular part or a particular group, no risk of persecution in that country. Applicants from these countries will have their case certified as unfounded, and so have no right of appeal in the UK. This is known as a non-suspensive appeal, because appeal does not suspend removal. This certification is discussed below, and detention at Oakington is discussed in chapter 15. Under the New Asylum Model, people who are in this group are designated 'NSA' – non-suspensive appeal – and may be detained or not, pending the decision on their claim and removal.

Selection for Harmondsworth or Yarl's Wood is not based on a statutory presumption of an unfounded claim, but on a departmental list which may change frequently, compiled under the authority of a ministerial authorization to discriminate on the basis of nationality, Race Relations Act 1976 s 19D, as explained in chapter 8. This list is of countries from which applications may be deemed suitable for quick decision. The list includes some countries for which claims may be certified as NSA, but also some that are not. This usually means refusal as shown by the Asylum Statistics; for instance, in the first quarter of 2006 there were 330 initial decisions at Harmondsworth of which 1 per cent were granted asylum. Claims at Harmondsworth and Yarl's Wood are to be decided in three days. This system is sometimes known as the 'super-fast track'. It is geared to fast processing through the appeals system as well as the initial decision. Harmondsworth has hearing rooms as well as the detention facilities, so that the whole process from arrival through appeal can take place on the premises. Time limits for appeal then allow two days for notice of appeal, two days for a respondent's notice, and the hearing must be fixed within two days after that (Immigration and Asylum Appeal (Fast Track Procedure) Rules 2005, SI 2005/560).

Engagement of the appeals as well as decision-making system means that the Ministry of Justice, formerly Department of Constitutional Affairs, is also engaged in the business of fast processing of asylum seekers. The DCA Department report 2006/07 says:

We continue to work closely with the Home Office in integrating the appeals system as part of the NAM...Processes have been reviewed and amended in line with the principles of end-to-end case management by Home Office caseworkers. (4.9)

Concerns about the fairness of this system have been expressed by UNHCR, BID and the Joint Committee on Human Rights. The UNHCR has commented that the two day time limit for appealing is too short, and runs the risk of returning someone to persecution and thus contravening the Refugee Convention (Asylum and Immigration Tribunal – Fast Track Procedure Rules, Response to Consultation CP(R) 05/05 Department for Constitutional Affairs). Some key findings of the BID research were:

- 77 per cent of detainees did not have publicly funded representation at their appeal hearing
- There was inadequate time to prepare the case
- Claims of torture were made but not investigated
- Detainees did not know why they were in the fast track or what it entailed
- 60 days after the appeal hearing, one third of the detainees were still detained. (2006:8)

The Joint Committee on Human Rights concluded:

226. We are concerned that the decision to detain an asylum seeker at the beginning of the process simply in order to consider his or her application may be arbitrary because it is based on assumptions about the safety or otherwise of the country from which the asylum seeker has come. It is self-evident that some asylum seekers – most obviously torture victims and those who have

been sexually abused – are unlikely to reveal the full extent of experiences to the authorities in such a short-time period, and that this problem will be exacerbated where they are not able to access legal advice and representation, and the support of organisations able to help them come to terms with their experiences.

227. We are also concerned that although fast track detention for anything more than a short, tightly controlled period of time is unlawful, some asylum seekers find themselves detained at the beginning of the asylum process for periods in excess of this. The act of claiming asylum is not a criminal offence and should not be treated as such. If asylum seekers are detained at the beginning of the asylum process, then the period of detention should be limited to a maximum of seven days.

228. We recommend that asylum seekers who are detained as part of the fast track and super fast track processes should be provided with free, on-site legal advice – for example, on the model previously provided by the Refugee Legal Centre and the Immigration Advisory Service at Oakington – to ensure that victims of torture and other forms of abuse are identified and taken out of the process; and that claims for asylum are properly considered. (10th report 2006–07: Treatment of Asylum Seekers)

The lawfulness of the fast track was challenged by the Refugee Legal Centre, but the Court of Appeal held that although the system was not operating with sufficient flexibility, and improvements should be made, it was not *inherently* unfair and therefore could not be said to be unlawful (*R (on the application of the Refugee Legal Centre) v SSHD* [2004] EWCA Civ 1481 at para 25). IND's operational instructions were revised to respond to the Court of Appeal's comments, to make provision for such contingencies as for example the illness of the applicant, non-attendance or lateness of representative and the need for more evidence to be gathered. However, the matter arose again in *R (on application of Sidibe)* [2007] EWCA Civ 191. The applicant's solicitors had applied on at least three occasions within a few days to have the case taken out of the fast track. An expert confirmed that there were complex issues that needed more evidence, but the Secretary of State still refused to take the case out of the fast track, apparently on the basis that the right of appeal (within the fast track) would be enough to deal with issues. Moses J held that this was not so. The right of appeal could not replace taking the case out of the fast track, which, following evidence given in the *Refugee Legal Centre* case, should have been done as soon as it was apparent that more evidence was needed. See chapter 18 for the other extraordinary breach in this case.

Harmondsworth is intended only for single men, interpreted by the Minister for Citizenship and Immigration as 'men who have no dependants on their claim' (HC Debs 16 Sept 2004 col 158WS). The claimant argued in *Kpandang v SSHD* [2004] EWHC 2130 Admin that his detention in Harmondsworth was unlawful partly because he had a partner and child. McCombe J was persuaded that 'single' meant that there were only detention facilities for men on their own, not that it referred to their marital status. He also held that short detention in reasonable circumstances would not in general be a breach of Article 8 and was not in this situation given other justifications for detaining the claimant (see *R (on the application of Saadi) v SSHD* [2002] UKHL 41, discussed in chapter 15).

The 2003 report into conditions of detention at Harmondsworth by the Chief Inspector of prisons found that the centre was 'unsafe'. There was a hunger strike in May 2004 in protest at the length of detention, poor legal advice and assaults by staff. Although the legal process is fast, once the claim has been denied and the appeal lost, the claimant may then face a considerable period in detention before being removed. BID found that two months' detention following failure of the claim was common, and reported an instance of 10 months of such detention (BID to Des Browne, Minister for Citizenship and Immigration 15 March 2005).

There were disturbances at the centre on 19 and 20 July 2004 when a detainee, Sergey Baranuyck, was found hanged in a shower room. A report into the disturbances by Sue McAllister, Head of Security Group, H M Prison Service found, ironically, that the open and unstructured nature of the detention for 501 young men, without the usual system of earning privileges associated with prisons, was in part to blame for the tensions in the centre (HC 1265, November 2004). A further report by the Chief Inspector of Prisons in July 2005 found that there had been some improvements but that shortcomings remained, including in reception procedures and access to competent legal advice. There was another suicide at Harmondsworth on 19 January 2006, the thirteenth in immigration detention in the UK since 2000.

Yarl's Wood is for women and families. Research into the experiences of women there suggests that there are serious problems with the fairness of the system, for instance:

Applications to be taken out of the Detained Fast Track were rejected in the following cases: a complex case involving torture, suicidal tendencies, sexuality, and a lack of medical evidence; sexual violence; exceptional circumstances based on sexual assault; pregnancy (the appellant was 26 weeks pregnant). (Cutler 2007)

There are many examples of very poor practice. For instance, one woman's claim based on forced marriage, rape and threat of FGM was adjourned for one hour to be examined by the detention centre doctor. She was refused the same day at the hearing where the medical evidence was not considered (2007:11). The data gathered by BID suggests that women asylum seekers in Yarl's Wood are placed in a position where they will fail at every stage. Legal representation is available at public expense to all women for their initial asylum claim, using a rota system maintained by the LSC. Representatives without a fast-track contract cannot undertake fast-track work using legal aid, although privately charging lawyers can and do. In BID's experience, the quality of legal representation on the rota is very varied. Allocation to a lawyer on the rota is administered by the Home Office; women cannot choose whom to approach. Should women be unhappy with the quality of work or the decision not to represent them at their appeal, the timetable continues, leaving women without representation and vulnerable to refusal and removal.

It is notable that, in BID research on Harmondsworth and Yarl's Wood, there is a surprisingly low instance of applications to take cases out of the fast track. The fast track is a Home Office administrative procedure which has become too closely associated or confused with legal status or rights. As Farbey says, 'there is no difference between asylum claimants in Harmondsworth and elsewhere, save that the Home Office has decided that Harmondsworth cases can be speedily processed' (2004:199). These claimants are subjected to a different set of appeal procedure rules, with shorter time limits for action to be taken. The judicial process has therefore been changed according to the view taken by one party of the merits of the proceedings.

12.4 'Clearly unfounded' – non-suspensive appeal

Under Nationality, Immigration and Asylum Act 2002 s 94(2) the Secretary of State has the power to certify that an asylum claim is 'clearly unfounded'. The result is that there will be no appeal in the UK. These are known as 'non-suspensive appeals' (NSAs), i.e. the appeal does not suspend the removal. As the claim will be refused (because the

Secretary of State is saying it has no merit) the asylum seeker faces removal. An appeal from abroad, especially in a country where the person fears persecution, is worthless.

The statute offers no further guidance on the meaning of 'clearly unfounded'. Case law has established that 'clearly unfounded' means 'bound to fail' (*R v SSHD ex p Thangasara and Yogathas* [2002] UKHL 36, concerning an earlier similar provision) or that the case is 'unarguable' (*R (on the application of Razgar) v Secretary of State for the Home Department* [2003] EWCA Civ 840, not overturned by the House of Lords). This is a demanding standard. The SSHD should consider whether the claim is either partially or wholly credible in the round, and 'whether, if eventually believed in whole or in part, it is capable of coming within the Refugee Convention. If the answers are such that the claim cannot on any legitimate view succeed, then the claim is clearly unfounded, if not, not' (*ZL and VL v SSHD* [2003] 1 All ER 1062). This means that where there is a factual dispute, or any evidence is still awaited, the claim cannot be certified. Given the acknowledged difficulty in making a decision in asylum claims, one might expect that, if this standard were rigorously applied, there would be few certificates. Instead, many cases coming before the higher courts are challenges to certificates that the case is 'clearly unfounded'. This is a dangerous power, particularly in the 'refusal culture' which seems to persist in the Home Office (see e.g. Refugee Council 2007). The Asylum Statistics do not record how often this power is used, as NSA cases are recorded in the same total as those who choose not to appeal.

12.4.1 'Safe' countries of origin

Some countries are treated as 'safe', so that if an applicant is from one of these countries the Secretary of State must certify their claim unless satisfied that it is not clearly unfounded (s 94(3)). Once again, the consequences are that there is no appeal in the UK.

The basis upon which a country or part of a country is designated as 'safe' is that the Secretary of State is satisfied that there is 'in general' in that State or that part of the state 'no serious risk of persecution' (s 94(5)). Blanket statements of safety sit rather uneasily with the requirement to investigate whether the particular applicant is at risk. Returning someone before their appeal is heard to a country where they fear persecution risks a breach of the principle of *non-refoulement*.

In making the decision to designate, the Secretary of State:

(a) shall have regard to all the circumstances of the State or part (including its laws and how they are applied), and

(b) shall have regard to information from any appropriate source (including other member States and international organisations). (s 94(5C))

This requirement was inserted by the Asylum (Procedures) Regulations 2007, SI 2007/3187, implementing Council Directive 2005/85/EC of 1 December 2005 on minimum standards on procedures in member states for granting and withdrawing refugee status (the Asylum Procedures Directive). The Directive permits certification only where 'it can be shown that there is generally and consistently no persecution...no torture or inhuman or degrading treatment or punishment and no threat by reason of indiscriminate violence in situations of...armed conflict'. Designation of safe countries of origin was a matter upon which European member states were unable to agree. Within Europe there has been strenuous opposition to the concept of safe countries of origin and accelerated or suspensive procedures (see ECRE March 2005 and Statewatch 2004). The new subsection requires the Secretary of State to consider a broad base of evidence, whereas the section as originally enacted made no specifications as to how the Secretary of State should reach this view. Still the Directive's standard is more demanding.

Subsection (3) says:

If the Secretary of State is satisfied that an asylum claimant or human rights claimant is entitled to reside in a State listed in subsection (4) he shall certify the claim...unless satisfied that it is not clearly unfounded.

The use of the word 'shall' means that the Secretary of State is obliged to certify the claim unless satisfied that there are reasons to the contrary. The burden of proof is therefore on the claimant to show that the claim is not clearly unfounded. In *ZL and VL v SSHD and Lord Chancellor's Department* [2003] 1 All ER 1062 the Court of Appeal set out the decision-maker's process of reasoning to certify a claim clearly unfounded:

(i)   consider the factual substance and detail of the claim

(ii) consider how it stands with the known background data

(iii) consider whether in the round it is capable of belief

(iv) if not, consider whether some part of it is capable of belief

(v)   consider whether, if eventually believed in whole or in part, it is capable of coming within the Convention. (para 57)

They concluded that there was 'no intelligible way' of certifying a claim from a listed country except by this same process (para 58). *Koceku* (below) clearly demonstrates that in every case a view must be taken of the merits of the case, even when the applicant comes from a listed country.

There is a power in s 94 to add to or remove from the list by Order made by the Secretary of State. The grounds for addition are that the Secretary of State is satisfied that:

(a) there is in general in that State or part no serious risk of persecution of persons entitled to reside in that State or part, and

(b) removal to that State or part of persons entitled to reside there will not in general contravene UK's obligations under the Human Rights Convention (s 94(5)).

States designated under Orders now in force are:

- Albania, Jamaica, Macedonia, Moldova, Bolivia, Brazil, Ecuador, South Africa, Ukraine (Asylum (Designated States) (No. 2) Order 2003, SI 2003/1919),
- India (Asylum (Designated States) Order 2005, SI 2005/330),
- Mongolia (SI 2005/3306),
- Bosnia-Herzegovina, Mauritius, Montenegro, Peru, Serbia (SI 2007/2221).

The 2004 Act contains a further power for the Secretary of State to certify a state or part of a state safe in relation to a group of people (s 27(5), inserting s 94(5A) in the 2002 Act). The power was used for the first time in December 2005 to designate Ghana and Nigeria safe for men, and in 2007 also in respect of men: Gambia, Kenya, Liberia, Malawi, Mali and Sierra Leone.

Criticisms could be and have been made of the inclusion of a number of these countries. For instance, it is difficult to reconcile the inclusion of Albania with the UK government's commitment to improve its policy and practice in relation to the protection of women trafficked for sex, Albania being one of the major centres of organized crime of this kind. Certification of an Albanian case was successfully challenged in *R (Koceku) v SSHD* [2003] EWHC 2063 in which Newman J said that the evidence of a sufficiency of protection in blood feud cases fell short of a standard which would make Mr Koceku's case unarguable. There had been conflicting findings in relation to protection in similar Albanian cases in the very recent past.

In *A v Secretary of State for the Home Department* [2003] EWCA Civ 175 the Court of Appeal found the Jamaican appellant at risk of her life and of degrading treatment, giving rise to breaches of Articles 2 and 3 if she were to be returned. The speed with which a claim may be refused and the person returned without an appeal hearing may give rise to real risks in individual serious cases such as that of A. In *Atkinson v SSHD* [2004] EWCA Civ 846 (see chapter 13) the Court of Appeal held that there was at least an arguable case that the criminal justice system offered insufficient protection for the applicant in Jamaica. The claim should not have been certified.

12.4.1.1 *Challenging designation*

There are two levels of decision which may be challenged. One is the specific decision to certify the particular claim, as in Atkinson's case, as clearly unfounded. The more fundamental challenge is to the designation of a country within s 94. The designation of Bangladesh was successfully challenged in *R (on the application of Zakir Husan) v SSHD* [2005] EWHC 189 (Admin). Wilson J held the inclusion of Bangladesh to be irrational and therefore unlawful in the light of a volume of evidence about widespread human rights violations in the country. The more or less unanimous picture painted by CIPU reports at the time of the designation of Bangladesh was that violence in politics was pervasive, the use of torture was widespread, abuse of children and violence against women and religious minorities was common and widespread and corruption endemic (*Husan* para 55). Bangladesh was removed from the list of safe countries on 22 April 2005 (Asylum (Designated States) (Amendment) Order 2005, SI 2005/1016).

The arguments in *Husan* raised some important and interesting questions about the basis for designating a country as 'in general' one in which there is no serious risk of persecution. The Secretary of State relies in part on the low number of successful asylum claims from a country in determining whether it can be designated. Wilson J exposed the fallacy in this reasoning. He pointed out that poor economic conditions might well drive some people to make asylum claims which would be refused, but that this did not indicate a low risk of persecution in the country. It was disclosed that in Parliament a minister had replied that concerns about human rights in Bangladesh, did not mean that 'the vast majority' of Bangladeshi nationals were at risk of having their human rights abused, apparently confusing the question of whether there was in general a serious risk of persecution with a risk of general serious persecution. The Minister advanced the reason for designation that 'it gives people the message that it is not worth coming unless they believe that they have a genuine claim' (para 21). The certification process does not, of course, test the genuineness of the applicants' beliefs.

In the case of Sri Lanka, the government removed the designation without litigation specifically on that point, though there had been many challenges to the certification of individual Sri Lankan claimants. The designation of Sri Lanka followed a peace accord in that country, but conflict broke out again very shortly after the order was made. In 2004 the UN Human Rights Committee called on the Sri Lankan government to cease using confessions which have been extracted by torture (Advocacy.net news bulletin no.23, 2 November 2004). Human rights groups continued to press that Sri Lanka was not a safe country. On December 2006 the government repealed the designation of Sri Lanka on account of the deteriorating situation there.

In *ZL and VL v SSHD and Lord Chancellor's Department* [2003] 1 All ER 1062 the Master of the Rolls held that the inclusion of a country in the so-called White List did not mean that there was no risk of any breach of Convention rights. It seems to be easier to identify what inclusion in the List does not mean rather than what it does mean. Persecution is only in the most extreme cases a phenomenon encountered 'in general' in a country. This is inherent in the concept of discrimination. In *Husan* the evidence was that Bangladesh ranked worst in the world on a Corruption Perceptions index (UK Foreign and Commonwealth Office 2004) and was either second or fourth worst in the world for violence against women (Immigration and Refugee Board of Canada). The widespread nature of torture and police brutality and corruption meant that any individual could be at risk. So whatever a country is in which there is 'in general' no serious risk of persecution, it is not this, following *Husan*.

An earlier challenge to the inclusion of India failed (*R (Balwinder Singh) v SSHD and Special Adjudicator* [2001] EWHC Admin 925) on the basis that, although Sikhs may be persecuted, they were too small a percentage of the population to mean there was a risk of persecution 'in general'. 'In general' did not mean 'recurring', 'ongoing' or 'predictable'. It referred to the spread of persecution over the population.

Burton J also found that there was nothing illegal in the Secretary of State having a policy of this kind, and that this did not interfere with each case being decided on its merits.

The first challenge of this kind was in *R v SSHD ex p Javed and Ali* [2001] Imm AR 529 in which the designation of Pakistan under an earlier statute was found to be unlawful. The claimants relied in particular on the House of Lords' judgment concerning women in that country in *Shah and Islam* (see chapter 13) and the recorded position of Ahmadis there. These were evidence of persecution of women and religious minorities. The challenge raised a constitutional question. The Secretary of State argued that the designation could not be challenged as it had been made by affirmative resolution in Parliament, which was argued to be a proceeding in Parliament. To interfere with it would therefore be a breach of Article 9 of the Bill of Rights 1689 which prohibits proceedings in Parliament from being questioned in the courts. The Court of Appeal did not accept that argument. By approving the Order, Parliament had not debated its justification in detail or examined the evidence for it. Even though the Order was made by affirmative resolution it was still delegated legislation and as such open to judicial review in the usual way. Having disposed of the constitutional point the Court of Appeal found that, on the evidence concerning women and Ahmadis, the Secretary of State's decision to include Pakistan in the White List was irrational.

12.5 Credibility

Credibility is the term used to refer to whether or not the decision maker believes the applicant is telling the truth about their claim. An assessment of an applicant's credibility is made by the Home Office, and then upheld or overturned by the immigration judge at the appeal. Arguably, the subject of credibility could fill a chapter on its own, or be dealt with in the next chapter, or chapter 14, or this one, or not at all. In determining refugee claims the question of credibility is both everything and nothing. It is not an aspect of the refugee definition to be satisfied, like the matters covered in the next chapter, and yet the majority of asylum claims which are lost are lost precisely because of adverse findings on credibility – in other words the decision-maker does not believe the applicant's story.

Credibility can be considered alongside 'well-founded fear' as discussed in chapter 13. A fear will only be well founded if it is genuine. As the main source of evidence is usually the asylum seeker themselves, the assessment of whether that person is to be believed is crucial. If the decision-maker does not believe the asylum seeker's account, they are found not to be credible and their claim will fail. Difficulties arise where decision-makers disbelieve asylum seekers too readily and make negative credibility findings very early on in the process without assessing all the evidence.

What must be credible is the main part of the asylum seeker's story, as explained further below. Unfortunately, the issue of credibility has become entangled with the question of assessing whether they are afraid. This issue is discussed further in the next chapter, where it is contended that decision-makers should not be looking to establish that the refugee has a subjective state of trepidation about what they might face if returned to their home country. This is not what proves they are at risk. It is not appropriate to require the decision-maker to assess the inner state of a person whose culture and circumstances may be very far from their own. Hathaway and Hicks (2005, see further reading for chapter 13) describe how this impossible quest leads decision-makers to attempt to 'objectify' the asylum seeker's state of mind with questions such as 'did you claim asylum at the first opportunity?'. The implication is that, if not, the asylum seeker was not genuinely afraid. Thus the assessment of credibility may be bound up with a search for subjective fear, a search which arguably should not be undertaken.

A very important principle in asylum law is that, although the asylum seeker has to prove their case, there is no requirement for their evidence to be corroborated from another source, as there would be in a civil case (*SSHD v Karakas* [1998] EWCA Civ 961). The standard of proof is a reasonable degree of likelihood (see *Sivakumaran and Karanakaran*, chapter 13). This is a particularly important principle, given that an asylum seeker may well have quickly fled their country in fear of persecution and not have been in a position to collect relevant documentation before their departure. Furthermore, when travelling clandestinely in order to avoid the authorities, it would not be desirable to be holding information on their person, such as an arrest warrant, which would identify them as wanted by the authorities if they were stopped en route. It is often the case, therefore, that the asylum seeker's evidence consists of their written statement and objective country information but little else. They should not be penalized for this.

The case of *Chiver* (10758) is an authority on the proper approach to credibility. The adjudicator in that case pointed to the discrepancies in the respondent's story in order to, in the words of the tribunal:

list the matters which were adverse to the respondent's case and to reflect his belief that they did not affect the kernel of his story. He adopted the approach which is urged upon adjudicators i.e. to weigh up the evidence and to indicate that which is believed and that which is not.

From this it may be gleaned that some inconsistencies are not fatal to the claim. The question is whether the immigration judge believes the core of what is claimed, or, in the oft quoted words in *Chiver*, whether 'the centerpiece of the story stands'. In the same case the tribunal pointed out that there may be perfectly valid and understandable reasons for exaggeration or not telling the truth, which do not mean the asylum claim is not valid. For instance, a claimant may embroider their story if they fear it is not strong enough or change facts which they fear will be thought implausible. Gorlick (2002) quotes Hathaway as making the same point, that dishonesty, though not to be encouraged, is explicable for instance 'when bad advice is received from traffickers or others viewed by an asylum seeker as an expert'.

The case should be looked at in the round, and all the relevant circumstances taken into account (*Karanakaran*, see chapter 13). In *AA (Turkey) v SSHD* EWCA Civ 6/11/07 (Lawtel unreported) the Court of Appeal held that even if an asylum seeker's real motive for leaving his country had been to avoid military service, that would not relieve the decision maker of the obligation to consider all matters relevant to the risk of ill-treatment.

Immigration judges are warned about judging facts to be implausible. Hathaway (1991:81) points out that it is not in the nature of repressive societies to behave reasonably. Decision-makers should not place weight on their own subjective and culturally bound views about a claimant's demeanour or way of giving a statement or evidence.

This was evident in *HK v SSHD* [2006] EWCA Civ 1037 where the court characterized the facts as 'unusual and remarkable'. Nevertheless, the evidence was consistent and there was no contradictory evidence. The court gave important guidance:

Inherent probability, which may be helpful in many domestic cases, can be a dangerous, even a wholly inappropriate, factor to rely on in some asylum cases. Much of the evidence will be referable to societies with customs and circumstances which are very different from those of which the members of the fact-finding tribunal have any (even second-hand) experience. Indeed, it is likely that the country which an asylum-seeker has left will be suffering from the sort of problems and dislocations with which the overwhelming majority of residents of this country will be wholly unfamiliar. (para 29)

The mere concept of inherent improbability is inappropriate where one has no real grasp of what would be inherent in a situation. The Court of Appeal in *Gheisari v SSHD* [2004] EWCA Civ 1854 took a slightly different but related tack, saying that just because something is inherently improbable does not mean it is not true.

It is legally permissible to find the claimant's account inherently implausible, even though such a conclusion should be reached with extreme care. In *MM (DRC – Plausibility) Democratic Republic of Congo* [2005] UKIAT 00019 the appellant claimed to have escaped leaving his clothes in the hands of a solider who was restraining him, and then have vaulted a six-foot wall while six other soldiers were outside the house in which he and his family had been seized. His advocate at the tribunal advanced possible explanations, but the tribunal held that, where there were possible explanations, these should be advanced by the claimant, not speculated upon by his representative. In the absence of such alternative explanations the adjudicator had not been wrong to find this account inherently implausible, and to do so it did not need to be outside the realm of human experience, thus declining to follow an Australian decision, *W148/00 A v Ministry for Immigration and Multicultural Affairs* [2002] FCA 679.

In *MM* the tribunal gave further guidance on the treatment of the claimant's evidence. A decision-maker should be wary of relying on the demeanour of a witness. Conclusions drawn from this are too likely to be subjective and rely on interpretation of behaviour. It is the *content* of evidence rather than the way it is given that should inform credibility.

It is difficult to overturn credibility findings on appeal, because appeals are restricted to points of law, and it is difficult to establish that an immigration judge's decision on credibility amounts to an error of law. However, in *NM (Afghanistan) v SSHD* [2007] EWHC 214 (Admin) the court held that the immigration judge's finding on credibility was not soundly reasoned because he had made an error in interpreting the legal relevance of the claimant's passport application, and it could not be ruled out that his understanding of these events had affected his view of the claimant's credibility. This is not to say that reasons must always be given for all aspects of a credibility finding. As the Court of Appeal said in *B v SSHD* [2006] EWCA Civ 922, 'inadequate reasons may be a guide but they are only a guide to the ultimate question which . . . is whether or not the decision is one which the tribunal was entitled to reach on the evidence which was before it' (para 18).

In *Koca v SSHD* [2005] CSIH 41, the court held that the Adjudicator should have put to the appellant the discrepancies upon which she based her adverse credibility findings.

12.5.1 Credibility and expert evidence

In *Slimani* 01/TH/00092 in a starred determination the tribunal restated the principle that decision-makers should give reasons for finding evidence, in this case expert evidence, to be implausible. The issue of credibility is bound up with the conduct of hearings and the whole question of fairness in the decision-making process. Expert evidence should be assessed on its merits.

The Amnesty International report on initial decision-making noted a practice of forming a negative view of the claimant's credibility based on a subjective response to the claimant, then discounting other evidence in the light of that view. This practice appeared in the decision of an adjudicator in *Mibanga v SSHD* [2005] EWCA Civ 367. The Court of Appeal found that the adjudicator should have looked at all the evidence, including that from the Medical Foundation and a professor with extensive knowledge of the Democratic Republic of Congo, before forming a view of the claimant's credibility. It was not appropriate to treat the claimant as not credible and then discount other evidence on the basis of that. *Mibanga* was distinguished in *SA (Somalia) v SSHD* [2006] EWCA Civ 1302 where the medical report did no more than repeat the claimant's explanation for the scars. The immigration judge formed a negative view of the claimant's credibility and the medical report did not provide independent evidence of that.

AJ Cameroon [2005] UKIAT 00060 warned against immigration judges making their own assessment of scars. In the rare case where an immigration judge 'has specific skills, qualifications, knowledge and experience, then he or she should disclose them to the parties and make clear what use, if any, it is intended to put them to in the course of the hearing and determination process' (para 34). An immigration judge should not conduct physical examinations in the hearing. Conversely, a medical expert should not draw conclusions on credibility (*HH (Ethiopia) v SSHD* [2007] EWCA Civ 306). Given the nature of assessing credibility, this conclusion is less obvious than that in *AJ Cameroon*. Particularly in cases where the effects of trauma are to be reckoned with, there would be an argument that a psychological expert would be better placed than a court to assess credibility.

The Medical Foundation and other organizations which support torture victims say that insufficient attention is given to the effects of trauma on memory when assessing inconsistencies. The UN Committee Against Torture also advise that these effects should be taken into account. The tribunal in *XS (Serbia and Montenegro)* [2005] UKIAT 00093 held that psychiatric reports should not be dismissed because the symptoms were 'self-reported'. The weight to be given to psychiatric evidence will depend upon the authority of the witness and their independence.

Expert evidence about conditions in a country may be very significant to the claim. The tribunal in *LP (Sri Lanka CG)* [2007] UKAIT 00076 held that significant weight should be given to evidence from the British High Commission as it was 'compiled by professional diplomats who are skilled and trained in the observation and acquisition of knowledge in the countries in which they are based' (para 205).

12.5.2 **Section 8 AITOC and the immigration rules**

The immigration rules in HC 395 para 339L, implementing Article 4 of the Qualification Directive, provide a demanding standard for credibility. Where aspects of the person's statements are not supported by documentary or other evidence, those aspects will not need confirmation when all of the following conditions are met:

(i) the person has made a genuine effort to substantiate his asylum claim...;

(ii) all material factors at the person's disposal have been submitted, and a satisfactory explanation regarding any lack of other relevant material has been given;

(iii) the person's statements are found to be coherent and plausible and do not run counter to available specific and general information relevant to the person's case;

(iv) the person has made an asylum claim...at the earliest possible time, unless the person can demonstrate good reason for not having done so; and

(v) the general credibility of the person has been established.

How this rule operates depends very much upon where the emphasis is placed. It could be treated as giving the asylum seeker the benefit of the doubt. Alternatively, it could run counter to the case law discussed above in almost every respect. According to UNHCR Handbook para 196, the applicant should be given the benefit of the doubt in establishing their claim where supporting evidence is not available.

Asylum and Immigration (Treatment of Claimants etc) Act 2004 s 8 creates a new obligation for a 'deciding authority' to take into account as damaging the claimant's credibility factors which that authority 'thinks' are deliberately misleading. It further sets out a list of behaviours which *shall* be treated as designed to conceal information or mislead. These include failure to produce a passport, destruction of documents and failure to answer a question, in each case without reasonable explanation. Other matters are listed without provision for a reasonable explanation: production of a document which is not a valid passport as if it were and failure to claim in a safe third country or make a claim before an immigration decision or arrest under an immigration provision.

This extraordinarily draconian provision (so says Macdonald 2005:818) contradicts the core principle that an evaluation of all the facts is necessary, and deception about one matter does not necessarily mean that the claim itself is false. In *SM Iran* [2005] UKAIT 00116, an early case on the use of s 8, the tribunal made it clear that it was not going to be overly bound by this parliamentary attempt at inroads into the decision-making process. The Adjudicator stated that he had taken account of all relevant matters under s 8 'including all matters pertaining to her account of travelling from Iran to the UK'. The Secretary of State submitted that s 8 should be taken as the starting point for credibility, but the tribunal disagreed. It said that s 8

has the incidental effect of interfering with the well-established rule that the finder of fact (in this case, the Adjudicator, or immigration judge) should look at the evidence as a whole, giving each item of it such weight as he or she considers appropriate. That is unfortunate, and may in some circumstances be difficult to manage...it is inevitable that the general fact-finding process is somewhat distorted, but that distortion must be kept to a minimum. There is no warrant at all for the claim...that the matters identified by section 8 should be treated as the starting point of a decision on credibility. The matters mentioned in s 8 may or may not be part of any particular claim; and their importance will vary with the nature of the claim that is being made, and the other evidence that supports or undermines it. (paras 7 and 9)

The tribunal treats the factors listed in s 8 as just part of the overall assessment of evidence, and refuses to allow the section to create a blanket presumption against the asylum seeker.

12.6 Asylum appeals

As explained at the beginning of this chapter, an appeal against the refusal of an asylum claim is made by appealing the underlying immigration decision on asylum grounds. The appeal system and grounds in outline have been discussed in chapter 8.

There are differences of principle, however, between appeals on asylum grounds and other appeals. The appeal process, as mentioned at the beginning of this chapter, is in a sense an extension of the asylum decision process. The tribunal also carries the obligation of *non-refoulement*, and there is some obligation in the direction of a more inquisitorial process, rather than being simply an arbiter between two arguments. This should not be taken to the point of excessive intervention in cross-examination, taking hostile points against the appellant which the Home Office had not thought fit to raise (*XS Serbia and Montenegro* [2005] UKIAT 00093). The procedure of the hearing is governed by the Asylum and Immigration Tribunal (Procedure) Rules 2005, SI 2005/230 as amended.

As the House of Lords said in the case of *Bugdaycay v SSHD* [1987] AC 514, an asylum claim involves matters of such great importance that judicial bodies should subject each case to 'the most anxious scrutiny'. Evidence should be admitted of 'any matter which the tribunal thinks relevant to the substance of the decision, including evidence which relates to a matter after the date of the decision' (2002 Act s 85(4)). This is particularly important and relevant in asylum claims where the question to be determined is what may happen to the asylum seeker in the future.

Asylum appeals have the particular characteristic that the determination of claims is not an establishment of facts but an assessment of risk and 'there is a two way obligation of fairness' (Thomas 2005). The claimant alone possesses all the relevant knowledge about their asylum claim, but the state is better placed to investigate conditions in the country of origin.

12.7 **Evidence**

We have already considered the question of credibility, which is an aspect of the assessment of evidence. This section will consider the admission of late evidence, the treatment of expert evidence, and the evaluation of evidence about the claimant's country of origin.

12.7.1 **Late evidence**

Although matters up to the date of the hearing may in theory be relevant in an asylum claim, as in other litigation the parties are still required to comply with procedure rules and serve evidence on the other side within a specified time before the hearing. This time is set by the tribunal giving directions. Often it is not practical to have all evidence before the hearing, due to the length of time it takes for medical reports to be prepared. This is exacerbated by the fact that the asylum process has been speeded up considerably, so getting a report before a hearing is a challenge in itself.

The procedure rules say that the tribunal 'must not consider any written evidence which is not filed or served in accordance with those directions unless satisfied that there are good reasons to do so' (r 51(4)). The 'anxious scrutiny' which should be applied to asylum appeals is relevant in determining whether such good reasons exist. So said the tribunal in *MD Pakistan* [2004] UKIAT 00197 in which the appellant was present and ready and willing to give oral evidence. Although his statement had been filed late, there was no prejudice to the Home Office in admitting the statement. In *SA Sri Lanka* [2005] UKIAT 00028 the tribunal held again that the anxious scrutiny required in an asylum claim meant that the adjudicator should have admitted a medical report which had a bearing on the appellant's credibility. The Home Office had not sent a representative to the hearing but the tribunal held that by this omission they had deprived themselves of the opportunity to comment on it, and the appellant should not be penalized on that account.

12.7.2 **Fresh evidence or fresh claim**

The points above raise the question of finality in legal proceedings. When does the asylum claim cease? If it is focused on future risk, and there is a substantial change in the asylum seeker's country of origin the day after she has lost her appeal in the tribunal, what then? What if new evidence comes to light before she is removed which substantiates the risk she feared? Although the tribunal is concerned with the risk to the appellant of persecution on return, the state of affairs which is under consideration is that at the date of the hearing. If this were not so, the matter could go on being re-opened indefinitely. However, the decision must be made on the best evidence as to the facts, and new facts may come to light.

Since the creation of the single-tier appeal tribunal in 2005, all appeals must be on a point of law. There is no appeal on a question of fact. This makes it particularly difficult to argue that any challenge can be made solely on the basis of evidence that was not before the immigration judge, as evidence usually contributes to a finding of fact rather than law. Sometimes, different evidence may be used to show an error of law (Symes 2005). In *AR (Christians – risk in Kabul) Afghanistan* [2005] UKIAT 00035 the tribunal ruled that the test for material error law is not whether the Adjudicator 'could have' reached a different conclusion but whether the documents *would properly* have led him to a different conclusion on the whole of the evidence which was before him (Symes 2005).

As discussed in chapter 8 in relation to *E and R v SSHD* [2004] EWCA Civ 49, a mistake as to fact may, in certain circumstances, amount to an error of law and thus be appealable, particularly in asylum cases. In that case the Court of Appeal said that the sort of mistake of fact that would give rise to this conclusion would occur when there was:

- a mistake as to existing fact;
- of which evidence was uncontentious and objectively verifiable;
- when the appellant or their advisers were not responsible for the mistake;
- and the mistake played a material though not necessarily decisive part in the tribunal's reasoning.

Evidence of such a mistake could be admitted, usually on the principles derived from the case of *Ladd* v *Marshall* [1954] 1 WLR 1489. These are: that the fresh evidence could not have been obtained with reasonable diligence for use at the trial (here, the tribunal hearing); if given, it would probably have an important influence on the result; it is apparently credible thought not necessarily incontrovertible (*E and R* para 23). These principles may be departed from in asylum cases in exceptional circumstances when the interests of justice so require (*E and R* para 91). In these cases the human rights reports produced after the date of the hearing added to the tribunal's understanding of the position as it was at the date of the hearing. They did not concern matters arising later.

Sometimes it will be appropriate, after an asylum claim has been refused and an appeal lost, to make a fresh claim for asylum. This will only be considered when new submissions are significantly different from the material which has been previously been considered, as prescribed in para 353 of the immigration rules:

The submissions will only be significantly different if the content

1) Had not already been considered;
2) Taken together with the previously considered material created a realistic prospect of success, notwithstanding its rejection.

Collins J added in the case of *R (Rahimi) v SSHD* [2005] EWHC 2838 (Admin) that 'the realistic prospect of success test is a low one. It really amounts to little more than there is a reasonable chance that the claim might succeed' (para 12). In this case a newspaper article carrying a request for disclosure of the whereabouts of the claimant had been published after the adjudicator had refused the claim. Collins J thought that given the grey area between prosecution and persecution in Afghanistan, the claim should be investigated again.

Given the length of time spent in the UK by many asylum seekers whose claim has failed, and the developments that can happen in that time, the question of the threshold for a fresh claim is an important one. As there is no right of appeal in these cases, the only avenue to challenge refusal is judicial review. There is now a clear line of Court of Appeal decisions on the right approach, which is not to ask whether they think the new claim is a good one, but 'whether there is a realistic prospect of an adjudicator, applying the rule of anxious scrutiny, thinking that the appellant will be exposed to a real risk of persecution on return'. Secondly, the court must consider whether the Secretary of State has satisfied the anxious scrutiny requirement in evaluating the facts and the legal conclusions to be drawn from them (*WM (DRC) and DR (Afghanistan) v SSHD* [2006] EWCA Civ 1495).

A fresh claim may be on the basis of a feared breach of human rights as well as an asylum claim. One of the drawbacks is that an asylum seeker may wish to present new evidence of the effect of return on their health, but, as we have seen in chapter 4, health risks abroad are subject to a very high threshold, both of harm and risk of harm.

For a full account of the law relating to evidence in asylum appeals, reference should be made to a practitioner work such as Macdonald.

12.7.3 Country of origin information

The availability, reliability, relevance, and scope of information about an asylum seeker's country of origin are enormously important in asylum decisions and appeals. The claim is that the asylum seeker fears persecution in their country of origin. To succeed, they must be able to show, as required by the Refugee Convention, that their fear is well-founded. To substantiate or refute this there must be evidence of relevant state practices, and this may be gleaned from governmental reports and non-governmental organizations, particularly those that monitor human rights.

12.7.3.1 *Country reports*

Common sources relied on are the Home Office's own country reports, the human rights reports from the US Department of State, Amnesty International, Human Rights Watch. It is rare for such a report to mention the asylum seeker personally, although this may happen, and there may be references to others with whom she is associated. The main value of country information from the asylum seeker's point of view is to establish the likelihood of what will face them on return, given what can be shown of how their country treats others like them. It is rare that an asylum seeker will have resources to compile substantial country information on their own behalf, and although independent experts may be instructed, the asylum seeker will often be reliant on information produced by organizations who do not have them or their case in mind.

The Home Office has its own country information unit which produces reports about countries of origin of asylum seekers. Since the revival of the list of safe countries of origin, the collection of country information has a further importance in that it may inform a decision to designate a country under s 94 of the 2002 Act. In recognition of this, the 2002 Act provided for a new Advisory Panel on Country Information, but in the case of *Husan* it was disclosed that the panel did not consider themselves sufficiently resourced to engage in the question of designation, and declined to do it.

Unfortunately, Home Office country reports have often not been suitable to bear the weight placed upon them, and this has been compounded by their being inappropriately used. In 2003 the Immigration Advisory Service carried out an analysis of 15 Home Office country reports and found that the majority were unreliable. There were multiple inaccuracies, mis-quoting and omission of relevant information. The Home Office relies mainly upon other source material rather than its own researchers in the field, and the IAS research found that the tendency was to be selective in a way that put a positive slant on the material from other sources. There was also a tendency to use Home Office opinion in the reports, which claim to be factual (Carver 2003). A second IAS research project in 2004 examined the text of twenty-three country reports and compared them with their source material. There was an improvement from the previous year, but still over-reliance on one source and poor sourcing generally (Carver 2004). For a robust approach by ECtHR to assessment of background material see *Said* v *Netherlands* App. No 2345/02.

12.7.3.2 *Country guidance cases*

A further development in the search for consistency in relation to conditions in a country is the designation of 'country guidance cases'. The authoritative beginning of this idea is with the Court of Appeal in *S v SSHD* [2002] EWCA Civ 539. As Laws LJ pointed out in that case, the notion of a precedent which is binding as to fact is 'foreign to the common law' (para 26). For this reason alone, the proposition should be treated with caution that findings of fact made in one case about say, Zimbabwe, should be binding in another case. However, one can readily see that asylum cases present the law with a new phenomenon. It is not common in other areas of law that litigants make comparable assertions about the same background situation. Asylum law may be an appropriate field for the development of a new principle. Laws LJ continued, that in the context of asylum claims, the unusual idea of a factual precedent 'may be benign and practical' (para 28). He advanced two reasons for adopting the practice: the waste of judicial and other resources in hearing evidence about similar factual issues repeatedly, and the need for consistency in decision-making, which is an aspect of justice as is the right of the individual to be heard on the particulars of their claim. The latter principle gave rise to a number of provisos, which should be strictly applied if factual precedents were to be allowed as a possibility:

- In making a decision which is intended to give guidelines on conditions in a country, the tribunal must apply the duty to give reasons 'with particular rigour'.
- Such a decision must be 'effectively comprehensive. It should address all the issues capable of having a real as opposed to a fanciful bearing on the result, and explain what it makes of the substantial evidence going to each such issue'.
- The facts of an individual case must still be examined.
- Country guideline cases may provide a backdrop against which that individual examination takes place, recognizing that 'the impact of the political reality may vary as between one claimant and another'.

The practice of promulgating and following Country Guideline cases (designated CG in the case name) grew up quickly after *S*. The Immigration Advisory Service carried out research and consultation on the use and nature of country guideline cases. Their work reveals many concerns including the following:

- Country guideline cases may be out of date for the case in hand, or worse, based on obsolete material.
- Factual findings specific to a particular claimant may be elevated into country guidance.
- Country guideline decisions may not be referenced properly, so that a future claimant is unable to distinguish their case from the CG because they cannot identify the evidence.
- 'the judiciary operate under severe time constraints and a reference to a Country Guideline case is sometimes used as an alternative to giving reasons rather than an aide to decision-making' (p. 20).

- Some country guideline cases have been designated where the dismissal of the claim was based on a *lack* of evidence.
- Even in a CG case, evidence was sometimes used and dismissed selectively without objective reasons being given, particularly by preference being given to government reports over other sources. (IAS 2005)

The IAS challenged the concept of country guideline cases as importing an artificial degree of certainty 'on an uncertain and often rapidly changing country situation'. Thomas criticizes the CG system as 'naïve' – different conclusions may be drawn from similar facts (2005:476). Even if one accepts the concept, the IAS research suggests that the reality does not match up to the cautious standards set by the Court of Appeal in *S*.

The tribunal has embraced the notion of country guideline cases. There are now hundreds in relation to particular issues such as 'risk on return – Ivory Coast' which are listed on the AIT website. The tribunal's practice direction goes much further than *S* in relation to their weight as precedents. It says that the most recent CG case 'shall be treated as an authoritative finding on the country guidance issue identified in the determination . . . so far as that appeal:

(a) relates to the country guidance issue in question; and

(b) depends upon the same or similar evidence'. (4 April 2005, para 18.2)

Even more unequivocally: 'any failure to follow a clear, apparently applicable country guidance case or to show why it does not apply to the case in question is likely to be regarded as grounds for review or appeal on a point of law' (para 18.4 endorsed in *R & others v SSHD* [2005] EWCA Civ 982). The exception is when there is other, inconsistent authority that is binding on the tribunal.

This approach is moving the CG system into something like a more specific form of 'White-listing'.

12.8 **Refugee status**

In the cases where refugee status is granted (10 per cent of initial decisions in 2006 and 22 per cent of appealed cases) the Refugee Convention and now the Qualification Directive set out the legal consequences of recognition. Refugees have a right to the issue of a travel document, an important right bearing in mind that they may well not have a passport of their country of origin or be able to travel using it. They are entitled to social rights on favourable terms and the intention of the Convention is that they should be integrated into the host society. The rights listed in the Convention include civil and political rights and fundamental freedoms such as that of religion and religious education (Art 4). The Directive concentrates on social and economic rights: employment, education, accommodation, health care and social welfare. Denial of fundamental rights would be unconstitutional in the EU, but social and economic rights have very limited protection. Some social rights in the Directive are granted on the same terms as to nationals – e.g. education for children. Some are on the same terms as other third country nationals – e.g. accommodation. For a really comprehensive account of Convention provisions, see Hathaway 2005.

12.9 Cessation

The Refugee Convention Article 1C makes provision for refugee status to end in certain circumstances. Most refer to the voluntary actions of the refugee. The exception is Article 1C(5), that 'because the circumstances in connection with which he has been recognized as a refugee have ceased to exist' he can no longer 'refuse to avail himself of the protection of the country of his nationality' or, if stateless, his former residence. The host state bears the burden of proving this, and refugees should not be subject to continual examination of their status as this undermines the very security the Convention aims to give (see the UNHCR Handbook para 135). These conditions are reproduced in the Qualification Directive, and in the new immigration rules implementing it. The rules include that there has been a 'significant and non-temporary change' in the conditions in the refugee's country of origin. The Directive and rules omit one provision of the Convention, which is that there are 'compelling reasons arising from previous persecution' for not returning to the country of origin. This means that the Directive and rules do not give the refugee the opportunity to argue against losing their refugee status because of the severity of their previous experience.

UK practice used to be to grant indefinite leave to remain to those granted refugee status. On 30 August 2005, UK policy changed to giving five years' leave instead. At the end of that period the need for protection will be reviewed and leave may be renewed if protection is still needed. The Qualification Directive provides that only a three-year residence permit need be given to refugees and their families (Art 24).

12.10 Subsidiary protection

Many signatory states to the Refugee Convention make provision for a safety net status where a person is held not to qualify for asylum, but there are compelling reasons why they should not be returned to their home state. The Refugee Qualification Directive 2004/83 provides for a form of 'subsidiary protection' (Art 18) and this is now incorporated into the immigration rules as humanitarian protection.

Prior to the Qualification Directive, this was the status granted in the UK to give protection where removal created a risk of breach of Articles 2 and 3.

It now provides the subsidiary protection required by the Directive, the terms to qualify for it have been harmonized with the Directive, and it is fully incorporated in the immigration rules at paras 339C–N. These rules and the API make it clear that humanitarian protection is treated in many ways like asylum, and is a fallback status for an asylum seeker whose claim has failed. The Directive requires that a year is the minimum leave given as humanitarian protection. In the immigration rules, five years is the norm, as for asylum. The rights that go with humanitarian protection are less than for refugee status in the Directive. In the immigration rules, both are unrestricted in employment and have a right to a travel document.

Principles of internal flight and sufficiency of protection (see next chapter) are applied in considering whether to grant humanitarian protection (API).

Exclusions also apply, but are more severely drawn than for refugee status (see chapter 14). People who would be excluded by Article 1F are excluded, but so is a person who has committed a 'serious crime' whether political or not. This exclusion will become statutory under the Criminal Justice and Immigration Act. Persons excluded from humanitarian protection may be considered for a six-month period of discretionary leave.

It is still possible on human rights or other grounds for the Secretary of State to grant leave outside the rules. Where this is because of family ties or private life in the UK, the leave granted will be discretionary leave, the conditions for which are set out in policy and guidance. In general, discretionary leave may be given to avoid breaching the person's Article 8 rights in the UK, in case of medical or severe humanitarian risks which would breach Article 3 and in very limited circumstances where other human rights violations are feared on return. Other exceptional cases should, according to the API, be considered for leave outside the rules rather than discretionary leave. The initial grant of discretionary leave is normally three years but may be less in specified cases. It is less secure than humanitarian protection, as it will not lead to settlement until six years have elapsed, and there will be a review after three years which may result in the end of the leave. The API from October 2006 provides that discretionary leave will not be granted 'on the basis that, for the time being, practical obstacles prevent a person from leaving the UK or being removed, for example, an absence of route or travel document'. See the discussion of the case of *Khadir* in chapter 15 for the significance of this.

There is a potential contradiction in that Article 8 claims are generally based on strength of family ties in the UK, which would generally become stronger with the passage of time. This was addressed in *R (on the application of Shahid) v SSHD* QBD Admin 13 October 2004. Gibbs J held that it was reasonable to grant three years' discretionary leave instead of indefinite leave to remain. If there was no significant change in circumstances the leave would be extended at the end of three years and the claimant could eventually expect to obtain indefinite leave to remain. Its grant would enhance his enjoyment of his Article 8 right, but the lack of it did not interfere with it beyond the allowable interference under Article 8.2.

Leave outside the rules is now more circumscribed than was Exceptional Leave to Remain, which was the general form of leave available outside the rules until April 2003.

The diagram on the next page gives an outline of the asylum decision process, including the outcomes.

12.11 Safe third country

Finally, we consider the application and development of safe third country provisions. Where these apply, an asylum claim need not be heard in the UK at all. The basic contention is that the claimant may be safely sent somewhere other than their country of origin or where they fear persecution. Where an asylum seeker has travelled through another country which might have heard their claim then the safe third country provisions may mean that they are removed without going through any of the asylum claim process, except the initial screening interview, which identifies safe third country cases. The notion of 'burden-sharing', now a key element in the development of

Table 14 Asylum determination process

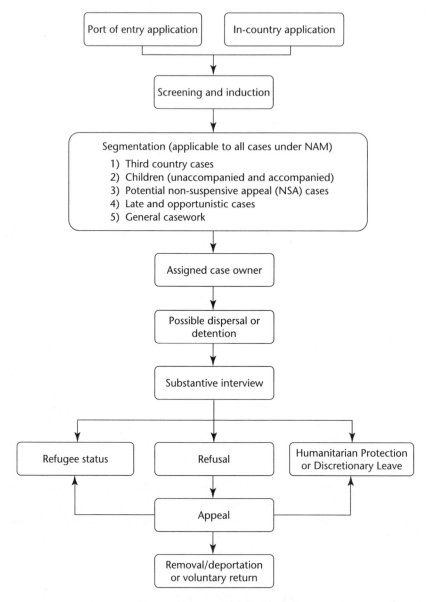

NB: This diagram does not include the appeals process.

Reproduced with consent from 'The Operation of the Asylum Determination Process' ICAR (2007)

policy in Europe, has always been a function of international refugee law. Indeed, one of the preambles to the Refugee Convention is to this effect:

the grant of asylum may place unduly heavy burdens on certain countries, and that a satisfactory solution of a problem of which the United Nations has recognized the international scope and nature cannot therefore be achieved without international co-operation.

In addition to 'burden-sharing' the safe third country provisions also enact the idea that 'refugees who come directly from their country of origin are entitled to greater rights than those who may be forced by circumstances, or may elect, to adopt a more circuitous route to safety' (Tuitt 1996:111). The use of safe third country provisions is widespread. For instance, on 29 December 2004 Canada implemented a safe third country agreement with the USA, thereby closing its land border to most asylum claims and effecting a significant reduction in asylum claims overall. The Canadian Council for Refugees refers to this as 'the government's unstated purpose' (2005:26). The third country means one that is neither the refugee's home state nor the country where they have sought asylum, and the fact it is safe means that it will not be a breach of Refugee Convention Article 33, the obligation of *non-refoulement*, to send them there.

12.11.1 Development of safe third country provisions

Prior to any statutory provisions the decision to remove an asylum claimant was a matter of administrative discretion, subject only to the obligation of *non-refoulement* under Refugee Convention Article 33. The case of *Musisi* v *SSHD* [1987] AC 514 established that the doctrine of *non-refoulement* applies to indirect as well as direct return. In that case the appellant sought asylum from Uganda, but had travelled to the UK from Kenya and applied to enter as a visitor. The immigration service proposed to remove him to Kenya, but there was evidence from that country that they would not accept him and would in fact send him back to Uganda where he feared persecution. The House of Lords found that although the decision on this point was within the discretion of the Secretary of State, he had failed to consider the question adequately, having not addressed the question of danger. *Yassine* v *SSHD* [1990] Imm AR 354 was the first reported case of the UK refusing to deal with an asylum application on the basis that the applicant was in transit to another country which would admit him. In the 18 years since then, safe third country provisions have become a key element in refugee law and practice, though purely in terms of numbers their effect is not substantial. Refusals on safe third country grounds constituted 1,690, that is 8 per cent of the 20,930 initial decisions made in 2006 (Asylum Statistics UK 2006 Table 4.1).

Protection against indirect *refoulement* as it arose in *Musisi* found its way into the immigration rules as an obligation to return the asylum seeker to a country through which they had travelled, if it was safe to do so. This set the basic principles of safe third country decisions, which still underlie the provisions that are in place today:

- the applicant has not travelled directly from the country of persecution;
- there is another country to which they could be sent as they could have made their asylum claim there; and
- this would be considered safe in the sense that the life or freedom of the asylum applicant would not be threatened (within the meaning of Article 33 of the Convention) and the government of which would not send the applicant elsewhere in a manner contrary to the principles of the Convention and Protocol.

It may be apparent that using this rule requires a lot of fact-finding on the part of the Secretary of State. Information is needed about the third country, not only about its systems of refugee protection, but also about the asylum claimant's travel route and their experiences. The Secretary of State had a discretion under this rule but one which it is difficult to exercise properly.

The Secretary of State was under no obligation to consult the authorities of the third country before returning an applicant (para 345) to them, and they were under no obligation to deal with the claim. So for some years there was a phenomenon known as 'refugees in orbit' whereby asylum claimants were shunted from one unwilling country to the next and back again. Both Tuitt (1996:119) and Macdonald (2001:547) suggest that this might constitute inhuman or degrading treatment contrary to Article 3 ECHR.

The first statutory provision to endorse removals to a safe third country was the Asylum and Immigration Appeals Act 1993, which allowed the Secretary of State to certify that a country was one which respected the Refugee Convention and was therefore safe for the applicant. Following many legal challenges to these certificates the 1993 Act was succeeded by the Asylum and Immigration Act 1996, in which s 2 provided that if the Secretary of State certified that the safe third country conditions were met the claimant could be removed to European or designated countries *before* any appeal took place. The conditions were similar to those now found in the Procedures Directive regarding nationality, threats to life and liberty for a Convention reason and *non-refoulement*.

Challenges to safe third country certificates by judicial review were a forum for examining the compatibility of refugee law in European member states. These questions can no longer be litigated, as the combination of statute (AITOCA 2004) and a binding EU Regulation (Dublin II) creates an obligation to treat EU member states as fully compliant with the Refugee Convention. Immigration and Asylum Act 1999 s 11, as amended by Nationality, Immigration and Asylum Act 2002 s 80, contained a deeming provision which entailed that member states of the European Union were *'to be regarded as'* places in which the safe third country provisions were met. This in turn was replaced by the current provision.

12.11.2 Current legislation on safe third countries

Asylum and Immigration (Treatment of Claimants, etc) Act 2004 Sch 3 contains provision for three lists of safe third countries and a fourth provision enabling certification in relation to an individual. The only one of these which is active is the first list, which consists of 28 other countries of the European Economic Area, i.e. all except Liechtenstein. These countries are deemed to be safe places to return an asylum claimant whom the Secretary of State certifies is not a national of that country. They are deemed to be safe in three respects:

- the applicant will not face persecution contrary to the Refugee Convention in that country
- that country will not send the applicant to another country where there was a risk of such persecution
- that country will not send the applicant to another country if the removal would give rise to a risk of human rights violations.

The Secretary of State is also obliged to certify that a human rights appeal concerning the immediate consequences of removal to that country would be unfounded, unless s/he is satisfied that it would not be. This refers to any other human rights implications of removal aside from the possibility of onward removal from the destination state, for instance a claim that family or private life in the UK will be infringed by the removal (Art 8), or that the applicant faces a risk of degrading treatment in the receiving state (Art 3). The effect is that anyone who may be returned to a European country will be returned without an appeal unless the Secretary of State is persuaded that there would arguably be a breach of human rights in the UK in doing so.

There can be no judicial review of the safety of the First List country for refugee or human rights Convention purposes as the statutory presumptions put these matters beyond challenge. The Parliamentary Joint Committee on Human Rights doubted the compatibility of these provisions with the UK's obligations under the Human Rights Act and ECHR in 'precluding any individual consideration of the facts of a particular claimant's case and conclusively ousting the jurisdiction of the courts to hear a claim that removal to a third country on the First List would breach the claimant's rights because of the risk of onward removal' (Session 2003–04 Thirteenth Report (HL paper 102, HC paper 640)). The government's rationale was that the first list is intended to apply to countries which are signatories to the ECHR, so they may be assumed to comply with the requirement not to *refoule* in breach of human rights (HC Standing Committee B col. 355 22 January 2004). However, the High Court in *Nasseri v SSHD* [2007] EWHC 1548 (Admin) made a declaration of incompatibility in relation to Schedule 3 para 3 which deems the destination state safe. The claimant feared that if he were returned to Greece under Schedule 3 he would be at risk of return to Afghanistan. Although Greece had changed its procedures so that this risk was reduced by the time of the hearing, the claimant's contention was that this was irrelevant, because the Secretary of State was prohibited by para 3 from considering whether Greece was safe or not. The court accepted this. The ECtHR held in *Assenov v Bulgaria* (1999) 28 EHRR 652 that failure to conduct an adequate investigation into the risk of loss of life or torture or inhuman and degrading treatment was a breach of Article 3. Paragraph 3 therefore put the Secretary of State in breach of Article 3 because it prevented any such investigation. *Nasseri* followed *TI v UK* [2000] INLR 211 where the ECtHR held that international agreements such as the Dublin Convention (see below) could not absolve states of their responsibilities under the ECHR.

There is no indication yet as to how the government is going to deal with this declaration of incompatibility.

If and when orders are made to create second and third lists in AITOC Schedule 3, they will be of countries designated safe for Refugee Convention purposes only. In the case of the second list the Secretary of State will be obliged to certify human rights claims. The Third List allows the Secretary of State to designate countries for the purposes of the Refugee Convention only. A return to a country in this category may still be individually certified as safe for human rights purposes. All these three provisions also debar appeal on the safety issues from abroad, and any immigration appeal in the UK. Where a claimant has travelled through a country which might be regarded as safe (e.g. Canada or Switzerland (API Feb 2007)) but which is not in the first list, claims may still be certified on a case-by-case basis under Part 5 of Schedule 3.

The 2004 Act repeals the safe third country provisions in the 1999 and 2002 Acts, though not s 94 of the 2002 Act regarding certification of human rights claims and its consequences. Notwithstanding the repeal, the Asylum and Immigration (Treatment of Claimants, etc.) Act 2004 (Commencement No. 1) Order 2004, SI 2004/2523 para 3 states expressly that certificates under the 2002 and 1999 Acts continue to be valid.

12.11.3 Dublin Convention and Dublin II

This increasingly unchallengeable system of certification and removal without appeal is a manifestation of the Common European Asylum System. The European Union attempts to prevent the phenomenon of 'refugees in orbit' by ensuring that at least one member state accepts an application for asylum, stopping asylum seekers moving around the European Union in search of the country which seems to them to offer the best prospects and precluding multiple claims by one person in different member states. The first mechanism adopted across the whole Union to do this was the Dublin Convention (OJ C 254 19.8.1997), which came into force in 1997. The Dublin Convention had no direct effect in the UK as it was a Treaty entered into under the Third Pillar of the European Union. In *R v SSHD ex p Behluli* [1998] Imm AR 407 the Court of Appeal confirmed that the Convention could not give rise to any direct rights or obligations in national law. It was a mechanism that could be used to implement a removal, for instance in the UK when the Secretary of State certified under the 1996 Act.

Council Regulation (EC) No 343/2003 OJ 2003 L 50/1 has replaced the Dublin Convention and is directly effective and directly applicable in national law without implementing measures (EC Treaty Art 249(2)). The Regulation, known as 'Dublin II', came into effect on 1 September 2003. Its purpose, like that of the Dublin Convention, is to establish the criteria and mechanisms for determining the member state responsible for examining an asylum application lodged in one of the member states by a third country national. Dublin II, in its Recitals, confirms 'the principles underlying' the Dublin Convention, and its provisions are very similar. The criteria for deciding which state takes responsibility for the asylum claim include for instance where a claimant has a family member who has been recognized as a refugee or is an asylum seeker and is legally resident in a member state, that state will be responsible for the claim, providing the persons concerned agree (Arts 7 and 8). Unaccompanied minors should be dealt with in the country where they make their application (Art 6). Also a member state which issues a residence permit or visa will be responsible normally for a claim from the holder of that permit or visa (Art 9). Where there is evidence of illegal entry into a member state, the state so entered remains responsible for processing the asylum seeker's claim for 12 months. After that, or in the event of there being no evidence of illegal entry, the member state in which the asylum seeker was living for the last five months is responsible (Art 10). The underlying principle is that except where these and other provisions apply to determine a responsible state, the claim should be processed in the first member state at which the asylum seeker lodges an application (Art 13).

In *R (on the application of Mosari) v SSHD* [2005] EWHC 1343 Lightman J held that where the claimant had entered Hungary as a minor with his adult cousin, and made an asylum application there, Hungary remained the country which had responsibility under Dublin II to determine which state should hear the asylum claim. The fact that the claimant was now living with his uncle in the UK since his clandestine entry here did not mean that the UK had to take responsibility under Article 6. His original entry to the EU and first claim was made in Hungary, and family life here would not disturb that unless to proceed with the return to Hungary was disproportionate. Lightman J held that it was not.

Article 15 provides that 'Any member state…may bring together family members, as well as other dependent relatives, on humanitarian grounds based in particular on family or cultural considerations'. This at first sight appears to be a powerful route for an asylum seeker to argue for family unity, not necessarily in the country which would otherwise be responsible for deciding their claim. However, in *R (on the application of G) v SSHD* [2005] EWCA Civ 546 the Court of Appeal held that Article 15 did not create a right for asylum seekers, but was only intended 'to regulate the relationship between two or more member states' (para 25). Similarly, in relation to procedural provisions such as time limits for action, in *Omar v SSHD* [2005] EWCA Civ 285 the court held that these did not have direct effect as there were no clear words to create the rights which would then flow for the asylum seeker. Mr Omar could not insist that the UK take responsibility for his claim when there was a delay in transferring responsibility back to Italy.

The operation of Dublin II relies in part on the fingerprint database known as Eurodac, discussed in chapter 5. *Mota v SSHD* [2006] EWCA Civ 1380 illustrates the workings of these systems. The appellant arrived in the UK in 2005 and claimed asylum. A fingerprint match revealed that she had claimed asylum in the Netherlands in 2003. She claimed that in the intervening period she had been back in Sierra Leone, but suffered atrocities which made her flee and renew her claim for asylum. The Dublin Regulation provides that, if the claimant had left the EU for more than three months, then the responsibility for the claim lapsed. The two governments did not accept that she had left the EU. This meant that her claim would still be the responsibility of the Netherlands. The court held that this finding was not irrational and she could be returned to the Netherlands. Importantly for her, the Dutch asylum authorities would not be bound to deny that she had returned to Sierra Leone by having accepted responsibility for her claim.

The combination of European developments and UK legislation has created a system which leaves very little opportunity for an asylum seeker to have their claim heard in the UK if they have travelled through Europe. Macdonald refers to 'a lava flow of presumptions of safety and relentless removal of in-country appeal rights' (2005:795).

12.11.4 Challenging certificates and deeming provisions

The certification of a claim as clearly unfounded, the designation of some states as safe, and the statutory deeming of third countries as safe are all methods which prevent the individual claim from being fully examined on its merits and entail the asylum seeker being removed without an appeal. In the case of safe third country provisions, the asylum seeker is removed without the claim even being considered at all. The capacity to challenge these provisions is clearly important.

Challenges to the designation of safe countries of origin has been discussed above. Currently these are possible as the designations are made by secondary legislation, and, despite the attempt of the Secretary of State to argue that delegated legislation was immune from challenge if made by affirmative resolution (*Javed and Ali*), designations remains challengeable on general judicial review grounds. Originally, safe third countries were deemed safe by executive certificate, and then these were challengeable also. For instance, in *Adan and Aitseguer* the House of Lords held that the Secretary of

State had to satisfy himself of the safety of the destination for the two asylum seekers. Accepting assurances from the receiving state did not fulfil this requirement of the 1996 Act. He could not be satisfied if he did not have the evidence. Once third countries were deemed safe by statute where a certificate was issued (1999 Act s 11), the question was whether anything of *Adan and Aitseguer* survived. In *R (Yogathas) and R (Thangarasa) v SSHD* [2002] 3 WLR 176 certifications were challenged, for Yogathas under the 1996 Act and Thangarasa under the 1999 Act. In relation to Thangasara, Lord Bingham acknowledged that in relation to the certification of a European country 'the argument which succeeded in *Adan and Aitseguer* [2001] 2 AC 477 is effectively blocked'. Simon Brown LJ's words in *Ibrahim* [2001] Imm AR 430 CA had to be regarded as conclusive:

Parliament has...in unambiguous terms, dictated that henceforth France, amongst other member states, is to be regarded as a safe third country. Of course the Secretary of State is not bound to certify in every case, but where he chooses to do so, in my judgment that certificate cannot be impugned on the grounds that France after all is not properly to be regarded as a safe third country.

The 2004 Act took this a step further by taking out the requirement for certification and just deeming EU states to be safe. However, the discussion of *Nasseri* above shows that, while refugee claims can be excluded, human rights claims, because of the enforceable obligations under the ECHR and Human Rights Act, cannot.

12.12 **Conclusion**

The majority of the provisions discussed in this chapter are procedural – none of them concern the requirements that must be fulfilled under the Refugee Convention to establish a refugee claim. The procedural hurdles to be crossed are just as much of a challenge to establishing a refugee claim as satisfying the legal definition.

QUESTIONS

1 Is it appropriate to see the Home Office as the opponent in asylum appeals, or is this unnecessarily confrontational?
2 How would you explain to an asylum seeker detained in Harmondsworth the meaning of their detention?
3 What would be your priorities for change in the asylum system?

 online resource centre For guidance on answering questions, visit www.oxfordtextbooks.co.uk/orc/clayton3e.

FURTHER READING

Amnesty International (2004) *Get it right: how Home Office decision-making fails refugees*, Amnesty International UK.

Asylum Aid (1995) 'No Reason at all'.

—— (1999) 'Still no Reason at all'.

Bail for Immigration Detainees (2006) 'Working against the clock: Inadequacy and injustice in the fast track system'.

Barnes, J. (2004) 'Expert Evidence The Judicial Perception in Asylum and Human Rights Appeals' *International Journal of Refugee Law* vol. 16, no. 3, pp. 349–357.

Canadian Council for Refugees (2005) 'Closing the Door on Refugees: report on safe third country agreement 6 months after implementation', CCR August.

Carver, N. (2003) *Home Office Country Assessments: An Analysis* IAS September.

—— (2004) *Home Office Country Reports: An Analysis* IAS September.

Cohen, J. (2001) 'Questions of Credibility: Omissions, Discrepancies and Errors of Recall in the Testimony of Asylum Seekers' *International Journal of Refugee Law* vol. 13, no. 3.

Constitutional Affairs Committee Second Report 2003–04, *Asylum and Immigration Appeals* HC 211.

Cornelisse, G. (2004) 'Human Rights for Immigration Detainees in Strasbourg: Limited Sovereignty or Limited Discourse?' *European Journal of Migration and Law* 6: 93–110.

Costello, C. (2005) 'The Asylum Procedures Directive and the Proliferation of Safe Country Practices: Deterrence, Deflection and the Dismantling of International Protection?' *European Journal of Migration and Law* vol. 7, no. 1, March 2005, pp. 35–70(36).

Doughty Street Chambers, *Blackstone's Guide to the Asylum and Immigration Act 2004* (Oxford: OUP), Chapters 8 and 9.

ECRE March 2005, Comments on Amended proposal for a Council Directive on minimum standards on procedures in member states for granting and withdrawing refugee status, as agreed by the Council on 19 November 2004.

Ensor, J, Shah, A. & Grill, M. (2006) 'Simple Myths and Complex realities – seeking truth in the face of section 8' *Journal of Immigration, Asylum & Nationality Law* vol. 20, no. 2, pp. 95–111.

Good, A. (2004) 'Expert Evidence in Asylum and Human Rights Appeals: An Expert's View' *International Journal of Refugee Law* vol. 16, no. 3, pp. 358–380.

Gorlick, B. (2002) 'Common Burdens and Standards: legal elements in assessing claims to refugee status' UNHCR Working paper no. 68.

Hathaway, J.C. (2005) *The Right of Refugees under International Law* (Cambridge: Cambridge University Press).

Head, M. (2004) 'The Global "War on Terrorism": Democratic Rights under Attack' in Brownsword, R. (ed.) *Global Governance and the Quest for Justice* (Oxford: Hart).

Home Affairs Committee report on asylum applications *Asylum Applications*, Second report of 2003–04, HC 218, 26 January 2004.

House of Commons Public Accounts Committee *Improving the speed and quality of asylum decisions*, Fourth Report 2004–05 HC 238.

Joint Parliamentary Committee on Human Rights *The Treatment of Asylum Seekers*, Tenth Report of 2006–07 HL Paper 81 HC 60.

Joint Refugee Council, Scottish Refugee Council and Welsh Refugee Council submission to House of Commons Home Affairs Committee inquiry on EU issues September 2006.

Lambert, H. (2006) 'The EU Asylum Qualification Directive, its impact on the jurisprudence of the United Kingdom and international law' *International and Comparative Law Quarterly* 55(1).

Medical Foundation (2004) *Right first time,* (Smith, E.).

National Audit Office (2004) *Improving the Speed and Quality of Asylum Decisions*, report by the Comptroller and Auditor General HC 535 Session 2003–04 23 June 2004.

Refugee Council (2007) New Asylum Model.

Rhys-Jones, D., & Verity-Smith, S. (2004) 'Medical Evidence in Asylum and Human Rights Appeals' *International Journal of Refugee Law* vol. 16, no. 3, pp. 381–410.

Statewatch (2004) EU divided over list of 'safe countries of origin' – Statewatch calls for the list to be scrapped.

Symes, M. (2006) 'The Refugee Qualification Directive' Electronic Immigration Network.

Thomas, R. (2005) 'Asylum Appeals: The Challenge of Asylum to the British legal System' in Shah, P. (ed.) *The challenge of asylum to legal systems* (London: Cavendish).

UNHCR (2005) Provisional observations of UNHCR on Amended proposal for a Council Directive on minimum standards on procedures in member states for granting and withdrawing refugee status.

Woodhouse, S. (2004) *The Annual Report of the Certification Monitor.*

Yeo, C. (ed.) (2005) *Country Guideline cases: benign and practical?* (London: IAS).

13

The refugee definition

SUMMARY

This chapter examines the definition of a 'refugee' found in Article 1A of the UN Convention Relating to the Status of Refugees 1951. Although at the time of drafting the Convention this paragraph may not have been the main preoccupation of contracting states, every phrase of it has now been extensively examined in courts and tribunals worldwide. The case law relating to the main aspects of the Article is discussed, and some of the controversies which surround refugee definition.

13.1 Definition of 'refugee'

Refugee status is determined by applying the definition found in Article 1A(2) of the Refugee Convention, which says that a 'refugee' is a person who:

Owing to a well-founded fear of being persecuted for reasons of race, religion, nationality, membership of a particular social group, or political opinion, is outside his country of nationality and is unable or, owing to such fear, is unwilling to avail himself of the protection of that country; or who, not having a nationality and being outside the country of his former habitual residence...is unable or, owing to such fear, is unwilling to return to it.

As explained in chapter 12, this definition is now applied in the EU as interpreted by European Directive 2004/83, referred to here as the Qualification Directive. The Directive is implemented in the UK by the Refugee or Person in Need of International Protection (Qualification) Regulations 2006 SI 2006/2525. The legal relationship between the Directive and the Convention is yet to be fully explored in the courts, but the EC Treaty Article 63(1) stipulates that measures shall be adopted on asylum 'in accordance with the Geneva Convention' and so it may be that, in case of any provision in the Directive which gave less protection to refugees, the Convention would take precedence (see Gil-Bazo 2005, Lambert 2006). The domestic regulations may make more generous provision than the Directive (preamble para 8) which only lays down minimum standards.

The Qualification Directive provides for refugee claims only from third country nationals and those who are stateless. The UK's implementing regulations apply to anyone who is not a British Citizen but, as explained in chapter 12, the safe third country provisions effectively debar a claim from an EEA national. The rest of this chapter consists of an exploration of this definition as it has been interpreted by courts and tribunals.

13.2 **The fear**

The centrality of the requirement of fear places a greater emphasis on the experience and circumstances of the individual than the refugee protection measures which preceded the 1951 Convention. Arguably, the fear has both a subjective and objective aspect. The *UNHCR Handbook* paras 37–50 suggests that both are necessary.

13.2.1 **Subjective fear**

The subjective aspect is the refugee's own experience of fear. Paragraphs 40 and 41 of the UNHCR Handbook discuss the way in which the subjective element may be evaluated, and what it may contribute to the possibility of attaining refugee status. These paragraphs suggest that the requirement of subjective fear gives scope for taking account of the effect of circumstances on an individual. For instance, 'one person may have strong political or religious convictions, the disregard of which would make his life intolerable; another may have no such strong convictions' (para 40). Therefore similar circumstances may bear differently on different people. The assessment of the subjective state of fear, according to para 40, involves engaging in 'an assessment of the personality of the applicant...since the psychological reactions of different individuals may not be the same in identical conditions'. However, tribunals tend to steer away from too intense a psychological scrutiny of the subjective fear. The proper and usual approach was expressed as follows by the tribunal in *Asuming v SSHD* (11530):

we understand 'fear' in an asylum claim to be nothing more nor less than a belief in that which the appellant states is likely to happen if he returns to his country of origin...one should not approach the issue on the basis of a need to assess whether a person is 'afraid' in the sense of being fearful rather than courageous.

In law and practice subjective fear is secondary to objective fear. The objective aspect of the fear is the question of whether or not it is well-founded, i.e. whether or not the events that the claimant fears are indeed likely to come about.

Hathaway says that 'the use of the term "fear" was intended to emphasize the forward-looking nature of the refugee claim, not to ground refugee status in an assessment of the claimant's state of mind' (1991:75). This approach supports the purpose of the Convention which is to protect people from actual persecution and was used and approved in the leading tribunal case of *Gashi and Nikshiqi* [1997] INLR 96. The same standard of proof applies to the subjective and objective aspects of fear (*Asuming*). The third colloquium on challenges in international refugee law produced the Michigan Guidelines on Well-Founded Fear (adopted 28 March 2004). These took a further step in this same direction by suggesting that the different psychological effects of the same circumstances should be considered not in relation to establishing the 'fear' but only in relation to persecution. The Guidelines in effect endorse *Gashi and Nikshiqi* and Hathaway's earlier work, but more strongly, saying not only that there is no need to look for a state of trepidation, but that doing so is harmful, discriminatory and wrong (see Hathaway and Hicks 2005). For a contrary view, see Tuitt (1996:96–97) who argues that the central importance accorded to the test of objectively well-founded fear may be seen as part of a legal trend which enables the state to make generalized statements about safety which defeat an asylum claim.

We can summarize by saying that the subjective aspect of the fear is an anticipation that persecution would result if the asylum seeker returned to their home country. In general it will not come into question where there is evidence that the fear is well founded.

13.2.2 **Objective fear**

The applicant has the burden of proving that their fear is well founded, i.e. that there are objective grounds for believing that the fear will materialize. In proving that they face a risk of persecution in their country of origin the refugee faces substantial difficulties. Not only are they outside their country of origin, in an unfamiliar environment, without access to common reference points, witnesses or documents, but also, communication with their country of origin may be difficult or impossible. The very nature of their claim means that governmental sources in their own country will not be willing to provide supporting evidence. The refugee is not likely to have substantial documentary evidence proving their claim, they may not even have documents proving their identity. On the other hand, the consequences of refusing a valid claim could be extremely serious. As the tribunal said in *Asuming*, 'Asylum cases differ from most other cases in the seriousness of the consequences of an erroneous decision, in the focus of the decision on the future, and the inherent difficulties of obtaining objective evidence'. In such a situation, the question of what standard of proof must be reached by the asylum claimant is all important. Are they required to prove beyond reasonable doubt that they will be persecuted on return (the criminal standard) or on balance of probabilities (the civil standard) or on the lower standard that there is a risk of persecution or a reasonable likelihood (the standard formerly used in the 1993 Act in relation to whether torture may have occurred)?

13.2.2.1 *Standard of proof*

It is settled law since the House of Lords' judgment in *R v SSHD ex p Sivakumaran* [1988] AC 958 that the asylum seeker should be required to establish a reasonable degree of likelihood that their fear will materialize i.e. that persecution will take place. The standard of proof to be applied was variously described in that case as 'a reasonable chance', 'substantial grounds for thinking', 'a serious possibility', and 'a one in ten chance'. Lord Keith's formulation 'reasonable degree of likelihood' is generally taken to express this standard.

What has happened in the past is an important indicator of what may happen in the future. The Qualification Directive says:

The fact that an applicant has already been subject to persecution or serious harm or to direct threats of such persecution or such harm, is a serious indication of the applicant's well-founded fear of persecution or real risk of suffering serious harm, unless there are good reasons to consider that such persecution or serious harm will not be repeated. (Article 4.4)

In the case of *Kaja* (11038) an experienced tribunal convened for the purpose of resolving the question held that the *Sivakumaran* standard of proof should be applied to the question of whether past events had taken place as well as to whether persecution would take place in the future. So, if the applicant claimed that they had been beaten in custody and that this would recur, both matters need to be proved to be a reasonable likelihood. In fact, the tribunal said, past events and future risks were all part of the same question which should be approached as a question of reasonable likelihood. To divide past events from assessment of future risks is artificial as assessment of future risk will depend in many cases to a great extent on an evaluation of what has happened in the past. *Kaja* has been relied upon since as authority for the proposition simply as stated above, that the lower standard of proof should be applied to past events as well as the chance of future occurrences. Brooke LJ in *Karanakaran* [2000] Imm AR 271sug-gested that this is an oversimplification of the tribunal's judgment which amounts to mis-stating it, and that the decision should be applied using its full reasoning. This was that a decision-maker in an asylum claim will be faced with four kinds of evidence:

1. evidence whose validity they are certain about;
2. evidence they think is probably true;
3. evidence to which they are willing to attach some credence, but would not go so far as to say that it is probably true; and
4. evidence to which they are not willing to attach any credence at all.

The contentious area is the third category of evidence, as this falls below the standard of proof which would warrant reliance upon it in a civil claim. The tribunal's view in *Kaja* was that the asylum decision-maker should not exclude such evidence from their mind.

Karanakaran steers decision-makers away from a mechanistic approach to the stand-ard of proof in *Sivakumaran* and *Kaja*. It is not that the asylum seeker must prove the matters alleged to the standard of reasonable likelihood. In itself this can become a rather meaningless word game, as though the phrase had the precision of a percent-age and as though events and risks could be proved to a quantifiable degree. A refugee claim is not like a civil claim in which there are two competing sets of evidence, one of which the judge must prefer. A refugee claim is not an adversarial process at all. Rather, although *Sivakumaran* and *Kaja* represent appropriate standards if standards are required, and for this purpose the Court of Appeal follows *Sivakumaran* and approves *Kaja*, the inherent uncertainty of future possibilities and of the evaluation of evidence must be understood. Assessing an asylum claim is not a matter simply of fact-finding but, crucially, of evaluation. It must be approached as a whole, as a public law enquiry into the need for protection rather than as an exercise in proving facts to a standard. The application of this approach is a question of assessing the evidence in every case. Evidence of likelihood involves evidence of context and surrounding factors which may suggest for instance trends of behaviour by police or security forces. Asylum cases therefore rely not only on evidence concerning the particular applicant, but also on evidence of what has happened to people who are in a comparable situation to the applicant and of trends for instance, in political repression as may be relevant in the country concerned. As discussed in the previous chapter, these kinds of evidence are procured by using expert evidence and regularly produced reports on the overall situ-ation in particular countries by organizations such as Human Rights Watch, Amnesty International, the US State Department, and the Home Office's Country Information and Policy Unit (CIPU). In chapter 4 we mentioned that the same standard of proof is used in asylum and Article 3 ECHR cases. This is the prevailing view, though there are arguments to the contrary. Two cases in the Court of Appeal which dealt with a failed asylum claims show that whatever the general situation, the ultimate question is whether there is a real risk (as the test is phrased in the Article 3 context) to this applicant. In *Hariri v SSHD* [2003] EWCA Civ 807 the Court of Appeal said that the appellant's case depended entirely on whether he would suffer ill-treatment as a member of a class, either of draft evaders or of those who had left Syria without authority. Therefore the question of whether there was generally a pattern of ill-treatment of such people was crucial to establishing whether there was a real risk to the appellant. The tribunal was therefore not wrong to look for 'a consistent pattern of gross and systematic violation of fundamental human rights' in order to establish whether there was a real risk. However, there are clear risks of over-applying such a formulation, identified by Sedley LJ in *Batayav v SSHD* [2003] EWCA Civ 1489: 'Great care needs to be taken with such epithets. They are intended to elucidate the jurisprudential concept of real risk, not to replace it' (para 38). He then used the example of a car with faulty brakes, quoted in chapter 4. Even if the brakes only fail one time in ten, most people would think there was a real risk of travelling in such a car. There do not have to be frequent or routine brake failures for this to be the case. In *AA (Involuntary returns to Zimbabwe) Zimbabwe CG* [2005] UKAIT 00144, which concerned the risk to failed asylum seekers on return to Zimbabwe, the tribunal followed *Batayav* and reiterated the warning against over-formulation. It noted that in *Batayav v SSHD (No. 2)* [2005] EWCA Civ 366 the Court of Appeal had taken *Hariri* too far in looking for 'conditions in that system that are universal' (para 5) in order to establish risk. The tribunal gives a helpful explanation of how the approach has to be different in different cases in order to answer the crucial question of whether there is 'real risk' to the appellant. The courts are moving in the direction of preferring the concept of 'real risk' to 'reasonable degree of likelihood'. This is not with any intention to change the standard of proof, but in order, as explained by Macdonald (2005:688) to avoid straying into calculations of probability rather than staying with the question of danger to the applicant.

13.2.3 Timing of fear

The well-founded fear must, at the time of the claim, be an operative cause of the asylum seeker's being away from their country of origin. In the case of *Adan* [1998] Imm AR 338, the House of Lords considered whether historic fear, i.e. fear in the past, would be sufficient to found refugee status, and concluded that it would not. Article 1(A)(2) says that it is 'owing to a well-founded fear' that the refugee 'is' outside their country of nationality. In Mr Adan's case, he could not, at the time of his claim, avail himself of the protection of his country (Somalia) as there was no effective government to offer that protection. However, the initial fear which had caused him to flee had subsided as President Barre had fallen and the risk to him of persecution was accordingly lessened. The House of Lords said that there were two parts to a refugee claim, the 'fear test' and the 'protection test', and held that Mr Adan could not obtain refugee status because the fear did not still exist, even though no governmental protection was available and there were risks to him consequent on the continuing civil war.

In *In re B; R v Special Adjudicator ex p Hoxha (UNHCR intervening)* [2005] UKHL 19 the House of Lords considered an argument centred on the cessation clause in Article 1C of the Refugee Convention. As discussed in the last chapter, this clause provides for the ending of refugee status when there has been such a radical change in the circumstances in the refugee's country of origin that they can no longer fail to avail themselves of their country's protection. There is an exception in Article 1C where a refugee is able to 'invoke compelling reasons arising out of past persecution'. In this case the refugee status is not ended. The appellants in *Hoxha* had not obtained refugee status because of the changed circumstances in Kosovo. They argued that the persecution they had suffered in the past was nevertheless so severe that they should not be obliged to return. The House of Lords rejected this argument. An exception to the cessation clause could not be used to achieve refugee status for someone who had not achieved it on their asylum application. Their fear was not current, as was required in order to obtain protection.

13.2.4 **Refugee *sur place***

The opposite situation also arises, where a refugee has left their country of origin without fear for some other purpose, e.g. a holiday or study, but during their absence an event such as a change of government takes place which causes them to fear persecution should they return. In this case the fear is the operative cause of their remaining outside their country of nationality, even though it was not the cause of their leaving it. They are thus entitled to claim refugee status and are referred to, following the French, as a refugee *'sur place'*.

It follows that if events since the applicant's arrival in the UK may give rise to a well-founded fear, these events may take place not only in the applicant's home country but equally in the UK, in fact they may be the actions of the applicant themselves. This was established by the Court of Appeal in *Danian* [2000] Imm AR 96, in which it was confirmed that refugee status could be granted after the applicant was at risk of persecution in his country of nationality because of his activities in the UK. This possibility is affirmed in the Qualification Directive Article 5.

This decision does not necessarily mean that a person may create their own refugee status cynically by undertaking political activities in the UK when they have no genuine political motive. This question has been considered in a number of cases since *Danian*. The Court of Appeal in *Iftikhar Ahmed v SSHD* [2000] INLR 1 explained that *Danian* simply brings the decision back to the essential question, 'is there a serious risk that on return the applicant would be persecuted for a Convention reason?' That risk may be created by the applicant's own cynical or unreasonable conduct but may still be real. The evaluation of how real it is would of course be affected by some doubt as to the applicant's own credibility. In *Danian* itself the Court endorsed the view of the UNHCR:

it should be borne in mind that opportunistic post-flight activities will not necessarily create a real risk of persecution in the claimant's home country either because they will not come to the attention of the authorities of that country or because the opportunistic nature of such activities will be apparent to all including to those authorities.

It follows that it is a mistake to dismiss the claim without considering the effect of activities in the UK on the applicant's prospects on return (*R v IAT ex p Mafuta* [2001] EWCA Civ 745).

Mr Danian himself ultimately lost his appeal when the case came back to the tribunal, after the Court of Appeal decision. The tribunal considered that lack of good faith undermined the credibility of a well-founded fear of persecution. It took the view that if Mr Danian's motives were cynical, then he did not have a fear, and on the facts of his political involvement in the UK, the Nigerian authorities would not impute to him a political opinion. This option is left open by the Qualification Directive, which says that member states may introduce a presumption against the grant of refugee status where the risk is 'based on circumstances which the applicant has created by his own decision' (Article 5.3). The UK government made it known that it would not instate such a presumption, and there is none in the implementing rules or regulations.

13.2.4.1 *Rejected asylum claims*

A related issue is the effect of the asylum claim itself on what treatment the individual might face on return. The Home Office occasionally accepts as a matter of policy that returning people to particular countries may not be possible because the fact of having made an asylum claim may bring reprisals from their home government. In the case of Libya the Home Office adopted a policy of this kind in 2001 (see *Hassan* [2002] UKIAT 00062). More recently, the only country to which as a matter of policy removals have not been taking place has been Zimbabwe (letter Des Browne to Keith Best IAS published 12 July 2004). Amid protest, in November 2004 the Home Office lifted this moratorium. In Zimbabwe some politicians welcomed the move, but Information Minister, Jonathan Moyo, considered that returnees should be treated with suspicion as they could be 'trained and bribed malcontents', sent to disrupt the election (newsvote. bbc.co.uk 17 December 2004). The resumption of returns caused not only a political storm, but also scores of asylum seekers to go on hunger strike in detention. Numerous applications were lodged for judicial review of removal directions. Eventually the Home Office was forced to concede that removals to Zimbabwe could not continue at least until the hearing of a test case. Interestingly, on the same day that the Home Secretary was compelled to this position, the European Parliament issued a far-reaching resolution on Zimbabwe, calling for the strengthening of sanctions and condemning the regime but making no reference to the return of failed asylum seekers (7 July 2005).

All pending judicial reviews were stayed, and a case considering the evidence of the treatment of returnees came before the tribunal. At the third tribunal hearing and after two Court of Appeal hearings, the tribunal held that there was no means of distinguishing between people being returned because asylum claims had failed and being returned for other reasons. Those at risk would be those who would be of interest to the security services because of outstanding criminal matters or histories of political or military involvement, including those with civil society associations that had attracted adverse interest from the government. People in these groups would be identified by the intelligence services at Harare Airport and taken away for a second stage of questioning. At that stage the risk of ill-treatment arose (*HS (Zimbabwe)* [2007] UKAIT 00094) for such people, who were not necessarily failed asylum seekers. In the meantime, removals to Zimbabwe are still suspended, and the unsuccessful appellant is seeking leave once again to appeal to the Court of Appeal. Each time there is a decision in these cases, there is a wave of protest in the UK at the prospect of people being forcibly returned to Zimbabwe.

Comparable arguments were made in the case of failed asylum seekers returning to the Democratic Republic of Congo, and the High Court asked the Home Office (*R (on application of Lutete)* [2007] EWHC 2331 (Admin)) to suspend removals to DRC while this matter was under consideration. The tribunal eventually decided that there was insufficient evidence that people returning were at risk simply by virtue of being failed asylum seekers (*BK (DRC CG)* [2007] UKAIT 00098). As signatories to the Refugee Convention and with intelligence personnel active in the UK, the DRC government could be taken to know that asylum procedures were conducted in private and did not involve public denunciation of the state of origin. The accounts of failed asylum seekers would by definition have been disbelieved and so would not have brought discredit on the DRC government.

In addition to general country policies, it may be necessary to argue that the return of a particular failed asylum seeker is not safe. This has often arisen in relation to the return of Kurds to Turkey as there are concerns about the authorities' treatment of them on arrival. In *Degirmenci v SSHD* [2004] EWCA Civ 1553 the Court of Appeal held that there needed to be a full assessment of the evidence relating to the treatment on return of a failed asylum seeker such as the appellant. Where, for instance, as in *Yapici* (below) the appellant had left the country in breach of reporting conditions, this would increase the risk of their coming to the notice of the authorities.

13.3 **Persecution**

The concept of persecution is central to the recognition of refugee status. It is not conclusively defined, and in fact the UNHCR Handbook expressly avoids attempting to lay down any such definition, saying that whether threats or actions will amount to persecution 'will depend on the circumstances of each case' (para 52) and 'it is not possible to lay down a general rule as to what cumulative reasons can give rise to a valid claim to refugee status' (para 53).

The Qualification Directive Article 9 says that to amount to persecution acts must be 'sufficiently serious by their nature or repetition' to constitute 'a severe violation of basic human rights' particularly those which are non-derogable under the ECHR (see chapter 4), or must be an accumulation of measures, including violations of human rights, which is severe enough to affect an individual similarly to a severe violation of non-derogable rights. The second paragraph of the Article is an important development in refugee law in Europe:

2. Acts of persecution as qualified in paragraph 1, can, inter alia, take the form of:

  (a) acts of physical or mental violence, including acts of sexual violence;
  (b) legal, administrative, police, and/or judicial measures which are in themselves discriminatory or which are implemented in a discriminatory manner;
  (c) prosecution or punishment, which is disproportionate or discriminatory;
  (d) denial of judicial redress resulting in a disproportionate or discriminatory punishment;
  (e) prosecution or punishment for refusal to perform military service in a conflict, where performing military service would include crimes or acts falling under the exclusion clauses as set out in Article 12(2);
  (f) acts of a gender-specific or child-specific nature.

We shall return to this list as the matters arise.

One approach to identifying persecution, in a line of cases of which *Jonah* [1985] Imm AR 7 is the oft-quoted authority, has been reliance on the dictionary definition: 'to pursue with malignancy or injurious action'. However, this requires a focus on the motive and actions of the persecutor. It might be said that a person tortured once in a police station and then released has not been 'pursued' and that a person who would be prosecuted for any expression of their sexuality is not the target of malignancy but of government policy. Whereas the dictionary definition would work for some cases, it does not for others. This approach has been falling into disuse in favour of an emphasis on the acts or their effects rather than the motive. The Qualification Directive does not attempt to define persecution as such, but only acts of persecution, as described above.

The tribunal in *Gashi* adopted the submission of the UNHCR that: 'for the Convention to be a living instrument of protection, the term "persecution" must be interpreted in a manner that best achieves its humanitarian object and purpose'. The tribunal went on to say that 'it would be a mistake to attempt a definition of persecution which could in any way restrict its power to meet the changing circumstances in which the Convention has to operate'. A simple formulation is that persecution = serious harm + failure of state protection (set out in this way by the Refugee Women's Legal Group (*Women as Asylum Seekers* 1997:9)). This is a workable formulation which underscores the crucial aspect of state responsibility and has been used by the courts, for instance by Lord Hoffmann in *R v IAT & SSHD ex p Shah and Islam v IAT* [1999] 2 AC 629.

There must be an analysis of whether what is feared in a particular case is persecution. However, the decision-maker does not so much *define* persecution as *identify* it. The difference is that a definition is an attempt to provide in the abstract a statement that will apply in a wide range (preferably all) circumstances, whereas identification starts with a set of circumstances and asks whether these amount to persecution. This might be similar to a doctor who considers the patient's symptoms in the light of all available knowledge and then decides whether they have the disease, rather than trying to list an exhaustive set of symptoms and then asking whether the patient fits into them.

The Qualification Directive approach to acts of persecution is consistent with the commonly used starting point proffered by Hathaway:

The sustained or systemic violation of basic human rights demonstrative of a failure of state protection in relation to one of the core entitlements which has been recognized by the international community. The types of harm to be protected against include the breach of any rights within the first category, a discriminatory or non-emergency abnegation of a right within the second category or the failure to implement a right in the third category which is either discriminatory or not grounded in the absolute lack of resources. (1991:112)

The three categories to which he refers he sets out in the following way:

Category one:
Freedom from arbitrary deprivation of life, from torture, cruel, inhuman or, degrading treatment or punishment, from slavery, imprisonment for breach of a contractual obligation, retroactive criminal prosecution, freedom of thought, conscience and religion, and the right to be recognized as a person in law.

Category two:
Freedom from arbitrary arrest and detention, right to a fair trial, equal treatment including in access to public employment, freedom of expression, assembly and association, of movement inside a country, to leave and return to one's country of origin, to form and join trade unions, to take part in public affairs and vote, and protection for privacy and the family.

Category three:
The right to work, including just and favourable conditions of employment, to an adequate standard of living including food, clothing and housing, to the highest attainable standard of health, to education, and to engage in cultural, scientific, literary, and artistic expression.

This human rights approach to persecution was broadly adopted by the UNHCR and from them by the tribunal in *Gashi and Nikshiqi*. It has been used and endorsed by the higher courts for instance the House of Lords in *Horvath v SSHD* [2000] 3 All ER 577 and *Sepet and Bulbul v SSHD* [2003] UKHL 15. It is an extremely useful framework though not final or definitive, and it has some limitations (see for instance Wilsher 2003). Goodwin-Gill proposes a formulation of 'reasons, interests and measures': the reasons for persecution would be race, religion and so on; the interests affected would be fundamental ones such as life and liberty; and the measures are the infliction of harm, arbitrary arrest and so on (2007:132). Again, this formulation steers away from focusing on persecution as a special kind of activity, but rather emphasizes the actual consequences and the denial of rights.

Whatever approach is taken to identifying persecution, it requires both 'serious harm' and a failure of state protection.

In the leading case of *Horvath*, Lord Hope said: 'The general purpose of the Convention is to enable the person who no longer has the benefit of state protection against persecution for a Convention reason in his own country to turn for protection to the international community'. This is known as the principle of surrogacy. The underlying idea is the fundamental breakdown in the relationship between citizen and State, so that the citizen can no longer rely on the State for the protection which is their due, and must look instead to the international community. This may entail that the state is actively the persecutor, as when the police routinely torture people in their custody. Alternatively, it may entail that others perpetrate the serious harm, as when skinheads attack Roma people, but the state fails to protect them. When persecution is carried out in this way by non-State actors, further legal problems arise, and these are discussed below.

Professor Hathaway's reference to the 'systemic violation' of rights suggests that the violation is part of the functioning of the State system, the State endorses the violations, implicitly by not providing redress or explicitly by for instance oppressive legislation, or covertly, by promoting brutal interrogation by security services.

This may be distinguished from, although it is connected to, the question of whether ill-treatment must be *systematic* to amount to persecution. This is sometimes used in the same way as 'systemic', but may also be used to mean 'repeated' or 'persistent', which will often be appropriate but not always. Where the violation feared is sufficiently serious, e.g. killing or torture, there is no necessity for repetition in order for this to be persecution.

The Qualification Directive follows the earlier EU Joint Position of 4 March 1996, in saying that acts feared will be persecution if sufficiently serious by reason of 'their nature *or* their repetition'. Either severity or repetition is required, but not both.

The authorities on a single instance of ill-treatment as persecution were comprehensively reviewed in the case of *Doymus* 00/TH/01748, expanding upon the Court of Appeal judgment in *Demirkaya* [1999] Imm AR 498, where Stuart-Smith LJ said:

At one end of the scale there may be arbitrary deprivation of life, torture and cruel, inhuman and degrading treatment or punishment. In such a case the conduct may be so extreme that one instance is sufficient, but less serious conduct may not amount to persecution unless it is persistent. (para 15)

That a single violation of a first category right would constitute persecution is so, not only in common sense (a single threat to life is enough) but also by reference to the human rights instruments from which these standards are derived. For instance 'no one shall be subjected to torture or to cruel, inhuman or degrading treatment or punishment' (Art 9 ICCPR as well as Art 3 ECHR). This does not allow an exception if the torture happens only once, and case law under these Articles treats single acts of torture or cruel, inhuman or degrading treatment, or punishment as violations. The tribunal in *Doymus* cited other academic writers, the UNHCR and case law of other jurisdictions also as authorities that, while persistency is a usual characteristic of persecution, it is not an inevitable one.

There is no requirement to be 'singled out' for persecution (*R v SSHD ex p Jeyakumaran* [1994] Imm AR 45). If the persecutory treatment is for a reason included in the Convention (see below), the fact that others who share the same characteristic are treated similarly may be evidence that supports the asylum claim but it does not detract from it. As Lord Lloyd said in *Adan* at 348: 'It is not necessary for a claimant to show that he is more at risk than anyone else in his group, if the group as a whole is subject to oppression'. Conversely, there is no need for all those sharing the characteristic to be persecuted (*Shah and Islam*). However, in situations of civil war, there will not be a refugee claim where *all* sections of society are similarly in fear (*SSHD v Adan* [1999] 1 AC 293). Macdonald points out that there are a number of countries which have been in a state of armed conflict for many years (2001:507). Examples are Sri Lanka, Algeria, or Angola. Refugee claims from these countries are assessed in the normal way, and give rise to questions of whether there is persecution for a Convention reason. The House of Lords required, for a successful claim, that where society had broken down into continual conflict 'the individual or group has to show a well-founded fear of persecution over and above the risk to life and liberty inherent in civil war' (*Adan* 349).

The final form of the Qualification Directive does not contain an earlier proposed clause which would have made it irrelevant that the applicant comes from a country where there is large-scale oppression.

13.3.1 Severe ill-treatment

A single instance of sufficiently severe ill-treatment may, as discussed in *Doymus* and *Demirkaya*, amount to persecution. A single instance of loss of life is a severe violation of human rights, and a single instance of torture is severe enough; these absolute rights admit of no justification or derogation. This was made very clear by the House of Lords in *R v SSHD ex p Sivakumar* [2003] 1 WLR 840 where even the applicant's suspected involvement in terrorism could not justify the appalling torture he had experienced. The recent attempts by many governments to justify torture have already been discussed in chapter 4.

The UN Convention against Torture and Other Cruel Inhuman or Degrading Treatment Article 1(1) defines torture as:

An act by which pain or suffering, whether physical or mental, is intentionally inflicted on a person for such purposes as obtaining from him or a third person a confession, punishing him for an act which he or a third party has committed or is suspected of having committed, or intimidating him or a third person, or for any reason based on discrimination of any kind, when such pain or suffering is inflicted by or at the instigation of or with the consent of public officials or other person acting in an official capacity.

This Article has not been widely referred to in refugee cases, though it was used as guidance by the High Court in *R v SSHD ex p Javed and Ali* QBD (Admin) (2001) The Times, 9 February. It suggests that not only the conduct but also who carried it out and the reason are significant in determining whether it amounts to torture. However, Goodwin-Gill and McAdam (2007:96) point out that there is no need for an asylum claimant to prove any particular intention on the part of their persecutor, nor that any particular person carries it out. Indeed, as *Sivakumar* makes plain, intention may be irrelevant, and the discussion below will show that who carries it out is less important than whether the state can provide protection.

In *Doymus* the tribunal recognized that it was not just the level of ill-treatment that was relevant but also the psychological effects. The applicant had described being stripped naked, sprayed with cold water from a hose, and beaten with a stick while his hands were tied behind his back. The tribunal held that this was likely to 'give rise to feelings of fear, anguish, and inferiority capable of humiliating and debasing him and possibly breaking his physical and moral resistance'. This would be a breach of Article 3 ECHR or Article 9 ICCPR, it was degrading treatment, and it was unnecessary to determine whether it amounted to torture. The judgment in *Doymus* thus links an act of persecution explicitly to human rights norms. In *Demirkaya* the Court of Appeal expressly disapproved trying to categorize behaviour such that a particular level of ill-treatment would amount to persecution. The question should be looked at in the round. 'Is this person at risk of persecution for a Convention reason?' The Court said that this was a question of fact.

In a case such as *Doymus* there is no examination of the motives of the police. It was an essential and undisputed element of Mr Doymus' claim that he was at risk because of his political affiliations, and the precise anticipated motives of the police on any particular occasion do not require inquiry. All the more so is this the case as torture cannot be justified and so even if their motive was to preserve law and order this would not prevent the feared action being persecution. If motive is unimportant, rape and other serious sexual assault receive anomalous treatment in refugee law.

13.3.1.1 *Rape and other sexual violence*

The Qualification Directive and UK implementing regulations include, in their list of possible acts of persecution, 'acts of physical or mental violence, including acts of sexual violence'. Although this is not new in law, in practice there has been a persistent failure at all stages of asylum decision-making to recognize rape and other sexual violence as forms of persecution. In order to address this and other gender issues, guidelines on gender have been produced by the Refugee Women's Legal Group in 1998, the Immigration Appellate Authority in 2000 and UNHCR in 2002.

The Immigration Appellate Authority's Asylum Gender Guidelines were in principle established as guidance for tribunal decision-making, and contained a section establishing the severity of sexual violence as a form of torture or cruel inhuman or degrading treatment or punishment. Cited in support of this argument were the Statutes of the International Tribunals for Former Yugoslavia and Rwanda, which list rape as a crime against humanity, and the Article 3 ECHR case of *Aydin v Turkey* (1997) 25 EHRR 251 para 83 in which the Court said:

Rape of a detainee by an official of the State must be considered to be an especially grave and abhorrent form of ill-treatment given the ease with which the offender can exploit the vulnerability and weakened resistance of his victim.

The IAA gender guidelines are referred to in the current (October 2006) Home Office guidance on gender issues in asylum claims but they have in reality been quietly dropped. They no longer appear on the AIT website, and a Parliamentary Question on 7 February 2007 (HL 1596) elicited the response that the gender guidelines were out of date, replaced by case law, and non-binding in any event. The Parliamentary Under-Secretary of State reassured the questioner (Lord Hylton) that judges had the benefit of the Judicial Studies Board (JSB) Equal Treatment Benchbook 'when conducting hearings and considering appeals involving vulnerable individuals', but this gives no guidance on rape and sexual violence as a form of persecution. The Home Office guidance, represented by the API, was not considered an adequate substitute by researchers (Ceneda and Palmer 2006).

The research conducted by Ceneda and Palmer suggested that non-recognition of sexual violence as persecution remains a substantial problem in asylum claims. There are many ways in which sexual violence is not recognized as persecution. Often the harm to the asylum seeker is minimized. Also there is much confused thinking about the motivation of the persecutor. This may be illustrated by the case of *R v Special Adjudicator ex p Okonkwo* [1998] Imm AR 502, where Collins J supported the distinction made by the adjudicator between rape committed 'merely to seek sexual gratification' and rape committed for some other motive. If it was 'merely to seek sexual gratification' then it was a common crime on a par with assault, and would not amount to torture unless repeated. It was argued for the applicant that rape constituted torture in part because the psychological effects can be similar to those referred to in *Doymus*, namely of fear, anguish, humiliation, and inferiority, and also because of the severity of the physical ill-treatment. The IAA Asylum Gender Guidelines para 2A.18 quoted Assistant Commissioner Wyn Jones of the Metropolitan Police: 'We want to kill the myth that rape is sexually motivated – it is usually intended to inflict violence and humiliation'. No reasoning of this kind appears in the current guidance. A fundamental disagreement about the nature of rape and other sexual violence affects whether it will be regarded as persecution. Of course the necessary element of state involvement must exist, but even this is not simple to identify. A crime which is investigated and punished is not persecution, a rape by a police officer of a person in detention which is part of a state-endorsed routine method of humiliating prisoners would surely be persecution. In *Okonkwo* the situation was between these two extremes as the assailant was an army officer who had threatened the applicant. She had suffered violence on other occasions from the authorities. She was not in detention at the time of the rape, but was attacked by the roadside and left there. The location and the lack of formal relationship between the assailant and applicant influenced Collins J in his agreement with the adjudicator. However, this leaves out of account the exercise of power by a member of the military forces and the lack of redress.

The reasoning in *Okonkwo* has been followed in later cases, for instance in *Farhat Saeed Chaudhary* 00/TH/00304 in which the adjudicator found and the tribunal accepted that rape by police could have been for sexual gratification and was therefore not persecution. Again in *R v IAT ex p Arafa Shaban* [2000] Imm AR 408 the motive of the rapist who was a member of the ruling political party, the applicant being associated with the opposition, was regarded as relevant. The question of whether a police officer who rapes is abusing power was considered more fully in *Muriu* 00/TH/02139 but no conclusion was reached as evidence of the rape was not considered strong enough. In *Bajraktari* [2001] EWHC Admin 1192 Harrison J found that rape did not constitute torture because it was not used to extract information.

The case law in this area in the UK has been slow to recognize the political nature of much sexual violence. Even systematic rape by armed forces has not necessarily been recognized as persecution, as in *R (N) v SSHD* [2002] EWCA Civ 1082, where the claimant had suffered double rape by armed forces who took away her son (and had probably killed him).The adjudicator had found that the rape was for sexual gratification, and once again this argument prevailed even before the Court of Appeal, who saw the situation as one of uncontrolled lawlessness by soldiers and did not construe this in the light of discrimination. The UNHCR Global Consultations Summary Conclusions on gender-related persecution say that one of the main problems facing women asylum seekers is 'failure to recognize the political nature of seemingly private acts of harm to women' (para 4). As appears from this, the recognition of sexual violence as persecution is bound up with the recognition of gender-based persecution, which is discussed further in relation to the Convention reason for persecution at 13.6 below. A fundamental issue is that much violence perpetrated on the basis of gender is socially sanctioned either by law or by practice, whether or not it is violence committed by a sexual act. Recognition of an asylum claim on such a basis therefore involves a political judgment which may go against the tide of public thinking either in the country of origin or the host country or both, or may involve disapproval of the values in another country. An example of increasing importance is the practice known variously as female genital cutting or mutilation, or female circumcision (FGM). Case law concerning this practice went in all directions until the Court of Appeal in *P and M v SSHD* [2004] EWCA Civ 1640 accepted that forcible subjection to female genital mutilation was severe ill-treatment which, combined with the absence of state intervention to prevent or punish it, amounted to persecution. This has now been put beyond doubt in the House of Lords' judgment in *SSHD v Fornah* [2006] UKHL 46, in which Lord Bingham described FGM as 'an extreme and very cruel expression of male dominance'. This case is discussed further at 13.6.4.1 below.

The use and effects of sexual violence as a weapon of war is simply and eloquently described in an obiter passage of the judgment of Baroness Hale in *In re B(FC) (Appellant) (2002) R v Special Adjudicator ex p Hoxha (FC) (Appellant)* [2005] UKHL 19. She explains that the effect may be compounded by a society which

adds to the earlier suffering she has endured the pain, hardship and indignity of rejection and ostracism from her own people. There are many cultures in which a woman suffers almost as much from the attitudes of those around her to the degradation she has suffered as she did from the original assault. (para 32)

13.3.2 Second category rights

In relation to violations of rights in Hathaway's second category, for instance detention, ill-treatment in detention short of torture, or denial of a fair trial, international human rights' instruments give states some limited power to derogate or to justify infringements. For example, detention may be justified for one of a number of listed reasons in Article 5 ECHR. This is reflected in refugee law. The leading case which demonstrates this is *Sandralingham and Ravichandran* [1996] Imm AR 97, CA.

Key Case

Sandralingham and Ravichandran [1996] Imm AR 97, CA

This case arose from periodic round-ups by the Sri Lankan police of young Tamil men and their detention for questioning, sometimes for periods of days. The appellants had been so detained, and had also been ill-treated in custody. They alleged that ill-treatment in custody and arbitrary arrest and detentions each separately constituted persecution. It was accepted that the situation had improved since the time when they were detained. There was therefore no reasonable likelihood of repetition of ill-treatment in detention and so this part of the claim fell out of the picture.

In considering detention as possible persecution, the Court of Appeal held following factors were relevant:

(i) the frequency of round-ups and the length of the detentions resulting;

(ii) the situation prevailing in Colombo at the material time and the Sri Lankan government's undoubted need to combat Tamil terrorism;

(iii) the true purpose of the round-ups and the efforts made to arrest and detain only those realistically suspected of involvement in the disturbances.

The Court of Appeal endorsed the respondent's argument that

young male Tamils are not arrested and detained because they are Tamils but rather because they may have been involved in some outrage. The round-ups are not arbitrary. The very fact that the particular sub-groups identified by the Amnesty Report are especially vulnerable to arrest shows that the true objective of the round-ups is to combat terrorism rather than discriminate against Tamils as such. (at 108)

It accepted that the authorities' attempts to control disorder had affected Tamils the most because more of the disorder had occurred in areas where Tamils lived. Detention of excessive length could amount to persecution, repeated detention of the same person could amount to persecution if it was not justified by an appropriate level of suspicion of that individual's having committed a criminal offence, and ill-treatment in detention would normally amount to persecution. However, if innocent people were accidentally caught up in a legitimate policing exercise, this was not persecution even if they were likely to be of a particular minority. This last point shows that it is difficult to consider persecution separately from the reason for the persecution. The separation is indeed artificial though necessary for the purposes of analysis and discussion. The reason for persecution is discussed below under the heading of 'Convention reason'.

In *Ravichandran* Staughton LJ said that 'Persecution must at least be persistent and serious ill-treatment without just cause'. It is apparent how this arises from the facts of *Ravichandran* in which a single instance of detention was not held to be persecution, but persistent or repeated detention might be, but the statement should not be taken out of context to require that persecution must *always* be persistent. The Qualification Directive list of acts of persecution includes 'legal, administrative, police, and/or judicial measures which are in themselves discriminatory or which are implemented in a discriminatory manner'.

13.3.2.1 *Prosecution or persecution?*

Continuing the consideration of second category rights, it is undeniable that the state has a right to prosecute its citizens, even a duty to do so in order to maintain law and order for the benefit of others. The UNHCR Handbook puts it in this way:

Persecution must be distinguished from punishment for a common law offence. Persons fleeing from prosecution or punishment for such an offence are not normally refugees. It should be recalled that a refugee is a victim – or potential victim – of injustice, not a fugitive from justice. (para 56)

However, prosecution may amount to persecution in certain circumstances. If a punishment is excessive, this may turn prosecution into persecution. For instance, it may be within lawful bounds of State action for there to be some penalty for adultery, but stoning to death goes beyond that (*Shah and Islam*).

The discriminatory application of the law may also turn prosecution into persecution, as suggested in the quotation above from *Ravichandran*. If people had been detained *because* they were Tamils, then this could have amounted to persecution. The Handbook gives the example of prosecution for an offence of public order for the distribution of pamphlets, which could be 'a vehicle for the persecution of the individual on the grounds of the political content of the publication' (para 59). In *Sivakumar* in the Court of Appeal [2002] INLR 310 Dyson LJ used the following words which were quoted with approval by the House of Lords:

Where a person to whom a political opinion is imputed or who is a member of a race or social group is the subject of sanctions that do not apply generally in the state, then it is more likely than not that the application of the sanctions is discriminatory and persecutory for a Convention reason. (para 30)

The House of Lords added the caveat that this should not be used to suggest a rebuttable inference in the legal sense. In *Asante* [1991] Imm AR 78 the tribunal found that the reason for prosecution was the political opinion imputed to the applicant, and this rendered the prosecution persecutory for Convention purposes.

The issue is less clear when an individual is not targeted for enforcement for a discriminatory reason, but enforcement of the law has a discriminatory impact. On the face of it the claims of Turkish Kurds for refugee status on account of conscription into the military raise this issue as a significant proportion of the work of the military may be engaged in action against the minority to which they belong. However these claims have on the whole not been successful. This is dealt with further below in relation to the Convention reason for persecution and the implications of objection to military service.

Prosecution may also amount to persecution where there is a lack of due process or fairness in the criminal process. Hathaway says that where 'the decision to prosecute, the process under which the charge is heard, or the nature of the sentence imposed is politically manipulated' (1991:172) then the prosecution may found a refugee claim. The allegations were of this kind in *Khan v SSHD* [2003] EWCA Civ 530 where the appellant fled Bangladesh after a violent demonstration, as a result of which he had been charged and a warrant issued for his arrest. He believed that he would not be granted bail, would be detained in inhuman and degrading conditions for a long period of time, and would not receive a fair trial. The adjudicator had held that what he feared was prosecution rather than persecution, but the Court of Appeal agreed that the case must be reconsidered by the IAT when Mr Khan was able to prove that he had been sentenced to 10 years' imprisonment in his absence. Where an individual is prosecuted for exercising fundamental human rights, then the prosecution may well be persecutory, but this will depend additionally on whether, in the circumstances, some curtailment of freedom is justified in the public interest, and if so, whether the curtailment imposed by the criminal law has exceeded what is justified. In Mr Khan's case there may have been grounds for charging a public order offence, but this could not justify an unfair trial. The Qualification Directive recognizes this form of persecution by listing 'prosecution or punishment which is disproportionate or discriminatory' including if through 'lack of judicial redress'.

As mentioned earlier in relation to failed asylum seekers, many cases have concerned the question of whether dissidents will attract the attention of the authorities on return and so be at risk. In *Yapici* v *SSHD* [2005] EWCA Civ 826 the Court of Appeal held that a proper decision must have regard to the effect of the appellant's leaving the country in breach of reporting conditions. Although the appellant was in breach of an administrative requirement, his reason for being in breach and the fact that it could bring him to the notice of the authorities were relevant to whether he would be at risk on return.

13.3.3 Discrimination as persecution

The violation and threatened violation of rights in Hathaway's third category gives rise to difficult questions in refugee claims. The Refugee Convention protects against persecution, but not against discrimination in delivery of social rights. In an age of bitter inter-ethnic wars and discrimination against minorities so fundamental that in some cases they have been obliterated from social and political life, when does one become the other? This is one of the challenges to the international framework of human rights and refugee protection which was probably not contemplated in this form when the Convention was first drafted.

A formative case on this issue is *Gashi and Nikshiqi*.

 Key Case

Gashi and Nikshiqi [1997] INLR 96

The appellants in this case were ethnic Albanians from Kosovo in Serbia. They had evaded military service, and their claim was based in part on the consequences for them of this evasion if they were to return and in part on the level of discrimination they would face as ethnic Albanians in Kosovo. There was an abundance of evidence before the tribunal about the situation of ethnic Albanians in land, such as Kosovo, under Serb control. The government policy was referred to as 'Serbianization', implemented by, for instance (quoting from the tribunal's summary of evidence):

> the removal of senior Albanians in the courts and public sector generally and restrictions in even the most menial of employment, e.g. street vendors. 80% of Albanians lost their posts...There is no control or evidence of any intended control by the central authority of the police in Kosovo and the police are all Serbians. There is a systematic state policy which, it is said, permits this police misbehaviour. In day to day life

> Albanians are harassed, subjected to house searches, beating, torture at police sta-
> tions, constant checks carried out at random without any recourse to courts with an
> effective system to provide adequate remedies and protection to ethnic Albanians.
>
> As a consequence the tribunal found that Mr Gashi and Mr Nikshiqi, in addition to prosecu-
> tion for draft evasion, faced physical abuse, inability to obtain employment, and constant
> and persistent harassment by police uncontrolled by government.

In considering whether this would amount to persecution the tribunal drew on the
internationally accepted view of the Convention as a living instrument. It said 'it would
be a mistake to attempt a definition of "persecution" which could in any way restrict its
growth to meet the changing circumstances in which the Convention has to operate'.
The prospects faced by Mr Gashi and Mr Nikshiqi amounted to persecution. The tribunal's decision adopts the reasoning of the UNHCR on the question of discrimination
without alteration. *Gashi and Nikshiqi* was by no means the first case to recognize denial
of third category rights as a basis for refugee status, but the extensive judgment made it
an authoritative and important turning point in this respect.

Where discrimination in social rights is feared, the decision as to whether this
amounts to persecution necessarily involves an assessment of the action taken by the
government to protect its citizens. Although each case can only be decided on the risk
to the particular applicant, it will be apparent that these are highly political decisions.
The recognition of an asylum claim is an acknowledgement that this individual is not
being protected by their own government, and particularly when discrimination is the
basis of the claim, this involves, in effect, judgments about the functioning of that society. These issues arose in the return of Serbs to Croatia after fighting in the war there
against Croatians. The Croatian government was showing commitment to promoting
a peaceful co-existence between Serbs and Croats and preparing legislation to that
end, but how would Serbs actually be treated? See *Protic* 01/TH/00098 and *Mrvaljevic*
00/TH/02863 for two different outcomes from tribunals which had to consider this
issue. Before conflicts in the former Yugoslavia, there was a short period when the
British media was full of reports of Roma people fleeing severe discrimination in eastern
European countries (see, for instance, report in Patrin Web Journal, 22 October 1997).
The British Home Office Minister, Mike O'Brien, appeared on television to say that the
majority of these claims would not be entertained as it was the job of the asylum seekers' own governments to resolve issues of discrimination, and they would not interfere
in the internal matters of another state.

On the whole, applications from European Roma continued to be turned down,
though it has been questioned by academic commentators (see, for instance, O'Nions
1999) whether claims have been genuinely considered on an individual basis as
required by the Refugee Convention. This scepticism as to whether Roma claims have
been treated with the seriousness that they deserve is indirectly supported by recent
cases in the ECtHR finding breaches of fundamental rights of Roma. For instance, in
D.H. v Czech Republic (Application no. 57325/00) Judgment 15 November 2007 the
ECtHR found by 13 votes to four that there had been discrimination against Roma children in the provision of education by placing the majority of them in special schools
for children with learning disabilities or particularly low intelligence. In *Kalanyos v
Romania* (Application no. 57884/00) Judgment 26 July 2007 the houses of Roma people

were burned down after threats to do so and the prosecution of the attackers was closed down partly on the basis that the Roma had brought it on themselves. The families affected lived in stables without heat or water as no alternative housing was provided. The case was settled because the Romanian government accepted that, by failing to act to protect the Roma and then by failing to provide any redress, there had been violations of Articles 3, 6, 8, 13 and 14 of the ECHR. None of these of course are findings of persecution as the ECtHR is not concerned with that. Nevertheless the level of severity of suffering of Roma people at the hands of or with the connivance of the state received recognition in these cases.

The prospect of countries of origin of most Roma claimants becoming members of the EU at the time the asylum claims were being heard is likely to have been a factor in the view taken of them. Since their accession to the EU such claims would have been even more problematic, and since 10 October 2006 are no longer possible on the face of the Refugee Directive 2004/83, which provides for refugee claims only from third country nationals and those who are stateless. This may be an issue which tests the compatibility of the Directive with the Refugee Convention.

The emphasis in the Qualification Directive is on non-derogable rights, but there is scope for persecution to arise from 'an accumulation of various measures, including violation of human rights, which is sufficiently severe as to affect an individual in a similar manner to' severe violation of basic human rights. The Directive allows for claims based on discrimination, but only with reference to 'legal, administrative, police or judicial measures'. This seems to indicate a retreat at European level from countenancing claims with an economic basis, though some have succeeded in the past. The UNHCR Handbook suggests that discrimination may amount to persecution where:

measures of discrimination lead to consequences of a substantially prejudicial nature for the person concerned, e.g. serious restrictions on his right to earn a livelihood, his right to practise his religion, or his access to normally available educational facilities. (para 54)

The question according to the tribunal in *Gujda* (18231) was whether the denial of social rights, to education, housing, and so forth, is such that it interferes 'with a basic human right to live a decent life'. It must also be grounded in discrimination, not an absolute lack of resources in the state; citizens of countries where the majority live in extreme poverty cannot claim asylum on this basis. In *Harakal (also known as Harakel) v SSHD* [2001] EWCA Civ 884 the Court of Appeal found that a lifetime of serious discrimination should be taken into account in allowing the asylum claim of a Roma from the Czech Republic. The Court of Appeal described it as 'significant discrimination in all facets of his life throughout his life'. In *Chiver* (10758) the asylum application succeeded before the adjudicator where the claimant was a miner from Romania who had refused to take government orders to take part in breaking up anti-government demonstrations. He was dismissed from his job as a result, and refused a work card. Without this he was unable to obtain a job or any state benefits. He went on hunger strike, and was arrested and beaten by a policeman. His claim was based substantially on the denial of the right to a livelihood, and succeeded on this. It is noteworthy that although discrimination amounting to persecution is on the whole a more recent use of the Refugee Convention, a claim like this is a classic refugee claim such as might have been envisaged by the drafters of the Convention. It is one in which the State makes normal life impossible for a political opponent.

13.3.4 **Effective state protection**

So far we have been considering the serious harm aspect of persecution. This is closely bound up with the second aspect, that of lack of state protection. Assessing state protection requires consideration of three questions:

- Who will perpetrate the feared harm?
- What kind of protection is available against that?
- What kind of body is capable of delivering effective protection?

13.3.4.1 *Perpetrators – agents of the state*

This is the most obvious situation, where the feared persecution will be carried out by those who are part of the state machinery. Examples are the police, the military, security services or perhaps a combination of branches of government, such as when the judiciary implement discriminatory laws passed by the legislature. An agent of the state remains an agent of the state for Convention purposes even though their actions do not necessarily reflect official government policy. For instance, the Turkish police who tortured Mr Doymus were not necessarily implementing a policy which the Turkish government would acknowledge; in fact, rather the reverse, as Turkey is anxious to improve its human rights record. However, if such actions are not controlled and prevented then they amount to persecution by the state. Where there is proper redress for such incidents then there would be no fear of repetition and thus no reasonable likelihood of persecution in the future. The crucial question is whether the individual can obtain protection. This was confirmed in the case of *Svazas v SSHD* [2002] 1 WLR 1891, a case of maltreatment by the police of a person in custody. The majority of the court held that there was a spectrum of state responsibility, involving questions such as the seniority of the person involved, and what redress was possible.

13.3.4.2 *Perpetrators – non-State actors*

Goodwin-Gill and McAdam point out that 'neither the 1951 Convention nor the *travaux preparatoires* say much about the source of the persecution feared by the refugee, and no necessary linkage between persecution and government authority is formally required (2007:98). The UNHCR Handbook at para 65 says: 'where serious discriminatory or other offensive acts are committed by the local populace, they can be considered as persecution if they are knowingly tolerated by the authorities, or the authorities refuse, or prove unable, to offer effective protection.' Thus, persecution may be accepted as such when carried out by, for instance, members of a different ethnic group from the asylum claimants, if the State is not able to protect them. This was the situation in *R v SSHD ex p Jeyakumaran*, in which Tamils resident in Colombo were the victims of reprisals by local Sinhalese (majority ethnic) residents, and were not protected by the State. Although the victims were not 'singled out' for persecution by the government, the High Court held that they were nevertheless persecuted, as the State failed to protect them.

This is by way of example only. A person may be persecuted by a member of the same group as themselves as the Sri Lankan cases of Tamils fearing Tamils clearly demonstrate.

In this sense, persecution by State and non-State agents is quite similar. If the individual can be protected then ill-treatment may have occurred, but it is not persecution. If there is no effective protection then there may well be persecution whether the actions are those of State agents or not, although in cases of sexual assault there is an anomalous tendency to regard the absence of official relationship as fatal to the claim of persecution even before deciding the protection question.

13.3.4.3 *What protection is available*

The leading case on the question of persecution by non-State actors is the House of Lords case of *Horvath v SSHD*.

 Key Case

Horvath v SSHD [2000] 3 All ER 577

The appellant was a Roma from the Slovak Republic who based his asylum claim on fear of violence by skinheads and on discrimination in employment, the right to marry, and education. The tribunal concluded that any failure of these social rights in his case did not amount to persecution. The Court of Appeal agreed, and the appeal went to the House of Lords only on the question of the failure of state protection against the skinhead violence.

Three questions were considered by the House of Lords.

First: does the concept of 'persecution' refer simply to serious harm, or does it necessarily incorporate a failure of State protection?

Second: the refugee definition requires that a person is 'unwilling' to avail himself of State protection. Does this mean that they fear being persecuted precisely because they have gone to the police?

Third: if persecution implies a lack of State protection, what is the test for determining whether there is sufficient protection against a person's persecution in the country of origin? Is it sufficient that there is in that country a system of criminal law which makes violent attacks by the persecutors punishable and a reasonable willingness to enforce that law on the part of the law enforcement agencies? Or must the protection be such that it cannot be said that the applicant has a well-founded fear? The first alternative focuses on whether the State is doing its best, the second on whether risk is actually minimized or eliminated for the applicant.

Lord Hope said that the proper approach to this task was not 'to construe its language with the same precision as one would if it had been an Act of Parliament' but rather to give the words 'a broad meaning in the light of the purposes which the Convention was designed to serve'. He identified the key relevant Convention purpose as

> to be found in the principle of surrogacy. The general purpose of the Convention is to enable the person who no longer has the benefit of protection against persecution for a Convention reason in his own country to turn for protection to the international community. (at 383)

This approach is known as the protection theory. It is to be contrasted with the attribution theory which has been followed in some other European countries according to which persecution is not recognized as such unless it can be attributed to the State. This way of setting out the issue by Lord Hope at an early stage in the judgment seems to be a classic endorsement of the protection theory. However, there is a curious contradiction. The House of Lords found, in relation to the three questions that:

1. persecution included by definition a failure of State protection,
2. that the applicant needed to be unable or unwilling to avail themselves of the protection of the State because they feared persecution for doing so, and

3. that a system with a reasonable willingness to enforce it was sufficient for protection.

The net result of this is much closer than Lord Hope's statement suggests to the attribution theory. The effect is not to focus on the failure of state protection for the asylum seeker, but rather on whether the State should be regarded as culpable, which, judging by the preamble to the Convention, is not its purpose. As Lord Hope stated in the beginning, the purpose is to protect where State protection has failed. The focus in *Horvath* has turned from the refugee to the State.

Despite the contrast Lord Hope draws with interpretation of statute, the case of *Horvath* does seem to illustrate the risk of overdefining. Its effects have been mitigated and refined in later decisions. Schiemann LJ in *Noune v SSHD* The Times 20 December, 2000, CA made these points in relation to *Horvath:*

As a study of the many judgments and speeches in that case shows, the law in relation to persecution by non-state actors was unsettled and difficult to understand...[if it was interpreted to mean]...that where the law enforcement agencies are doing their best and are not being either generally inefficient and incompetent (as that word is generally understood implying a lack of skill rather than a lack of effectiveness) this was enough to disqualify a potential victim from being a refugee [this would be] an error of law. (para 28)

Schiemann LJ goes on to say that the crucial question is whether there was a reasonable likelihood of the appellant being persecuted for a Convention reason. This case too concerned the sufficiency of State protection, but the Court of Appeal, while bound by *Horvath*, came back to that central question of the risk to the appellant. *Horvath* has been more explicitly followed in other cases, for instance *Banomova v SSHD* [2001] EWCA Civ 807 CA in which on comparable facts the Court of Appeal held that the police were willing to protect the appellant who had withdrawn her complaint after death threats and so, following *Horvath,* there was sufficient protection.

On the other hand in the case of *R (Bodzek) v Special Adjudicator* [2002] EWHC 1525 Admin an adjudicator's decision that there was no evidence that the Polish State was unwilling to protect a Jewish family who had been the target of anti Semitic attacks was held to be Wednesbury unreasonable. They had suffered from acts of personal violence, vandalism, and graffiti of their property for 10 years, and had been forced to move house. They complained that the police response was inadequate as no attempt was made to identify the perpetrators. The adjudicator had accepted that the State was not unwilling as it was difficult to pursue a prosecution when the identity of the assailants was not known. The applicants' case was that it was a policing job to investigate and identify the assailants, and they had given what information they could. *Horvath* was followed by the Administrative Court, which on the evidence of years of police inaction, held it could not be rational to say that the State was not unwilling to act.

The Court of Appeal in *Bagdanavicius v SSHD* [2003] EWCA Civ 1605 emphasized that punishment after the event was not sufficient protection. Also the Court incorporated the principle from the ECtHR case of *Osman v UK* (1998) 29 EHRR 245 that where the authorities were or should have been aware of the applicant's particular protection needs but failed to do anything about it, then there was a failure of state protection. These points bring the questions back in the direction of the situation of the particular applicant, though without changing the main findings in *Horvath.* Furthermore, the House of Lords in *Bagdanavicius* gave such an unqualified endorsement of the application of the *Horvath* approach to an Article 3 case that it is clear there is no retreat from it ([2005] UKHL 38).

A number of cases before and after *Horvath* elaborate the requirement for both willingness and effectiveness. The Federal Court of Canada in *Annan v Canada (Minister for Citizenship and Immigration)* IMM 215–95 said that 'pious statements of intent' about outlawing genital mutilation had not resulted in any action to do so and so not in protection for the asylum claimant. The Court of Appeal in *R (on the application of Atkinson) v SSHD* [2004] EWCA Civ 849 held that a lack of effectiveness would entail a systematic failure applying to individuals in the same group as the applicant, here, people who were or were seen to be informers for the People's National Party. It was not just a failure in relation to some individuals.

In *P and M v SSHD* the IAT held that evidence, that the police prosecuted due to public pressure after a woman had been killed by her husband and another had been seriously burned with acid, suggested there was State protection against domestic violence. The Court of Appeal said this was to 'miss the point'. Where the police had to be compelled by such extreme circumstances to act (para 26), this did not amount to protection.

The requirement for an effective legal system has been taken as a starting point by some decision-makers: if there is an effective system then this applicant would not be at risk. This has some resonance with the s 94 provisions discussed in the last chapter by which the Secretary of State may determine that in a particular country 'there is in general no serious risk of persecution'. The Court of Appeal in *Mishto v SSHD* [2003] EWCA Civ 1978 advised against taking this approach. In this case the adjudicator had considered the protection system for women in Albania and concluded it was sufficiently effective, therefore whatever the strength or weakness of the appellant's case, there was no real risk to her so he did not need to investigate the facts in order to find against her. The Court of Appeal held that in this particular case there was no injustice done to the applicant, but as a rule this approach would be unwise. General conditions in a country must be evaluated in the light of the circumstances of the particular applicant. The tribunal in *Hussein v SSHD* [2005 CSIH 45] had taken a similar approach. The Court of Session's decision illustrated how the general meshes with the particular and cannot be considered aside from it. The appellant stated that he had not proceeded with a complaint to the police about shooting at his house because a bribe had been required. The tribunal found that Pakistan had a sufficiently protective legal system, but made no findings on whether the bribe had been requested by a single corrupt officer or whether the appellant could not expect protection without a bribe because of the system. In the latter case there would be no effective protection. The Court on appeal held that it was essential to go back and investigate this question. In *DK v SSHD* [2006] EWCA Civ 682 the Court of Appeal held that evidence about the capacity of the KDP police to protect DK from being killed in a blood feud had not been properly considered. The question was not whether they had provided a sufficiency of protection within their capacity but whether the KDP police were actually capable of providing DK with adequate protection. *DK* is another case which shifts the focus from the State's performance to the individual's protection. Following *Noune*, it was not necessary to show that the state machinery had collapsed before being able to claim refugee status (para 27).

The question of non-State actors was a question which divided European countries in the course of the negotiations over the Qualification Directive. France and Germany have not in the past recognized persecution by non-State actors, which was one of the reasons for challenges to France and Germany as safe third countries (see chapter 12). Belgium and Greece have also been found to differ from the UK in this respect. However, the Qualification Directive 2004/83 recognizes persecution by non-State actors where the state is unable or unwilling to protect (Art 6), though differences may remain over the meaning of this. Article 7 states that there will be protection when reasonable steps are taken to prevent the suffering or persecution by, *inter alia*, the operation of an effective legal system, in effect following *Horvath* and leaving open the questions considered above.

13.3.4.4 *Sources of protection*

The final question here is whether protection must be offered by the State itself, or whether it may be offered by an entity which is capable of providing protection. *R (on the application of Vallaj) v Special Adjudicator and Canaj v Secretary of State for the Home Department* [2001] INLR 342 CA concerned the proposed return of the appellants, who were Kosovar Albanians, to Kosovo. The court held that UNMIK (the United Nations Interim Administration Mission in Kosovo) supported by KFOR (the internal security force in Kosovo) had an international law obligation to protect Kosovans, which it was in fact discharging with the host country's consent, and this was enough to satisfy the Convention requirement for protection.

The Qualification Directive, followed by the UK's implementing regulations, goes further than *Vallaj and Canaj*. The Directive allows that protection may be provided by 'parties or organisations, including international organisations, controlling the State or a substantial part of the territory of the State' (Art 7.1b). The European Council on Refugees and Exiles (ECRE) is disturbed by this inclusion on the grounds that such authorities 'are not and cannot be parties to international human rights instruments and therefore cannot be held accountable for non-compliance with international refugee and human rights obligations' (ECRE information note October 2004). This argument was considered by the tribunal in *DM (Majority Clan Entities can Protect) Somalia* [2005] UKAIT 00150, which concluded that all that was essential was effective protection. It could, in that case, be provided by a majority clan which had a militia. Somalia was a state in international law, and even if the function of government was fragmented, if a majority clan militia could provide protection, issues about the effectiveness of government would not need to be decided. Although drug barons or armed militia might be less effective than an army and police subject to law, this went to the question of effectiveness, and did not demand the existence of protection by the state.

13.4 **Internal relocation**

The concept of internal flight or internal relocation completes the consideration of persecution and State protection. Simply put, the internal flight or relocation doctrine, also called the internal protection alternative, is an assertion that, although they risk persecution in their home area, the asylum seeker, instead of going abroad, could find safety somewhere else in their own country. If established, then the asylum claim will be lost as there is no well-founded fear of persecution. The Michigan Guidelines on the Internal Protection Alternative (the product of an international consultation and colloquium in 1999) say that internal protection analysis must be 'directed to the identification of a present possibility of meaningful protection within the boundaries of the home state' (para 8).

The foundational case in relation to internal relocation is that of *Robinson* [1997] 3 WLR 1162.

 Key Case

Robinson [1997] 3 WLR 1162

The appellant was a Tamil from northern Sri Lanka and had connections with the LTTE (Tamil Tigers). He claimed asylum in the UK following the assassination of the President of Sri Lanka by Tamil militants in May 1993, but his claim was refused. The Special Adjudicator held that, while he might risk persecution in an area controlled by the Tamil Tigers as he might be recruited against his will to support them, he could safely return to Colombo as it was controlled by the Sri Lankan authorities. He was in Colombo at the time of the President's assassination and had been briefly detained there. The Special Adjudicator did not expressly consider whether it was *reasonable* to expect the appellant to relocate in Colombo on the basis that this was an unreviewable matter of the Secretary of State's discretion.

The Court of Appeal decided that appellate authorities do have jurisdiction to consider the reasonableness of the internal flight alternative. As for the question of what is reasonable, that must be decided by looking at all the circumstances.

The Court of Appeal took guidance from the Australian case of *Randhawa* 124 ALR 265, suggesting that factors to be taken into account in determining whether it was reasonable to expect the appellant to relocate would include, for instance, the accessibility of the 'safe' part of the country, any danger or hardship of travelling there, the quality of internal protection in the country, i.e. does it meet 'basic norms of civil, political and socio-economic human rights'? To this one might add that safety of re-entering the country at all is relevant for internal flight as for any return (*Degirmenci v SSHD* [2004] EWCA Civ 1553).

The question to be answered was, it suggested, that posed in the Canadian case, *Thirunavukkarasu* (1993) 109 DLR (4th) 682, namely: 'would it be unduly harsh to expect this person, who is being persecuted in one part of his country, to move to another less hostile part of the country before seeking refugee status abroad?' The Canadian court had given the following examples:

While claimants should not be expected to cross battle lines or hide out in an isolated region of their country, like a cave in the mountains, a desert or a jungle, it will not be enough for them to say that they do not like the weather in a safe area, or that they have no friends or relatives there, or that they may not be able to find suitable work there.

These are extremes to illustrate the principle, which has been expanded upon in English case law referred to by the Court of Appeal. Nolan J in *R v IAT ex p Jonah* [1985] Imm AR 7 considered that it was unreasonable to expect a senior Ghanaian trade union official to go back to what was in effect a hideaway, a very remote village accessible only by a 15-mile walk through the jungle. On the other hand, in both *R v SSHD ex p Yurekli* [1991] Imm AR 153 (CA) and *R v SSHD ex p Gunes* [1991] Imm AR 278 the courts held that it was not unreasonable to expect Turkish Kurds to relocate in a part of Turkey away from the villages where they faced persecution. In *El-Tanoukhi v SSHD* [1993] Imm AR 71 the Court of Appeal held that it was not unreasonable to expect a claimant who lived in a part of Lebanon under Israeli control to relocate in a different part of Lebanon.

Since *Robinson*, case law has not changed the basic question of whether it would be unduly harsh to expect the claimant to relocate. A number of principles have developed which concern the quality of life and of protection that the claimant should be expected to accept in the area of relocation.

13.4.1 Replicating persecution in 'safe haven'

The internal protection alternative must not be used so as to require the refugee to live in a way that replicates the persecution they flee if they live normally, exercising basic human rights. The case of *Iftikhar Ahmed* is discussed below in the context of religious persecution. It was held on the facts that Mr Ahmed would continue to proclaim his Ahmadi faith wherever he went. There would therefore be a reasonable likelihood of persecution in any part of Pakistan. The Court of Appeal held that no internal protection alternative was viable. The court held in *Hysi v SSHD* [2005] EWCA Civ 711 that the tribunal had given insufficient consideration to whether it would be unduly harsh to expect a young man to return to Kosovo and hide his mixed ethnicity. The court thought that the Australian case of *Appellant S 395 v Minister for Immigration and Multicultural Affairs* [2004] INLR 233 cited the correct principle:

It would undermine the object of the Convention if a signatory country required [refugees] to modify their beliefs or opinions or to hide their race, nationality or membership of particular social groups before those countries would give them protection.

In *HC v SSHD* [2005] EWCA Civ 893 the Court of Appeal held that the adjudicator, in considering that the appellant could return to a different part of Lebanon, had failed to take sufficient account of the cumulative effect of being homosexual and a Palestinian refugee. She had also not taken into account significant evidence of conditions in that country for homosexuals when holding that he would be safe in a place other than the refugee camp where he grew up.

However, where the internal protection alternative obviates the direct persecution but could be seen as condoning it, the result may be different. This is illustrated in the case of *AE Sudan* [2005] UKAIT 00101. The appellant was internally displaced because of the activities of government backed militias, who were carrying out so-called ethnic cleansing, i.e. killing, raping and destroying the homes of whole populations of a particular ethnicity. The AIT held that even though to live in a part of the country where he would not be persecuted by the militia was doing what the militia wanted, as he could be safe there he would not be able to claim refugee status outside Sudan. This was so even though he could not be said to be obtaining the protection of his government, as the government allowed the militia action and it was not through their protection that he could live elsewhere, but simply because the militia did not operate there. This decision is in conflict with the UNHCR Guidelines on Internal Protection 23 July 2003:

Where internal displacement is a result of 'ethnic cleansing' policies, denying refugee status on the basis of the internal flight or relocation concept could be interpreted as condoning the resulting situation on the ground, and therefore raises additional concerns.

13.4.2 **Past persecution by the State**

Is internal protection automatically debarred when past persecution was by the State? The Michigan Guidelines on the Internal Protection Alternative (para 16) say that there should be 'a strong presumption against finding an "internal protection alternative" where the agent or author of the original risk of persecution is, or is sponsored by, the national government'. UNHCR Guidelines 2003 take a similar position.

The authority now is *Januzi, Hamid, Gaafar and Mohammed* v *SSHD* [2006] UKHL 5 in which Lord Bingham said 'there is no absolute rule' or presumption (para 21). He referred to the spectrum of State responsibility we noted earlier in the case of *Svazas*, and said that the relationship between the State and the act(s) of persecution must be assessed: 'The more closely the persecution in question is linked to the state, and the greater the control of the state over those acting or purporting to act on its behalf, the more likely (other things being equal) that a victim of persecution in one place will be similarly vulnerable in another place within the state' (para 21). Lord Hope said that 'where the state is in full control of events and its agents of persecution are active everywhere' internal relocation is obviously not an option (para 48).

The severity of past persecution has repeatedly been argued to have a bearing on this question. Amnesty International evidence to the New Zealand Refugee Status Appeals Authority suggested it should (see Symes and Jorro p. 219). The reasons for this are indicated by Elias J, in *R v IAT ex p Sellasamy* CO/3238/99:

the fact that on his return he is protected by a state which has, albeit through a different agency and in a different area, inflicted great pain and humiliation on him, is potentially highly material to the question of whether it would be unduly harsh to expect him to return. (para 33)

Such a person might have developed a 'distrust of the country itself and a disinclination to be associated with it as its national' (Grahl-Madsen, quoted in *In re B & R v Special Adjudicator ex parte Hoxha* [2005] UKHL 19). This point remains open to date. A somewhat comparable argument was made unsuccessfully for Mr Januzi, but this was based on the severe effect of persecution on him rather than the severity of what he experienced.

13.4.3 **Risks in site of internal protection and basis of comparison**

A case can be made that the Refugee Convention sets the standard of protection that is appropriate for a refugee. This standard should therefore be available in the site of alternative protection. The Michigan Guidelines and a number of New Zealand authorities support this view (see Symes and Jorro p. 218). However, in *E v SSHD* [2003] EWCA Civ 1032 the Court of Appeal held that what is required in the site of relocation is protection from persecution, not delivery of other human rights. The House of Lords in *Januzi, Hamid, Gaafar and Mohammed* agreed. It endorsed the UNHCR Guidelines in saying that relocation

requires, from a practical perspective, an assessment of whether the rights that will not be respected or protected are fundamental to the individual, such that the deprivation of those rights would be sufficiently harmful to render the area an unreasonable alternative. (para 28, in [2006] UKHL 5 para 20)

The Refugee Convention requires delivery of political and socio-economic rights, and integration into the host state. However, in internal relocation, the question would be whether what is lacking is the 'the real possibility to survive economically'. The Refugee Convention was not intended to define rights in the claimant's home country.

In reaching its conclusion the Court was supported by the Qualification Directive which, as it said, imposed a 'standard significantly lower' than the Michigan Guidelines and New Zealand cases would require (para 17). The decision must take account of the effect on the individual, but is not linked to a particular human rights standard.

This case disposes of a further question which has hovered over internal protection cases: the basis of comparison in assessing internal protection is between the proposed location and the refugee's home area, not with the country of asylum. The latter question is relevant to a human rights claim, and humanitarian leave may be granted where return to another area is considered to breach human rights.

The appeal of Mr Januzi was dismissed, but the appeals of Messrs Hamid, Gaafar and Mohammed were sent back from the House of Lords to the tribunal for decision. In the space of 18 months, the cases have gone back up the appeal chain and have been heard again in the House of Lords. The cases are politically sensitive ones as they concern the situation of people from Darfur. While, on the one hand, the situation in Darfur has caused alarm worldwide and has been characterized as one of the greatest human rights disasters of the present age, on the other hand the question of whether such a situation can or should be contained within Africa, what kind of material standards a rural Sudanese person can expect, and whether refugee camps are tolerable places, all raise issues that go to the heart of global inequities.

 Key Case

AH (Sudan), IG (Sudan), NM (Sudan) v SSHD **[2007] UKHL 49**

All three appellants were black Africans formerly living in Darfur in western Sudan. They had been victims of serious persecution by Arab bands known as the Janjaweed, persecution which the government of Sudan had connived in or at the very least not restrained. It was accepted that by reason of the well-known facts about the desperate situation of black Africans in Darfur, all of the appellants were prima facie entitled to international protection. The Secretary of State's case was that they could safely return to Sudan provided that they return not to Darfur but to Khartoum. The appellants' case was that they would still be in danger of Refugee Convention persecution in any part of Sudan; alternatively, even if they were not in danger of persecution if returned to Khartoum, it would be unduly harsh under the rules to require them to return there. They were village people and subsistence farmers. If they returned to Khartoum they would be in a camp outside the city in conditions of urban or sub-urban poverty. In the judgment one expert is quoted as follows:

> In the Al-Fatah camp where the victims of forced relocation were living at the time of my visit, I was struck with their most desperate situation and appalling conditions of extreme poverty. They had scarcely been able to erect makeshift huts from plastic sheets and cardboard as they had been left without any building material. While there was a water bladder no food or other life-sustaining goods had been provided...The camp is situated some 50km outside of Khartoum in the desert, where without water agricultural activities are impossible. (para 43)

The AIT held that they would not be at risk of persecution anywhere in Sudan, and conditions in Khartoum would not be unduly harsh because they were no different from the conditions of rural poverty elsewhere in squatter camps and slums. The appeal continued to the Court of Appeal and House of Lords on the question of whether return to Khartoum was unduly harsh.

The Court of Appeal held it would be unduly harsh to expect them to relocate to Khartoum, including a principle that 'Traumatic changes of life-style, for instance from a city to a desert, or into slum conditions, should not be forced on the asylum-seeker'. (para 33)

The House of Lords overturned the Court of Appeal's decision and allowed the Secretary of State's appeal. Their only criticism of the tribunal's decision was that it came close to equating the standard of what was unduly harsh with a breach of Article 3. It did not actually do so, but this would have been an error. The Court of Appeal had introduced questions that were not necessary into the consideration of internal flight. The proper approach remained that in *Januzi*:

The decision-maker, taking account of all relevant circumstances pertaining to the claimant and his country of origin, must decide whether it is reasonable to expect the claimant to relocate or whether it would be unduly harsh to expect him to do so. (para 21)

Lord Bingham agreed that 'enquiry must be directed to the situation of the particular applicant, whose age, gender, experience, health, skills and family ties may all be very relevant'. However, this did not mean that certain considerations should be mandated, prohibited or prioritised:

There is no warrant for excluding, or giving priority to, consideration of the applicant's way of life in the place of persecution. There is no warrant for excluding, or giving priority to, consideration of conditions generally prevailing in the home country. (*AH* para 5).

13.4.4 Safety of home area

Finally, if persecution has ceased in the home area, refugee status is not available, even if conditions remain risky elsewhere in the country (*Canaj and Vallaj v SSHD and Special Adjudicator* [2001] INLR 342). However, risks elsewhere in the country may make the home area inaccessible and thus invoke the doctrine of *non-refoulement*. This issue arose in numerous cases of planned return to the Kurdish Autonomous Area of Iraq (KAA) as there were no direct flights to the KAA and an asylum seeker would need to travel through Baghdad. In *Osman Mohammed v SSHD* [2002] UKIAT 05816 the appellant feared persecution by Iraqi security forces. His appeal was dismissed mainly because the KAA was found to be a State-like entity capable of providing protection. The question of safe routes of return is considered in more detail in chapter 18.

13.4.5 Summary and burden of proof in relation to internal flight

As the internal flight alternative is raised by the Secretary of State, it could seem appropriate that the Secretary of State would have the burden of proving that it would *not* be unduly harsh to return the claimant. This is strongly suggested by the Michigan Guidelines (para 14). Alternatively, if the Secretary of State raises the point, does the burden then shift to the claimant to show that it would be unduly harsh, and if so, to what standard of proof? The Court of Appeal in *Karanakaran v SSHD* [2003] 3 All ER 449 held that there was no standard of proof in the civil sense, as discussed above in relation to establishing a well-founded fear of persecution. The claimant did not have to prove to a certain standard that particular events were likely to occur, but the decision-maker should take into account all the evidence and decide whether it was unduly harsh for the claimant to return to a different area. This point was refined by Sedley LJ in *Salam Jasim v SSHD* [2006] EWCA Civ 342 where he said that

Once the judge of fact is satisfied that the applicant has a justified fear of persecution or harm if returned to his home area, the claim will ordinarily be made out unless the judge is satisfied that he can nevertheless be safely returned to another part of his country of origin. Provided the second issue has been flagged up, there may be no formal burden of proof on the Home Secretary (see *GH* [2004] UKIAT 00248); but this does not mean that the judge of fact can reject an otherwise well-founded claim unless the evidence satisfies him that internal relocation is a safe and reasonable option. (para 16)

The risks of persecution in the claimant's home area must be considered first, because it is against these that the proposed location must provide protection. Symes and Jorro (p. 221) point out that this means a claim should not be certified as unfounded (see chapter 12) on the basis of internal protection.

Reading case law on internal flight can be confusing. Who is arguing what? It may be seen like this:

Step 1: Asylum claim is assessed and risk is found of persecution in home area.

Step 2: Secretary of State asserts that the claimant would not face persecution in another area of their home country.

Step 3: Secretary of State, looking at all relevant factors, determines that it would not be unduly harsh for the claimant to return to a different area.

Step 4: In reply the claimant *may* argue that there is a risk of persecution elsewhere.

Step 5: Whether or not there is a risk of persecution elsewhere, the claimant may additionally argue that it would be unduly harsh to return them to that area.

Step 6: Undue harshness is assessed, bearing in mind whether the risks in the alternative site would amount to indirect *refoulement*, and the effect on them individually, as set out in *AH, IG and NM (Sudan)*.

Step 7: The refugee claim may succeed if the claimant would face persecution in their home area *and* it would be unduly harsh to force them to return elsewhere.

In the event of the asylum claim failing for lack of a Convention reason, the Secretary of State may argue that although the claimant faces a risk of inhuman treatment in their home area (in breach of Art 3) they would not do so in another area, and so should return there. An outstanding question is whether the claimant may then argue, and whether the secretary of State has to consider, whether return to that area would be unduly harsh for reasons falling short of breaches of Article 3. If so, must these involve discrimination or other human rights breaches?

13.5 Causal link

Returning to the Article 1A definition, we see that a refugee is one who is 'outside his country of nationality, and owing to a well-founded fear of being persecuted *for reasons of...*', and then the list of Convention reasons appears. This apparently simple connecting phrase has significance in the case law of the Convention and in the determination of who is a refugee. The UK's implementing regulations follow the Convention quite closely, but the Qualification Directive requires only a 'connection' between the Convention reason and the persecution. The tribunal in *SB (Moldova CG)* [2008] UKAIT 00002 accepted that it was sufficient that the persecution was related to the Convention reason.

The persecution must be carried out for one of the Convention reasons, but as the UNHCR Handbook points out 'Often the applicant himself may not be aware of the reasons for the persecution feared. It is not, however, his duty to analyze his case to such an extent as to identify the reasons in detail' (para 66). The reasons in detail in fact may not all be important as there is no requirement that the persecution is carried out solely for Convention reasons (see *SB (Moldova CG)* [2008] UKAIT 00002). Reasons may in reality be very mixed and the personal motivation of the persecutor is not generally regarded as the key to this (see Goodwin-Gill and McAdam 2007:101). For instance, in the case of *Sivakumar* referred to above, the House of Lords were aware that the persecutors might have the suppression of terrorism among their motives for torturing the appellant. However, the reason that he was tortured was a mixture of his ethnicity and supposed political stance. Thus it may be seen that the law of the Convention is not concerned with the personal motivations of the persecutor. These are an aspect of individual criminality but are not connected with the failure of the state to protect which is the phenomenon that Convention decision-makers are concerned to identify. The relevant reason for the persecution is the structural reason in that society, not the personal reason of the persecutor. Again we can see that the case of sexual attacks is treated quite differently as in *Okonkwo* and the cases following discussed above, the supposed personal motive of the persecutor was regarded as overriding. Musalo (2003) proposes that some of this inconsistency in relation to gender-based claims would be resolved by a more widespread adoption of what she calls a 'bifurcated approach' to causation – namely, that there will be persecution for a Convention reason if either the ill-treatment or the failure of protection is for a Convention reason.

The question of the causal link, or *nexus,* was considered at length by the House of Lords in *Shah and Islam*. It considered the Canadian approach which is to use the 'but for' test, as in UK discrimination law. This is by asking the question: 'but for their gender, would these people be persecuted?' It is tempting to say that this is sufficient, and that in *Shah and Islam* (see below) the two women would not have been persecuted but for their gender. However, this approach is not favoured as, following its use in tort law, it brings with it the question of how much of the cause the Convention reason needs to be i.e. 60 per cent, 40 per cent, etc. (see discussion in Hathaway and Foster 2003). This is a fruitless path which, it is suggested, it is better not to tread.

Lord Hoffmann suggested that drawbacks in the 'but for' test were revealed by the example of women raped in a situation of general lawlessness. The women would not be raped but for their gender but the reason for this treatment would also be the breakdown in law and order, and not their gender. This analysis is open to question in that men are subject to rape, but the power imbalance between men and women suggests that women are more likely to be raped, therefore one might argue that women would not be raped but for this imbalance which is left uncontrolled by the breakdown of law and order. They would not be raped but for their gender not because they are women but because they are women in a society where lawlessness exposes them to the underlying power imbalance. Nevertheless, one can disagree with the example and still see the point Lord Hoffmann is making, which is that causation should be sought at the structural level, in the lack of protection. He demonstrates this with the example of a Jew in Germany punished for failing to obey the racial laws, who is thereby persecuted for their race. The reason for this is that there is no State protection against such punishment and the state's lack of protection is also grounded in race. Whether the individual who initiates the prosecution hates Jews or not is irrelevant. Whether there are additional reasons, such as conducting a census, for identifying Jews is irrelevant. The reason in that society that that person is suffering that treatment is that they are a Jew.

The effects of taking a subjective approach to causation are illustrated in the case of *Omoruyi v SSHD* [2001] Imm AR 175 in which the appellant sought asylum following death threats from the Ogboni cult as he refused to comply with their demands in relation to his father's burial. The Court of Appeal found against the appellant on the grounds that the Ogboni were not motivated by the appellant's religion (Christianity) to persecute him but by his non-compliance with their requirements. Anyone else who had similarly failed to comply would be treated in the same way. Simon Brown LJ said: 'The Nigerian State Authorities in the present case were not unable or unwilling to protect the appellant because of his being a Christian but rather because he was at risk for having crossed this particular cult'. Simon Brown LJ thus looked for motivation first in the non-State persecutors and secondly in the state, and finding none, concluded that there was no causal link to the appellant's religion. Hathaway and Foster (2003) provide a different analysis of this decision. The question, they suggest, should be 'why is the applicant in the predicament he is in?' rather than 'why does the persecutor wish to harm the applicant or the state refrain from protecting him?'. The answer then would be 'because he was a Christian'. Hathaway and Foster contrast *Omoruyi* with the similar Australian case of *Okere v MIMA* 157 ALR 678 (Aust Fed C Sept 21 1998). In this case the court held that the causal nexus was satisfied. It noted that religious persecution often takes indirect forms, and if this form of causation were not accepted:

Persons who have a well-founded fear of persecution for reasons of their refusal to work on the Sabbath could be found not to have a well-founded fear of persecution for reasons of their religion; the persecution feared by them would be related to their refusal to work and not to their religion.

Lord Hoffmann in *Shah and Islam* also identified a fallacy which had confused the Court of Appeal, namely the idea that all members of a group have to be persecuted in order for the reason for persecution to be membership of that group. The reason these two women were persecuted was because they were women in society which discriminates against women. Not all women in the society need to be discriminated against for this to be the case.

The question of causal nexus was briefly considered by the House of Lords in *Sepet and Bulbul*. The result is not entirely clear. Lord Bingham reiterated the generally accepted view that the motive of the perpetrator is not the reason. The question is, 'what is the real reason?'. It is not clear how the real reason is ascertained, though the question may be approached consistently with *Okere*. In *Gaoua v SSHD* [2004] EWCA Civ 1528 the Court of Appeal held that the question of what was the real reason for the risk of detention and persecution upon return could be answered in the following way. If it was because he was perceived to hold radical opinions, this would found an asylum claim.

If it was 'just' to obtain information about Algerian terrorists in the UK, then 'arguably' it would not. This case should be compared with *Sivakumar* (above).

The question of causal nexus may be simplified under the Qualification Directive, but will still overlap with a key question in refugee law, identification of the Convention reason for the persecution.

13.6 Convention reason

Persecution only gives rise to refugee status if it is 'for reasons of race, religion, nationality, particular social group or political opinion'. The first three reasons can be briefly dealt with, the other two require closer examination.

13.6.1 Race

Convention law does not require a technical definition of race. The Handbook says that race 'is to be understood in its widest sense to include all kinds of ethnic groups that are referred to as "races" in common usage' (para 68). It is not impossible for there to be persecution of members of the same race for reasons of race. The Federal Court of Australia in the case of *Perampalam* v *Minister for Immigration and Multicultural Affairs* (1999) 55 ALD 431 notes that the LTTE (Tamil Tigers) would approach Tamils for financial support. The implication is that pressure could be brought to bear.

The Handbook also emphasizes the seriousness of racial discrimination, and that where such discrimination interferes with the exercise of fundamental rights, or has serious consequences, this is likely to amount to persecution. Goodwin-Gill comments that 'Persecution on account of race is all too frequently the background to refugee movements in all parts of the world' (2007:70). For instance, Buxton LJ identified the persecution in Darfur which has given rise to many asylum claims as 'one of the most serious and extensive examples of racial persecution to have occurred in recent years' in *AH (Sudan), IG (Sudan), NM (Sudan) v SSHD* [2007] EWCA Civ 297.

It may be recalled that the European Commission on Human Rights found the state's action in passing racially discriminatory legislation capable in itself of amounting to a violation of Article 3 ECHR (*East African Asians v UK* (1973) 3 EHRR 76). Claims of persecution of Roma have been accepted as being for reasons of race (e.g. *Horvath, Harakal*), although also commonly Roma cases have failed, and in the case reports the emphasis is rather on questioning or establishing the seriousness of the violations of other human rights (to physical security, housing, etc). The racial dimension, rather than being seen as an aggravating factor, seems invisible.

13.6.2 Religion

Religion is widely defined in the Qualification Directive, to include atheistic beliefs and both participation in and abstention from worship. The definition of religion has not been a major issue in asylum case law. More common issues have been what degree of self-restraint might be expected of the asylum seeker, what level of constraint is acceptable by a government, and therefore what kinds of religious activities should be absolutely free from state interference.

Although Hathaway places freedom of religion in his first category of rights, both the International Covenant on Civil and Political Rights (Art 18) and the ECHR (Art 9) allow some limitations by the state on that freedom where these are prescribed by law and 'necessary to protect public safety, order, health, or morals or the fundamental rights and freedoms of others' (ICCPR Art 18(3).

The ICCPR Article 18 also provides: 'No one shall be subject to coercion which would impair his freedom to have or to adopt a religion or belief of his choice'. The freedom therefore includes the freedom to change faith, or to hold a different faith from the official state religion, and this has arisen in numerous cases, for instance *Beshara* (19443) concerned a Christian under pressure to convert to Islam. Mr Beshara lost his claim because the tribunal were satisfied that the Egyptian government took steps to protect its citizens from undue pressure by religious groups.

There are a number of cases regarding those of the Ahmadi faith, regarded variously as a sect of Islam or as a separate faith, since they follow a man they believe to be a later prophet. These cases cover many of the issues which arise in claims of refugee status for reasons of religion. In *Ahmad v SSHD* [1991] Imm AR 61 the Court of Appeal had held that the state of the law was not in itself persecution. Proclaiming the Ahmadi faith was illegal under the terms of a Presidential Ordinance no XX of 1984, however, Slade LJ accepted the Secretary of State's evidence that 'most Ahmadis live ordinary lives, untroubled by government, despite the existence of the Ordinance'. Mr Ahmad failed in his claim. This had been based partly on the assertion that if he did proselytize he would be subject to persecution. However, the Court of Appeal held that there was insufficient evidence to show that he would do in future what he had not done before. This raises the question, considered but not decided in the earlier case of *Mendis v SSHD & IAT* [1989] Imm AR 6, as to whether a claimant could be expected not to speak out, which could mean not exercising a fundamental human right. The problem from the State's point of view, as Balcombe LJ pointed out in that case, is the asylum claimant could create their own asylum claim by insisting on their right to voice unwelcome views if they return home.

The case of *Ahmed (Iftikhar) v Secretary of State for the Home Department* [2000] INLR 1, was somewhat different in that Mr Ahmed had suffered intense harassment personally before leaving Pakistan and regarded proselytizing as an essential element of his religion. The Court of Appeal accepted that he would not be likely to desist. It referred to *Ahmad* and to *Mendis* but distinguished this case because Mr Ahmed had already demonstrated what he would do and it was not a question of speculation, nor of the state of the law in itself being regarded as persecution. He did not fear prosecution under the Ordinance, but rather a continuation of the harassment he had already experienced. The State was unlikely to protect him from this. If the state did intervene at all it would be to prosecute him rather than protect him. The case of *Danian* should be used to decide that even if Mr Ahmed's behaviour was thought unreasonable, the real question was whether he was likely face persecution on return. It is, of course, highly relevant that in the behaviour which some may think unreasonable he was exercising a fundamental right. He was therefore accorded refugee status.

The ICCPR and ECHR refer to freedom to *manifest* one's religion or beliefs. The case of *Ahmed* shows that how the belief is manifested may to an extent be determined by the requirements of the particular belief. This will still not prevent state authorities from curbing religious expression where the permissible reasons in the ICCPR and ECHR apply.

13.6.3 **Nationality**

This Convention reason is given a loose interpretation, not restricted to citizenship, as in the Qualification Directive Article 10(1)(c) which includes 'cultural, linguistic or ethnic identity, common geographical or political origins or its relationship with the population of another State'. The UNHCR Handbook notes that in conflict within a state where there are 'two or more national (ethnic, linguistic) groups...It may not always be easy to distinguish between persecution for reasons of nationality and persecution for reasons of political opinion'.

Persecution on grounds of nationality could include where citizenship is denied to a minority. Though Czech and Slovak Roma have been in this position (see O'Nions 1999) once again there was little evidence of this being used to their advantage in asylum claims.

13.6.4 **Particular social group**

This Convention reason has given rise to more litigation than any other and it is more open to interpretation than the preceding ones. It has the capacity to some extent to enable the Convention to meet needs not originally envisaged, but is not a cure-all or catch-all category. As the tribunal said in *Montoya* [2002] INLR 399 para 24:

> The convention is not intended to protect all suffering individuals, only those who can show that the risk of persecution in their case is for an enumerated Convention ground. If ignoring this principle the PSG grounds were read too widely, the enumeration of grounds would be superfluous; the definition of 'refugee' could have been limited to individuals who have a well-founded fear of persecution without more.

As a general starting point for determining whether a claimant comes within a social group which could be protected by the Convention, it is useful though not essential to consider the principle of *ejusdem generis*. In other words, to construe particular social group as being of the same kind as the other Convention reasons. This does not mean that social group repeats the other reasons, but that by having regard to the defining characteristics of the other reasons it may be possible to identify a social group for Convention purposes.

To use the *ejusdem generis* rule it is therefore necessary to identify the key characteristics of the other Convention reasons. The US Board of Immigration Appeals in the case of *Acosta* (1985) 19 I and N 211 did this as follows:

> Each...describes persecution aimed at an immutable characteristic: a characteristic that either is beyond the power of the individual to change or is so fundamental to individual identity or conscience that it ought not to be required to be changed...The shared characteristic might be an innate one such as sex, colour, or kinship ties, or in some circumstances it might be a shared experience such as former military leadership or land ownership.

Very similar qualities were identified in *Attorney General for Canada v Ward* (1993) 2 SCR 689, an application by a member of the Irish National Liberation Army for asylum in Canada. The Supreme Court built on what was said in *Acosta,* and suggested the following 'working rules' for identifying a particular social group:

(1) groups defined by an innate or unchangeable characteristic;

(2) groups whose members voluntarily associate for reasons so fundamental to their human dignity that they should not be forced to forsake the association;

(3) groups associated by a former voluntary status, unalterable due to historical permanence.

None of this should be regarded as cast in stone, and exceptionally cases may well find social groups outside these descriptions. However, what we shall refer to as the *Ward* criteria have been extensively relied on by the courts.

The leading case in the UK on identifying particular social group is *Shah and Islam*, to which reference has already been made in the context of causal nexus. The case resolved a number of disputed points in relation to the identification of social group.

 Key Case

Shah and Islam v SSHD [1999] 2 AC 629

Mrs Shah's husband was violent and turned her out of their home in Pakistan. She arrived in the UK and gave birth to a child shortly afterwards. She was afraid that her husband might accuse her of adultery and denounce her under Sharia law for the offence of sexual immorality. The court accepted evidence from an Amnesty International report on the position of women in Pakistan that the legal system discriminated against women in particular in its rules of evidence, and for the most severe charges of sexual immorality the evidence of women would not be heard. Arrests on such a charge could be made without preliminary investigation and could result in prolonged detention. For those convicted 'there is the spectre of 100 lashes or stoning to death in public' (549e).

Mrs Islam also had a violent marriage, but she had remained in it for 20 years. She was a schoolteacher. One day, a fight broke out at the school between two young supporters of rival political factions. She intervened and one faction became hostile and accused her of infidelity. These accusations were repeated to her husband who was a member of the same political faction. Mrs Islam's husband assaulted her and she was admitted to hospital twice. She left her husband and stayed briefly with her brother, but unknown men then threatened him and she could not stay.

It was clear in practical terms that these women faced persecution for reasons of their gender. However, gender is not a Convention reason. The Court of Appeal held that they were not members of a particular social group. One reason for this was a doctrine propounded that the members of the group must associate with each other, there must be some cohesiveness, interdependence or co-operation, this was what made them a *social* group. None of the possible ways of defining a group of which Mrs Shah and Mrs Islam were members produced groups with this characteristic. The House of Lords dealt with this unambiguously. Contact among group members was not required. The examples given in *Ward* of characteristics which might form a social group (e.g. language, sexuality) do not suggest such contact. The groups are social groups in the sense of being recognizable in the context of the society in which they arise (per Lords Hoffmann, Hope and Millett at 571a and 569e).

The second reason that the Court of Appeal held that the women were not part of a social group was the difficulty of defining the group without reference to the persecution. It is settled law, e.g. in *Savchenkov* [1996] Imm AR 28, that the group must exist independently of the persecution, and groups such as 'women subject to death by stoning for adultery' or 'women subject to domestic violence without redress' incorporate the persecution into the definition.

The problem was resolved by asking what was the reason for the persecution. It was because they were women, but not only this. They were still women after fleeing to the UK but did not still anticipate persecution. The reason was that they were women in a society which discriminates against women. This was not to use the persecution as a way of defining the group, but to use discrimination, and to acknowledge that women may be perceived as a group in a society which discriminates against them. This may be further explained by taking another example which was used, that of left-handed people in a society which discriminates seriously against left-handedness. It may readily be seen that, in such a society, left-handed people would be regarded as a group in a way that they are not in a society which does not so discriminate.

To summarize, the group is a social group in the sense of being a group in the context of a society. It is necessary first of all then to ascertain the society within which the group appears. The group may (but need not) be identified by discrimination against them in relation to a characteristic identified in the *Ward* criteria. There is no need for social cohesiveness in the group. The upshot in *Shah and Islam* was that the social group was found to be 'women in Pakistan', or 'women in a society that discriminates against women'.

13.6.4.1 *Gender-based persecution*

In the absence of gender as a listed reason in the Convention itself, case law has developed ways of including gender-specific persecution, and *Shah and Islam* was a significant step in this process. Women have faced enormous difficulty in establishing asylum claims. As discussed earlier, decision-makers at all levels have been very slow to recognize the political uses of rape and its place in the persecution of women, and the nature of much gender-based persecution of women has not been recognized. A crucial issue is that the forms of persecution particularly suffered by women and the forms of political activity they frequently engage in has often not been recognized. The Home Office's Guidance on Gender Issues in the Asylum Claim sets out some of the issues. For instance:

A woman may experience

i) gender-specific persecution for reasons unrelated to gender (e.g. raped because of her activity in a political party)

ii) non-gender-specific persecution for reasons relating to her gender (e.g. flogged for refusing to wear a veil)

iii) gender-specific persecution because of her gender (e.g. female genital mutilation).

In connection with political opinion the API identifies that:

gender roles in many countries mean that women will more often be involved in low level political activities, for instance hiding people, passing messages or providing community services, food, clothing or medical care. Decision-makers should beware of equating so-called 'low-level' activity with low risk.

The production of this guidance for the first time in 2004 was welcomed in many quarters. It followed years of lobbying by NGOs and others. As discussed above in relation to sexual violence, the guidance is more limited than other versions that have been in existence, although it has been revised since the version criticized by Ceneda and Palmer. More crucially, though, their research revealed a widespread failure to follow the guidance. Decisions still failed to recognize rape as persecution, the political activities of women as political, or the possibility of applying *Shah and Islam* to identify a particular social group of women, persecuted for reasons connected to their gender (Ceneda and Palmer 2006).

The reported cases show that attempts to follow *Shah and Islam* have gone in all directions in the tribunal. To succeed, a woman must still show that she is a member of a particular social group which can be defined without reference to the feared persecution. This requires evidence of the situation of women in a comparable situation to herself in the society she is in. In some cases, single women have been found to be members of a particular social group. For instance, in *Kaur* [2002] UKIAT 03387 the tribunal considered the case of a woman from rural India who had had an adulterous relationship in the UK which resulted in the birth of a child, and noted evidence that honour killings were still common in rural India; it concluded, 'looking at the Appellant's background in rural India in the light of the social, cultural and religious mores, women in the Appellant's circumstances are identifiable as a particular social group'.

In *P and M* v *SSHD*, P had been subject to serious violence by her husband including death threats and received no state protection. Her husband was a police officer who had friendships with high-ranking police officers. The evidence was that violence against women was taken as normal in Kenya, and that death or life-threatening injuries would have to occur before police would take action. The particular social group was 'women, who are disadvantaged in Kenya because of their position in society' (para 21, quoting the adjudicator).

R (N) v *SSHD* [2002] EWCA Civ 1082 was mentioned earlier in the context of rape. The Court of Appeal saw no merit in the argument that women in that locality where rape was common and uncontrolled were a social group. They saw the situation as one of general lawlessness by soldiers and did not construe this in the light of discrimination.

Claims based on FGM may succeed where societal discrimination and lack of protection is proved. In *P and M* the Court defined the particular social group of which M was a part as women in Kenya, particularly Kikuyu women under 65. They had immutable characteristics of age and sex which existed independently of persecution and could be identified by reference to their being compelled to undergo FGM (para 41). The appellant's father had joined the Mungiki sect which enforces FGM, and his behaviour had become more aggressive following this. He and about twenty other members of the sect had performed a forced FGM on the appellant's mother, who died as a result. He then married another member of the sect who insisted that the appellant and her sister should be circumcised. Both refused. Five members of the sect were involved in raping M and violently assaulting her. Her sister was forcibly circumcised and M was told she would be next.

In the light of *P and M*, it was surprising that another FGM case, that of *Fornah*, went as far as the House of Lords (*Fornah v SSHD* [2006] UKHL 46).

 Key Case

***Fornah v SSHD* [2006] UKHL 46**

In 1998 the Appellant and her mother were living in her father's family village to escape the civil war, and she overheard discussions of her undergoing FGM as part of her initiation into womanhood. In order to avoid this she ran away, but she was captured by rebels and repeatedly raped by a rebel leader, by whom she became pregnant. An uncle arranged her departure from Sierra Leone to the UK. She feared that if she was returned she would have nowhere to live except her father's village, where she feared she would be subjected to FGM. It was common ground that FGM constitutes persecution if the appellant was found to be a member of a particular social group. The Secretary of State argued that women in Sierra Leone could not be a social group because the cutting only happened once, and once it was done such women could no longer be in fear of persecution. But to hold that uninitiated women were the social group would be to define the group by the (fear of) persecution, therefore they could not be a social group for Convention purposes.

Baroness Hale pointed out the fallacy: 'It is the persecution, not the fear, which has to be "by reason of" membership of the group...[and]...It is well settled that not all members of the group need be at risk' (para 113). She defined the group as 'Sierra Leonean women belonging to those ethnic groups where FGM is practised' (para 114) although she added that 'it matters not whether the group is stated more widely, as all Sierra Leonean women, or more narrowly, as intact Sierra Leonean women from those ethnic groups. For all of them, the group has existence independent of the persecution' (para 114).

The House of Lords found that Ms Fornah was a member of a particular social group, though they defined it in a variety of ways. Lord Bingham's approach was interesting:

women in Sierra Leone are a group of persons sharing a common characteristic which, without a fundamental change in social mores is unchangeable, namely a position of social inferiority as compared with men. (para 31)

Here he refers to an 'unchanging' characteristic as being not something innate or historical, or essential to human life, as the *Ward* criteria might indicate, but rather he refers to the power of social values to create a situation from which one cannot escape. The essential unchanging characteristic of course is the gender of the woman, which, in the context of Sierra Leonean society, entailed, their Lordships found, being subjected to institutionalized discrimination, of which FGM was an extreme expression. Lord Bingham found the social group, on the basis of this reasoning, to be women in Sierra Leone. Most of their Lordships added some further qualifying characteristic such as not having undergone FGM (being 'intact' or 'uninitiated').

The discrimination in *Shah and Islam* was in part because of the law itself, which was discriminatory. In many cases, however, the question is not the law but the practice. In *P and M*, P could not obtain protection because of social attitudes and the power and practice of the police, not because violence was formally legal. In *RG (Ethiopia) v SSHD* [2006] EWCA Civ 339 the societal discrimination against women was combined with the non-enforcement of the law, and with a particular law which provided immunity from prosecution for rapists if their victims could be persuaded to marry them. The court followed *P and M* in saying that societal discrimination and lack of police protection were crucial, and found that young women in Ethiopia were a particular social group.

The Court of Appeal in *Liu v SSHD* [2005] EWCA Civ 249 said that 'the need to establish a particular social group should not become an obstacle course in which the postulated group undergoes constant redefinition' (para 12). The Court remitted the case to the tribunal for reconsideration with guidance as to the treatment of Chinese women giving birth or becoming pregnant in breach of China's one-child policy. Relying on cases in Canada and Australia, the court was of the view that the current direction of development was in favour of finding a particular social group in such cases. They also said that persecution may form part of the means of identifying the group, though not the sole means.

In *NS (Afghanistan CG)* [2004] UKIAT 00328 the tribunal found that lone women in Afghanistan are at risk of abuse, without adequate judicial redress and protection, and that the appellant could establish a fear of persecution as a member of the particular social group of women in Afghanistan (see Women's Asylum News issue no. 49 February 2005). There was a striking finding in *HM (Somalia)* [2005] UKIAT 00040. The tribunal said:

What then is the cumulative picture? Women in Somalia form a PSG not just because they are women, but because they are extensively discriminated against. Second the measures of discrimination to which women in Somalia are exposed include legislative, judicial and police or militia discrimination in the way in which women can obtain and suffer from seeking protection from the (regionalised or local) clan-based authorities. Thirdly, the serious harms they face from male sources arise in the context of very limited ability by these authorities to protect them. Finally, the measures of discrimination they face are extensive, intense and sustained. (para 35)

As a young, single woman the appellant faced real risk of persecution 'by reason of her membership of a particular social group, namely women'. However, in *AI (Nigeria) v SSHD* [2007] EWCA Civ 707 the Court of Appeal rejected an argument on behalf of a young single woman with a child. She might well face discrimination, but this did not amount to persecution. This case illustrates a point that was accepted in *Fornah*, that the persecution can play a part in identifying the particular social group, provided it is not the defining factor.

13.6.4.2 *Social perception*

The UNHCR Guidelines identify two approaches to the recognition of a particular social group. One is the 'protected characteristics' approach, which we have used and referred to as the application of the *Ward* criteria. The other is based on social perception. They recommend the adoption of a single standard that incorporates both approaches (2002 para 10). Social perception adds an important element in that there may be persecution of a particular social group that does not meet the *Ward* criteria. Goodwin-Gill and McAdam suggest that there is a value in recognising 'groups in society, in the ordinary everyday sense'. By way of example they refer to 'the landlord class, the working class, the ruling class' (2007: 85). Even without the connection to fundamental characteristics required by the *Ward* criteria, the identity of the group might be well-known and acknowledged in society. The social perception approach does also take account of irrational prejudice as a basis for persecution.

However, a requirement for recognition *by* the society in which the persecution arises would present serious pitfalls. For instance, it is unthinkable that Pakistani society, whether government or otherwise, should be required to identify women in that country as discriminated against and thus a social group. Opinion on the matter would obviously be divided. The particular social group is a legal construct in the hands of the decision-maker in the refugee claim, not a naturally arising phenomenon. Its identification is a matter for those decision-makers *in the context* of the society in which it is said to arise. In non-state actor cases it cannot be acceptable to identify a social group simply on the attribution of some members of society. It does seem right, and in accordance with *Shah and Islam,* to say that the group should be identifiable within that society, and of course that will often mean that members of that society would be able to identify the group. However, to say that they must be identified *by* that society is open to the (perhaps mis-)interpretation that if the society is unaware of what it is doing to a group of people then they cannot be a social group. It introduces an unnecessary element of subjectivity and risks replicating the very discrimination from which the asylum claimant seeks redress. The Australian case of *S v MIMA* [2004] HCA 25 sets out the difference between recognizing a group in the context of that society (here, young, able-bodied men in Afghanistan, who might as a consequence be subject to forcible recruitment by the Taleban), and their recognition as a group *by* that society. The latter was an unnecessary requirement, they thought, for a refugee claim. The Qualification Directive seems to require the group to be recognized using *both* approaches. It says that a group shall be considered to form a particular social group where in particular the *Ward* criteria are met, and 'that group has a distinct identity in the relevant country, because it is perceived as being different by the surrounding society'. The UK implementing regulations repeat the two approaches, though say that groups will be recognized 'for example' where these are met, instead of 'in particular', which softens the requirement to apply both approaches. Lord Bingham in *Fornah* regarded an interpretation of the Directive which would require both the *Ward* criteria *and* the social perception approach as wrong. In the House of Lords' judgment the group is recognized in the context of the society, but the group that would be recognized *by* the society is uninitiated women, who were regarded as particularly inferior.

The tribunal in *SB (Moldova CG)* [2008] UKAIT 00002 noted that this view of Lord Bingham was obiter, and said that authority and sense required that the two approaches both be used. A group must usually be recognizable in the context of its society *and* meet the *Ward* criteria.

Having considered some of the follow-on from *Shah and Islam* and the construction of social group, we shall now consider some other particular social groups, and other issues in relation to defining social groups will arise in these contexts.

13.6.4.3 *Sexuality*

Shah and Islam expressly laid the foundation for resolving some of the inconsistencies that had bedevilled claims of asylum based on sexuality. Claims from homosexuals had been denied and granted on the basis of particular social group, but there had been no authoritative judgment on the matter. The issue was and is seriously in need of clarification as, according to Outrage!, fourteen gay asylum seekers committed suicide between 2001 and 2004 rather than return after the failure of their claim (uk.gay.comUK 17 December 2004). Although the comments of their Lordships in *Shah and Islam* must be regarded as obiter they said, and it is the inescapable conclusion of their reasoning in the case, that homosexuals may constitute a social group if, as a group defined by their sexuality, they suffer discrimination. Sexuality is clearly within the *Ward* criteria, either as an innate or unchangeable characteristic or else as something fundamental to human dignity which a person should not be required to forsake, depending on the view one takes of sexuality. It was mentioned in *Ward* as a possible basis for a claim based on social group.

This is now confirmed by the Qualification Directive, which says 'depending on the circumstances in the country of origin, a particular social group might include a group based on a common characteristic of sexual orientation'(Article 10(1)(d)). This would not include acts considered criminal in the national law of member states. So, for instance, a common sexual orientation as a paedophile would not constitute a particular social group.

Both before and after the Qualification Directive, discrimination needs to be established in the context of the particular society in which the claim arises. In the case of *Jain v SSHD* [2000] INLR 71 the Secretary of State accepted that following *Shah and Islam* practising homosexuals in India formed a particular social group. Homosexual intercourse was a criminal offence, and although the social climate was changing, and prosecution was less likely, that atmosphere of discrimination would have other consequences such as the appellant not being able to engage in a sexual relationship with a normal degree of openness.

However, in *R v Special Adjudicator ex p T* [2001] Imm AR 187 the applicant was accepted to be a member of a social group, but there was no likelihood of persecution unless he 'flaunted' his sexuality. Homosexuality was a criminal offence in Pakistan but prosecution was not common. It was argued for T that criminalizing his private life was a breach of Article 8 ECHR. This has been held to be so in the case law of the ECHR, (e.g. *Dudgeon v UK* (1981) 4 EHRR 149 and *Modinos v Cyprus* (1993) 16 EHRR 485) but the High Court held that this did not constitute persecution. In this case it seems, although it would be rash to draw extensive conclusions from it, that membership of a particular social group defined by discrimination + arguable breach of a qualified right does not = persecution. As we discussed at the beginning of this chapter, the use of human rights to identify persecution does not mean that refugee law is interchangeable with a system of human rights protection. In *The Queen on the application of M v IAT (SSHD interested party)* [2005] EWHC 251 (Admin) the appeal was limited to the question of violation of Article 8, the asylum claim having failed. The appellant's argument was that he would have unacceptably to curb his homosexual behaviour (thus violating Art 8) if he were to return. Henriques J found that he could return to Kenya because in his particular situation the persecutory acts had only been suffered at or near his home, and he could live elsewhere without fear.

In *SSHD v Z, A v SSHD, M v SSHD* [2002] Imm AR 560 Schiemann LJ emphasized that such cases are very 'fact sensitive' and that general pronouncements about particular countries should be avoided. In *MN Kenya* [2005] UKIAT 00021 the tribunal held that in order to make a proper determination on whether there was a real risk that the appellant would be persecuted on return, it was necessary to find out what a natural expression of his sexuality would be. Some people wish to keep their sexuality private; for others, it is a central aspect of the identity they want to be known. Once this is ascertained, it is necessary to find out how a person living in the way that would be natural to them would be treated in that country.

In *R (Dawkins) v SSHD* [2003] EWHC 373 Admin, again a human rights claim after an asylum claim had failed, Wall J held that the existence of law criminalizing homosexuality in Jamaica could not found a human rights claim where there was no likelihood of substantial discrimination or violence and abuse. See also *R (on the application of Bazdoaca) v SSHD* [2004] EWHC 2054 (Admin) for a similar assessment of Moldova. These cases suggest that a certain level of interference with the right to a private life will not be enough warrant a claim for protection in another state. Similarly in *V (Ukraine)* [2003] UKIAT 00005 the tribunal considered that in the cities of Ukraine the applicant would have no problem unless he deliberately advertised his sexuality.

There is some parallel here with claims based on religious practice, although it seems that more latitude is allowed to the state in relation to restricting sexual expression.

In T an argument was made for the claimant similar to that in *Iftikhar Ahmed,* namely that if he would in fact express himself in a way that would draw opprobrium upon him, then there was a reasonable likelihood of persecution. It may be recalled that in Mr Ahmed's case this argument succeeded, as he could not be expected to moderate his religious expression more than he was accustomed to doing. However, the court held that T could not expect the same level of tolerance of his sexual behaviour in Pakistan as he had experienced in the UK, and could be expected to act accordingly. The Court of Appeal in Z v *SSHD* [2004] EWCA Civ 1578 accepted that the implication of *Danian v SSHD* [1999] INLR 533 and *Ahmed v SSHD* [2000] INLR 1 was that an asylum claim could be established where to live in their own country a person would be required to modify their behaviour to a level that constituted persecution. It seemed that they were willing to apply the logic of Ahmed to the situation of a homosexual compelled to hide their sexuality or relationship. Similarly in an Iranian case, *J v SSHD* [2006] EWCA Civ 1238, where the issue was how overt the individual would be about their sexuality, the question was not what they *could* do but what was *likely* to happen.

The question of risk of persecution for homosexuals in Iran has been hotly contested in the tribunal, but has now been settled at this judicial level by *RM and BB (Iran)* [2005] UKIAT 00117 and *HS (Iran)* [2005] UKAIT 00120. The tribunal in *RM and BB* found that there was a real risk that homosexual activity, which is a crime according to the Islamic Punishment Act, would be punished by lashings and/or imprisonment. This was confirmed in *HS (Iran)* where the tribunal made unequivocal findings that the appellant, who had already been ill-treated in prison and subjected to assaults because of his sexuality, would face prosecution and severe penalties including imprisonment and lashings and would be likely also to experience further serious ill-treatment in custody. The tribunal noted that recent executions of homosexual young men could not with certainty be attributed to their sexuality, but the appellant did not have to prove that he would be killed in order to succeed, as he did in his refugee claim.

Cases on homosexuality differ widely, not on the identification of social group, which is now greatly simplified, but on the question of the likelihood of persecution and the threshold of treatment which will warrant such a finding.

13.6.4.4 *Families*

Cases which seek to identify a family as a particular social group have raised some difficult issues. Clearly, the first element in the *Ward* criteria is satisfied. There is an innate characteristic which is the blood tie, or there is a characteristic so fundamental that the person should not be required to change it in marriage or a comparable relationship. Lord Bingham in *K v SSHD* [2006] UKHL 46 (heard and decided with *Fornah*) said 'the family is the quintessential social group'(para 3). There is an argument, not yet concluded, that a particular social group must have a civil or political status, and the family does have civil status in that its ties are recognized and even created by law. Article 23 International Covenant on Civil and Political Rights says: 'The family is the natural and fundamental group unit of society and is entitled to protection by society and the State'. However, although cases on family as a social group often repeat the assertion that a family can be deemed a particular social group for Convention purposes, in fact such claims have often failed.

One reason, which is now disposed of in the UK by *K*, was the argument that if Y is persecuted for being a family member of X, X must have been targeted for a Convention reason in order for Y to claim the family relationship as a Convention reason. This mistaken reasoning was followed on the authority of *Quijano v SSHD* [1997] Imm AR 227 in which the first person in the family was targeted because he had refused to co-operate with a drugs cartel, which was not a Convention reason. When other members of his family were then persecuted by the drugs cartel, they were persecuted for being members of a family rather than for refusing to take part in drug-dealing, but the Court of Appeal held that as the original reason was not a Convention reason, although a family could in theory be a particular social group, here they would not be so for Convention purposes. The House of Lords in *K* preferred the earlier case of *R v IAT ex p De Melo* [1997] Imm AR 43 in which, on judicial review, Laws J found two sisters to be members of a particular social group as the family members of a Brazilian farmer who had refused to grow drugs.

In *K* the appellant feared persecution because her husband had been detained and ill-treated, and after his detention the Revolutionary Guard had visited their home and raped her. She and her family were royalists associated with the late Shah of Iran. The adjudicator had not found evidence that the husband's persecution was for a Convention reason. The House of Lords held that this was an unnecessary requirement. Likewise, it was unnecessary that all members of the family should be at risk for the same Convention reason or that all members of the family should be at risk at all. The reason in K's case was that she was a family member of her husband. Lord Rodgers of Earlsferry said:

Even if Mr K was detained for completely valid reasons, singling out the members of his family for mistreatment simply because they are members of the family of a detainee would amount to persecution for the purposes of the Convention. (para 63)

It may be that *K* will have an impact on the blood feud cases, some of which have succeeded but many failed. For instance in *Hurtado* [2002] UKIAT 03158 there were ninety-two members of each family who had been killed in a feud that had gone on since 1983, for obscure reasons, possibly connected with an argument over a bunch of bananas. The tribunal commented: 'The Hurtado family were simply an ordinary family which had got involved in a feud'. Then less surprisingly: 'It would be artificial to regard it as a particular social group'. Then somewhat confusingly: 'Even if the family was a group, the fear of persecution was not because of membership of the group but because of fear of reprisals'. This latter seems to say that fear of persecution is because of fear of persecution, unless it is meant to imply a degree of responsibility for the consequences of continuing the feud. In a number of cases, a 'straightforward blood feud' has been said not to give rise to a particular social group. This means where no other Convention reason can be identified behind the feud, and may well be different after *K*.

It is certainly a mistake to require that all members of the family be at risk in order to qualify as a particular social group. This was already the case following *Shah and Islam*, and *K* reinforces the point.

13.6.4.5 *Other status*

There is a wealth of case law relating to a wide range of possible social groups. Here we seek to give an understanding of some further categories which demonstrate general principles.

The quotation given earlier from *Acosta* is a principle that those people protected from persecution are those who cannot, if they remain in their homeland, make a choice which would prevent the treatment they fear. This issue has been discussed in relation to persecution for reasons of religion or as a member of a particular social group defined by sexual orientation. It was addressed directly in *Ouanes v SSHD* [1998] Imm AR 76, a Court of Appeal case concerning an Algerian midwife who, as she was required to do, gave contraceptive advice as part of her practice. As a result of doing so she received threats from religious fundamentalist groups opposed to this advice. The question was whether her employment was something so fundamental to her conscience that she should not be required to change it. The leading judgment was given by Pill LJ who said at 82:

A common employment does not ordinarily have that impact upon individual identities or conscience necessary to constitute employees a particular social group within the meaning of the Convention. I accept the possibility that fellow employees may constitute a particular social group if, by reason by the nature of their employment or the addition of other links to those of employment, the above principle applies. Employment as a member of a religious order could be an example.

Examples of others who have applied on the basis of particular social group are a Colombian landowner (*Montoya*), a wealthy educated Sierra Leonean mine owner (*Diallo* 00/TH/01231), a rich Lithuanian entrepreneur (*R v Special Adjudicator ex p Roznys* [2000] Imm AR 57). The words of Burton J in the last-named case probably sum up the courts' and tribunals' approach: 'I do not consider that it is arguable that possession of money puts you into a particular social group, namely a particular social group with money as opposed to those who do not have money'. *Montoya* 'seeks to clarify post-Shah and Islam criteria for establishing whether there exists a particular social group'. In that case the adjudicator had accepted the existence of a particular social group of private landowners, but the tribunal accepted the Secretary of State's view that Mr Montoya was targeted because he had money, and this, as expressed by Burton J, is not a social group.

The third limb of the *Ward* criteria, in the words of the Qualification Directive, sharing 'a common background that cannot be changed', opened the way to an important identification of a particular social group in the case of *SB (Moldova CG)* [2008] UKAIT 00002. The claimant was held to be a member of the particular social group of 'former victims of trafficking for sexual exploitation' in Moldova. She had given evidence against her trafficker in his prosecution in the UK. After his prison sentence he was now free, and she feared reprisals from his network if she were to return to Moldova. The tribunal confirmed that discrimination did not need to be an identifying characteristic of the group, providing it was formed according to the *Ward* criteria (here, common history) and (this being their interpretation of the Qualification Directive) the group was recognizable in that society. Evidence suggested this was the case in Moldova.

13.6.5 Political opinion

A political dissident was the typical figure of a refugee who was the focus of the Refugee Convention when it was first drafted and political dissent continues to play a significant part in establishing refugee claims. Political opinion as a Convention reason however goes much wider than this.

Political expression is valued as an essential requirement of democracy as without debate and freedom of political speech democracy cannot thrive. In the case law of the ECHR, political speech is protected more fully than other forms of expression as the court allows a narrower margin of appreciation to states which seek to restrict it (see, e.g. *Lingens* v *Austria* (1986) 8 EHRR 407). In refugee claims the question arises as to whether an opinion is political. Sometimes this is obvious, such as support for a political party. Sometimes it is less obvious, for instance a woman in Iran who refused to conform to a strict dress code and wore make-up was regarded by the tribunal in *Fathi and Ahmady* (14264) as expressing a political opinion.

Guidance was given in the tribunal case of *Gomez* 00/TH/02257 on the characteristics of a political opinion: 'To qualify as political the opinion in question must relate to the major power transactions taking place in that particular society'. This makes it clear that not only party politics is intended, so for instance attending an anti-globalization protest would be an expression of political opinion. Current Asylum Policy Instructions say that 'if a woman resists gender oppression, her resistance is political' (API Assessing the claim part II para 9.5).

A political opinion may be expressed or it may be imputed by the persecutor. Hence it is not the holding of the opinion which is the important point to establish, but how the claimant is perceived by the persecutor. This is not to reverse all that was said earlier about the motivation of the persecutor. A detailed enquiry into their motives is not required. What is required is to ascertain what is the reason for the persecution.

A number of relevant principles are cited in the case of *Noune* v *SSHD* [2000] All ER (D) 2163.

 Key Case

Noune v SSHD [2000] All ER (D) 2163 CA

The appellant was an Algerian worker with a responsible position in the national Post Office. She was approached on numerous occasions by masked men asking her to send messages to Japan and the Soviet Union, offering her 'protection' in return. She was threatened with violence or other serious consequences if she did not comply and the suggestion made to her was that it was her duty to help. Those who approached her wore religious dress, whereas her appearance and demeanour were of a Westernized woman. There was plentiful evidence of killings by religious extremists in Algeria, and there was evidence of 'Westernized' women being targeted, but no evidence that she had been threatened for this reason, rather for her non-co-operation.

The Court of Appeal held *inter alia* that:

(i) The motives of the persecutor may be mixed, and they can include non-Convention reasons: it is not necessary to show that they are purely political.

(ii) Political opinion may be express or imputed.

(iii) It follows that in order to show persecution on account of political opinion it is not necessary to show political action or activity by the victim: in some circumstances mere inactivity and unwillingness to co-operate can be taken as an expression of political opinion. (UNHCR Handbook para 80)

(iv) If it is shown that there is a reasonable likelihood that the persecutor will attribute a political opinion to the victim and persecute him because of it, the fact, if it be a fact, that the persecutor would be in error in making that attribution does not disqualify the victim from refugee status. (para 8)

The Court of Appeal held that the facts were capable of giving rise to a claim on the basis of political opinion and remitted the case to a tribunal for decision.

As referred to above, cases concerning witnesses of crimes and people refusing to co-operate with criminal activity have been argued under both social group and political opinion. For such claims to be seen as relating to the 'major power transactions in a society' the criminal activity in question must have a relationship to those power transactions. Like social group, political opinion must be construed in the context of the society in which it arises. In the UK for example, it would not constitute political opinion to refuse the request of a common criminal to kill for him. However, to refuse to do the same at the request of say, Special Branch, could be a political action and might suggest a political opinion. Goodwin-Gill suggested a wider definition of political opinion as one 'on any matter in which the machinery of the state, government and policy may be engaged'. This definition has been approved by the courts (Goodwin-Gill and McAdam 2007:87). The Qualification Directive definition is perhaps wider, as it includes holding an opinion, thought or belief on a matter related to the potential actors of persecution, which includes non-state actors (Article 10(1)(e)).

In *Acero-Garces* (21514) the appellant had witnessed the murder of a policeman and since then had been subject to serious threats and harassment. This had to be seen against the background in Colombia of the drugs cartels, in the words of the tribunal 'a power unto themselves. The links between the narcotic industry, crime and the government is very thoroughly documented'. The tribunal found that she risked persecution for reasons of political opinion, 'that the appellant is seen to be on the side of law, order and justice and against disorder, chaos and injustice; and it is these dark forces that control government'.

There was a different result in *Storozhenko v SSHD* [2002] Imm AR 329, CA. Here the appellant had witnessed drunken police officers driving a speeding car which knocked down and injured a young girl. When he remonstrated with them one of them hit in the face with a baton, breaking his jaw. He made a formal complaint at the police station but there was no action taken, and after this he began to receive serious threats and was attacked. The US State department report was critical of police corruption in Ukraine. The Court of Appeal accepted that he was being persecuted for attempting to bring a police officer to justice, but said it was 'manifestly artificial to talk in terms of imputed political opinion' (para 44).

The case of *Gomez v SSHD* is a starred appeal which sets out a number of points intended to clarify issues in these cases where some attitude may be imputed to the victim by a non-state perpetrator but it is arguable as to whether this is a political opinion. *Gomez* was heard before *Storozhenko* but would support the conclusion in that case.

The tribunal confirmed established case law that the fundamental rights of the victim must be protected. So a person should not be in fear because they have exercised the rights to freedom of thought, conscience, opinion, expression, association, and assembly. To qualify as political an opinion must relate to the major power transactions taking place in that particular society. Where a non-State actor is not itself a political entity the tribunal thought it would be difficult to regard an opinion imputed by them as political. This raises the further question as to whether the severe harm must be for a Convention reason, or the lack of state protection, or both, which is a difficult question, and is not resolved in *Gomez*. In *Gomez* itself, features of the Colombian context made it more possible than otherwise that criminal elements or guerrilla organizations would view the words or actions of those they persecuted as representing a political opinion. This was certainly true of FARC, the guerrilla organization being considered in this case.

Gomez disapproved of the attempt in *Acero-Garces* to create a fixed category of persons on the side of law order and justice. The tribunal said 'reference, Star Wars-style, to "dark forces" does not serve the interests of objective decision-making'. This should not have been regarded as a political position.

Where social group has been used in these kinds of situations it has tended not to be a successful argument, as for instance in *Savchenkov* [1996] Imm AR 28 CA the appellant argued unsuccessfully that he was a member of the group of individuals whom 'the mafia seeks to recruit and who refuse'.

13.6.5.1 *Conscientious objection*

Conscientious objection as a form of political opinion has generated a volume of case law from which certain principles may be distilled. Guidance is found in paras 167–174 of the UNHCR Handbook, though in places this is tentative and does not conclude that there will be a right to refugee status in all the circumstances raised.

There is a tension between the right of the state to demand military service from its citizens, and the right of the individual not to be forced to do something which goes against their conscience. All states have the right to demand military service from their nationals; some have a system of compulsory military service for all, some employ conscription only in times of war. In each case it is usually a criminal offence either to refuse to join up or to desert the armed forces. An exemption from prosecution and an alternative to military service is given in some countries to those who can establish a genuine conscientious objection to military action. However, by no means all states provide this, although the trend is moving towards doing so (see, for instance, Schnöring 2001). In a 1998 survey by War Resisters International, referred to in the UK's leading case on conscientious objection, *Sepet and Bulbul,* the following figures were given. 'Of 180 states surveyed, some form of conscription was found to exist in 95. In 52 of those 95 states the right of conscientious objection was found not to be recognized at all. In a further 7 of those 95 states there was no known provision governing a right of conscientious objection. In the remaining 36 states the right of conscientious objection appeared to be recognized to some extent' (para 18).

Prosecution for avoidance of normal military service is not regarded as persecution unless the punishment is disproportionate or is inflicted or impacts in a discriminatory way. For instance, some countries, including the USA, still maintain the possibility of the death penalty for refusal to serve. In some countries, avoiding military service for whatever motive is seen as political dissent which warrants severe punishment. Country guidance cases on Eritrea hold that people who will be perceived as draft evaders are at risk on return to Eritrea, and that 'the issue of military service has become politicised and actual or perceived evasion of military service is regarded by the Eritrean authorities as an expression of political opinion' (*IN (Draft evaders – evidence of risk) Eritrea CG* [2005] UKIAT 00106).

Refusal to undertake military action which is against international law can found refugee status. Lord Bingham in *Sepet and Bulbul* states established law in this way:

There is compelling support for the view that refugee status should be accorded to one who has refused to undertake compulsory military service on the grounds that such service would or might require him to commit atrocities or gross human rights abuses or participate in a conflict condemned by the international community, or where refusal to serve would earn grossly excessive or disproportionate punishment. (para 8)

This is partly endorsed in the Qualification Directive where the acts listed as persecution includes prosecution or punishment for refusing to perform military service which would entail committing war crimes, crimes against peace, crimes against humanity or against the purposes and principles of the UN or serious non-political crimes. The implication is that any punishment for refusal to perform such action would amount to persecution. The political opinion of the refuser would readily be imputed if not expressed. Earlier drafts of the Directive allowed for broader grounds of conscience to found a refugee claim, but these were lost in the negotiation process. The cases of *Radivojevic and Lazarevic* [1997] 2 All ER 723 concerned objection to military service in the former Yugoslavia in an action that was internationally condemned. However, it was held in the Court of Appeal (and this point not pursued to the House of Lords) that even in such a conflict the individuals themselves must object to the condemned action on principle, not just be 'opportunistic draft evaders' in order to obtain asylum. So at one end of the spectrum, refusing military service in violation of international law may found refugee status, and at the other, refusing military service because of a wish not to fight will not. In between are the contested areas.

In the case of *Sepet and Bulbul* the two appellants were Turkish Kurds who objected to military service for the Turkish government. They did so because they opposed the Turkish government's policy towards the Kurds, and feared that they might be sent to a Kurdish area and required to commit atrocities against their own people. Turkey provided no alternative to military service. Draft evaders were liable to a prison sentence of between six months and three years, which was not thought disproportionate.

Their claim was framed as conscientious objection, but it was clear that they did not have a conscientious objection to military service as such, but only in the present circumstances. Nevertheless, their objection was evidently a political opinion and could not unreasonably be regarded as a reason of conscience. The Convention reason was therefore established, but the question was whether imprisonment because of this political opinion could amount to persecution, when imprisonment for refusal not based on such an opinion would not.

The decision of the House of Lords illustrates one of the limitations of framing asylum law in human rights terms. Their Lordships considered the submission for the appellants that there was a recognized human right of conscientious objection, for instance implied in the Universal Declaration of Human Rights Article 18, which provides for a right to manifest belief. If there was such a right, then it could be argued that a discriminatory denial of the right could amount to persecution. However, their Lordships concluded that the weight of the evidence was that to date there is no such human right although there are developments in that direction.

The House of Lords and Court of Appeal each made the distinction between 'absolute' and 'partial' conscientious objectors. Absolute objectors would object to all military action for reasons of conscience. This would include people who were pacifists without a religious belief, and people whose pacifism arose from a belief system which normally entailed it, such as Quakers or Buddhists. There was authority to suggest that in the case of absolute objectors at least that prosecution could amount to persecution. This was accepted without question by the special adjudicator in the case of *Zaitz v SSHD* [2000] INLR 346. In the Court of Appeal, Buxton LJ distinguishes between conscientious objectors and others who desert or evade the draft. Only in the second case does he find the proportionality of the punishment to be relevant. In the case of conscientious objection, the implication is that any punishment at all could amount to persecution.

In its Resolution on the Annual Report on International Human Rights and European Union Human Rights Policy, released on 16 March 2000, the European Parliament called on 'the Council of Ministers and on European Union member states to grant asylum rights or refugee status to conscientious objectors and deserters from countries where the right to conscientious objection is not recognized...' (resolution A5–006/2000 para 68). Schnöring says that 'few governments have responded positively to this call' (2001:157), and as we have seen, the Refugee Qualification Directive does not go this far.

The House of Lords judgment in *Sepet and Bulbul* was not different in that respect. In the light of their finding that there was no human right of conscientious objection their Lordships considered that punishment for refusal of military service would *not* amount to persecution per se, reversing *Zaitz* to the extent that that case could be regarded as deciding otherwise.

Partial objection referred to people such as the appellants in these cases whose objection was a political one based on the practices and policy of the Turkish military, not on military action as such. In this case, the greater includes the less, because if there is no right of conscientious objection then even less will punishment of 'partial objectors' amount to persecution.

Not only *Zaitz* but a long line of tribunal cases had gone in opposite directions on the question of whether absolute conscientious objection can found a claim to refugee status. It is important, given that this is the first House of Lords authority on the issue, to note in what respects the case is binding. The appellants were partial objectors. The case must therefore be taken to decide that partial objection per se will not found a claim to refugee status. Comments that absolute objection does not give rise to a refugee claim must be regarded as obiter.

The starred tribunal case of *Foughali* 00/TH/01513 thoroughly explores the situations in which military service may give rise to a Convention claim. Although it must now be read in the light of *Sepet and Bulbul,* some issues are untouched, such as the finding that refusal to perform military service due to the repugnant nature of that service could found refugee status. This followed para 171 of the UNHCR handbook which suggests that where military action has drawn the condemnation of the international community, punishment for refusal may amount to persecution. In *Krotov v SSHD* [2004] EWCA Civ 69 the Court of Appeal considered a Russian soldier's refusal to participate in the Chechen war. The Secretary of State argued that the British asylum decision-making and appeal process could not be drawn into the kind of international judgments that would be required in order to grant refugee status on this basis. The Court of Appeal disagreed. They held that there were plenty of norms of international law to which reference could be made, and refugee status could be founded on objection to military service where that service would involve participation in acts which were contrary to basic rules of conduct as defined by international law. It was not necessary to wait for formal condemnation of the conflict by the international community. The claim could succeed if combatants could be punished for refusing to act in breach of basic rules of human conduct or if the genuine fear of such punishment was a reason for refusing to serve.

Not all cases of Turkish Kurds refusing military service will necessarily fail, even following *Sepet and Bulbul.* The case of *Aydogdu* [2002] UKIAT 06709 succeeded because the appellant left Turkey at a time when the military action he would have been called upon to undertake would have been condemned by the international community. This was in 1997–98 when, in the tribunal's words, 'The policy of the Turkish army, albeit against a determined and vicious enemy, did result in international condemnation as it involved a programme of compulsory village clearances and the large-scale displacement of the Kurdish civilian population' (para 18).

It is of course the case, as the Court of Appeal recognized in *Krotov,* that the question of international opinion on a war is a highly political matter. A number of American conscientious objectors to the war in Iraq have sought refugee status in Canada, where several have been refused at the first level of decision-making. Other soldiers who objected to the war but did not flee have been sentenced in the USA to imprisonment or hard labour (Amnesty International press release 13 May 2005).

A soldier cannot claim refugee status on account of risks from terrorists (*Fadli* v *SSHD* [2001] Imm AR 392). Being a soldier entails taking the risk of losing one's life in the service of one's country, and this is no different if the enemy is an internal one (here, the GIA, a fundamentalist group in Algeria). However, conditions of military service may be such as to amount to persecution if they are inhuman, as was acknowledged in *Foughali.*

13.7 Conclusion

This chapter has given an introduction to refugee law in the UK, but no more. This field is now so vast that a glance at some key issues and an examination of some of the key cases is all that is really possible in a small part of a larger book. The next chapter examines some of the legal restrictions upon refugee claims.

QUESTIONS

1 What are the benefits and the problems of operating with an international definition of who is a refugee?

2 Should gender be a Convention reason?

3 Is discrimination in relation to social rights a suitable basis for an asylum claim?

 online resource centre For guidance on answering questions, visit www.oxfordtextbooks.co.uk/orc/clayton3e.

FURTHER READING

Berkowitz, N. and Jarvis, C. (2000) *Asylum Gender Guidelines* (London: Immigration Appellate Authority).

Ceneda, S. and Palmer, C. (2006) 'Lip service or implementation? The Home Office Gender Guidance and women's asylum claims in the UK', RWRP at Asylum Aid.

Ceneda, S. (2006) 'The Role of Gender Guidelines in the Determination of Asylum Claims' *Immigration Law Digest* vol. 12 no. 2.

Chaudhry, M. (2007) 'Particular social group post *Fornah*', *Journal of Immigration, Asylum & Nationality Law* vol. 21 no.2 pp. 137–146.

Crawley, H. (2001) *Refugees and Gender* (Bristol: Jordan & Sons).

Gil-Bazo, M-T (2006) 'Refugee Status, subsidiary protection and the right to be granted asylum under EC law', Refugee Studies Centre, University of Oxford.

Goodwin-Gill, G. and McAdam, J. (2007) *The Refugee in International Law* (Oxford: Clarendon Press) 3rd edn.

Goulbourne, S. (2000) 'Refugees, state sovereignty, and the Geneva Convention' INLP vol. 14, no. 4, pp. 213–222.

Harvey, C. (2000) *Seeking Asylum in the UK: Problems and Prospects* (London: Butterworths).

Hathaway, J. (1991) *The Law of Refugee Status* (Ontario: Butterworths Canada Ltd).

—— (2002) 'The Causal Nexus in International Refugee Law' *Michigan Journal of International Law* Winter vol. 23, pp. 207–221.

—— and Foster, M. (2003) 'Membership of a Particular Social Group' *International Journal of Refugee Law* vol. 15, no. 3 477–491.

—— (2003) 'The Causal Connection (Nexus) to a Convention Ground' *International Journal of Refugee Law* vol. 15, no. 3 461–476.

—— and Hicks, W.S. (2005) 'Is there a subjective element in the refugee convention's requirement of 'well-founded fear?' *Michigan Journal of International Law* Winter vol. 26, pp. 505–525.

Kelly, N. (2001) 'The Convention Refugee Definition and Gender-Based Persecution: A Decade's Progress' *International Journal of Refugee Law* vol. 13, no. 4, 559–568.

Lambert, H. (2001) 'The Conceptualisation of "Persecution" by the House of Lords: *Horvath v SSHD*', *International Journal of Refugee Law* vol. 13, no. 1/2, pp. 16–31.

Millbank, J. (2004) 'The Role of Rights in Asylum Claims based on Sexual Orientation' *Human Rights Law Review* vol.4, no. 2, pp. 193–228.

Musalo, K. (2003) 'Revisiting social group and nexus in gender asylum claims: a unifying rationale for evolving jurisprudence', Spring, 52 *DePaul L. Rev.*, p. 777.

—— (2006) 'Claims for Protection Based on Religion or Belief' *International Journal of Refugee Law* (2004), vol. 16, no. 2, pp. 165–226.

O'Nions, H. (1999) 'Bona fide or Bogus? Roma Asylum Seekers from the Czech Republic' *Web Journal of Current Legal Issues* 3.

Pearce, H. (2002) 'An Examination of the International Understanding of Political Rape and the Significance of Labelling it Torture' *International Journal of Refugee Law* vol. 14, no. 4, pp. 534–560.

Schnöring, K. (2001) 'Deserters in the Federal Republic of Yugoslavia' *International Journal of Refugee Law* vol. 13, 153–173.

Shah, P. (2000) *Refugees, Race and the Legal Concept of Asylum in Britain* (London: Cavendish).

Stevens, D. (2004) *UK Asylum Law and Policy* (London: Sweet & Maxwell), Chapters 1 and 2.

Symes, M. and Jorro, P. (2003) *Asylum Law and Practice* (London: Lexis Nexis Butterworths).

UNHCR (2002) 'UNHCR Guidelines on International Protection', 7 May 2002, Membership of Particular Social Group and Gender-related Persecution.

—— (2003) 'Guidelines on Internal Protection'.

—— 'Handbook on Procedures and Criteria for Determining Refugee Status'.

Wilsher, D. (2003) 'Non-State Actors and the Definition of a Refugee in the UK: Protection, Accountability or Culpability?' *International Journal of Refugee Law* vol. 15, no. 1, pp. 68–112.

Yeo, C. (2002) 'Agents of the State: When is an Official of the State an Agent of the State?' *International Journal of Refugee Law* vol. 14, no. 4, pp. 509–533.

—— (2006) 'Qualification Directive: a new era?' *Immigration Law Digest* vol. 12 no. 3.

14

Criminalization and excluding an asylum claim

SUMMARY

This chapter is concerned with the process of increasing criminalization of migration and of making an asylum claim, and with the provisions whereby an individual can be excluded from refugee status because of their conduct. It shows how these powers have increased rapidly in recent years in the light of the objectives of deterring asylum claimants and combating terrorism.

14.1 Criminalizing asylum claims

There is a right in international law to seek asylum (UDHR 1948 Art 14, echoed in the European Charter of Human Rights) but, as we have seen, it is difficult to exercise within the law. In *R v Naillie* [1993] AC 674 HL the House of Lords held that arriving in the UK and requesting asylum without attempting to deceive did not make the defendants illegal entrants. However, in *Saadi v SSHD* [2002] UKHL 42 the House of Lords held that detention of asylum claimants was lawful 'to prevent unauthorized entry' (HRA Art 5(1)(f)). It did not go so far as to say that unlawfulness was contemplated. Indeed there was clear evidence that it was not. As Collins J said at first instance, the claimants were doing all they could to enter lawfully. The asylum seekers were detained pending determination of their claim, simply in order to facilitate immigration control (see chapter 15 for full discussion of the law on detention).

Scheimann J in1989 described the difficulties faced by asylum claimants in the face of visa regimes, carrier sanctions and now we would add border control measures such as the placement of airline liaison officers. As a consequence, he said, an asylum seeker has the option of:

1. lying to the UK authorities in his country in order to obtain a tourist visa or some other sort of visa;
2. obtaining a credible forgery of a visa;
3. obtaining an airline ticket to a third country with a stopover in the UK. *(Yassine v SSHD* [1990] Imm AR 354 at 359)

We might add a fourth option: clandestine entry.

We shall shortly examine some of the specific criminal measures which are in place, and shall see that these sanctions, the lack of lawful option as described in *Yassine,* and the acceptance that asylum seekers may be treated in a punitive manner even without any wrongdoing *(Saadi),* combine to create a murky zone between legality and illegality within which asylum claims are made. Among the results of this are that an asylum seeker may be convicted and punished for acting in a way they could not avoid, and that others who might help them gain entry are deterred from doing so through fear of the law. Equally troubling, the boundary between asylum seeker and criminal is blurred in the minds of officials who deal with them and of the public.

Though these risks have become heightened, they have always been present for refugees because of the secrecy in which some have been forced to leave their countries, and the difficulty of obtaining documents. The Refugee Convention therefore made provision for this.

14.2 **Article 31**

Article 31 of the Refugee Convention says that refugees coming directly from the country of persecution should not be punished on account of their illegal entry or presence, provided they present themselves without delay and show good cause for this. In the case of *R v Uxbridge Magistrates Court ex p Adimi, R v Crown Prosecution Service ex p Sorani, R v SSHD ex p Kaziu* [2000] 3 WLR 434 three people who travelled on false documents were prosecuted. The purpose of Article 31 was to provide immunity for genuine refugees whose quest for asylum reasonably involved a breach of the law. The court recognized that this could be a matter of necessity for a genuine refugee, and therefore the Secretary of State rather than the Crown Prosecution Service should decide when asylum seekers should be prosecuted for travelling on false documents. It was a matter relating to conduct of immigration and asylum, not to the need to punish criminal activity generally. They could use Article 31 to stay the criminal proceedings.

This means that where there are grounds to believe that Article 31 will apply, a prosecution should not be brought. A joint Memorandum of Good Practice for liaison between the police, IND, CPS and the Law Society concerning the prosecution of refugee claimants for offences concerning the use of false documents advises that if an immigration officer thinks that Article 31 might apply, a suspect should be granted police bail pending resolution of the asylum claim (Macdonald 2001:681).

Following the judgment in *Adimi,* a statutory defence to forgery, deception and falsification of documents was enacted in Immigration and Asylum Act 1999 s 31. It inserts the key provisions of Article 31 into the statute, with the effect that its provisions may now be relied upon as a defence. However, s 31 is more restricted than Article 31 and the *Adimi* judgment. For instance, the defence is available only to someone whose refugee claim succeeds, whereas *Adimi* applied Article 31 to asylum seekers. This is crucial to the effectiveness of Article 31 as otherwise any asylum seeker could be penalized before their claim is determined. It also has the effect that there is no defence for someone whose claim is made on what they themselves consider to be proper grounds, but who does not succeed in law. This elides the genuine but unsuccessful claimant with the dishonest one, and confuses deception in the means of obtaining entry with deception as to the substance of the claim. The Court of Appeal in *R v Kishientine* [2004] EWCA Crim 3352 made it clear that the criminal court could have no part in assessing the merits of the asylum claim so as to deal with any of these objections.

Article 31 refers to people 'coming directly' from the country of persecution, but the court in *Adimi* did not take this too literally. They held that there could be some element of choice by refugees as to their destination, and a short-term stopover on the journey could not be used to say that the refugee had not come to the UK directly. The Divisional Court in *R (on the application of Badur) v Birmingham Crown Court and Solihull Magistrates' Court* [2006] EWHC 539 (Admin) held that Article 31 would have permitted other considerations, for instance that the appellant was a minor at the relevant time, which might have had a bearing on whether he could have claimed asylum in a safe country. Section 31 does not allow for these factors. It limits the defence to situations where the defendant can show that in any third country at which they have stopped on the way to the UK they could not reasonably have expected to obtain refugee protection.

Section 31 as interpreted by the API takes a more restrictive approach than *Adimi* to the question of whether someone has presented themselves as soon as possible. UNHCR says that 'delay caused by an asylum seeker's wish to approach a lawyer or a voluntary organization first to seek advice is not unreasonable and should not preclude the protection of s 31'. They were concerned that account be taken of proper reasons for delay, such as the effects of trauma, language differences, lack of information, previous experiences which have resulted in a suspicion of authority, and a feeling of insecurity. UNHCR issued detailed advice on the API, but this has not been implemented, and the Home Office relies on the primacy of s 31 as statute over and above the provisions of the Refugee Convention. This view was confirmed in *R (on the application of Pepushi) v Crown Prosecution Service* [2004] EWHC 798 (Admin) where the court held that there is no scope to claim the protection of Article 31 Refugee Convention, even though the protection offered by Immigration and Asylum Act 1999 s 31 is explicitly narrower. Mr Pepushi had stopped in France and Italy long enough to claim asylum. Section 31 gave no scope to extend the defence. The court had an obligation to read the words of the statute which was intended to give effect to the Convention compatibly with the Convention; where this was not possible, parliamentary sovereignty entailed that the statute prevailed. Unlike the Human Rights Act, there is no provision for a declaration of incompatibility. The court in *Badur* held that s 31 could not apply to the offence of seeking to obtain entry by deception as set out in an earlier form in Immigration Act 1971 s 24(1)(a)(aa). The defence could only apply to offences to which it explicitly refers. Mr Badur should have been charged under s 24A(1)(a), but as he was not, the defence in s 31 did not apply. He should have had the benefit of Article 31.

The API take the view that Article 31 has no application to offences not mentioned in s 31. This is indicated in *Pepushi*, though obiter. The reason for this is that Article 31 is not incorporated into UK law; section 31 is the government's decision on how Article 31 should be used, and as legislation it is binding. That is not the implication of *Badur*.

The joint memorandum of good practice was never published (Macdonald 2005:979). It advises close co-operation between police, prosecutors and the immigration service, reliance on both Article 31 and s 31, and that prosecution should proceed only in the clearest of cases. The use of the Article as well as the section would have meant that prosecutions should not necessarily proceed where the strict terms of s 31 are not met. It is a question of whether prosecution is in the public interest. The need for this kind of guidance and co-operation to take place outside the court setting is apparent in *R v Makuwa* [2006] EWCA Crim 175. Here the court held that the defendant would need to give some evidence of being a refugee, which the Crown would then need to disprove.

If that burden was passed, then it would be up to the refugee, on balance of probabilities, to prove the other elements of the defence – that they could not have claimed elsewhere, or quicker, and so on. The court reached this view by deciding that the mischief addressed by s 31 was the use of false passports etc. It is perhaps surprising that the court did not think that the mischief addressed by the section was the wrongful punishment of people who had no choice but to enter the UK illegally to make a claim for international protection. The Joint Parliamentary Committee on Human Rights noted that 'a significant number of people have been wrongfully imprisoned' for offences to which s 31 should have provided a defence. Estimated figures ranged between 1, 000 and 5, 000 (Session 2003–04 Fifth Report HL paper 35 HC 304, para 10). People who were wrongly convicted and imprisoned have received average compensation of £40, 000 (Macdonald 2005:979).

14.3 Offences

Using deception may result in a number of criminal charges. The use of deception to seek or obtain leave to enter or remain in the UK or to seek the avoidance of enforcement or removal action is an offence contrary to Immigration Act 1971 s 24A (as inserted and amended by the 1996 and 1999 Acts), carrying a maximum penalty of two years in prison. The use of false or altered documents is an offence contrary to s 26(1)(d), and the Forgery and Counterfeiting Act 1981 is also quite often used in cases of alleged false documents. For an offence under Forgery and Counterfeiting Act s 3 in *R v Kolawole* [2004] EWCA Crim 3047 the court gave guidance that 'The appropriate sentence for using or holding with the intention of use one false passport, even on a guilty plea by a person of good character, should usually be within the range of 12 to 18 months' imprisonment'. This was because of the increase of public concern on these matters. The maximum sentence is 10 years.

14.3.1 Asylum and Immigration (Treatment of Claimants etc) Act 2004 s 2

A practice which has troubled the Home Office has been that of asylum seekers who destroy their documents while on their journey to the UK. This may be on the advice of agents who have organized their travel. While in broad terms the possible motivations for this can be guessed at, this does not give any indication in an individual case of why a person was so determined to conceal their identity, prevent the possibility of return, or otherwise conceal their means of travel, as the case may be. The desire to start a new life anonymously, or conceal a deception, or fear of persecution are clearly all possible motives.

In order to prevent this practice, the Asylum and Immigration (Treatment of Claimants etc) Act 2004 introduced a new offence of attending an asylum interview without a passport or similar document (s 2), unless it is produced within a three day grace period after the interview (s 2(3)(b)). Statutory defences include:

- To produce a false immigration document and to prove that this was used for all purposes in connection with the journey to the UK.

- To prove that he travelled to the UK without, at any stage since he set out on the journey, having possession of an immigration document.
- Reasonable excuse, which does not include destruction of the document unless that was for a reasonable cause or beyond the claimant's control.
- Reasonable cause in this context does not include delaying an asylum decision, increasing one's chances of success, or complying with the instructions of a facilitator (smuggler) unless it would be unreasonable to expect noncompliance in the circumstances (s 2(7)(b)(iii)). It is hard to imagine when it would be more reasonable to rely on a speculation about the needs of a system the asylum seeker has not yet personally encountered than on the advice of the person who has got them this far. The instructions to immigration officers implementing the section suggest that it would be unreasonable to expect noncompliance with advice where the asylum seeker has been threatened or intimidated so that this amounted to force.

In *R v Bei Bei Wang* [2005] EWCA Crim 293 the defendant had travelled for six months through several countries with an agent who had retained her passport at all points except for the moment of going through passport control. The Court of Appeal commented that her situation was not very different from that of someone who had not had possession of a travel document at all, or someone who travelled on forged documents. In the latter case, there would be a defence under Immigration and Asylum Act 1999 ss 2, and 31 would provide a defence to a different criminal charge in the event of a successful asylum claim. A lighter sentence was therefore appropriate.

The sentence was also reduced in *Lu Zhu Ai* [2005] EWCA Crim 936 in which the court reiterated the very specific purpose of this offence, the distinction between s 2 and offences of fraud etc, and, as in *Bei Bei Wang,* the significant deterrent element in the sentencing. The court also noted that it was difficult in these cases to take full account of individual circumstances. The components of the alleged offence could be considered, i.e. the journey and to what extent the defendant had control of their travel document, but the merits of their asylum claim could not be considered at all by the criminal court. This is different from establishing eligibility for the s 31 defence, where the Court of Appeal in *Makuwa* said that the jury would need to consider whether the defendant was a refugee, if the Crown disputed it.

The case of *Thet v DPP* began to set the limits of prosecutions under s 2.

 Key Case

Thet v DPP (2006) The Times, 1 November

The defendant had entered the country on a false passport which, after passing through immigration control, he handed immediately back to the person who facilitated his entry, as instructed. As a former political prisoner he had been unable to obtain a genuine passport in Burma. The Lord Chief Justice held that Mr Thet could rely on the defence in s 2(4)(c) – that he had a reasonable excuse for not being able to produce a document at interview of the kind referred to in s 2(1), namely one which is 'in force' and 'satisfactorily establishes his identity and nationality'. The court held that the passport referred to in s 2 is a valid passport, not a false one.

The prosecutor wanted to rely on statements in Parliament under the rule in *Pepper v Hart* [1993] AC 593 to show that there was a parliamentary intention to prosecute people who disposed *en route* of false documents. The Lord Chief Justice held that the section was 'ill-drafted but not ambiguous' and so there was no *prima facie* case for using *Pepper v Hart*. If there had been, it would have been at least arguable that, where a criminal statute was ambiguous, the defendant should have the benefit of the ambiguity.

Similar facts in *R v Mohammed and R v Osman* [2007] EWCA Crim 2332 gave rise to a finding that, where the defence in s 2(4)(e) was relied on, which is that the person never had an immigration document, the immigration document referred to need not be a genuine one. In other words, following *Thet*, a defendant cannot argue that they were never in possession of an immigration document throughout the journey because the only one they had was false. This would give a defence to a possessor of a false passport in circumstances where a possessor of a genuine passport would have no such defence, an unlikely proper effect of the statute, the court thought. The convictions were overturned because the jury had not been properly directed on whether the defendants' reasons for giving their passports back to the agents were reasonable ones (the same defence as *Thet*), but this was too late to be of benefit to the appellants, who had already served prison sentences. Indeed, Mr Osman had been served with a deportation order, and it was only by intervention of the Criminal Cases Review Commission that his conviction had come before the court.

This involvement of the criminal justice system in matters so closely connected with the substance of an asylum claim is problematic. The defences in s 2 and the existence of s 31 demonstrate recognition that any offence is connected with the circumstances of leaving and the reasons for it, and thus relevant to their asylum claim. Destruction of a passport makes it more difficult to return a person to their country of origin against their will. The s 2 offence is based on the proposition that it is not legitimate to obstruct one's return, an asylum claim having failed, even if that was based on fear of return rather than a cynical desire to obstruct the legal system. In other words, no relevant *mens rea* is required for the s 2 offence. The defendant is in an invidious position. If they have destroyed their passport in an attempt to ensure their own safety this fear is very relevant to the success of their asylum claim, but admitting its destruction will make them guilty of an offence and liable to imprisonment.

As Macdonald points out (2005:975), where the facts are in dispute, in the light of tightening controls by carriers the court may disbelieve a passenger's assertion that they never had a travel document. Although the offence is designed to curb destruction of documents before arrival, this is based on the assumption that the passenger did have such a document. If they actually did not, s 2 forces a possibly innocent person fleeing persecution to prove a negative in the criminal courts. Arriving without a travel document does not in itself amount to the offence of illegal entry, as there is in law no entry, nor is it an attempt to commit the offence of illegal entry as by definition it only arises at an interview. It does not target a person who attempts to remain hidden, but rather one who may have arrived by clandestine means but makes an application to regularize their stay. The underlying mischief is the destruction of travel documents but there is no requirement on the prosecution to prove this as the *actus reus* is simply presentation at interview without the document. The burden of proof is on the defendant to show they never had one.

The Parliamentary Joint Committee on Human Rights considered whether this reverse burden meets the requirements of Article 6(2) ECHR. They did not reach a concluded view on that matter, but accepted that in principle it could be justifiable to place the burden on the defendant of showing an excuse for the destruction of a passport. This was with the caveat that immigrants should have access to information on the effect of destroying travel documents, even on the advice of facilitators (para 23).

In addition to problems with the offence itself, there is the problem of its being wrongly used. We have already noted that many people, probably thousands, have been wrongly prosecuted for offences to which s 31 would have provided a defence. The Joint Parliamentary Committee on Human Rights, reporting on the Bill, voiced their concern (Session 2003–04 Fifth Report HL paper 35 HC 304, para 10) that like the offences of forgery and falsification of documents, s 2 might be wrongly used, thus penalizing even more asylum seekers and breaching Article 31.

The defence of never having had a travel document was introduced to go some way towards alleviating the Committee's concerns. Nevertheless, many of the people who have been convicted under s 2 were in comparable positions to Mr Thet. His solicitor commented:

this Act...had an effect of criminalising genuine asylum seekers who often can only leave their own country using a false passport for which they have had to pay an agent. Due to the power the agent has over them, they usually have to return the passport to the agent or destroy the passport on arrival in the United Kingdom. (Refugee Council briefing, October 2006)

The press reported 230 asylum seekers arrested and 134 convicted in the first six months of s 2 being in force ('Asylum seekers jailed for having no passports' The Guardian 18 March 2005).

14.3.2 **Those who assist or arrange entry**

The whole problem is contained in the rather bland heading to this section. Should it read 'those who assist unlawful immigration' or 'those who assist asylum seekers'? Section 25 Immigration Act 1971 would suggest both. As indicated by its high maximum sentence, this has been treated as one of the most serious immigration offences. In the Immigration Act 1971 it was originally titled 'Assisting illegal entry and harbouring'. It consisted then of knowingly being concerned in 'making or carrying out arrangements for securing or facilitating the entry into the United Kingdom of anyone whom he knows or has reasonable cause for believing to be an illegal entrant' and of harbouring such a person. The maximum sentence increased from seven to 10 years in 2000 (1999 Act s 29) and to 14 years in 2003 (2002 Act s 143). These sentences, and the powers in ss 25C and D to seize vehicles owned by a person convicted, are aimed at those who profit from arranging illegal entry, and show the prominent place that this offence plays in the government's campaign to prevent people smuggling and organized deception. It can be committed however simply by allowing an illegal entrant to stay in one's home. By its nature this offence may be committed abroad. Section 25(5) therefore provides for British nationals to be liable for the offence whether committed inside or outside the UK.

The Nationality, Immigration and Asylum Act 2002 greatly extended this offence and split it into three parts. The offence in s 25 is to do an act 'which facilitates the commission of a breach of immigration law by an individual who is not a citizen of the European Union'. The definition of immigration law is wide, covering any provision which controls entitlement to enter or be in a member state. This wide definition enables the development of immigration control into an international policing activity (as discussed in chapter 7). A British citizen in Albania organizing a marriage of convenience in Italy could be charged under this section. It would also catch an accountant in London preparing accounts for a Czech business to give a false impression that its main centre of operations was in Germany. The new offence in s 25B is assisting entry in breach of deportation or exclusion orders by European citizens. This closes the loophole which would otherwise have opened up after the creation of the specific offence in s 25 directed at facilitating entry by non-Europeans.

Section 25A has the extraordinary heading of 'helping asylum seeker to enter UK'. Amended again by the UK Borders Act 2007, the offence is 'knowingly and for gain' to facilitate the arrival or entry of someone the defendant knows or has reasonable cause to believe is an asylum seeker. There is a defence for someone acting on behalf of an organization which aims to help asylum seekers and does not charge for its services, but none for an individual. For instance, a married couple who facilitated the entry of the man's brother and his friend were each sentenced to two years' imprisonment for that offence. The fact that the two entrants claimed asylum the day after their entry was irrelevant (*R v Javaherifard and Miller* [2005] EWCA Crim 3231). This means that, in terms of criminal liability, issues such as the good faith of the asylum claim, its merits, or the defendants' beliefs in relation to those matters are not relevant, except perhaps as mitigation of sentence. This offence is not aimed at asylum seekers but at those who profit from their need to find a way into the UK. Controlling such commercial arrangements for illegal entry is a matter of some priority in the emerging immigration law of the EU (see generally chapter 5). Relevant European provisions here are Directive 2002/90 and Framework Decision 2002/946, and the UK has opted in, but the offences under the expanded s 25 go beyond what is required by European measures. Notably, the s 25A offence of 'helping an asylum seeker to enter the UK' does not entail that the entry be illegal, simply that the entrant is an asylum seeker, whereas the Directive and Framework Decision require criminal sanctions for the facilitation of entry or transit 'in breach of the laws of the state concerned', not penalties on the travel arrangements of asylum seekers per se. Directive 2002/90 Article 1.2 allows any member state not to apply sanctions where the 'aim of the behaviour is to provide humanitarian assistance to the person concerned'. The British defence is limited to organizations who do not charge for their services.

The facilitation offence in s 25 relates to assisting an illegal entrant. There is no requirement that the entrant themselves be guilty of or charged with a criminal offence. Illegal entry may be treated as a criminal offence, but usually immigration enforcement would be used, i.e. removal (see chapter 17). The criminal offence of illegal entry is more tightly drawn (s 24(1)(a)). To be guilty, the person must know that they are entering in breach of the law so this must be proved, and they must actually enter, although an attempt may be charged as such. Section 28 extends the time limit for prosecution from the usual six months to three years if the evidence of the alleged offence has come to light in the previous two months. If the prosecution is brought within six months, the burden of proof is changed from the normal criminal one; it lies on the defendant to show that they had leave to enter (s 24(4)(b)). Once a criminal conviction has been obtained, the illegal entrant is still present and the immigration situation still has to be dealt with, so there is no obvious benefit in incurring the expense of a criminal prosecution.

14.3.3 **Trafficking**

The offences under s 25 are committed by people who can claim in some way to be serving the interests of the person whose entry is arranged. Once this has happened, the entrant is free of the smuggler or agent if they have paid for their services. This is not so in the case of trafficking. Trafficking is defined in the United Nations 2000 Protocol to Prevent, Suppress and Punish Trafficking in Persons, especially Women and Children (the Palermo Protocol) Article 3 as:

the recruitment, transportation, transfer, harbouring or receipt of persons, by means of the threat or use of force or other forms of coercion, of abduction, of fraud, of deception, of the abuse of power or of a position of vulnerability or of the giving or receiving of payments or benefits to achieve the consent of a person having control over another person, for the purpose of exploitation. Exploitation shall include, at a minimum, the exploitation of the prostitution of others or other forms of sexual exploitation, forced labour or services, slavery or practices similar to slavery, servitude or the removal of organs.

The Joint Parliamentary Committee on Human Rights (26th report 2005–06) identifies some differences between people smuggling and human trafficking, which can be elaborated as follows:

Table 14A Smuggling and trafficking

Smuggling	Trafficking
The smuggled person in broad terms consents or agrees to what is done by the smuggler. They may have no control over specifics such as route or documentation, but they want to make the journey. Any deception is practised on third parties, such as an immigration officer	Trafficking is carried out by coercion or deception of the trafficked person
Relationship with smuggler ends when smuggled person reaches their destination	Trafficking entails subsequent exploitation of trafficked person
Smuggling entails movement across international borders	Trafficking can take place within and across national frontiers
Entry is illegal. If legal entry were possible, the smuggler would not be required	Trafficking may entail legal or illegal entry

People smuggling is treated as a criminal matter with a significant migration dimension. Trafficking entails human rights violations over and above the migration and criminal issues involved. Increasing international concern and domestic pressure has brought about an increase in criminal penalties, but a slower development of human rights protection. Nationality, Immigration and Asylum Act 2002 s 145 created a new offence of trafficking in prostitution, and marked the UK's first statutory attempt to control the growing sex industry. Locating it in a migration statute confused the issues, and s 145 was swiftly repealed and replaced by offences in the Sexual Offences Act 2003. This refocused attention on the trafficker rather than emphasizing the unlawful immigration status of the victim.

After the deaths of 23 Chinese cockle pickers who drowned in Morecambe Bay in February 2004, it was no longer possible to ignore other labour exploitation by traffickers and gangmasters. The Asylum and Immigration (Treatment of Claimants etc)

Act 2004 introduced a new offence of trafficking for exploitation. Exploitation includes slavery and forced labour, using threats or deception or someone's youth or vulnerability to force them to provide benefits or services, and encouraging the sale of human organs (s 4). The UK Borders Act 2007 amends this offence and that in the Sexual Offences Act 2003 so that acts abroad are included. Relevant legislation was also introduced outside the immigration sphere in the form of the Gangmasters (Licensing) Act 2004 which regulates the activities of those who employ casual migrant workers in agricultural work and the shellfish industry. The UK is bound by the Council Framework Decision 2002/629 on trafficking in human beings which requires the member states to have criminal penalties for trafficking offences.

Aside from pursuing criminal penalties, the UK government is under pressure from the Council of Europe, the European Union, Amnesty International, Anti-Slavery International and UNICEF UK to institute legal measures for the protection of victims. These would include automatic reflection periods, i.e. a period during which immigration enforcement will be held in abeyance while the victim considers their situation, and residence permits for trafficking victims. The Joint Parliamentary Committee on Human Rights published a report on human trafficking which strongly recommended these measures (26th report 2005–06). After a consultation during 2006 on tackling human trafficking, in March 2007 the UK government published its Action Plan, and the Home Secretary signed the Council of Europe's Convention on Action against Trafficking Human Beings. On 15 January 2008 the Home Secretary announced that the UK would ratify the Convention by the end of the year. The Action Plan states that, once the Convention comes into effect, reflection periods and residence permits will be made available, but no timescale is given for this. The UK has not opted into the European Directive on residence permits for trafficking victims (Directive 2004/81).

Remedies for victims of trafficking not only relate to immigration status. Compensation through the criminal compensation scheme is theoretically possible, but at the time of the Joint Parliamentary Committee on Human Rights report (October 2006) had never been awarded. An international protective status such as humanitarian protection or asylum is also theoretically possible. The ECtHR in *Siliadin v France* [2005] ECHR 545 held that Article 4 entailed a positive obligation to penalize slavery and forced labour. In that case a domestic worker had been held in conditions akin to slavery. The proposed withdrawal of the immigration rules concerning domestic workers (commented upon in chapter 11) has provoked concern about an upsurge of abusive practices in the UK, including from the Joint Parliamentary Committee on Human Rights in their report on human trafficking. Successful asylum cases are rare. One reason for this is indicated by the Joint Committee on Human Rights, which reports that 'evidence provided to us suggests that people who have been trafficked into the UK may not be asked appropriate questions by officials, and as a result will fail to be identified as victims' (para 145).

Through mistrust of officials, not understanding what is happening to them, fear of reprisals or of being returned to their home state, victims may also be unwilling to talk about being trafficked. The JCHR report cites instances of trauma to victims in giving evidence when their privacy was not respected. The Committee emphasizes the role to be played by support workers in this situation. It is not clear whether this understanding was present in the Court of Appeal in *IO (Congo) v SSHD* [2006] EWCA Civ 796. Social workers asserted that the appellant had probably been trafficked. All the circumstantial evidence pointed to this. The appellant herself denied it. The Court of Appeal held that there was 'real risk' that she had been trafficked, but that in order to treat this as established for the purposes of assessing her asylum claim it would have to be proved on balance of probabilities as it was against her own assertions. It is debatable whether this is a correct interpretation of the standard of proof of matters in the past, as expounded in *Karanakaran* and *Koyazia Kaja* (see chapter 13). However, the asylum claim would depend crucially on an assessment of future risk, which would be difficult to assess if the real risk was of matters denied by the appellant.

SB (Moldova CG) [2008] UKAIT 00002 is a significant decision for victims of trafficking, briefly discussed in chapter 13. The appellant was held to qualify for refugee protection because of the risks of reprisals she faced as a formerly trafficked person who had given evidence against her trafficker.

14.3.4 Immigration and criminal law

Immigration offences are not covered in detail in this book. Their prosecution is an aspect of criminal law rather than immigration law. Nevertheless immigration offences are created in immigration statutes rather than in criminal justice statutes, and immigration officers now have powers almost identical to those of the police in relation to immigration offences, illustrating that this kind of law enforcement is seen as an aspect of immigration control. We have briefly discussed a few of the offences that have direct relationship with other human rights issues, particularly asylum claims. However, the whole area of interaction between immigration law and criminal law raises human rights issues of various kinds. For instance, a person subject to immigration control is subject to double jeopardy in the criminal courts as they may be deported in addition to any other sentence. This issue is considered in chapter 16. Additionally, such a person may in the future lose their right to remain under provisions in the Criminal Justice and Immigration Bill 2007. There are numerous minor and regulatory immigration offences, many of which are rarely prosecuted. The majority of prosecutions in relation to immigration offences are under 2004 Act s 2. A new offence of failing to co-operate with removal action is considered in chapter 17. Offences which may be committed by employers and advisers and powers in relation to these are dealt with in chapters 11 and 8.

In accordance with the increased preoccupation with enforcement as a priority in immigration policy, the Immigration and Asylum Act 1999 gave enhanced powers to immigration officers very similar to those possessed by the police in the investigation of crime and the apprehension of suspects. The enhanced powers apply both to dealing with people suspected of immigration offences (Immigration Act 1971 Part III) and to the carrying out of immigration functions under Sch 2. Powers of entry, search of people and premises, seizure of documents, and fingerprinting apply in relation to investigation of immigration status and to investigation of criminal offences. Section 145 provides that in exercising any power to

(a) arrest, question, search or take fingerprints from a person,

(b) enter and search premises, or

(c) seize property found on such person or premises,

an immigration officer must have regard to specified codes of practice. These are the Codes of Practice issued in relation to the Police and Criminal Evidence Act 1984, as modified and specified by the Immigration (PACE Codes of Practice) Direction 2000 and the Immigration (PACE Codes of Practice No 2 and Amendment) Directions 2000.

PACE codes of Practice were revised with effect from 1 January 2006 by the PACE Codes of Practice Order 2005, SI 2005/3503.

We now move on to a quite different area of penalties relating to actual or alleged criminal activity – exclusion from an asylum claim.

14.4 Exclusion, expulsion, and anti-terrorism

The Refugee Convention provides both for the exclusion of individuals from initially obtaining refugee status (Art 1F), and the expulsion of recognized refugees and asylum seekers from the host state as a result of their actions there (Arts 32 and 33(2)). The significance of this area of law has increased rapidly in recent times as powers are interpreted and strengthened in the context of the escalation in international action and domestic legislation against terrorism. This began before 11 September 2001, but has accelerated since then.

Questions of exclusion from refugee protection are not only questions of refugee law. In *Gurung v SSHD* [2003] Imm AR 115 the tribunal adopted the summary conclusions from the Lisbon expert roundtable, held as part of the 2001 UNHCR Global Consultations on International Protection, to say that 'there is a need, in the interpretation and application of Art 1F, to draw on "developments in other areas of international law since 1951, in particular international criminal law and extradition law as well as international human rights law and international humanitarian law"' (para 34). In the domestic context, these refugee law provisions must also be read in conjunction with recent legislation on terrorism, the Terrorism Act 2000, the Anti-terrorism, Crime and Security Act 2001 and the Terrorism Act 2006.

Article 1F Refugee Convention makes exclusion from refugee status mandatory for a person with respect to whom there are serious reasons for considering that he has committed:

(a) A crime against peace, a war crime, or crime against humanity as defined in international instruments.

(b) A serious non-political crime outside country of refuge prior to admission to that country as a refugee.

(c) Acts contrary to purpose and principles of UN.

The tribunal decision in *Gurung* encouraged adjudicators to take the initiative in promoting a greater use of exclusion under this provision (paras 38 and 144). It referred to Lord Mustill's comment in the case of *T v SSHD* [1996] 2 All ER 865, that while the wording of Article 1F had not changed, the world around it had. It continued:

In the aftermath of the events of 11 September these thoughtful words remind us that, whilst there is nothing new about criminality, the precise forms and methods used by those who perpetrate violent acts or crimes continue to undergo change. (para 33)

The tribunal considered that the 'well-settled principle that the Refugee Convention is a living instrument' applied to the interpretation of exclusions as much as of the requirements to establish refugee status. In this respect too it must be interpreted 'so as to give a contemporary response to contemporary realities' (para 35). Immigration judges should be more ready to use the exclusion clauses, and it was not only allowable but actually their duty to raise Article 1F even where the parties had not, if its applica-tion to the facts of the case was 'obvious' (para 47). This approach was followed by the Court of Appeal in *A (Iraq) v SSHD* [2005] EWCA Civ 1438 in which the appellant's asylum claim had been based on fear of reprisals because he had personally tortured many people under Saddam Hussain's regime in Iraq. The court held that it was obvi-ous that he was liable to be excluded under Article 1F and the adjudicator should have raised it. *Gurung* (para 17) refers to a Home Office policy of considering exclusion where the asylum applicant is a member of an organization proscribed under the Terrorism Act 2000. The relationship between these provisions is discussed below.

This section on exclusions will begin by considering each of the Article 1F grounds in turn.

14.4.1 Article 1F(a): Crime against peace, war crime, crime against humanity

There are several international instruments which elaborate on the meaning of these crimes, and some are listed in Annex VI of the UNHCR Handbook. Examples are the 1948 Convention on the Protection and Punishment of Genocide and the four 1949 Geneva Conventions for the Protection of Victims of War. There has been very little UK case law concerning crimes against peace, war crimes, and crimes against humanity.

Article 6 of the Charter of the International Military Tribunal includes in the defi-nition of a crime against peace 'planning, preparation, initiating or waging a war of aggression, or a war in violation of international treaties, agreements or assurances'. The tribunal in *Amberber* 00/TH/01570 made it clear that just participating in such a war would not amount to a crime against peace. The tribunal emphasized that an act of aggression was an act by a state against the territorial sovereignty or political inde-pendence of another state (UN General Assembly Resolution 3314). Mr Amberber as an active member of an armed group (AAPO) in Ethiopia had not committed a crime against peace, even though he procured and supplied arms to other members of the group. His appeal against exclusion was allowed. The UNHCR Guidelines 1996 on the application of exclusion clauses say 'there are few precedents if any for exclusion of individuals under this category' (para 27). *Amberber* was followed in *PK (Sri Lanka – risk on return – exclusion clause) Sri Lanka* [2004] UKIAT 00089 where the parties and the tribunal agreed that the Adjudicator was wrong to apply Article 1F(a) where the claimant had been an active fighter in the LTTE. Although he had been responsible for the deaths of soldiers, there was no evidence that these killings were unlawful acts of war.

War crimes are crimes committed within the context of war, in violation of the law of war 'including the mistreatment of civilians and prisoners of war, or the infliction of unjustified property damage during wartime' (Hathaway 1991:216). Originally, they were conceived of as occurring only in wars between nations, but the International Criminal Tribunal for Former Yugoslavia established that they may also occur in inter-nal conflicts (UNHCR Guidelines para 30 and n 20, referring to *Dusko Tadic* case no IT 94 I T).

Crimes against humanity are defined in Article 6(c) of the Charter of the International Military Tribunal as:

Murder, extermination, enslavement, deportation and other inhumane acts committed against any civilian population, before or during war; or persecutions on political, racial or religious grounds in execution of or in connection with any crime within the jurisdiction of the Tribunal, whether or not in violation of the domestic law of the country where perpetrated.

Symes' *Case Law on the Refugee Convention* (2000) quotes an example from the Canadian case of *Sivakumar v Canada* (MEI) [1994] 1 FC 433 to show that private individuals may commit such a crime. Linden JA in *Sivakumar* refers to the *Flick Trial, US Military Tribunal at Nuremberg, Law Reports of Trials of War Criminals*, vol. IX, p. 1 when several industrialists were convicted of crimes against humanity for using slave labour in their factories. In their document Addressing Security Concerns without Undermining refugee protection the UNHCR concurred 'with the view that the 11 September attacks constituted a crime against humanity' (para 13). An individual will only be responsible however if they engaged in a positive act with a conscious intention (UNHCR Guidelines para 39).

The incidental killing of civilians during military action is neither a war crime nor a crime against humanity but the deliberate massacre of the people of a whole village could be both.

14.4.2 Article 1F(b): Serious non-political crimes

Until recently, this was the ground usually used for exclusion in the UK.

14.4.2.1 *Meaning of 'serious non-political crime'*

The leading case on the definition of serious non-political crimes is the case of *T v SSHD* [1996] 2 All ER 865, which concerned a member of an organization in Algeria that intended to secure power, was prepared to use violence to achieve its ends, and had been declared illegal in 1992. The special adjudicator found that the appellant was involved in and had had prior knowledge of a bomb attack on the airport in Algiers in which ten civilians had been killed, although there was a dispute about the level of intended damage and of the appellant's knowledge of that. He had also been engaged in planning a raid on an army barracks to seize arms in which one person had died. The question for the House of Lords was whether these offences were serious non-political crimes. This involved a consideration of what was meant by 'serious', what made a crime political and what degree of involvement in an offence was required to exclude the person concerned from refugee protection. The House of Lords endorsed the UNHCR Handbook's extended section on Article 1F exclusions (paras 151–161), which suggests that a 'serious' crime in this context 'must be a capital crime or a very serious punishable act' (para 155).

The question of the seriousness of the crime and its political or non-political character to an extent run together. The common law character of the crime must be weighed against its political nature. Some crimes are so serious that their common law nature outweighs any political motivation. So in this case, the killing of ten civilians was too great a crime to warrant being called 'political'. There also had to be a sufficient link between the political purpose to be served and the act carried out. Lord Lloyd suggested a test. First of all, for a crime to be political it must be committed for a political purpose, 'that is to say, with the object of overthrowing or subverting or changing the government of a state or inducing it to change its policy'. Second, there must be 'sufficiently close and direct link between the crime and the alleged political purpose. In determining whether such a link exists, the court will bear in mind the means used to achieve the political end, and will have particular regard to whether the crime was aimed at a military or governmental target, on the one hand, or a civilian target on the other, and in either event whether it was likely to involve the indiscriminate killing or injuring of members of the public' (at 787).

T's degree of involvement was held sufficient to exclude him from refugee status. He had not planted the bomb or carried out the raid, but he had planned the raid and was a political organizer for the group which planted the bomb. He had sufficient knowledge of the plan, even if it did not extend to details.

The approach of the tribunal to implementing these principles has not always been consistent. In *Hane* [2002] UKIAT 03945 the appellant was a Maoist Party member in Nepal who had been involved in an armed raid on a police station in which two policemen were injured. This was in the context, described by the tribunal, of a high level of violence between Maoists and State authorities. For a period of time reported by Amnesty International the official figures were 548 Maoists, three soldiers, and one policeman killed. The appellant was excluded from refugee protection by Article 1F, as the criminal nature of his act outweighed the political context in which it was committed. In *Mete* (17980) the appellant's account was disbelieved by the tribunal, but if he had stored arms for Dev Sol as claimed (grenades and a handgun), that would, in the view of the tribunal, have excluded him under Article 1F.

By comparison in *Gnanasegaran* [2002] UKIAT 00583 the appellant was an active member of the LTTE (Tamil Tigers) in Sri Lanka. He and two other members were wanted for the murder of one or two policemen. The tribunal concluded, following T, that this was a political crime. It concluded:

Disturbing though we find it in the circumstances of this case that 'the perpetrator of a repellent crime should insist on the hospitality and protection of any nation whose borders he can manage to penetrate' (from the judgment of Lord Mustill in T...) we consider that this appeal must be allowed.

The comparison of *Hane* and *Gnanasegaran* illustrates the old adage that 'one person's terrorist is another's freedom fighter'. Indeed, Lord Mustill in T used the concept of 'terrorism'; however, there is no internationally accepted definition of terrorism, and the definition in the Terrorism Act 2000 is extremely wide. It is probably more useful and accurate in the application of Article 1F to apply the wording of the Article and to use the test propounded by Lord Lloyd (above). The tribunal in *Gurung* also advised a cautious approach to the notion of 'terrorism', and identifies particular differences between serious nonpolitical crimes and terrorism. For instance, a serious common law robbery or a murder are not terrorism but are serious non-political crimes. The loose use of the word 'terrorist' to describe the appellant without considering the elements of Article 1F was held not to be a sound legal basis for exclusion (*Jesuthasan* 01/TH/01444), though, as will be seen in relation to Article 1F(c), that is changing. In terms of labelling 'terrorists' as excluded under Article 1F(b), there is a fundamental contradiction in that definitions of terrorism refer to its political purpose, and it is generally understood to have one. Terrorism Act 2000 s 1 refers to a 'political, religious or ideological' purpose. The excluded crimes in Article 1F(b) are by definition non-political, so suggesting that the excluded person is a 'terrorist' muddies the water considerably. The phrase 'non-political' does not on the face of it refer to crimes which have a religious or ideological purpose, though it is apparent that the crimes under discussion here do so. Without that, there would be no refugee status as the claimant would be fleeing prosecution not persecution (as the adjudicator had found initially in *Hane*). The argument is that the common law element outweighs the religious or ideological element. The Qualification Directive says that 'particularly cruel actions, even if committed with an allegedly political objective, may be classified as serious non-political crimes'.

14.4.2.2 *Restrictive interpretation*

There are a number of general principles of importance in the application of Article 1F. It has generally been accepted that the Article should be construed restrictively because it deprives a person of protection who would otherwise qualify for refugee status. A decision to exclude them may expose them to persecution (UNHCR Handbook para 180). This principle of construing the Article restrictively was reconsidered by the tribunal in *Gurung*. It was still accepted, but with this qualification:

37. If the underlying purpose of the Refugee Convention is protection of human rights, then it is surely relevant, when applying the Exclusion Clauses, to take account of the extent to which those guilty of Art 1F crimes have violated the human rights of others. As set out in the Preamble, the objects of the Refugee Convention are not confined to protection of the rights of refugees; they begin by referring to the principle that 'human beings shall enjoy fundamental rights and freedoms without discrimination'. In our view, the greater the scale of the violation of the human rights of others by those who perpetrate acts or crimes proscribed by Art 1F, the less rationale there is for a restrictive approach. To take the example of an individual terrorist who exploded a nuclear device in a large city, in such a case we doubt that a restrictive approach should have any place at all.

This said, when the tribunal summarized its conclusions it started with the principle that exclusion clauses should be applied restrictively (para 151).

The tribunal in *AA* (see below) suggested a gloss on this principle in *Gurung*, namely that although the exclusion clauses should be interpreted restrictively, they should not be applied restrictively. This enabled an extension of the use of Article 1F(c) discussed below.

14.4.2.3 *Inclusion before exclusion*

Another established principle, though shaken somewhat by *Gurung*, was that inclusion should be considered before exclusion. In other words, that the question of eligibility for refugee status should be considered before the question of whether the person should be excluded from it. The Lisbon expert roundtable conclusions give a number of reasons for this:

- Exclusion before inclusion risks criminalizing refugees.
- Exclusion is exceptional and it is not appropriate to consider an exception first.
- Non-inclusion, without having to address the question of exclusion, is possible in a number of cases, thereby avoiding having to deal with complex issues (though one might also put this point the other way round).
- Inclusion first enables consideration to be given to protection obligations to family members.
- Inclusion before exclusion allows proper distinctions to be drawn between prosecution and persecution.
- Textually, the 1951 Convention would appear to provide more clearly for inclusion before exclusion...
- Interviews which look at the whole refugee definition allow for information to be collected more broadly and accurately.

We might add another reason, which is that the UNHCR Handbook advises striking a balance between 'the nature of the offence presumed to have been committed by the applicant and the degree of persecution feared' (para 156). This balance cannot be struck if the feared persecution has not been fully considered. However, the same roundtable discussion notes that this practice is declining in states, and in T Lord Mustill said that that the political or non-political character of the offence could not depend upon the consequences that the offender might suffer on return. In the UK the requirement for balance was excluded by Anti-terrorism, Crime and Security Act 2001 s 34, which says that exclusions from refugee status 'shall not be taken to require consideration of the gravity of events or fear' which might give rise to refugee status. This section is tucked away in a statute, rushed through Parliament in three months following the events of 11 September 2001, where refugee protection was not at the top of the agenda.

The Anti-terrorism, Crime and Security Act 2001 (ATCSA) introduced a power for the Secretary of State to certify that an asylum claim which was to be heard before the Special Immigration Appeals Commission is excluded under Article 1F or 33(2) (see below), which prevented the claim for inclusion in the Convention from being heard at all. The Immigration, Nationality and Asylum Act 2006 extends this to appeals before the Asylum and Immigration Tribunal, and thus to all asylum appeals. The statutes make no concession to the principle of 'inclusion before exclusion' as once the Secretary of State has certified, the tribunal must begin considering the statements in the Secretary of State's certificate. If the tribunal agrees with those statements it must dismiss the claim for asylum (before considering any other aspect of the case) (s 33 of the 2001 Act, replaced by s 55 of the 2006 Act).

This is both an extraordinary provision and extraordinary terminology. The phrase 'agrees with' suggests that the certificate contains an opinion rather than facts. Indeed the certificate is 'that the appellant is not entitled to the protection of Article 33 of the Convention' (s 55(1)) because the exclusions apply, which is a legal opinion. There is no scope for challenging the factual basis of the certificate as the only appeal is on a point of law. The only limitation is that where the Secretary of State certifies that Article 33.2 applies in the AIT, as opposed to SIAC, this must be on national security grounds.

14.4.2.4 *Standard of proof*

The standard of proof of allegations which would lead to exclusion is a matter of some importance, even more so following the statutory provisions just discussed, as its establishment will prevent the asylum claim from being heard. The decision in *Gurung* on this point gives grounds for concern that the paramountcy of refugee protection may be lost. The Article says that a person will be excluded if 'there are serious reasons for considering' that they have committed one of the acts discussed. The Lisbon Expert Roundtable says this should be interpreted as a minimum to mean 'clear evidence sufficient to indict', and that in view of the seriousness of the issues and the consequences 'appropriate procedural safeguards derived from human rights law' should be in place (para 17). The UNHCR also suggests that the standard of proof should be higher than 'reasonable suspicion' (Addressing Security Concerns without Undermining Refugee Protection para 17). The tribunal in *Gurung*, invoking the holistic approach in *Karanakaran*, declined to find that the Secretary of State has any legal burden of proof, i.e. that the matters must be proved to a certain standard. It concluded, 'there is no need to go beyond the words of Article 1F, i.e. "...serious reasons for considering..."' (para 95).

In so deciding, the tribunal in *Gurung* endorsed the tribunal's decision in *Thayabaran* (18737) that the Secretary of State bears an evidential burden, i.e. has the obligation to introduce evidence of the alleged actions. However, after that passage, the decision in *Thayabaran* goes on to refer to the distinction drawn by Lord Mustill in T between extradition and exclusion. The importance of this, it said, lay in the burden of proof. It continued:

> In asylum matters, as Lord Mustill said, there is a general duty not to expel unless the exclusion clause applies. In an asylum case (as distinct from an extradition case) it is the Secretary of State who is relying on the exclusion clause. We think that the usual principle 'he who asserts must prove' applies to this issue. The matter was not, however, the subject of argument before us, because Mrs Elam conceded on behalf of the Secretary of State that the respondent bore the burden of proof on this issue.

A similar position was taken in the earlier case of *Kathiripillai* (12250): 'One starts from the position that the burden of proving that the appellant loses the protection of the Convention under this article lies on the respondent'.

Gurung has precedent value as a starred determination 'for the purpose of giving guidance to adjudicators on the proper approach to the Refugee Convention's exclusion clauses at Article 1F' (para 1). It is also a decision of the President of the tribunal and two Vice Presidents and must be regarded as authoritative on this point. There would be an argument to say that the reasons for the approach in *Karanakaran* do not apply to Article 1F. This Article is not, like the refugee determination itself, concerned with speculation about future possibilities, it is concerned with events that have already occurred. The uncertain quality of evidence should not be allowed to dictate the standard of proof when the consequences of a wrong decision could be so serious. It is precisely these consequences which also guided the Court of Appeal in *Karanakaran* to take a holistic view of the assessment of the claim. Contrary to the view stated in *Gurung,* the principles in *Khawaja* [1984] AC 74 could apply to warrant a standard of proof at the higher end of the civil standard, for similar reasons (see chapter 17).

Attractive though this argument is, it is not in tune with current authority. In *Y v SSHD* [2006] UKSIAC 36/2004 the SIAC held that the *Karanakaran* approach applied to whether the appellant was a risk to national security (see chapter 16). This was enough to give 'serious reasons for believing' he could be excluded under Article 1F.

14.4.2.5 *Complicity*

The question of complicity is the question of how implicated the claimant is in the wrongful acts. In the case of T, although the appellant had not planted the bomb or carried out the raid, he had taken part in the planning and preparation of the latter and as a political organizer had at minimum an incriminating level of knowledge of the former. The degree of complicity which will result in exclusion is related to the nature and seriousness of the offence. Knowledge in advance that a demonstration may well erupt into stone-throwing and damage to property is a very different matter from knowledge in advance that a bomb will be planted in a densely populated area. Level of control in the organization may be taken into account. As mentioned above complicity normally entails 'a positive act and conscious intention' (UNHCR Guidelines para 39). This may be affected by duress. In the words of the Nuremberg Tribunal, 'The criterion for criminal responsibility…lies in moral freedom, in the perpetrator's ability to choose with respect to the act of which he is accused' (quoted in UNHCR Guidelines, para 38).

In *Gurung* the question of complicity arose directly as the main evidence against the appellant was his membership of a Maoist organization which used violent means. In the current climate in the UK this starting point raises very significant issues. Subsequent to T, the question in case law has generally been 'what was the claimant's relationship to the offence(s)?' Determination of the character of the offence(s) as political or not and of the claimant's relationship to the offence(s) has taken into account their membership of an organization. In fact it would rarely be the case that an offence would be considered political without the appellant being a member of a political organization.

The tribunal in *Gurung* poses a different question: 'is mere membership at the time of the commission of acts or crimes proscribed by Article 1F enough to entitle an adjudicator to conclude that an appellant is excluded...?' (para 103).

It notes that the consistent approach of previous case law is that mere membership is not enough. However, it seems to depart from that previous approach, suggesting that in certain circumstances membership might be enough. In so doing it endorses the following passage from the UNHCR's *Addressing Security Concerns:*

Where, however, there is sufficient proof that an asylum-seeker belongs to an extremist international terrorist group, such as those involved in the 11 September attacks, voluntary membership could be presumed to amount to personal and knowing participation, or at least acquiescence amounting to complicity in the crimes in question. In asylum procedures, a rebuttable presumption of individual liability could be introduced to handle such cases. Drawing up lists of international terrorist organisations at the international level would facilitate the application of this procedural device since such certification at the international level would carry considerable weight in contrast to lists established by one country alone. The position of the individual in the organisation concerned, including the voluntariness of his or her membership, as well as the fragmentation of certain groups would, however, need to be taken into account. (para 18)

The tribunal says that adopting this approach is necessary 'to reflect the realities of modern day terrorism' (para 106).

The UNHCR calls for an internationally agreed list of relevant organizations. There are indeed a number of initiatives at the international level which are aiming to produce international standards which will effectively combat international terrorism and prevent the refugee system from being used to assist its growth. The European Union has adopted a Proposal for a Council Framework Decision on Combating Terrorism (COM 2001 521), but there are still not effective international lists of organizations membership of which might warrant exclusion from the Refugee Convention.

14.4.2.6 *Effect of UK legislation*

In common with many other countries, the UK uses a national list in the form of organizations which are proscribed under the Terrorism Act 2000. The grounds for proscription are that the organization is concerned in terrorism (s 3) and this is defined as committing, participating in, promoting or encouraging or otherwise engaging in terrorism. The Terrorism Act 2006 adds that an organization promotes or encourages terrorism if it glorifies it. This means to praise or celebrate it in such a way as to give people to understand that such conduct should be emulated and presumably it is something which falls short of 'encouragement'. The commitment to this provision was part of the Prime Minister's statement on what action the government would take after the 7 July bombings in London.

In Sch 2 to the 2000 Act as it received Royal Assent was a list of Irish organizations including the Ulster Defence Association (UDA) and the Irish Republican Army (IRA).

These have been supplemented by Amendment Orders. The first one came into force on 29 March 2001 proscribing a long list of organizations including Al-Qa'ida, the LTTE and the PKK (Terrorism Act 2000 (Proscribed Organizations) (Amendment) Order 2001, SI 2001/1261). The second one, adding four more organizations, came into force on 1 November 2002, and includes by way of explanation:

The entry for Jemaah Islamiyah refers to the organisation using that name that is based in south-east Asia, members of which were arrested by the Singapore authorities in December 2001 in connection with a plot to attack US and other Western targets in Singapore. (Terrorism Act 2000 (Proscribed Organisations) (Amendment) Order 2002, SI 2002/2724)

These orders are an aspect of the UK's contribution to 'the war on terrorism'. As organizations, in the government's view, become implicated in such incidents, they will be proscribed in the UK. A statement made by the Prime Minister on 5 August 2005 on measures the government proposed following the bombings in London in July 2005 expressed an intention to proscribe more organisations, specifically Hizb-ut-Tahrir and the successor organization of Al Muhajiroun. These proposals were highly controversial, and in the event, a further fifteen Islamic organizations were proscribed, though not the two mentioned (Terrorism Act (Proscribed Organisations) (Amendment) Order 2005, SI 2005/2892). Four more organizations were added in 2006 and two more in 2007. What, however, is the meaning of 'proscription'? By Terrorism Act 2000 ss 11, 12, and 13 it is an offence to belong to a proscribed organization or to profess to do so, to invite support for a proscribed organization which is not restricted to money or other property, to arrange or support or address a meeting in order to support a proscribed organization, or to wear an item of clothing or display an article suggesting support for a proscribed organization.

Judging by the Home Office policy referred to in *Gurung*, in the context of Article 1F, the proscription of an organization is being used to provide *prima facie* evidence that the organization falls into the group membership of which, following *Gurung*, raises a presumption against the asylum claimant. There is a defence under Terrorism Act 2000 s 11(2) that the organization was not proscribed when the person charged became a member and that the person has not taken part in the activities of the organization since it was proscribed. The presumption of exclusion under Article 1F should be displaced by establishing the same facts.

There are dangers in making this link between membership of a proscribed organization and exclusion from refugee status, particularly on the basis of a national rather than an international list. The first is that the UNHCR refers to membership of an 'extremist terrorist group'. Although it quoted an obvious example of mass murder of civilians, in general it is not so easy to identify 'an extremist terrorist group'. Kirby J in the Australian case *of Applicant A v MIMA* 190 CLR 225 (Aust. High Ct, Feb 24 1997) famously said of particular social groups under the Convention that judges 'will recognize persecuted groups of particularity when they see them'. This approach has not been followed, and it is suggested that the 'I know one when I see one' approach to extremist terrorist groups also will not satisfy the rule of law. However, this is what is risked in the absence of any international definition, even of terrorism, let alone of 'extremist groups'.

There is an all too obvious danger that a national list will include groups for political reasons. Without scope to recognise that 'one man's terrorist is another man's freedom fighter', the Refugee Convention would be undermined, as persecution for reasons of political opinion is an archetypal qualification for refugee status. It is easy to recognize the events of 11 September 2001 as an atrocity, but it is not easy to derive a principle from this.

Already the proscribed list in the UK has the capacity to make a significant impact on refugee claims. As mentioned, the LTTE and PKK are included. Very many asylum claims from Sri Lanka are brought by LTTE members. Similarly, a large number of Turkish claims are brought by members of the PKK or indeed other proscribed groups. However, in cases such as *Gnanasegaran* referred to above, the applicant member of the LTTE was awarded refugee status even when he had committed very serious crimes because he faced ill-treatment for reasons of political opinion and his crimes were political ones. The connection of the events of 11 September 2001 with this aspect of refugee status is potentially very damaging to the whole refugee framework of protection. Taking UNHCR's whole document, rather than individual paragraphs, the implication is that membership of an 'extremist terrorist group' could be taken as *prima facie* evidence of a crime against humanity, i.e. using paragraph (a) rather than paragraph (b) of Article 1F. If the matter were approached like this, there would be less concern that people would be wrongly excluded from refugee status. Complicity in a crime against humanity is a very serious charge which could only be approached with great care and requiring significant proof. However, there is a danger that the approach in the UK as exemplified by the Home Office policy referred to in *Gurung*, will result in membership of a nationally proscribed organization (proscription being achieved simply by Order of the Secretary of State) being regarded as *prima facie* evidence of involvement in a serious nonpolitical crime. The contradiction here is apparent, that membership of a political organization is *prima facie* evidence of non-political criminal activity. There is a plausible confusion in the UK because membership of the proscribed organization is a crime, that this will be regarded as grounds for exclusion under Article 1F, even though the crime is clearly political.

14.4.3 Article 1F: Acts contrary to purpose and principles of UN

The purpose of this paragraph was summarized in the Canadian case of *Pushpanathan* [1998] 1 SCR by Bastarache J: 'The rationale is that those who are responsible for the persecution which creates refugees should not enjoy the benefits of a Convention designed to protect refugees' (para 63). There is no explicit restriction in this paragraph, or paragraph (a), to acts carried out before arriving in the country of refuge, although there is in paragraph (b). A likely reason for this is that the drafters of the Convention had in mind those people to whom this paragraph has traditionally been applied, namely 'only to those operating on a state level and perpetrating crimes of national or international significance' (Pretzell *et al* 2002:149 and UNHCR Guidelines 2003). Article 33.2 provides for exclusion of individuals on account of their actions after arrival in the country of refuge. It was probably not in the minds of the drafters that provision would be needed to exclude people who committed political crimes after arrival in the country of refuge (see Goodwin-Gill and McAdam for the drafting history). However, *Pushpanathan* countenanced some extension:

The category of persons covered by Art 1F(c) was not, however, restricted to persons in positions of power. Although it may be more difficult for a non-state actor to perpetrate human rights violations on a scale amounting to persecution without the State thereby implicitly adopting those acts, the possibility should not be excluded.

Article 1F(c) was a little-used provision, but it has recently been invoked far more and is being used to deny or revoke refugee status where refugees are suspected of international terrorist activity in the country of refuge. In *Singh and Singh v SSHD* (SIAC 31 July 2000) the Special Immigration Appeals Commission held that Sikh activists who were supporting armed struggle in India from the UK could be excluded from refugee status under Article 1F(c). They had conspired to commit acts of violence in India and had been involved in transporting explosives. The fact that these actions were in pursuance of a fight for self-determination did not provide a defence against exclusion. They could not have been excluded under Article 1F(b) because these acts were committed after arrival in the country of refuge. The SIAC found that as there was no express limitation of Article 1F(c) to individuals carrying governmental authority, none should be implied. The crucial finding was that the UN unequivocally condemns terrorism. The actions of Singh and Singh could be brought within the definition of terrorism in the UK (Terrorism Act 2000 s 1). Therefore terrorist acts such as these were contrary to the purpose and principles of the UN.

Singh was followed in the Immigration and Asylum Tribunal in *KK (Article 1F(c)), Turkey)* [2004] UKIAT 00101, a decision which bears close examination. The claimant had been active in Kurdish politics while living in Turkey, had been arrested, detained and interrogated on seven occasions, and had fled after being implicated in a serious bombing incident. He had been active in the PKK (Kurdistan Workers Party) and Dev Sol, which became DHKP-C. Both are proscribed organisations in the UK (see below). The Secretary of State accepted that he had a well-founded fear of persecution in Turkey because of his political opinions. Before his asylum claim was determined, KK was found guilty of arson and conspiracy to commit arson in relation to attacks in London on a Turkish travel agent and Turkish bank. No-one was injured in the attacks.

The Secretary of State sought to exclude him from refugee status under Article 1F(c). UNHCR argued that the crimes referred to in this paragraph are those with an international or global dimension, capable of affecting relations between states. The use should be exceptional and usually confined to those in positions of power or influence. Although it could be appropriate to broaden it to include individuals who committed acts of terrorism with international consequences, this should only be done in the most extreme cases. This follows *Pushpanathan.*

The tribunal held that the act was political, as it was continuing the fight against the Turkish government in which the claimant had been involved in Turkey. In the country of refuge no distinction should be drawn between common crime and political crime. The refugee would be subject to that legal system. The tribunal concludes:

there are some acts which, despite being political or politically-inspired, do not depend for their criminality on the individual matrix of power within a particular state. These acts, in our view, are those which are intended to be covered by Article 1F(c). That subparagraph does not apply to every crime, nor to every political crime. It applies to acts which are the subject of intense disapproval by the governing body of the entire international community. (para 85)

This is the crux of the tribunal's decision. The act that KK had committed came within the UK's controversial and wide definition of terrorism under Terrorism Act 2000 s 1. The UN condemned terrorism and so his action brought him within Article 1F(c).

KK was followed in *AA (Palestine)* [2005] UKIAT 00104 ILU vol.8 no. 12 in which the appellant had been arrested while on a suicide bombing mission. The tribunal criticized the adjudicator for not raising the question of Article 1F. Whether paragraph b or c would be applied would be left to the adjudicator, but the advantage to the Secretary of State in using paragraph c was evident here as the tribunal held that paragraph c contains no requirement that the crime in question be non-political in order to attract exclusion, therefore if an act is accepted to come within this paragraph there does not need to be any enquiry into whether the common law criminal element outweighs any political motivation. Ironically, this may result in a lesser crime giving rise to exclusion under Article 1F(c) than under 1F(b), even though the apparent intention is the other way round. The UNHCR Handbook and guidance was rejected even more emphatically than in *KK* as an authority on the interpretation of the Convention, and UN material condemning terrorism relied on instead.

The matter is put beyond doubt by Immigration, Asylum and Nationality Act 2006 s 54:

In the construction and application of Article 1F(c) of the Refugee Convention the reference to acts contrary to the purposes and principles of the United Nations shall be taken as including, in particular –

(a) acts of committing, preparing or instigating terrorism (whether or not the acts amount to an actual or inchoate offence), and

(b) acts of encouraging or inducing others to commit, prepare or instigate terrorism (whether or not the acts amount to an actual or inchoate offence).

Here, instead of enacting a domestic equivalent, as it did with Article 31 discussed earlier, Parliament has enacted a definitive interpretation of an international Convention. The effect is surely coming closer to the vision that Lauterpacht warned against, the international community becomes 'one of mutual insurance for the maintenance of established governments' (see previous chapter).

The tribunal in *KK* and *AA* rejected the argument that sentences served for offences committed served to expiate the crime so that the person would no longer be excluded from international protection.

KK was followed by the Court of Appeal in *MT (Algeria), RB (Algeria) & U (Algeria) v SSHD* [2007] EWCA Civ 808. It was argued for the appellants that acts in the country of refuge could not exclude a person from refugee status under Article 1F(c), but the Court of Appeal disagreed. The other issues which were considered at length in *Singh*, *KK* and *AA* concerning the nature of the acts and the person responsible were not argued in *MT*, nor in *Abu Qatada v SSHD* [2007] UKSIAC 15/2005, which came to the same conclusion. This nature of the acts was not even raised in the Court of Appeal, but in the case of *MT* at the SIAC stage (then known as *Y*), as in *Abu Qatada*, the Commission simply said that 'the acts which the SSHD relied on showed that the Appellant had been guilty of acts contrary to the purposes and principles of the UN' (*Abu Qatada* para 104, *Y* para 147). These deportation cases were based on national security assessments by the Secretary of State. By their very nature, such assessments do not necessarily require past actions to be proved against the appellant (see chapters 8 and 16), and in these cases there were no criminal convictions of any of the appellants in the UK. MT had been acquitted in the ricin plot trial, and there were two outstanding convictions of Abu Qatada in Jordan. However, Article 1F only requires 'serious reasons for believing' that acts contrary to the purpose and principles of the UN have been committed. The upshot of this seems to be that in the case of Article 1F(c) an individual may be excluded from refugee status on a far lower standard of proof than would be required in a criminal trial to convict them of the same matters. It is arguable whether this accords with the view of Goodwin-Gill and McAdam:

Article 1F(c) ought only to be applied, therefore, where there are serious reasons to consider that the individual concerned has committed an offence specifically identified by the international community as one which must be addressed in the fight against terrorism, and only by way of a procedure confirming to due process and the State's obligations generally in international law. (2007:197)

14.4.4 Article 33(2)

One argument against Article 1F applying to acts in the country of refuge is that, if it does, it duplicates Article 33(2), which certainly fills that role. Article 33(2) of the Refugee Convention provides an exception to the *non-refoulement* obligation. This is where there are 'reasonable grounds' for regarding the refugee as 'a danger to the security of the country in which he is' or in relation to a person 'who, having been convicted by a final judgment of a particularly serious crime constitutes a danger to that country'. This paragraph has also not been often used, but by way of example was held to go against the appellant in *A v SSHD* CA 16/2/2004. He had been convicted in the UK of a serious sexual assault on his daughter, and of the rape of a woman.

The effect of the exclusion is to allow *refoulement,* rather than, as with Article 1F, exclusion from refugee status. This provision is intended for use where a refugee engages in serious criminal activity in the host country. The emphasis is on danger to the country, i.e. conviction of a particularly serious crime should not of itself warrant exclusion if the person would not constitute a danger to the country. Goodwin-Gill says:

Application of Article 33(2) ought always to involve the question of proportionality, with account taken of the nature of the consequences likely to befall the refugee on return. The offence in question and the perceived threat to the community would need to be extremely grave if danger to the life of the refugee were to be disregarded, although a less serious offence and a lesser threat might justify the return of an individual likely to face only some harassment or discrimination. (1996:140)

If the state succeeds in arguing under Article 33(2) that a refugee ought to be returned, their actual return may still be prevented by Article 3 of the Human Rights Act. If their refugee status is revoked under Article 1F they lose any rights and privileges that go with that status. The Qualification Directive provides for refugee status to be revoked on grounds equivalent to Article 33(2). The Criminal Justice and Immigration Bill also proposes that a person excluded from refugee status under Article 1F or Article 33.2 may be designated, and lose the right to any protective status at all, if they cannot be returned to their country for human rights reasons.

14.4.5 UK legislation affecting Article 33.2

UK statute now contradicts Goodwin-Gill's principles in two ways. First, as mentioned earlier, ATCSA s 34 prevents precisely this question of proportionality from being taken into account in *refoulement* under Article 33(2) as well as exclusion under Article 1F. The tribunal in *A v SSHD* held that there was no reason to restrict the application of s 34 to terrorist cases. It is generally worded, and despite its inclusion in an anti-terrorism statute, there is no other evidence that it should be restricted to that context. The question under Article 33(2) was whether the appellant was a danger to the public.

Second, Nationality, Immigration and Asylum Act 2002 s 72(2) resiles entirely from the obligation to make the necessary judgment under Article 33(2) as to danger to the community. It says:

A person shall be *presumed* to have been convicted by a final judgment of a particularly serious crime and to constitute a danger to the community of the United Kingdom if he is –

(a) convicted in the United Kingdom of an offence, and

(b) sentenced to a period of imprisonment of at least two years. (emphasis added)

By s 72(11) this does not include a suspended sentence but does include a hospital order. The offence of belonging to a proscribed organization under Terrorism Act 2000 s 11 carries a maximum sentence of 10 years. This comes close to making membership of the LTTE, PKK, and so on grounds for *refoulement* without the commission of any serious non-political crime, although the presumption in s 72(2) is rebuttable.

The impact of s 72 took a further leap on 12 August 2004 with the coming into force of the Nationality, Immigration and Asylum Act 2002 (Specification of Particularly Serious Crimes) Order 2004, SI 2004/1910. This is made under the power in s 72(4) to specify further crimes, having the same effect as a conviction under s 72(2). The order specified 183 offences including not only rape, murder and stockpiling biological weapons, but also theft, entering a building as a trespasser intending to steal and aggravated taking of a vehicle. Section 72 is stated to be 'for the purpose and construction of article 33.2 of the Refugee Convention. The Parliamentary Joint Committee on Human Rights advised the government that the Order was incompatible with Article 33(2) of the Refugee Convention 'because it includes within its scope a number of offences which do not amount to "particularly serious crimes" within the meaning of Article 33(2)' (Joint Committee on Human Rights Session 2003–04 Twenty-second Report). As the Human Rights Committee pointed out, legislation which is designed to give effect to international obligations must be interpreted compatibly with those obligations. If the order is incompatible with the Convention then it follows that it is *ultra vires* the 2002 Act. The Committee made this finding, and went on to express doubts about the compatibility of s 72 itself with the Refugee Convention on the grounds that a presumption undermined the case by case basis of refugee determination, reversed the burden or proof as stated in Article 33.2, and precluded the application of a proper proportionality test to each case (paras 32–36). Goodwin-Gill and McAdam consider the section incompatible for these reasons (2007:183). The provisions also drew strong criticism from the UNHCR (see press release 7 November 2004), but the government was undeterred.

SB Haiti [2005] UKIAT 00036 was decided after the implementation of s 72 but on pre-2002 Act law, as the decision under appeal had been taken prior to the 2002 Act. Here, a history of repeated offending including burglary, theft, possession of an imitation firearm was held not in itself to constitute a danger to the community such as to deprive the appellant of the protection of Article 33, unless he had, following the words of 33.2, been convicted of a 'particularly serious crime'. This had to be taken literally, the tribunal thought, and none of the above offences would qualify. He lost his refugee status however because he had also committed an offence of wounding, which the tribunal thought was 'particularly serious'. Interestingly, this had been committed after receiving indefinite leave to remain as a refugee, and the tribunal did not think that should affect its view of the matter.

Section 72 seemed initially to make it easier to remove a refugee than another person convicted of a criminal offence. However, the field has been levelled by the UK Borders Act 2007 ss 32–39. As discussed in chapter 16, these sections make deportation automatic in many cases, including where a person has committed any of the crimes specified under s 72 and has received a custodial sentence of any length. Those denied refugee status have become a trial group for powers extended to others.

This section sets a disturbing precedent in legislating in contravention of the Convention, not only of its spirit, but also of its express terms in Article 33(2). As there is no international body charged with the enforcement of refugee law, there is no mechanism for striking down such a legislative provision. The combination of s 72 and the new re-interpretation of Article 1F(c) discussed above means that the potential sanctions against refugees and asylum seekers for criminal acts, even against property, are extremely serious.

Section 72 is also used in the Criminal Justice and Immigration Act as the basis for a new form of deprivation of rights: 'designation' by the Secretary of State, which deprives a person of leave to enter or remain, or prevents them from attaining it. In addition to people excluded from refugee status, people may be designated if they have committed an offence specified under s 72 and cannot be deported from the UK for human rights reasons. The effect will be to deprive the person of social benefits including housing, though some limited provision is made for accommodation and support through vouchers.

14.4.6 **Article 32**

This Article, in contrast to Article 1F and 33(2), gives a refugee protection against expulsion and in that respect complements Article 33(1), but its terms are surprisingly weak. It applies to recognized refugees, and says that they shall not be expelled save on grounds of national security or public order. Proper legal process for appeal must be allowed. In effect this makes a refugee in the UK liable to deportation like any other foreign national, but with a higher threshold to be reached by the state to justify expulsion. Also, this is not a *refoulement* provision. The state must allow the refugee a reasonable period within which to seek admission to another country.

14.5 **Conclusion**

The direction of change in Europe is towards curtailing asylum rights. European developments promise a less secure status for refugees and a greater willingness to exclude by reason of the threat posed by individuals. The UK, however, has already expanded the use of exclusion and even the defining conditions which enable it to take place. The linkage made between asylum and terrorism, has been demonstrated in this chapter not just to be political talk but a matter of law.

QUESTIONS

1 Why does the Refugee Convention exclude from protection those who have committed a serious non-political crime? Is there still a justification for limiting this exclusion to

non-political crimes? What would be the effect of excluding people from protection for any serious crime?

2 Why might an asylum seeker travel on a false document?

3 The offence under s 2 of the 2004 Act is committed in transit to or on arrival in the UK. How is its deterrent effect achieved?

 online resource centre For guidance on answering questions, visit www.oxfordtextbooks.co.uk/orc/clayton3e.

FURTHER READING

Bowring, B. and Korff, D. (2004) 'Terrorist Designation with regard to European and International Law: the case of the PMOI', Paper for International Conference of Jurists, 10 November 2004.

Brennan, R. (2006) *Immigration Advice at the Police Station*, 3rd edn (Law Society Publishing).

Bruin, R., and Wouters, K. (2003) 'Terrorism and the Non-derogability of *non-refoulement' International Journal of Refugee Law* vol. 15, no. 1, pp. 30–67.

Finch, N. (2002) 'Refugee or terrorist?' *Journal of Immigration, Asylum & Nationality Law* vol. 16, no. 3, pp. 144–147.

Gilbert. G, (2001) Current issues in the application of the exclusion clauses', UNHCR Global Consultations on International Protection.

—— (2003). 'Protection after September 11th' *International Journal of Refugee Law* vol. 15, no. 1, pp. 1–4.

Lindsley, F. (2003) 'Compensation and Prosecution – asylum seekers travelling on false documents after *ex p Adimi', Journal of Immigration, Asylum & Nationality Law* vol. 17, no. 2, pp. 144–147.

Pretzell, A., Krushnder, D., and Hruschka, C. (2002) 'Terrorism and the 1951 Refugee Convention' *Journal of Immigration, Asylum & Nationality Law* vol. 16, no. 3, pp. 148–165.

Saul, B. (2004) 'Exclusion of Suspected Terrorists from Asylum: Trends in International and European Refugee Law' Institute for International Integration Studies, Discussion Paper, no. 26, July 2004.

UNHCR (2002), *Addressing Security Concerns without Undermining Refugee Protection.*

—— (2003) 'Guidelines on International Protection: Application of Exclusion clauses: Article 1F of the Convention Relating to the Status of Refugees'.

Walker, C. (2007) 'The Treatment of Foreign Terror Suspects', *Modern Law Review* vol. 70, no. 3, pp. 427–457.

SECTION 6

Enforcement

15

Detention

SUMMARY

The deprivation of liberty is one of the most serious infringements of fundamental human rights. In immigration law, individuals may lose their liberty through the exercise of a statutory discretion by the Home Office or immigration officers, and so guidelines and safeguards for the exercise of this discretion are crucial. The statutory powers and executive guidelines are examined here, together with the human rights and common law rules which apply. Legal provisions are set in the context of empirical research into detention decisions. The use of detention is seen as an increasingly frequent phenomenon in the asylum process, and the former use of indefinite detention for foreign terrorist suspects is also considered.

15.1 Introduction

'In English law every imprisonment is *prima facie* unlawful, and...it is for a person directing imprisonment to justify his act'. These well-known words of Lord Atkin in the wartime internment case of *Liversidge* v *Anderson* [1942] AC 206 at 245 are still a proper statement of legal principle. Detention is not lawful unless authorized by law. This is the reverse of the usual rule in English law, whereby anything is lawful providing it is not specifically prohibited. Detention however interferes with one of the most basic human rights, that of physical liberty, and the advent of the Human Rights Act 1998 strengthens the common law by providing in Article 5 a statutory right which may only be infringed in prescribed circumstances. The deprivation of physical liberty is regarded as the most serious punishment available in the criminal justice system in the UK. Nevertheless, in the immigration and asylum system, detention may be imposed upon people who are not charged with any crime nor even suspected of committing one.

In this chapter we shall consider, first, human rights law having a bearing on immigration detention; second, who is detained in the UK presently under immigration powers; and third, the parameters of the domestic law power to detain.

15.2 Human rights standards

International human rights instruments show unanimity on the issue of detention. United Nations Declaration of Human Rights Article 9: 'No-one shall be subjected to arbitrary arrest, detention and exile;' International Covenant on Civil and Political

Rights Article 9(1): 'Everyone has the right to liberty and security of person. No one shall be subjected to arbitrary arrest or detention'; European Convention on Human Rights Article 5: 'Everyone has the right to liberty and security of person. No one shall be deprived of his liberty save in the following cases and in accordance with a procedure prescribed by law...'.

All these three international human rights documents demonstrate a concern with arbitrariness, a key principle in assessing the lawfulness of detention, and this is a matter of both the content and process of decision-making. The United Nations Human Rights Commission's Working Group on Arbitrary Detention sets out three criteria of arbitrariness:

- When there is no legal basis for the detention.
- When detention is imposed as a state response to the exercise of a fundamental right.
- When the total or partial non-observance of the norms of a fair trial is of such gravity as to make the resulting detention arbitrary.

The UNHCR Working Group visits countries to investigate their detention practice. They visited the UK in 1998 to examine the situation of migrants and asylum seekers in detention, and identified a number of concerns relating to

- reasons for detention,
- duration of detention,
- availability of independent review of detention,
- and limited consideration of other options before resorting to detention.

In terms of the qualities of arbitrariness identified by the UNHCR Working Group, these concerns in the UK mainly relate to the first criterion – the legal basis for detention. These themes have persisted in critique of the UK's detention practices. The organization Bail for Immigration Detainees (BID) identified governmental failure to address the recommendations of the Working Group, and made a submission in 2002 to the Working Group, inviting it to return to the UK for a further inspection.

The Human Rights Act principles, as contained in Article 5 ECHR, are concerned with similar issues:

- Detention must be for a reason specified in Article 5, and no other
- Only imposed through a procedure prescribed by law
- That law should protect the individual from arbitrariness, both in content and process
- The detained person has a right to reasons for their detention
- They must be able to challenge their detention.

15.2.1 Human Rights Act

Article 5 ECHR begins with a presumption of liberty: 'Everyone has the right to liberty and security of person'. The principles upon which this liberty may be curtailed, as contained in Article 5, may be summarized as follows:

- Article 5.1 'No-one shall be deprived of his liberty save in the following cases...'

In other words, detention must be for a reason specified in Article 5, and no other. Unlike the qualified rights in the Convention which may be interfered with in the interests of broad public policy objectives, the right to liberty may be interfered with for specified purposes only. Two of these relate to immigration: 'to prevent unauthorized entry' into the country; and 'detention of a person against whom action is being taken with a view to deportation or extradition' (Art 5(1)(f)).

- Article 5(1) '...and in accordance with a procedure prescribed by law...'

This has a similar meaning to that employed in other Convention Articles which require that a measure infringing a right must be 'prescribed by law'. This means that the detention is in accordance with substantive and procedural rules of national law (*Conka* v *Belgium* (2002) 34 EHRR 54), and that the quality of that law is compatible with the rule of law (*Amuur v France* (1996) 22 EHRR 533 para 50). It requires that the legal provision in question be accessible and precise.

This requirement is an aspect of lawfulness. Each of the listed reasons for detention in Article 5.1 is preceded by the word 'lawful'.

The second limb of lawfulness in the context of Article 5 is that the detention 'should be in keeping with the purpose of Article 5, namely to protect the individual from arbitrariness' (*Chahal v UK* (1996) 23 EHRR 413, *Amuur v France*, *Conka* v *Belgium*). The case law of the ECHR on the question of arbitrariness shares some of the principles identified by that the UN Working Group on Arbitrary Detention, for instance, procedural fairness, limits on the duration of detention, the legitimacy of reasons for detention, and the availability of review.

15.2.1.1 *Procedural fairness*

In *Conka v Belgium* the Court found a breach of Article 5.1 in that the reasons given for detention were misleading. Notices were sent to about 70 asylum seekers, requiring them to attend police stations to enable the files concerning their asylum applications to be completed. At the police station they were served with an order to leave Belgium, a decision for their removal to their country of origin and notice of their detention for that purpose. They were detained and removed.

The ECtHR found that this was a breach of Article 5.1 in that the wording of the notice which brought them to the police station was a deliberate ploy by the authorities to mislead the applicants in order to ensure the compliance of the largest possible number. The Court said that the action of the police in misleading asylum seekers about the purpose for which they were requested to attend the police station and thereby detaining them by deception could be found to contravene the principle against arbitrariness.

The mass nature of the deception practised by the police in this case attracted particular criticism by the Court. In addition to Article 5.1, the Court by a narrow majority found a violation of Protocol 4 Article 4, which prohibits collective expulsion of aliens.

Conka v Belgium has an uncomfortable echo in Weber and Gelsthorpe's research on UK detention decisions (2000). They discuss individuals called for interview to hear the final result of their asylum claim. No deception is alleged, but the statements of some immigration officers interviewed reveal a discomfort with lack of information. For instance:

What I remembered about the interviews and feeling uncomfortable about it was that often the asylum seeker would come to those interviews not realising what they amounted to, and then they would be detained. It sort of felt wrong to me. But you see if they were told they probably wouldn't have shown up. (p. 92)

15.2.1.2 *Limit on duration of detention*

In *Chahal* the European Court of Human Rights held that where a person was detained with a view to deportation, the principle of lawfulness required that the deportation proceedings should be 'prosecuted with due diligence' (para 113). If they were not, the detention would cease to be lawful. Mr Chahal had been in detention for four years by the time of his application to the ECtHR. Two further years were spent waiting for his case to reach the Court, bringing his total detention to six years, though the Court could only consider the legality of the first four. The domestic proceedings were complex, involving deportation proceedings, two refusals of asylum, two applications for judicial review, the second of which was also refused on appeal by the Court of Appeal, and then refusals of leave to appeal to the House of Lords by both its Judicial Committee and the Court of Appeal. The ECtHR commented that the case involved 'considerations of an extremely serious and weighty nature'. It went on to say, 'It is neither in the interests of the individual applicant nor in the general public interest in the administration of justice that such decisions be taken hastily' (para 117). While a lack of due diligence could give rise to a breach of Article 5.1(f) as a violation of the principle of lawfulness, the Court here held that there had not been undue delay on the part of the government.

In *Amuur* v *France* four asylum seekers were detained at an airport in the international zone. Their conditions were fairly comfortable, and they were free physically to board another flight out of France, although their safety in the event of this could not be assured. The government argued that this did not amount to detention. The Court said that such conditions were a restriction on liberty. This might be necessary to prevent unauthorized entry, but should not be unduly prolonged. In this case they were restricted for 20 days. This length of time turned a restriction into a deprivation of liberty, which is detention.

15.2.1.3 *Quality of legal reasons*

Article 5.2 requires that everyone 'should be informed promptly' in a language that they understand, of the reasons for their detention. The quality of legal reasons for detention also has a bearing on the question of arbitrariness.

In *Dougoz v Greece* (2002) 34 EHRR 61 the ECtHR considered the quality of the domestic law which authorized Mr Dougoz's detention, in the light of the Court's principles on arbitrariness and the rule of law. Mr Dougoz had been released from detention after a criminal sentence on the explicit view of the indictments chamber that he was not a danger, would be unlikely to commit further offences, and need not be detained. This being the case, his detention was not actually authorized by domestic law, and so would have fallen at the first hurdle. However, there was a purported authorization in domestic law, in that the Deputy Public Prosecutor offered the opinion that an executive rule, which enabled detention of those who were subject to expulsion by administrative order, could be applied by analogy. The ECtHR did not consider that the opinion of a senior public prosecutor 'constituted a "law" of sufficient "quality" within the meaning of the Court's case law' (para 57). This case has close parallels in the UK, as we shall see in discussion of detention after a prison sentence, below.

The quality of legal reasons may initially be accepted, but may become unlawful if the reasons cease to apply. In the case of *Chahal* the alleged threat to national security posed by Mr Chahal was accepted by the Court to be a sufficient reason, but to avoid arbitrariness there needed to be a check on the continuing application of this reason. This check was provided by the former advisory panel (see chapters 8 and 16).

15.2.1.4 *Review of detention*

The availability of review is a separate heading of challenge under the ECHR, as Article 5.4 provides:

Everyone who is deprived of his liberty by arrest or detention shall be entitled to take proceedings by which the lawfulness of his detention shall be decided speedily by a court and his release order if the detention is not lawful.

In the case of *Chahal v UK* the former advisory panel procedure was held to be a sufficient guarantee against arbitrary reasons, in that the panel could review the grounds for detention and check that it was still warranted in the interests of national security. There was therefore no breach of Article 5.1. However, it did not satisfy the requirements of Article 5.4 as the panel did not have the qualities of a 'court'. It lacked the normal qualities of judicial procedure, the right to representation, to notice of the case against the appellant, and so on. Even allowing for the need of the state for secrecy in national security matters, some fairer procedure could be devised. This decision led to the demise of the advisory panel and the creation of the Special Immigration Appeals Commission (see chapter 8).

15.2.1.5 *Use of the Human Rights Act*

A judgment in the High Court illustrates that beginning with the obligation in s 3 Human Rights Act and fundamental nature of the right to liberty can influence an outcome (*R (on the application of Amirthanathan)* [2003] EWHC 1107 (Admin)). The principle of proportionality inclined the judge in this case to find the detention unlawful.

 Key Case

R (on the application of Amirthanathan) [2003] EWHC 1107 (Admin)

It is Home Office policy not to detain a person pending an appeal (and see Immigration Act 1971 Sch 2 para 29). The claimant's solicitor had indicated an intention to appeal, and had 10 days within which to lodge the appeal. Before the appeal could be lodged the claimant was detained. He was released three days after the appeal was lodged. Singh J held that detention was disproportionate.

On reaching the Court of Appeal, *Amirthanathan* was joined with the case of *Nadarajah* (see below). The question of proportionality in relation to Article 5(1)(f) was taken further. Counsel for the appellants argued that the application of proportionality in *Saadi* meant that detention needed to be proportionate to the reasons for it, that is, in these cases, where detention in Article 5(1)(f) terms was 'with a view to deportation', proportionate to the assistance with removal that it afforded (*Nadarajah & Amirthanathan v SSHD* [2003] EWCA Civ 1768 para 46). The Court of Appeal disagreed. The ECtHR in *Chahal* had held that detention did not need to be reasonably necessary for the purposes of deportation; the court thought this disposed of an argument which related the proportionality of the detention to the reason for it.

In both *Amirthanathan* and *Nadarajah* the Court of Appeal found that the detentions fell foul of Article 5 because acting on a policy that was undisclosed did not comply with the requirement that the detention be prescribed by law; the policy was not accessible (paras 67, 69 and 72).

In *R (on application of Hindawi & Headley) v SSHD* [2006] UKHL 54 the House of Lords, overturning the Court of Appeal, unanimously found that the right of prisoners who were subject to a deportation order to have their case referred to the Parole Board came within the ambit of Article 5. Denying referral to the Parole Board on grounds of their nationality (as prisoners subject to deportation, which British national prisoners were not) was discrimination contrary to Article 14. It was objectively unjustifiable, as individual decisions about prisoner release were for the body experienced in this task, and were not (interestingly) 'political' decisions to be made by a government minister.

15.2.2 Detention of asylum seekers

Additional human rights considerations apply in the detention of asylum seekers. Article 14 of the Universal Declaration of Human Rights provides that the 'right to seek and enjoy asylum' is a basic human right. Clearly, a person should not be detained *for* seeking asylum. In the absence of lawful routes to enter and claim asylum, it is sometimes difficult to see the difference between being detained as an illegal entrant and being detained as an asylum seeker. As UNHCR acknowledges, asylum seekers 'may not be in a position to comply with the legal formalities for entry' and may be 'forced to arrive at, or enter, a territory illegally' (Guidelines on applicable Criteria and Standards Relating to the Detention of Asylum Seekers (February 1999). Detention of asylum seekers as illegal entrants, though widely accepted in Europe, looks like a *prima facie* breach of Article 31 of the Refugee Convention (see chapter 14).

Additional humanitarian reasons may apply in the case of asylum seekers, who may have been tortured or come from a war zone or have otherwise already suffered in detention.

The UNHCR Guidelines say that, in exceptional circumstances, asylum seekers may be detained, subject to strict compliance with principles of non-discrimination and against arbitrariness. The 15th meeting of the Standing Committee in June 1999 suggested that exceptional reasons, which should be 'clearly prescribed in national law', would be:

(a) to verify identity;
(b) to determine the elements on which the claim for refugee status or asylum is based, but not 'for the entire status determination procedure, or for an unlimited period of time';
(c) in cases where asylum-seekers, acting in bad faith, have destroyed their travel and/or identity documents or have used fraudulent documents intentionally to mislead the authorities of the State in which they have claimed asylum;
(d) to protect national security and public safety.

Unaccompanied minors and pregnant and nursing mothers should not be detained, and alternatives to detention should be actively sought in the case of unaccompanied elderly people, those who have suffered torture or trauma, or who have a mental or physical disability. People in these groups should only be detained after medical advice that detention would not adversely affect their health or well-being.

The Guidelines advise that asylum seekers should not be detained in prisons, and that where this is unavoidable they should not be detained with those who are detained for criminal justice reasons, i.e. convicted or remand prisoners. Basic hygiene, medical, exercise, and legal facilities should be provided. There should be segregation of women and men and the opportunity for religious activity and contact with friends and relatives. While the guidelines do not have any binding effect, Simon Brown LJ in *R v Uxbridge Magistrates' Court ex p Adimi, R v Crown Prosecution Service ex p Sorani, R v SSHD ex p Kaziu* [2000] 3 WLR 434 at 444 said that they should be given 'considerable weight'.

15.3 Who is detained in the UK?

In the first decade after the Immigration Act 1971 came into force, the power to detain, granted by that Act, was used mainly as a way of enforcing a refusal of leave to enter. For instance, a visitor or student who had been refused at the port might be detained overnight (see for example Weber and Gelsthorp 2000). Lengthy detention beyond this was rare.

From the mid-1980s the number of asylum applications began to rise, and the Home Office was not able to process asylum applications quickly enough to prevent a backlog arising. A survey by the Joint Council for the Welfare of Immigrants revealed an increasing resort to detention as a matter of course to manage asylum applications (Ashford 1993). From a few hours to resolve some outstanding point, or to effect removal, immigration detention quite commonly extended to weeks or months. It is still the case that, although asylum seekers number less than a quarter of people removed from the UK each year, they constitute around three-quarters of the people in immigration detention.

Only limited weight should be placed upon these figures. The way that asylum and detention statistics are collected and presented makes it difficult to draw conclusions about the way that individuals pass through the system (see ICAR Statistics Paper 1 Peach and Henson 2006). For instance, the figure for asylum detainees makes no distinction between those who are detained pending their claim and those whose claim has failed and who are detained pending removal. The percentage which asylum detainees represent of the total should be seen in the light of the rapidly falling number of asylum claims made in the years shown.

In 1989, Kurdish detainees went on hunger strike in protest at their mass detention on arrival. One detainee, who was released and subsequently detained again after refusal of his asylum claim, was suffering from a profound depression at the prospect of return to Turkey and set fire to himself with fatal consequences (see Shah 2000:167).

Table 15 Asylum seekers as percentage of immigration detainees

Snapshot figures in September of these years	Total immigration detention	Detainees who had sought asylum at some stage	Asylum-related detainees as % of total
2005	2,220	1,695	76
2006	2,010	1,455	72
2007	2,321	1,625	70

This protest and tragic death were unfortunately not the last. Since 1989 there have been 10 suicides of asylum seekers in detention (ncadc.org.uk 6 December 2007). This figure in itself is the tip of an iceberg of self-harm. Information about the level of self-harm in immigration detention has been revealed by answers to questions raised by non-governmental organizations under the Freedom of Information Act. For instance, to NCADC, 'in the 14 months from April 2006 to June 2007 there were 251 attempts to self-harm that required medical treatment' and to Medical Justice Network. Sometimes, deaths have sparked large-scale protests in removal centres, which have brought the death to public attention (see for instance irr.org.uk 26 July 2004, 30 June 2005, accessed 20 December 2007). There have been other protests too about conditions in immigration detention, such as lack of legal advice and medical care. These have occasionally persuaded the Home Office to some temporary change of policy, but the trend continues to be one of increasing use of detention. The number of detention places available has increased to 2,418, and a new centre is being built near Gatwick, in order to 'send a very clear message' to new arrivals (Immigration Minister 24 July 2007, www.whitehallpages.net, accessed 20 December 2007). There was fierce opposition in Parliament about this kind of message when Nationality, Immigration and Asylum Act 2002 s 66 renamed detention centres as 'removal centres'. The concern was about the impression given to newly arrived asylum seekers of the way that their claim was regarded. It was too late to oppose the change, as it was revealed in the House of Lords that the name change had already taken place before the clause had even been debated in Parliament.

Other immigration detainees include those who have served a criminal sentence and are to be deported, and people arrested for removal after overstaying their leave or perhaps working in breach of a condition.

Table 15A Circumstances in which an asylum seeker may be detained

---

AN ASYLUM SEEKER MAY BE DETAINED

---

1. **ON ARRIVAL**
   - (A) if claims asylum:
     Pending decision whether to grant leave to enter
     If either
     - Claim can be decided quickly, or
     - To verify identity, risk of absconding etc.
   - (B) if does not claim asylum but enters clandestinely or on false docs:
     Pending a decision whether to remove

2. **ON A LATER CLAIM**
   As for 1A

3. **ON REFUSAL OF CLAIM**
   Pending a decision to remove

4. **ON LOSING APPEAL**
   Pending a decision to remove

5. **ON DECISION TO REMOVE**
   Pending removal

6. **ON SETTING REMOVAL DIRECTIONS**
   Pending removal

Most of the 10 immigration removal centres are for men only, but three include facilities for women and children. The Home Office research publication examines in detail a sample of 'the illegally resident population in detention', and finds that the majority are young men, but otherwise generalizations were hard to make. The report gives an idea of the human experience behind the figures. Three-quarters of those interviewed had worked illegally in the UK. Around half were in detention as a result of a raid on their workplace, for most it was their first immigration detention and they were previously not in contact with the Home Office (Home Office online report 20/05). The researchers attempted to distinguish between those illegally resident and asylum seekers whose claim had failed, but this distinction was difficult to make.

Other material about who is detained using immigration powers emerges from the case law discussed below. For instance, legal challenges to the detention of families with young children tell us a lot about the way that the power to detain is used and about their experience of detention.

15.4 Statutory basis of powers to detain

The power to detain for immigration purposes is found in Immigration Act 1971 Schs 2 and 3 and in Nationality, Immigration and Asylum Act 2002 s 62. No distinction is made in the statutes between asylum seekers and others. Powers to detain are possessed both by immigration officers and by officials in the Home Office, though as a matter of policy, the immigration officer's power to detain is normally exercised by a Chief Immigration Officer. In broad terms we can think of there being three stages at which detention may occur:

- Before a decision is made to grant leave to enter
- In order to remove someone
- To effect a deportation after the recommendation of a criminal court.

In terms of the legality of detention under domestic law, there are three main questions to consider:

- Does the power to detain exist in this situation? In other words, is the decision made 'pending examination' (before a decision to give leave is made), or pending removal or a decision to remove or deportation?
- Are there sufficient *reasons* to exercise the power?
- How long has this person been detained already?

Immigration officers have powers to detain which follow from their border control functions. They may detain pending examination, pending a decision whether to remove, and pending removal (Sch 2 of the 1971 Act). The original division of powers in the 1971 Act (see chapter 7) which made the Secretary of State responsible for 'in-country' decisions and immigration officers responsible for decisions on entry has, as we have seen, been largely eroded, and the Secretary of State now has similar powers (s 62(1) and (2)).

These powers have been augmented in the UK Borders Act 2007 by a power for a designated immigration officer to detain someone for three hours at a port if they think that person may be arrestable under criminal law powers of arrest. This may have nothing to do with any immigration matter, and is a pure extension of immigration officers' powers into the criminal sphere.

Until the 2002 Act the Secretary of State only had power to detain pending deportation (Sch 3 to the 1971 Act) and this power remains.

Part 4 of the 2002 Act containing these new powers of detention displays some quite obscure drafting; for instance, that the power to detain is exercisable when the Secretary of State has reasonable grounds to suspect that he may make a decision to give or refuse leave to enter or a decision whether to give directions for removal. This is strange indeed, raising the Kafkaesque spectre of detention ending at the point where the Secretary of State decides not to make a decision, or of a person being detained when the Secretary of State reasonably suspects that he is about to grant leave to enter (s 62(7), read with s62(1) and (2)), suggesting a kind of introspective self-policing by the Secretary of State. However, the intention of the drafting seems to have been to make the power to detain as wide as possible without necessarily invoking these bizarre extremes. They were explained by the Parliamentary Secretary to the Lord Chancellor's department during the Standing Committee stage of the 2002 Bill as an attempt to simplify the process (House of Commons Standing Committee E 14 May 2002 cols 233–234).

15.4.1 Detention on arrival – pending examination

This power to detain 'pending examination and pending a decision to give or refuse leave to enter' (1971 Act Sch 2 para 16.1) may be exercised by immigration officers or the Secretary of State whenever the decision or examination takes place. In other words, a person may be detained on arrival, perhaps as a clandestine entrant at a port, but they may also be detained at any stage before leave to enter is given. An asylum seeker may wait many months or even years for a decision on their application for leave to enter. The power to detain continues throughout this time. Although it is a discretion which must be exercised in accordance with proper criteria, the statutory power to detain persists. They may be required to report regularly to a police station in the meantime, and for many asylum seekers the day of reporting is an anxious time, as it presents an opportunity for them to be detained.

The power to detain pending examination is mitigated by the Human Rights Act, even aside from the question of criteria for its exercise. The only relevant specified reason for detention in Article 5 is 'to prevent his effecting an unauthorized entry'. The

Table 16 Powers to detain on arrival

Person arriving	May be detained in these circumstances
Entry clearance holder	Only if leave is cancelled and reasons exist*
Non-visa national visitor, requiring leave on entry	If further investigations needed in order to decide whether to grant leave to enter, and if reasons exist*
Claims asylum on entry	In order to decide whether to grant leave to enter and either claim can be decided quickly or reasons exist*
Clandestine entrant	Pending decision whether to remove, and reasons exist*
Arriving on false documents	Will depend on application made and nature of documents. May transfer into criminal remand if prosecution brought

* 'Reasons exist' refers to an assessed risk of absconding, the need to verify identity etc.

first House of Lords' decision on the Human Rights Act was concerned with whether this permitted detention simply in order to process an application.

 **Key Case**

R v SSHD ex p Saadi, Maged, Osman and Mohammed [2002] 1 WLR 3131

This case was a challenge to the regime at the Oakington Reception Centre which represented a significant plank of government policy. Oakington was specifically for new arrivals in the UK who did not come within the existing criteria for detention, because there was no risk of any kind attached to their being at liberty. The regime at Oakington was described in the Home Office Operational Enforcement Manual as 'relaxed' (para 38.1). It was a kind of 'soft' detention. However, residence there was compulsory (by an amendment to Immigration Act 1971 Sch 2 para 21), and there could be no doubt that in terms of Article 5 it amounted to a deprivation of liberty. The new Oakington criterion, as announced in Parliament, was that 'it appears that their application can be decided quickly' (HC written answers 16 March 2000 col 263). It was apparent from guidance issued on applications at Oakington that the expectation of dealing with a claim quickly arose chiefly from judging it ill-founded.

In the *Saadi* case the appellants were Iraqi Kurds who claimed asylum on arrival. The House of Lords proceeded on the footing that all were detained under Immigration Act 1971 Sch 2 para 16(1) 'pending examination'. The detention was lawful in domestic law without consideration of the Human Rights Act. The question in the House of Lords was whether detention for the purpose of enabling a speedy decision, in other words purely for operational reasons, could come within the language of Article 5(1)(f). At first sight, the detention was not in order to prevent an unauthorized entry. As Collins J said in the High Court:

Once it is accepted that an applicant has made a proper application for asylum and there is no risk that he will abscond or otherwise misbehave, it is impossible to see how it could reasonably be said that he needs to be detained to prevent his effecting an unauthorised entry. He is doing all that he should to ensure that he can make an authorised entry. (para 29)

The House of Lords rather surprisingly resorted to the principle of sovereignty, which statute and human rights law are to a degree designed to mitigate, and quoted *Oppenheim's International Law*:

The reception of aliens is a matter of discretion, and every state is by reason of its territorial supremacy competent to exclude aliens from the whole, or any part, of its territory. (para 31)

This, for the House of Lords, was the starting point. If this is the starting point then, so reasoned Lord Slynn, every entry is unauthorized until it is authorized. The entry of the appellants was therefore, quite simply, unauthorized because it had not been authorized. The House of Lords was influenced in its decision by considerations of proportionality. Lord Slynn, giving the only reasoned judgment, said that the methods of selection of Oakington cases '(are they suitable for speedy decision?)', the objective of speedy decision-making and 'the way in which people are held for a short period...and in reasonable conditions' were not arbitrary or disproportionate and therefore did not fall outside the Article 5 requirements of lawfulness (para 45). He accepted the 'need for highly structured and tightly managed arrangements' in the interests of speed (para 46).

Table 17 Short-term and fast-track detention and removals, 2005 and 2006

Centre	Total principal applicants 2005	Number removed	Total principal applicants 2006	Number removed
Oakington	5,330	1,010	2,030	490
Harmondsworth	1,495	985	1,205	780
Yarl's Wood	230	125	375	205

Source: Home Office Asylum Statistics 2006

Oakington has a reputation as 'the most benign of all immigration detention centres' (Prisons and Probation Ombudsman 2005). It was all the more disturbing then when a BBC programme 'Detention Undercover: The Real Story' revealed 'a sub-culture of abusive comment, casual racism, and contempt for decent values'. A report followed by the Prisons and Probation Ombudsman which made recommendations for 'establishing a more just and proper system'. While the report notes the many good qualities of Oakington and its staff, it draws an interesting conclusion:

the very purpose of immigration detention is to exercise coercive power over foreigners prior to their removal from the country. It is perhaps not a surprise that this function, combined with the attitude towards asylum-seekers and other would-be immigrants of some sections of the media, can become a breeding ground for racist and abusive word and deed.

The ECtHR Grand Chamber confirmed the House of Lords' decision by a majority of 11 to 6 (*Saadi v UK* [2008] ECHR 79 (29 January 2008)). They also confirmed the House of Lords' decision that there was a breach of Article 5.2 – the right to reasons for detention.

In the Cambridge research, which took place before the Oakington regime began, 4.4 per cent of immigration officers interviewed said that they detained someone to 'expedite a claim'. Since the House of Lords' decision, acceptable short-term detention to make speedy decisions at Oakington is now treated as 14 rather than seven days, though this was criticized by the JCHR in their report on Treatment of Asylum Seekers (Session 2006–07). A boundary was set by the case of *Conka v Belgium* in which administrative convenience had been taken to an extreme and this was a breach of Article 5.1. The UNHCR Guidelines specifically exclude administrative convenience from being a legitimate basis for a detention decision.

The Oakington criterion refers to speed of *deciding* a claim, and there is no reason why someone should not have their claim speedily decided and then leave Oakington on temporary admission. The development of the fast-track procedures, discussed in chapter 12, makes it clear that Oakington was the beginning not only of quick decision but also quick removal. The Oakington regime remains somewhat different, but the detained fast track is intended to be a process in which the asylum seeker does not leave detention at any point.

15.5 Detention pending removal or deportation

In the 1971 Act, as originally enacted, the power to detain pending removal was a power to detain someone 'in respect of whom directions may be given' (Sch 2 para 16(2)). In other words, someone who had already been deemed subject to removal, and before the Immigration and Asylum Act 1999 this meant someone upon whom notice had been served that they were deemed an illegal entrant. The 1999 Act, as well as widening the grounds for removal (see chapter 17), also amended para 16(2) to permit detention where there were 'reasonable grounds to suspect' that a person might be subject to removal. This means that, even where the removal decision has not been taken, for instance because the claim is not decided, or it is not clear to which country the claimant may be removed, they may still be detained. The discretion must still be exercised in accordance with the criteria discussed below. We consider first whether the power exists, then whether the discretion to use it should be exercised.

The jurisdiction to detain pending removal raises some crucial questions, in particular whether detention is lawful when there are obstacles in the way of removal. 1971 Act Sch 2 para 16 permits detention when there are reasonable grounds for suspecting that a person may be removed. However, what if the person may be removable at some point, but at present is not?

It is a breach of the Refugee Convention (Article 33) to remove an asylum seeker from the UK until their claim has been determined. This is confirmed in Nationality, Immigration and Asylum Act 2002 s 77, which prevents removal while an asylum claim is pending. As we have seen in chapter 12, an exception is made when an asylum seeker can be returned to a third country which is deemed safe. Where an asylum seeker is detained before their claim is finally determined, it could be argued that, as the removal cannot be implemented, detention on this basis is unlawful. An argument to this effect was made in the case of *Samateh* [1996] Imm AR 1 in the context of deportation. However, the Court of Appeal found that the power to deport subsists even when it cannot be implemented, and so detention was lawful. The 2002 Act makes it clear that it is only the removal itself which cannot happen while the claim is pending. Removal directions can be issued, and other preparatory steps taken (s 77).

In a Privy Council case, *Tan Te Lam and others v Superintendent of Tai A Chau Detention Centre and others* [1996] 4 All ER 256), the applicants were among those who fled from Vietnam to Hong Kong in the late 1970s, the 1980s and early 1990s. They were of Chinese ethnic origin, and under the agreed repatriation arrangements it was the policy of the Vietnam government not to accept repatriation of non-Vietnam nationals. Therefore, although they were detained pending removal under the Immigration Ordinance of Hong Kong, as non-Vietnamese nationals they would not be removable. The Privy Council said that this was not an aspect of the discretion to detain, it went to the question of jurisdiction to detain in the first place (at 266j). There was no jurisdiction to detain 'pending removal' people whom there was no power to remove. This must be distinguished from the position in *Samateh*, where there was jurisdiction to remove, even though it could not at present be exercised.

The UK is one of the few Western democracies which does not place a statutory limit on the length of time that at least certain categories of people may be detained for immigration reasons. This was one of the concerns of the UNHCR Working Group. In the body of case law challenging the length of detention, considered separately below, it has been considered that the lengthy detention may undermine the jurisdiction to detain, so that if obstacles to removal persist for too long a period, the power to detain a person expires, and they must be released (see Macdonald 2005:1139). However, in *R v SSHD ex p Khadir (Appellant)* [2005] UKHL 39, Lord Brown of Eaton-under-Heywood, giving the only reasoned judgment, found that the *'Hardial Singh* line of cases' (see below) referred to the exercise of the power to detain and not to its existence. In other words, length of detention affects the exercise of the discretion to detain, which becomes unreasonable if it goes on too long. It does not affect the power to detain; ' "pending" in paragraph 16 means no more than "until"' (para 32). The House of Lords regarded *Tan Te Lam* as an exception in this respect 'because there was simply no possibility of the Vietnamese government accepting the applicants' repatriation' (para 33).

The question of length of detention is affected by practical obstacles to removal. Many cases have been brought by people who have been detained in order to be removed, but whose removal could not then be arranged. *Appellant A v SSHD* [2007] EWCA Civ 804 followed *Khadir* in that there must be 'some prospect' of A being removed within a reasonable period in order for the power to detain to exist. The level at which this prospect may be doubted is set extremely high. In *Appellant A*, after two years of lawful detention, A was detained for 19 months during which he could not be removed because no airlines were willing to take enforced removals to Somalia, and he was not willing to go. The parties were agreed that this degree of practical obstruction and length of time did not affect the *existence* of the power to detain but only its exercise. There was still 'some prospect' of A being removed.

15.6 Detention after court recommends deportation

The third basis is detention by the Secretary of State after the recommendation of a criminal court that the person be deported, providing the person is not on bail or in prison already by virtue of the judgment of the court (1971 Act Sch 3 para 2(1)). The paragraph says that the person shall be detained unless the Secretary of State directs release. This might be thought to create a presumption in favour of detention. If this were the case the Secretary of State might be able to argue that when someone had served their sentence no decision would need to be taken about their liberty, they would just stay in detention until they were deported. However, this was found not to be the case in *R (on the application of Sedrati, Buitrago-Lopez and Anaghatu) v SSHD* [2001] EWHC Admin 418, in which Moses J granted a declaration that Sch 3 para 2 created no presumption in favour of detention upon completion of a sentence of imprisonment. Such a presumption would breach Article 5, and Moses J interpreted the statute so as to uphold Convention rights. Therefore the Secretary of State must actively decide in each case whether the prospective deportee should be detained.

This is a ruling which clearly goes to the jurisdiction to detain, as demonstrated in *R (on the application of Vovk and Datta) v SSHD* [2006] EWHC 3386 (Admin). Mr Vovk was sentenced to 28 days in prison for using a false identity to gain employment. After his release date he was detained for a further six weeks *before* being given notice of deportation which authorized his detention for that purpose. Mr Datta received an eight-month prison sentence for using a false passport. He was also detained past his release date and later served with a notice authorizing his detention pending deportation. The High Court held that, until the decision had been made and notified to the two claimants, their detention was unlawful.

In *Vovk and Datta* the Secretary of State argued that the claimants knew they were recommended for deportation, so it must have been obvious to them why they were not released. This is similar to *Dougoz* in the ECtHR which we considered earlier. In that case the state relied upon the opinion of the prosecutor that an executive power which did not apply to the situation could be relied on by analogy to detain the claimant after his due release date. In *Vovk and Datta* there was not reliance on an opinion having been formed by any particular individual, but rather an expectation that executive power of an unidentified sort would be sufficient.

In the case of automatic deportations under the UK Borders Act 2007, the Secretary of State seems to acquire the power that he aspired to in *Vovk and Datta*. Section 36 of the 2007 Act provides that a person who has already served their term of imprisonment may be detained 'while the Secretary of State considers' whether the automatic deportation provisions apply. Section 34 provides that a deportation order is made 'at a time chosen by the Secretary of State'. The JCHR pointed out the scope that this gave for detention in breach of Article 5. There is no requirement for the decision to be made even within a reasonable period, let alone a specified one.

15.7 **Exercise of the discretion**

Where the statutory power to detain exists, it is still a discretion, which should only be exercised upon specified criteria otherwise it risks breaching the principle against arbitrariness. Immigration statutes are silent on the question of what criteria should lead to detention. Statutory criteria would be more publicly accessible, so providing a greater degree of compliance with the rule of law and thus the requirement of lawfulness in Article 5. Statutory criteria would be subject to parliamentary debate and thus democratic control over change. They would also be more readily enforceable (see BID Submission to the UN Working Group on Arbitrary Detention). As it is, the statutory discretion is exercised on the basis of guidance and policy.

15.7.1 **Status and nature of guidance**

Although guidance does not have statutory force, failure to have regard to established guidelines gives grounds for challenge in administrative law (*R v SSHD ex p Khan* [1985] 1 All ER 40). Non-compliance with the detention criteria has been held to be a reason to grant a declaration that continued refusal of bail was unlawful. *R v SSHD ex p Glowacka and Brezinski* CO/4237/95, CO/4251/95 was an application for leave to move for judicial review of decisions to detain. Owen J granted leave saying 'when there has been, on the face of affairs presented by the Applicant, clear breach, perhaps even an ignorance of the policy which has been declared by the Secretary of State, there is a public reason for granting leave'.

The challenge in *Saadi* was not to non-compliance with criteria, but to the application of a new criterion. Thus the House of Lords' judgment deals with the Home Office's entitlement to have a policy rather than the detainee's capacity to challenge failure to comply with that policy. In this context it says, *obiter*, 'the Home Office is entitled to adopt a policy in relation to procedures to be followed, a policy which may be changed from time to time as long as it does not conflict with relevant principles of law' ([2002] UKHL 41 para 11). Their Lordships did not elaborate on what these relevant principles are, but the principle against arbitrariness is undoubtedly one.

The government is entitled to adopt a policy to deal with asylum claims, and so the existence of a criterion referring solely to asylum seekers is not unlawful or objectionable.

The application of a more punitive criterion to asylum seekers is of much more doubtful legality (see, for instance, Art 31 Refugee Convention) but the House of Lords' and ECtHR judgments in *Saadi* do not regard the Oakington criteria as punitive.

Guidance to immigration officers on detention decisions may be found in the IND Operational Enforcement Manual, Chapter 38. The heart of the instructions is a list of factors to take into account in making a detention decision (38.3). In revisions of Chapter 38, the discretionary nature of the decision to detain is far less prominent, the implications of Articles 5 and 8 are set out more fully and precisely (38.1.1.1 and 2). Officers are advised:

In order to be lawful, immigration detention must be for one of the statutory purposes for which the power is given and must accord with the limitations implied by domestic and ECHR case law.

Much depends on the immigration officer's perception of the width of their discretion. Weber and Gelsthorpe found that 38 per cent of officers thought they did not have a wide discretion, whereas 28 per cent thought that they did. As the researchers comment, within an organization decision-making rapidly becomes routinized so that decision-makers easily lose sight of the amount of discretion they actually (or theoretically) hold. Local practices develop, and this may account in part for the very different detention figures between different ports of entry. For instance, 32 per cent of all arrivals were detained overnight at Manchester's Terminal 2 as compared with 1.5 per cent at London Heathrow's Terminal 1(Weber and Gelsthorpe 2000). This disparity is noted by Macdonald as grounds for concern about the arbitrariness of the UK's detention practice (2001:790).

15.7.2 Content of guidance

The three main approved policy reasons for detention, as set out in the 1998 White Paper, Fairer, Faster and Firmer – A Modern Approach to Immigration and Asylum, (Cm 4018) crystallize out in the detention policy as six approved reasons for detention:

   (a) The person is likely to abscond if given temporary admission or release
   (b) There is currently insufficient reliable information to decide on whether to grant temporary admission or release
   (c) Removal from the United Kingdom is imminent
   (d) The person needs to be detained whilst alternative arrangements are made for their care
   (e) Release is not considered conducive to the public good
   (f) The application may be decided quickly using the fast track procedures.

In order to be lawful, detention must not only be based on one of the statutory powers and accord with the limitations set by human rights law, but must also be for one of these reasons. The decision to detain must also be taken in accordance with the principles which are set out in Chapter 38:

   1. There is a presumption in favour of temporary admission or temporary release.

2. There must be strong grounds for believing that a person will not comply with conditions of temporary admission or temporary release for detention to be justified.

3. All reasonable alternatives to detention must be considered before detention is authorised.

4. Once detention has been authorised, it must be kept under close review to ensure that it continues to be justified.

5. Each case must be considered on its individual merits.

These principles give due priority to the presumption of liberty. Particular factors which must be taken into account are also set out as follows:

- What is the likelihood of the person being removed and, if so, after what timescale?
- Is there any evidence of previous absconding from detention?
- Is there any evidence of previous failure to comply with conditions of temporary admission or bail?
- Has the subject taken part in a 'determined attempt' to breach the immigration laws (examples given here include attempted or actual clandestine entry)?
- Is there a history of complying with requirements of immigration control (e.g. by applying for a visa, further leave etc)?
- What are the person's ties with the UK? Are there close relatives (including dependants) here? Does anyone rely on the person for support? Does the person have a settled address or employment?
- What are the individual's expectations about the outcome of the case? Are there factors such as an outstanding appeal, an application for judicial review or representations which afford incentive to keep in touch?

Puzzlingly, all the above are listed as factors '*for detention*', which rather undermines the clarity of legal principle with which Chapter 38 began.

Ultimately, the above enquiries must, if the person is to be detained, crystallize into one or more of the six listed reasons for detention which are ticked on a standard form (OEM 38.6.3). These reasons, and 14 listed factors which are used to determine whether the reason exists, were referred to in *Amirthanathan* and *Nadarajah* as 'an important part of the published policy' (para 55).

The policy also lists those who are said (OEM 38.10) to be unsuitable for immigration detention:

- the elderly, particularly where supervision is required;
- pregnant women, unless there is the clear prospect of early removal and medical advice suggests that there is no question of the baby arriving before this;
- people with serious disabilities;
- people with serious medical conditions or mentally ill;
- unaccompanied children and young people under 18;
- where there is independent evidence that they have been tortured.

What was meant in this situation by independent evidence of torture was considered in *R (on the application of D and K) v SSHD* [2006] EWHC 980 (Admin).

R (on the application of D and K) v SSHD [2006] EWHC 980 (Admin)

D and K both sought asylum on arrival in the UK and were detained in Oakington. The Detention Centre rules contained two provisions for medical examination on arrival. First, all detainees should be medically screened including an assessment for risks of self-harm within two hours of their arrival. Secondly, all detainees must have a physical and mental examination by a medical practitioner within 24 hours of arrival. The Secretary of State initially argued that this did not constitute independent evidence of torture, but Davis J held that the emphasis placed upon the need for medical examination must mean that it was an essential part of the assessment as to whether a person was suitable to remain in fast-track detention. In that case it must be capable of constituting independent evidence of torture. The Secretary of State agreed.

This is an important outcome for detainees, who are not in a position to substantiate their claim of having been tortured in any other way at such an early stage after arrival, and it underscores the importance of the provision of medical services in detention centres.

Those with a violent or serious criminal background are, according to 38.10.1, among the very few immigration detainees who may or should be held in prison. Others include 'where there is specific (verified) information that a person is a member of a terrorist group or has been engaged in terrorist activities'. The implication of the word in brackets is that this information has been verified from another source.

The fact that these listed factors and reasons exist does not mean that the detention decision can be reduced to a box-ticking exercise. The five principles stated earlier are addressed to lawfulness as opposed to arbitrariness, and without adherence to these principles oppressive practice may occur. This was amply demonstrated in *Karas and Miladinovic v SSHD* [2006] EWHC 747 (Admin).

Karas and Miladinovic v SSHD [2006] EWHC 747 (Admin)

Mr Karas had lost his asylum claim, but made a request to have a fresh claim considered in 2001. Time passed. He married Ms Miladinovic. His solicitors wrote making representations about his family life and asking for her to be added to his asylum claim. There was no response. He continued to report weekly to the Croydon immigration office as he was required to do. Ms Miladinovic became pregnant. On 10 October 2004 he reported as usual. Unbeknown to him or them, on that day removal directions had been faxed to Heathrow for a flight at 7.40 a.m. on 12 October. At 8.30pm on 11 October the couple were detained by immigration officers at their home and told that they were to be removed the next morning. It turned out that Mr Karas' claim had been refused by fax sent to his solicitor shortly before the close of business on 11 October, four hours before the couple were detained.

Munby J. held that 'detention in the circumstances of this case was...oppressive, unreasonable and unnecessary' (para 65). It was done as it was in order to prevent the claimants from obtaining legal advice or being able to apply to a judge (para 81). The guiding principles of policy in chapter 38 require detention to be used as a last resort. This detention was used in the opposite way – as a pre-emptive strike.

This case gives a flavour of what is meant by arbitrariness. There was no guiding rationale for the detention apart from to catch the claimants unawares and get them on the plane. It also gives an insight into practices which often do not reach the law reports. Munby J endorses the words of Collins J in a 'strikingly similar' case, *R (Collaku) v Secretary of State for the Home Department* [2005] EWHC 2855 (Admin):

The Home Office practice involving delay in deciding a claim but then of arresting and serving the refusal at one and the same time with a view to removal within a day or two, often at weekends and frequently early in the morning, is one that is to be deplored. This court has deplored it on many occasions. It leads to unnecessary applications to the duty judge. It has the effect of preventing those who are to be removed from seeking proper legal advice to which they may be entitled and, even if the Home Office takes the view that there is no conceivable merit to be both found in any possible challenge, this is not the way to go about it. A reasonable time must be provided to enable representations to be made, if any are to be made, certainly to enable advice to be sought if the person to be removed wishes to obtain it. Quite apart from anything else, the approach to the duty judge will almost inevitably result in an order preventing the removal until the matter can be sorted out, either the following day or the next working day, when an application can be put before the Administrative Court. The result is that the flight ticket has to be given up – it is often more than one ticket because frequently an official will accompany the person to be removed – so public money is inevitably wasted. (para 14)

The Operational Enforcement Manual Chapter 44 says that a minimum of 72 hours including at least two working days must elapse between service of removal directions and the removal itself.

The policy and guidance found in the Operational Enforcement Manual do not represent the total policy in relation to detention. Where statements and usual practices are communicated to practitioners they are entitled to rely upon these. In *R (on the application of Nadarajah)* [2002] EWHC 2595 Admin, Stanley Burnton J found that detention was unlawful because the claimant had been detained although the Home Office knew that his solicitor was about to apply for judicial review, and they had made it known that in these circumstances five days would be allowed for the application to be lodged. It had not communicated a further aspect of the policy, which was that it acts more quickly in the case of second or third applications, as this was. The Court of Appeal agreed with the High Court. The case was joined with *Amirthanathan* in the Court of Appeal because both concerned unlawfulness through a departure from published policy. The policy in issue in *Amirthanathan* was not to suspend detention where an intention was expressed to apply for appeal or review, but only when the application was actually made. The effect of such a policy is to detain someone for a few days until their solicitor commences proceedings, and then be obliged to release them because removal is not imminent. Macdonald says that 'the distress, disruption and cost of such a practice hardly seems sensible'. In *R (on the application of Mpasi) v SSHD* [2007] EWHC 2562 (Admin) the judge found that the policy referred to in *Nadarajah* was lawfully applied to Mr Mpasi. On the facts of that case the Secretary of State was entitled to maintain a position that removal was imminent until not only judicial review action had been commenced, but the grounds had been received.

From March 2007 there is a new a detailed policy in the OEM Ch 44 concerning when removal will and will not be suspended on threat or commencement of judicial review, with limited reference to detention practice. The Home Office's governing principle is probably reflected in 44.4: 'Where possible, detention should be maintained pending the outcome of the judicial review'.

15.7.2.1 *Application of criteria*

D and K, in the case of that name discussed above, both bore physical scars consistent with torture, and their medical examination confirmed this. They were not, however, released speedily when that was revealed to be the case. In 2000 the evidence of Amnesty International and the Medical Foundation was that those who have suffered torture were still being detained (Dell and Salinsky 2000).

There is also evidence that other groups who should very rarely be detained, according to the instructions, are being detained in circumstances which are not justified as being exceptional. These detainees include pregnant women and the mentally ill. (See, for the effect of such detention on mothers and babies, 'A Crying Shame: Pregnant asylum-seekers and their babies in detention' (2002) and, for the impact on mental health, 'A Second Exile: the Mental Health Implications of Detention of Asylum Seekers in the United Kingdom' (1996) and 'Fit to be Detained? Challenging the detention of asylum seekers and migrants with health needs' (2005).)

15.8 **Detention of families**

Prior to 2001, established policy in relation to the detention of families was that it should generally be avoided, and should, if at all, take place 'only to be as close as possible to removal so as to ensure that it lasted no longer than a few days' (Cm 4018 para 12.5). There is evidently far less risk of a whole family absconding, even prior to removal. In October 2001, a policy change was announced that would allow detention of more families. A letter from the Home Office to various representatives organizations, on 25 October 2001 announced an increase of family detention provision. The detention criteria for families were to be brought more closely into line with the criteria for detention of people without children, although the Home Office also stressed that this would only be where it was considered necessary, particularly in view of the possible breach of Article 8 (see Cole 2003).

The reason for the policy change was obscure, but it is apparent from case law that the current OEM reflects present policy: 'families can be detained on the same footing as all other persons liable to detention' (38.9.4). The increase in detention of children, with and without their families, has been provided for by an increase in the provision of family units, so that family places in 2005 reached 456. 286 family beds have been opened at Yarl's Wood, the detention centre previously destroyed by fire, and this has become the main centre for detention of families.

S, C and D (by their litigation friend S) v SSHD [2007] EWHC 1654 (Admin) gives an insight into how this may work in practice.

 **Key Case**

S, C and D (by their litigation friend S) v SSHD [2007] EWHC 1654 (Admin)

S had lived illegally in the UK for about three years and came to the attention of the immigration service when she was arrested for a minor offence. She claimed asylum and was asked to report to Gatwick airport with her two children. She was told that they would be detained in Oakington for 14 days. Despite anticipating detention she and the children went to Gatwick as requested. They were detained in Oakington. Her claim was assessed as suitable and refused, but they were not then released. There had been a decision to remove her and the reason given was that it was likely the family would abscond. They were transferred to Yarl's Wood removal centre, and detained for a total of four months, then released. D had his first birthday in detention. His progress was so hampered by poor nutrition that he developed rickets and anaemia.

The court held there were no grounds to anticipate they would abscond. Their addresses had been verified, C was in school, and they had supportive relationships. There was a breach of Articles 5 and 8.

In December 2003 the government began to publish statistics on children in detention in the quarterly figures. The figures show that at any one time there are scores of children in detention. Inevitably, figures only show those children who are detained with their families, as those whose age was disputed would be shown as adults. For families who contacted Bail for Immigration Detainees (BID), the average length of detention was 49 days (BID press release 9 November 2004).

15.8.1 Detention of unaccompanied children

The UNHCR Guidelines and the UN Working Group on Arbitrary Detention both state that children should not be detained.

The UN Convention on the Rights of the Child (CRC) Article 22 says:

States Parties shall take appropriate measures to ensure that a child who is seeking refugee status or who is considered a refugee in accordance with applicable international or domestic law procedures shall, whether unaccompanied or accompanied by his or her parents or by any other person, receive appropriate protection and humanitarian assistance in the enjoyment of applicable rights set forth in the present Convention and in other international human rights or humanitarian instrument to which the said States are Parties.

The UK has entered a reservation to the Convention in relation to immigration and asylum matters, and this has implications for a number of aspects of the UK's treatment of asylum-seeking children, although this reservation does not prevent the Children Act 1989 from applying to children in immigration detention, which means that Local Authority obligations continue to apply to them. In *S, C and D (by their litigation friend S) v SSHD* [2007] EWHC 1654 (Admin), discussed above, the judge held that the UK's reservation to the UN Convention on the Rights of the Child, excluding protection in relation to immigration matters, could not apply to conditions for detaining a child (para 49). As mentioned in chapter 9, it seems that the government is contemplating withdrawing the reservation.

An opinion on the reservation given in November 2001 by Nicholas Blake and Sandhya Drew for Save the Children says, in relation to detention in Oakington, that 'it is inconceivable that the best interests principle could contemplate even a short-term detention of child asylum seekers for administrative convenience whilst their protection claims are processed'. However, the reservation in their view supplanted the best interests principle. The policy paper issued by the government on 31 January 2008 refers to a pilot scheme for alternatives to detention for families with children (*Better outcomes: the Way Forward. Improving Care of Unaccompanied Asylum Seeking Children*).

15.8.2 Age disputes

An unaccompanied person under 18:

(i) will not generally be detained or subject to fast track procedures;

(ii) if their asylum claim is refused will only be removed from the UK if adequate care and reception arrangements are in place in their country of return;

(iii) may benefit from being looked after by local authorities under the Children Act

(R (on the application of I and O) v SSHD [2005] EWHC 1025 (Admin) para 32)

Therefore procedures for resolving whether someone is over 18 are crucial. Furthermore, the age assessment process itself can compound the suffering of a traumatised young person; see *R (on the application of T)* v *London Borough of Enfield* [2004] EWHC 2297 (Admin) for a disturbing account of this. It should be borne in mind that the fact of dispute does not necessarily reflect on the asylum seeker's good faith, as the measuring, recording and concept of age may be treated differently in their country of origin from the UK. It is the UK's measure which is determinative.

Home Office guidance on the measurement of age and conduct of age disputes is that:

- A claimant *must* be given the benefit of the doubt with regards to their age unless their physical appearance *very strongly* suggests that they are aged 18 or over.
- 'Merton compliant' (see below) Social Services age assessments should be regarded as authoritative.
- Paediatricians' reports *must* be considered.
- Unaccompanied minors must only be detained in very exceptional circumstances and then only overnight, with appropriate care, whilst alternative arrangements for their care and safety are made (Asylum Process Manual and OEM ch 38).

'Merton compliant' local authority age assessment is that which follows the judgment in *R (on the application of B)* v *Merton LBC* [2003] 4 All ER 280, namely:

- A local authority must make its own decision and not simply adopt the stance of the Home Office.
- There must be adequate information to make this assessment.
- This will include asking the child about their education, family, activities and history.
- The assessment cannot normally be made on the basis of physical appearance alone except in an 'obvious' case.

By way of example, A arrived at Heathrow from Afghanistan. He did not know his precise age, but his mother had informed him he was 14 years old. The social services department assessed his age in a cursory fashion, without giving reasons, as adult. A was detained as an adult but eventually determined to be 16. In a consent order signed on 8 October 2004 the Secretary of State accepted that he had unlawfully detained A for 12 days, and accepted that he was liable in damages for that unlawful detention (*In the Matter of an application for judicial review between R (on the application of A) and SSHD* CO/2858/2004).

The policy paper '*Better outcomes*' proposes setting up regional centres for age assessment. A key interest of the policy appears to be consistency, and it contemplates though is not certain about the use of X-rays.

Despite the general agreement that detention is inappropriate for children, it appears to be happening on a significant scale. A report for Save the Children, based on 32 case studies of children detained either with their parents or on their own where age was disputed, found that the length of detention varied from 7 to 268 days, with half detained for more than 28 days (Crawley and Lester 2005). Inspection reports have been critical of the detention of children, for instance in Tinsley House and Dungavel removal centres (HMIP 2005). The January 2008 policy paper suggests that children may be removed from the UK, which under present policy is deferred until they are 18.

15.8.3 Detention of children and families and Article 8

The detention of children is clearly an interference with private and/or family life. In *R (Konan) v SSHD* [2004] EWHC 22 Admin the six-month detention of a mother and her two-year-old daughter was unlawful. The detention was in breach of policy and of common law rules as the removal could not be effected because judicial review of it was pending. Detention was also a *prima facie* breach of Article 8. The court held that if and to the extent that proportionality applied, the Secretary of State's policy should be taken as representing his view of what is proportionate.

In *S, C and D*, discussed earlier, the damage to baby D's health through conditions of detention was held to be a breach of his right to respect for private life, namely his physical integrity, which suffered through denial of medical and nutritional care.

In *Mayeka and Mitunga v Belgium* (application number 13178/03) Judgment 12 October 2006 the ECtHR found violations of Articles 3, 5.1, 5.4 and 8 in the detention of a five-year-old girl in adult detention facilities without the company of any adult known to her. Travelling with a relative she was due to join her mother who had been granted asylum in Canada. During the child's two months of detention a legal tangle surrounding the child in Belgium even entailed her being deported, unaccompanied, back to the Democratic Republic of Congo before she was finally able to join her mother. The violations were of the mother's Articles 3 and 8 rights as well as the child's, since not knowing what was happening to her child and being unable to influence the course of events from Canada, despite daily telephone calls, was acutely distressing.

15.9 Length of detention

As mentioned at the start of this chapter, one of the concerns of the UN Working Group on Arbitrary Detention is that in the UK there is no fixed statutory limit on the length of time a person can be detained. In July 1997 a research report considered treatment of asylum seekers in 12 countries including the UK. It found 'the UK detains more people, for longer periods, with less judicial supervision than any other country we considered'. Clearly, the combination of no time limit and limited judicial control is a disturbing one from a human rights point of view. As we have seen, the length of detention is no longer regarded, following *Khadir*, as something which can undermine the power to detain. It only affects whether, as a matter of discretion, the detention should continue.

However, it is still the case that, if the purpose for which detention is authorized ceases to apply, then the detention is no longer authorized. This was the case in *R v Special Adjudicator and SSHD ex p B* [1998] INLR 315 in which the Secretary of State was initially in doubt as to the applicant's true identity, and this was one of the reasons for detention. However, after the applicant had provided convincing proof of this, his detention became unlawful.

There is also an implied limitation of a reasonable time to achieve the purpose sought by the detention, as was held in *R v Governor of Durham Prison ex p Hardial Singh* [1983] Imm AR 198, although, as mentioned in relation to *Chahal v UK*, a substantial period of time may still be lawful if this is necessary to complete legal proceedings.

In *Hardial Singh*, Woolf J said 'if there is a situation where it is apparent to the Secretary of State that he is not going to be able to operate the machinery provided in the Act for removing persons who are intended to be deported within a reasonable period, it seems to me that it would be wrong for the Secretary of State to exercise his power of detention' (at 200). In that case, Woolf J directed the applicant's release, finding that 'the Home Office have not taken the action they should have taken and nor have they taken that action sufficiently promptly' (at 202). Mr Singh had been in detention for five months and had attempted to take his own life. The court similarly intervened in the case of *Wafsi Suleman Mahmod* [1995] Imm AR 311 in which Laws J held that 10 months was too long to try to persuade Germany to take back a man granted asylum in Germany who had been convicted of a criminal offence whilst on a visit to the UK. The Home Office activity during the 10 months was described as 'nothing but fruitless negotiations'.

In *Tan Te Lam*, in which the applicants had been in detention for 44 months, Lord Browne-Wilkinson summarized the law as follows:

First, the power can only be exercised during the period necessary, in all the circumstances of the particular case, to effect removal. Secondly, if it becomes clear that removal is not going to be possible within a reasonable time, further detention is not authorised. Thirdly, the person seeking to exercise the power of detention must take all reasonable steps within his power to ensure the removal within a reasonable time.

The Court of Appeal applied these principles in *R (on the application of I) v SSHD* [2002] EWCA Civ 888. Although lengthy detention of itself is not a reason for release, the length of time a person has already been in detention was a factor referred to in earlier internal instructions as being relevant to whether detention should be continued, and this was found to be so by the Court of Appeal. The appellant was an Afghani asylum seeker who had been found guilty of a criminal offence. Like the applicants in *Sedrati, Buitrago-Lopez and Anaghatu*, Mr I was detained under 1971 Act Sch 3 para 2 after the end of his criminal sentence and pending deportation. However, in his case removal was not practically possible as there were no flights from the UK to Afghanistan. Bearing some similarity to *Mahmod,* the Home Office was engaged in activity which might still have resulted in his removal in that they were engaged in negotiations with countries neighbouring Afghanistan for the return of Afghani asylum seekers whose claims had failed. The *Hardial Singh* point, the second in Lord Browne-Wilkinsons's formulation in *Tan Te Lam*, was the crucial one for Simon Brown LJ in the Court of Appeal. Was it going to be possible to remove Mr I within a reasonable period of time, bearing in mind the time he had already spent in detention? Simon Brown LJ held that the Home Office's 'hope' that negotiations with neighbouring countries would bear fruit was not sufficient, given the time that Mr I had already spent in detention. By the time the case came before the Court of Appeal he had been in administrative detention (i.e. after the end of his criminal sentence) for 16 months. He should therefore be released. Dyson LJ thought that the time already spent in detention was enough to justify release.

Appellant A was distinguished from *I* in that the danger to the public posed by A was greater than that posed by I, and this was a factor which weighed in the exercise of discretion to release or to continue to detain.

The question arises whether the condition of being *subject to* detention but not actually detained (like Mr Khadir) can also go on too long, and whether, if detention ceases because it has gone on too long, liability to detention also ceases. The House of Lords' judgment in *Khadir* suggests not. Their Lordships' interpretation of the 'the *Hardial Singh* line of cases', contrary to the understanding of Macdonald (2005:1139) is that they do not affect jurisdiction to detain but only its exercise. The effect of this is that temporary admission can go on for as long as it takes to arrange a removal, as long as there is 'some prospect of achieving this'. This represents a fairly low test for the Secretary of State. Moreover, if someone is actually detained for an unreasonable period, they can expect to be released from detention, but not from liability for detention. In October 2005 a Home Office minister indicated that 21 Iraqis would be released from detention, as it was not currently possible to arrange their return to the Kurdish Autonomous Area. Their release however is on bail, confirming the effect of *Khadir* and s 67(2).

The UK is a party to the International Covenant on Civil and Political Rights, Article 9.1 of which provides that 'no one shall be subjected to arbitrary arrest or detention'. The UK has not accepted the right of individual petition for breaches of the Covenant. However, Australia has done so, and in the case of *A v Australia* (1997) 4 BHRC 210 was found to be in breach because of a lengthy detention. The UN Human Rights Committee said, 'detention should not continue beyond the period for which the State can provide justification'.

15.10 **Alternative to detention – temporary admission**

The practical meaning and importance of cases like *Khadir* cannot be understood without appreciating the growing and important part played in present-day immigration control by the status of temporary admission.

Wherever there is a power to detain there is also power to grant temporary admission (Immigration Act 1971 Sch 2 para 21 and Nationality, Immigration and Asylum Act 2002 s 62(3)). People are temporarily admitted when their applications for entry or asylum claims have not been determined. Once a claim is determined and refused, the person who was seeking asylum may remain on temporary admission. They were initially liable to detention pending examination. They are now liable to detention pending either a decision to remove or removal, and thus may still be kept in the state of temporary admission.

Temporary admission is granted for a fixed period which may be renewed. The person admitted must report back to the Home Office or immigration service at the expiry of the period. At this point there is a risk of detention, and there is no right of appeal against a refusal to extend temporary admission, because in itself it is not a status awarded, it is more like being on licence while being theoretically subject to a prison sentence. The challenge at that point is to the decision to detain, which would be by way of judicial review (though see below for forms of challenge to detention).

Temporary admission may be subject to residence or employment restrictions and requirements to report to the police or an immigration officer (1971 Act Sch 2 para 21(2)). Residence restrictions may include the requirement to reside in accommodation provided under Immigration and Asylum Act 1999 s 4 or Nationality, Immigration and Asylum Act 2002 s 26. A prohibition on employment is now routinely imposed on those whose asylum claim has not yet been determined. The practice whereby this was lifted after six months has been discontinued, though application may be made to lift it after a year. The restrictions may be varied, and the power to detain continues throughout the period of temporary admission. If a person is re-detained, although a breach of conditions is not specifically required by the schedule, the lack of such reasons would give rise to a finding of arbitrariness (see Macdonald 2001:780) unless, as is common, it is to carry out removal.

Temporary admission is a curious kind of limbo status, and this is where its importance lies. The person on temporary admission has no appeal rights, and only very minimal welfare rights. These are largely dependent on the stage of their asylum claim, and a person whose claim has failed may be temporarily admitted but without welfare support of any kind. Some rights to health and social assistance depend upon the claimant being 'lawfully present', and the government has maintained that people on temporary admission are not 'lawfully present' for these purposes. For a time, there was a legal fiction that people temporarily admitted are not present at all, let alone lawfully. This was scotched in *Szoma v Secretary of State for the Department of Work and Pensions* [2005] UKHL 64, in which their Lordships held that the appellant was lawfully present. The Court of Appeal in *MS (Ivory Coast)* [2007] EWCA Civ 133 gave a useful account of the difference between having discretionary leave and being temporarily admitted, showing the importance of the differences and the disadvantages of temporary admission.

The extended use of temporary admission contributes to the creation of a group of people without rights of any kind. Many people are in an uncertain situation; typically, their asylum claim has failed, but for practical reasons they cannot be returned to their country of origin. Prior to 2002, many people in this position would have been granted exceptional leave to remain (ELR). This status could, after some years, allow reunion with family members, and eventually indefinite leave to remain. It allowed the person to work and claim benefits. Although by nature temporary and insecure, it could be extended and could eventually bring security. This is the background to the case of *Khadir*.

Key Case

Khadir v SSHD [2005] UKHL 39

Mr Khadir's asylum application had been refused but he could not be returned to the Kurdish Autonomous Area of Iraq as there were no direct flights, and any travel via Baghdad would not be safe. The British government had been in negotiation with Turkey over the return of Iraqi Kurds, but they were not enthusiastic to permit travel of Kurdish people through their territory, and discussions had stalled. Usual practice at that time would have been to grant exceptional leave to remain, on the basis that return was not safe or possible. The Home Office's initial refusal to do so was quashed in the High Court. Mr Khadir was not in reality subject to removal and therefore it was not lawful to detain him. If there was no basis for detention there was no basis for temporary admission. His status should change to ELR.

When the High Court decision was given, the government was in the process of drafting the 2002 Bill and took the opportunity of inserting s 67(2) and (3). Section 67(2) provides that a reference to a person who is liable to detention shall be taken to include a person if the only reason why they cannot be removed is because of a 'legal impediment' concerning the UK's obligations under an international agreement, or practical difficulties in arranging the removal. This means that a person in Mr Khadir's situation may continue to be treated as liable to detention. In other words, they may remain on temporary admission despite the fact they cannot at present be removed. The subsection removes the obligation to grant ELR (now discretionary leave). The House of Lords held that the subsection was not even necessary. A person who could not for practical or legal reasons be removed was still liable to be removed and thus the power to detain existed. Section 67(3) gave s 67(2) retrospective effect. The draconian nature of this provision became irrelevant once it was found to have always been the case anyway.

The result dovetails with the Asylum Policy guidance on the grant of discretionary leave, which replaced ELR in 2003 (see chapter 12):

Discretionary leave is not to be granted on the basis that, for the time being, practical obstacles prevent a person from leaving the UK or being removed, e.g. an absence of route or travel document.

Another kind of legal obstacle to removal has arisen in the case of Sri Lanka. The ECtHR has received a number of applications from Sri Lankan Tamils whose asylum claims have been turned down but who still fear return to Sri Lanka. The court has written to contracting states asking them not to issue removal directions for Sri Lankan Tamils until these claims can be deal with (letter 23 October 2007, disclosed on www.biduk. org). The effect of s 67(2) is that people in a similar position are still liable to detention until the case in the ECtHR is resolved, but they can argue that discretion should be exercised to release them.

Lord Brown raised a question, 'how the fact that someone has been temporarily admitted rather than detained can be said to lengthen the period properly to be regarded as "pending...his removal"' (para 31). Ironically, this is one effect of this judgment, as it is possible for people to be maintained for even longer periods in the limbo state of temporary admission, yet without the Home Office being required to concede that removal is unrealistic, and grant a more beneficial status. The periods spent on temporary admission can be far longer than any reasonable (and thus lawful) length of actual detention. On release from such excessive detention, however, removal would still be possible in law, and this appears to be Lord Brown's point. Length of time was not intended to displace the removal. Compatibility with Article 5 was not considered by the court, as physical liberty was not in issue.

The importance of *Khadir* may now be appreciated. If they had accepted that length of detention affected the jurisdiction to detain, that would mean that temporary admission also could expire simply through length of time. There would come a point when a challenge in judicial review would accept that the jurisdiction to keep someone on temporary admission had expired because it had gone on too long. If length of time only affects the discretion to detain, as the House of Lords found, then there is always jurisdiction to detain while ever there is 'some prospect' (see above) of effecting a removal. Thus temporary admission, which subsists along with the jurisdiction to detain, may continue even while it would be a wrong use of discretion to actually detain the person.

As we have seen, in the context of European law the ECJ was not prepared to regard someone on temporary admission as not having entered (C–357/98 *R v SSHD ex p Yiadom* [2003] ECR I-9265). She had been present in the UK for months and this was regarded as unreal. We have also seen that time spent on temporary admission may count towards a period of residence for nationality (see chapter 3).

15.11 Judicial supervision

The availability of judicial safeguards is central to the lawfulness of detention. There must a possibility of bringing such arguments before the court. There are mechanisms for review of detention. The major criticism by the UN Working Party and others is that none is automatic.

15.11.1 Right to reasons for detention

Notice of reasons for detention may help the detainee to challenge the decision. The Human Rights Act gives a right in primary legislation to reasons for detention in Article 5.2: a detained person 'shall be informed promptly, in a language which he understands, of the reasons for his arrest'. There is an obligation in secondary legislation to give reasons on initial detention, and monthly thereafter (Detention Centre Rules 2001, SI 2001/238 r 9) As mentioned above, the UNHCR Guidelines on Applicable Criteria and Standards relating to the Detention of Asylum Seekers carries similar advice. The Home Office produces a checklist of reasons, reflecting the criteria in the OEM. This is given by immigration officers to detainees, with boxes ticked to show which standard reasons for detention apply in their case.

These standard forms were first introduced during the period of the Cambridge research project referred to above, and were discussed with immigration officers during the research. There were doubts about whether they reflected all the reasons that were actually used. As the research had already shown that reasons outside the criteria were being employed, this may suggest that the form was an attempt to ensure that only sanctioned reasons were actually used. However, there was also confusion about whether the form was additional to oral reasons or replaced them, and some thought it more appropriate to write a paragraph on the actual case. There is scope then for doubting whether the real reasons are actually disclosed by the checklist even though in most cases these standard reasons are now routinely given.

Failure to use appropriate reasons may invalidate the detention if it can be shown that there were in fact no sustainable reasons for it. For instance in *C, S and D*, standard reasons that they were likely to abscond was ticked, but this was contrary to all the available evidence.

15.11.2 **Bail**

A crucial safeguard for anyone in detention is the possibility of applying for bail. A bail application may, but need not, address the question of the lawfulness of detention. There may be jurisdiction to detain but in a bail application the argument is principally that the discretion to detain should not continue to be exercised in the particular case; the applicant should therefore be released. The question of the lawfulness of detention may be closely intertwined with such an argument, but it is not necessary to attack the jurisdiction in order to make a bail application.

Immigration and asylum detainees have a right to apply for bail, but unlike the position in criminal cases there is no automatic bail hearing. The Immigration and Asylum Act 1999 contained a scheme for a system of automatic bail hearings, but this was never implemented and was repealed by s 68(6) of the 2002 Act. The reason given for this repeal was that the appellate authorities (i.e. tribunals and adjudicators) would be unable to cope with the volume of work (Standing Committee E col 256). However, this is puzzling as the bail hearings were to have taken place before magistrates (s 44 of the 1999 Act 'to the court'). There is no statutory presumption of a right to bail, but the Chief Adjudicator's Guidance notes to adjudicators confirm that there is a common law presumption. This means that the burden of proof to show that bail should not be granted rests on the Secretary of State. The standard of proof is the balance of probabilities.

15.11.2.1 *Eligibility to apply for bail*

The right to apply for bail is found in Immigration Act 1971 Sch 2 paras 22 and 29 and Immigration and Asylum Act 1999 s 54. The exception is that those detained pending examination under 16(1) do not have a right to apply for bail until they have been in the UK for seven days (paragraph 22 (1B)).

15.11.2.2 *Power to grant bail*

An immigration officer of ordinary rank does not have power to grant bail. Under paras 22, 29, and 34 bail may be granted by a chief immigration officer or an immigration judge. However, the Nationality, Immigration and Asylum Act 2002 s 68 takes away the power of the chief immigration officer to grant bail to anyone who has been detained for more than eight days, and gives it to the Secretary of State. This changes the previous position in which anyone who could detain could also release on bail. Immigration judges retain the power to grant bail, however there may be difficulties in obtaining legal aid to be represented before them.

15.11.2.3 *Conditions for the grant of bail*

Bail may be granted on condition that the person bailed reports at a specified time and place, usually a police station or the immigration officer. Bail will be made subject to recognizances. These are pledges of money which will be forfeited if the person does not report to bail. Under Immigration Act 1971 Sch 2 para 22(1A) the applicant for bail must provide their own recognizance. This may be for a nominal sum such as £10 where a person has no assets, as may often be the case particularly if they are an asylum seeker. In addition, if it appears necessary to ensure that the person will answer to bail, further recognizances may be taken from people who are willing to stand as surety for a fixed sum proportionate to their means. The Chief Adjudicator's guidelines for adjudicators make it clear that sureties are not essential, and should not be routinely required. Adjudicators are reminded that 'asylum seekers rarely have relatives or friends in the UK who can act as sureties'. Sureties may be required 'if that will have the consequence that a person who might not otherwise be granted his liberty will be granted it' (*R v SSHD ex p Brezinski and Glowacka* CO 4251/1995 & CO 4237/1995, unreported, 19 July 1996). Conditions may be fixed such as that the bailee resides in a certain place, and other conditions may be imposed, but only if they are strictly necessary. The Secretary of State may pay for travelling expenses incurred in meeting reporting restrictions or bail conditions (2002 Act s 69).

15.11.3 **Habeas corpus**

The lawfulness of detention may be challenged by the prerogative writ of *habeas corpus*. This is an ancient remedy which has been regarded as constitutionally important as it is a means whereby a court can inquire into the reasons for any detention and order immediate release. The basis of the jurisdiction is 'a detention or imprisonment which is incapable of legal justification' (*Halsbury's Laws* vol. 1(1), para 208). Although a foreign national has as much right as a subject to apply for *habeas corpus* (see *Khawaja v SSHD* [1984] AC 74 at 111: 'He who is subject to English law is entitled to its protection') it is of little use in challenging immigration detention. The reason for this is there is nearly always a jurisdiction to detain, i.e. the basic statutory precondition is in existence. The question is usually how that jurisdiction has been exercised. This is a matter for judicial review, not *habeas corpus*. The amendment brought in by Immigration and Asylum Act 1999 s 140(1), permitting detention where there is a reasonable suspicion that directions for removal may be given means that it is even more unlikely that jurisdiction can be questioned.

Where there is a question of the jurisdiction to detain this can be argued in both judicial review and *habeas corpus* proceedings and where appropriate both sets of proceedings can be pursued simultaneously. The relationship between the two was considered by the Court of Appeal in *R v SSHD ex p Sheikh* [2001] Imm AR 219 who pointed out that *habeas corpus* proceedings may be brought at any time that an applicant is detained, and are not subject to the strict time limits applicable in judicial review. Furthermore, *habeas corpus* is a writ of right, whereas permission must be sought for judicial review. Where the challenge is really to the underlying immigration decision, e.g. the refusal of leave to enter, then judicial review is the appropriate procedure, not habeas corpus (*R v SSHD ex p Muboyayi* [1991] 4 All ER 72). Finally, Macdonald's view on the 1999 Act amendment was that 'this change sounds the death-knell for habeas corpus in removal cases, save where there is no reasonable suspicion (i.e. *mala fides* is alleged) or where detention is excessively lengthy (the *Hardial Singh* situation)' (2001:762) This latter point would now be displaced by *Khadir*.

15.11.4 **Other legal routes to challenge detention**

A decision to detain is not a decision relating to entitlement to enter or remain the UK, and is not appealable under Nationality, Immigration and Asylum Act 2002 s 82. The most common route to challenge the legality of detention has been judicial review. However, now both the benefits and limitations of the Human Rights Act and the increased use of administrative detention have given impetus for the use of private actions. In these damages can be claimed on a broader basis and there is greater scope for disclosure of evidence and cross-examination. Two important cases in this developing area will be discussed here.

 **Key Case**

Youssef v Home Office [2004] EWHC 1884 QB

This was an action for false imprisonment by reason of the length of the detention and the unrealistic prospects of removal. Reading the judgment gives a rare insight into negotiations conducted between the UK and a foreign government. The claimant was a leading member of Egyptian Islamic Jihad, which mounted high profile terrorist attacks. He claimed asylum and was excluded under Article 1F, but faced likely torture on return. For comment on the political process see, e.g. The Guardian 16 November 2004.

Three months before the refusal decision in December 1998, Mr Youssef had been detained under Special Immigration Appeals Commission Act 1997 s 3(2)(a), for reasons of national security. Even though the case predated the Human Rights Act, his removal to Egypt would have been a breach of Article 3, following *Chahal v UK* (1997) 23 EHRR 413, as there was a reasonable likelihood of torture or other inhuman or degrading treatment on his return. The UK government sought assurances from the Egyptian government of fair treatment for Mr Youssef but these were not forthcoming. A key issue in the case was whether there was any realistic prospect of obtaining such assurances, so as to justify Mr Youssef s continuing detention until 9 July 1999, when negotiations were accepted to have failed and Mr Youssef was released.

Mr Youssef was initially detained pursuant to statutory authority. Detention remained lawful while it was reasonable for the UK to be negotiating with the Egyptian government, but would cease to be so, following *R v Governor of Durham Prison ex p Hardial Singh* [1984] 1WLR 704, when there was no realistic prospect of his being removed. The decision on this was for the Secretary of State. He argued that the standard by which the reasonableness of his view should be judged was the *Wednesbury* standard, but the court disagreed. 'Where the liberty of the subject is concerned the court ought to be the primary decision-maker as to the reasonableness of the executive's actions, unless there are compelling reasons to the contrary...' although '[T]he court...should make allowances for the way that government functions and be slow to second guess the executive's assessment of diplomatic negotiations' (paras 62–63). In following this case, courts have asserted their obligation to consider the lawfulness of detention even in judicial review, affirming that this is a matter which they are competent to judge.

In *ID and others v Home Office, BID & ILPA intervening* [2005] EWCA Civ 38 the Court of Appeal reinstated particulars of claim which had been struck out in the lower court, allowing the appellants to proceed with an application for false imprisonment. A family on arrival in the UK had been detained in Oakington for a week. Following *Saadi* they could not succeed in any action challenging that detention. The court in *C, S and D* followed *ID* as authority that detention of families in Oakington was not unlawful per se. However, their claim was then refused, and they were moved to Yarl's Wood detention centre. The fire there started the night that they arrived. They lost their possessions, and were lucky to escape with their lives as they had been locked in and the guards forgot to let them out. In a state of shock, they were then transferred to Harmondsworth. The Court of Appeal held that their action in tort concerning the latter two periods of detention should be heard by the courts. The Home Office had argued that immigration officers were immune from suit in making decisions pursuant to statute. The Court of Appeal (Brooke LJ giving the only reasoned judgment) considered the limited immunities from suit still available in the case of decisions to detain, and concluded that there was no such immunity for immigration officers.

The Home Office relied also on an argument that 'the power of a state to control immigration...extends beyond the simple control of entry to encompass the treatment of aliens and the control of their activities while they are present or resident in the State (para 71). This amounted to an attempt to argue that foreign nationals are not subject to the same law as nationals and do not have full redress in the courts. This argument was dealt with in *Khawaja* [1984] AC 74 and so the Court of Appeal held in *ID*. The Court also rejected an argument that the claim was an abuse of process: 'there is nothing in the slightest bit peculiar about an individual bringing a private law claim for damages against an executive official who has abused his private rights' (para 57).

ID is an important decision. Although for the particular claimants it was only the beginning of the road to having that action heard, the court's approach on the principles re-opens the way to redress for unlawfully detained claimants, which seemed to be closing down.

15.12 Detention centres

15.12.1 Detention centres as public authorities

The management and running of detention centres, and of transport and escort services to effect removals, are increasingly contracted out to private bodies. An important question in terms of redress is whether these contractors act as public authorities for the purposes of the Human Rights Act 1998. These questions were relevant, though for the most part not contentious, in *R (on the application of D and K) v SSHD* [2006] EWHC (Admin) 980. GSL UK (formerly Group 4 Total Security) were the contractors running Oakington, and they accepted that they were bound by the Detention Centre Rules and were a functional public authority for the purposes of the Human Rights Act (see chapter 4). GSL contracted out the provision of medical services at Oakington to a company called Forensic Medical Services ltd, a subsidiary of another company called PCFM. There was a failure to provide medical services according to the standard in the Detention Centre Rules, but this failure had been known to all parties for a long time. GSL said they were not funded to provide it. However, theirs was the obligation to ensure compliance with the contract, and so declarations were made against GSL and the Home Office, though not against PCFM.

Bacon (2005) examines the growth in involvement of private prison companies in running immigration detention centres. At that time, seven of the 10 removal centres were run by private companies, but only 10 per cent of prisons. She cites the attractiveness of immigration detention to such enterprises, it being less regulated than prisons in the criminal justice system, and thus offering more opportunities for increasing the profit margin. Her suggestion is interesting, that the profit motive is powerful, and it may be that the agenda of private companies is driving the increase in immigration detention just as much as government policy.

15.12.2 **Detention and accommodation**

The government's early plans to provide large accommodation centres for asylum seekers pursuant to their power in Immigration and Asylum Act 1999 s 4 have run aground on planning objections and local opposition.

A fall in asylum claims is also cited as a reason for not pressing ahead (HC 9 June 2005 WA col 653).

The conceptual and practical blurring between detention and accommodation is likely to manifest in new and smaller centres designed to house asylum seekers from claim to removal. For an understanding of accommodation as a form of support for asylum seekers, reference should be made to reading listed below.

15.13 **Indefinite detention in the 'war on terror'**

In a sense, this final subject does not belong in a textbook on immigration and asylum law. The detention without trial of foreign nationals that took place from 2001 to 2005 would be more appropriately located in a book on civil liberties. It has a place in this chapter because immigration powers were used to justify it. When that foundation in immigration law was held by the House of Lords to be a misuse the provisions were declared unlawful. Nevertheless, these provisions in the Anti-terrorism, Crime and Security Act 2001 (ATCSA) were not an aberration. They were only the most extreme end of a number of measures we have noted already in this chapter, the designated status currently before Parliament in the Criminal Justice and Bill, and UK Borders Act provisions for detention pending automatic deportation, both lead towards a limbo without rights for foreign nationals whom the government wishes to deport but currently may not. The use of special advocates and of closed material has been adopted from Special Immigration Appeals Commission procedures to apply to control orders, the successor to ATCSA detention.

The Anti-terrorism, Crime and Security Act 2001 was the UK Parliament's legislative response to the attack on the World Trade Centre on 11 September of that year.

The government claimed that intelligence information suggested that there were people operating within the UK who had international terrorist connections, but against whom there was insufficient evidence to bring a prosecution. Against British nationals operating in such a way there would be no sanction. Foreign nationals could be deported on the grounds that their deportation was conducive to the public good (see *Rehman* v *SSHD* [2001] 3 WLR 877) but not if a person faced torture or inhuman or degrading treatment or punishment contrary to Article 3 EHCR (*Chahal v UK* (1996) 23 EHRR 413) in the destination country. ATCSA s 23 gave a power to detain a foreign national who could not be deported if the Secretary of State reasonably believed their presence in the UK to be a risk to national security and reasonably suspected that person of international terrorist activities or connections.

The provision clearly breached Article 5.1 as detention was not pending deportation or extradition or a criminal trial. Accordingly, the UK government derogated from Article 5 to the extent that it would be breached by this Act (Human Rights Act 1998 (Designated Derogation) Order 2001). This meant that Article 5 was suspended to the extent that it conflicted with 2001 Act provisions, both for the purposes of action in Strasbourg (Art 15 ECHR) and under the Human Rights Act (HRA s 1(2)). The validity of the derogation was challenged by the first twelve people to be detained under s 23. The challenge initially came before the Special Immigration Appeals Commission (SIAC) who granted a declaration under Human Rights Act 1998 s 4 that the detention power was incompatible with Article 14 ECHR.

The Court of Appeal overturned SIAC's declaration (*A, X, Y and others v SSHD* [2002] EWCA Civ 1502). Its approach follows in the footsteps of the House of Lords in the national security case of *Rehman*, considering that in measures concerning 'a public emergency threatening the life of the nation' it was appropriate to accord deference to the Home Secretary who is in a special position to be able to assess the evidence and take the decision. It was therefore prepared to accept the Home Secretary's assertion that only the detention of non-nationals was necessary.

The UK's continued detention of eleven men under these powers attracted criticism from the committee of Privy Counsellors (the Newton Committee) convened to review the legislation, the Parliamentary Joint Committee on Human Rights (in its Fifth, Sixth and Eighth Reports of 2003–04), The UN Human Rights Committee, the European Commissioner on Human Rights (Opinion 1/2002, August 2002), and many NGOs and other commentators.

The House of Lords overturned the Court of Appeal's decision in a momentous judgment (*A v SSHD* [2004] UKHL 56). Nine judges sat in the Lords, demonstrating the constitutional importance of the issue. They reiterated the fundamental constitutional importance of the right to liberty, and that the law applies equally to all.

They noted that SIAC had found as fact that 'there are many British nationals already identified – mostly in detention abroad – who fall within the definition of suspected international terrorists, and...there are others at liberty in the UK who could similarly be defined' (para 32). Also, 'allowing a suspected international terrorist to leave our shores and depart to another country, perhaps a country as close as France, there to pursue his criminal designs, is hard to reconcile with a belief in his capacity to inflict serious injury to the people and interests of this country' (para 33). These points had been made by the European Commissioner for Human Rights and by the Newton Committee, who recommended the repeal of these powers and their replacement with measures 'to deal with all terrorism, whatever its origin or the nationality of its suspected perpetrators'. The lack of rational connection to the aim to be achieved made the measures both disproportionate and discriminatory.

The derogation was not, they thought, limited to what was strictly required by the exigencies of the situation. Lord Bingham of Cornhill referred to the very strict bail conditions upon which one detainee had been released. These were less draconian than detention, but presumably considered sufficient. As the derogation was discriminatory and so in breach of Article 14, it was also in breach of Article 26 ICCPR and thus not consistent with the UK's other international obligations, as required by Article 15.

Lord Hoffmann alone found that there was no threat to the life of the nation warranting derogation under Article 15. The life of the nation should not be equated with individual human lives, but rather with the values and practices that constitute the collective life. 'Terrorist violence, serious as it is, does not threaten our institutions of government or our existence as a civil community', he said, and most memorably: 'The real threat to the life of the nation, in the sense of a people living in accordance with its traditional laws and political values, comes not from terrorism but from laws such as these' (paras 96 and 97).

The majority found that s 23 was disproportionate and thus in breach of Article 15, and discriminatory and thus in breach of Article 14. They issued a quashing order in relation to the derogation order and a declaration of incompatibility in relation to s 23. Only Lord Walker of Gestingthorpe dissented.

The government's response to the House of Lords' judgment has already been discussed in chapter 1. The detainees' bail conditions were swiftly transposed into control orders under the 2005 Act. A special provision exempted them from judicial oversight (PTA 2005 s 3(1)(c)).

A number of control orders have now been challenged in the House of Lords and the most draconian were found to be in breach of Article 5. These entailed confinement alone to a one-bedroomed flat in an unknown area for 18 hours a day, limited telephone and no internet access, no visitors who had not been vetted by the Home Office, a limited radius of travel, a prohibition on attending any gatherings of people except once a week in an approved mosque, wearing an electronic tag at all times and reporting to a monitoring centre on leaving and returning to the flat. The majority of the House of Lords thought that this amounted to a deprivation of liberty rather than merely a restriction on liberty. Baroness Hale said that the whole condition of someone's life had to be taken into account, and life under these control orders was similar to being in an open prison, but without association with other prisoners. None of the permitted reasons in Article 5.1 existed, so the control order breached the right (*SSHD v JJ* [2007] UKHL 45). In other cases of lesser restriction, no breach of Article 5 was found (*SSHD v MB and AK* [2007] UKHL 46).

It may be doubted whether such a draconian system would have come into being without the more severe detention regime first being imposed on foreign nationals. Finnis has doubted whether the ATCSA provisions were ever necessary. His view is that deportations of those detained were never so out of the question that detention could not have been justified. In the light of the case law studied in this chapter, the reader may form their own view.

This section would not be complete without a reference to *The Queen on the application of Abbassi v Secretary of State for Foreign and Commonwealth Affairs* [2003] UKHRR 76, a challenge to the Foreign Secretary's exercise of prerogative in interceding for the British prisoners held in the American military base in Guantanamo Bay, Cuba. The case in essence concerns the impotence of the British government to intervene in the affairs of another nation and of the citizen to challenge that. However it proceeded on the accepted basis that the detainees had access to no legal review of their detention, that detention was indefinite and that they had no access to legal advice or representation. Within the confines of the legal principles available to it, the Court of Appeal could only reiterate the primacy of liberty, and that every detention is a *prima facie* breach of law (para 60). They were powerless to intervene as the matter was in the political, not the legal sphere. As discussed in chapter 1, the impasse resulted in a break with constitutional convention when Lord Steyn spoke in a non-judicial setting to criticize the detentions (The Independent 26 November 2003). There was a similar outcome for three non-British residents of the UK who had indefinite leave to remain, two as refugees. The High Court held that even the risk of torture to them, of which there was objective evidence, did not generate a right for the UK to intervene. Remedies under the International Law Commission's Articles on State Responsibility only entailed that States should work together to eradicate the breach of international law that torture represented, not that the UK could intervene directly with the US to prevent it in an individual case (*R (on application of Al-Rawi) v FCO and SSHD* [2006] EWHC 972 (Admin).

15.14 Conclusion

We end this chapter as we began, *Liversidge* v *Anderson* dealing with wartime internment, and *A* v *SSHD* dealing with internment in a different kind of public emergency. In *Liversidge* v *Anderson*, although the House of Lords found for executive, the case is remembered more for Lord Atkin's dissent than it is for its ratio. As *A* v *SSHD* takes its place in legal history it will be interesting to see whether the majority or the dissent leaves a stronger print on history. The 8:1 decision that the detentions were unlawful has given the case a claim to be 'one of the most constitutionally significant ever decided by the House of Lords' (MLR Belmarsh special issue p. 654). Lord Bingham's leading judgment carefully marshalls international law to reach the majority conclusion, and this is important not only for the outcome but also because it shows that the UK is subject to international restraints upon government. The minority view which has had impact though is not Lord Walker's dissent on the outcome but Lord Hoffmann's on the emergency threatening the life of the nation. To reach this view he invokes the common law, not human rights, and his ringing statement 'the real threat to the life of the nation…' has been more quoted than the pages of closely reasoned judgment which subject to the UK to international human rights law. The subject matter is not accidental. Reviewing *Saadi, Khadir* and judgments of the lower courts we may detect the persistence, appearing in many forms, of resort to a power which is resistant to restraint. This chapter has shown that although *prima facie* unlawful, detention is on the increase, and even statutorily enshrined human rights can be defeated by a judicial assertion of the State's power to control aliens. The administrative power to detain pending determination of a claim has grown far beyond its original use for visitors overnight, and become the foundation for a whole new system of detention. Perhaps what this chapter really illustrates, although indirectly, is that the political context of the law is sometimes the most influential factor.

QUESTIONS

1 Does the House of Lord judgment in the case of *Saadi* recognize the right in Article 14 UDHR to claim asylum?

2 Is it appropriate that the decision to detain should be a discretionary one without statutory criteria to guide its exercise?

3 Should asylum seekers have an automatic bail hearings as criminal suspects do?

online resource centre For guidance on answering questions, visit www.oxfordtextbooks.co.uk/orc/clayton3e.

FURTHER READING

Amnesty International (1996) *Cell Culture: The Detention and Imprisonment of Asylum Seekers in the United Kingdom* (London: Amnesty International).

Bacon, C. (2005) 'The evolution of Immigration detention in the UK: the involvement of private prison companies,' *Refugee Studies Centre*, Working Paper no. 27.

Bail for Immigration Detainees (2002) *Immigration Detention in the United Kingdom, Submission to the United Nations Working Group on Arbitrary Detention* (London: BID).

—— (2005) *Fit to be Detained? Challenging the detention of asylum seekers and migrants with health needs* (London: BID).

Black, R., Collyer, M., Skeldon, R. and Waddington, C. (2005) *A Survey of the Illegally Resident Population in Detention in the UK*, Home Office research paper 20/05.

Blake, N., Buchan, S., Kawani, F., Owers, A. (1997) *Providing Protection: Towards fair and effective asylum procedures* (Justice, ILPA and ARC).

Burnham, U. (1998) 'Negligent False Imprisonment: Scope for re-emergence?' *Modern Law Review* vol. 61, no. 4, p. 573.

Cohen, R. (1994) *The Frontiers of Identity* (London and New York: Longman), Chapter 4.

Cole, E. (2003) 'The Detention of Asylum-seeking families in the UK' IANL vol. 17, no. 2, pp. 96–113.

Dell, S., and Salinsky, M. (2001) 'Protection not Prison: Torture Survivors Detained in the UK' Medical Foundation for the Care of Victims of Torture, September 2001.

Fenwick, H. (2002) 'The Anti-terrorism, Crime and Security Act 2001: A proportionate response to September 11th?' *Modern Law Review* vol. 65, no. 5, 724–762.

Finnis, J. 'Nationality, Alienage and Constitutional Principle' *Law Quarterly Review*, vol. 123, July 2007, pp. 417–445.

Macdonald, I., and Webber, F. (2005) *Macdonald's Immigration Law and Practice*, 6th edn. (London: Butterworths), Chapter 17.

McLeish, J., Culter, S., Stancer, C. (2002) *A Crying Shame: Pregnant Asylum Seekers and their Babies in Detention* (Maternity Alliance, BID, LDSG).

Modern Law Review (2005) 68(4) Cases Section: Special Issue on Belmarsh.

Poole, T. 'Harnessing the Power of the Past? Lord Hoffmann and the *Belmarsh Detainees* Case' *Journal of Law and Society* vol. 32, no. 4, pp. 534–561.

Pourgourides, C. K., Sashidharan, S. P., Bracken, P. J. (1996) *A Second Exile: The Mental Health Implications of Detention of Asylum Seekers in the United Kingdom* (Birmingham: Northern Birmingham Mental Health Trust).

Sawyer, C., and Turpin, P. (2005) 'Neither Here Nor There: Temporary Admission to the UK' *International Journal of Refugee Law*, vol. 17, no. 4, December 2005, pp. 688–728.

Shah, P. (2002) *Refugees, Race and the Concept of Asylum* (London: Cavendish), Chapter 8.

Sharpe, R. J. (1989) *The Law of Habeas Corpus* (Oxford: Clarendon), pp. 117–123.

Smith, K. (1999) 'The reality of detention: a reaction to the Immigration and Asylum Bill' *Immigration and Nationality Asylum Law and Practice* vol. 13, no. 3, pp. 96–99.

Tomkins, A. (2002) 'Legislating against Terror: the Anti-terrorism, Crime and Security Act 2001' *Public Law* Summer, pp. 205–220.

UNHCR (1999) *Revised Guidelines on Applicable Criteria and Standards Relating to the Detention of Asylum Seekers.*

Wadham, J. (2002) 'Why Lawyers should be ashamed of the latest ruling on internment' *New Law Journal* vol. 152, no. 7054, p. 1633.

Weber, L., and Gelsthorpe, L. (2000) *Deciding to Detain: How Decisions to Detain Asylum Seekers are Made at Ports of Entry* (Cambridge: Cambridge Institute of Criminology).

16

···

Deportation

SUMMARY

This chapter gives a brief history of the power of deportation, then discusses in some detail the application of the main ground which remains after recent legislative changes: that the deportation is conducive to the public good. There is discussion of this ground in the light of recent legislative changes, and its use in national security cases. The chapter concludes with some points on particular issues which arise in considering the effect of deportation on family and private life.

16.1 Introduction

Deportation has a long history. The word conjures up images of forced removals, divided families, and poor conditions on board crowded ships. Deportations still take place, though they are now not a common legal means of removing someone from the UK; the usual route is the newer power of administrative removal, which is dealt with in the next chapter. Deportation has traditionally offered more rights to the person removed than does the process of removal, though these have gradually been eroded almost to vanishing point. The process of extradition, which may have an interaction with asylum claims but which arises in relation to non-immigration criminal issues, will not be considered in this book. Supervised and voluntary departures are considered later in this chapter.

16.2 What is deportation?

Deportation is a process of enforced departure from the UK, pursuant to an order signed by the Home Secretary, which also prevents the deportee from returning to the UK unless and until the order is revoked. In this respect it may be distinguished from the other forms of enforced departure. Although removal, supervised and voluntary departure affect the ability of the individual to return to the UK, unlike a deportation order they do not have any continuing legal force beyond the departure date. Paragraph 362 of the immigration rules sets out the effects of a deportation order:

(i) it requires the person who is the subject of the order to leave the UK

(ii) it authorizes that person's detention until they leave the UK (subject to a common law restraint on the length of detention, as discussed in the previous chapter)

(iii) it prohibits that person's re-entry for as long as the order is in force

(iv) it invalidates any leave to enter or remain given to the person before the order was made or while it was in force.

The first formal step in the deportation process is the notice of decision to deport, which gives the reasons for the decision, the country to which it is proposed to deport the person, and notice of appeal rights. Appeal is against the notice of decision to deport. Once the deportation order is signed it becomes valid and there is no further appeal, though it may be possible to appeal a refusal to revoke the order (Nationality, Immigration and Asylum Act 2002 s 82(2)(k)).

Entry while the deportation order is still in force makes that person an illegal entrant (Immigration Act 1971 s 33A).

16.3 **History and development of the power to deport**

The origin of the power to deport was arguably in the prerogative of the Crown to regulate the entry and stay of aliens. As a prerogative power can only be used in relation to aliens (*R v IAT ex p SSHD* [1990] 3 All ER 652: see chapter 1), in this early stage Commonwealth citizens could not be deported. The law regulating deportation began to develop when the exercise of the power was first controlled by statute in the Aliens Act 1905. Under the statute deportation could only take place after conviction of an imprisonable offence, or if a magistrates' court certified that the person had been sentenced elsewhere for an extradition offence, or had:

Been found in receipt of any such parochial relief as disqualifies a person for the parliamentary franchise, or found wandering without ostensible means of subsistence, or been living in insanitary conditions due to overcrowding.

Criminality, poverty, and the spread of disease have often been mixed in with immigration policy, as discussed in chapter 1. The operation of appeal boards was suspended in 1914, and although for a short time there was a review panel, its decisions were unpopular with the Home Office and it was abolished again. Effectively, from 1914 to 1955 people who were to be deported had no access to appeal or independent review.

We have seen that the Commonwealth Immigrants Act 1962 marked an historic shift in the relationship between the UK and its Commonwealth citizens. Not only did it provide the first powers to refuse them entry, it also provided the first powers to deport Commonwealth citizens, though originally this too was only for criminal offences on the recommendation of a criminal court (s 6). The 1962 Act s 7 provided protection against deportation for anyone who could prove they had been ordinarily resident in the UK for five years prior to conviction. This exemption was preserved by the Immigration Act 1971 for existing residents, but otherwise abolished. Recently the importance of long-term residence has again been recognized in Europe, both in debates in the Council of Europe and in increased protection for long-term residents in EU law (see chapter 6). In the UK, long residence rules (discussed in chapter 7) may give settled status but no longer give any protection against deportation.

The Immigration Appeals Act 1969 widened powers in relation to Commonwealth citizens by giving the power to the Secretary of State to deport Commonwealth citizens who were in breach of their conditions of admission (s 16), again with an exemption for those who had been ordinarily resident for five years. The power to impose conditions was only introduced by the 1962 Act. This was a significant step as it developed deportation as a means of enforcing immigration rules, not only a means of excluding people who were considered socially undesirable. The Immigration Act 1971 made the position of aliens and Commonwealth citizens broadly the same, in that deportation became possible for both groups for breach of condition or overstaying, when conducive to the public good and after recommendation by a criminal court (s 3). This power applied to all those who were subject to immigration control, and aliens and Commonwealth citizens were not separately treated by the Act, though there were some Commonwealth citizens who were exempt (see below). From that time onwards, apart from the exemptions, the distinction between Commonwealth citizens and aliens for deportation purposes has vanished. The main distinction now is between EU nationals and others.

The Immigration Act 1988 s 5 restricted the possible grounds for appeal against deportation for people who had been in the UK for less than seven years. After this change, people who had been in the UK less than seven years who were being deported for breach of condition or overstaying could not argue their case on the merits of whether they should be deported, but only on whether there was power in law to deport them. This restriction was interpreted strictly, as demonstrated in the case of *Harjinder Kaur Singh* TH/26/1199 where the tribunal found the appeal was limited to whether there was power in law to deport. The manner in which that power was exercised was outside their jurisdiction and if the Secretary of State had failed to have regard to his policy on domestic violence, there was nothing they could do about that.

The Asylum and Immigration Act 1996 added a further ground for deportation – obtaining leave to remain by deception. Despite the widened grounds and the restricted appeal rights, a person who was to be deported still had greater rights than one who was to be removed in that they had a right to appeal from inside the UK which the person to be removed did not. The Immigration and Asylum Act 1999 translated most of the grounds for deportation into grounds for removal, thereby further reducing appeal rights and substantially eradicating the distinction between deportation and removal. It is an open question whether this reduction in rights was balanced in the 1999 Act by the introduction of the human rights appeal which applies to removal as well as deportation (see, for instance, CM below).

In summary, until the implementation of the 1999 Act, the scope of the power to deport increased, while the rights of people who were to be deported decreased. In the Nationality, Immigration and Asylum Act 2002 a new right of appeal was introduced against a decision to deport following the recommendation of a criminal court (s 82(2)(j)). Interestingly, the Bill which preceded the 1999 Act included this right of appeal, but it was removed by a late amendment sponsored by the government in the House of Lords.

The latest chapter in the development of deportation powers began in 2005 with the Prime Minister's statement following the bombings in London that year. He proclaimed a 'list of unacceptable behaviours' and an intention to make these grounds for deportation and speed up the deportation process. The Home Secretary consulted on the list, which would be taken to demonstrate an indirect threat to national security. It included writing, producing, publishing or distributing material; public speaking including preaching; running a website; using a position of responsibility to express views which the government considers 'foment terrorism, justify or glorify terrorism, foster hatred which may led to intra community violence in the UK' and expression of 'what the Government considers to be extreme views that are in conflict with the UK's culture of tolerance' (*Exclusion or Deportation from the UK on non-conducive grounds*: consultation document, October 2005). In the event these ideas fed into the creation of new offences in the Terrorism Act 2006, but were not explicitly linked to deportation.

In May 2006 the press disclosed that, over a seven-year period, 1,000 foreign national prisoners had been released without being considered for deportation (see chapter 2 for discussion of the incident). This turned out to be due to failures of management, organization and communication within the Immigration and Nationality Directorate. It was not that it would have been appropriate to deport all these prisoners, but rather that whether they should be deported had not been considered. Over 100 were the subject of a court recommendation. As a response the government announced that there would be automatic deportation of serious offenders, a proposal which was supported by the House of Commons Home Affairs Committee (Fifth report 2005–06). The Committee also recommended that the court's powers of recommendation should be abolished, as they served no useful purpose as the decision was always ultimately that of the Home Secretary. These powers are currently under review. The immediate result was a significant rule change in July 2006. Until this time, the power of deportation, even in its earliest forms, was a discretion exercised on the merits of the case. From the inception of the present immigration rules until July 2006 a deportation decision required consideration of the all the mitigating factors, including specific listed circumstances such as age, length of residence in the UK, etc. (see chapter 18).

Rule change HC 1337 on 20 July 2006 abolished consideration of these factors in favour of a presumption that a deportation which the Secretary of State considered to be conducive to the public good would be in the public interest. Most recently, UK Borders Act 2007 ss 32–39 create a statutory obligation to make a deportation order in many criminal cases, and deem these to be conducive to the public good. The age-old discretion is now limited by statute and the rules, as explained more fully below.

16.4 Rationale for deportation

The power to deport is most commonly used in relation to people who have been convicted of a criminal offence. The traditional and liberal view is that its use is not intended to be a further punishment for the criminal offence, but should only be considered when the person's continued presence in the country impinges on the life of the public in a way that is contrary to the public interest (Immigration Act 1971 s 3(5)(a) and *R v Nazari* [1980] 3 All ER 880). Every society contains a certain level of criminal activity and so crime in itself does not warrant deportation. The Court of Appeal in *Raghbir Singh* [1996] Imm AR 507 said that the Secretary of State should consider 'whether it is bad for the country for him to remain'. The rule change in 2006 and provision for automatic deportation in the UK Borders Act 2007 demonstrated that this is not the view espoused by the current government. Present executive policy tends more towards the view that any non-British person who commits a criminal act should be removed. This view is an example of a policy which tends to creating categories of 'belongers' and 'non-belongers'. It is not really a penal policy as such, in that it regards criminality as secondary to nationality. It has echoes of the ATCSA experiment discussed in the last chapter, treating criminal matters as immigration matters wherever possible. Regarded as a penal policy, it could be summarized as 'out of sight, out of mind', rather like transportation of British subjects who had committed criminal offences to North America or Australia in the eighteenth century.

At the other end of the spectrum of opinion, it would be said that removing the criminal from society does not address the causes of crime and the wrongdoing of a non-citizen is no greater than the wrongdoing of a citizen. The possession of citizenship (and so exemption from deportation) is an irrelevant technicality given that one may apply for naturalization and so become a citizen after three years' residence in the UK, or on the other hand have lived here all one's life and still not have citizenship. The discrimination which results from the deportation of the non-citizen, combined with the harm to family and social networks, is a greater fracturing of the social fabric than the continued presence of someone who has committed a criminal offence. Punishment as meted out by the court is already intended to deter others and prevent re-offending and if it fails to do so that is a matter for criminal policy, not immigration control.

Whether or not one adopts the latter view, the option of 'out of sight, out of mind' presents significant problems in a globalizing world. For the most part neither the UK nor other countries any longer have domination over territories remote from themselves to which they can transport wrongdoers (although 'out of sight, out of mind' is perhaps now practised with a different groups of people, subject to extraordinary rendition or detention in military bases). Deportation is not to a remote place but usually to the deportee's country of nationality. However they may not have lived there for a considerable period of time, perhaps for the whole of their adult life. Which country should take responsibility? Increased international co-ordination of policing raises also the question of international co-ordination of criminal justice systems, but social attitudes to crime also differ widely. Deportation, if it is a solution at all, is only a local solution, and engages the question of how the destination state will treat the deportee. Indeed the punitive attitude of the destination state is now sometimes argued in deportation appeals as a reason why the person should not be deported (see, for instance, M v SSHD [2003] 1 WLR 1980 para 10 and Oviasoghie v SSHD [2002] UKIAT 06038 para 12). Deportation is frequently sought as a solution to national security threats, but, as discussed later in this chapter, this route has been fraught with difficulties for the government. As most potential deportees of this kind are suspected of *international* terrorism, their geographical location may not be a major factor in their operations.

If deportation is not a punishment, the philosophical basis for it is hard to find in an age where there is not a no-(white)man's land to which the criminal can be transported. It is sometimes viewed as a sanction for a kind of breach of hospitality, but where a person has spent all their working life in the UK and contributed as much as many citizens, this does not hold up.

16.5 Exercise of the power to deport

Section 5(1) Immigration Act 1971 expresses the power to make a deportation order as a power of the Secretary of State. However, in accordance with the *Carltona* principle (*Carltona Ltd* v *Commissioner of Works* [1943] 2 All ER 560 CA), properly authorized officials may carry out the function of the Secretary of State and in doing so their actions count as the actions of the Secretary of State. In the context of deportation, the *Carltona* principle authorizes deportation action to be taken by officials of the Home Office. This would not automatically be taken to include immigration officers, who, as we have seen, are a separate service within the Home Office, and in the case of deportations would have been involved in the investigation of the case. In 1988 the Secretary of State authorized certain nominated immigration officers of the rank of inspector also to make deportation decisions. This delegation was challenged in the case of *Oladehinde and Alexander* v *Secretary of State for the Home Department* [1991] 1 AC 254, but the House of Lords upheld the delegation. The court's concern about procedures being properly applied was met by the practice of making written records of the decision-making process, ensuring that immigration officers who had been involved in the investigation process were not involved in the deportation decision, and referring to the Home Office any proposed deportation where the person has compassionate circumstances or has been in the UK for a long time.

Deportation orders are usually signed by the Home Office Immigration Minister, but the Immigration Directorate Instructions (IDI Ch 13 s 1 para 6 May 2007) say that contentious cases may be signed by the Home Secretary. The Home Secretary has normally signed personally deportation orders which are made on what we may loosely call national security grounds. These grounds are discussed more specifically below. The Nationality, Immigration and Asylum Act 2002 s 97 brings together all immigration decisions made on these grounds, and provides that there will be no right of appeal to the tribunal if the Secretary of State certifies that the decision was taken by them personally wholly or partly in the interests of national security or the relationship between the UK and another country (s 97(2)). Section 99 allows the Secretary of State to issue a certificate under s 97 while an appeal is pending and thereby to prevent the appeal from continuing. In these certified national security cases, appeals are made instead to the Special Immigration Appeals Commission (see chapter 8).

16.6 Who may be deported?

Section 3(5) Immigration Act 1971 says that 'a person who is not a British citizen' may be deported. Here the term 'British citizen' has the meaning given to it by s 2 Immigration Act, as substituted by British Nationality Act 1981 s 39. It therefore includes not only those who have British citizenship but also Commonwealth citizens who retained right of abode when the British Nationality Act 1981 came into force, as discussed in chapter 3, namely those who married a British man before 1 January 1983, or who had a UK born parent.

There are other exemptions also. By Immigration Act 1971 s 7 Commonwealth and Irish citizens who were ordinarily resident in the UK on 1 January 1973 (the date that the 1971 Act came into force) and meet a further residence condition are exempt from deportation. The case of *Lawrence Kane* v *SSHD* [2000] Imm AR 250 confirmed that the only further residence condition which can now be applied is that the proposed deportee had been ordinarily resident for five years before the decision to deport was taken (s 7(1)(b) and (c)). The other basis for exemption in s 7(1)(a), which was residence in the UK at all times since the 1971 Act came into force, ceased to have independent effect at the end of 1977.

Unusually in counting periods of residence, according to Immigration Act s 7(2), remaining 'in breach of immigration laws' counts towards this five-year period. Case law has established that this only applies to people who overstay their period of leave, and not to those who entered illegally in the first place. Time spent in prison however does not count (*Lawrence Kane*). Section 8(3) provides an exemption from deportation for diplomats and their families.

The point which is sometimes a difficult one to grasp is that even people who have indefinite leave to remain and are settled may be deported unless they are exempt under s 7. There used to be an exemption for Commonwealth wives of Commonwealth men settled in the UK before 1973, but this was abolished by s 1 Immigration Act 1988. The abolition of this security for Commonwealth women was in breach of a guarantee which had been given by s 1(5) of the Immigration Act 1971, that Commonwealth citizens would be no less free to come and go after the 1971 Act than they were before. The 1988 Act repealed that section and caused a furore by removing the rights of Commonwealth citizens. However, without constitutional protection, given the UK's doctrine of the legislative supremacy of Parliament, such promises cannot be relied upon. Even the Human Rights Act does not act as a constitutional guarantee of the right to family life of Commonwealth citizens living in the UK (see generally chapter 9).

As discussed more fully in chapter 6, EEA nationals are only liable to be deported on the limited grounds allowed by Directive 2004/ 38. Developments in both EU and domestic law leave little room for doubt that EEA nationals have greater protection. Deportation of EEA nationals is an exception to the underlying right of freedom of movement and as such should be interpreted restrictively (Case 41/74 *Van Duyn v Home Office* [1974] ECR 1337). No such right can be claimed by non-EEA nationals. On the other hand, a non-EEA national to be deported from the UK will almost invariably have indefinite leave to remain. A question to bear in mind as we examine the case law is whether such leave to remain in the UK carries any protective power comparable with European freedom of movement.

16.7 Grounds for deportation

After overstaying and breach of condition became grounds for removal instead of deportation, there remained three grounds in the Immigration Act 1971 for deportation:

- the Secretary of State deems the deportation to be conducive to the public good (s 3(5)(a));
- being a family member of a deportee (s 3(5)(b));
- the recommendation of a criminal court sentencing a person over 17 (s 3(6)).

In case law and literature prior to the 1999 Act, deportations under what is now s 3(5)(a) are referred to as 's 3(5)(b)' deportations, and what is now s 3(5)(b) was s 3(5)(c).

16.7.1 Conducive to the public good

It has been noted in the historical introduction to this chapter that deportation conducive to the public good has a long history. The provision in the Aliens Act

1905 for deportation on grounds of criminal convictions or destitution is on the basis that it is not in the public interest for such persons to remain. Even before that, Finnis regards it as 'a constitutional principle that foreigners may be expelled for misconduct of sufficient weight' (2007:418), although our discussion of the sources of immigration law in chapter 1 tells us that the scope and origin of this principle is open to debate.

The meaning of this phrase and the necessity to establish it as the basis for deportation will rarely be relevant after the commencement of UK Borders Act 2007 ss 32–39. At the time of writing, on the authority of *EO (Deportation appeals: scope and process) Turkey* [2007] UKAIT 00062, the meaning of the 2006 rules is that the decision as to whether the deportation is conducive to the public good still has to be made, and the presumption contained in those rules only applies once that decision has been made. We shall therefore examine the meaning of 'conducive to the public good' rather briefly, with the understanding that a detailed consideration of its components may be of decreasing relevance.

The power to deport on s 3(5)(a) grounds is a broad one, not confined to any one interpretation of the meaning of the public good. In *Raghbir Singh* it was said that the ground 'covers a whole range of circumstances limited only by conventional public law and *Wednesbury* rules and the doctrine in *Padfield* v *Minister of Agriculture*,' i.e. normal administrative law limitations of reasonableness and impartiality.

The commission of criminal offences is the most common basis for deportation conducive to the public good. Until the implementation of UK Borders Act 2007 ss 32–39 this requires evaluation of the seriousness of the offence, the likelihood of re-offending and any deterrent effect on others. After the implementation of ss 32–39, the sentence awarded will be the only criterion. Likelihood of re-offending and deterrence are only included in the deportation decision to the extent that they are already taken into account in the sentence.

Case law has been divided on the question of whether the seriousness of the offence alone warrants deportation. For a time, it seemed that the influence of European law suggested that seriousness of the offence would only very rarely be enough on its own to warrant deportation. Now, case law is swinging the other way. As a reminder from chapter 6, in European cases, deportation is only justified when:

The personal conduct of the individual concerned must represent a genuine, present and sufficiently serious threat affecting one of the fundamental interests of society. Justifications that are isolated from the particulars of the case or that rely on considerations of general prevention shall not be accepted. (Directive 2004/38 Art 27.2)

By comparison with non-European cases, in *R v Abdi* [2007] EWCA Crim 1913 the underlying attitude of the court seems to be that the claimant would not have any grounds to defend his deportation after a sexual assault upon an eight-year-old boy, although the decision was not precisely on that point. The court does distinguish between serious and less serious offences, as in *R v Ahaiwe* [2007] EWCA Crim 1018, where the court held that an offence of using a false passport to gain employment, and for which the applicant was sentenced to seven months' imprisonment, was not serious enough in itself to warrant deportation.

A recent case decided under the pre-2006 version of the rules illustrates the issues which arise in deportation cases, the differences in approach that have prevailed, and a fairly classic judgment by the Court of Appeal.

 **Key Case**

GO (Nigeria) (Appellant GO) [2007] EWCA Civ 1163

The appellant was born in Nigeria. He first came to the UK in 1986, and after a trip to Nigeria in 1989, in 1990 returned and married a British citizen, obtaining leave to remain on that basis. The leave became indefinite in 1992. They had three children.

In 1992 the appellant was convicted of five offences of dishonesty on two separate occasions. In 1997 he was convicted of fraud in Denmark. In 1998 he was convicted of 20 offences of dishonesty in Australia. In 1999 he was convicted of a further seven offences of dishonesty in the UK, and nine more in 2004. He was sentenced on this occasion to three and a half years' imprisonment, half of it suspended. The Secretary of State decided to deport him. On appeal the immigration judge had to decide whether the deportation was conducive to the public good. In so doing, she drew a distinction between offences which struck 'at the heart of the community' such as those involving 'violence, sex, arson, drugs or terrorism' and offences of dishonesty, which she described as 'anti-social offences causing inconvenience and financial loss'.

The Court of Appeal held that this was an error of law, agreeing with the judge who reconsidered the matter that the sentence of three and a half years should have been taken into account as an indicator of the seriousness of the offence, and that the 'search for offences which "in themselves merit deportation" was misguided. What was required was an assessment of the appellant's offending, of his immigration history, of links with the UK (including but not confined to the links with his family) and then a balancing exercise' (para 19). The deportation was upheld.

The decision of the immigration judge, even though ultimately overturned, makes a distinction that has commonly been made, between offences which strike at the heart of the community and those which do not, usually regarded as relatively minor offences of dishonesty. For instance in *Goremsandu* [1996] Imm AR 250 the Court of Appeal held that the appellant's incest with his daughter was 'sufficiently morally repugnant to the accepted standards of morality' that his 'continued presence was not acceptable'. The judge's mistake in *GO*, according to the appeal court, was not the distinction she made between different kinds of offences, but disregarding the sentence as a measure of severity, and overweighting the *type* of offence as a factor, rather than making an overall assessment of the appellant's history of offending. The immigration judge gave an accurate account of her duty when she said 'what I have to consider is not whether he is a good or savoury character, but whether deportation would be conducive to the public good' (CA para 8). A highly significant factor in *GO*, as in any deportation case, was the risk of his re-offending. This includes not only the risk of whether he will, but also the seriousness of that for the public good, should it occur.

GO (Nigeria) is factually not an unusual deportation case. The decision-maker must weigh up the seriousness of the offence, the risk of re-offending, and the effect on the deportee and their family life.

Cases pre-dating the 2006 rules still have some authority, and reference may be made to, for instance, dicta in *Marchon* [1993] Imm AR 384 and *Samaroo* [2001] UKHRR 1150 for a view commonly taken of the seriousness of drugs offences. In *Samaroo* the Secretary of State explained the justification for a policy of deporting drugs offenders.

The purpose of the policy was to protect UK residents from the harm of drugs offences, and to give a deterrent signal to other would-be offenders. The protective purpose is warranted if there is a serious risk of the individual re-offending. The deterrent purpose was not evidenced, and following *Huang and Kashmiri* [2007] UKHL 11 it may be that the need for such a policy would be subjected to greater scrutiny on a future occasion. This puts a great divide, after the implementation of ss 32–39, between human rights cases and non-human rights cases. In the latter, where the deportation is for a specified offence, there will be no opportunity for examining the policy, its application to the individual, or reasons for it, except by way of judicial review; but the main policy is contained in statute, which is immune from review.

The assessment that deportation is conducive to the public good may be based on reasons other than criminal offences. Deception of the Home Office resulting in a grant of leave (*Kesse* [2001] EWCA Civ 177) and abuse of the institution of marriage (*ex p Cheema* [1982] Imm AR 12) are reasons that have been used in the past. Both these would now be subject to other statutory procedures for removal rather than deportation. *Ex p Cheema* defines marriages of convenience, confirming *ex p Ullah* [1982] Imm AR 124 in which the applicant was deported for entering into such a marriage, thereby abusing an institution which is 'one of the cornerstones of our society'.

These kinds of deception would now bring liability for removal either for obtaining entry by deception or obtaining leave to remain by deception. This became a specific ground for deportation in 1996, thus removing any need for the Secretary of State to prove that deportation was conducive to the public good, and on 2 October 2000 obtaining leave in this way became grounds for removal.

16.7.2 Future of deportation 'conducive to the public good'

At the time of writing, UK Borders Act ss 32–39 are not yet in force, so deportations are governed by the 2006 version of the immigration rules. The substance of the 2006 version of para 364 is as follows:

- where a person is liable to deportation
- the presumption is that the public interest requires it.
- SSHD will consider all relevant factors in each case BUT
- only in exceptional cases will public interest in deportation be outweighed
- EXCEPT where deportation is contrary to Human Rights or Refugee Convention.

EO (Deportation appeals: scope and process) Turkey [2007] UKAIT 00062 is the authority on interpretation of these rules. The tribunal held that the first point, 'where a person is liable to deportation', entails a decision that the deportation is conducive to the public good, as a person is not liable to deportation until that decision has been made. Therefore the presumption that deportation is in the public interest replaces the previous mandatory weighting of personal factors, but only comes into play once it has been determined that the deportation is conducive to the public good or the court had recommended it and it has been decided that neither the Human Rights nor the Refugee Convention would be breached. Old case law on conducive to the public good therefore, according to EO, still has relevance to all deportation decisions.

16.7.2.1 *UK Borders Act 2007 ss 32–39*

Section 32 provides that, where a person is sentenced to a period of imprisonment of at least 12 months, or is sentenced to a period of imprisonment of any length but has committed an offence specified under Nationality, Immigration and Asylum Act 2002 s 72(4), their deportation is automatically deemed to be conducive to the public good and the Secretary of State is obliged to make a deportation order. The main exceptions are where deportation would breach a person's ECHR rights or their rights under European Community law or breach the Refugee Convention, or the person was a minor at the date of conviction. The exceptions do not mean that no deportation order will be made (s 33), but rather that there is no duty to make the deportation order. In the case of a minor there is also no presumption that the deportation is for the public good. It is strange that the presumption of being conducive to the public good stands in the case of a proposed deportee protected by Community law, as in such a case Community law will prevail (see chapter 6).

Once the UK Borders Act provisions are in force, although it is proposed to end the use of deportation as a recommendation of the sentencing court, and the Secretary of State will make the deportation decision, in actuality the sentence of the court will be a decisive factor. This provision goes in exactly the opposite direction to the development of EC law, in which, as we have seen in chapter 6, deportation must be based on the personal conduct of the individual and the risk they present to society, and is a last resort for very serious reasons, in fact intended to be rare where the individual has lived in the host country for more than five years.

Once UK Borders Act ss 32–39 are implemented, the Secretary of State only has discretion to decide whether deportation is 'conducive to the public good' in cases of minors or where the proposed deportee has not received a prison sentence of the kind covered by the section, or in cases not based on a criminal convictions. The old case law will in theory apply where the deeming provisions do not. Where Article 8 is raised in opposition to the deportation the court or tribunal will still have to decide whether the deportation is necessary in a democratic society, as required by Article 8.2. The approach under the 2006 rules and then the 2007 Act will need decisions of the higher courts in order for the matter to be fully resolved.

16.7.3 **Political reasons**

Interestingly, the deeming sections in the UK Borders Act will not necessarily apply to deportations under s 3(5)(a) where the ground of the decision is that deportation is conducive to the public good as being in the interests of national security or of the relations between the UK and any other country (Nationality, Immigration and Asylum Act 2002 s 97(2)). The reason for this is that these deportations are not necessarily based on criminal convictions but on the Secretary of State's assessment of the risk that the person poses to national security. Before the 2002 Act the national security ground also included 'other reasons of a political nature'. Unlike other deportations under s 3(5)(a), national security appeals do not go through the ordinary appeal process, but only to the Special Immigration Appeal Commission (SIAC). The Secretary of State also has power to take proceedings out of the ordinary appeal process and transfer them to SIAC if he or she certifies that the decision was made wholly or partly in reliance on information which ought not to be disclosed for reasons of public interest or national security or relations with other states (s 97(3)).

As in other areas of law, where the question of national security arises, the balance between the state and the individual shifts further towards the State, involving curtailment of the rights of the individual. The curtailment of access to the courts meant that in the past there was little case law on deportation on national security or political grounds. However, developments in the last few years have brought political and national security deportations more into the public and legal sphere. First, the judgment of the European Court of Human Rights in the case of *Chahal v UK* (1997) 23 EHRR 413 was critical of UK procedures in national security cases. As a consequence, the UK government was obliged to set up the Special Immigration Appeals Commission (SIAC), to meet the Court's concerns. Second, the growing involvement of all three branches of government (executive, judicial, legislative) in defining and controlling terrorism has brought a spotlight onto the question of exclusion from the UK for reasons connected with national security. This is not a new phenomenon following the US President's declaration of a so-called 'war on terrorism' in September 2001, although the Antiterrorism, Crime and Security Act 2001 was expressly a response to that declaration. As we shall see below, some developments pre-date 11 September 2001, but the pace of them has been increasing.

16.7.3.1 *Basis of political deportation*

Although so-called 'political' or 'national security' deportations are treated differently from others, the formal grounds for such a deportation are still that the deportation is conducive to the public good. The bases of national security and international relations may overlap. The Secretary of State is not obliged to settle the allegations in such a way that they fit into one or another category (*SSHD v Rehman* [2001] 3 WLR 877discussed below). Simply stating that the deportation was 'in the interests of national security, namely the likelihood of your involvement in terrorist activity' was held to be giving sufficient reason in *Jahromi v SSHD* [1996] Imm AR 20 where the Home Office gave evidence that further disclosure would jeopardize intelligence sources.

Before the changes following on the case of *Chahal v UK* (1997) 23 EHRR 413, there was no right of appeal at all to a judicial body against a political or national security deportation. The Special Immigration Appeals Commission (SIAC) which resulted from this case has already been described in chapter 8, and the first case in the SIAC holds an important place in the development of the law on national security deportations.

16.7.3.2 *Rehman's case*

 Key Case

SSHD v Rehman [2001] 3 WLR 877

Mr Rehman was a Muslim minister of religion who had limited leave to remain under the immigration rules in that capacity. He was married and had two children born in the UK. He was refused indefinite leave to remain on the grounds that the Secretary of State was satisfied that Mr Rehman was involved with an Islamic terrorist organization, that in the light of that association his continued presence in the country represented a danger to national security.

The Secretary of State added that his deportation from the UK would be conducive to the public good in the interests of national security because of his association with Islamic terrorist groups. The organization was named, though the Secretary of State's view was formed on the basis of information received from confidential sources.

The SIAC found that the evidence did not establish the acts alleged, namely that Mr Rehman had recruited British Muslims to undergo militant training, or engaged in fund-raising for Lashkar Tayyaba (LT), or knowingly sponsored individuals for militant training camps. It was accepted that he had provided sponsorship, information, and advice to people going to Pakistan for training. Such training he had regarded as purely religious and developmental. It had not been proved that he was aware of any militant content in such training.

In addition to the question of the jurisdiction of the Commission, two questions of law were appealed to the Court of Appeal and House of Lords. The first was the standard of proof to be applied. The SIAC took the view that these were serious allegations which had important repercussions for the individual involved and which impugned his good character. For these reasons, a standard of proof such as that laid down in *Khawaja* [1984] AC 74 should be applied, that is, a high civil standard of proof. It was in using this standard that they found that the matters alleged against Mr Rehman, as above, were not proved. The Court of Appeal and House of Lords approved the standard as applied to the appellant's actual involvement in alleged terrorist activities, but found that the question of danger to national security required an all round assessment of the situation, not just a finding of, as it were, guilt or innocence in relation to past events. The Court of Appeal said: 'it is necessary not only to look at the individual allegations and ask whether they have been proved. It is also necessary to examine the case as a whole against an individual and then ask whether on a global approach that individual is a danger to national security' ([2000] 3 All ER 778 at 791). The House of Lords approved this view and said that the Secretary of State was 'entitled to have regard to precautionary and preventative principles rather than to wait until directly harmful activities have taken place' (para 22). In fact the idea of a standard of proof was, said Lords Steyn and Hoffmann, not really appropriate to a case where the central question was not, as in a civil or criminal trial, whether something had happened in the past, but rather whether something was likely to happen in the future. It was an evaluation of risk. The effect of this is that the Secretary of State is entitled to make a decision, based on evidence which s/he is not obliged to disclose, that an individual who cannot be proved to have taken part in any unlawful activities, should be deported because there is, in the words of Lord Slynn, a 'real possibility' that their presence may in the future constitute a danger.

The second issue in the appeals was the question of the definition of national security. First, there was the question of whether the SIAC had jurisdiction to engage in the question of defining national security. The House of Lords held that this could be within the jurisdiction of a judicial body; it was a question of construction and therefore a question of law. The area of contention between the parties was whether activities in the UK which furthered the cause of an organization abroad which could use violence which was not directed at the UK could be said to endanger the security of the UK. For the purposes of the case, SIAC adopted the position that:

A person may be said to offend against national security if he engages in, promotes or encourages violent activity which is targeted at the UK, its system of government, or its people. This includes activities directed at the overthrow or destabilisation of foreign governments if that foreign government is likely to take reprisals against the UK which affect the security of the UK or its nationals. National security extends also to situations where UK citizens are targeted wherever they may be.

SIAC accepted the appellant's argument that for an activity to endanger the national security of the UK there must be some direct link between the activity and a danger to the UK. The House of Lords and Court of Appeal rejected this view. They adopted the approach of Auld LJ in *Raghbir Singh* [1996] Imm AR 507, who said at 511, 'all sorts of consequences may flow from the existence of terrorist conspiracies or organizations here, whether or not their outcome is intended to occur abroad. Who knows what equally violent response here this sort of conduct may provoke?', and of Lord Mustill in the asylum case of T [1996] Imm AR 443, that 'terror as a means of gaining what might loosely be described as political ends poses a danger not only to individual states but also to the community of nations'. Lord Slynn said:

It seems to me that, in contemporary world conditions, action against a foreign state may be capable indirectly of affecting the security of the United Kingdom. The means open to terrorists both in attacking another state and attacking international or global activity by the community of nationals, whatever the objectives of the terrorist, may well be capable of reflecting on the safety and well-being of the United Kingdom or its citizens...To require the matters in question to be capable of resulting 'directly' in a threat to national security limits too tightly the discretion of the executive in deciding how the interests of the state...need to be protected.

This approach is an international one, in which the fight against terrorism is seen as something in which nations have a common interest. National security is bound up with international security, thus promotion of terrorism against any state is capable of being a threat to the security of the UK, and in the context of terrorism the Secretary of State was not necessarily wrong to justify a decision on national security by reference to damage to relations between countries.

The House of Lords made a distinction between deciding what national security is, which the courts could decide, and what is *in the interests of national security,* which they regarded as a matter for the Secretary of State to decide. In the words of Lord Hoffmann: 'the question of whether something is "in the interests" of national security is not a question of law. It is a matter of judgment and policy' (para 50). Such judgments should be made by someone who was democratically accountable, not by the courts.

The deference shown to the Secretary of State's view on what is in the interests of national security, combined with the abandonment of a standard of proof, to an extent undermines the jurisdiction of the SIAC. They can indeed review all questions of law, fact, and exercise of discretion, but issues of what is in the interests of national security are to be regarded as an exercise of discretion concerning risk, not one of establishing facts, and this is a discretion which the Secretary of State is best placed to exercise.

Macdonald commented on this case at the Court of Appeal stage: 'Not since the majority decision *Liversidge and Anderson* has the executive been given such deference; one can hear the Secretary of State saying "I can make national security mean anything I want it to mean"' (2001:724).

Macdonald was commenting in May 2001, and his comparison with *Liversidge and Anderson* [1942] AC 206 was prophetic. That decision is often explained on the basis that it was taken during wartime, when the government needs to be given more scope to act as it sees fit, even in breach of people's ordinary civil liberties. The response of the UK and USA to the attack on the World Trade Centre on 11 September 2001 was to legislate in way that is reminiscent of war time in the extent of inroads made into civil liberties.

This approach to the standard of proof and assessment of national security risk is similar to that used in refugee claims to assess future risk should the asylum seeker return to their country of origin, and the authority on that point, *Karanakaran*, is used also in national security appeals. For instance in *Y v SSHD* [2006] UKSIAC 36/2004, SIAC held the proceedings were not civil proceedings, requiring acts to be proved on a balance of probabilities. 'They are public law proceedings the focus of which is risk, that is an evaluation of what harm may happen in the future' (para 128). This draws directly on *Karanakaran*. Y was arrested on suspicion of being concerned in the instigation, preparation or commission of acts of terrorism. He was tried as a defendant in the 'ricin' or 'poisons plot' trial but acquitted on all charges. Like other potential deportees on national security grounds, he did not hear all the evidence against him, as some was considered in 'closed' sessions of the SIAC. He was shown to be linked to militant organizations in Algeria, indeed facts related to this had formed the basis of his asylum claim which had succeeded on appeal some years earlier. Y could be shown to have connections and associations with people who were found culpable. For instance, he ran the bookshop at the mosque associated with extremist activity, and appeared to have photocopied the poison recipes. As the SIAC said, in isolation, each matter might be explicable as 'innocent'. Crucially, they decided that treating the matters as separate was not the right approach. They should be regarded cumulatively, and in that way they built a picture of someone the Secretary of State could legitimately regard as a risk. This makes it clear that the assessment of national security cases now is the opposite end of the spectrum from criminal trials, and it does not follow the *Khawaja* approach that would require a high standard of proof because of the serious consequences for the individual. The risk to society is seen as more serious.

Deportation on national security grounds has been used for proceeding against numerous people suspected of terrorist activities but who have not been convicted of, and often not even charged with, criminal offences in the UK. The deportation of Abu Qatada was held lawful on this ground by the SIAC (*Omar Othman (aka Abu Qatada) v SSHD* [2007] UKSIAC 15/2005). The nature of SIAC proceedings and evidence is discussed is chapter 8, and the reliance on assurances of fair treatment in the country to which the person is deported is discussed in chapter 4.

Procedural rules have developed restrictively in national security cases. In *N v SSHD* [2005] UKSIAC 18/2002 the SIAC held that the relevant circumstances for deciding whether a deportation order ought to be revoked were to be assessed at the date of the deportation decision, not the date of the hearing. In a non-political deportation on public good grounds, heard by the AIT, under Nationality, Immigration and Asylum Act 2002 s 82(2)(k), evidence is assessed at the date of the hearing. The effect of this is that in a political or national security case, the judicial body does not have an opportunity to decide whether facts subsequent to the decision bear out the initial assessment that the person was a danger. The Immigration, Asylum and Nationality Act 2006 includes a provision that deportation orders may be made on the grounds of threat to national security while an appeal is pending or may be brought, in contrast with other deportations in which no order may be made until the appeal process is exhausted (s 7, excluding application of s 79 of the 2002 Act).

The London bombings on 7 July 2005 provoked further legislative proposals, and the government published a consultation paper suggesting that the power to deport on national security grounds should include 'indirect threat', apparently not taking into account that the House of Lords had already sanctioned this in *Rehman*.

16.7.4 **Family members**

Apart from deportations conducive to the public good, the only other people who may be deported since the implementation of the 1999 Act are family members of people who are deported under s 3(5)(a). Note that these deportations now take place under s 3(5)(b) of the 1971 Act, whereas in case law prior to October 2000 they will be referred to as s 3(5)(c). 'Family members' are defined by the 1971 Act s 5(4), as amended by the 1996 Act, as the husband or wife and children of the person to be deported. 'Children' include adopted children. When parents are unmarried, children are regarded as children of only their mother. Although the entry of second or further wives is not permitted under the Immigration Rules, in the context of deportation polygamy is recognized, as 'wife' includes each of two or more wives.

Paragraphs 365–368 of the Immigration Rules give guidance on the deportation of family members, including civil partners, though these are not mentioned in the Act. According to these paragraphs, the Secretary of State will not normally decide to deport the partner of a deportee where they have qualified for settlement in their own right or have been living apart from the deportee. If a child is living apart from the deportee either with their other parent or because they have established themselves on an independent basis, the Secretary of State will not normally decide to deport the child. This is also the case where the child married before the deportation 'came into prospect'. There are additional factors to be taken into account in the deportation of family members, and these are set out in para 367 as follows:

(i) the ability of the spouse or civil partner to maintain himself and any children in the United Kingdom, or to be maintained by relatives or friends without charge to public funds, not merely for a short period but for the foreseeable future; and

(ii) in the case of a child of school age, the effect of removal on his education; and

(iii) the practicality of any plans for a child's care and maintenance in this country if one or both of his parents were deported; and

(iv) any representations made on behalf of the spouse or child.

In *Njuguna v SSHD* [2001] EWCA Civ 688 the Court of Appeal held that these questions were irrelevant in relation to a five-year-old child. He was not, in any event, going to be able to make a life independently of his mother in the UK. If she were deported, he would be too, and issuing a notice and order in relation to him was simply taking the legal power which inevitably followed from his mother's deportation.

According to s 5(3) of the 1971 Act, a deportation order may not be made against family members if more than eight weeks have elapsed since the principal deportee left the country. Again, this in practical terms only applies where the family member has a viable life in the UK aside from their deported relative.

16.7.5 **Criminal court's recommendation**

Section 3(6) of the 1971 Act gives the power to the Secretary of State to deport following the recommendation of a criminal court. The power to make such a recommendation is a sentencing power which may be exercised by the courts in relation to a non-British citizen over the age of 17 who has been convicted of an offence which is punishable with imprisonment. Appeals against the recommendation itself are appeals against sentence and are made through the criminal appeals process.

The decision whether to follow the recommendation is a separate step, and this is the responsibility of the Secretary of State. The recommendation of the sentencing judge, prior to the UK Borders Act 2007, did not bind the Secretary of State. Case law held that he or she has a different constitutional role in the decision-making process and is better placed to take a wider policy-based view of whether deportation is the right course (*R v SSHD ex p Dinc* [1999] Imm AR 380 CA).

16.7.5.1 *Criminal courts and deportation*

The general powers of the criminal courts include sentencing for immigration offences. On the other hand, people who are liable to deportation for an offence which has nothing to do with immigration may not have a flawless immigration history. There is plenty of scope for confusion here. Macdonald used some choice words to describe an aspect of the problem:

Matters have not been assisted by the tendency of the courts to describe any non-citizen guilty of an offence under the Immigration Act as an 'illegal immigrant'. The phrase is meaningless and has pejorative connotations of status that may be misleading. A student who fails to get the Department of Employment's permission before getting a summer job, a husband who forgets to apply in time for permission to remain with a wife, an alien who fails to inform the police of a change of address, are doubtless all guilty of offences which may be described as regulatory, but it would be as inappropriate to describe them as 'illegal immigrants' as it would be to describe the company which fails to make expeditious VAT returns as an illegal business. (1995:489)

Deportation for an immigration offence is not appropriate unless it would be warranted in accordance with the proper criteria for deportation discussed below. Some immigration offences are relatively trivial and the fact that they are immigration offences does not justify deportation.

16.7.5.2 *Guidelines*

Guidelines for the criminal courts in exercising their power to recommend deportation were set out initially in *R v Caird* (1970) 54 Cr App Rep 499, CA and developed in *R v Nazari* [1980] 3 All ER 880.

The first guideline is that criminal courts are concerned with the potential detriment to the UK of the person remaining in the country. This has been regarded as nothing to do with their immigration status as the detriment is through criminal activity. However, in *R v Benabbas* [2005] EWCA Crim 2113 the Court of Appeal held that where deportation was for an immigration offence, immigration status is 'not entirely irrelevant: it is part of the defendant's personal conduct...a matter of public interest' (para 40) and 'detriment is intimately bound up with the protection of public order afforded by confidence in a system of passports' (para 41). Here the offence was of using a stolen and forged French passport contrary to Forgery and Counterfeiting Act 1981 s 3, and the recommendation was held to be warranted. The risk of re-offending is a key matter to be assessed, and the court will also have regard to the nature of the offence and the defendant's past record.

Second, the court in *Nazari* thought that they should not be concerned with the political situation or regime or any political threat in the defendant's home country.

The Home Office rather than the criminal court was the place to assess such matters. It will readily be seen that concerns about what the defendant may face in their home country may be asylum issues, and the Secretary of State's decision to deport can be appealed on asylum grounds under s 84 of the 2002 Act. Issues concerning the political situation in the defendant's home country would be addressed in that appeal. However, the Human Rights Act affects this stance by the courts. As public bodies under s 6, they are obliged not to act in a way which is incompatible with the defendant's Convention rights. If there is clear evidence that deportation would expose the defendant to a risk for instance of torture, inhuman or degrading treatment or punishment, contrary to Article 3, then a recommendation for deportation would be a breach of s 6 and appealable within the criminal appeal system on human rights grounds.

Third, following *Nazari* the courts were to have regard to the effect of a recommendation for deportation on innocent third parties. The emphasis here was on the harm and distress caused to others, e.g. dependent children or spouse, by the deportation. One might expect this consideration to be expanded by the application of the Convention right in Article 8, to respect for private and family life.

However, the Court of Appeal in *Carmona v R* [2006] EWCA Crim 508 held that the criminal court's recommendation was not an interference with the right. The actual question of interference arises only when the Secretary of State decides to implement it. Furthermore, as the criminal court was not in a position to assess any breach of the appellant's rights abroad, they could not assess them at all, and it would accordingly be irrational to consider the less directly engaged rights of family members. In so deciding they took into account that there is now a right of appeal against the Secretary of State's decision, whereas at the time of *Nazari* there was not. The court also held that there was no difference between the standards applied to European nationals and non-Europeans. Leave to appeal to the House of Lords has been sought.

16.7.5.3 *Relationship between the Secretary of State's decision and the court's recommendation*

Until the Nationality, Immigration and Asylum Act 2002, case law developments on the question of deportation on the basis of criminal convictions took place mainly in the civil jurisdiction as appeals against deportation conducive to the public good. The 2002 Act granted a right of appeal against the recommendation of the criminal court, and this, perhaps combined with the different provisions of the legal aid scheme in the criminal courts, has meant that more recent cases exploring deportation have taken place in the criminal appeal courts, as shown by the examples above of *Carmona, Abdi, Benabbas* and *Ahaiwe*. In *Abdi* the court commented on what it perceived as the likely lawfulness of the Secretary of State deciding to deport. This shows a tendency to conflate the two jurisdictions, which is unsurprising in the light of the UK Borders Act.

The earlier case law on the relationship between the Secretary of State's decision and the court's recommendation now looks quite ironic in the light of that Act. The court in *Nazari* said that when a court made a recommendation for deportation, all it was doing was giving an opinion that it would be to the detriment of the country for the accused to remain. The Secretary of State then has regard to 'a larger canvas of factors' (*M v SSHD* para 24) when making the decision whether to deport. These include policy issues, perhaps in relation to deterrence, and the position in the country to which the defendant would be deported. The court in sentencing will now have to reckon with the opposite situation, that if it hands down a prison sentence of more than 12 months to a foreign national, it is automatically at the same time compelling the Secretary of State to deport the defendant, unless human rights or asylum considerations prevent that. In the present state of the law, *Carmona* may be relied upon to exonerate the sentencing court from considering or taking responsibility for any human rights violation, which, the court thought, would be more appropriately assessed at the end of the sentence in the light of circumstances known then. In the case of a 12-month sentence, after deducting automatic remission and perhaps time on remand, the question may become more immediate for the sentencing court and may even affect sentencing practice.

16.8 **Revocation**

A deportation order does not expire after a period of time. It runs until it is revoked unless the person who is the subject of the order becomes a British citizen (1971 Act s 5(2)). However it may be revoked on application in accordance with paras 390–392 of the Immigration Rules. The factors which will be taken into account are:

(i)   the grounds on which the order was made;

(ii) any representations made in support of revocation;

(iii) the interests of the community, including the maintenance of effective immigration control; and

(iv) the interests of the applicant, including any compassionate circumstances.

Paragraph 391 provides that the deportation order will not normally be revoked unless the applicant has been away from the UK for at least three years, unless in the most exceptional circumstances. In *Wiafe* (17224) 17 years of prior residence and her children and other family members in the UK did not count as an exceptional circumstance. These factors would have already been taken into account in the decision to deport. In *Jain* (HX00597) the detriment to the applicant's business because of his inability to attend to it personally also did not count as an exceptional circumstance. The tribunal took the view that he had an opportunity to avoid that by leaving voluntarily at an earlier stage.

Paragraph 391 also provides that revocation will not normally be authorized unless there is a change of circumstances or fresh information coming to light, either of which might materially alter the situation. The passage of time in itself may amount to a change of circumstance, but as is clear from the above, less than three years is not normally long enough. Annex A to the Home Office's internal guidance on deportation provides guidance on the periods which could be regarded as normal before revocation. It suggests three years for people deported under the old s 3(5)(a) for overstaying or breach of condition and their families, and 10 years for people convicted of serious offences. These are defined as offences of violence, persistent, or large-scale burglary or theft, blackmail, forgery, drug offences, and public order offences including riot and affray.

Under s 82 of the 2002 Act there is a right of appeal against the refusal to revoke a deportation order, but under s 92 this right may only be exercised from outside the country unless it is based on asylum or human rights grounds that have not been certified as clearly unfounded. Until the deportee actually leaves, time does not start to be counted towards the time before which an application can be made to revoke. From this point of view there may be nothing to be gained by attempting to stay longer, although occasionally successful public campaigns are mounted to avoid deportation even at this late stage (see, for instance, 'Resistance from Below' in *No-one is Illegal* (Cohen 2003)).

Revocation of a deportation order does not entitle the successful applicant to enter the UK. It only means that an application may be made for leave to enter under the immigration rules and this will be considered on its merits. If for some reason the order is not enforced, IDI Ch13 s 5 provides that consideration can be given to revoking it.

16.9 Supervised and voluntary departures

Once a person is aware that they may be subject to deportation, if there are no strong grounds to challenge the deportation they may wish to leave the country as quickly as possible to avoid a deportation order being made. This may happen with a greater or lesser degree of official involvement. It is possible for a person to leave of their own accord and at their own expense at any time after they become aware that they may be subject to deportation. This may be before or after notice of intention to deport has been served. Informing the Home Office of their travel plans will avoid any further action being taken and so avoid the making of a deportation order.

If the deportation order is made and the person is not aware of it, but leaves after it was made, they are still regarded as deported, and the order will have the same validity as if the Home Office had enforced the order (IDI Ch 13 s 1 para 9.1). If they leave before the order is made, even without contact with the Home Office, any deportation order made after that date will be invalid.

Alternatively a person may sign a formal disclaimer of appeal rights and agree to leave, which gives rise to the possibility of the immigration service paying for their passage (Immigration Act 1971 s 5(6)). This is known as 'supervised departure' (IDI Ch 13 s 5 para 9.2).

There are no immigration rules concerning these procedures, although supervised departure was included in the rules until 2 October 2000. In reality of course someone cannot be prevented from leaving of their own accord, and in a sense no rules are required. The International Organisation for Migration operates voluntary return programmes for 'irregular migrants' as well as people whose asylum claims have failed.

Where voluntary procedures avoid a deportation order being made they also avoid a prohibition on re-entering the UK. However, it is possible that the person's passport may be endorsed to show that the decision to deport was made and served, and this may affect future applications to enter under para 320 of the Immigration Rules.

QUESTIONS

1 The European Court of Human Rights in the case of *Maaouia v France* said that deportation is not a criminal penalty imposed upon a foreign national. It is not a punishment for a crime for which they have already served a prison sentence, but is an administrative matter. Consider the arguments for and against that view.

2 Is it justifiable to treat European nationals more favourably in the context of deportation?

online resource centre   For guidance on answering questions, visit www.oxfordtextbooks.co.uk/orc/clayton3e.

FURTHER READING

Bevan, V. (1986) *The Development of British Immigration Law* (Croom Helm), pp. 305–309.

Clery, E., Daniel, N., and Tah, C. *The Voluntary assisted return and reintegration 2003: an evaluation*, Home Office RDS 2005.

Cohen, S. (2003) 'Resistance from below', in Cohen, S. (ed.) *No-one is Illegal* (Stoke on Trent: Trentham Books).

Dembour, M.-B. (2003) 'Human Rights Laws and Nationality in Collusion: The Plight of Quasi-Nationals at Strasbourg', *Netherlands Quarterly of Human Rights,* vol. 21, no. 1, pp. 63–98.

Farbey, J. (2007) 'Foreign National Prisoners: Current Law and Practice' *Journal of Immigration, Asylum & Nationality Law* vol. 21, no.1 pp. 6–13.

O'Nions, H. (2001) 'The Human Rights of Deportees in the English Legal System' *Journal of Civil Liberties* 691, pp. 3–17.

Shah, R. (2007) 'The FNP Saga' *Journal of Immigration, Asylum & Nationality Law* vol. 21, no.1, pp. 27–31.

17

Grounds for removal

SUMMARY

This chapter describe the grounds in law for exercising the power to remove a person from the UK. The development of the definition of an illegal entrant is described, and the inclusion within the removal power of many people who formerly could only be deported.

17.1 Introduction

The power of removal is the clearest possible demonstration of the Crown's power to control the entry of foreign nationals, though this does not mean that it is an untrammelled power. It is exercised within a statutory framework, principally that of the Immigration Act 1971, amended and supplemented by the Asylum and Immigration Act 1996, the Immigration and Asylum Act 1999, the Nationality, Immigration and Asylum Act 2002 and the Asylum and Immigration (Treatment of Claimants etc) Act 2004. The power is tempered by human rights and asylum considerations; nevertheless, in 2006, 63,865 people were removed from the UK.

Directions for removal may be given without, necessarily, any kind of judicial process. A person may be put onto an aeroplane or a ship and taken to another country without any opportunity to object in advance to this course of action. Because of the abrupt and potentially speedy nature of this process, and its lack of judicial oversight, it can be described as 'summary removal'. It is difficult to imagine a more dramatic exercise of power by the executive over the individual, but its power may be mitigated by a right of appeal. Where there is an existing entry clearance or work permit then there are in-country rights of appeal, and when human rights or asylum claims are made, but only if this claim is not certified as clearly unfounded by the Secretary of State (Nationality, Immigration and Asylum Act 2002 Parts 4 and 5). There are other limited appeal rights, but these may only be exercised after removal. As a consequence, resort has often been made to judicial review, which suspends the implementation of removal.

By returning to the UK after being removed, a person is not in automatic breach of a legal provision, as they would be when subject to a current deportation order. However, the removal and the reasons for it are discretionary reasons for refusing entry on a subsequent occasion (HC 395 para 320: see chapter 7).

17.1.1 Terminology

There is scope for a great deal of confusion in the use of the term 'removal' and associated phrases. One use of the term 'administrative removal' is to refer to removal on the grounds which used to be grounds for deportation, discussed below. This distinguishes it from removal of illegal entrants and those refused entry. Another use of the term 'administrative removal' is to refer to all removals, using 'administrative' to distinguish it from deportation which has an enduring legal effect. Finally, all enforced departures including deportation end in removal, as this term is used to describe the actual embarkation on transport which takes the person away, and all such departures are preceded by removal directions. These are served on the captain of a ship or aircraft or on a train operator and on the person themselves, telling them when and where to report in order for their removal to take place. The term 'removal' is used in this chapter to refer to all removals as distinct from deportations. The term 'administrative removal' is not used. In a later section removal directions are discussed specifically.

17.1.2 Expansion in use of the power to remove

The power of removal has existed in its present form since 1 January 1973 when the Immigration Act 1971 came into force. The Act made Commonwealth citizens and aliens subject to the same legal regime, and this included the power to remove anyone who had entered in breach of immigration laws (Sch 2 and s 33). *Azam v SSHD* [1974] AC 18 confirmed that this statutory power applied even to Commonwealth citizens who had entered before the Act came into effect, and who would have been immune from removal or deportation under the previous law.

The power to remove was implemented straight away. Evans charts the growth in the use of the power of removal from 80 people in the first year of operation to a peak of 910 in 1980, dropping again to 640 in 1981. The starting figure of 80 was, he points out, a significant increase on the steady annual figure of around 60 people removed each year from 1968 to 1972. The increased number of removals in this period reflects expansion of the law governing removal at that time. The 1971 Act extended power to Commonwealth citizens, and after the implementation of the Act the courts took hold of the concept of 'illegal entrant' and extended it, as discussed below, in a way not foreseen by Parliament. In 1983 the House of Lords put the brake on this expansion.

17.1.3 Policy on removals

Developments in policy and practice have had at least as significant an impact on removals as developments in law. The growth in numbers of asylum seekers has been accompanied by a rise in the numbers of removals. The number of people removed as illegal entrants doubled from 1987 to 1988 and the UK Immigration Advisory Service suggested that the increase in removals was part of an attempt to curtail asylum appeals (Dummett and Nicol 1990:255). By the time of the most recent published annual figures the number of removals had shot up to 63,865 (Control of Immigration Statistics 2006 Home Office August 2007), a higher figure than the previous two years, though not the highest ever.

A desire to process asylum claims quickly and to remove unsuccessful applicants are significant policy drivers behind the law and practice on removal. This is borne out by the steady reduction in appeal rights against removal, particularly the powers to certify human rights and asylum claims. It was considered in the Home Affairs Select Committee Report on Asylum Removals that the integrity of the asylum process relies on the capacity to effect the removal of those whose claim has failed (e.g. para 8). The Committee's report also describes the practical and legal complexities of effecting removals, and although asylum policy may drive the law, in 2006 only 16,330 of the 63,865 people removed had sought asylum at some stage (2006 Statistics para 6.3). These practicalities were also discussed in chapter 2.

On 16 September 2004 the British Prime Minister promised to double the number of failed asylum seekers removed by the end of 2005, though the statistical basis for this was not clear. On the other hand, there continue to be important questions about whether removals to certain countries are safe and feasible. The UNHCR made statements advising that returns to Somalia and Iraq were unsafe (16 June and 22 October 2004: unhcr.org.uk), but the Home Office declined to undertake that removals would not take place to these countries, and continued to consider them on a case by case basis. The only country to which, as a matter of policy, removals have not been taking place in recent times has been Zimbabwe, as discussed in chapter 13.

The manner in which removals are carried out is also an issue of public concern. The Medical Foundation published a report detailing excessive force used, sometimes resulting in injury. As a consequence, CCTV cameras were to be installed in the vans used to carry out removals (news.bbc.co.uk 5 November 2004).

17.2 Grounds for removal

There are two sets of powers of removal; Immigration Act 1971 Sch 2 paras 8 and 9 gives power to immigration officers to remove people who have been refused leave to enter (para 8) and illegal entrants (para 9). Immigration and Asylum Act 1999 s 10 gives power to remove people who have overstayed the limit of their leave, or have breached conditions of leave or obtained leave to remain by deception. It also gives power to remove the families of such people.

We shall consider each of these grounds in turn. The main legal controversies have surrounded the question of who is deemed to be an illegal entrant.

17.2.1 Illegal entrants

The way that provisions concerning illegal entrants are enacted suggests a lack of importance, and it is extraordinary that powers of such a draconian nature are almost incidental in statute. The reasons are historical, but the many legislative changes since 1971 have not addressed this. The definition of an illegal entrant is found in s 33, the definition section of the 1971 Act, and the power to remove an illegal entrant is in Sch 2. A power which forms a major plank of immigration control would be more appropriately located in the body of the statute. However, the power to remove was envisaged as an administrative matter, an action which could be taken speedily by immigration officers without judicial involvement.

An 'illegal entrant' is defined in s 33(1) of the 1971 Act, as amended by the Asylum and Immigration Act 1996, as a person:

 (i) unlawfully entering or seeking to enter in breach of a deportation order or of the immigration laws; or
 (ii) entering or seeking to enter by means which include deception by another person.

A person may be termed an 'illegal entrant' without actually entering, as s 33 covers those who 'seek to enter' as well as those who actually do. A person may be apprehended, say, at a port, and may be subject to removal as an illegal entrant if they were seeking to enter in breach of immigration laws but had not yet done so. A clandestine entrant may come within this category. Where someone presents documentation or makes an application, the nature of that documentation or application is crucial as a lawful applicant with entry clearance has a right of appeal if refused. An illegal entrant has no such right of appeal against refusal of leave, except on human rights or asylum grounds (2002 Act s 84). Secondly, a person may be deemed an illegal entrant if they do actually enter illegally. We shall consider shortly what this means. Thirdly, an illegal entrant is a person 'who has so entered'. The effect of this is that there is no cut-off date for designation as an illegal entrant. Under the Commonwealth Immigrants Act 1962 a person who remained undetected for 24 hours could not be removed; the 1968 Act extended this to 28 days but there are no such periods of grace in present law. Now, a person may live for years in insecurity, not knowing whether they will be subject to enforcement action. While a long residence in this country may affect whether enforcement action is taken or is successful (see chapter 7), the possibility of that action remains until their status is regularized. There are a number of ways in which a person may be considered to enter illegally.

17.2.1.1 *Entering without leave*

'Entering in breach of the immigration laws' was initially interpreted as meaning simply 'entering without leave'. The immigration laws were primarily concerned with the regulation of entry, so someone who entered in breach of those laws entered without having gone through that regulatory process. Specifically, 1971 Act s 3(1)(a) states:

Except as otherwise provided by or under this Act, where a person is not a British Citizen (a) he shall not enter the UK unless given leave to do so in accordance with this Act.

Entry without leave by someone who needs leave is therefore a breach of immigration laws in that it is a breach of s 3 of the 1971 Act. Entry without leave does not require any particular state of mind or of knowledge in order to result in a person being an illegal entrant. The Court of Appeal in *R* v *Governor of Ashford Remand Centre ex p Bouzagou* [1983] Imm AR 69 rejected the submission that any *mens rea* was required. The breach of immigration laws does not need to be deliberate or even known to a person in order for them to have entered without leave and thus be deemed an illegal entrant.

This kind of illegal entry includes clandestine entrants who arrive in the back of lorries or land by night in a small boat on a secluded beach. It also includes people who mistakenly enter without leave, even if the mistake is that of the immigration officer. This surprising conclusion was reached in the case of *Rehal* v *Secretary of State for the Home Department* [1989] Imm AR 576 CA. Mr Rehal was a British overseas citizen. The immigration officer, glancing at his British passport, thought he was a British citizen and waved him through. Without a stamp in his passport, Mr Rehal had no leave to enter. The immigration officer's invitation for him to pass through was not a grant of leave but a (barely considered) decision that he did not need leave.

The same result comes about when the mistake, though still not the fault of the passport holder, is in the passport rather than the action of the immigration officer. This was apparent in the case of *Mokuolo and Ogunbiyi* v *SSHD* [1989] Imm AR 51 CA in which the passports of two Nigerian sisters mistakenly stated that they were British citizens.

Accordingly, they were not granted leave to enter on the assumption that they did not need it. Although, like Mr Rehal, they were not guilty of any deception or wrongdoing, they, like him, were found to be illegal entrants.

The Court of Appeal's decision in *Rehal* turned on the meaning they gave to 1971 Act Sch 2 para 6, the obligation to make a decision within 24 hours, failing which the entrant has six months' deemed leave. It applies where a person 'is to be given' limited leave. The Court of Appeal interpreted this to mean where the immigration officer intends to make a decision on the question of leave. This means that if the immigration officer has not thought about it because for instance as in Mr Rehal's case they did not realise it was necessary to do so, the deemed leave provision does not apply, so the person is considered an illegal entrant. Macdonald puts forward an alternative and surely preferable interpretation that the words 'is to be given' refer to someone who needs leave, i.e. does not have right of abode (1995:70). This objective interpretation would bring within para 6 those who are deemed illegal entrants through the immigration officer's mistake. This otherwise seems an injustice, as at the time of arrival at the port there was no difference in law between Mr Rehal and any other lawful applicant for leave to enter.

Leave to enter is normally endorsed on a passport, and since the Leave to Enter and Remain Order 2000, SI 2000/1161 will often have been granted by entry clearance in advance (see chapter 7). Therefore the question of proof that it exists is reasonably straightforward except that since the Leave to Enter and Remain Order leave to enter need not always be given in writing and need not be given to the traveller personally. It may be granted by fax or e-mail or for a visitor even by telephone (art 8) and in the case of a group travelling together it might for instance be endorsed on a passenger list rather than a document produced by an individual (art 9). In these cases the burden of proof is on the person claiming that they have leave to enter to prove that is the case (art 11). This reverses the burden of proof at precisely the point at which the entrant is most vulnerable, but it is unlikely that an oral grant of leave will often be given.

Section 11(5) of the 1971 Act provides that an air or sea crew member who seeks to remain beyond the time allowed (s 8(1)) will be treated as seeking to enter the UK. If they do so in breach of immigration laws they will be regarded as an illegal entrant.

17.2.1.2 *Entry in breach of a deportation order*

The s 33 definition of an illegal entrant includes someone who enters in breach of a deportation order. This means that any person who is the subject of a deportation order is subject to removal as an illegal entrant if they enter the UK while the deportation order is still in force against them. The order is in force unless it has been revoked. A deportation order completely prohibits re-entry, whether or not the person would normally require leave to enter, e.g. if they were an EEA national they would otherwise be able to enter without leave, but as a deportee they are an illegal entrant if they do so (*Shingara v SSHD* [1999] Imm AR 257 CA).

If the person who is the subject of the deportation order had leave when the deportation order was made the leave is invalidated by the deportation order. See, for instance, the case of *Dinc* [1999] Imm AR 380 CA, discussed in the last chapter, where the respondent had indefinite leave to remain. Any leave granted during the currency of the deportation order, whether to enter or remain, is also invalidated (1971 Act s 5). The result of this is that if someone enters while a deportation order is in force against them, they enter without leave. This is the case whether they enter clandestinely or whether, by mistake or deception, they manage to obtain an apparent leave, as any such leave will have no effect.

It might therefore be objected that these words are redundant in the definition of an illegal entrant. A person subject to a deportation order is without leave anyway. This argument was advanced for the appellants in *Khawaja v SSHD* [1984] AC 74 as evidence that 'in breach of the immigration laws' should be given a narrow interpretation, i.e. restricted only to those who entered without leave. If it was open to a wider interpretation, there would be no need to specify 'in breach of a deportation order', as that would be included. However, the House of Lords rejected that argument, and while the inclusion of entry in breach of a deportation order may, strictly speaking, be redundant, it still stands.

17.2.1.3 *Entry by deception*

As indicated earlier, the possibility of becoming an illegal entrant by deception was at first a common law development. It was not in the contemplation of Parliament at the time of the passing of the Immigration Act 1971 that illegal entrants would include anyone other than those entering in breach of a deportation order or without leave (see, for instance, discussion in Grant and Martin, *Immigration Law and Practice* (1982) and Evans, *Immigration Law* (1983)). Support for this view could be obtained from the terms of the criminal offence of illegal entry, the relevant part of which only refers to entry in breach of a deportation order and entry without leave (1971 Act s 24). The courts however began to interpret 'in breach of the immigration laws' as including people who had passed through immigration control and had obtained leave to enter, but had done so by deception. In a series of cases, leave obtained by deception contrary to s 26(1)(c) was treated as invalid. Section 26(1)(c) sets out a criminal offence, committed where a person:

Makes or causes to be made . . . a return, statement or representation which he knows to be false or does not believe to be true.

The courts thereby created a relationship between the definition of an illegal entrant and the criminal provisions of the Immigration Act. The statute already provided a sanction for an offence under s 26, but the courts intertwined this offence with the administrative enforcement provisions. They decided that leave obtained in this way was obtained 'in breach of the immigration laws' and therefore not leave which would entitle a person to enter.

This judicial invention was ratified by the House of Lords in July 1980 in *Zamir* [1980] 2 All ER 768. This case represented a low point for the peace of mind and security of immigrants. Their Lordships held that leave granted through the use of deception was not leave granted in accordance with the Immigration Act and could rightly found a removal as an illegal entrant. Even more disturbingly, they considered that the duty of a potential immigrant was a 'duty of candour', analogous to the duty of utmost good faith imposed upon parties in the law of contract. This meant that the applicant must disclose all potentially relevant information, and was under a duty to volunteer information, not just to answer questions. This put the applicant in the position of being responsible for deciding what was relevant, and risking being removed as an illegal entrant if they made a wrong judgment on that matter.

This decision 'provoked widespread academic criticism and a storm of protest from the ethnic communities and bodies concerned with improving race relations'

(Evans 1983:314). It was reversed in important respects by the House of Lords in *Khawaja* [1984] AC 74 which held that there was no duty of utmost good faith. There must be actual or attempted deception before illegal entry could be established, not just a failure to interpret correctly the requirements of the immigration rules. This judgment put beyond doubt that entry obtained by deception could give rise to removal as an illegal entrant, but tempered the more extreme aspects of the *Zamir* judgment. The House of Lords found that the burden of proof that the person was an illegal entrant was upon the Secretary of State, and the standard was the civil standard, but this should be interpreted as being at the high end of the balance of probabilities, bearing in mind the serious consequences for the individual and the quasi-criminal nature of the allegations. Importantly, the House of Lords in *Khawaja* reversed the 'hands-off' approach which had characterized earlier judicial decisions concerning illegal entrants. The courts had shown a tendency not to investigate the facts, and in judicial review held that such investigation was outside the court's scope of enquiry as the jurisdiction is one of review of the decision-making process, not an appeal on the merits. The House of Lords in *Khawaja* held that the fact that someone was an illegal entrant was a matter which determined whether or not there was jurisdiction to act. Such 'jurisdictional facts' *did,* they said, come within the scope of the court's inquiry. The court would therefore examine for itself the evidence as to whether the person was an illegal entrant.

Following *Khawaja,* the inclusion of a person who gained entry by deception in the definition of illegal entrant was here to stay. Obtaining entry by deception became more explicitly part of the statutory definition with the Asylum and Immigration Act 1996. The offence was created of using deception to obtain or seek to obtain leave to enter or remain in the UK (amending Immigration Act 1971 s 24, renumbered again by Immigration and Asylum Act 1999 so the offence is now found in 1971 Act s 24A). An offence under that section, like an offence under s 26(1)(c) is 'in breach of immigration laws' and so makes the perpetrator an illegal entrant as found in *Khawaja.*

However, the way was still open for dispute on a number of issues which inevitably arise in the determination of questions surrounding deception. These included the effect of deception by a third party, the use of false documents, the relationship between any deception and the leave granted, and what conduct may give rise to a finding of deception, in the absence of a duty of utmost good faith.

Third party deception and use of false documents
The Asylum and Immigration Act 1996 resolved the question of the effect of deception by third parties by adding to the definition of illegal entrant in s 33(1) para (b): 'entering or seeking to enter by means which include deception by another person.' This addition to s 33(1) puts beyond doubt that deception by a third party will make the entry illegal and means that earlier case law on this point no longer has any effect. Deception by a third party includes for instance preparing a false passport or a false offer of housing or employment.

The use of invalid documents is also covered by the statutory provisions introduced by the 1996 Act. If the entrant produces a false document knowing it to be false, this is deception contrary to s 24A(1). If they are not aware of its falsity but this is the result of the deliberate act of a third party, the deception is covered by s 33(1).

Relationship between deception and leave granted
The effect of the deception is a matter of some importance. At one extreme, some acts of deception might be about a quite peripheral fact, which had very little bearing on

the decision to grant entry. It would be inappropriate then to regard entry as illegal. At the other extreme, misrepresentation about a central fact such as whether the sponsor and applicant did in fact intend to marry could easily be a deception which would render the entry illegal. The question to be addressed is whether, to make an entry illegal, the deception has to be the effective cause of leave being granted, or just a factor which contributed to the decision.

The question of the effect of the deception was addressed authoritatively in *Khawaja* in which the court held that the deception should be the effective means of obtaining leave in order for the entry to be regarded as illegal. It relied on the earlier case of *R v SSHD ex p Jayakody* [1982] 1 All ER 461 in which the Court of Appeal had held that in order to render the entry illegal the fraud should be the decisive factor in the application. In other words, if there had been no deception then the application would probably have been refused. In *Bugdaycay* v *SSHD* [1987] 1 AC 514 the House of Lords said that the question was, if the true facts were known, whether the decision-maker would have been 'bound to refuse' the application. However, in *Bugdaycay,* the House of Lords also held that an applicant could not legitimize their entry by arguing that if they had put forward the true facts leave would still have been granted. In that case a person who applied as a visitor had not disclosed that he intended to apply for asylum. If he had applied for asylum he would not have been able to be removed. However, the House of Lords held that his argument could only be seen in the light of the application which he did in fact make, and that was deceptive, and so he was treated as an illegal entrant. The judgment seems to proceed on the basis that an applicant should not be allowed to get away with deception, but if the deception did not make any difference it is hard to see how it is effective in the *Khawaja* sense. Although *Bugdaycay* did not expressly overturn *Khawaja*, it did depart from that reasoning, and an approach more consistent with *Bugdaycay* is the one that has been followed since then as the courts have developed an approach requiring deception to be material rather than decisive. For instance, in *Sukhjinder Kaur* v *Secretary of State for the Home Department* [1998] Imm AR 1 (see below) the appellant argued that alternative financial sponsorship was available and so she would still have qualified for entry as her husband's wife, but the Court of Appeal did not accept this argument.

In *Durojaiye* v *Secretary of State for the Home Department* [1991] Imm AR 307 the Court of Appeal considered that giving false answers to questions about a student's attendance at college was 'material in the sense that it was likely to influence their decision'. This is not the same as saying that they were a matter without which a different decision would necessarily have been made. In *R v Secretary of State for the Home Department ex p Castro* [1996] Imm AR 540 at 544, the High Court considered that 'it may be sufficient for the Secretary of State to show that the deception was material in the sense that it was likely to influence the decision whether to grant leave to enter'. However, although this point has been summarized in the headnote of the case it does not seem to form part of the *ratio* as the judge found that the more stringent test of effective cause was satisfied. This judgment should therefore be treated with caution in this respect. *Sukhjinder Kaur* was not a case about illegal entry but about refusal of entry to a person who held entry clearance. The applicant had not disclosed that her husband was in prison at the time of the application, but had said he was living at his home address. The Court of Appeal held that this non-disclosure was material because it was 'likely to influence' the outcome of the application in that it affected whether her husband would be able to support her financially. The Court of Appeal accepted that *Khawaja* did not apply as this was not an illegal entry case. The duty for the appellant to disclose that her husband had been arrested arose, they pointed out, from the immigration rules, which impose a duty to disclose material facts (then para 17, the equivalent of present-day para 321). The case therefore turned on the question of what was material as this is what should have been disclosed. Here the Court of Appeal did not make any distinction between illegal entry and refusal of leave to enter. Ward LJ said: 'I agree that the time has come when we should put that [the *Jayakody*] test to rest', without referring to the context of refusing leave to enter, but also without stating that the Court regarded the two legal strands as interchangeable on this point. He followed *Bugdaycay* and *Durojaiye*, using the line of authority concerning materiality in illegal entry.

Since *Khawaja* the different statutory formulation goes some way to resolving the question. At the time of *Khawaja* a person was an illegal entrant by deception if they made representations which they knew to be false (1971 Act s 26(1)(c)). The causal relationship with the leave then granted was matter for the courts to consider. Since the 1996 Act, however, the relevant sections (24A and 33(1)) both refer to entry obtained or sought 'by means which include' deception. The use of the word 'include' suggests that there might be other factors also at work in the grant of leave. In other words that this is not a case where, apart from the deception, the decision-maker would have been 'bound to refuse'. On the other hand 'by means' implies that the deception is operative. It takes effect to bring about the grant of leave and has a bearing on the decision. The net result of this is that in order for the deception to give rise to a finding of illegal entry, it must have played a part in the decision to grant entry, but need not necessarily have been the only factor. Macdonald considers that the current statutory formulation of 'by means which include' is a decisive shift in the direction of materiality and away from the *Jayakody* test (2001:749).

Conduct – deception by silence

Before the 1996 Act, in order to show that silence was a deception giving rise to illegal entry it would have to be shown that there was a representation by silence, for instance presentation of a passport (e.g. *R v Secretary of State for the Home Department ex p Kuteesa* [1997] Imm AR 194) in order to bring the case within s 26(1)(c). However the current sections do not require that. The issue is only whether entry was gained or sought by means which include deception.

If the applicant says nothing about a relevant matter it may be because they are deliberately concealing it, or it may be because they are not aware that it is relevant and have not been asked about it. In the latter case there is no deception. Which of these is the case is matter of inference for the tribunal from available evidence. To establish illegal entry from a failure to mention something it needs to be established how much the applicant should have been expected to say. As there is not a duty of candour, what can the applicant be expected to know is relevant?

In *Cendiz Doldur v SSHD* [1998] Imm AR 352 the Court of Appeal held there was no duty on the applicant to disclose his marriage on arrival when he was not asked about it or about any change of circumstances. He was still dependent in fact on his father and could not be expected to know that this did not mean that he was still dependent in law after he had married. In the case of *Kuteesa* the applicant obtained leave to enter for two years as a student, subject to the condition that he was not to take employment. He decided not to enrol on the course for which he had been given leave, but enrolled on a later course and worked in the meantime. Shortly before he was due to start the new course his father died, and he went home to Uganda for the funeral. On his re-entry to the UK, he produced his passport and a letter from the college saying:

This student is going home as a result of a bereavement in the family and will be returning to college to continue his studies. I confirm that [there is] a place reserved for him.

The High Court held that by his silent presentation of his passport he had made a representation that he had previously fulfilled his conditions of entry. As this was false, contrary to s 26(1)(c), he was an illegal entrant. He argued that if he had revealed the true facts he would still have been granted leave to enter as to refuse would have been unreasonable. However, Harrison J disagreed. He found that the immigration officer would have refused leave to enter if he had known the full history. This was at least in part because the applicant had had leave to enter as a student on a previous occasion and worked in breach of conditions. The argument in this case illustrates how engagement with the question outlawed by *Bugdaycay* (whether leave would have been granted had the true facts been known) merges into the question of materiality (what was relevant) and even, in this case, what would have been a proper exercise of discretion.

Unlike Mr Doldur, Mr Kuteesa had done something (presented his passport) which was a positive action and could thus amount to a representation. However the case turned more on what the entrant in each case could be expected to have known was relevant, i.e. an investigation of their state of mind. This kind of reasoning survives the amendments made by the 1996 Act as the question of whether there has been deception must involve the question of the entrant's state of mind. In *Durojaiye* the passport holder obtained leave to remain, then left the country and returned again. The Court of Appeal held that the presentation of the passport on re-entry amounted to deception as the passport holder was aware that the leave stamped in it had been obtained falsely.

Standard of proof

The burden of proof that a person is an illegal entrant is on the Home Office. The standard of proof, first laid down in *Khawaja,* has been developed but not substantially altered by subsequent cases. It was said to be the civil standard, i.e. on the balance of probabilities, but at the higher end of that scale in view of the gravity of the matters in question. If the person is found to be an illegal entrant they are liable to detention and removal from the country; as liberty is at stake the burden of proof should be strictly applied.

This standard was reiterated and applied in *Doldur.* No one apart from Mr. Doldur himself knew exactly what was in his mind when he entered the UK. The Secretary of State could not prove that it was 'an irresistible inference' that he knew that his marriage was relevant to his entry to the UK, and so the allegation could not be proved to the required standard. In his judgment in *Doldur* Evans LJ relied on *R v SSHD ex p Rahman* [1997] 3 WLR 990 in which the standard of proof was that 'the degree of probability was so great as closely to approximate the criminal standard'.

However, an inference against the applicant may be drawn from the evidence if it meets the standard. For instance, in *Kesse* TH/00419, the appellant had obtained entry on the basis of marriage to a person who was subsequently found to have never been married. The tribunal upheld the finding of deception, using the standard of proof laid down in *Khawaja* and endorsed in *Doldur,* and which they described as being 'a high degree of probability'.

R (on the Application of Ullah) v SSHD [2003] EWCA Civ 1366 provided a more recent example of the application of this standard of proof. The case had proceeded without the benefit of a witness statement from the person who would have been the appellant's first wife had that marriage been valid. The Court of Appeal held that the Secretary of State could in theory proceed without such a statement, but in this case there was insufficient evidence to meet the high standard of proof that the appellant must have known of the invalidity of his marriage.

In the context of standard of proof, reference should also be made back to the section on entry without leave, as in the case of visitors who claim to have been granted oral leave to enter, or passengers who claim that their leave was granted as part of a group or for some other reason to a person other than themselves, the burden of proof is in effect cast on the traveller.

17.2.2 **Refused leave to enter**

As we have seen, a greater number of people are removed after being refused leave to enter than as illegal entrants. The Immigration Act 1971 Sch 2 para 8(1) says that where a person arriving in the United Kingdom is refused leave to enter then they may be removed on the direction of an immigration officer. This rather stark provision, read in isolation, could give an impression that anyone refused leave could just be returned forthwith to the country from which they came. This is a possibility, but not in every case, as some people refused leave to enter have a right of appeal which they may exercise in the UK. The Nationality, Immigration and Asylum Act 2002 s 92 repeats earlier provisions in giving a right of appeal in the UK to a person who holds an entry clearance or work permit. It also gives a right of appeal in the UK against refusal of leave to enter to an EEA national or their family member who claims that the refusal would breach their rights of entry or residence under European Community law and to someone who has made a human rights or asylum claim while in the UK. Section 78 provides that people who by s 92 have a right of appeal exercisable in the UK may not be removed while their appeal is pending. There is a further caveat to this, however, which is that s 94 gives power to the Secretary of State to certify asylum and human rights claims as 'clearly unfounded' in which case the appellant will lose their right of appeal in the UK, and be removable. Certificates of this kind will be issued automatically in the case of the listed states (see chapter 12). The 2002 Act therefore creates a kind of 'to and fro' motion, as in the following example:

> X applies for leave to enter as visitor – refused – no right of appeal (s 89) – X is removable
>
> X claims removal breaches Refugee Convention – appeal s 92(4) – X is not removable (s 78)
>
> Secretary of State is satisfied that X is entitled to live in Mongolia, certifies claim clearly unfounded s 94 – X is removable

An asylum seeker who may be returned to a safe third country may be removed without their asylum claim being considered (see chapter 12). If an asylum seeker is wrongly removed pending appeal, the court may be prepared to grant an injunction to compel the Secretary of State to return the claimant to the UK so that his rights could be preserved pending the outcome of his appeal (e.g. *R (on the application of T) v SSHD* [2004] EWHC 869 (Admin)).

Removal under Immigration Act 1971 Sch 2 para 8 is therefore not necessarily permitted straight away, and whether it is permitted is not necessarily apparent immediately. A swift removal might take place for instance in the case of a non-visa national applying unsuccessfully to enter as a visitor or student, and who has no asylum or human rights claim. On the other hand there may be a lengthy process, perhaps an asylum claim with an unsuccessful appeal, and a person who is given temporary admission while their application is being processed and who has been in the UK for months or years without leave ever having been granted, is still subject to removal at the end of that process. In this case the directions for removal would be made by the Secretary of State under Sch 2 para 10, and the Secretary of State will have responsibility in any case where more than two months have passed since the refusal of leave (paras 8 and 10). Under the 1999 Act removal directions could not be given (Sch 4 para 10) while an appeal was pending, however the 2002 Act has reversed this and permits removal directions to be given even while they cannot be carried out (s 78). This is an example of the policy of the 2002 Act to streamline and speed up removals as far as possible.

17.2.3 Expansion in grounds for removal

The courts had expanded the definition of 'illegal entrants', but from 1 January 1973 until 2 October 2000 those subject to removal were restricted to illegal entrants and people refused entry at the port. On 2 October 2000 Immigration and Asylum Act 1999 s 10 came into effect, and changed a number of grounds for deportation under Immigration Act 1971 s 3(5) into grounds for removal.

In the 1971 Act as originally passed, breach of condition and overstaying were grounds for deportation (the old s 3(5)(a)). Deportation carried a full right of appeal while summary removal attracted a right of appeal only from out of the UK, i.e. after the event. There was a rationale for that distinction as the original target of the removal provisions was those who were refused entry at the port and people who had arrived clandestinely but were apprehended soon after arrival. People who had overstayed or breached their condition have had some period of residence, and some connection with the UK, perhaps brief, but perhaps of many years. It would therefore be legitimate to treat them differently. However, in practice this rationale broke down because the courts developed the category of illegal entrant to include a person who had entered using deception. This could include a person whose original leave had been gained years earlier. This put a person deemed an illegal entrant and an overstayer in a much more similar position.

Parliament's response to this was to level down the rights of overstayers to those of illegal entrants, influenced no doubt by the policy imperative of moving people though the system more quickly. The levelling down happened in two stages. First, as discussed in chapter 16, the Immigration Act 1988 s 5 limited appeals for people who had overstayed or breached condition, and had been in the UK for less than seven years, to the grounds that that there was 'in law, no power to make the deportation order for the reasons stated in the notice'. In other words, they could only appeal on grounds that they had not, in fact, overstayed or breached their conditions. This took away the right to be heard on all other circumstances of their case.

The second stage of levelling down came with the Immigration and Asylum Act 1999 s 10 which made those who had overstayed, breached condition, or obtained leave by deception (a ground for deportation added by the Asylum and Immigration Act 1996) subject to removal and not deportation. Appeal rights would therefore only be on the restricted grounds, however long the person had lived in the UK, and could only be exercised from outside the UK. These provisions and the changes are discussed in more detail below.

17.2.3.1 *Obtaining leave to remain by deception*

This ground for removal was introduced into 1971 Act s 3 as a new ground of deportation by the 1996 Act but was changed into a ground for removal along with overstaying and breach of condition by 1999 Act s 10.

It refers to situations where, for instance, a person obtains indefinite leave to remain by misrepresenting at the end of their first year of leave that their marriage is still subsisting whereas in fact it has broken down, as for instance in *R* v *SSHD ex p Chaumun* CO/3143/95 (unreported). The 2002 Act s 74 has tightened this provision further by substituting a new s 10(1)(b): 'he uses deception in seeking (whether successfully or not) leave to remain'. It is difficult to see what is achieved by this attempt to cast the net even wider, as a person who did not succeed in obtaining leave to remain would presumably be without leave and so removable on another ground, probably overstaying. The words 'uses deception in seeking' revive the debates about the role of the deception in seeking leave. As phrased here, the intention would seem to be to catch *any* level of deception, no matter how material it might or might not be to the application. In application this provision should be treated as analogous to the illegal entry provisions, given that the consequences are similar. It does not cover third party deception; the words 'he uses' refer only to the applicant, so a person who was not aware for instance of the falsity of some evidence could not be removed under this provision.

17.2.3.2 *Overstaying and breach of condition*

As mentioned above, these two grounds, related to breaches of limited leave, were formerly grounds for deportation and are now, under Immigration and Asylum Act 1999 s 10 grounds for removal.

Staying beyond the time allowed by a grant of limited leave is a factual matter. There may be issues of proof, for instance of the duration of the leave, but there is little scope for legal interpretation. The only issue of interpreting the statute is a matter of making sense of what would otherwise be nonsense, making use of the golden rule of interpretation. The statute says 'having only a limited leave to enter or remain, he...remains beyond the time limited by the leave' (1999 Act s 10). This must mean 'having had', otherwise the leave has not yet expired and no overstaying has taken place (Macdonald 2001:756). It is strange that the opportunity was not taken in the re-enactment of this provision in the 1999 Act to correct the wording of the 1971 Act, which was the same.

A person does not stay beyond the time allowed and become an overstayer by applying for a variation of their leave and then staying for that application to be heard, provided they applied during the currency of the original limited leave. Immigration Act 1971 s 3C (as substituted by the 2002 Act s 118) continues the original leave until the end of the period set for appealing against a decision on the variation application. If an appeal is made, the same section continues the leave while the appeal is pending. It is only once these time limits are exhausted and the applicant has been unsuccessful that they may be treated as an overstayer.

Section 10 of the 1999 Act extends removal to the breach of conditions imposed under 1971 Act s 3(1)(c). The only conditions which may be imposed are: restricting employment or occupation, requiring the subject to maintain and accommodate himself and any dependants without recourse to public funds, and registration with the police. The Home Office policy statement (see chapter 9) that short-term recourse to public funds as a matter of necessity will not attract penalties is an appropriate approach in all cases of breach. Where private or family life would be interfered with by a removal, then the removal would in any event have to be proportionate under Article 8, and a trivial breach should not attract the sanction of removal.

The case of *Sabir* [1993] Imm AR 477 held that past breaches of condition could give rise to liability for deportation, but this could hardly be the case when overstaying is in the past and has been in effect cancelled out by a fresh grant of leave. It seems appropriate for breach of condition and overstaying to be treated similarly in this respect, and the statute does use the present tense, suggesting that overstaying or breach should be current to attract the penalty. This should all the more be the case now that the sanction is summary removal.

Where breaches of condition or overstaying are not disclosed in a further leave application, this may constitute obtaining leave to remain by deception and result in removal under s 10. Where they are disclosed, they should simply be taken into account as part of all the circumstances in the decision to grant or refuse leave on this occasion.

Family members of the person removed may also be removed, providing notice of this is given to them no more than eight weeks after the departure of their relative. Immigration and Asylum Act 1999 s 10 makes this provision in relation to s 10 removals. This was extended for the first time to illegal entrants by the Nationality, Immigration and Asylum Act 2002 s 73, inserting a new para 10A into 1971 Act Sch 2.

17.2.3.3 *Breach of conditions of temporary admission*

The High Court in *Yilmaz v SSHD* [2005] EWHC 1068 (Admin) reconsidered the question of whether someone who breaches their conditions of temporary admission becomes an illegal entrant. A person who is on temporary admission is at liberty instead of in detention (see chapter 15), and is awaiting leave to enter. Earlier cases had suggested that someone who breaks their conditions of temporary admission becomes an illegal entrant as they have destroyed the condition which makes them not an entrant at all (e.g. *R v IAT ex p Akhtar* [1993] Imm AR 424). However, when a claimant sought to be treated as an illegal entrant so as to obtain the benefit of a policy which applied to them and not to those awaiting grant or refusal of leave to enter, the court held that there was a discretion not to treat them as such. In *Yilmaz* the claimant argued that discretion should be exercised *not* to treat him as an illegal entrant. However, Beatson J held that becoming an illegal entrant was the normal consequence of breach of conditions of temporary admission. The common thread with cases suggesting discretion was that the claimant sought to have it exercised in their favour, and this would not be allowed.

17.3 Effect of leave obtained in breach of immigration laws

When the courts first began to find that leave obtained in breach of s 26(1)(c) was obtained in breach of immigration laws and thus grounds for finding the holder to be an illegal entrant, they also developed the doctrine that the leave so obtained was void. However, as with the doctrine of a duty of utmost good faith, this was to import into immigration law a concept deriving from the law of contract, and was removed in *Khawaja* where Lord Bridge said at 119:

It is for the immigration authorities to decide whether or not to seek to secure summary removal of an illegal entrant by invoking their powers under Schedule 2. If they do not do so, leave to enter stands.

This point, however, is a rather esoteric one, because once notice is given to a person that they are deemed to be an illegal entrant, any leave that they have no longer has effect. Also, leave obtained by deception is obtained 'in breach of immigration laws', and residence in breach of immigration laws is not effective for all purposes.

The House of Lords in *Shah v Barnet London Borough Council* [1983] 2 AC 309 held that residence in breach of immigration laws could not be relied upon to establish ordinary residence. This was in the context of entitlement to a student grant, and not an immigration case, but is applied in the immigration context where ordinary residence is required to establish settlement. The decision in *Shah* could have meant that an illegal entrant could never become settled, but in fact there are established concessions, which became rules in 2003 (see chapter 6), which give an opportunity for settlement to people who have been resident for many years.

Nationality, Immigration and Asylum Act 2002 s 11 defines residence 'in breach of immigration laws' for the purposes of calculating entitlement to apply for British citizenship by naturalization or registration to include a resident 'who does not have leave to enter or remain'. A clandestine illegal entrant therefore cannot count their residence towards an application for nationality. What of an illegal entrant whose leave was obtained unlawfully? Following *Khawaja* their leave is in existence, but following *Shah* it does not count towards ordinary residence. A letter from Beverley Hughes, Minister of State in the Home Office, to Fiona Mactaggart MP, 18 July 2002, helps to clarify the policy behind the section. Clandestine entrants and overstayers will be treated as in breach of immigration laws. People on temporary admission or in detention will not be treated as being in breach of immigration laws. Therefore, a refugee who made an illegal entry but then a successful claim for asylum, will not be obstructed in making a nationality application on account of their illegal entry or time spent on temporary admission.

The case of *Chaumun* applies the principles of *Khawaja* and *Shah* to leave to remain, as distinct from leave to enter. The applicant's leave to remain was obtained by forging a letter from his ex-wife. The High Court held that this was leave obtained in breach of s 26(1)(c) and, thus, was 'in breach of immigration laws'. The residence which followed could therefore not be counted as ordinary residence, and he was therefore not settled. As a consequence his second wife could not apply to remain with him in the UK. Both were liable to be deported, although now they would be liable to removal under Immigration and Asylum Act 1999 s 10, Mr Chaumun for obtaining leave to remain by deception and Mrs Chaumun for overstaying.

17.4 EEA nationals and removal

As EEA nationals may enter as of right on production of a passport or identity documents in order to exercise Treaty rights it is rare that an EEA national may be deemed an illegal entrant. In C–215/03 *Oulane* the ECJ held on a reference for a preliminary ruling that detention of a European national with a view to deportation was an unjustified restriction on free movement where his offence was principally lack of documentary proof of his status. So, while an EEA national may be deported as discussed in the previous chapter on public policy grounds, removal is only likely to occur if the EEA national enters in breach of an exclusion or deportation order (*Shingara v SSHD* [1999] Imm AR 257 CA).

17.5 **Conclusion**

Removal is a major plank of government immigration policy. There are 'targets' for removals, questions by Opposition MPs about number of removals, and promises to do more. The law on removal is a battleground. It is often tortuous and technical and its implementation may cause enormous human distress. It is a major practical challenge for enforcement agencies. Removal began as a mean of administrative enforcement, but its reach has grown to include people who enter by deceit and long-term residents of the UK. Some of the tension surrounding removal is explained not only by what is at stake for individuals, but also by what is revealed by the challenges under Article 8, namely that what is at stake for the government is the maintenance of a firm immigration policy.

QUESTIONS

1 Was it appropriate for the courts to develop the definition of 'illegal entrant' to include someone who entered by deception? What would have been the alternative?

2 Mrs Mahmood (refer back to chapter 4) was a British citizen. Do you think that this should have affected the decision to remove Mr Mahmood?

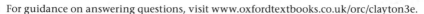 For guidance on answering questions, visit www.oxfordtextbooks.co.uk/orc/clayton3e.

FURTHER READING

Evans, J.M. (1983) *Immigration Law,* 2nd edn (London: Sweet & Maxwell), Chapter 6.

Fasti, M. (2002) 'The restrictive approach taken by the European Court of Human Rights: deportation of long-term immigrants and the right to family life, Part 1: integrated aliens and family rights: involution versus evolution' (2002) IANL vol. 16, no. 3, p. 166; Part 2: 'Consensus enquiry and security of residence of long-term immigrants in Europe' vol. 16, no. 4, p. 224.

Joint Council for the Welfare of Immigrants (2006) Seddon, D. (ed.) *Immigration, nationality and refugee law handbook,* Chapter 33.

Rogers, N. (2003) 'Immigration and the European Convention on Human Rights: are new principles emerging?' *European Human Rights Law Review* 1, pp. 53–64.

18

Defences against removal and deportation

SUMMARY

This chapter considers the arguments that can be made to prevent someone from being removed from the UK. It begins with the legal arguments based on immigration rules, policies or human rights, and concludes with the question of viability of return, an increasingly litigated issue as practical obstacles to return may sometimes have legal consequences. An asylum claim may often in form be an argument against removal, but this ground is not considered here as it has already been fully covered in chapter 13.

18.1 Introduction

The material in this chapter follows on from the previous two, in that it is assumed that the legal ground for the deportation or removal, as set out in those chapters, has been established, and the question now is whether any argument can be advanced to weigh against the grounds in law to deport or remove. As all deportations may end in removal, for ease and brevity this chapter proceeds by using the term 'removal' to refer to all cases of enforced departure, except where the context or law requires a distinction.

18.2 Immigration rules

The immigration rules set out the factors which should be taken into account that may militate against a decision to remove. There are no immigration rules relating to the removal of illegal entrants or to port removals. The rules apply to situations where, within the law, the person to be removed could have spent some considerable time, maybe years, in the UK, and have established ties. Although in practice this may equally be the case for illegal entrants or those subject to 'port removals', their situation is not recognized by the rules. Neither those subject to port removal nor illegal entrants have received leave to enter, which perhaps makes it more controversial for the immigration rules to explicitly cater for their continued presence, though the Human Rights Act and policies outside the rules make none these distinctions.

The rules require the decision-maker to take into account all relevant factors. In the case of proposed administrative removals under 1999 Act s 10, i.e. for overstaying, breach of condition, obtaining leave to remain by deception, and families of those people, these must include the following (HC 395 para 395C):

(i) age; length of residence in the UK; strength of connections with the UK: this covers, for instance, family ties and business or employment interests; personal history, including character, conduct, and employment record; domestic circumstances;

(ii) previous criminal record and the nature of any offence of which the person has been convicted: this should only include unspent convictions under the Rehabilitation of Offenders Act 1974;

(iii) compassionate circumstances; and any representations received on the person's behalf.

There is no indication of what weight should be given to the person's circumstances, simply that 'regard will be had' to them.

In *CM Jamaica* [2005] UKIAT 00103 the tribunal held that these factors are wider than those normally considered under Article 8, in particular by including the strength of ties with the UK, domestic and compassionate circumstances. It meant that the interests of other family members were to be weighed in the balance, which, as we have seen in chapter 4, is not necessarily so in Article 8 claims. This was reaffirmed in *CW Jamaica* [2005] UKIAT 00110.

Prior to July 2006 these factors had to be taken into account in deportation cases. However, the rule change discussed in chapter 16 substituted these considerations with a presumption that if a deportation is conducive to the public good then it is in the public interest. Only in exceptional circumstances will the public interest in deportation be outweighed by individual factors. There is one provision remaining in the deportation rules from the pre-2006 version, which is that the aim is an exercise of the power of deportation which is consistent and fair as between one person and another, although one case will rarely be identical with another in all material respects (para 364). The presumption and the deeming provisions of the UK Borders Act probably leave less scope for inconsistency in any event. The Operational Enforcement Manual 36.1.2 says that the factors listed in para 395C must still be taken into account in a deportation decision, but only in an exceptional case will they outweigh the presumption in favour of deportation. The 2006 rule seems to hover uneasily between retaining the power for the Secretary of State to decide each individual case on its merits, which arguably must be done in order to avoid fettering a discretion, and creating a policy of general application.

18.2.1 **Long residence**

The long residence rules are of continuing importance. As with the factors in para 395C, these apply whether or not a person has a family in the UK and so add a significant protection outside the Human Rights Act in limited circumstances. These rules have been described in detail in chapter 7.

In cases of removal as opposed to deportation, while immigration offences may have been committed, the grounds for removal relate to immigration status rather than to the desirability or otherwise of the individual's continued presence in the UK. The only public interest in removing them, which may be set against their interest in staying, is the interest in maintaining firm immigration controls and being seen to be doing so. As this is the case, the long residence rules have an important application in cases of removal as the objective of showing firm immigration control is, by the very nature of the rules, accepted as being limited.

18.3 Policies

The decision to remove or deport a person is a discretionary one. An individual may have stayed beyond their leave or entered in breach of immigration laws, but this does not oblige an immigration officer to order their removal. Government pronouncements announcing targets for removal are open to the charge that they have lost sight of the principle that each case is decided on its particular merits. Where policies exist, discretion must be exercised in accordance with them and not arbitrarily (*Abdi v SSHD* [1996] Imm AR 148 CA).

The Operational Enforcement Manual (OEM), available on the Home Office website, gives guidance on the conduct of deportations and removals, and contains most of the relevant policy. Its 93 chapters include one called 'Extenuating Circumstances' (Chapter 36) which now collects in one place at least reference to most of the policies which might protect a person from removal or deportation. Publication of a policy gives rise to a legitimate expectation that it will be applied fairly and rationally in the applicant's case (*Khan v IAT* [1984] Imm AR 68 CA). Where policies have not been published there can be no legitimate expectation generated. Nevertheless, policy should still be fairly and rationally applied (*R v SSHD ex p Amankwah* [1994] Imm AR 240 and *Rashid v SSHD*). In *Baig v SSHD* [2005] EWCA Civ 1246 the Court of Appeal held that they did not just need to consider whether the Secretary of State had taken the policy into account, but the court itself could apply the policy on appeal. This was held not to be the case in *AG (Kosovo) v SSHD* [2007] UKAIT 0082, but the Court of Appeal in *AB (Jamaica)* [2007] EWCA Civ 1302, while referring to both these cases, held it could apply the policy to a fairly clear-cut case.

18.3.1 Families

Where a person faced with removal has a family in the UK, the principal policies which provide guidance on the decision are DP3/96 and DP069/99. These policies are still referred to in OEM Chapter 36, although much of their content is overtaken by the Human Rights Act. In certain instances the Act and policies may complement one another.

DP3/96 applies to illegal entrants and deportees, but not to others refused entry. Where the facts permit, this limitation may result in applications for judicial review in which the applicant, as we have seen in *Yilmaz*, seeks to be treated as an illegal entrant in order to receive the benefit of these policies. In *Olawale* [2001] Imm AR 20 and in *Khaled Ahmed* [2002] Imm AR 427 the High Court confirmed that the Secretary of State had a discretion where the facts allowed, and was not obliged to treat the applicant as an illegal entrant. There would be a difficulty for the Home Office in extending the policies to people who have received so-called 'port refusals', as to do this would be to accept the delay in the system as a factor whose effects must be reckoned with, not just cured. Since the implementation of the Human Rights Act 1998, not benefiting from DP3/96 is less significant. The Court in *AB (Jamaica)* considered that DP3/96 was 'tougher' than Article 8 (para 28).

DP3/96 also applies to removal for overstaying and breach of condition under s 10 (confirmed in *MA Algeria* [2005] UKAIT 00127). The central advice in DP3/96 is contained in the following:

As a *general rule*, deportation action…in non-criminal cases or illegal entry action should not be initiated in the following circumstances…

(a) where the subject has a genuine and subsisting marriage with someone settled here and the couple have lived together in this country continuously since their marriage for at least 2 years before the commencement of enforcement action; *and*

(b) it is unreasonable to expect the settled spouse to accompany his/her spouse on removal.

It is for the settled spouse to make the case that it would be unreasonable for them to leave, and that the Home Office will take into account strong family ties in the UK, length of residence in the UK (more than ten years), and that significant impairment or danger to life or health would result from removal.

This is general guidance only, and removal may still take place even when there is a qualifying marriage. This part of the guidance concludes: 'for instance, a particularly poor immigration history may warrant the offender's enforced departure from the UK notwithstanding the factors referred to above'. Although it contains some ambiguity, the gist of the policy is that a person will not normally be removed for overstaying, illegal entry or breach of condition where its conditions are met. Reference to its terms remains in OEM Chapter 36 without distinguishing between deportation and removal, though the policy itself does not appear. The terms are loosely stated and do not include the presumption against removal that is the clear intention of the policy.

The status of DP3/96 in relation to deportation is unclear after the introduction of the presumption into the rules in 2006. DP3/96 introduces the opposite presumption to that in the rules, in other words a presumption against deportation where there is a marriage of more than two years. In *EO v SSHD* [2007] UKAIT 00062 the Home Office argued that the rule change in July 2006 did not make a substantive change in the rules, only one of emphasis or clarity. The tribunal did not accept this argument. Chapter 36 retains the position that the change was only one of emphasis concerning cases of criminal convictions, and confusingly repeats both the presumption in favour of deportation and that the seriousness of the offence should be balanced against family ties. The best that can be said is that this chapter of the OEM is currently rather muddled. It and the rules will need further amendment when the deeming provisions of the UK Borders Act come into force, and in the meantime the policy is unclear.

Issues also remain about the scope of DP3/96. In *CH v SSHD* [2007] EWCA Civ 792 the court held that the policy could not apply where the sponsoring spouse had died before the two-year period expired. OEM Chapter 36 applies the equivalent of DP3/96 to unmarried partners, but civil partners are not mentioned. As rule changes in December 2005 brought civil partners into the immigration rules, an application of policy which does not respect such relationships when it comes to removal cannot be maintained, and the word 'marriage' should be interpreted accordingly.

DP069/99 (amending DP5/96) gives guidance on removal when the person to be removed has children. The factors to be taken into account are: the length of the parents' residence without leave; whether removal has been delayed by protracted and repetitive representations, or by the parents going to ground; the age of the children, or whether the children were conceived at a time when either of the parents had leave to remain; whether return to the parents' country of origin would cause extreme hardship for the children or put their health seriously at risk. The policy says that enforcement will not generally proceed against families where the children were born here and are aged seven or over, or where the children arrived in the UK at an early age and have lived here for seven years or more. However, in *R (on the application of Onwumere) v SSHD* [2004] EWHC 1281 (Admin) the claimant had a child born in the UK who was older than seven when enforcement proceedings began as well as two younger children. He claimed the benefit of DP5/96. The court held that the Secretary of State was correct to treat the scales as starting evenly balanced and to weigh in them the interests of the children and the interests of immigration control. The claimant's poor immigration history could be taken into account according to the terms of DP5/96, and it was not disproportionate to expect him to leave and apply for entry clearance from Nigeria. In *Baig v SSHD* [2005] EWCA Civ 1246 the interests of four children in living in the UK, the only country they had known, were held to be outweighed by the couple's 10-year history of irregular immigration status. They had entered on false passports, and did not effectively seek to regularize their status, as although they made an application to be regularized as overstayers they had not attended interviews to pursue that application. They had travelled since on false passports, and the father had been detained, but managed to avoid deportation although a deportation order was made against him in 2000.

Policies on marriage and children are of less importance since the Human Rights Act, as the Act encompasses all family situations as well as the factors set out in DP3/96 and DP069/99. In the last two mentioned situations, Article 8 did not improve the appellants' cases.

18.3.2 People over 65

There was formerly a policy not to remove people over 65. This was revoked on 28 October 2004, and now each case is to be looked at on its merits (*R (on the application of Doka) v IAT, SSHD interested party* [2004] EWHC 3072 (Admin). Home Office guidance says 'age by itself is not a realistic or reliable indicator of a person's health, mobility or ability to care for themselves'. It is for the individual to show that they should not be removed (OEM 36.8).

18.4 Human rights appeals

The argument that removal will breach Convention rights is now the most important basis of challenge. There is, as we have seen, no right to reside in the country of one's choice, or at least there is no such right for non-nationals of that country. The deportation *per se* does not therefore infringe a protected right. The Convention rights most likely to be engaged by the threat of removal are Articles 3 and 8.

18.4.1 Article 3

Article 3 protects against torture, inhuman or degrading treatment or punishment, and will most often be engaged when an asylum claim has failed even though it is established that the asylum seeker may face ill-treatment on return. The use of Article 3 in this context has been discussed in chapter 4. There may also be Article 3 issues outside what is, in effect, the substance of the asylum claim. For instance, in *R (on the application of Ahmadi) v SSHD* [2002] EWHC 1897 (Admin) the applicants at first alleged that their return to Germany would breach Article 3, not because they feared that Germany would return them to Afghanistan, the country they originally fled in fear of persecution, but because of the conditions in the refugee centres in which they were living in Germany. This part of the claim was ultimately not pursued before the High Court. *AK*, discussed below, unsuccessfully alleged treatment contrary to Article 3 at the border to the Palestinian Territories.

Apart from the use of Article 3 in asylum claims, the Article most often engaged in removals is Article 8, the right to respect for private and family life, home and correspondence.

18.4.2 **Article 8**

Reference should be made to chapter 4 for discussion of Article 8 and for the relationships which constitute family or private life. Here we consider the issues arising from deportation and removal. The proper approach to an alleged breach, as set out by the Immigration Appeal Tribunal in the case of *Nhundu and Chiwera* (01/TH/000613) at para 24, is:

Article 8 is to be analysed according to a step-by-step approach, asking first whether there is an existent private or family life, second whether there is an interference with that private or family life, third whether that interference pursues a legitimate aim, fourth whether it is in accordance with the law and finally whether it is proportionate.

This step-by-step approach, approved by the House of Lords in *Razgar*, will be followed here with application to removal.

18.4.2.1 *Interference*

The most obvious and damaging interference with family life by a removal is the break up of the family. It can also be argued that the upheaval and disruption of support networks, wider family relationships and so on is an interference with family and private life. If other family members are removed the upheaval to the whole family must be considered as the potential breach, though, depending on how obiter points in *AB* are taken up, perhaps only in relation to the Article 8 rights of a person who is the named subject of removal (see below and chapter 4).That removal constitutes such an interference was made clear by the tribunal in *Baljit Singh* [2002] UKIAT 00660. The tribunal in that case did not claim to lay down a general rule of this kind, but given the nature and effects of removal only in rare instances could it be otherwise. *Nhundu* makes this point, saying that where a family is established removal will constitute an interference with family life. What respect for family life requires when a family is already living in a country together may be different from what is required before they have made a home together. This does not mean that ultimately the family may not be required to leave, but that it will be a rare case in which the choice of separation or of uprooting and losing support networks, perhaps jobs, schooling, friends, and family, cannot be argued to be an interference with family life. This is not always the approach taken in tribunals. For instance in *SS Hussain v SSHD* [2004] EWCA Civ 1190 the children's six- to 12-month separation from their step-father was not considered to be a relevant interference because it would not be long enough to result inevitably in family break-down. The opportunity to apply for entry clearance, and its impact in a particular case, is better regarded as a matter which goes to proportionality (see below).

The ECtHR does not hesitate to find an interference in removal cases, and in *Shevanova v Latvia* found that a deportation order amounted to an interference with private life even though it was never enforced, because of the uncertainty and insecurity it created.

Once it is accepted that there is an interference, consideration must move to whether it is justified under Article 8 para 2, which states:

There shall be no interference by a public authority with the exercise of this right except such as is in accordance with the law and is necessary in a democratic society in the interests of national security, public safety or the economic well-being of the country, for the prevention of disorder or crime, for the protection of health or morals, or for the protection of the rights and freedoms of others.

18.4.2.2 *Legitimate aim*

The identification of the legitimate aim is a necessary first step in applying Article 8.2 (see chapter 4 for full discussion of this point). In the case of deportations it is usually possible to cite 'prevention of disorder or crime' or 'protection of health or morals' as public interests served by the deportation. In removals the legitimate aim may be less easy to identify. Removal is directed towards immigration enforcement, but this is not listed in para 2 as a legitimate aim. In *Abdulaziz* the ECtHR accepted that the immigration policy which restricted entry of spouses was for the 'economic well-being of the country'. It is rarely possible to show that the removal of a person who was making an economic contribution fulfilled this aim, particularly where removal would result in the loss of the only income and therefore leave a family reliant on state support. The approach that is usually taken is to say that the maintenance of an immigration policy *per se* is for the economic well-being of the country. It is therefore not that the individual must be removed for the public good, but that they must be treated as one of a group in relation to whom there is a policy that serves that aim. This has repercussions for the question of proportionality if the harm to the individual is to be weighed against the need for the policy, but not a specific ill that would result from their remaining.

The courts and tribunals commonly hold, as did the tribunal in *Baljit Singh*, that the family interests must be weighed against the interest of the government in 'maintaining effective immigration control'. While this may sometimes be used as shorthand for the reasoning above, there is a danger in so doing as the discussion all too easily slips into circularity. The reason there is a case before a tribunal is that there is some breach of immigration law. If the maintenance of immigration control is used *per se* to justify an interference with a right, the individual may easily end up with an unwinnable argument. Indeed, this is often the case. One of the many examples, illustrating also the limits of the application of Article 8, is *SO (Nigeria)* [2005] UKAIT 00135. Here, the appellant had a substantial life in the UK. He had entered legally, but as his marriage had not worked out he had no right in immigration law to remain. He employed 16 people and was a well-regarded Christian lay minister. The tribunal gave extended reasons as to why any economic disadvantage to others from his removal was speculative and irrelevant, but did not appear to consider how removing a productive and socially useful person served the economic well-being of the country. Simply the fact he had no immigration right was enough. Even more starkly, in *AY Ivory Coast* [2004] UKIAT 00205 the tribunal held that the Secretary of State provisionally discharged the burden of proof to show that the removal was proportionate by 'relying upon the substantial weight to be accorded to a firm and fair immigration policy' (para 22).

In principle, Convention rights should produce the opposite starting position. The rights are protected, and the legitimate interference in para 2 of the qualified rights is the exception. Of course, the tribunal still must be satisfied that the rest of para 2 is met.

18.4.2.3 *In accordance with the law*

Interferences are nearly always in accordance with the law in immigration cases, though the legal source should be identified. In *Estrikh v Latvia* [2007] ECHR 57 the ECtHR held that a deportation was not in accordance with the law because it had taken place on the day that the applicant lodged an appeal against the deportation, in contravention of the Criminal Procedure Code, which, as in the UK, deemed that the order was not final until appeals had been exhausted. A person cannot be removed while they still have an appeal pending which should be heard in the UK, and this includes human rights appeals (Nationality, Immigration and Asylum Act 2002 s 78). Section 78 does permit enforcement steps preparatory to removal to be taken, and there is a growing body of case law and policy concerning whether a person may be detained when all appeals have been exhausted but a judicial review is either possible or pending. This area of developing law may entail examination of what is in accordance with the law or prescribed by law.

18.4.2.4 *Proportionality*

This is generally the substantive issue and is a matter which can only be decided on a case-by-case basis. The decision-maker must weigh carefully the harm done to the individual by the interference against the public interest pursued. The task of considering proportionality follows on from the application of the test which the European Court of Human Rights has on the whole taken seriously, that of 'necessity in a democratic society', equating it with a 'pressing social need' (*Sunday Times v UK* (1979) 2 EHRR 245). The State must show that the interference is not just useful or desirable but necessary, then argument will centre chiefly on the question of whether the proposed interference with a right is proportionate to the legitimate aim pursued.

As discussed in chapter 4, the proper approach to the question of proportionality has been debated since even before the commencement of the Human Rights Act. The debate has in principle been settled by the House of Lords' decision in *Huang and Kashmiri v SSHD* [2007] UKHL 11, though there has been continuing discussion of the meaning and application of that case (see for instance Chowdhury, Clayton and Vaughan in chapter 4 reading list). Subsequent Court of Appeal decisions interpreting and applying *Huang* have been removal cases, and there is no basis in their Lordships' judgment for distinguishing in law between entry cases (which technically were the cases before the Appeal Committee) and removal cases.

The question of proportionality must be assessed by reviewing all the information about the effect of the prospective deportation or removal on the family or private life of the individual concerned. This includes the duration and quality of their relationships and the kind of contact upon which the relationships are now based, for instance is the person living with family members? In the case of private life a range of factors may be taken into account. *AG (Eritrea) v SSHD* [2007] EWCA Civ 801 is a leading case interpreting and following the House of Lords' decision in *Huang*.

   **Key Case**

AG (Eritrea) v SSHD [2007] EWCA Civ 801

The appellant was a young man who had suffered adversity as a child and come to the UK aged 14. He had built up a circle of relationships, was committed to his education, and was in individual and group psychotherapy to deal with the effects of his earlier life. His conscientious attempts to contribute to society and to recover from trauma were aspects of his private life. The immigration judge found that interference with this private life for the permitted aims in Article 8.2 was not necessary. The Court of Appeal commended the immigration judge's approach.

The hallmark of proportionality decisions relying on Article 8 in the ECtHR is their very detailed discussion of the facts, and their weighing of the elements of the applicant's life against the specific interest of the State advanced to support the expulsion. They do not rely on any presumption, and in each case a balance is struck to determine whether the harm done to the applicant is proportionate to the public interest served by the expulsion.

A factor which is an essential consideration is whether the family could live together elsewhere. This consideration derives from entry cases, but is also applied in removal cases. It was posed in *Mahmood* as the question of whether there were insuperable obstacles to the family living together elsewhere. The Court of Appeal in *Husna Begum v ECO Dhaka* [2001] INLR 115 warned against elevating this idea into a rule of law, but this still seemed to happen in the period before the House of Lords' decision in *Huang*. The implication is that a lesser level of distress and inconvenience will not figure in the proportionality exercise. The sponsor having refugee status would, one might imagine, be a clear case of insuperable obstacles to return. However, it was not always so regarded. In *Kilala v SSHD* [2002] UKIAT 05220 the appellant's wife had been recognized as a refugee from the Democratic Republic of Congo. Only a year after this recognition, the tribunal said that this did not mean there were insuperable obstacles to the couple returning. The situation there might have changed. This in effect required the applicant to argue their spouse's refugee status all over again. By comparison, in *Soloot* 01/TH/001366 the tribunal found that there were insuperable obstacles to the couple returning to Iran. The appellant's wife was a recognized refugee, so clearly she could not return as she would be at risk. The appellant himself would face criminal penalties for his manner of leaving Iran, and would not be able to make an application for entry clearance there.

The proper approach now is referred to in *Huang* as the question of whether 'the life of the family cannot reasonably be expected to be enjoyed elsewhere' (para 20). This requires that all the factors related to the possibility of family life elsewhere should be taken into account, rather than that the family should be required as an essential legal threshold to overcome all obstacles except those which are actually impossible to overcome. Having said this, the ECtHR sometimes uses the words 'insuperable obstacles', but does not consistently apply that requirement in a rigorous way.

Many Article 8 cases opposing removal are of former asylum seekers whose claim has failed. Former traumas, even though they have not, for whatever reason, been found to substantiate an asylum claim, may still be relevant in the question of proportionality, which should take into account *all* relevant factors. In *AG (Eritrea)* the fact that the appellant was recovering well from trauma played a part in establishing his private life and was considered as part of the proportionality question. In *MT (Zimbabwe) v SSHD* [2007] EWCA Civ 455 the court accepted that 'because of shared experiences in Zimbabwe and the recovery from those experiences by mutual life together continuing in the UK, Ms T was more than normally emotionally dependent on Mr G and his family' (para 26).

Removals that do not follow upon a deportation order are, in essence, regulatory in the sense that they are conducted in order to enforce immigration control. In *Shevanova v Latvia* the applicant had committed various immigration offences, such as having a false stamp placed in an invalid passport, failing to apply for regularization of her position in Latvia, and concealing her Russian citizenship. She had lived in Latvia for around 30 years. The ECtHR held that her offences were not criminal but regulatory, and making a deportation order against her was disproportionate even though it was not enforced. Interestingly, they held that the legitimate aim was the prevention of public disorder, as enforcing immigration control was for this purpose.

ECtHR case law on deportations demonstrates the fact-specific nature of these decisions. Factors which should be taken into account in any expulsion for a criminal offence challenged under Article 8 are given in *Boultif v Switzerland* [2001] ECHR 497:

- the nature and seriousness of the offence committed by the applicant;
- the length of the applicant's stay in the country from which he or she is to be expelled;
- the time elapsed since the offence was committed and the applicant's conduct during that period;
- the nationalities of the various persons concerned;
- the applicant's family situation, such as the length of the marriage, and other factors expressing the effectiveness of a couple's family life;
- whether the spouse knew about the offence at the time when he or she entered into a family relationship;
- whether there are children of the marriage, and if so, their age; and
- the seriousness of the difficulties which the spouse is likely to encounter in the country to which the applicant is to be expelled.

Üner v The Netherlands [2006] ECHR 873 added two more considerations:

- the best interests and well-being of the children, in particular the seriousness of the difficulties which any children of the applicant are likely to encounter in the country to which the applicant is to be expelled; and
- the solidity of social, cultural and family ties with the host country and with the country of destination.

There are numerous earlier cases assessing some of these factors, though trends are not always easy to identify precisely because decision-making is so fact-specific. Long residence in the state is often regarded as very important. See, for instance, *Beldjoudi v*

France (1992) 14 EHRR 801 in which a life of crime was not sufficient to outweigh the fact that the applicant had spent almost all his life in France, and had a French wife with whom his marriage would probably be destroyed if he were deported. On the other hand, in *Boughanemi v France* the retention of links with Tunisia meant that the deportation was proportionate, though in other respects the facts were quite similar. Warbrick (1998) criticizes the decision on this basis. *Beldjoudi* is probably more indicative of the court's approach. The seriousness of a crime is a relevant factor, but again it must be weighed against other considerations. In *Bouchelkia v France* (1998) 25 EHRR 686 the applicant had lived in France since the age of two, and was living with his family of origin, but the ECtHR held that his deportation following conviction for rape was proportionate.

The approach of the ECtHR ranges between a search for principles respecting the lives of integrated aliens, to that exemplified in the minority judgment of Judge Pettiti in *Beldjoudi* that only Article 3 was capable of interfering with the State's right to deport an alien. There is however a development towards considering the actual harm which would be inflicted by continuing residence, rather than just looking at a criminal history. Rogers (2003) identifies a trend towards a more realistic assessment of the difficulties facing family members required to relocate and that *Boultif* gives some indication of this. She says: 'The judgement is significant for its recognition that in cases where there are real barriers such as lack of ties for some of the family members or language difficulties, the Court is likely to conclude that the family cannot be expected to follow the deportee' (p. 62).

In the case of *Kaya v Germany* [2007] ECHR 538 the applicant's cruelty to his partner and another woman and his attempt to shift responsibility to a co-defendant suggested to the court that even though all his offending happened in a short period of time it was not 'mere juvenile delinquency' and he was not someone who was taking responsibility for his actions. Although he was born and brought up in Germany his removal to Turkey was not a violation of his right to respect for private life. By contrast, Mr Maslov's offences, though they were many, within a short period of time and 'of a certain gravity', were typical of juvenile delinquency and to deport him was a breach of Article 8 (*Maslov v Austria* [2007] ECHR 224). Both *Kaya* and *Maslov* concerned second-generation immigrants, in relation to whom one can say that, but for the particular provisions of nationality law into which they were born, they would be nationals of what is in reality their home state, and so not deportable.

The ECtHR in *Üner v Netherlands* expressly addressed the question of whether there should be particular protection for established residents. They say that in their view the usual principles for considering expulsion cases which raise Article 8 issues apply whether the person is a recent arrival, a long-term resident, or even born in the state. In Recommendation 1504 (2001) on the non-expulsion of long-term immigrants the Parliamentary Assembly of the Council of Europe recommended that member states move towards guaranteeing that long-term migrants who were born or raised in the host country will not be expelled under any circumstances, and that long-term residents will only be expelled in the most severe cases. The Court in *Üner* considers this recommendation, but nevertheless holds that even when a non-national 'holds a very strong residence status and has attained a high degree of integration, his or her position cannot be equated with that of a national'. The court reiterated what was said in *Maaouia*, that expulsion is not a double punishment. This is perhaps a surprising emphasis for the court following the Parliamentary Assembly's recommendation and secondary legislation in the European Union enhancing the rights of European citizens against expulsion. Following established authority and guidance in *Huang*, the Strasbourg cases 'are of value in showing where, in many different factual situations, the Strasbourg court, as the ultimate guardian of rights, has drawn the line' (para 18).

In the UK, the judgment of the Court of Appeal in *B* v *Secretary of State for the Home Department* [2000] Imm AR 478 is illuminating as an example of the court addressing the questions of legitimate aim and proportionality. B was an Italian national from Sicily who had been in the UK since he was seven years old. He was convicted of sexually assaulting his daughter and assaulting his son. His wife divorced him and he had no contact with his children. His parents had other children in the UK on whom they could rely if he were no longer in the country. He had some relatives in Italy and business skills and the capacity to work. The case for deportation of B was made on the grounds of the seriousness of the offence. It was accepted that B's opportunities for re-offending were limited and that it was unlikely that he would do so, therefore although the Secretary of State argued that his deportation was 'for the prevention of crime' this was not based on likelihood of his re-offending.

The Court of Appeal accepted that there could be cases of 'sufficiently serious offending, with or without a propensity to re-offend', which would warrant deportation, but decided that this was not such a case. The legitimate aim of prevention of crime could therefore not justify deportation, as the evidence was that he was unlikely to re-offend.

On the question of proportionality the court said that, although the offence was serious, deportation in this case was 'more akin to exile'. It was therefore disproportionate. Little identifiable public good would be achieved, and the harm to the individual was great. *B* was decided before the Human Rights Act came into effect; however, as the case concerned a European national, Article 8 ECHR was directly applicable as a principle of European law. The more generous approach in *B*, although a UK case, is consistent with the ECJ's use of Article 8. In Case C-60/00 *Carpenter*, a factual situation similar to many non-European Article 8 claims, the ECJ did not regard the immigration breach as particularly worth dwelling on by comparison with the disproportionate upheaval in the appellant's family life. The maintenance of immigration control for its own sake, where no other damage was anticipated, was not regarded as important enough to outweigh fundamental rights.

In *Mert v SSHD* [2005] EWCA Civ 832 the deportation order had been made six years earlier, but not carried out. The Secretary of State argued that if the deportation order was once appropriate it could not become inappropriate through passage of time. The Court of Appeal held that the adjudicator had carried out a proper proportionality exercise. He had taken account of the importance of the Secretary of State's policy of deterrence, but held that 14 years' residence, children born in the UK, a strong family life, and six years since the deportation order was made, meant that to carry out a deportation would be disproportionate.

Even after the implementation of UK Borders Act ss 32–39, deportations where human rights are claimed to be infringed (a significant number, as many potential deportees have at least a private life in the UK) will require an exercise of judgment by the Secretary of State. The starred tribunal decision in *Noruwa* 00/TH/2345 was an appeal against a refusal to revoke a deportation order which, like the making of a deportation order, is a discretion. The tribunal explained that, in addition to considering on appeal whether a discretion should have been exercised differently, the human rights appeal adds jurisdiction to decide that a deportation was disproportionate and therefore unlawful. An appeal on a question of proportionality was 'a genuine appeal – not merely a review of whether the Respondent's conclusion on proportionality was open to him' (para 54). This is the conclusion of the House of Lords in *Huang*. Following *Huang*, respect and weight is accorded to the Secretary of State's view as to the necessity of the deportation for reasons of public policy to the extent that the content or context warrants it, but it is not given an automatically greater weight than other evidence (para 16). Issues of deterrence and punishment are well within the court's normal field of expertise and so not a matter on which the Secretary of State's view should be given special preference. Evidence as to the individual's propensity to offend and what might prevent that are routine considerations in the criminal courts. The consistent application and rationality of policy are also within the domain of the judiciary (e.g. *R v SSHD ex p Amankwah* [1994] Imm AR 240 and *Wheeler v Leicester City Council* [1985] AC 1054). It is arguable that in the post-Human Rights Act era the UK courts will be called upon more and more to follow the practice which has developed in some other countries, of assessing social information as evidence. For instance, they might be invited to consider the statistical evidence of the effectiveness of deportation as a deterrent. Some dicta in *Huang* suggest that the need for the policy is outside the remit of courts in judicial review, but no view is expressed on whether such issues could be considered in the appeal courts and tribunals.

18.4.2.5 *Other family members*

The question of whether the rights of other family members must be taken into account in a human rights appeal has been discussed in chapter 4.

18.5 Removal directions

At some point, either at the same time as or, more usually, after the decision to remove or the deportation order, the person who is to be removed receives a copy of removal directions. These are instructions by an immigration officer or the Secretary of State to the captain of a ship or aircraft to remove the person in question to a country or territory:

(i) of which s/he is a national or citizen;

(ii) in which s/he has obtained a passport or identity document;

(iii) in which s/he embarked for the UK; or

(iv) to which there is reason to believe s/he will be admitted (Immigration Act 1971 Sch 2 para 8).

Removal directions have no duration or continuing legal effect beyond the moment when they are put into practice. They are enforceable in the very real sense that a person may be arrested and detained in order to give them effect. In law they are themselves a form of enforcement (see, for instance, Burnton J in *SSHD v Kariharan* [2001] EWHC Admin 1004 likening them to a bailiff's warrant).

Removal directions could be appealed under 1971 Act s 16 and 1999 Act s 66, but only on the grounds that there was no power in law to issue them on the grounds stated. Additionally, this right of appeal could only be exercised from outside the UK unless there was an asylum claim. Deportees and those refused entry also had an appeal against destination.

These limitations on appeals against actual physical removal were particularly problematic where a lengthy claim, perhaps for asylum, ended unsuccessfully. If it had taken years to process, the asylum seeker could hardly be expected to refrain from making relationships in that time, but their asylum claim would have dealt with the risk in their country of origin, and not any developing private and family life reasons for needing to remain in the UK. There would then be no forum for arguing these points, as the appeal against removal directions could only deal with the jurisdictional matter, and there would rarely be any dispute that the person was in fact an illegal entrant or perhaps an overstayer. An answer seemed to be provided by Immigration and Asylum Act 1999 s 65, which gave a right of appeal on human rights grounds against 'any decision under the Immigration Acts relating to that person's entitlement to enter or remain' in the UK. If the issue of removal directions was such a decision then there could be a human rights appeal against it.

The Court of Appeal in *Kariharan v SSHD* [2002] EWCA Civ 1102 followed the interpretative obligation in HRA s 3 by giving a meaning to s 65 which upheld Convention rights, interpreting a 'decision...relating to...entitlement' broadly, so as to allow the possibility of a human rights appeal. It found that removal directions were discretionary and, as such, were capable of being determinative of entitlement to enter or remain. It did not consider that the comparison with a bailiff's warrant was altogether apt because of this continuing discretion. The Court of Appeal's judgment therefore gave the right to an appeal on human rights grounds against directions for removal. The Secretary of State appealed to the House of Lords, but even before that could be heard, Nationality, Immigration and Asylum Act 2002 s 82 reversed *Kariharan* by specifying 'immigration decisions' against which appeals can be made. Section 82(2)(g) and (h) permits an appeal against a 'decision that a person is to be removed by way of directions'. This means that all that is appealable is the initial immigration decision which results in the liability for removal, not the removal directions themselves.

As the 2002 Act does not include removal directions in its list of appealable decisions, the former rights of appeal against removal directions have also gone. There is no challenge to validity or destination. Directions are sometimes issued which are actually invalid but now there is no power in the statute to declare them so. For instance, directions must specify a country to which the person can be returned, and must specify the time and date of removal (1971 Act Sch 2 para 8) and there is a problem if these are wrong or non-existent. The only remedy is judicial review, though this is also on the ground of illegality. In *KF (Iran)* [2005] UKIAT 00109 a notice of decision to remove indicated that the appellant would be removed to Iran, though directions had not actually been given to this effect. It was not certain that Iran could receive him. The tribunal followed *SSHD v Zeqaj* [2003] Imm AR 298 – the destination was not appealable. However, the destination did have to be stated as, otherwise, there was no basis for assessing risk to the appellant of return, under either the Refugee Convention or the Human Rights Act. If the destination was invalid under the 1971 Act the Secretary of State would have to issue a new removal decision, and this would attract a fresh right of appeal.

In *MA (Statelessness; removal; KF applied) stateless* [2005] UKAIT 00161 the appellant's asylum claim failed. Saudi Arabia was his country of habitual residence. His father was Somali, his mother Yemeni; the appellant was stateless. The decision being challenged was to remove him to Yemen. The tribunal held, following *KF*, that the destination was relevant to whether the removal would breach the appellant's human rights as any risks in Yemen would need to be assessed. However, if they were satisfied that there were no such risks, they had to assume that Yemen was a country 'to which there was reason to believe the appellant would be admitted'. Travel documents would have to be arranged, and there would have to be negotiations with the Yemeni Embassy. If all this proved non-viable, then he would not be removed as Yemen could not be compelled to accept him, but the tribunal could not deal with the practicalities.

18.6 **Viability of return**

Many of the more recent legal issues concerning return and removal have concerned the viability of return. As a thematic briefing for the Independent Asylum Commission relates, there may be practical and institutional barriers to removal. These include:

- lack of travel documents and identification
- lack of institutional co-ordination
- lack of an international airport, safe route or carrier (ICAR 2007).

Not all of these issues come before the courts or tribunals or have a legal dimension, but they are at least as important as legal issues in explaining why, although someone may be an illegal entrant or their asylum claim may have failed, they cannot necessarily be removed from the UK. The gap between the numbers of people who have no right in law to remain and the numbers removed is not just due to government inefficiency or non-compliance by those to be removed.

The safety of route of return has come before the Court of Appeal.

 **Key Case**

Gedow, Abdulkadir and Mohamed v SSHD **[2006] EWCA Civ 1342**

This case concerned return to Somalia. The international airport at Mogadishu was closed, and the last enforced departure to Somalia had been in May 2004. The only place a plane could land to return unsuccessful asylum seekers would be an airstrip, and no international flight would do this. The Home Office position had for some time been that returns to Somalia were not suspended, but in reality very few were practical. The airport in Mogadishu re-opened on 15 July 2006 after being closed for 11 years (www.azworldair-ports.com, accessed 18 December 2007).

The appellant Gedow did not fear ill-treatment after arriving home; the issue was what he would face at the airport and on the journey home. The Court of Appeal held that, when the Secretary of State did actually issue removal directions (which had not yet been done at the time of the hearing, because they were impractical), sufficient time must be allowed for the appellant to arrange safe conduct for himself home from the airport. So he must know the date, time and location of his arrival well in advance. However, in a case such as this, where no removal directions had been set, the court could not speculate about the practicalities of arrival nor assume that these would breach Article 3. The Secretary of State should act in a way that made it possible for the appellant to protect himself.

In *GH v SSHD* [2005] EWCA Civ 1182 the court held that, where removal directions are given as part of, or incidental to, an appealable decision, or where the Secretary of State adopts a routine procedure for removal or return so that the method or route is implicit in the decision to remove, the directions may also be considered as part of the appeal. Normal practice is to give the removal directions well after any appealable decision. *GH* concerned an Iraqi Kurd who, it was decided, could live safely in the area of northern Iraq from which he came, but who argued that he would face risks when travelling within Iraq from the point of arrival to his home area. As no removal directions had been set, the court held that this question was 'academic'. Note that in cases of internal relocation, discussed in the context of asylum claims in chapter 13, risks in travelling to the new safe area may be taken into account to determine that the proposed relocation is 'unduly harsh'. In these cases such as *GH*, we are considering a different situation, where the appellant is held *not* to be at risk in their home area. Then risks on travelling there will only engage the UK's legal system of protection if they amount to a risk of violation of Article 3 (e.g. torture on return at the airport) or if, once removal directions have been set, they are so unreasonable as to be challengeable by judicial review.

In *AK v SSHD* [2006] EWCA Civ 1117 in a similar vein the court held that as there were no proven obstacles to the appellant's re-entering the Palestinian Territories via Jordan, even though he might encounter some difficulty, this was not a matter the court could engage with. Inconvenience is not an objection to removal unless it amounts to treatment in breach of Article 3 (also in *MA (Palestinian Arabs – Occupied Territories – Risk) Palestinian Territories CG* [2007] UKAIT 00017).

A further practical difficulty in the way of removal may be obstacles to obtaining travel documents. Asylum and Immigration (Treatment of Claimants etc) Act 2004 s 35 makes it a criminal offence for an asylum seeker to fail to comply, without reasonable excuse, with obtaining a travel document. Guidance to immigration officers suggests that reasonable excuse would be something like a need for emergency medical care or transport problems which prevented a person from getting to an interview. This does not include the claimant's fear of contact with authorities in their home country. This was confirmed in *R v Tabnak* [2007] EWCA Crim 380 in which the Court of Appeal endorsed the Home Office interpretation of reasonable excuse, as in the guidance. It must be something which made the asylum seeker unable to comply, not unwilling. The criminal court was not able to assess risks in the country of return, which would have already been assessed by the immigration authorities and perhaps a tribunal.

There is a possible maximum prison sentence in the UK of two years for failure to co-operate. OEM 85 1.1 advises that action under s 35 should not be started while an individual has an outstanding appeal, but should be continued if further representations are made after action has been commenced under s 35. It is obvious also that steps to obtain a travel document from the appellant's embassy should not be taken before an appeal has been concluded if there is any chance of risk to the appellant. In *R (on the application of Sidibe) v SSHD* [2007] EWCA Civ 191, Home Office officials had taken the claimant to the Guinean embassy to arrange travel documents, despite the fact that there were serious allegations of the risk he faced as a member of the military, an expert's report was pending on the risk to him, and his appeal had not yet been heard. Moses J made it clear that this was highly irregular and that it would be necessary to discover why it happened because if there was no good reason for it to be done that raises doubts as to the bona fides of those responsible for this applicant in the circumstances of his particular case, and may indeed add force to the contention that he was deliberately exposed to a risk by those responsible for his detention. (para 4)

The case law on practical obstacles to return is the tip of an iceberg. Under the water are many other factors which do not readily enter the court room. In addition to all the human reasons that an asylum seeker whose claim has failed may have for not wanting to return to their home country are the interests of the country of return. It is easy to lose sight when studying the UK's system that the return of an asylum seeker is an international action. The country of return may have social, economic or political reasons for not wanting to accept the returnee. As the ICAR report says, 'in times of conflict they may be reluctant to re-admit supporters of resistance groups' or they may fear that returnees will not be absorbed economically, or compromise fragile security situations.

The other major issue which follows is what status an asylum seeker can have once the legal process has ended unsuccessfully, where the UK is unwilling to give any leave to remain, but return cannot be achieved. Issues about lack of status and resulting destitution underlie some of the cases dealing with the feasibility or otherwise of return. Reference should be made to discussion of temporary admission in chapter 15.

18.7 **Conclusion**

Arguments against removal are among the most crucial to the individual of any immigration case that comes before a decision-maker. They are also among the most common. Defences to removal have been restricted in the immigration rules, and policies have been overtaken by the Human Rights Act, the effectiveness of which depends largely on judges' willingness to take charge of the concept of proportionality. Powers to remove are wide-ranging and still, in essence, discretionary. The appellant is therefore still aiming an unpredictable shot at a moving target. This is not to say that the matter is a lottery. There are important guiding principles in the Human Rights Act and still, to a lesser extent, in policies. In sense though, the whole legal edifice has been overtaken by events in relation to removal. The most influential issues are the practical ones. Why is it that people are willing to undergo significant hardship in the UK in order to avoid removal? Why is it that such a small percentage of people with irregular immigration status are in fact removed? There is a suspicion that the plethora of legal powers are a kind of window dressing, an attempt to persuade a doubtful publicthat the government not only can but also should control who lives in the UK.

QUESTIONS

1 What would be the legitimate aim in Article 8.2 in the case of *Baig*? How would you argue for and against the right to respect for family life in that case?

2 Should removal directions be appealable? If so, on what grounds?

3 Is there any point in having policies such as DP3/96 after the Human Rights Act?

 For guidance on answering questions, visit www.oxfordtextbooks.co.uk/orc/clayton3e.

FURTHER READING

Sherlock, A. 'Deportation of Aliens and Article 8 ECHR' (1998) 23 ELR, pp. 62–75.

Warbrick, C. 'The Structure of Article 8' [1998] EHRLR 1, pp. 32–44.

INDEX